The KREMLINOLOGIST

Johns Hopkins Nuclear History and Contemporary Affairs

Martin J. Sherwin, *Series Editor*

The KREMLINOLOGIST
LLEWELLYN E THOMPSON
America's Man in Cold War Moscow

Jenny Thompson and Sherry Thompson

JOHNS HOPKINS UNIVERSITY PRESS

Baltimore

© 2018 Johns Hopkins University Press
All rights reserved. Published 2018
Printed in the United States of America on acid-free paper
9 8 7 6 5 4 3 2 1

Johns Hopkins University Press
2715 North Charles Street
Baltimore, Maryland 21218-4363
www.press.jhu.edu

Library of Congress Cataloging-in-Publication Data
Names: Thompson, Jenny, 1949– author. | Thompson, Sherry, 1954– author.
Title: The Kremlinologist : Llewellyn E Thompson, America's man in Cold War
    Moscow / Jenny Thompson and Sherry Thompson.
Description: Baltimore : Johns Hopkins University Press, [2018] | Series:
    Johns Hopkins nuclear history and contemporary affairs | Includes
    bibliographical references and index.
Identifiers: LCCN 2017017066 | ISBN 9781421424095 (hardcover : alk. paper)
    |ISBN 9781421424545 (pbk. : alk. paper) | ISBN 9781421424101 (electronic)
    | ISBN 1421424096 (hardcover : alk. paper) | ISBN 1421424541 (pbk. : alk.
    paper) | ISBN 142142410X (electronic)
Subjects: LCSH: Thompson, Llewellyn, 1904–1972. | United States—Foreign
    relations—1945–1989. | United States—Foreign relations—Soviet Union. |
    Ambassadors—United States—Biography. | Soviet Union—Foreign
    relations—United States. | Cold War—Diplomatic history. |
    Diplomats—United States—Biography. | World politics—1945–1989.
Classification: LCC E748.T518 T56 2018 | DDC 327.7304709/04—dc23
LC record available at https://lccn.loc.gov/2017017066

A catalog record for this book is available from the British Library.

*Special discounts are available for bulk purchases of this book. For more information, please contact Special Sales
at 410-516-6936 or specialsales@press.jhu.edu.*

Johns Hopkins University Press uses environmentally friendly book materials, including recycled text paper
that is composed of at least 30 percent post-consumer waste, whenever possible.

For our families

Contents

Acknowledgments

We do not belong to an academic institution, and therefore our project was self-funded. Our older half-sister, whose life was a black hole of sorrow, died in a nursing home, bedridden by the toxic effect of drugs given to combat mental illness. She left us a small inheritance that enabled us to move forward with the research for and writing of this book. And so we dedicate it to our parents and to her.

We are extremely grateful to the University of Wisconsin at Madison and the Department of State for putting the Foreign Relations of the United States (FRUS) series of historical documents online, as well as to other institutions, like the presidential libraries, that have also made so much available, including the presidential recordings at the University of Virginia's Miller Center and the amazing collection of oral histories at the Foreign Affairs Oral History Program of the Association for Diplomatic Studies and Training. We could not have attempted this project if we'd started ten years sooner. The developments of the Internet and, along with it, Google, Skype, and e-books were essential. Technology has completely revolutionized research by making it more democratic, because primary source documents are available to everyone.

What was more important, and much more enjoyable, were the amazing and wonderful people who encouraged and cajoled us, made essential introductions, translated documents, argued, critiqued, confided, remembered, and shared both wisdom and memories. In particular, we want to express our appreciation to our husbands for their support and patience throughout this long project, as well as to Donald Lamm, David Langbart, Priscilla McMillan, and Martin J. Sherwin, who also believed in us from beginning to end. Our profound thanks go to our editor, Elizabeth S. Demers, at Johns Hopkins University Press, and to our copy editor, Kathleen Capels, both of whom meticulously went over our manuscript and improved it. We are also indebted to Barbara Stetzl-Marx from the Boltzmann Institute, one of the first people to take us seriously and who generously invited us to participate in the conference she organized on the Vienna summit. We are grateful to the *Foreign Service Journal* for publishing our article on the Trieste negotiation in 2008.

We also want to thank those who gave up their time to read all or part of the manuscript and who offered us their invaluable comments and suggestions:

Avis Bohlen
William Burr
Raymond Garthoff
Susan Herter
Sergei Khrushchev
David M. Miller
James Nathan
Svetlana Savranskaya

William Taubman
Brian VanDeMark
Peter Vujacic
Steven Vujacic
James Wade
Kenneth Weisbrode
Vladislav Zubok

We would also like to acknowledge the many people who helped in various other ways, talking to us and clarifying or adding information:

Georgi Arbatov
Francis Bator
Günter Bischof
Art Buchwald
Richard Davies
Hugh de Santis
David Eisenhower
Halvord Ekern
Theodore Eliot
Wendy Hazard
Gregg Herken
James Herschberg
Tom Hughes
Edward Hurwitz
Stuart Issacoff
Kempton Jenkins
Rada Khrushcheva
Edward Kilham
David Klein
Harriet Klosson
William Knight
Georgi Kornienko
Mark Kramer
Janet Lang
Wolf Lehmann
Irving R. Levine
Frank Lindsay
John Mapother
Robert Martens

Jack Matlock
Martha Mautner
David A. Mayers
James McCargar
Robert McNamara
Timothy Naftali
James Nathan
Isaac Patch
Olga Pavlenko
Vladimir Petchantov
Oliver Rathkolb
Jonathan Rickert
Walter Roberts
Dean Rusk
Daniel Shorr
Marshall Shulman
Sim Smiley
Theodore Sorensen
Gerald Stourzh
Viktor Sukhodrev
Horace Torbert
Eugene V. Thaw
Vladimir Toumanoff
Masha Troyanovsky
Hans Tuch
Stewart Udall
Leonard Unger
Giles Wittel

Last, but not least, we would like to show our appreciation for archivists at the various libraries, who were so helpful:

Paul Barron, and especially Jeffrey Kozak, who finally found the C. B. Wright interview with Llewellyn E Thompson after a seven-year search, George C. Marshall Foundation Library

Mary Burtzloff, Dwight D. Eisenhower Library

Ashton Ellett, Richard B. Russell Library for Political Research and Studies, University of Georgia

Charlene Hester, Lyndon B. Johnson Library

Vasilii S. Khristoferov, Central Archive of Russia's Federal Security Service

David Langbart, National Archives, College Park

Jennifer Pino, Howard Gottlieb Archival Research Center, Boston University

Stephen Plotkin, John F. Kennedy Library

Konstanin Provalov, Department of Historical Documentation, Russian Foreign Ministry

Mikhail Prozumenshchikov, Russian State Archive of Contemporary History (and also thanks to Tatiana Kireeva for her help in translating Russian archive documents)

Many other archivists at the following institutions were also helpful: National Archives, College Park; National Security Archives, George Washington University; Seeley Mudd Manuscript Library, Princeton University; and the Library of Congress.

Notably, we do not include the Central Intelligence Agency, which has been stalling for a decade and still has not honored our Freedom of Information Act request.

We have done our best to remember everyone who helped us during the fifteen years our project took, but please forgive us if we have left anyone out.

Introduction

Llewellyn E Thompson
A Cold War Owl in the Cause of Peace

A long, lean, graceful, and absurdly quiet man, Llewellyn E Thompson Jr. is and was a mystery. He was sociable and made friends easily, yet he was reserved and self-effacing. He gained respect from his subordinates but was never domineering. He was a ladies' man, but not a playboy. He joined and stayed in the Foreign Service both to feed his desire for adventure and from a deep sense of duty.

Those in the inner circle of the administrations he served were well aware of his accomplishments, but he is often overlooked by historians, because he purposely left little documentary evidence and never wrote a memoir. No one could boast of being very close to him, though people from completely opposite ends of the political spectrum lauded him and claimed him as their own. Scholars have even cited the same event to label him either a Hawk or a Dove. As his daughters, seeking to understand his work, we discovered that he was both and neither, so we appreciate the moniker given to him by British correspondent Henry Brandon and call him the Cold War Owl.

We started off by scratching at the surface of his era, in an effort to discover who this person really was and what he actually did, so that we could build a frame on which to hang our memories. We were not trying to prove a thesis or further a professional career. We wanted not only to get to know him, but to also make him known to our children and grandchildren because, when all is said and done, he was an American in the traditional sense, when character meant more than personality. We were never really certain, until the book was done, that we *would* finish, but we believed the effort was worth our investment of time, energy, and personal resources. We were prepared to face the possibility that we might not like what we found out about our father. What amazed us was the extent to which he was involved in the administrations of John F. Kennedy, Lyndon B. Johnson, and even Richard M. Nixon. What motivated us to continue at various points—when dropping the project looked like an option—was the encouragement of those who knew Thompson and agreed that a biography of the man was badly needed. Their time and contributions made giving up impossible.

This search was also a self-educating process. When we started, we imagined writing a book with no references, but we soon realized that it could be dismissed as just a hagiographic account by two daughters, so we decided to document our findings. This was often difficult with no research assistance, but we have done our best with our references and citations. Undoubtedly there have been mistakes, for which we apologize in advance.

One day shortly before his death, we found our father cleaning out his desk and admonished him for disposing of personal papers, suggesting it was possible that someday we would write a book about him. Thompson looked over the rim of his glasses dubiously and told us that if we got the inclination, we would find everything we needed in the National Archives, where he was sending most of his papers. We have spent over fifteen years stealing patches of time to do just that. Fortunately, our mother, who was more optimistic, saved a trove of personal letters, a partial diary, clippings, photos, and other documents. And then there were our own recollections and understanding: his advice to us, family discussions, comments, and overheard conversations.

Guided through the archives by brilliant Sherpa archivists, we found a paper trail to the events of his career, but we never lost sight of the pitfalls of relying too heavily on the written record. In uncanny ways, we found the history we were researching metamorphosing into the present, often in a more terrible aspect. For example, the covert organizations that sprang up to fight the Cold War could be counted on one hand, but today, thousands of government organizations and private companies spend unidentifiable sums of money fighting the War on Terror. The problems of interagency rivalry and coordination that existed in the beginnings of organizations like the CIA are thus much worse.

Sometimes, when many of the half-truths, political spins, malformed opinions, and misconceived politics have passed through the sieve of time, a picture emerges that poses questions not "askable" before. Events shaped to fit an image that the majority of people accepted as reality now appear in a different light. The affair involving a U-2 spy plane is one such example.

Our correspondence put us in touch with all types of people engaged in re-creating history, a sort of time travel. "Find the dots and then join them," advised journalist, historian, and author Priscilla McMillan. The dots are there, but there are infinite ways to connect them. We were amazed at the meticulous effort of many scholars to find the straightest line between the dots, while others took lengthy and questionable detours. It was a surprise to learn that the truth of history can be a malleable thing.

Now we have pieced Llewellyn Thompson's story together sufficiently enough to tell it, in the hopes that it will spark interest in serious scholars of diplomacy to give our father the attention he merits. As we went deeper into our research and reflected on our experiences of and with him, we saw that we held the clue that could help others understand him. We could bring the "persona" into the picture, and this could add to a more comprehensive picture of the turbulent years from America's emergence as a world power through the decades of the Cold War.

We hope you'll find it a good story, one that chronicles a journey from the dust of the Old Santa Fe Trail to the inner circles of the White House and the cobblestones of Red Square. Thompson's story also confirms the power of personal diplomacy, patience, and the cultivation of a deep understanding of and empathy for the other.

PART I

Expectations and Education

The Beginning

Both matter and radiation possess a remarkable duality
of character, as they sometimes exhibit the properties
of waves, at other times those of particles.
—WERNER KARL HEISENBERG,
The Physical Principles of the Quantum Theory

People are both packets of personality and a continuation of an ancestral wave. To understand who an individual person is, you must look at the wave they are on. The Thompson "wave" can reliably be traced back to Scotch-Irish Presbyterian origins.[1] In the late 1600s, increased land rents and religious restrictions impelled a great number of people in northern Ireland, including the Thompsons, to emigrate to the colonies. Once in America, as land in the east became scarce, they moved west. "Clannish, aggressive, violent, and devoted to their livestock,"[2] some of these Protestant migrants underwent a religious conversion along the way and became Baptists, the Thompsons among them.

In the early 1700s, a number of these Baptists moved through the Cumberland Gap to Kentucky, and it was here that Llewellyn Thompson Jr.'s great-great-grandfather David was born in 1760. David possessed a restless streak that seemed to have been passed on to succeeding generations. He joined George Rogers Clark on a number of expeditions at the turn of the nineteenth century before finally settling down in Crab Orchard, Kentucky.

There was something restless about his grandson, too. In 1842, David Thompson II shed these roots and moved to Missouri, where he married Frances Penney, aunt to the famous retailer J. C. Penney. David was a handsome, bearded man with a high forehead and slightly receding hairline, a Thompson trait. He had a fierce look in his clear blue eyes and did not smile often. In 1849, he and a younger brother set off for California's Gold Rush to seek their fortune, but they had to turn back when David's brother became ill.

The Civil War caused a split in the Thompson family. Most of the Thompson brothers fought on the Confederate side, but some broke with tradition and joined the Union forces. No records show that David II owned any slaves, but he nonetheless chose to fight for the South. Showing a capacity for leadership, he soon became a captain in the Caldwell Minutemen in 1861. David was captured by the federal militia when he returned home on a recruiting mission. His fifteen-year-old daughter Sally visited him in prison,[3] and she tried to convince Captain Isaac Newton Hemry, his custodian and fellow Missourian, to let him go. In the process, Sally and Isaac fell in love. Despite her father's disapproval, they married. When asked why he allowed it, David explained, "I know when I'm whipped."[4]

David's youngest son, Llewellyn Thompson Sr.,[5] was named after a fellow Confederate soldier who died fighting beside David. Llewellyn Sr. resembled his father—the same receding hairline, long nose, high forehead, and determined look. Although not bearded, he sported a hefty mustache for most of his life. Llewellyn Thompson Sr. heard the "call" and became a "hardshell Baptist" minister, probably early on in his life. This strain of Baptists was more relaxed in terms of ritual but rigid in their interpretation of the Bible. They owned no church; their ministers preached in the open air or in borrowed buildings. Thompson Sr. traveled and preached. By the time he was thirty-three, he had already acquired a reputation as a minister. His travels took him to Volga, West Virginia, where he met the woman who became his wife, Lula Lorena Butcher.

The Butcher side of the family was more difficult to track down genealogically. Lula's father, Eli Esceridge Butcher, was a Confederate. Captured twice by Union soldiers, he somehow managed to talk his way out of imprisonment. He was a kind, courtly gentleman—a saddlemaker, not a fighter. While Llewellyn Thompson Jr. shared a name and a physical resemblance with his father, many who knew them thought that, in character, he was more like his grandfather, Eli Butcher. For instance, on one Memorial Day celebration, the main speaker asked if there were any Civil War veterans in the audience. Eli and a man named Troup, a Union veteran, came to the front. Eli greeted Troup cordially, and "people in the audience knew that they were witnessing a very fine end of a difference of opinion."[6]

As fate would have it, Eli Butcher was also a member of the hardshell Baptist church. One day he took his two daughters to hear this new itinerant preacher. It must have been quite a sermon, because Llewellyn Sr. and Lula married a few days later. Shortly after their marriage, the couple joined a wagon train and retraced the steps of Kit Carson down the Santa Fe Trail from Missouri to Trinidad, Colorado. Llewellyn Sr. homesteaded a sheep ranch near there, in partnership with Judge Julius Caldeen Gunter, later governor of Colorado.

Lula, in exchange for consenting to an expedited marriage, insisted that her older sister, later known as Aunt Jenny, move in with them.[7] So, a year later, Eli Butcher, by then a widower, made the trip west with his eldest daughter to join Llewellyn Sr. and Lula on their ranch in Colorado. Nine months after the couple's marriage, their oldest son Eldridge arrived. Lula was pregnant with their second son, MWood,[8] when Llewellyn Sr. sold his share of the ranch and moved 100 miles east to Las Animas, Colorado, in 1899, to set up a small farm on his own. One day a Basque sheepherder from France, Mike Nalda, came looking for work. He could barely speak English, but Nalda and Llewellyn Sr. formed a lasting partnership.

Llewellyn Sr. and Nalda began to piece together parcels of land for a sheep and cattle ranch in Lincoln County, New Mexico, where land was cheap. Memories of the Lincoln County range wars, which culminated with Sheriff Pat Garrett shooting Billy the Kid in 1881, were still fresh in that rough and wild place, and there was no love lost between the cattlemen and the sheepherders. Despite this, Nalda and Llewellyn Sr. eventually accumulated 163 sections of remote and rugged land, mostly covered in blue grama and buffalo-grass, crisscrossed with arroyos that formed easily in the tough-looking but extremely fragile landscape.[9] A small ranch in those dry parts was meaningless, and working even a large one like theirs did not ensure success or income.[10] Their sprawling Diamond T ranch stretched from East Vaughn to a few miles northwest of Corona, the closest town to the ranch's headquarters. It's hard to imagine commuting from Las Animas, about 340 miles north by horse or carriage, the way Llewellyn Sr. did several times a year.

Las Animas in those days was hardly the "city of lost souls"—the original name bestowed on it by Conquistadores. Located along the Arkansas River, now it is a quiet town of well-acquainted neighbors, since no interstate highway passes near it, but then it was a hub on the mountain spur of the Santa Fe Trail and became a regional railhead for cattle and other goods. Llewellyn Sr. became a successful and respected member of the community. Besides ranching, he eventually started an insurance company and was president of the First National Bank of Las Animas. During the Great Depression, he had to double up as the bank's janitor, in order to make ends meet.

Lula, who did not want to live on the ranch, preferred to reside in a more important town like Las Animas. She soon covered her small mud-brick adobe home with clapboard, to make it easier to maintain and look more presentable. The house had a parlor, a dining room, three tiny bedrooms, a large kitchen with a bathtub behind the stove (the only source of heat), and, later, a small indoor lavatory. In the back there was a smokehouse, an arbor, a storage house with a canvas roof that they called the "tent house," and a sort of garage where Eli Butcher kept his bee business, the Virginia Butcher Apiaries.

Llewellyn E Thompson Jr. was born in Las Animas on August 24, 1904—the same year the railroad came to Corona. Thompson was called Wally in his youth, but he did not like that name and, as soon as he left Las Animas, he took on the nickname "Tommy." Three years after Llewellyn Jr., Gunter arrived, named after his father's former partner. Lastly, a girl, Mary Virginia, was born in 1909. All five children lived with their parents, together with Aunt Jenny and their maternal grandfather Eli, in the same small house. J. C. Penney Jr., Llewellyn's cousin, was a frequent visitor. Aunt Jenny taught school, organized the town library, and raised money for educational endeavors.[11] Lula cooked, but her sister Jenny was the one who directed the children's education and upbringing.

As a boy, Thompson built the town's first radio, from a mail-order kit. He raised rabbits in a hutch in back of the house, with his sister's help. It was his first attempt at running a business and keeping accounts. It was also his first disappointment, because, despite his meticulous accounting and planning, he was not able to find enough buyers. Soon he had more rabbits than he knew what to do with. At the Las Animas drug store, Thompson had his first experience with "love"—and, perhaps, diplomacy. Having saved some money from his rabbit business, he invited a girl he had a "hankering for" to have a soda. The girl ordered not only a soda but a large ice cream, which wiped out his savings. He could not afford to order anything himself and had to be content to sit opposite her and watch her gobble up his earnings.

From left to right, siblings Gunter, Mary Virginia, and Llewellyn Thompson Jr. in front of hutches for Llewellyn Jr.'s first business attempt, raising and selling rabbits, at their family's home in Las Animas, Colorado, circa 1925. Thompson Family Papers.

One summer, when the boys were working at the Diamond T ranch, Thompson, who was often ill, needed to have his tonsils removed. He was only nine when his father put him on the train at a rail stop on the ranch to make his way alone to the hospital in Trinidad, Colorado, 400 miles to the north. There he checked in, had his tonsils removed, and then took himself back to the ranch. In later years, when he was ill, he shocked his wife when he asked her to leave his bedside, because he did not want her to sit there and watch him suffer. Illness was something you faced alone.

If you sneeze when you drive into Corona, you will have passed through it by the time you open your eyes, but in those wide-open spaces, time and distance seem to acquire different qualities. Corona was vital to the surrounding ranches. It was a street of buildings lined up opposite the railroad tracks, and it has barely changed since those days. There is a post office, a general store, a guest house, and a drug store that, for a long time, housed the only telephone in the area.[12] Today, a paved road takes you from Corona to the entrance of the ranch, 28 miles away. From there to ranch headquarters, it is another eleven and a half miles, so you can imagine how long it must have taken on horseback, over a rugged track. When his daughter Sherry took up riding years later, Thompson told her he could not understand how someone could want to ride a horse just for fun.

The area surrounding Corona is slightly hilly, full of juniper and piñon pines. It has a cozy, protected feeling, but it soon flattens out completely—so flat that it is said you can see for another 100 miles if you stand on a tin can. Imagine being in the middle of the sea, but instead of blue waves you see clumps of green—sometimes almost blue—grass, mixed with browns and yellows, and it goes on forever. You might think you could just run or gallop through it, but you soon discover that the ground is hard and uneven, full of small plants with sharp points. Dispersed throughout are cholla cacti, with purple flowers sprouting at the end of their thin, prickly fingers—little soldiers to keep you on your guard. Even though flat, the land is actually high desert, at an altitude of 6,820 feet, making the clouds seem lower and the stars at night breathtakingly close. Most of the ranch is a place of stark beauty and utter desolation that attests to a person's vulnerability and keeps one's notion of self-importance within reasonable proportions.

One winter, Llewellyn Sr. was out riding the fenceline, carrying mending tools. He got caught in an unexpected whiteout snowstorm, far from headquarters, and became disoriented. Close to frozen and with no shelter anywhere in the vast, flat grassland, he eviscerated a cow and crawled inside the corpse to try to survive the night. The next morning, happy to be alive and even happier to find his horse still living, he climbed onto the saddle and passed out. Coming to, he found himself along a fenceline he recognized. The horse had found his way back home and saved Llewellyn Sr.'s life.

The house at headquarters, which had originally been built by Comancheros,[13] probably in the early 1900s, was a low, lime-plastered, Hispanic-style structure, with a columned porch that ran the length of the front of the house, giving it a stately air. It lay in the shadow of a tall, wood-paddled windmill that brought precious water to the place. A few big cottonwood trees helped shade the house, a long, low bunkhouse, and the barns and the sheep corral, all of which were constructed from unhewn logs and rocks, the latter painfully cleared by hand from the nearby fields. The graffiti drawn by a lonely itinerant cowboy is still visible on the stones of the old barn: "Ramon" and "1917" appear near a crude sketch of a girl in pigtails.

Mike Nalda managed the ranch and made it successful, gaining a reputation among the locals for his uncanny understanding of sheep. The Naldas lived in the headquarters house, and Llewellyn Sr. stayed with them when he visited from Las Animas to keep an eye on things. When the boys came, they were relegated

Llewellyn Thompson Jr. (*far left*) and ranch hands in front of the bunkhouse at his family's Diamond T ranch in New Mexico, circa 1925. Thompson Family Papers.

to the bunkhouse. It was here, among the taciturn ranch hands and cowboys, that Thompson first learned the fine art of playing poker, a skill that would serve him well in the Foreign Service. He also learned a little Spanish and French from the Basque cowboys. Together they mended fences, dug wells, sheared sheep, branded calves, hung jerky on the fence to dry, and drove livestock to the Corona railroad station. These experiences would later help him connect with Nikita Khrushchev, who grew up in the Ukraine, the son of peasant farmers.

As Llewellyn Sr. advanced in age, he decided to give half of the ranch to Mike Nalda, both in gratitude and as payment for his years of service through good and bad times.[14] He drew a line approximately in the middle of the map of the ranch, splitting it between the half that held the headquarters house and barn, and the half that had the most productive land and water, guessing that Nalda would take the house and forego the best land. And so he did. Nalda was happy with the arrangement and continued to run both his and Thompson's stock together, for a percentage of the profits.

As Nalda was aging, too, he brought his brother Pete from France to help. He wanted someone he could trust, who also had good livestock skills and was able to speak French. When asked why he never learned English after all those years in America, Mike replied that the sheep didn't speak English, either. In September 1945, Pete announced that he would go back to France. Mike, unable to run the entire ranch without Pete, informed the Thompsons that they would have to run their half themselves. The Thompson brothers and their father decided to sell the ranch, rather than force one of the boys, most likely MWood, to take it on. They sold their half of the ranch to Mr. T. T. Sanders from Roswell, New Mexico, on a handshake deal that called for installment payments. Their judgment of Sanders proved to be correct, and he ultimately paid off his debt in 1952.

Sanders persuaded Pete Nalda to stay on and run the ranch, with tragic consequences. Pete's young nephew, Gratien, was awakened in the night by a bandit brandishing a knife. Not finding any money in the house, Luis Campos and his accomplice, Valeriano Alaniz, made Nalda write out four checks at gunpoint. They then forced Pete and Gratien out into the night. Hearing one of the men say "this is the time to kill them," Pete took off running in one direction, and Gratien in the other. Gratien felt the bullets whizzing by and just kept running until he reached headquarters, telling Mike Nalda what had happened. Pete lay dead in the arroyo. The banditos went into town and tried to cash the checks at the local bank, where they were immediately apprehended. Alaniz was eventually hanged. Campos spent the rest of his life in jail in Texas.[15]

Ranching is an enterprise of boom or bust, and it seemed to be more bust in Thompson's childhood. He worked continuously from the age of twelve at odd jobs, including as a janitor, hardware store clerk, and ticket agent for the Santa Fe Railroad. Thompson's father did not give up on his preaching, continuing until his death in 1953. He would preach in someone's house, after which the host would serve an enormous Sunday lunch for everyone.[16] Apart from Sunday services, Thompson and his brothers participated in Bible readings every morning before breakfast and as the last thing at night, just before bedtime. Having had enough Bible reading as a boy to last him a lifetime, Thompson never went to

any church unless forced, and he was always reluctant to discuss his feelings on the subject of religion. His early upbringing, however, must have helped form the principles and morals that guided him throughout his life.

Llewellyn Thompson Jr.'s parents and siblings, circa 1925. *From left to right, seated*, Eldridge, Mary Virginia, Llewellyn Sr.; *standing*, Ruth, Llewellyn Jr., MWood, Gunter, and Lula. Thompson Family Papers.

Thompson's closest companion was the youngest of his siblings, his sister Mary Virginia. Both were musical. He played the violin and she the piano, and together they improvised tunes to the silent films at the local theater. Thompson and MWood were similar in character and were also very close. Each loved to fly fish, and they both had a quiet demeanor and easy sense of humor. Their eldest brother, Eldridge, was a high school football star, big both physically and in personality. He was a big talker, too. He moved to Texas, was the most financially successful of the brothers, and was never short on advice for anyone. Thompson's young daughters were fascinated by this gregarious Texan, so unlike their own father, and took to calling him "Big Shot." The youngest brother, Gunter, was the black sheep of the family. When he married Unarose, a Catholic, his father never quite forgave him.

For anyone living in large, hectic cities and looking at life in Las Animas and Corona through a telescope, it has a soothing, uncomplicated feel to it, but turning the telescope around and looking at Las Animas through the other end, from the point of view of someone who grew up there, it could easily have felt like the smallest, most abandoned corner of the planet. The possibility of being trapped there frightened Thompson, a young man with adventure in his heart. The University of Colorado, in Boulder, proved to be his opening to the world.

When Thompson Sr.'s boys graduated from Bent County High School, he gave them each $1,000 ($10,000 today) as a grubstake in life, and he did not dictate how it was to be spent. Three of the boys used it to go to college, but Gunter, in typical fashion, soon blew it all on "a car, girls, and loose living." In keeping with biblical tradition, Thompson Sr. took back his prodigal son and sent Gunter on to further his education, too.

Thompson Jr. followed his brother MWood into the Delta Tau Delta fraternity. Although Llewellyn was interested in science, he majored in economics, thinking he might go into business. He washed dishes and played a little poker to help pay his way through college, until he became manager of his fraternity chapter house and thus earned his room and board. He later claimed that he first learned about diplomacy and how to run an embassy during the summers, when he and a friend, Bill Plested, turned the place into a boarding house for rich girls escaping the Texas heat.

One vacation, Bill took Thompson home with him to work at his father's mining company near Trinidad. Bill's father worked the boys half to death, but this connection turned out to be a good investment on Thompson's part. He and Bill were later caught making bathtub beer in the basement of the fraternity house. Since this was during Prohibition, the boys were arrested and the incident written up in the *Denver Post*. Luckily, Bill's uncle was a well-connected lawyer and had the boys' records expunged, but the university suspended them for a semester.[17]

During that time, as penance and to get away from their fathers' disapproving looks, Thompson and Bill went to Seattle to work for a logging and lumber company. He corresponded with his sister, Mary Virginia, and sent her little presents. She kept him informed of her progress in school and all the gossip in Las Animas. On New Year's, Mary Virginia wrote, "I'm sorry you had to stop school because if any of us deserves an education, you do," and said how sad it was that Thompson and Bill had a lonely Christmas dinner in a Seattle hotel. She hoped that he would be able to come back and somehow graduate. He did come back in April, only to find her very ill. She died of consumption at the age of sixteen. It was a grievous experience. Thompson had lost his closest friend, and his mother, Lula, never quite recovered.

Bill and Thompson returned to the University of Colorado. They were not allowed to graduate with their class, however, and received their diplomas by mail in 1927.

2

Into the World

Integrity and good judgment make a good diplomatic
officer. But how does a young man develop good
judgment? Part of it is inherent, some comes from
education—but experience is the real proving ground
for good judgment.
—LLEWELLYN THOMPSON, *Family Weekly*,
   January 20, 1963

His time at the University of Colorado whetted Thompson's appetite for the world
beyond. After graduation, he thought he might get to see more of it by traveling
northwest and seeking employment in an import-export company in Seattle, but
he was rejected for lacking "foreign experience." Somewhat at a loss for what to do next, he
boarded a steamer and headed south to Los Angeles. In one of those mysterious coincidences, he sat next to a retired consul for the US Department of State.[1] In the ensuing conversation, Thompson expressed worry that he would end up in an office, as an accountant,
all his life. The consul suggested that if he wanted adventure and travel, he should join the
Foreign Service. Thompson took his advice. Armed with a reference from his father's ex-
partner, Judge Gunter, he headed for Washington, DC, saving money by staying in "Delt"
fraternity houses along the way. A recommendation from the Atchison, Topeka, and Santa
Fe Railway Company, where he had worked as a boy, got him temporary employment in
the Interior Department until he gained admission to the Foreign Service school at Georgetown University in Washington, DC, in order to prepare for the entrance exam.

A job at the accounting offices of Price Waterhouse supported him during his studies.
Thompson sat for the Foreign Service exams in spring 1928 and, contrary to the norm,
did better in the written section than the oral part.[2] He was one of only 34 out of 185
applicants to pass. It was lucky that he did, because the Great Depression was just months
away, and he would be the only member of his family to be employed when it hit. He
formally entered the Foreign Service in January 1929, and in September he took up his
first post as vice consul to Ceylon (now Sri Lanka). He was twenty-five years old. Charles
"Chip" Bohlen was another twenty-five-year-old who joined the Foreign Service that

year, but Thompson would not meet him for another ten years, establishing a friendship that would last for the rest of their lives.

Ceylon

Thompson was in Las Animas when the letter came telling him of the posting. Young and overconfident, one of the first things he did was to contest the $200-per-month compensation the State Department offered. Given the cost of living in Ceylon, he argued, his room and board alone would be well over half that amount. It was the first time, but not the last, when Thompson struggled to persuade the department to give him a reasonable subsidy. On this occasion, he succeeded in getting it raised by 10 percent.

His great adventure began when he boarded the SS *George Washington* in New York City, headed for the port of Cherbourg in France. A letter of introduction from Ruth B. Shipley, the State Department's chief of passports, to Norman Armour, in the American embassy in Paris, got him an invitation to lunch.[3] Shipley had asked Armour to cheer up the young man, because Ruth thought Armour, who had spent some time in Ceylon, was "the best the Service affords," and knew that poor Thompson would soon meet "the worst." She was referring to Thompson's boss-to-be, Ambassador Stillman Eells (pronounced "eels"), whose disagreeable name was coupled with an unsavory reputation. To buoy Thompson up, Armour shared his own good memories of his time in that country's capital, Colombo, and told him, "While it may be that 'all of nature pleases and only man is vile,' your future chief may not be as bad as he sounds."[4]

Thompson did not seem to be in a hurry to reach Ceylon, as it took him almost two months to arrive there. In France, he made his way from Paris to Marseilles, where he boarded a drab-looking liner, the *André Lebon*, in September 1929. Spewing black smoke from its twin stacks, this vessel took him through Italy's Straits of Messina, past the grumbling and burping Stromboli volcano. From there it stopped in Port Said, Egypt. Waiting for the ship to be cleared to go through the Suez Canal, Thompson had enough time to ride a camel, see the pyramids, and take photos. Once the ship arrived in India, he boarded a smaller schooner, appropriately called *The Chance*, and sailed into Colombo's harbor on September 23.

One of his first official duties was to present his credentials. He wore shoes shined to a mirror finish, striped trousers, a coat with tails, a vest, a striped tie, and a starched white shirt. He sent a photo of himself to his parents, obviously proud, but with the comment on the back that he hoped he didn't look "quite as goofy" as this picture made him out to be.

Ruth Shipley turned out to be right. Stillman Eells's only interest in life was slowly drinking himself to death and, as long as Thompson didn't bother him, all went well. Besides the consular paperwork, Thompson helped Americans who had run into problems in Ceylon. Shortly after his arrival, Thompson's interest in science paid off.[5] An American businessman had refused to pay an extortionate hotel bill for the bathtub he had ruined by taking a sulfur cure for a skin disease. His boat was about to leave, and the authorities would not release the luggage they had confiscated in lieu of payment. Thompson went to

Llewellyn Thompson Jr. in Colombo, Ceylon, circa 1930, during his first Foreign Service posting. Thompson Family Papers.

a pharmacy, bought some sodium borate, and in less than an hour had the bathtub shinier than ever. The distraught American caught his boat, and Stillman Eells pretty much let Thompson run the consulate after that.

In 1929, Ceylon was still a British colony, and it was a place of stark contrasts—rich tea planters and rubber barons alongside indentured Indian Tamil laborers. There was some self-government and a new constitution, but elected officials in the governmental assembly barely outnumbered official appointees, leaving the British still firmly in charge. Thompson would not forget this firsthand experience with colonialism. Thompson's life in Ceylon at first was like a nineteenth-century fairy tale—fancy women in silk dresses and Brits in pith helmets drinking cocktails on the large pillared verandas of the Galle Face Hotel. They played tennis and croquet at their clubs, wearing white suits or Bermuda shorts and knee-high socks. Thompson began filling his photo album with pictures of damsels and curious-looking expat characters out of a Graham Greene novel.

The strange local sights intrigued him most, and he made a list of the words and images he encountered, including women carrying large *chatties* (pots), working elephants, monkeys, snake charmers, and darting geckos. The famous Bo (Bodhi) tree, planted in 288 BC, and the majestic, dome-shaped rain trees seemed otherworldly. He was fascinated by the indigenous funerals. He watched catamarans navigating canals put in by the Dutch during their own colonial period in the seventeenth century. He lived in a large wooden house with slow-moving ceiling fans, all his needs attended to by native servants. They prepared spicy curries, which he loved. It was a complete change from Las Animas and thoroughly enjoyable, at first.

Eventually, the routine became monotonous. There was little Thompson could do to actually prove his worth to the State Department in this sleepy outpost. Although Mr. Eells gave him glowing evaluations, Thompson's reports were classified as "no rating," simply because there was nothing of substance to report. Now coping with the Great Depression, the department could not afford to transfer him, making Thompson despair that his career might end up like that of Mr. Eells. He put a good spin on those stagnating days by saying that running the consulate gave him a decision-making role far earlier than most of his contemporaries.[6] The long wait, however, would prove to be detrimental to his health. He developed excruciating stomach pains and soon had a hard time finding anything he could eat. He had developed stomach ulcers, which were so bad they bled. This condition remained with him throughout his life, and Thompson blamed the curries he had eaten with so much enthusiasm. He began losing both weight and the cheerful look he had arrived with. During those seemingly endless months of waiting, Thompson worked on his French, looked into astrology, and began exploring Buddhism, a totally new religious perspective for him. He filled numerous journals with annotations on his discoveries and received counsel from an American *bhikkhu* named John Silva, who gave him affirmations and meditations and advised him to "eat cooling foods during the hot spell."[7]

Eells finally managed to get out of Ceylon, and his replacement took pity on Thompson, recommending the young vice consul be transferred to a post with a more temperate climate. Reassigned to Geneva, Switzerland, in March, he boarded another dreary-looking boat (the SS *President Adams*) in Bombay, India. In September 1933, Thompson was finally able to get home leave, the first in four years. He brought back a set of ebony elephants as a present for his parents, which Lula proudly displayed in her parlor.

Geneva

Ceylon gave Thompson practical experience, and Geneva helped forge his political awareness. Two of the most important ideologies of the century—Fascism and Communism—were on the rise. Franklin D. Roosevelt (FDR) had just been elected for his first term as president. Thompson's new posting occurred right after Hitler was named chancellor of Germany and just before the United States recognized Stalin's nascent Soviet state. Geneva was the seat of the League of Nations, established as part of the peace treaty that ended World War I. The League's purpose was to prevent wars, assure collective security, and arbitrate international disputes. The ideas were noble, but their implementation was impossible.[8] America had never ratified the Treaty of Versailles and was not an official member of the League, despite Woodrow Wilson's passionate support for both. Nonetheless, the United States kept a close watch on the League's activities.

Thompson's new boss, Consul Prentiss B. Gilbert, influenced his career more than any other person.[9] Gilbert had gained a reputation for imperiousness, with some calling him "consul-general." Along with other young Foreign Service officers, such as Jacob Beam and

—CHAQUE SOLDAT DE MON ARMÉE PORTE LE BATON DE MARÉCHAL DANS SA GIBERNE !

EVERETT   BIGELOW   RIDDLEBERGER   THOMPSON   BEAM   LAWTON   GILBERT

James Riddleberger, Thompson benefited greatly from Gilbert's "school for ambassadors." Part of the training included a weekly Saturday night poker game, where the consul "hectored them on every draw and bid with a kind of gleeful sadism."[10] Gilbert mercilessly forced his protégés to rewrite reports over and over, until he

"Gilbert's School for Ambassadors," cartoon by Derso et Kelen, 1935. Copy in Thompson Family Papers.

was satisfied it was impossible for anyone in Washington, DC, to misconstrue their meaning. Under Gilbert, Thompson embraced a "light touch" in foreign policy, where the United States would "prod but not dictate."[11]

Sooner or later everyone who was anyone—prime ministers, ambassadors, financiers—came through Geneva to transact business.[12] The politics, the activity, and the mountains and cool air were all welcome changes for Thompson. Despite the better climate and food, his stomach pains continued. As "health" was one of the criteria in efficiency reports that determined the trajectory of one's career, he never mentioned his ulcer attacks. Gilbert's first impressions of Thompson were disappointing, but he revised his opinion when he discovered that Thompson's occasional lack of energy and taciturn character were the results of terrible pain. Gilbert was amazed that Thompson had shown such fortitude without complaint.[13]

Switzerland did not eliminate Thompson's ulcer entirely, but it did improve his general spirits as he enjoyed the thriving nightlife of Geneva. The city exposed Thompson to the cosmopolitan and educated society of Europe, as well as to its rich culture. He absorbed everything like a sponge and soon had little trouble fitting in with the international set. In summers he frequented the Lake Geneva beaches, and in winters he climbed the Swiss slopes "with the élan of a mountain goat and skied down with grace and wild abandon. All these pursuits gave Thompson the reputation of a ladies' man (which he well deserved) and of a playboy (which he did not)."[14]

Gilbert soon observed that the people Thompson dealt with valued his tact and seriousness. Gilbert assiduously took to polishing his diamond in the rough and gave him increasingly more-responsible duties. Thompson responded well to Gilbert's severe tutoring, and in less than a year, Gilbert switched Thompson and Riddleberger, giving Thompson the more challenging work of reporting on the League of Nations and assigning Riddleberger to regular consular tasks. In 1936, Gilbert selected Thompson to represent the United States at the International Labour Organization (ILO), an agency of the League. It was set up to promote social justice, fair wages, and humane working conditions, but the ILO would prove as ineffectual at this as the League was at maintaining peace.

The first woman appointed to a US cabinet position, Frances Perkins, secretary of labor under FDR, had finally "shepherded" the United States into the ILO.[15] It was one of the very few international organizations America participated in during the 1930s, since, after the Depression, the United States was more interested in domestic social programs and public works. The League's director general wrote that Thompson,[16] "as the first officer of the United States Mission in Geneva who was assigned responsibility for discussing [the many difficult questions that faced the ILO during that period,] made an outstanding contribution to their solution . . . and served the cause of international understanding."[17]

Over the three-year period when he was there, Thompson's work at the League changed from being primarily procedural and academic to becoming more political. He impressed Gilbert and his fellow delegates by handling ILO issues with "shrewdness and tact."[18] As a result, his efficiency reports steadily improved. But Gilbert inexplicably added unhelpful caveats to these reports, which impeded Thompson's progress. While Gilbert wrote that the quality of Thompson's drafting of reports was "most notable" for its improvement, he also often made references to the latter's delicate health.[19] Feeling stuck in Geneva and unaware of Gilbert's unhelpful evaluations, Thompson assumed he lacked the necessary "old boy" connections to get ahead. He embarked on a campaign to boost his career, seeking recommendations from businessmen, academics, and government officials.[20]

Thompson's letter-writing campaign eventually paid off, resulting in his promotion to consul in 1937. Even Gilbert, just before being transferred to Germany, managed to give Thompson an unqualified "excellent" on his last efficiency report.[21] Howard Bucknell, Thompson's new boss in Geneva, recognized Thompson's skills and sent him to ILO conferences in Prague and London, but Thompson began to fear he might become typecast as an expert in labor relations or economic matters. Fortunately, more letters and Bucknell's praiseworthy reports finally got him assigned to Washington, DC, at the end of 1938, after ten years of serving abroad.[22]

3 ≋

To Moscow

In Russia, everything is true except the facts.
—A. T. CHOLERTON, *London News-Telegraph*
   correspondent, 1930s

After a short visit with his family, Thompson arrived at the State Department's Office of European Affairs (EUR) in January 1939 and was promoted three months later.[1] He was happy to be working with James C. Dunn, who had written one of the letters to get him out of Geneva. Heading the League of Nations desk at EUR, Thompson could sense his career finally gaining momentum. He settled into a comfortable apartment on Sixteenth Street in Washington, DC. It had an enormous fireplace and high ceilings, and it was just across the hall from his friend Jacob Beam.[2]

In Europe, Hitler had taken over Austria and the Sudetenland.[3] In August 1939, Hitler signed a nonaggression pact with the Soviets, in order for the two of them to divide Poland, unleashing a terrible force on the world. Britain declared war on Germany on September 3. The League of Nations expelled the Soviet Union over its invasion of Finland in November 1939.[4] Shortly thereafter, the State Department sent Thompson to the Army War College for special training. He was one of four officers who made up the first group from the State Department to attend the War College's Strategic Studies program.[5] He wrote home that he had a new duty, but his brothers concluded that it must be secret, because he demurred from telling his family anything about it.[6] The intensive course covered politics and foreign policy through the lens of both historic and current conflicts.[7] Not only did Thompson get a broader and different perspective on world affairs from the one he got internally at the State Department, but he also recognized that the Strategic Studies program helped to bridge a divide, and lack of respect, between the army and the department.[8]

Robert F. Kelley, a staunch anti-Bolshevik and head of the Eastern European Division of EUR, ran the State Department's program to train Soviet experts. Thompson's friend Edward Page was a product of this program, as were future friends and colleagues George Kennan and Charles Bohlen, all of whom were already on site in Moscow under Ambassador William C. Bullitt. Although not a Kelley boy, Loy Henderson was also in Moscow at that time. Thompson had arrived at the State Department too late to be included in this group, making another difference between his training and that of the other "Kremlinologists." FDR wanted to develop a relationship with Moscow, so he abolished the anti–Soviet leaning Eastern European Division in 1935, and with it went Kelley.

The early years, after the United States opened its embassy in Soviet Moscow in 1933, had been "immensely exciting."[9] Stalin allowed the new American diplomats access to Kremlin officials, Soviet citizens, and cultural luminaries. "This embassy," Bohlen enthused, "is like no other embassy in the world." These were the outrageous days portrayed in the party scene of Mikhail Bulgakov's novel, *The Master and Margarita*. Ambassador Bullitt ordered Charles Thayer to teach the Red Army to play polo, and the entire embassy staff taught them baseball. Kennan remembered those years as the "high point of his life . . . in comradeship, in gaiety, in intensity of experience."

The period from 1936 to 1938, however, saw a complete reversal. The Stalin purges effectively stopped all contact between Americans and Soviets until those restrictions eased when the two sides became allies during World War II. The greatest period of terror, or *Yezhovshchina*,[10] would color every aspect of Soviet life and hang like a maleficent mist over the country for most of the twentieth century. It affected people's behavior toward each other and forced them to become participants in a collective paranoia that was impossible to shake off. This atmosphere sealed the Soviet experts' disillusionment with Stalin.[11] The 20 million deaths during his regime were profoundly terrible and certainly affected the way the diplomats regarded Stalin.[12]

Despite the evidence, many influential people would still not grasp its horror. Unlike Ambassador Bullitt, Joseph Davies, his successor, never strayed from his support of Stalin's regime. He wrote *Mission to Moscow*, a book defending Stalin and the purge trials, whose victims Davies believed were truly traitors. Yet these events were abhorrent to anyone who was there and could see for themselves what was happening. Bohlen, who had returned to Moscow under Davies, recalled witnessing the 1938 Bukharin show trial, where the judge read out sentences for the eighteen defendants—"to be shot, to be shot, to be shot, . . ."—and later wrote, "By the time of the last 'to be shot' I felt that the top of my head was coming off."[13] Bohlen's brother-in-law, Charles Thayer, even claimed that being transferred to Nazi Germany in 1938 was, at first, a welcome change from the horrors of Moscow. The experience confirmed Kennan's belief that the Soviet system was completely untrustworthy. As he would later put it in his "Long Telegram," ideology was reduced to "the fig leaf of [the Soviets'] moral and intellectual respectability."[14]

As the Kremlinologists left Moscow one by one, the State Department needed replacements and selected Thompson, although he spoke no Russian.[15] Keen to do political work, he was single, available, and eager to travel. Thompson started on his round of farewell parties in Washington, DC, as well as making a shopping trip to New York City to buy "supplies." On the advice of his friends, he bought a set of kitchen utensils and a uniform and shoes for his prospective Russian maid.[16] He would later wish his luggage had instead been filled with woolens for himself. At one farewell party, he was presented with various poems from female well-wishers:

From Omsk to Kiev, just wait and see if
The Soviet girls don't go frantic. . . .
With women he beats the Red Army;
So our hearts belong to Tommy.[17]

Another one went:

Oh, there is no joy in Washington since Thompson went away. . . .
But Moscow called, and Steinhardt too. He saw where Duty lay.
So Thompson went to Russia, even though it's far away.[18]

Getting to Moscow

Moscow was indeed far away, and traveling there was no easy task. To avoid the war zones in Europe, Thompson sailed across the Pacific to Vladivostok, in the Soviet Union. He took advantage of his westward route from Washington, DC, to stop over at Averell Harriman's Sun Valley resort in Idaho for a bit of skiing, and then head to Las Animas to see his family.[19] He sailed from San Francisco on the SS *President Cleveland* and was supposed to travel via Harbin, China, but that area was under quarantine, so he went through Japan.

He arrived in Vladivostok, "Ruler of the East," in January 1941, just as FDR was being sworn in for his third term as president. This city is a protected port in southeastern Siberia. Although its mountain backdrop and sea views make it quite beautiful in the warmer months, it was cold, foggy, and miserable in the dead of winter. As one naval officer colorfully put it, "If one were called upon to give Mother Earth an enema, [this] would unquestionably be the appropriate spot."[20]

The war was not going well in Europe, leaving an air of uncertainty hovering over everything and adding to the general gloom. The State Department detained Thompson for a time in Japan, because they wanted to pass secret instructions on to Angus Ward, the American consul in Vladivostok, regarding Soviet relations with the Germans and the Japanese.[21] The department was concerned that Germany, the Soviet Union, and Japan would form a "Eurasian bloc," and they believed the Soviets were supplying the Germans via Vladivostok.[22] In addition to secret papers, Thompson was escorting a supply of various nonfreezing but highly critical items to Moscow: chocolate, liquor, tobacco, and toilet paper. He would have to cover roughly 6,000 miles and seven time zones in just over ten days on the Trans-Siberian railway.

The temperature dropped with every mile that separated the train from the coast. Passing the permafrost near Skovorodino, the temperature fell to more than −60°C, or −76°F. The train crossed the vast steppes, so barren and flat that it seemed as if the cars were moving in slow motion. The topography changed at Lake Baikal, which took a day to pass, with the cars traveling along cliff-hugging tracks above the huge, mountain-rimmed lake, the deepest in the world. The train went on, past beautiful wooden architecture in Irkutsk, and then to Novosibirsk, the administrative center of Siberia and a quintessentially Soviet city.

It would be here that, twenty years later, Thompson would have one of his more difficult meetings with Nikita Khrushchev.

The train broke down frequently, and at one point the cars were without heat for days, forcing the passengers to huddle, fully dressed, in their bunks in order not to freeze to death. Luckily the samovar in each carriage provided *kipitok*, or boiling water, for tea. Thompson had time to observe Russians closely and, when it was warm enough to expose his hands, he worked at learning the Cyrillic alphabet. On the rare occasions when the train had a functioning dining car, it served greasy soups and cloudy, orange-colored beer. Thompson participated in the typically Russian custom of sharing food with others in the compartment, until boredom and vodka would induce some of the passengers to sing and play the balalaika.[23] He saw many of the different types and ethnicities that made up the vast Union of Soviet Socialist Republics (USSR), and he practiced his meager Russian.

Eleven days later, Thompson finally arrived at the Yaroslavsky railroad station in Moscow and made his way to the Mokhovaya, a severe-looking, five-story apartment building on a large square just across from the Kremlin. This building housed the American Chancellery offices and living quarters. It was snowing lightly, and bundled elderly women, or babushkas, in felt boots used twig brooms to endlessly sweep snow off the roads and sidewalks. The profound dullness of everything was powerful. Even the air smelled different. The type of fuel used by the trucks and the dampness of the snow added to it. Bathing facilities were not readily accessible to the average Russian, so people's body odors were strong too, occasionally masked by strawberry perfume. It was something to get used to.

Thompson arrived in 1941. He was to be second secretary, under Laurence Steinhardt, who had replaced Davies as ambassador. Bohlen had left the year prior to Thompson's arrival, and this was the first of many times Thompson would follow in Bohlen's footsteps. Thayer, a larger-than-life character, had returned to Moscow from Germany to be in charge of agricultural reporting, and he proved to be a great friend to Thompson. Thayer had a wicked sense of humor and the irreverent attitude toward life possessed by men who cheated death.[24] He had an extra helping of the adventurous streak shared by Thompson and most of the men who ended up in Moscow.

Like Bullitt and Davies before him, Ambassador Laurence Steinhardt was a complicated character, full of misspent energy. Moreover, his wife made the already difficult lives of his staff and their spouses wretched.[25] Thompson thought that her behavior warped the judgment of people in the embassy about the ambassador himself. The Soviets largely ignored Steinhardt. Stalin derided him as a coward for wanting to flee Moscow at the first sniff of war. On the other side of Steinhardt's ledger, in Thompson's opinion, was his relatively good grasp of the realities of Soviet policies.[26]

In Moscow, Thompson did what he had done in Colombo and in Geneva: he went outside the chancellery and began familiarizing himself with the "special political conditions" prevailing in the Soviet Union, trying to get to know as many people as he could. This was in contrast to the time period of Stalin's purges, when Americans had had no contact with ordinary Soviets. Thompson shared an apartment with another junior officer, Frederick Reinhardt. By now, they knew enough Russian so the two of them could go out and listen

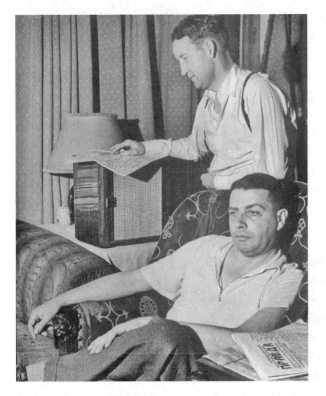

Llewellyn Thompson Jr. (*standing*), during his time as second secretary, and Charles Dickerson at Spaso House, the US ambassadorial residence in Moscow, USSR, 1941. Margaret Bourke-White, *Life* Picture Collection / Getty Images (50878022).

in the marketplace, in the restaurants, and on the Arbat to gather information.[27] Thompson observed that Russians would read the newspapers carefully for hints of the party line, in order to stay safe, so he diligently pored over all the newspapers and radio transcripts. As a result, he became the chancellery's chief political reporting officer.[28]

A couple of months after Thompson's arrival, FDR signed the Lend-Lease Act on March 11, 1941. The United States had not yet entered World War II, but it agreed to send over $50 billion in matériel and supplies to those countries actively fighting the Germans. The Soviet Union would not participate in this aid until the Germans betrayed and attacked them. In August 1941, Roosevelt and Winston Churchill drew up the Atlantic Charter, a joint declaration of Allied goals for the war. The main thrust of the charter was to ensure "self-determination" for all nations, allow no seizure of territory, and ensure that any territorial disputes would be postponed until the warring countries reached the peace table. All other considerations would have to defer to the principal objective of the war, the defeat of Germany.[29] The charter was later signed by all the Allies—including the Soviets, once Germany attacked them. Nonetheless, the Atlantic Charter would prove to be a high-minded but virtually powerless document.

There were warnings that the Germans would turn on the Soviets, and, though Stalin did not heed them, Ambassador Steinhardt did. He became obsessed with the idea that Germany would strike Moscow at any moment. Steinhardt cabled the State Department in March and stated that he was putting evacuation plans into effect. He had a makeshift bomb shelter built in the basement of his residence and had his officers take a stockpile of food, tents, medicine, and booze to the newly acquired ambassadorial dacha near Tara-sovka, about 20 miles away. Thus the Americans "enjoyed the exhilaration of roughing it in the gentle Russian spring countryside."[30] Then he planned for a more drastic evacuation to Kazan, on the Volga River.[31] He had boxes of food and drink hidden among the crates containing embassy archives and put Thayer and Assistant Military Attaché Joseph Michela in charge of their delivery to Kazan. To the amazement of Muscovites at the train station, and to the Americans' embarrassment, one of the "archive" boxes fell on the platform and began oozing brandy.[32] The rest of the less important embassy files were left in Moscow, which would later prove to be a tragic decision. Hitler attacked the USSR in summer 1941, and German forces descended on Moscow that December.

The Germans Attack

On June 22, 1941, as the last snows were turning to mud, the Germans initiated Operation Barbarossa and attacked the Soviet Union. At first, an incredulous Stalin ordered his troops not to shoot back, although he did evacuate Lenin's body to Siberia for safekeeping.[33] By June 28, the Germans captured Minsk. In response, Stalin made the horrific call for a scorched-earth policy to burn crops and destroy anything that could conceivably be used by the advancing German army. This decimated the basic staples that the Russians would need that winter. In the villages, peasants were reduced to shooting crows for food.[34]

In Moscow, the people prepared for war. They didn't just fortify defenses and camouflage their troops. They also booby-trapped some of the buildings and, perhaps expressing a Potemkin flair, camouflaged the entire city.[35] Their efforts were a tour de force, practically turning the entire place into a stage set: "The wall of the Kremlin had been painted to look like a whole series of different buildings. . . . Lenin's Tomb was completely covered with an imitation dwelling house. Blank walls had windows painted on them and in other places windows were painted over."[36]

Now that the Soviets were fighting the Germans, FDR wanted to make sure Stalin didn't change his mind. Roosevelt was eager to show him how advantageous it was to align with the Allies, so he sent his adviser, Harry Hopkins, to make arrangements for a Lend-Lease supply mission to Moscow. W. Averell Harriman, a rich, ambitious protégé of Mrs. Eleanor Roosevelt, had gotten himself appointed the US Lend-Lease representative in London, and he attached himself to the Hopkins mission. Harriman and Lord Beaverbrook, the British supply minister, descended on Moscow in September 1941 for what was to become known as the First Moscow Conference.[37] Chief of Naval Operations William H. Standley, who would later become Ambassador Steinhardt's successor, was included in the group.

Thompson, part of the welcoming party, watched in horror as Soviet antiaircraft guns fired by mistake at the B-24 bombers carrying the delegation.[38] Everyone breathed a sigh of relief as the two slightly shaken VIPs emerged from the plane to an honor guard reception. Their arrival reflected the hot and cold atmosphere of the entire conference. The delegation proceeded to their hotel, where they feasted on "caviar, cold fish, roast beef, and some kind of Jell-O business and cake for dessert," after which they were to call at the ambassador's residence, Spaso House.[39]

Steinhardt opposed giving generous aid to the Soviets. He believed that the Red Army would collapse and precious US matériel would end up in German hands.[40] Hopkins had warned Harriman about Steinhardt's opposition and told him the Soviet leadership did not respect Steinhardt. So Harriman and Beaverbrook decided that they would meet with Stalin alone. Stalin was open and charming in their first meeting, candidly describing the military situation and expressing his appreciation of their nations' assistance. In the next meeting he was petulant, complaining that "the paucity of your offers clearly shows that you want to see the Soviet Union defeated." In the third meeting, Harriman, on FDR's instructions, asked Stalin to promise to allow freedom of worship, so Roosevelt would not lose the Catholic vote. Stalin refused. The meeting then became less formal and more convivial. Perhaps buoyed by the prospect of a successful outcome, Beaverbrook took it upon himself to suggest that Stalin invite Churchill to Moscow. As the evening wore on, Harriman and Stalin exchanged rather nasty comments about each other's respective envoys, Stalin being particularly hard on Steinhardt.[41] In his briefing to FDR after the trip, Harriman reported that Steinhardt's usefulness in Moscow might have ended, which led to Steinhardt's resignation. Harriman was kinder to the embassy staff and singled out Thayer and Thompson for particular praise.[42]

The Beaverbrook mission had effectively left the embassy out of the whole conference. Privately, Thompson thought they were missing a rare opportunity to advance American interests by not asking for any quid pro quo for Lend-Lease aid. The Lend-Lease operations they had just negotiated were to be overseen by Colonel Philip Faymonville, assigned to head the US supply office in Moscow and organize the station in Vladivostok, where half the supplies would be shipped. He was unabashedly pro-Soviet and almost universally disliked by the Americans in Moscow. Faymonville pitted himself and the Lend-Lease office against the ambassador, the embassy, and the military, but most especially against Joseph Michela, the military attaché, whose pleas for information and access would not move Faymonville one iota.

4

The Siege of Moscow

When a Russian woman was asked if Communism was
worth all this sacrifice, she replied: "Whether or not one likes
Communism, the fact remains that for over twenty years we have
fought, bled, hungered, and died for it. Having paid such a price,
we are now damned if we'll let anyone take it away from us."
—ALICE MOATS, *Blind Date with Mars*

The State Department struggled under FDR, who left his secretary of state and his
ambassadors in the dark, preferring instead to use personal envoys like Harry Hopkins and Averell Harriman when dealing with the Soviets.[1] The Moscow embassy
suffered because of this. Both Roosevelt and Stalin ignored the first ambassadors under whom
Thompson served in Moscow. Stalin was only interested in talking to the people responsible
for the cornucopia of Lend-Lease aid, which was overseen by Colonel Philip Faymonville.

FDR's marching orders to Faymonville were clear: keep the Soviets in the fight and give
them what they want. The embassy's military attaché was infuriated, because Faymonville
refused to use his leverage to ask the Soviets for military information or access to the front.
Thompson knew this was not an idle issue. The Americans wanted feedback on how some of
their newer tanks and other Lend-Lease equipment worked in actual battle. They also wanted
a look at captured German equipment, and they wanted information on German battle tactics, all of which could make a material difference for Allied troops in Europe.

If the embassy did get any information, it was outdated by the time its cables reached
Washington, DC, making the Moscow mission even less influential. The embassy's sense of
isolation and irrelevance only got worse after it was evacuated to Kuybyshev. This same period would add to Thompson's experience and career, however, since he stayed in Moscow.

Evacuation

The Germans began their offensive against Moscow with heavy bombing raids. They shelled
the city with improvised bombs made of explosives in concrete casings, designed to save
metal and cause as many civilian casualties as possible. In one of the first raids, a bomb fell
in Mokhovaya Street, halfway between the Kremlin and the American embassy. It merci-

fully harmed no one, but it left a large crater—a message that no one was exempt. The raids turned into a siege, with the Germans pounding the Soviet capital nightly, while the Soviets fought back, bringing down 10 percent of the German aircraft. This defense was so effective that the bombers began to come less frequently, but they still continued.

By October, the German army had penetrated the Soviet lines and started toward Moscow, making evacuation a reality. Thompson distributed first aid kits, offered typhus and tetanus shots to the American community, and then shared a magnificent last meal with the embassy's staff and correspondents at the National Hotel.[2] They heard the thud of a bomb hitting far away, or so they thought. When they left the hotel, they saw that a huge, 2,000-pound dud had fallen just outside. If it had exploded, none of them would have finished their lunch.[3]

The next day, Foreign Minister Vyacheslav Molotov summoned the British and American ambassadors and informed them that the foreign colony was to join the Soviet government's evacuation to Kuybyshev (not Kazan, where the US ambassador had originally planned to flee when he had preempted the official evacuation), although Stalin and Molotov would remain in Moscow.[4] Thompson volunteered to stay behind, to take care of US interests and those of Britain and other Allies.[5] His friend, Third Secretary Frederick Reinhardt, also stayed to help him. On October 15, Thompson called the American press corps together to tell them that they would be evacuated by train that night, along with American embassy and military staff, including the Lend-Lease office.[6]

Sleet had turned to fat flakes of snow as the caravan of cars crept out of Spaso House toward the railroad station, their headlights dimmed for the blackout. The darkness was pierced by an occasional flash from trolley cars, packed mostly with bundled-up women carrying shovels to dig antitank trenches on the outskirts of the city.[7] The scene at the station was not one of panic, but it was still a confusion of anxious would-be refugees, punctuated by the din of antiaircraft guns and intermittent bombers overhead. Thompson checked off the passengers, in order to be sure they, their food, and their luggage were all on the right train, which, amazingly, they were.[8] In addition to the American and other foreign diplomats, the train trailed a couple of cars loaded with prisoners for the gulag. They could barely make out the steeple of Kazan station through the gloom. It wasn't until 1:30 a.m. that the train, with its unlikely cargo, finally pulled out. Thompson and Reinhardt headed slowly back over the now snow-packed and silent streets for what would be a ten-month siege. It took the train five days to make the normally eighteen-hour trip to Kuybyshev.[9] The passengers ran out of food, resorting to an unseemly raid on the chicken coops of a small collective farm along the way.[10]

Thompson camped out in Spaso House. It was located on a square of the same name in the Arbat district, about half a mile from the embassy chancellery, and had been built by a textile industry magnate who became known as the "Morgan of Moscow," an ideal residence for the capitalist world's representative. Built in New Empire style, its two wings flanked a curved and columned center portico. It was anchored inside by an 82-foot-long, domed grand hall, surrounded by marble Ionic columns and balustrades on the balconies above, all overshadowed by an enormous crystal chandelier.[11] But this grand lady had seen better days.

A 1,000-pound bomb had blown out many of the windows in a structure that already had a leaky roof and intermittently functioning plumbing, heating, and electricity.[12]

"Black snow" fell from the chimneys of government buildings, where functionaries were destroying papers, and from private buildings, where citizens were burning anything the invading Germans might use to identify them as Communist Party members.[13] Ordered to incinerate the embassy documents the ambassador had not sent to Kazan, Thompson spent his first day in charge of Spaso House stationed over his own bonfire. The American papers included confidential files of US citizens (and their families) who had relinquished their passports after being lured to the Soviet Union. Some came during the Great Depression, for jobs to help fulfill the Soviet Five-Year Plan. Others were drawn to the progressive state by an ideology that promised new beginnings. After seeing the reality of life under the Soviets, however, most tried to leave, making arduous journeys to the embassy in Kuybyshev to get their passports reinstated. Because their proof-of-citizenship papers had been burned with the other embassy files, those who didn't have alternate proof were turned away. Some ended up in the gulag, and a few were even executed. Thompson's future father-in-law had also toyed with the idea of going to the Soviet Union during those Depression years. He told his daughter that they might be going to a place where she could pursue her interest in ballet with the best teachers in the world.[14] Luckily, he changed his mind.

The city's water supply was one of the Germans' targets, so Thompson filled the bathtubs in Spaso House with water and made "ice cubes" by filling metal trash cans and putting them outside to freeze. A bomb went through both the roof and the back seat of an old Rolls Royce that Charles Thayer had acquired and left parked in the backyard as a last-ditch escape vehicle. Given the questionable plumbing, Thompson painted over the car windows, dug a pit below the bomb-hole in the seat, and created what had to be the most luxurious latrine ever.[15] Later, as the Germans added light incendiary bombs to their bigger explosives, everyone, including young boys, took to the roofs to grab the bombs and throw them down into the snow.[16] On more than one occasion during the siege, Thompson had to put out incendiary bombs that landed on the Spaso House roof.[17]

Thompson found it easier to engage with ordinary Russians during this shared crisis, and he practiced speaking their language with them whenever possible, including during a couple of nights in makeshift air raid shelters deep in the subway. At the height of the raids, 750,000 people slept in the metro stations. Thompson was in the habit of wearing a little enameled American flag pin on his lapel, which stimulated conversation. Some felt let down by the great Red Army, because the Germans had pushed it back close to Moscow. Others anticipated Russia's defeat and just wanted the bombing to stop, even reproaching Thompson for Lend-Lease's aid, thus prolonging the war. Despite this, it was clear that they hated the Germans even more than the Bolsheviks or the bombs.[18]

Usually, however, Thompson and Reinhardt took bravely to their beds during the nightly blackouts. These were so severe that Thompson recalled, "You couldn't even light a cigarette on the street for fear of being shot at by some eager guard."[19] It wasn't all blackouts and outhouses, though. Every Saturday afternoon, Thompson showed American films to whoever else was around. The Bolshoi Ballet had a reduced company that valiantly performed, over and over, the one ballet they were able to stage. Thompson claimed he saw *Swan Lake* 179 times, memorizing every step and note—and proved it years later to his aspiring-ballerina daughter, on whose behalf he suffered through yet many more *Swan Lakes*.[20]

One of the dancers was a friend of his, and more than a friend. Nina Borisovna was a slender reed of a woman, with pronounced cheekbones, a high forehead, and an angular face. Her large mouth smiled easily, and her delicate hands made flowing movements as she talked. She was no beauty, but Thompson liked her. She was serious and knowledge-able, and she made him feel at ease. They spent the better part of four years together. Nina belonged to an "extraordinary institution" (as Thayer called it), peculiar to Moscow. It was a group of mostly women who were allowed to associate with foreigners, in exchange for periodic reports to the secret police. They had the benefits of small luxuries, an active so-cial life, and uncensored information about events outside their borders. Most of them were ballerinas, actresses, or artists. This practice, which existed before the great purges, was reinstated as the regime became liberalized to maintain the war effort.

The foreign community formed a uniquely close group with the Russians they met. They shared each other's company, along with their sorrows and their pleasures. Thomp-son knew, of course, that Nina would have to report to the security police. Those were strange times, under the intense atmosphere of a terrible war, in a country that was wracked by the fear unleashed during the purges. Extreme misery and hardship alternated with exorbitant joy, in a way that is difficult for anyone to understand who has not lived under such circumstances.[21] The intensity of this experience stayed with Thompson throughout his life, and he spent his last days reminiscing about them. Nina and her friends in the corps de ballet helped Thompson meet other dancers, artists, musicians, and writers, giv-ing him a look at the often-suppressed but still vibrant cultural life in Moscow. Thompson gained valuable insights into how artists were controlled in the Soviet Union, as well as how internal Soviet bureaus operated. The contacts he made helped him to understand the potential and the importance of cultural diplomacy, which he would later champion.

Nina also put Thompson in touch with a high-ranking official in the Soviet military, who believed that keeping the Americans in the dark about what was happening on the front was detrimental to the war effort. He was able to pass on information to Thompson about which towns had fallen to the Germans and which had been retaken by the Red Army. His facts were confirmed as accurate by later official communiqués, and Thompson was thus able to provide military intelligence to the Americans long before the embassy in Kuybyshev did. This communications channel went both ways as, once its accuracy had been determined, Thompson was able to "try out and receive suggestions that could not have safely been made officially."[22]

Russians who fraternized with Westerners often paid for their relationships. Nina spent nine years in Siberia after the war, returning to Moscow only after Stalin died. When Thomp-son saw her again, years later, her time in exile was evident. Most of her teeth had been re-placed by steel ones and her hair had gone gray, but she was still buoyant, agile, and good company. She would become friends with Thompson's wife, Jane, and join their inner circle, with the unspoken understanding that she still had to report to the secret police.

Thompson may have been in a war zone, with his life in danger, but conditions in Kuybyshev were, in some ways, worse.[23] The weather was already freezing cold, and embassy personnel were isolated in a backwater town, crowded in temporary quarters, where the running water did not reach the second floor. Not doing much of anything, Ambassador Steinhardt gave up and departed after only a month, leaving the vice consul in charge.[24] Back in New York City, on December 1, Steinhardt answered a letter from MWood Thompson, assuring him that his brother was all right and that he'd found Thompson's health and spirits "satisfactory" when he had spoken to him last.[25] Coincidentally, on that same day in Moscow, Thompson wrote to the State Department that the Germans would either have to capture the city within the week or have to wait until spring. Exactly one week later, on December 7, 1941, Japan attacked Pearl Harbor and America was officially at war. The US mission to the USSR was headed by a thirty-seven-year-old second secretary in Moscow (Thompson), and only a vice consul in Kuybyshev. If the Germans were to take the city, these men would now be the enemy.

Moscow Saved

The Battle of Moscow lasted six months and covered a territory the size of France. More Soviet soldiers died in that battle alone than all the British, French, and Americans forces in World War II combined.[26] The Germans managed to get within six miles of the Kremlin before the Soviets—thanks in large part to reinforcements led by General Georgy Zhukov, and a with little help from the coldest winter in forty years—turned them back. It was the first time during the war that the Germans had been forced to retreat. Today, there is a haunting sculpture of three huge, rust-colored, steel tank stoppers to mark that spot. It is sobering to see just how close they came to taking the city. The people of Moscow were jubilant. Their beloved city was saved, even though it suffered staggering military losses and over a thousand civilians in the city had died.[27] Cyrus Sulzberger of the *New York Times* was the first Western correspondent to venture back from Kuybyshev that December. He described the German retreat as a trail of tanks and other vehicles that were abandoned when their fuel ran out, with burned houses and corpses left behind in the hurried march.[28] Meanwhile, the battles of Stalingrad and Leningrad raged on, and the Soviets would continue to fight bravely. Soviet losses in those cities climbed to over 2 million.

Government officials and the diplomatic corps remained in Kuybyshev as the Soviets mounted a counteroffensive. There was still no American ambassador in the USSR, and Stalin was in Moscow. Thompson, as the highest-ranking US official in Moscow, became the conduit for messages between FDR and Stalin. Thompson called it "a kind of post office job," but that treated the experience too lightly. It would make a difference later that Thompson actually conducted business face to face with the amber-eyed Stalin. He described Stalin as a man with "tremendous personal charm and understanding, but who viewed all moves by the capitalists with suspicion and mistrust."[29] As an example, FDR sent notice that the United States would have to ship forty locomotives that Stalin was expecting via an alternate sea route, because of intense German submarine attacks.[30] Stalin's interpreter translated the word "engine" with the words "prime mover." Thompson had a hard time convincing Stalin that the word meant "locomotive" and had to take personal responsibility for this assurance. As soon as he could, he wired Washington, DC, just to be "damn sure." It taught Thompson the role that nuances in language played in Soviet suspicions and paranoia, since "they expected every encounter to be some kind of maneuver and would not believe any conclusion drawn for them."

Thompson dealt more often with Molotov, the Soviet minister of foreign affairs. Molotov, whose nickname was "Mr. Nyet," was a rectangular block of a man, seemingly with no neck, as his scowling, round face appeared to rise from between his shoulders. He was relatively small, but he made up for it by exuding a kind of sinister power. Dealing with this man under these circumstances also proved to be useful to Thompson eventually.

After the battle for Moscow, life lightened up a bit. Although the government did not come back until the following year, the city had become relatively safe. The German armies were already in retreat when Anthony Eden, the British foreign secretary, secretly visited Stalin to form an Anglo-Soviet alliance and make sure that Stalin did not conclude a separate peace treaty with Hitler. Since Thompson oversaw British interests as well as American ones, he received the British leader and looked out for his safety and comfort. There was a food shortage for ordinary Russians, but foreigners received rations, and the embassy larder had an ample supply of canned goods.[31] Thompson, using some of these stores, laid out a table full of *zakuski* under the big chandelier.[32] Eden, quintessentially British—a tall, slender, impeccably dressed man with a trim military mustache—chatted easily with his military entourage and the handful of Americans who had come from Kuybyshev. Eden had made a tour of the front and was able to see what the war in the East was really like.[33] This rankled a bit, since no American was permitted to get close to it yet.

Thompson first learned what Eden and Molotov had discussed when he went to see a forthright Molotov at his Kremlin office—the British-Soviet war effort and postwar Europe. The Soviet government was the victim of aggression and wanted its frontiers, which had been defended with so much bloodshed, "reconstituted as they existed before the German invasion."[34] The next day, Eden corroborated Molotov's statements. Stalin was determined to retain the territory secured under his pact with Hitler and proposed two agreements: one on military cooperation, and the other, a Soviet-British treaty for the settlement of postwar Europe.[35] Eden told Thompson that Stalin implied an additional expansion to the west, but Eden assured Thompson that the British would not agree to any postwar reorganization without consulting the United States first.[36] It was unusual for an officer of Thompson's rank to be briefed by someone in Eden's position, and this only happened because the American was in Moscow, rather than in Kuybyshev.

A New Ambassador

Shortly after the German invasion, Stalin signed an agreement with Poland that allowed the release of tens of thousands of Polish prisoners from the gulags, in exchange for their promise to fight for the Soviets.[37] By 1942, when Stalin no longer wanted or needed them for cannon fodder, he signed another agreement, which marched them all out of the country to other Allied fronts.[38]

That year also saw many changes at the US embassy and in Thompson's daily life: pregnancy scandals, the departure of Reinhardt and Thayer, and the arrival of a new ambassador. In the winter, Reinhardt had to leave Moscow rather suddenly. His young Russian mistress became pregnant, and he decided to get her out. They were escorted from Moscow to the Iranian border by one of the military attachés, but their timing was bad and she gave birth on the Soviet side. This complicated matters, because the exit visa was for two individuals, not three. They had to wait in Baku until Loy Henderson, head of the EUR desk at that point, got permission for the baby to leave with them by withholding something the Soviets wanted.

The new ambassador, Rear Admiral William H. Standley, having witnessed the treatment of his predecessor during the First Moscow Conference in 1941, also found himself marginalized, despite his best efforts. He was hampered by an embassy spread out in two locations and by the widening divide between FDR's view of relations with the Soviets and his own. As a result, Roosevelt bypassed Standley, too, sending "personal emissaries" and all communiqués for Stalin through Thompson, who was in Moscow.[39] Thompson had to do a delicate dance to "avoid any impression on Standley's part that he was usurping his position in any way."[40] He made a special effort to keep the ambassador abreast of everything that was going on.[41]

A Cheshire cat of a man by the name of James McCargar arrived that spring, on his way to his post at the Lend-Lease office in Vladivostok. McCargar had an easygoing manner and a roundish face that was consumed by an infectious, enormous, snaggletoothed smile. Because of the conflict in the Pacific arena, he came by way of Trinidad, Brazil, Liberia, Nigeria, the Sudan, Egypt, Baghdad, Tehran, and Baku; by rail from Baku to Kuybyshev; and from there to Moscow, where he was supposed to board the Trans-Siberian Railway for Vladivostok. But he ended up staying in Spaso House for most of the summer.

Thompson's experiences were changing him. He was becoming more circumspect and less the carefree young man. McCargar observed that even in relaxed settings, like outings at the ambassadorial dacha, he could only get a "pleasant smile" out of Thompson: "He was never outspoken, always choosing his words carefully. Even when speaking offhandedly, his words carried weight."[42]

A House Divided

Although the US embassy was still in Kuybyshev, both the military and the naval attachés moved their offices back to Moscow that spring. It fell upon Thompson to feed, house, and entertain them, as well as to transmit their cables. The attachés were obliged to report through him, which they initially resented, since he was of considerably lower rank than they, putting him in the awkward position of having to defend his responsibilities. His Army War College experience proved to be useful in befriending them, and in the end they accepted the situation with better grace. More delicately, he was the liaison officer between them and Colonel Faymonville.[43] Faymonville had become a political and philosophical outcast among the embassy community. His attitude became a sort of proxy for the debate in the embassy about what the US policy toward the Soviet Union should be—that of unconditional friend or that of wary associate. Thompson, like others in the State Department who had served in Moscow, particularly Loy Henderson and George Kennan, worried about the postwar repercussions of the alliance. FDR and Hopkins, however, were focused on maintaining the Soviets' help in defeating Hitler. Bohlen, who was chief of Eastern European Affairs,[44] felt that the administration's "soupy and syrupy attitude toward the Soviet Union" came, in part, from a sort of collective guilt complex over Russia's immense human sacrifice and America's slow entry into the war.[45]

The Soviets continued to routinely deny any US embassy requests, as well as the embassy's access to top Soviet officials or information from the front, and Standley did nothing. He was ineffectual because he was circumvented by other representatives from the American government and, consequently, ignored by Stalin. In June 1942, Thompson's frustrations spilled over into a long personal letter to Standley, in which he encouraged the ambassador to pressure the Kremlin to deal with the embassy directly and stop going through Faymonville and the Lend-Lease office. He also mentioned a rumor he had heard—that the Allies were planning to open a second front, to relieve the pressure on the Soviets. Thompson said that if this were true, it could be used to entice cooperation from our "allies," the Soviets. The rumor was partly true, as Molotov had secretly been to Washington, DC, earlier that month and persuaded FDR to make a public statement implying he would open a second front, even though Roosevelt had no intention of doing so at that moment.

Early in July 1942, Ambassador Standley finally complained to Stalin about the lack of Soviet cooperation and asked that the Soviet government deal with the US embassy on everything except Lend-Lease business. Although Standley's request was completely ignored, the American embassy did see a distinct improvement in the attitude of Soviet officials, as well as some progress on the "protection cases." These were instances of American citizens, or their Russian families, who were being detained by the Soviets.[46] One of them was an American Communist named Isaiah Oggins, whom Thompson would meet later that year.

With the threat of a German occupation of Moscow clearly gone, Thompson moved out of Spaso House and into a walk-up apartment behind the Mokhovaya chancellery. The canteen remained in Spaso House, under Thompson's supervision, with the help of the two Chinese-Soviet housemen named Chin and Tung, affectionately referred to as "Chin and Tonic." Thompson pooled everyone's monthly ration tickets to purchase supplies at the Kremlin commissary. These consisted of three kilos each of fish (with caviar substituted when fish was not available), cabbage, and potatoes; four liters of vodka; and a more or less unlimited amount of wine. In summer they augmented this with vegetables from the dacha's garden. Thompson had occasionally bought extra food with money from his own pocket, since he'd only been given a stipend for the small number of diplomats in his charge, but now that more and more military personnel and VIPs were coming in, expecting to be fed, the expense became untenable. Thankfully, Standley helped him obtain an extra allotment for this purpose. The canteen was an important part of the mission's culture, where everyone from junior clerks to the ambassador, when he was in town, would participate in

Llewellyn Thompson Jr. (*sixth from right*), with other US embassy staff and military attachés, in front of the Kremlin, Moscow, USSR, 1940s. Thompson Family Papers.

animated, broad discussions that ranged from local gossip to international politics to the mysteries and frustrations of Soviet life.[47] Thompson later mused that his experience running a girls' boarding house back in Colorado helped him in figuring out the logistics of bedding down and feeding everyone, as well as controlling the rivalries.

Thompson also organized entertainment, in part to give the otherwise unoccupied military staff something to do besides going through their vodka allotment. They skied in the Lenin Hills and made a skating rink in the yard in the winter, they worked in the garden and played tennis in summer, and they threw parties. One memorable event was described as being "set up by that indefatigable entrepreneur and diplomat, Tommy Thompson." The star was a gypsy, reportedly married to a Soviet general. Lalya Chernaya (meaning "black") was "an appropriate nom de étage."[48] She was very dark, with flowing black hair and jet black eyes, and sang wild songs, "whirling about in flamboyant dances, castanets clacking, filling the great rotunda with reverberating sound. . . . Then there were stunts— Gypsy magic and tricks. After the performers departed, it was discovered that the medicine cabinets were bare of soap, toothbrush paste, and pills. Tommy's favorite bedroom slippers were missing, too, though not taken from his feet, although it was later said these worthies undoubtedly would have removed his sox without unlacing his shoes." Thompson's parties became so well known that even the normally dour and stony-faced Molotov managed to joke that there were only ten swans in the performance of *Swan Lake* that week, rumor having it that the American embassy had demanded a couple of large birds for some affair.[49]

The parties were a wholly useful and necessary function—that of pooling and checking intelligence on the developments, mood, temper, and direction of a country where normal sources did not exist. In such a society, sometimes unexpected, tiny clues fit in with other pieces of the jigsaw puzzle, producing a recognizable picture.

The Second Moscow Conference

In August 1942, Averell Harriman headed back to the USSR for the Second Moscow Conference, this time with Winston Churchill. Loy Henderson, who had previously served in Moscow under Bullitt, joined their convoy in Cairo, as part of his inspection tour of American embassies. The purpose of Harriman and Churchill's visit was to break the bad news to Stalin that there would be no second front at that time. One joke going around Moscow went: "Why don't all the clocks in the world keep the same time? Because in Moscow they all say 'Now' and in London they all say 'Not yet.'" Churchill, in a dreadful gaffe, made the V for victory sign on his arrival (which looked like the gesture for "two"), giving the Soviets a false moment of hope for a second front.[50]

The first meeting went better than expected. Churchill was brilliant at stoking Stalin's ego while persuading him that the Allied advances in Africa were the priority.[51] That meeting gave way to difficult ones, with Stalin being demanding and insulting. As expected, these led to a final, more pleasant, get-down-to-business meeting, followed by a lavish banquet in what had been the ballroom of Catherine the Great. At one point Stalin made a toast to intelligence officers, "whose work is important but who themselves remain unknown." The American naval attaché, Captain Jack Duncan, rose and responded: "I can answer that toast to intelligence officers, because I'm one of them. If we make mistakes, it is because we know only what you tell us—and that's not much."[52] Stalin roared with laughter and strode over to Duncan's seat to toast him, later walking out arm-in-arm with him. It's uncertain, however, if Churchill succeeded in mollifying Stalin during the conference. Meanwhile, Russians were dying in astonishing numbers while waiting for that second front.

Henderson, on his inspection tour, found the Kuybyshev embassy in disarray. There was no proper inventory of American possessions, and they didn't even have the most basic office supplies to organize the documents they had brought with them. Analysis was pointless, because it took three to five months for mail to get to Washington, DC. They could not find local employees to work in the office because, as Henderson wrote in a stunning example of understatement, "the fact that four out of five of the Soviet research workers who were employed by the Embassy prior to the purge of 1937 have been arrested and sent to prison or perhaps in certain instances executed without public trial . . . discourages other Soviet citizens from accepting employment of such a nature with the embassy." Henderson added that, because the US government bypassed the ambassador, it handicapped him in his dealings with Stalin and the Soviet government.[53]

Spy Alliance

As Henderson filed his inspection report from Kuybyshev, the head of the British intelligence office in the Soviet Union, under the pseudonym Colonel Alexander Hill, was hatching a plan to recruit Thompson as his American counterpart in Moscow. The British Foreign Office had been coordinating spying missions in Nazi-held Europe with the Soviet secret police agency, the OGPU (later known as the NKVD), and Hill thought they could improve on the arrangement by enlarging it to include the Americans. He knew Thompson socially, had introduced him to his chief Soviet contact, and recommended that Thompson be enlisted. Hill described Thompson as "alive and a real go-getter" and hoped that his appointment could preempt America's Office of Strategic Services (OSS) from sending someone who might not have "knowledge of Russia."[54] The OSS liked the general idea and followed up on it, keeping FDR fully informed. Thompson apparently was not drafted, however. A year later, the OSS appointed its own man to set up an office in Moscow, but the ship convoy he was on was sunk.

Late in 1943, General "Wild Bill" Donovan, head of the OSS, traveled to Moscow himself. He, Bohlen, and an American general met with top-ranking Soviet intelligence officers to talk about how to get both Soviet and American spies behind enemy lines. Concerned about the prospect of a Soviet station in Washington, DC, J. Edgar Hoover killed the idea of mutual offices the following March. Nevertheless, missions and conversations between the American and Soviet intelligence agencies continued until at least November 1944.[55]

More Visitors

Later in fall 1942, FDR sent another personal emissary, Wendell Willkie, to meet with Stalin.[56] FDR left Standley out of the meeting, and Willkie refused to brief the ambassador. Willkie's visit was the last straw. Standley returned to Washington, DC, to demand that all future communiqués go through him. Hopkins and Roosevelt seemed to accede to Standley's terms, promising to keep him informed and giving him a letter instructing Faymonville to report only to the "chief of mission." But, unbeknownst to Standley, they secretly told Faymonville to ignore these instructions.[57]

While Ambassador Standley was in Washington, DC, he asked Henderson to stay on as chargé d'affaires until Standley's return in January 1943. The working arrangement Thompson had successfully choreographed with Standley did not work with Henderson. The latter acknowledged that Thompson's duties during the siege of Moscow were greater than anticipated, but thought him presumptuous to offer information or advice, seeing it as a "tendency toward prima donna–ism." Henderson, who was staunchly anti-Bolshevik, wrote in Thompson's efficiency report that Thompson did not understand internal Soviet policies or the workings of the Soviet government as he should.[58] On the contrary, Thompson spent a great deal of time over the next two years studying, thinking, and writing about the internal workings of the Soviet system and then discussing it with the three men he would remain close most of his life: Averell Harriman, Charles Bohlen, and George Kennan. By the time it was Harriman's turn to write Thompson's efficiency report, it read, "Mr. Thompson has built up a sound knowledge of many aspects of Soviet life and the Soviet system."[59]

Early in December, General Patrick J. Hurley, former secretary of war under Herbert Hoover, stopped in Moscow on his way to China, hoping to extract an assurance from Stalin not to interfere in the conflict between Chiang Kai-shek's Nationalist Party and Mao Zedong's Chinese Communists.[60] Hurley, whose birthplace was listed as "Indian Territory, US,"[61] saw in Thompson a kindred spirit from the American West, and they became friends during the month that Stalin kept Hurley waiting for an audience. Hurley spent ten days of that time in Stalingrad, the only American to visit the front, where he reputedly let out an Indian war whoop as bullets whistled by and shells burst over the command post.[62] When he returned, he described to Thompson the remains of the horses and soldiers, frozen in "grotesque postures," in a battlefield that "formed a superb and ghastly picture of the horrors of war."[63] But the tide was beginning to turn in favor of the Soviets. As the Soviets pushed the Germans out of Stalingrad, Ambassador Standley returned and finally moved the remaining embassy personnel back to Moscow in January 1943.

The Face of the Gulag

The day of Hurley's return from the front, on December 8, 1942, Thompson and a colleague went on a mission to Butyrka Prison to see one of the "protection cases."[64] Isaiah Oggins was an American Communist and Soviet spy who was no longer considered trustworthy by the Soviets and was thus serving eight years in the gulag at Norilsk.[65] Standley insisted on access to him, so Oggins was brought from Siberia to be interviewed. Although it seemed at first as though he might be released, Oggins ended up just being a pawn in a terrible game.

It was one thing to hear or read about the gulag, and quite another to stare it in the face. Butyrka Prison had an infamous reputation, and many, once they entered through its doors, disappeared without a trace. The prison was filled with the terrible stench of fearful, beaten men, who were cramped in small spaces. The interview room was down several dark corridors. Oggins, who was near starvation, walked in with difficulty. What Thompson did not know was that Oggins had already been in Moscow for several months, getting medical treatment and being fed before seeing the State Department men. Sitting across the table from Oggins, Thompson sensed the desperation in the man and asked him if he wanted to obtain an American passport. Amazingly, the NKVD officer who was present did not object, and perhaps for the first time in four years, Oggins allowed himself hope. He said he could not survive in jail and asked the Americans to keep in touch with him. Thompson recommended to the US government that they try more assiduously to get Oggins back, but it turned out to be a futile gesture.[66]

At one point, Thompson permitted himself a moment of optimism, hoping that Stalin might ease his paranoia once his people had proven their loyalty in the battles of Moscow and Stalingrad, for "never had any people given their blood, sweat, and tears in such profusion," but by the time of his visit with Oggins, he doubted that Stalin would ever change.[67]

In May, the embassy was informed that Oggins would be shipped back to the gulag to serve the rest of his term.[68]

That same month, Joseph Davies arrived to entertain Stalin with a film produced from Davies's book, *Mission to Moscow*. He also carried a not-so-secret personal letter from FDR to Stalin, asking him to receive this emissary privately. Davies was to reassure Stalin that he would continue to get whatever he needed from Lend-Lease.[69] Stalin put on a glittering state dinner for Davies, which was written up in the American press. Stalin, "dressed in a smart light gray semi-military jacket and trousers and black boots, sat at the center of a long table as host at the dinner." Thompson sat with the military and Lend-Lease personnel and watched in horror as the film portrayed victims of the purge trials as guilty. Standley had to watch a parade of Soviet officials who had refused him an audience pass through Davies's guest house for "long and friendly" talks with the American author.[70]

Shortly after the Davies visit, Thompson was granted leave, which he took in London. McCargar, sent out of the USSR over a pregnancy scandal, was travelling with him. Thompson said to McCargar, "I thought you were married." McCargar replied that he was and recalled that Thompson, after a few moments' thought, and as though with a sigh, said, "You best be careful."[71] McCargar expressed his curiosity at Thompson's choice of London as a holiday destination in the middle of the war, but Thompson replied that he thought London was the "most exciting city in the world."

The Germans in Retreat

There are only two peoples now. Russia is still barbarous,
but it is great. The other young nation is America.
The future is there between these two great worlds.
Someday they will collide, and then we will see struggles
of which the past can give no idea.
—ALEXIS DE TOCQUEVILLE, *Democracy in America*

After his temporary break in London, Thompson returned to Moscow with Averell Harriman's delegation, to participate in a foreign ministers' conference on how to wind up the war.[1] It is worthwhile taking a close look at one of these journeys, because it helps to explain what travel was like in those days. Flying then was like taking a car trip today. There were frequent stops for refueling and for eating lunch and dinner, as well as occasional overnight stays in one or two places. Travelers entered into a kind of limbo that could last for days or even weeks.

Harriman and his entourage used a four-engine propeller plane that looked like a monstrous, shiny swallow. It flew at about 190 miles per hour, and at an altitude low enough for passengers to observe the scenery below in detail. When Thompson boarded the plane there were already ten passengers on it, including Harriman, his daughter, and Robert P. Meiklejohn, his faithful, diary-writing assistant. Much of the plane was taken up by Harriman's and his daughter's ample luggage—seventy-five pieces altogether.[2] Surf was breaking along the fifty-foot cliffs as they landed beside pastoral green fields on the northwest coast of Cornwall. They lunched at the Great Western Hotel, where they heard that Italy had declared war on Germany. After a walk and a fine lobster supper, Thompson and his fellow passengers reboarded their plane at 10:52 p.m. There was a full moon as the plane headed south toward Algiers, and it landed twelve and a half hours later, after a quick refueling stop in Morocco. Harriman and his daughter were whisked away to stay at General Eisenhower's villa; the lesser folk, including Thompson, lodged in town. They all had to wait for Secretary of State Cordell Hull and Treasury Secretary Henry Morgenthau to arrive before flying to Moscow together. Thompson spent some of the time walking through the winding streets of Algiers, passing sunken ships in the harbor and other vestiges of war all around. American and British military personnel and cars were everywhere, while trolleys ran alongside, with people hanging all over them.

The convoy set off the next evening. It consisted of Harriman's aircraft and two additional planes for Secretary Hull and his staff. They headed for Cairo, spent the night there, and left the following morning for Tehran, a six-hour flight. Tehran was also full of American trucks, as it was a staging area for US Lend-Lease supplies destined for the Soviets.[3] The mountains could be seen in the distance, embracing the city like big brown arms. The houses of the wealthy and the palaces had high walls around them, but inside they were full of lush gardens and flowers, whose perfume rose above the barriers and mingled with the smell of manure left by the horse-drawn *droshkies*. Along the sides of the street, water from the mountains ran through open ditches, called *jubes*, to the south, where it sank below the sands. Late at night, the sound of running water had a soothing effect. Thompson discovered that the inexplicable lines of holes in the ground they had seen as the plane landed were *quanats*, an underground water system of channels that convey water from aquifers in the highlands. He was fascinated by these waterworks, which reminded him of the intricate irrigation system of *acequias* brought to the high deserts of southern Colorado and New Mexico by the Spanish Moors.

The group flew off at seven a.m. the next day. The three metallic swallows made their way over the Caspian Sea, past the city of Baku, and on toward the Volga River. Once they had passed the Volga, Thompson explained that the extremely large farms below were the result of collectivization, and that the vegetable gardens the passengers noticed behind each little house consisted of the only land these farmers had of their own, which not only provided them with their own produce, but also vegetables to sell on the black market. As the aircraft neared Moscow, the passengers noticed that four Soviet fighter planes appeared to escort them. The trip had taken thirty-five and a half hours, lasting over five days. Foreign Minister Molotov and other Soviet officials, along with representatives from the American and British embassies, met the planes.[4] A guard of honor lined up and played the American and Soviet national anthems. As the group split up, they saw British Foreign Secretary Anthony Eden's plane arrive, and the Soviets began their welcoming ceremonies all over again.[5]

The Third Moscow Conference

The October 1943 conference resulted in a declaration of objectives called the Moscow Pact.[6] In it, the Allies agreed to continue to work together toward a German surrender and disarmament, to void the annexation of Austria, to rid Italy of Fascism, to secure peace, and to establish an international organization of member nations to maintain global peace and security. The Moscow Conference delegation included Bohlen, who accompanied Secretary of State Hull as an interpreter. Harriman was there because of his experience in the previous two Moscow conferences, as well as to help Hull, in whom FDR did not have complete confidence. When the conference ended, Harriman stayed on as the new ambassador to the USSR, replacing Standley.

When Harriman agreed to take the post, he did several smart things. First, he insisted that he have complete authority to overhaul the embassy's personnel. Then he had all the military attachés and Faymonville recalled, having seen how destructive the internecine battles between them and the embassy had been. Finally, he asked for permission to select an expert on the Soviets as his counselor. Harriman did not get along with Loy Henderson, who was in that position at the time, possibly because Henderson held a negative attitude toward the Soviets.[7] The ambassador wanted Chip Bohlen, but Bohlen did not have the rank required for such a post. Harriman eventually got his next-best choice, George Kennan.[8]

Harriman had Bohlen stay on in Moscow, and this was when Thompson became close to all three men, especially Bohlen. Looking back at his relationship with Kennan, Thompson described him as a "paradox." Kennan was a "charming, lovable man, sentimental yet ruthless." He was also "aloof," a "one-man show." He had great sense of history and a broad perspective. He was often wrong in the short term, but right in the long run. He was a poor administrator yet refused to delegate authority. Kennan was brilliant at tossing out ideas, but not capable of choosing among them. He had a good intuition and was "exceedingly perceptive," but he was not the sort of person who should have the responsibility for carrying out policy. Working with Bohlen helped Kennan, since Bohlen "was practical and knocked many extreme ideas out of Kennan's head."[9]

The Russians Advance

By the end of 1943, the war situation had changed. A Soviet victory at the battle of Kursk marked the moment the war turned irrevocably against the Germans and the beginning of the Soviet push west. It was almost inevitable that the Soviets would end up deep in Eastern Europe.[10]

Life in Moscow was close to normal, and although travel outside of the city for foreigners was still limited to a forty-mile radius, Thompson and friends from the embassy went off on trips to explore the countryside. The Russians in the villages and on the collective farms welcomed the exotic Americans, especially when they came bearing small gifts from the commissary. Inevitably, the vodka came out, giving the Americans a candid view of the contradictions of Soviet life—their generosity and joy in life amid the devastation left by the German invasion. For Bohlen, it was a change from the Moscow he had known in the previous decade.

Ambassador Harriman rarely used his office in the chancellery, instead setting up his embassy at Spaso House, where he spent much of the day in bed.[11] Harriman had come to Moscow without his wife, so his daughter Kathleen served as his hostess. She was adventurous, vivacious, and liked to ski. Harriman also skied, although not as well as his daughter. He enlisted Thompson and the embassy's second secretary, Isaac Patch, to accompany them to the Lenin Hills, where Harriman insisted on leading the schuss. Sometimes Harriman got going too fast and crashed into the woods, where Thompson and Patch collected him, and then up they'd all go down the slopes again.[12] Kathleen ran the household, and she even took on some of the basic ambassadorial duties.

In January 1944, Harriman delegated his daughter to accompany a Soviet investigating committee to Katyn, in order to determine who was to blame for the massacre of thousands of elite Polish officers.[13] It was a weighty responsibility for a twenty-five-year-old. Twenty foreign journalists went along, too. Predictably, the Soviet commission concluded that the prisoners had been murdered *during* the German occupation. After viewing exhibits of planted evidence, Ms. Harriman endorsed the committee's findings, but Thompson and most of his colleagues in the embassy, including down to the clerks, believed that it had been the Soviets who had done so.[14] The ambassador, however, accepted his daughter's view and reported what FDR wanted to hear, that "in all probability the massacre was perpetrated by the Germans."[15] Harriman's initial purpose in Moscow had been to create a good atmosphere for Soviet-American relations, so Roosevelt could later make plans for postwar settlements that were favorable to the United States, but over the course of his tenure, Harriman learned that what his staff had told him was true—you could not store up good will for later use in Moscow.

On June 14, 1944, a few weeks after the Allies started a long-sought second front with the invasion of Normandy, Thompson accompanied Harriman to Tashkent and Alma Alta (in today's Uzbekistan and Kazakhstan) to meet Vice President Henry A. Wallace, who was on his way to China. Wallace belonged to the pro-Soviet current in American foreign policy, and his visit to Central Asia and Siberia confirmed his opinions. The Soviets even convinced him that the inmates of a gulag camp in Siberia were volunteer laborers.[16] Harriman and his party, including Thompson, met Wallace in Tashkent, where they visited collective farms and experimental seed collection stations. When the visitors asked why all the shops were closed, they received evasive and unconvincing explanations. Thompson, however, informed them that the stores had all been shuttered for the duration of the foreigners' stay, so they would not see how little was available in the way of consumer goods. He told them that the Soviets did not allow foreigners to make unescorted trips, in order to orchestrate the visitors' impressions. Harriman reported to the State Department that the vice president's knowledge of scientific agriculture impressed the Soviets and said that his visit made a substantial contribution to good Soviet-American relations, but he did not mention Thompson's observations.[17]

Earlier that year, a young war correspondent, William L. White, befriended Thompson and asked him to share stories of the siege of Moscow. Uncharacteristically, Thompson did so, but under the condition that the young man not reveal his source. The journalist went home and wrote a book that incorporated some of Thompson's stories, attributing them to a fictional character with "one blue eye and one brown, and six fingers on his left hand."[18] He also included an account of the Katyn massacre, describing it as the killing of Poles by the Soviets. The book was panned and its author was vilified. American journalists were even pressured to sign a petition against their colleague.[19] The United States was not ready to hear the truth about its ally.

Stalin Goes West

In one of their long conversations together that year, Bohlen and Thompson talked about how "the Soviet regime would be unable to resist the temptation to communize the states of Eastern Europe no matter how friendly they were to the USSR, because [the Soviets] could not tolerate even the slightest deviation from the party line."[20] It had become clear that the Soviets would only accept a Communist Poland, underlined by Stalin's cynical refusal to allow the Red Army to come to the aid of the Polish resistance during the Warsaw uprising against Hitler—despite the Red Army's immediate proximity. Moreover, he did not even allow American or British aircraft to use Soviet air bases to drop supplies for the beleaguered fighters. The Poles bravely held out, but Stalin could see that dismembering their resistance was useful for his own future plans. Nearly 200,000 citizens of Warsaw were killed, and the Germans expelled the entire surviving population, nearly 1 million people, to concentration camps. By the time the Red Army took over the city, it was completely deserted.[21] In June 1944, "the Red Army drove nearly five hundred miles across Belorussia and Poland,"[22] with FDR and Churchill getting what they wanted: decisive help in defeating the Germans. Yet Stalin would extract the highest price he could, holding that the victor had an inevitable right to impose its system on whatever territory its army occupied.[23] So much for the Atlantic Charter.[24]

Perhaps as a show of solidarity with their allies, Vyacheslav Molotov, Deputy Foreign Minister Andrey Vyshinsky, and Maxim Litvinov, Molotov's predecessor, made an unusual appearance at the US embassy for the Independence Day luncheon on July 4, 1944. Thompson and one other officer were there, but all the others, including Kennan and Bohlen, had gone to the ambassadorial dacha for the holiday.

Thompson learned in September that he would receive his dream assignment, as second secretary in the embassy in London. Harriman was adamant, however, that Thompson not leave until his replacement was in transit, since Thompson was acting as the "liaison with the British, [who were] requiring consultation with the Russians on international questions."[25] Thompson's presence would be "more keenly missed than any other officer," due to his capacity for "careful, accurate, and tactful handling" of those cases. Presumably, Harriman was referring to the OSS-NKVD talks (see chapter 4), which went on until November of that year. Before he left Moscow, Thompson would see two other major events take place: the Rumanian armistice, and the Fourth Moscow Conference.

The Rumanian Armistice

Thompson attended the preliminary meetings regarding a Rumanian armistice and said it was a fascinating and revealing experience. Since the Americans' objective was to set up free and independent countries in Eastern Europe, it was also "a story of failure."[26] The Red Army was still in Rumania, grabbing everything from art to coal to industrial machinery. One hope was that the armistice would bring this pillage to a halt, but it became clear that the Soviets considered Rumania their business, and democracy was not on their agenda.[27]

The meeting did not start until almost 11 p.m. It was held at the Spridonovka Palace, in a large white room with light glaring from the chandeliers. Individuals from the four countries that were represented—the USSR, the United States, the United Kingdom, and Rumania—sat around a large round table, presided over by Molotov and the other members of the Soviet delegation. Thompson and Meiklejohn sat at a small table behind the

American delegation, with the British representatives opposite them. A large painting, portraying the signing of the British-Soviet Mutual Assistance Treaty, stared down at them—a reminder of just whose side they were supposed to be on. The participants did not sign the armistice document until 5 a.m. the following morning. The Rumanians were required to pay over $1 billion in reparations, a lot for a small, war-torn country to bear. The agreement also created an Allied Control Commission—headed by a Soviet general— that the USSR would use to consolidate its power in Rumania. Thompson, looking back, believed that the early demobilization of nearby American troops and a return toward isolationism after World War II affected the situation unfavorably for the Rumanians. Frank Wisner, destined to become one of the central figures in the CIA, was in Rumania with the OSS at the time and witnessed the Soviet military occupation, forever marking his opinion of the Bolsheviks and influencing his future efforts to fight Communism covertly after the war ended.[28]

The Fourth Moscow Conference

Increasingly alarmed by Red Army advances into Eastern Europe, Churchill went to Moscow on October 9, 1944, for a fourth Moscow Conference. Once again it involved Harriman, but, on FDR's instructions, he was there simply as an observer. The bilateral meeting, code-named "Tolstoy," was therefore substantively between Churchill and Stalin, with Molotov and Eden mopping up. Harriman relied on his friend, the British prime minister, to fill him in. Churchill's first meeting with Stalin was supposed to create a coalition government for Poland, to be made up of members from its current two bodies: Poland's government-in-exile in London, and the Lublin Committee, installed by the Soviets. But this was not to be, and that country's government would become a Soviet creation.

The rest of Churchill's agenda was to secure British interests in Greece and then let Eden and Molotov settle the questions of Yugoslavia, Bulgaria, and Hungary. At dinner that evening, after getting Stalin to agree to receive the exiled Polish leader, Churchill delivered his "percentages agreement" proposal to Stalin. On a piece of paper, Churchill scrawled a list of European countries and the percentage of agreed influence the USSR and Great Britain would each have in them: Rumania 90/10, Greece 10/90, Yugoslavia 50/50, Hungary 50/50, and Bulgaria 75/25. Churchill slid it over the table to Stalin, who put down a blue check mark and pushed the paper back to the center of the table, where it continued to lay. Churchill, aware that this might be seen as a shameful arrangement, hesitated for days before he informed Harriman, who then cabled FDR, explaining that Churchill would "try to work out some sort of spheres of influence with the Russians, [with] the British to have a free hand in Greece and the Russians in Rumania and perhaps other countries."[29]

Thompson and Kennan were troubled by seeing Stalin's reach growing. If Churchill saw the Moscow agreement as a temporary tactic, Stalin would instead have viewed any tacit or explicit agreement that favored his national interests as permanent. It certainly would have been reasonable for Stalin to conclude that he was dealing with kindred practical politicians, whose narrow national interests he could appeal to. The difference was that "the 'national interests' of Britain in Greece included objectives like getting the ouzo concession for Harrods [a department store] and Greek support (optional) of British policies after the war; whereas the 'national interests' of Russia in Poland, for example, was quite simply everything that Poland had. Everything Poland produced, everything it aspired to do and be, was subject to Soviet preference."[30]

Thompson Explains the Soviet System

Thompson spent most of the summer before his departure from Moscow in 1944 pondering the events of the previous four years. He felt that his government did not really understand how the Soviet system worked. This put the United States at a disadvantage when dealing with an inscrutable regime. He set out to write a paper explaining it all, and, realizing that he lacked Kennan's ability to pack his thoughts into forceful expressions, asked his friend to look it over and, as Kennan phrased it, "polish it up."[31] Thompson's forty-page document, entitled "The Concept and Structure of Soviet Foreign Policy," was intended to illuminate the "peculiarities that pertained to Soviet foreign relations [and were] often overlooked or misunderstood."[32] Thompson wanted the pro-Soviet Roosevelt administration to realize their assumption that the United States and the Soviets operated from a similar world view was mistaken.

The new Socialist regime of the 1917 Russian revolution had been billed as a communal, and fair, economic system and society: in the words of Karl Marx, "from each according to his ability, to each according to his needs." Its fundamental ideology projected the inevitable progression of Communism throughout the world, so that the mere existence of any non-Communist state became a self-defined enemy. The cause warranted any means used to achieve its aims. Problems arose when that archetype collided with reality. The Soviet regime transformed this broad general doctrine from a revolutionary ideal to an imperative for survival, with the abiding goal being to preserve the ruling elite.

Thompson described the Soviet Union under Stalin as "a phenomenon very different from America or Britain: it was a totalitarian state, endowed with an all-explanatory, all-consuming ideology, committed to the infallibility of government and party, still in a somewhat messianic mood, equating dissent with treason, and ruled by a dictator who, for all his quite extraordinary abilities, had his paranoid moments." This fear meant that even when the Soviets had a legitimate objective, they seldom openly declared what it was, because they thought others would "try to thwart" that effort. The Soviets, Thompson said, had two foreign policies: one "actual," and the other "declared." He noted that, like other nations, the Soviets' declared policy professed adherence to certain general principles, as well as to specific objectives. The difference was that, where the United States, for instance, tended to subordinate short-term objectives in order to uphold national principles (such as allowing America's Communist Party members freedom of speech), the Soviets often did the opposite, appearing to contradict their national ideology in order to achieve short-term goals. For example, the USSR declared its support for policies such as "freedom of the press, freedom of religion, and non-interference in the affairs of other states . . . to which it was actually [ideologically] opposed."

Thompson said it was very hard to understand the "actual foreign policy" of the Soviets, since "secrecy and mystery make it difficult to judge what [it] is at any given time." Beyond such broad overall desires as security and economic stability, "it would appear that Soviet policy is based more on concrete and specific objectives than on general principles." According to Thompson, the USSR's strategy regarding specific objectives (as opposed to general principles) was "dynamic," replacing either obsolete or attained goals with new ones. The Soviets also repeatedly held out the possibility of cooperation with other states if the Soviets were granted "one last demand." This practice was later dubbed "salami tactics," where opposition to a particular goal is cut off, slice by slice. To illustrate his point, Thompson recalled that "incorporation [of the Baltic states] into the Soviet Union was not mentioned until Soviet troops were already in control of those countries."

As for the disparity between their declared and actual policies, the Soviets might proclaim adherence to the general principles of the Moscow Conference's charter in order to attain some immediate objectives, such as agreeing to a coalition government in Poland, while their long-term design was very different. As another example, one of the Soviets' declared principles was to support Communist movements in other countries, but they seemed to give more weight to their own national considerations than to international ones. Their backing of Communists in Poland was not to advance international Communism, but rather to protect Soviet national security. Consequently, Thompson concluded that world revolution was not an objective of the Soviets' then-current actual policy, even if global Communism remained as their long-term goal.

Thompson's conclusions contradicted the compelling idea behind the containment policy that the United States would shortly adopt. Throughout his career, Thompson maintained that America should encourage the Soviets' movement toward national interests, which were flexible, rather than their efforts toward ideological domination, which were not: "When determining the policy of any dictatorship, including the Soviet Union, it is important to distinguish between the effect that policy has upon the regime [i.e., the leadership] rather than on the state. While actual Soviet objectives might not be clear to outsiders, there appears never to be any vagueness in the minds of the leaders as to what they want." This, he observed, gave the Kremlin an advantage over the governments of other nations, which were handicapped "by the slowness of the democratic process."

Thompson devoted the rest of his paper to outlining the structure of the Soviet state and its effect on foreign policy. For example, contrary to what one would expect, their Foreign Ministry was the least important organ of the government in determining foreign policy. The Kremlin did that.[33] Soviet diplomats were not the ones who kept their government informed, but rather the news agency TASS, which tended to report what the Kremlin wanted to hear. Thus the USSR's leadership was not always well informed.[34] He also pointed out that the difficulty in dealing with the Soviet government in general stemmed from "the universal tendency of Soviet officials to evade personal responsibility." The drastic penalty for mistakes meant that only those high up in the Communist Party could make difficult decisions. When something could not get done lower down in the bureaucracy, this did not necessarily reflect a sinister purpose—it was just the way the system worked. In terms of arriving at agreements, he said that the Soviet government focused on getting "the best deal for itself, so they [*sic*] seldom negotiate in what the West would call good faith." "Furthermore," he wrote, the Soviets do "not bank good will for future deals."

Opposition to the regime was not a problem, because it was literally eliminated. Foreign Affairs Minister Vyshinsky himself said that the "Soviet system is based on combination of persuasion and force."[35] Thompson clarified that it was the Communist Party that provided the persuasion and the secret police (the NKVD) that supplied the force.[36] Soviet public opinion was ignored until after the fact. Then their government displayed "extreme sensitivity to criticism." Once a decision had been announced by the Communist Party, all its members were obliged to accept it and endeavor to carry it out. Deviation was subject to severe retribution. Any individual, even a foreigner, who openly opposed any part of the policy was immediately considered to be an enemy of the state and branded as "fascist or reactionary."

During World War II, the Soviet government had to appeal to national and religious feelings and downplay Communism to guarantee its citizens' full support. "After the hardships of war their immediate desires are material but they doubtless also feel they are entitled to a greater share in shaping [their country's destiny]," Thompson wrote. "Millions of Soviet men and women who so courageously bore the suffering of the war and so heroically contributed to the victory cannot now just be left to one side and will have to be brought into the Party, in which case it will cease to be the compact disciplined body it has been."

Thompson ended his paper by saying: "It might never be possible to have an intimate relationship or close cooperation with the Soviet Union such as the US enjoys with Great Britain. . . . Cooperation at the top level for the achievement of broad major objectives is possible if each side will take account of the limitations and peculiarities of the other." He spent the rest of his career pursuing those objectives and trying to explain each side to the other.

Thompson's tour of duty in Moscow had made him part of the exclusive club of men who spoke Russian and had Soviet experience, making him valuable to his government. He gained credibility with the Soviets for having stayed in Moscow during the Germans' siege of the city. Most importantly, during the war, the Communist Party apparatus's defenses were down and the people had a moment of openness, since "Russia was too busy with its survival to try to hide what it was in its essence."[37] Thompson gained rare insight, an "increment of understanding," by being able to see behind the curtain.[38] His departure from Moscow also marked the end of his education and the beginning of his attempts to influence policy. The paper Thompson asked Kennan to look over was a first step in that direction. Kennan returned this document, untouched, to Thompson almost a year later. A shortage of officers at the mission had prevented him from working on it, Kennan explained, but he advised Thompson to fix it up himself and put it on record with the department.

6 ≋

Conferences

If historians cannot solve their problems in retrospect, who
are they to blame Roosevelt, Stalin, and Churchill for not
having solved them at the time?
—ARTHUR M. SCHLESINGER JR.,
   "Origins of the Cold War"

Though it left Thompson with only a week at home in Las Animas after nearly four
years in Moscow, he followed Harriman's advice and stopped in Washington, DC,
for consultation at the State Department. It had been difficult for Thompson to
leave Nina. He had proposed marriage to her in order to get her out of the Soviet Union,
but she refused. She did not want to leave her country, and she understood that their relationship would not necessarily work elsewhere. Kennan promised to keep an eye on her.[1]
Thompson flew out of Moscow with Harriman in October 1944, making the trip to the
United States in a record fifty-six hours and fifty-nine minutes.[2] Anyone leaving Moscow
felt the accumulated tensions evaporate and a feeling of liberation take over. Still, Thompson had promised Nina that he would return.

Yalta

In November 1944, Thompson eagerly anticipated his move to the embassy in London.
He arranged to have a Studebaker Champion Deluxe two-door sedan in "channel-mist"
green shipped there.[3] His fantasy of tootling around the English countryside in his shiny
new car would have to wait, however, for soon after Thompson arrived in Washington,
DC, the State Department postponed his London appointment. They needed him to fill in
for Bohlen, who had been assigned as liaison between the White House and the State Department.[4] Thompson spent the next six months as assistant chief of the Eastern European
Division, with two of those months as acting chief, since the head of EUR was attending
the Yalta summit, which took place in February 1945.[5] Yalta, the next in a series of summits to shape the postwar world, was later criticized for sealing the postwar indenture of
Eastern Europe to the Soviet bloc. This criticism was unfair. Like Russian matryoshka dolls,

one summit nested in another, the first one dictating the shape of the last one. By the time the Allied leaders met in Yalta, the Soviets could not have been evicted from Eastern Europe without direct military confrontation.[6]

FDR wanted the Soviets to attack Japan, as well as to cooperate in creating a new international body, the United Nations, to replace the moribund League of Nations. He hoped that the conference could eliminate the Eastern European countries as a source of conflict between the United States and the Soviet Union.[7] Churchill wanted to ensure that Germany wasn't eviscerated, as it had been by the Treaty of Versailles after World War I. He also wanted to restore France as a major European power, as well as focus on the fate of Poland. Since Britain had committed itself to the liberation of Poland from the Germans, it would be dishonorable to surrender Poland's freedom to the Soviets.[8] Stalin wanted to retrieve territory his country had lost after World War I, and to establish a wide belt of Soviet-controlled states on his border, including Poland, which he saw as an "invasion corridor" for German aggression.[9] He wanted a cushion around him, to serve as padding against an increasingly hostile Western world. Moreover, he sought to extract maximum reparations, in order to rebuild his own battered and bloodied nation.

From these starting points came the various Yalta deals. The eastern part of Poland went to the Soviet Union, virtually following the dividing line established under Stalin's earlier pact with Hitler.[10] As compensation, Stalin proposed tacking territory in eastern Germany onto Poland, but his proposal for a Polish-German border along the Oder and Neisse Rivers came to naught. FDR wanted this issue postponed until the final peace conference, which never came, so the Oder–Neisse line would resurface in each of the following crises over Germany and Berlin. Additionally, Stalin managed to wrest effective control of Poland in exchange for an agreement to hold "free and unfettered elections [there] as soon as possible" and vague language enlarging that country's government to include representatives of other political groups. The elections provision would not protect Poland, but it did insulate FDR and Churchill politically.

The Anglo-American conferees felt encouraged when Stalin signed on to the Declaration on Liberated Europe, drafted by the State Department, which was meant to guarantee "sovereign rights and self government" in all liberated countries.[11] The summit participants created zones of occupation for Germany, giving France a zone carved from the British and American ones.[12] In retrospect, perhaps the most shameful deal made at Yalta was confirmation of a military agreement for the forceful return of freed citizens and prisoners of war (POWs) to their countries of origin. Many thousands of men, women, and children who were unfortunate enough to have fallen under German control were sent to their deaths or to the gulag, because Stalin regarded the POWs as deserters and everyone else as traitors.[13]

Although history marks Yalta as a defeat for the West, Stalin did not come away feeling victorious. The Americans thought they'd done very well at Yalta, especially by getting the Soviets to sign the Declaration on Liberated Europe. Time would prove both sides wrong. Looking back, Thompson supposed that "sometimes it is necessary to follow a foreign policy even if you know it is not going to succeed."[14] At the time, Thompson watched the

Soviets reveal their "actual" foreign policy with "the ink barely dry on the Yalta agreement."[15] Contrary to the Declaration on Liberated Europe, the Soviets soon installed a Communist government in Rumania and refused to consult with the other signers on the fate of Bulgaria, as called for in the declaration. Officials in London and Washington, DC, speculated on why Stalin ignored the declaration. Thompson's conclusion was bluntly realistic, "My own guess was that Stalin thought [the declaration] was a device to save face for us and that we did not really expect him to carry it out."[16] Stalin had projected his own mindset onto the Allies and presumed that they would subordinate a public statement of principles to the practical understandings between them.

Early that April, the Polish ambassador came to see Thompson to deliver a note for the Secretary of State. He told an alarming story of sixteen Polish underground leaders who had gone to a suburb of Warsaw to meet with a "Soviet general" and never returned. The general lured these leaders of the Polish underground—which was loyal to that country's government-in-exile—out of Poland a few at a time. He told them that their request to meet with the exiled government in London had been granted, and he wanted to discuss their participation in a coalition government, per the declaration. By the time the "general" was done, most of the principals of the underground, along with two representatives from each of the Polish political parties (except the Communist one) and an interpreter, had been ensnared.[17] They were abducted to Moscow and "interrogated" at the Lubyanka prison. But at the time, no one knew their fate. Thompson did not forget about the missing Poles, as the story of that incident left a deep impression. Even twenty years later, he urged historian Arthur Schlesinger Jr. to include the event in his "Origins of the Cold War" article.[18]

Birth of the United Nations

Eight days after the Polish ambassador's visit to Thompson, FDR died suddenly, in Warm Springs, Georgia. This occurred before Roosevelt could witness the birth of the United Nations (UN), and only a few weeks before Hitler's suicide, but certainly after Stalin's true intentions became apparent. As the untested Harry Truman took office, some in the new president's administration were concerned over what would happen. Would he change US foreign policy? Would he go forward with the UN conference in San Francisco?[19]

Because of his League of Nations and ILO experience, Thompson was named as political and liaison officer to the two-month-long conference. In late April 1945, he, along with approximately 3,500 other delegates, descended on San Francisco for one of the largest international assemblies ever held.[20] It took eighty planes and nine trains, plus thirty hotels and three clubs, to accommodate them all. Thompson dealt with the Soviet, Yugoslav, Ukrainian, Byelorussian, and Czechoslovak delegations, as well as the French-speaking ones. He acted as an interpreter, including for meetings between Molotov and Secretary of State Edward Stettinius. Thompson's supervisor, John D. Hickerson, the acting director of EUR, was impressed by Thompson's "objectivity and integrity of mind [in dealing with Soviet-US political issues] which were not always easy to maintain when a subjective approach would have been easier and probably more popular."[21]

At that time, any hint of criticism of the Soviet Union was simply not acceptable to the press.[22] The media was so "euphoric about Soviet intentions" that journalist Walter Lippmann walked out of a briefing in a huff, furious over a statement implying that the Soviets might be acting in bad faith over Poland.[23] Secretary of State Stettinius met with Molotov in San Francisco and asked about the missing Polish underground leaders. Later, Molotov hosted a dinner, during which he finally revealed their whereabouts. When greeting Stettinius, Molotov casually told him that "those sixteen Poles" had been arrested by the Red Army. He then quickly turned to the British ambassador, leaving Stettinius standing there, nonplussed yet still smiling from the greeting.[24]

On May 8, 1945, the UN delegates and the entire world celebrated VE day, the end of the war in Europe. That same month, Bohlen left the UN conference to accompany Harry Hopkins to Moscow, in order to meet with Stalin in an attempt to mend deteriorating relations and untangle the impasse on the composition of the Polish government in advance of the next summit in Potsdam.[25] Stalin would not tolerate a government unfriendly to the Soviets in Poland, but he finally agreed to let five non–Lublin party Poles participate in what would be the Provisional Government of National Unity, a lukewarm compromise, but enough to allow Truman and Churchill to recognize it.[26] The missing Poles went on trial between the time of the Bohlen-Hopkins trip and the opening of the Potsdam summit. It was a quick trial, in which they had no opportunity to mount a defense and no witnesses were called. Some died in prison, a few were released, and some were rearrested in Poland, while a few others fled to the West.[27] The UN Charter was signed on June 26, 1945, at the War Memorial in San Francisco by all of the original members of the conference, except Poland.

Potsdam

The Potsdam conference was the final matryoshka doll summit. Stalin was the only one left of the original "big three." Truman had replaced FDR, and, in the middle of the conference, Clement Attlee took over for Churchill, who had lost his election because of domestic policies.[28] Potsdam was supposed to lay the basis for a peace settlement with Germany and structure the politics of a new postwar world. In general, the Soviets got what they had asked for all along—a protective shield. All territory east of the Oder River and the Adriatic Sea and north of Greece fell into their sphere. The rest of Europe came under the influence of the Western powers. It was essentially the percentage deal that Stalin had worked out with Churchill in October 1944. As Stalin had said: "Everyone imposes his own system as far as his army has [the] power to do it. It cannot be otherwise."[29] Yet when the delegates left Potsdam, the world had changed, more than anyone realized. It had entered the atomic age.

Thompson, Bohlen, and Charles Yost were among the thirty-six Americans from the State Department who attended the Potsdam conference. Thompson took minutes of the plenary meetings of the heads of states and the foreign ministers, which took place at the Cecilienhof Palace. Everything from the dark English Tudor furniture inside to the dripping ivy outside conveyed a somberness and seriousness, perhaps underscoring suspicions that were becoming increasingly palpable. A conspicuous floral red star—consisting of red geraniums, pink roses, and hydrangeas—greeted everyone as they passed through the central courtyard. Anyone hoping Truman would take anything but a Rooseveltian stand toward the Soviets would have been disheartened to see the pro-Soviet Joseph Davies, the author of *Mission to Moscow*, sitting next to him for most of the conference.[30]

The president and the rest of the American contingent, including Thompson, stayed in a suburb of Berlin, perhaps appropriately called Babelsburg. Truman resided in a large villa, known as the "little White House," which he was told had belonged to a Nazi filmmaker who was sent to Siberia. In truth, it belonged to a respected German publisher and his family, who had been evicted by the Soviets to accommodate Truman.[31] Thompson and Bohlen talked for hours about the growing influence and intransigence of the Soviet Union. The two friends concluded that wherever the Red Army's soldiers were, the Soviet system, with its highly structured authoritarian control, would be imposed, even after the USSR signed the hopeful Joint Declaration of Liberated Europe.[32] They were right, but Austria would be the exception.

The delegates to Potsdam easily agreed on some points, such as denazification and the expulsion of all Germans from Eastern Europe. They also agreed to set up the Council of Foreign Ministers and to prepare a peace settlement for Germany, which was to be accepted "when a government adequate for the purpose is established." In the meantime, the delegates finalized occupation zones for postwar Germany. The Western zones would later become the Federal Republic of Germany, and the Soviet sector, the German Democratic Republic. The bifurcation of Germany would be mended some fifty years later, but none of the men at Potsdam would live to see it.

Settling the new borders with Poland proved to be more difficult, and the discussions on reparations were "endless, tortuous, complicated, and confused."[33] Part of the reason may have been language. The expression "basis for negotiations," which was agreed to at Yalta, "got us in trouble," Thompson said. "The Soviets thought that when we agreed to take their proposal that the Germans pay ten billion dollars in reparations as a basis for discussion at the next meeting, they assumed we had agreed to this figure and that the next meeting would discuss how it was to be paid."[34] The Americans and the British did not want to become responsible for paying German reparations because, as Thompson put it, they preferred not to "pour money into one side of Germany and let the Russians suck it out the other."[35] Instead, conference attendees decided that each power would obtain payments from their respective zones. In addition, the Soviets would receive 10 percent of the German industrial capital in the Western zones, once the Allied Control Council determined the permitted level of German industry for peacetime, never mind that the Red Army was already hastily dismantling all the machinery and equipment from German industries in all the zones.

The Potsdam summit showed Thompson how the Soviets had masterfully exploited ambiguous language to their benefit. In the last hectic hours of the conference, the Repatriations Commission allowed the Soviets to slip a clause into the agreement that included Austrian properties under the heading of "German assets" from which the Soviets could draw reparations. As a result, the Austrians would watch in bitter acquiescence while the Soviets extracted millions of dollars in tribute because the US commissioner—described by Charles Thayer as "a Texas oil magnate"—was "impatient to wind up and go home."[36] The American negotiators understood the term German assets to mean war booty. They failed, however, to get a clear definition of what war booty was.[37] Thompson later pointed out the mistaken US tendency to accept vague agreements when negotiating with the Soviets. He would remember this when he sat at the head of a negotiating table in Austria a few years later.

Perhaps the single most important event taking place during the timeframe of the summit passed by almost unnoticed at Potsdam. Shortly after Truman arrived at the conference, he received news of the successful atomic test at Alamogordo, New Mexico, not far from the Thompson ranch. After much debate, Truman decided he would have to tell Stalin about the bomb and mentioned it to him, almost as a by-the-way comment. Stalin's low-key reaction made Truman think he had not fully understood the importance of the news, but Stalin most likely already knew about the Manhattan Project through his spies.[38] Stalin was jolted by the bombs dropped on Hiroshima and Nagasaki shortly after the conference, however, and he thought that the atomic bomb robbed him of what he had earned during the war—his right to primacy in the postwar world.[39] Not only did this new type of bomb alter Stalin's calculations as to what he could achieve in the Far East, but it also made him press his own scientists to provide him with his own atomic bomb.[40] It must have been clear to him that the Americans were going to exploit their nuclear monopoly. They no longer needed him to defeat Japan and, moreover, they wanted him to stay out of the Pacific front altogether. This, combined with the Americans' refusal to provide large, low-interest loans to the Soviets and the cancellation of Lend-Lease, only confirmed Stalin's distrust of his erstwhile ally.

In his long paper written in 1944, Thompson still hoped that Stalin's relaxed internal controls might continue after the end of World War II. This would leave the possibility open for some kind of cooperation between the Americans and the Soviets. Now it was clear that these two wartime allies were headed for confrontation. Thompson called what happened in Eastern Europe after the war a "failure of our policy. . . . Our objective there was the establishment of governments that were free and independent." But he defended the role of the State Department, citing the circumstances and the correlation of events at that time. At the Potsdam summit, Stalin tried to get out of every agreement he had made at Yalta. There was little the West could do except watch as Stalin contravened all the deals that would allow Eastern Europe to decide its fate through free elections.[41] After speculating as to why Stalin had signed the Declaration on Liberated Europe at Yalta, Thompson said, "The Russians have shown that texts are no obstacle if they decide they do not want to live up to an agreement."[42] Or, as Stalin himself stated: "A declaration I regard as algebra, but an agreement as practical arithmetic. I do not wish to decry algebra, but I prefer practical arithmetic."[43]

By the time the peace agreements for the former Axis satellites were being drafted, it was already too late to rescue them. The State Department found itself in the position of applying triage, trying to salvage what little it could in Eastern Europe, such as establishing embassies and consulates in these Eastern bloc nations, in order to keep them less isolated. Thompson was not sanguine that they would get very far, but at least the State Department would focus attention on what was happening to the people in those countries.[44]

State Department historian G. Bernard Noble wrote to Thompson and other conferees in 1954, seeking official and personal papers related to the conference.[45] Although giving Noble one of his own papers on a negotiating position regarding Germany at the Potsdam summit could have made him look good, Thompson replied by stating that he strongly felt it would be a mistake to include subordinates' memoranda or personal letters.[46] Some of the material, he said, could be taken out of context. Thompson later wrote, in response to a similar request, "I have long thought there has been a tendency on the part of historians to give undue weight to written documents." He then cited the Potsdam papers, adding: "One prolific young man sent [Noble] dozens of documents, none of which I feel sure had been read by anyone of importance on the delegations. On the other hand I doubt if James Dunn, who was the principal advisor to the Secretary of State, had submitted any written memoranda. It would have been easy to have been misled by this documentation."[47] The Soviet armies had anchored the landscape Stalin desired. The Western allies were exhausted and not about to restart the war in order to save Eastern Europe, especially since the reality of the Cold War was only just beginning to unfold for an American public still smitten with their wartime ally, the Soviets.[48]

It's easy now to feel outrage over the millions of people displaced by World War II and the diplomatic maneuvers in its aftermath; repulsion at the allocation of spheres of influence, drawn up practically on the back of a napkin; and disgust for allowing Stalin almost everything he demanded. But all of this happened while most of Western Europe and America were still in a battle to the death with Hitler, the outcome of which was by no means certain, and the Allies feared Stalin might stop fighting on their side. They needed the Red Army to win the war. The bloody burden being borne by Soviet soldiers and citizens was one that the West was, for the most part, spared. If it weren't for the Soviets' sacrifices against the Germans, would the Allies have been willing or able to bear the additional suffering that would have inevitably come upon them? Truman dropped two atomic bombs on Japan, reasoning that this would shorten the war in the Pacific and spare American lives, despite some in the US government believing that the Japanese were likely to surrender regardless.[49] If the war in Europe had not been curtailed by the efforts of the Red Army, what might have happened?

On the plane ride home from the Potsdam conference, Thompson and Bohlen had a long talk about the atomic bomb and the power and security it gave to the Americans. They speculated about what methods the United States might use to press the Soviets to withdraw to their own frontiers and came to the conclusion that a threat of force was not the answer. For them, "it does not take years of diplomatic experience to realize that bluff on dimensions of this nature would be too risky and unproductive for any country including the US."[50] It was obvious that diplomacy would play a vital role in future US-Soviet relations. Thompson and Bohlen saw eye-to-eye on this and were growing closer.

Shortly after Thompson got back to Washington, DC, he received a disappointing letter—in two aspects—from another of his friends, George Kennan, who was still in Moscow. One, Kennan wrote that he was planning to leave the Foreign Service for "urgent and compelling reasons," which only he could judge, and ominously ended his missive with, "If I were not to do what I propose to do at this time, I would be of no great value to anyone in another ten or twenty years." Two, he returned the long paper Thompson had written the year before, explaining that although he had not had time to work on it, he thought the paper was a really "valuable document and should not go unused."[51] Six months later, on February 22, 1946, Kennan sent his famous Long Telegram to the State Department (see chapter 7). It would change everything.

7

The Hot War Ends and the Cold War Begins

From Stettin in the Baltic to Trieste in the Adriatic an
"Iron Curtain" has descended across the Continent.
—WINSTON CHURCHILL, speech,
  Fulton, Missouri, March 1946

Thompson finally left for "the most exciting city in the world" a year after his original appointment there.[1] He arrived in London as the Japanese formally surrendered, on September 2, 1945, which would have certainly made it the most exciting time to be in that city, especially with his new Studebaker. The war was really over. London bore many scars from World War II. Physically, it was drab and gray and smelled of dust, and many neighborhoods were nothing but rubble. But the capital was also coming back to life in spirit, almost as though all the joy that had been shuttered for the duration of the war burst forth. Thompson got to know some of the OSS people who were still in London through Charlotte Gilbert, the widow of his old boss, Prentiss Gilbert.[2]

Thompson had only been in London for a month when he learned that important changes had also taken place at home. Although Thompson knew the sale of his family's ranch was imminent, it was still "quite a shock" when this finally happened. He wrote to MWood that he couldn't help but feel a pang that the tie had been cut. He was happy for his brother, however, and offered "to take an interest in anything he selected to do next."[3]

Thompson became a political advisor to James Dunn, the US deputy to the Secretariat of the Council of Foreign Ministers, which had been set up during the Potsdam conference. The first meeting took place in London, at Lancaster House, from September 11 to October 2, 1945.[4] Bohlen, along with most of the US delegation, came over on the RMS *Queen Elizabeth*.[5] Thompson met the ship when it docked.[6] The London conference, however, was contentious and not very productive.[7] The emerging bipolar nature of the world was evident, as the Soviet Union found itself not only standing alone against a Western phalanx, but also as the subject of greater criticism than at any time since 1941.[8]

As part of the Council of Foreign Ministers, Thompson worked on the final treaty for Italy. As he recalled: "[The] Russians and Americans locked horns for days . . . doing the groundwork. One of the stumbling blocks was a phrase: the Americans insisted on the wording 'Allied and associated powers,' the Soviets on 'Allied powers.'" Neither side budged. Then, at a tea interval one day, Thompson took a young Soviet diplomat aside and told him confidentially what the *real* problem was. In a brief history of US internal politics, Thompson explained that the American phrasing was no booby trap, but was intended to get the treaty though Congress. Historically, he said, America was against "entangling foreign alliances," and the United States had not even agreed to the word "allied" in the World War I peace treaty. This private explanation soon changed the Soviets' public stand. "But I laid my reputation on the line," said Thompson, since, "if it had turned out otherwise, they'd never have trusted me again."[9] Another difficulty was one of the outstanding questions that had to be settled before an Italian peace treaty could be finalized: Trieste, a disputed border territory between Italy and Yugoslavia. As best they could, the commission of experts from the four main powers adhered to the ethnic balance between Slavs and Italians in establishing the boundary between Italy and Yugoslavia, but both of these nations claimed the city of Trieste, and there was no way out of the impasse.

Rather than attend the next Foreign Ministers Conference in Moscow in December 1945, Thompson and Philip Mosely, another political advisor, went on an information-gathering tour of central and southeastern Europe.[10] Thompson observed that the closer they got to the Soviet Union, the less interest they found in Communism.[11] He and Mosely went to Vienna to determine what neither the Potsdam nor the Moscow conferences had been able to make clear—the exact extent of German assets in Austria. This information was needed to fulfill Soviet requisites worked out at the Potsdam summit, in preparation for a final treaty with Austria.[12]

The Iron Curtain Descends

As Thompson had predicted, Soviet soldiers returning home openly talked about the difference in living standards between the USSR and Europe. As a result, Stalin clamped down. On February 9, 1946, he gave a speech at the Bolshoi Theater, making it clear that he was not only going to insulate the Soviet Union with a buffer zone of satellite states, but also isolate his citizens by reversing all the liberalizations he had allowed during World War II. Thompson speculated that had Stalin not shown all his cards at that time and instead "pretended he was a good boy. . . there would have been a real possibility of Communists coming to power either in France or Italy or both."[13] He believed Stalin did *not* play nice because it would have obliged him to liberalize his country internally, in order to convince the rest of the world that he was "good." This would have degraded the roles of the Communist Party and the secret police and, consequently, the basis of his own power. In other words, Stalin was protecting the interests of the regime, rather than the state.

A few weeks subsequent to Stalin's speech, and a few months after returning Thompson's forty-page paper, written in 1944, to him (see chapter 5), Kennan finally unleashed his own ruminations in what would become known as the Long Telegram.[14] In it, Kennan discussed the same issues Thompson had in his earlier paper: the main factors that motivated Soviet foreign policy, the background that led to the postwar Soviet outlook, the paranoia of that country's leadership, and Stalin's fears of "capitalist encirclement." Kennan went on to discuss the practical application of Soviet foreign policy on what he termed the "official and the unofficial level" (what Thompson had called the Soviets' "declared" and "actual" policies). Their conclusions differed, however. Kennan stated that the United States was facing "a political force committed fanatically to the belief that with the US there can be no permanent *modus vivendi*," and that the Soviets' power would only feel secure if "our traditional way of life [were] destroyed. The only way they have learned to seek security [is] in [the] patient but deadly struggle for total destruction of rival power, never in compacts and compromises with it."

Thompson, on the other hand, thought that understandings between the two nations could be reached, despite obstacles. While the West saw Soviet Communist agitation as a threat, the Soviet government had similar thoughts about the advocacy of democratic principles. In order to advance, Thompson wrote: "We will have to endeavor to disabuse them of their suspicions and at the same time resolutely oppose them when they step over the bounds of sound and decent relations. Weakness in such cases will only mislead them and make the solution of these problems infinitely more difficult."[15] As long as the United States was clear on what concessions it was prepared to make and which principles it was determined to uphold, the Soviets would respect their rival. Otherwise, he continued, "there is the danger that our opposition to any given Soviet action will simply be interpreted as unfriendly and this will strengthen the hands of those within the Soviet Union who are opposed to collaboration with us."

The differences between Thompson's paper and Kennan's telegram raise the question, what might have changed had Thompson, instead of Kennan, been in Moscow when the Treasury Department (not the State Department, as many think) asked the embassy for an interpretive analysis of Soviet foreign policy? Kennan wrote his analysis just after Stalin's Bolshoi Theater speech, which signaled a "return to Communist orthodoxy in both internal and external affairs."[16] Thompson set down his views before the war ended, when even Litvinov still believed that the Soviet Union would follow a universalist policy.[17] By the time Kennan penned his assessment, there were people in Washington, DC, who were ready to listen. The US government would use Kennan's telegram and, fifteen months later, his "X Article" to justify an American foreign policy on "containing" and possibly "rolling back" Communism.[18] Thompson thought the Long Telegram and the "X Article" were very important, for they shattered the prevailing "unrealistic illusions" about the Soviet Union at that time.[19] The emerging Hawks in Washington, DC, found in Kennan's telegram the manifesto they needed to pursue a military and defensive solution toward the expanding outreach of Communism. Coincidentally, the Soviet chargé d'affaires in the US capital, Nikolai Novikov, sent a cable to Moscow that virtually mirrored Kennan's Long Telegram. Novikov depicted the United States as "driven by an insatiable urge for world domination which could only be contained by a superior force."[20]

The Cold War Begins

In February 1946, news also broke about a Soviet defector to Canada, who provided the first incontrovertible proof of a massive network of Soviet spies in Canada, the United States, and Britain. Their target, among others, was getting information on the atom bomb out of the Manhattan Project laboratory in Los Alamos, New Mexico.[21] Sergei Kudriavtsev, who would reappear several times in Thompson's life, was one of the Soviet military intelligence (GRU) agents responsible for setting up that spy network.[22]

It was in this atmosphere that the second session of the conference of foreign ministers met, this time in Paris, from April 25 to May 15, 1946, in order to draft the final peace treaties with Rumania, Finland, Hungary, Bulgaria, and Italy. The impasse over Trieste again blocked closure on the Italian treaty, which was not signed until February 10, 1947. The ministers designated the area around that city as the "Free Territory of Trieste,"[23] to be run internationally until a solution could be reached. Thompson did not know it then, but Trieste would become an important part of his career.

Eastern Europe

Thompson expected to continue on in London, but the State Department had other plans for him, as the chief of E-EUR in Washington, DC. Thompson was becoming an Eastern European specialist, with particular expertise on Poland. He left for the US capital that spring, making a stopover in Moscow for about ten days, where he saw his old State Department colleagues and Nina, and then traveled on to Warsaw and Berlin, before finally reporting for duty in Washington, DC, on July 12, 1946.[24] He moved into a tiny house in the capital, on Dent Place in Georgetown. Thanks to a new governmental pay act, his salary was increased.[25]

On December 11, he received the Medal of Freedom, the highest civilian honor that can be bestowed in the United States, for protecting US and British interests in Moscow during the siege of that city, "at frequent risk to his life."[26] Not wanting any elaborate show, he requested the ceremony to be quietly conducted by Undersecretary of State Dean Acheson, in his office. For Thompson, recognition by his superiors was enough, but he was happy to present the medal to his proud parents in Las Animas at their golden wedding anniversary, in January 1947. All the family converged, dressed to the nines, with his mother looking like a tiny, gray-haired debutante, wearing a dress trimmed with gold and sporting a corsage as big as her head. One hundred and forty-five guests came to the party, which lasted until ten p.m. Thompson, however, had to leave early to go back to Washington, DC. MWood drove him to the station in La Junta, Colorado, where a train took him to Denver to catch his plane.[27]

Kennan also returned to Washington, DC, instead of resigning from the State Department, as he had told Thompson he would. The changing attitude in the capital was reflected in Kennan's mood.[28] His newfound fame got him reassigned to the National War

College, an institution set up to teach and prepare State Department officers and military men for the Cold War ahead. Thompson, who had participated as a guinea pig in the Army's first educational attempt for State Department officers, had been an enthusiastic supporter of the program. He was pleased to see this practice continue.[29]

Kennan occasionally asked Thompson to jointly lecture with him. In an off-the-record talk they gave to a press group, Thompson expressed disappointment that the Soviet regime was reverting to controlling its people by force, as "they [Stalin and his circle] are reasserting the role of the party and conducting purges to remove anyone who does not hew to the party line."[30] He gave as examples the purge of the Communist Party in the Ukraine, the harassment of intellectuals, and the recent removal of Marshal Georgy Zhukov.[31] The immensely popular Zhukov was a potential threat to Stalin.

Kennan said that if US policies were wise and not provocative, "we should be able to contain them [the Soviets] both militarily and politically for a long time to come."[32] When asked if military power ought to be used against aggressive expansion by the USSR, he demurred, saying that he did not think this would occur, as long as the Soviets were faced with "a superior force." He dismissed the notion that the United States might interfere in Soviet spheres of influence, saying, "If every free and indigenous movement [in Eastern Europe] happens to be anti-Russian that is not our fault." He protested that "if we were actually running around supporting people, financing movements, doing various things, it would be a different thing." Despite this assertion, Kennan soon set up an organization that would try to do just that.

8

The Truman Doctrine

Expansion proved to be the other side
of the coin of containment.
—ROBERT C. TUCKER,
  "Emergence of Stalin's Foreign Policy"

The general hope was that when the peace treaties for the former Axis countries were finally signed in Paris on February 10, 1947, this would alleviate the growing friction between the United States and the USSR, but Thompson did not think so.[1] Stalin would do whatever was necessary to secure the Soviet Union. Surrounding himself with sympathetic nations was not enough. He needed to control every aspect of these countries' governments and policies—so much so that he stayed aloof from Communist leaders Mao Zedong and Josip Broz Tito, because he could not exert enough control over them.[2]

The United States had cut its economic and military aid to Europe, just as FDR had indicated at Yalta. Stalin hoped that this meant America's return to isolationism, but several practically simultaneous factors influenced US foreign policy in the opposite direction: the Truman Doctrine, Kennan's formulation of "containment," the Marshall Plan for European economic recovery, and the North Atlantic Treaty Organization (NATO). The shift in American policy, in reaction to a perceived Soviet threat, set the stage for the United States' own empire building in the name of security.[3]

The Making of the Truman Doctrine

Thompson was involved in events that led to the speech by President Truman in which he pledged American support for "free peoples who are resisting attempted subjugation by armed minorities or by outside pressures," which many historians mark as the beginning of the Cold War.[4] Thompson never liked the term Cold War. He thought it would be better to call the conflict with international Communism the "Hundred Years' War," to prepare Americans for what he foresaw. He feared that they were unfitted by temperament for a conflict that might last generations.[5]

On February 21, 1947, Thompson was in his office looking forward to the weekend when his boss John Hickerson, the director of EUR, came in to brief him on a crisis developing in Greece and Turkey. Earlier that day, the British ambassador had delivered a note to Undersecretary of State Dean Acheson (because of Secretary of State George Marshall's absence), stating that British aid to Greece and Turkey would end, because Clement Attlee's Labour government had run out of money. The United Kingdom's withdrawal from Greece was another card in the collapse of the British Empire. Would the Americans take over? Hickerson told Thompson and his colleague Tom Wailes to participate in a Saturday working group to assess the situation—the first in a series of meetings to formulate support for Greece and Turkey. Kennan was not present at this meeting.[6]

Greece was in the middle of a civil war, with the Communist side being supplied by Tito's Yugoslavia. Turkey was vulnerable to pressure to accept a Soviet base on the Bosphorus Strait. The United States faced a monumental decision. Should America fill the void the British were leaving in Greece with economic and/or military aid (requiring Congressional approval, which would be difficult, with the United States wanting to contract into an isolationist posture), or should it stand back and watch Greece and Turkey fail and become vulnerable to Soviet encroachment?[7]

Hickerson met with Loy Henderson, head of the State Department's Near East and Asia (NEA) division, Acheson, and others that Monday to go over what Thompson and Wailes had worked on over the weekend and draft a memorandum to the president. The Special Committee to Study Assistance to Greece and Turkey now included Kennan. After a "long and energetic discussion," they concluded that the government should, in principle, provide that aid. Hickerson offered that it could be "presented to Congress in such a fashion as to electrify the American people." Thompson, Kennan, and John Jernegan (from NEA) prepared a memorandum for Secretary Marshall, setting forth the committee's recommendations.[8]

Truman approved the decision on Wednesday, and Secretary of State Marshall met with Congressional leaders the following day. Noticing that they were not responding to Secretary Marshall's "low-key" presentation, Acheson gave an impassioned plea of his own in support of the plan, invoking the specter of "Soviet domination of Europe, the Middle East, and Asia."[9] He voiced what would become the domino theory, although the metaphor he used was "like apples in a barrel infected by one rotten one, the corruption of Greece would infect Iran and Egypt, and to Europe through Italy and France."[10] He went so far as to liken the Greek crisis to Armageddon.[11] Acheson had shared FDR's optimism about the Soviet Union until mid-1946, when he became thoroughly disabused of this perception. Bohlen's observation that Kennan's illusions about the Soviet Union had been deep, and therefore his disillusionment was equally deep, also applied to Acheson.[12]

Senator Arthur H. Vandenberg took the lead in approving aid, "subject to the condition that the matter be presented . . . in the same geo-political terms."[13] As a Democrat, Truman faced a Republican Congress that had just won substantial legislative margins in a midterm election and was hostile to foreign aid, so Vandenberg further advised the president to make a personal appearance before Congress, in order to present the case to its members and the public "almost" as frankly and forcefully as Marshall and Acheson had.[14] Some say Vandenberg advised Truman to "scare the hell out of the country."[15]

At 10:30 a.m. on Friday, February 28, Acheson gathered a large group, including Thompson, in Secretary Marshall's conference room to give them instructions. He wanted the report presented to Congress and to the public in the "fullest and frankest terms." That afternoon, Francis Russell, director of the Office of Public Affairs, summarized Acheson's review of the situation. The Soviets "were maneuvering" in all parts of the world. Communist activity was growing in Turkey, Hungary, Austria, Italy, and France. Secretary Marshall believed that the world had arrived at an unparalleled point in history. It was not just the problem of bailing out the British or giving aid to US allies. Everything necessary to hold a non-Communist position in the Near East should be done.[16] The subcommittee, including Thompson, then formulated most of the themes that found their way into President Truman's message to Congress.[17]

Russell wondered about putting forward American involvement in Greece as a new US foreign policy—going to the assistance of free governments everywhere. Although Thompson thought it a good point to back "any government that was a democracy," he envisioned what the Soviet reaction to such a move would be. They would say that the United States was "pulling Britain's chestnuts out of the fire" and warn the United Kingdom against tying itself to the United States. They would also claim that America was supporting a reactionary government in Greece as part of a new anti-Soviet campaign. Turkey, Thompson suggested, should be downplayed, as assistance there could be seen as an "encircling" move on the part of the United States. The Soviets would cite all this as an excuse for any anti-Western actions. Adverting to Kennan, Thompson said that if the British departure left a vacuum in Greece, that could draw in the Soviet Union. Therefore, helping Greece financially was precisely the way to *avoid* war. Thompson did not want anyone to regard US intervention as an aggressive measure, and he suggested clarifying that there was no intention of sending US troops to Greece.[18]

After an hour and a half, the participants broke up into subgroups to work out the details of the subcommittee's report. Thompson was assigned to the public information group, to craft the sales pitch to Congress.[19] He suggested that Kennan be included as part of this working meeting in Russell's office, but he never was.[20] Later, Joseph Jones credited Thompson with "taking charge of the drafting of the most important parts of the report."[21]

The final report began, "A cardinal objective of United States foreign policy is a world in which nations shall be able to work out their own way of life free of coercion by other nations."[22] It then went on to present the rationale for US intervention, "It is the policy of the United States to give support to free peoples who are attempting to resist subjugation," underscored by stating that "this is not a new policy," as evidenced by the Atlantic Charter, the Declaration of the United Nations, and the Yalta summit. The report then professed that this policy would not increase world tension, but rather would enable an understanding where "the free countries of the world . . . can co-exist peacefully" with the Soviet Union. As drafts were passed around, somehow "it is the policy" changed to "it must be the policy," which led to the interpretation that it was a *new* policy.[23] This shift signaled a more provocative and confrontational attitude, thus changing a speech about aid to Greece into a universal doctrine.

On March 7, only a few weeks before the deadline for British withdrawal from Greece, Secretary Marshall, who was in Paris, on his way to Moscow, received a cable containing the draft speech. Bohlen, who was accompanying the secretary, said in his memoirs that he and Marshall thought "there was too much flamboyant anti-Communism in the speech." They made no substantive changes, however, accepting that the language was necessary to get it through Congress.[24] On Wednesday, March 12, 1947, the president appeared before a joint session of the Congress and delivered what came to be known as the Truman Doctrine.

In 1954, when Thompson was secretly in London negotiating the settlement regarding Trieste, Joseph Jones wrote to him, asking for his help on a book about those exciting days. Thompson declined, responding, "I have always felt that the responsibility in these matters is that of the top officers in the Department and that it is as wrong to ascribe credit to their subordinates as it is to attribute blame." In his letter to Jones, Thompson noted that while it was true in this case that the writing of policy preceded—and helped form—the basic policy decision, the "tail was wagging the dog in appearance only."[25]

Thompson said some years later that no one, including the president or the secretary of state, could explain how an idea was born, since "every day is a new situation; the action of one country affects others."[26] He asserted it was not the genesis of an idea per se, but the leadership, who chose *which* idea to act on, that mattered. The Truman Doctrine speech was less the product of a considered manifesto, created to guide future action, as it was the result of forming a practical answer to the crisis at hand. As Thompson wrote to Arthur Schlesinger Jr. in 1967, what was presented in that speech was not exactly a "choice between balance of power and universalism. My recollection is that in dealing with the day to day problems as they arose, not many were so conscious that they were making a choice between these two policies; rather, we were thinking more in terms of our obligation to the Poles, the dangers of further Soviet expansion, etc."[27]

The Truman Doctrine speech forcefully put the situation in Greece and Turkey into the context of a divided world, in order to obtain congressional approval. Unfortunately, once written, it no longer applied only to a specific problem, but instead became the focus of a general US policy that would drive events for years to come. When Congress appropriated funds for aid to Greece and Turkey, it also authorized covert funding to support non-Communist parties in France and Italy, which would be one of the United States' first salvos in the looming psychological war.[28]

When Jones was compiling his book, Kennan was attempting to redefine his role in these events and the ensuing policy. Kennan claimed to have objected to Truman's speech during its drafting.[29] The evidence, however, shows that all of Kennan's edits were either accepted or were insignificant.[30] Once Stalin had died and the Vietnam War had started, it is understandable that Kennan wanted to distance himself from the Truman Doctrine. Thompson never wrote his memoirs, so he was spared the temptation, but even as late as 1965, he repeated in a speech that he was "proud of having participated in those momentous days."[31] He thought the Truman Doctrine was the correct policy at that time and felt satisfaction in knowing that limits were finally being set. After Stalin's death, when Thompson tried to get the US government to see that the situation was now different, he would be reminded that changing an American administration's accepted orthodoxy is not easy.

The Making of the Marshall Plan

As the Truman Doctrine speech was being prepared, the Allies attempted once again to settle the final peace treaties for Austria and Germany at the conference of foreign ministers, which Marshall was attending. This conference achieved nothing but a postponement for yet another meeting. The inability of the Allies to resolve the German situation would insinuate itself throughout the Cold War and the rest of Thompson's career. The problem was that neither the Soviets nor the Western allies had a clear idea of what to do about Germany.

At first the United States was in favor of splitting the country apart, and even considered Treasury Secretary Henry Morgenthau's plan to strip Germany of all heavy industry and force it to return to an agrarian economy. When it became clear that a robust and re-industrialized Germany was needed to bring about the recovery of Europe, and that Western attitudes toward the Soviets were changing, the United States wanted to unite at least the Western nations' zones of occupation in Germany into an independent European state with a strong economy, which could also act as a buffer against any eventual Soviet military attack. The French also preferred to have the western part of Germany integrated into Western Europe, as a safeguard against a German military revival. The British were reluctant to attempt serious negotiation with the Soviets on German reunification.[32] The Soviet policy toward Germany was "shrouded in mystery."[33] On the one hand, Stalin had originally desired a united Germany, both to get maximum reparations payments and because he thought it might still fall under Soviet influence.[34] On the other hand, if that were not possible, he wanted Germany to be split apart, to keep it from ever causing harm again.

The Western allies were willing to agree to unite Germany, but only if free elections determined its government, something the Soviets were against unless they could control the results. If they couldn't have all of Germany, they at least did not want to lose the part they now occupied. Elections also held a danger, albeit a remote one, for the West: the Germans might choose a Socialist government and thus fall into an unacceptable bloc. This uncertainty resulted in a stalled agreement and the burden of continued financial support for an occupied Germany.[35] The unsettled situation also affected Austria, which was still under Allied control. Before the Soviets tackled the issue of Austria, they wanted to see what would happen to Germany. Reports of the dire situation in Western Europe and the lack of agreement over Germany resulted in the formation of the Marshall Plan.[36] If there had been no Truman Doctrine, there probably would not have been a Marshall Plan, and, like the former, it was not the inspiration of just one mind, but the product of many contributions.[37]

In 1947, the relief that a horrible war had ended was overwhelmed by the terrible reality of its consequences. Although the UN and the United States had pumped millions of dollars in aid into Europe, it was still not enough. As Thompson explained: "The destruction had been greater than [we had] thought. Probably the greatest basis of miscalculation was the intangible factors such as the breakdown of trade contracts between countries in Europe. . . . [There] was no credit mechanism in place, which meant that the people who had been doing business across frontiers no longer knew what the credit standing of another firm was. If they did make a deal, they couldn't be sure they could get their money back, etc. All this paralyzed Europe, so despite the enormous help pouring in, it was not curing."[38] There were also wrenching social consequences. Millions of displaced people were trying to find a home, food supplies were short, distribution systems no longer functioned, and unemployment was rampant.

As if that was not punishment enough, 1947 was the coldest winter since 1880, and this was followed by the hottest, driest summer since records began.[39] It was said at the time that the wheat crop in France was the smallest since the days of Napoleon.[40] The Americans tried to help by sending corn flour, but the French didn't know how to use it, resulting in almost inedible bread.[41] In the Soviet Union, over a million people died as a result of the famine, and there were even reports of cannibalism. There was a sense of hopelessness and impending disaster everywhere.[42] The frustration in Western Europe over this slow recovery made it ripe for Communism. Italy now had more Communist Party members than Poland or Yugoslavia, and France had over 900,000 Party members.[43]

Secretary of State George Marshall concluded that Stalin's indifference to the terrible economic conditions in Germany and Europe meant that Stalin understood a war-torn Europe made it vulnerable to his country's ideology. Marshall decided to set up an in-house think tank to help assess Soviet intentions and formulate strategy.[44] Impressed by Kennan and his Long Telegram, Marshall put Kennan in charge of it. The new Policy Planning Staff (PPS) of the State Department was formally established on May 5, 1947.[45] One of the first things Marshall asked Kennan and his staff to do was to come up with a plan to help Europe get back on its feet.[46]

Another major participant was William Clayton, assistant secretary for economics, who prepared a lengthy report for Marshall. He, too, had travelled to Europe that spring and was equally struck by the misery there. Thus what was even more important than his written report was the graphic description he gave to Marshall, Acheson, and other State Department officers, which left an enduring impression on them. Clayton predicted: "Without further prompt and substantial aid from the United States, economic, social, and political disintegration will overwhelm Europe. Aside from the awful implications which this would have for the future peace and security of the world, the immediate effects on our domestic economy would be disastrous."[47] Marshall then passed both Clayton's memo and report to Bohlen and asked him to draft the commencement speech Marshall planned to give at Harvard University in June 1947, which initiated what became known as the Marshall Plan. The formal plan began in April 1948, lasted for four years, and had Congressional appropriations of more than $12 billion in aid for Europe.[48]

The Soviets and Eastern European countries were not excluded from participating in the Marshall Plan, and a few of the latter showed real interest. The Polish Ambassador,

Josef Winiewicz, met with Thompson (representing EUR) and asked point blank if the plan was to include Eastern Europe or just Western Europe.[49] Thompson assured him that the idea was to develop a means for the recovery of Europe as a whole, but added that events seemed to divide rather than unite its various nations.[50] The Czechs went even further, wanting to be in Paris in July 1947, when the Soviets, the British, and the French met to implement the plan.

Everyone knew well before the meeting that Soviet participation was highly unlikely.[51] Molotov objected to the Marshall Plan, saying that it would affect the internal affairs of each country, and left the conference. Accepting US aid in a collective European plan that involved sharing resources would mean that the Soviets could lose their grip on all of their satellites in Eastern Europe, which was unthinkable. The publication of Kennan's "X Article"—advocating containing and possibly rolling back Communism—just at that time could not have helped. Stalin categorically forbade the Czechs from participating, and he then quickly took steps to ensure the complete Communist Party takeover of that government.[52]

Although the intent of the Marshall Plan was not to set barriers or prevent Soviet participation, it had this effect. Some saw that as an added bonus. Those who developed the plan certainly took no measures to facilitate Soviet acceptance of it, and at no time in the discussions did they introduce the idea that doing so might ease East-West tensions.[53]

In September 1947, even before the Marshall Plan had been approved by Congress, the USSR devised the Molotov Plan.[54] The Soviet government established the Communist Information Bureau (Cominform) to make sure the Communist parties of Soviet satellites and other countries did not veer from the policies it dictated. It provided all of them with a "clear cut ideological perspective on global confrontation with the US," signaling that, rather than turning to political realism, Stalin would use ideology to maintain iron-fisted control.[55]

Looking back on the period, Thompson noted: "Probably one of the most important things that we had to deal with was the psychological or the mental attitude of the people of Europe.... At that time people were talking about how long it would take the Soviets to reach Paris."[56] The move to counter a feared Soviet expansion did not stop with economic programs. By the following spring, Western powers took the first steps to establish a military alliance for the defense of Western Europe, which would become the North Atlantic Treaty Organization. The strengthening of NATO would later cause the Soviets to set up the Warsaw Pact, a mutual defense treaty between the Soviet Union and the other Communist states of Eastern Europe.[57]

By this time, Kennan's idea of containment as a US policy had earned the status of doctrine.[58] The problem was that Kennan had never actually explained how this containment was to occur, which, in turn, sparked debates—still going on—about exactly what he meant. As Thompson pointed out late in life, Kennan "shifted positions on issues so convincingly that he can be distorting."[59] When C. Ben Wright analyzed Kennan's spoken and written positions in the time period leading up to the Long Telegram and the "X Article," he came to the conclusion that Kennan certainly had not excluded military intervention in preventing Soviet expansionism, but thought the mere reality of superior American military power would be sufficient to allow political and diplomatic pressure to keep the Soviets in check.[60] Although Kennan later insisted that he had always meant political—not military—containment, his close colleagues believed otherwise and observed that "he never saw fit to correct them."[61] In 1947, Thompson certainly understood Kennan to mean "containment" as "military containment," which, Thompson again thought later, was sound—for that time period.[62]

The policy of containment was criticized by some, who thought it was not a forceful enough way to deal with the Soviets, but Kennan and the PPS were already working out other ways to secretly undermine the Communist bloc through covert actions directed by the benign-sounding Office of Policy Coordination (OPC). It was the beginning of rollback.

The Birth of Covert Operations

There were no organizations engaged in clandestine
activity when I entered the Foreign Service and I can only
regret that espionage and counter-espionage have become
prevalent throughout the world.
—LLEWELLYN THOMPSON, speech,
University of Colorado, June 6, 1969

In view of the increasing tension with the Soviet Union and to better deal with the resulting security issues, the National Security Act of 1947 created a presidential advisory
group, called the National Security Council (NSC), to coordinate between the executive branch, the Central Intelligence Agency (CIA), and the Joint Chiefs of Staff (JCS).[1]
The first resolution of the NSC (NSC 1/1) authorized US peacetime covert espionage.
Thompson and his colleagues in the State Department would all become involved in this in
one way or another. Kennan began a new organization, the Office of Policy Coordination,
that carried out covert operations behind the Iron Curtain. Frank Gardner Wisner (or
"Uncle Wiz," as the Thompson daughters came to know him), an attractive, energetic young
lawyer and former OSS officer, first led and sculpted the OPC. Charles Thayer began Voice
of America broadcasts in Russian to the Soviet Union. Chip Bohlen, with Thompson,
mined the Russian refugee community in New York City for information.[2]

The Slippery Slope to Covert Operations

In November 1947, a subcommittee of the NSC, the State–Army–Navy–Air Force–Coordinating Committee (SANACC), took up the thorny issue of how to conduct covert operations in peacetime.[3] James Forrestal, the first Secretary of Defense, was the godfather of
the documents that authorized the use of covert psychological warfare.[4] He and Kennan
were certain that Italy was the initial front in a Communist takeover of Western Europe,
and it became their first focus of attention.[5] A clandestine operation was mounted to help
Amedeo Francesco De Gasperi and his Christian Democrats win the Italian elections,
which they did.[6] De Gasperi would continue to use the threat of a Communist takeover as

a means of putting pressure on the United States over funding and later to try to get his way in the Trieste negotiations.

The Italian operation's success increased Kennan's interest in clandestine activity and raised the possibility not only of containing Communism, but of actually "rolling it back." Kennan and his Policy Planning Staff came up with a program to do just that, and in such a way as to be deniable by the US government.[7] The question was *which* government agency could actually carry out covert operations.[8] The military did not want control of subversive activities in peacetime, and the CIA (at that time) saw itself as an intelligence gathering organization, not one to conduct paramilitary activities.[9] In June 1948, the NSC created the Office of Policy Coordination (OPC) to carry out Kennan's plan.[10] Administratively attached to the CIA, it functioned under the supervision of the PPS.[11] The OPC kept some individuals in the State Department informed of its operations, and eventually the CIA took it over completely, but for at least four years, it engaged in clandestine activities with virtually no supervision or accountability, and with seemingly limitless funding.[12] The OPC's mission was to assist refugee programs; coordinate anti-Communist labor union activities in Western Europe; broadcast news stories behind the Iron Curtain; support resistance groups in Eastern Europe, in preparation for possible regime changes or a future "hot" war; and recruit and exploit defectors, displaced persons, and refugees.[13]

When asked to comment on the establishment of "freedom committees" as a means of bringing the refugees together, Thompson warned that "if the avowed purpose of these committees . . . is the overthrow of the governments now there, the [US] Government would be seriously handicapped in any relations with them, for by official relations [with the freedom committees] we would furnish an excuse to these countries for the breaking of relations [with us]." Thompson thought that being able to keep an official American presence in Soviet bloc countries was critical to the morale of their citizens, and he did not like the idea of the State Department sponsoring refugee groups who might jeopardize that. He did not, however, discount the value of "keeping tabs on them so as to be accurately informed of their activities and views."[14]

Kennan recommended that Wisner head the OPC and had himself appointed as its State Department representative; thus, in addition to his other functions, he played an important part in covert operations in 1948–1949.[15] Kennan later said, "It was the greatest mistake I ever made."[16] The OPC was very secret, and only three people had detailed knowledge of it and its operations.[17] Even the Secretary of State did not. Thompson was one of thirteen men who had general but not more-specific knowledge of OPC operations.[18]

Thompson and Bohlen gathered information from Russian émigré groups in New York City. It was evident to the two men that the information they obtained was hardly reliable, as each group had their own disparate interests and feuds. Thompson became even more convinced that the State Department should have nothing to do with the Russian émigré groups. In a meeting in February 1949, Kennan, Thompson, and Wisner made the decision to direct all exiles and refugees who were seeking support for their causes to the National Committee for Free Europe (NCFE) in New York City.[19]

The NCFE was a private organization created by the Council on Foreign Relations and supposedly funded by private contributions.[20] The idea was to support Communist refugees and provide them with constructive work until the destruction of the Soviet bloc, when they could then take part in a democracy in their own countries. Important Americans lent their name to its board: Allen Dulles, Henry Luce, and General Dwight Eisenhower, among others. In reality, NCFE monies came through the OPC, which oversaw and controlled its activities.[21]

Their most successful project was Radio Free Europe.[22] Staffed by émigrés, it broadcast anti-Communist propaganda into the Soviet satellite countries, and for many years it provided people behind the Iron Curtain with an alternative source of news. Another initiative of the NCFE was to grant young exile students generous scholarships to study at a college or university, presumably to have them on tap for any future action against the Communist bloc.[23] Although this never happened, it gave a number of refugees a chance to get a college degree. The NCFE's close relationship with the OPC meant it was also a recruiting ground for operations that included attempts at overthrowing governments, such as in Albania.

Albania

When Thompson met up again with James McCargar (the Cheshire cat from his Moscow days), he found himself uncomfortably involved in the beginnings of an OPC operation to overthrow the Albanian Communist regime—a tragic story of betrayal on many levels.[24] After leaving Moscow, McCargar had become an operative for the Pond—an even *more* super-secret organization than the OPC—led by the flamboyant and possibly mentally unstable John "Frenchy" Grombach.[25] When Thompson reunited with him, McCargar had already left the Pond and gone over to the OPC to work on the joint Anglo-American operations in Albania.[26]

Thompson attended a meeting between British Foreign Secretary Ernest Bevin and Dean Acheson, now the US secretary of state, where Bevin proposed nothing less than an American commitment to bring down the Enver Hoxha government, and even wondered aloud if there might not be some "kings around that could be put in" to replace Hoxha.[27] Acheson was agreeable, but Thompson, perhaps taken aback at the thought of plunking down a king in place of the dictator, pointed out that the Free Albania Committee would have a voice in forming any new government. Bevin, however, was skeptical and stated that "a person we could handle" would be better.

Wisner and the OPC took on joint operations with the British to infiltrate Albanian anti-Communist émigrés into the country, in order to help overthrow the regime. Thompson found himself involved further when McCargar asked to meet Lord Gladwyn Jebb, a member of the British Foreign Office's Russia Committee, in Thompson's office to explain the details of the mission. McCargar presented Jebb with a one-page paper summarizing operational actions. Jebb handed it back to McCargar "between two fingers as though it was something odious."[28] Jebb accepted the proposal but did not want to be on record for doing so. Thompson told McCargar that he disapproved of such operations, but he agreed to meet two of the delegates of the Albanian committee,[29] who were seeking State Department support to head a new Albanian government once the Communists were overthrown. Thompson listened but made it clear that the State Department could not help the committee and wanted to limit contact with them. He suggested that instead they get in touch with the NCFE.[30]

Thompson subsequently used his position at EUR to block McCargar's appointment as chief of (the CIA) station in Vienna. He told McCargar that "I don't want Foreign Service Officers doing that kind of work abroad." As McCargar described it: "This would have been covert operations . . . not necessarily blowing up things—that's not really an effective way of doing things. You get people out, you subvert people, you create a political movement of one kind or another—personnel intensive kind of work. The reason [Thompson] didn't like this was there were chances of whatever you were doing being blown and people would discover you were doing what diplomats were not supposed to be doing and you are under diplomatic cover. Tommy was quite right, although now it's honored in the breach rather than in the observance. Times have changed, but at the time this came up it was half a century ago and that wasn't proper. I was disappointed."[31]

Another of the early members of the OPC was an amazing character named Carmel Offie, Ambassador Bullitt's unlikely protégé in Moscow in the 1930s. He had been involved in one scandal too many to continue in the Foreign Service but had now joined the OPC. Offie, both a charming and an unsavory wheeler-dealer, was tailor made for the new school of covert operations (or for a bad movie about it).[32] Offie had spent time in the Albanian capital of Tirana after World War II, which made him theoretically suitable for the operation.[33]

Attempts to unseat Hoxha proved to be a disaster. All of the agents inserted into the country were promptly captured and executed, thanks to the notorious, high-ranking British intelligence officer turned Soviet spy, Kim Philby—who alerted the Albanians to the entire operation. Thompson's reservations about the whole business were justified. Its abject failure should have demonstrated that such a covert action, using paramilitary resources, would not bring about regime change. Instead, just as Thompson feared, it gave Hoxha the excuse to justify the total isolation of Albania from the rest of the world.

Strategy Planning

Thompson sat in on and contributed to meetings of the Policy Planning Staff and would eventually conclude that the problem with the PPS was that its head should not have been drawn into operations, the way Kennan had been. Instead, his role should have been kept separate.[34] The PPS was supposed to have figured out a long-range strategy for American foreign policy, but under the vague umbrella of containment, it actually ended up creating events and then reacting to them as they were happening.[35]

Thompson's understanding was that this policy of containment was to deter the further expansion of Communist regimes, in the hope that "once this was achieved, developments would take place within the Communist world which would make it easier to deal with."[36] Acheson, however, had no intention of waiting for "developments" to take place on their own. He felt that the vital ingredient in containment was military strength. Kennan, who had begun to waver after Albania, decided to leave the PPS, while Wisner led the OPC to even grander schemes. Kennan's position at the PPS was taken over by his deputy, Paul Nitze, who was more aligned with Acheson and also clearly understood that "policy" to mean "military containment." Nitze worried more about Soviet "capabilities" than "intentions" and argued in favor of the United States attaining superior military strength over the Soviets. He would get his way.[37]

Jane Monroe

Despite the seriousness of the events he was in the midst of, Thompson fell in love. His mother had given up hope that her forty-four-year-old son would ever marry, and she bought an extra plot in the Las Animas cemetery, next to the one for her and her husband, so that, when "his time came," he would not be alone. It was not that Thompson had no women in his life; there were several. Nina was still in Moscow, and there are traces in his papers of a woman in London who was quite important to him. All would soon fade from his mind, however. In summer 1948, Thompson made a sudden, rash, and precipitous decision to marry, scarcely seven days after meeting a young divorcée and her five-year-old daughter. Yet his courtship and marriage plans were intertwined with the worries and preoccupation of one of the initial battles of wills between the Soviets and the Americans— the first Berlin crisis (June 1948–May 1949).

The crisis was sparked by a dispute over the Allies' introduction of a new currency to replace the old, deflated Reichmark in the western zones of Germany. The Soviets responded by stopping all travel by land between the western zones of Germany and Berlin, as well as preventing all food supplies from the farm areas under Soviet control from reaching the non-Soviet sectors of Berlin. Trouble was already brewing in Berlin when Thompson received orders in spring 1948 to go to Rome to chair an internal State Department conference on problems with implementing the peace treaties with Italy (including Trieste), Hungary, Bulgaria, and Rumania.[38] After the conference, Thompson was to visit the chiefs of mission and report back to Washington, DC.[39] He would also have the opportunity to see his old boss, James Dunn, then the US ambassador to Italy. Thompson boarded the SS *Saturnia* in New York City on June 2, 1948, and stood on the deck as the big ocean liner pulled out of pier 96.[40]

Twenty-eight-year-old Jane Monroe and her young daughter, Fernanda ("Andy"), were on board the ship, intending to spend the summer on the Italian Riviera with Andy's paternal grandmother and namesake. Jane had been married to Robert Goelet, an unpromising young man who had vowed to give up an active social life in the jazz clubs of New

York City to become a gentleman farmer in Connecticut. His father headed one of the wealthiest New York families, and his godfather was Averell Harriman, but as Bobby soon demonstrated an incapacity for either work or family life, Jane asked for a divorce. Her ex-father-in-law had persuaded her to take this trip to Europe, hoping that his wayward son, also in Italy that summer, might get back together with her. Jane accepted the invitation to Italy, as she was fond of her ex-mother-in-law and wanted to tell her in person that she had decided to remarry, although not to Bobby. Out of two possible candidates, Jane had chosen a young Bostonian surgeon over a Venezuelan architect to be her next husband.

Most of Jane's childhood had been spent in New Jersey, but she preferred to say she came from Massachusetts, where she went to high school. Her mother, who lost her twin sister to pneumonia when they were both in an orphanage, became one of the first women to receive an advanced nursing degree. She married her chemistry professor, Kenneth Potter Monroe. Professor Monroe, a bright but highly strung man, battled mental illness for many years, which meant that Jane's mother often had to support the family of five.[41]

Jane wanted to be a ballerina, but she also loved painting and fancied herself an artist. Although her formal education did not go beyond junior college, she had a good dose of curiosity and was ambitious in her fields of interest. She possessed a natural sense of survival and a flair for pushing forward, even when the odds were against her. Her good looks got her modeling jobs, and she worked as a hostess during the 1939 World's Fair in New York City.

An artist friend of Jane's was on board the SS *Saturnia*. Kay Eichholz was escorting students from the Parsons School of Design for an "Italian experience." Her plan was to show some of her own paintings at the Venice Biennale, between stints of chaperoning her wards. Jane was to accompany Kay part of the time, to breathe in the bohemian atmosphere of the artistic world. Jane's ex-sister-in-law, Mimi Goelet, and Mimi's son Ogden were also on board, so the three women friends looked forward to an agreeable crossing together.

In those days, socializing and meeting fellow passengers was an integral part of the voyage. There were special trunks (in essence, miniclosets) specifically designed for ocean liners. Once opened, clothes hung neatly on one side, while smaller items rested in drawers on the other. Thompson traveled light as far as clothes went, but he came well prepared with reading material and papers to study for the conference. The US ambassador to Poland, Stanton Griffis, had cabled him to look up "an attractive young artist" traveling in third class on the liner. Thompson obediently did so the second day out. Kay, who had bribed her way out of third class and into first class to be able to lunch with Jane and Mimi, told them she had been invited to supper by "some State Department type." The next day, Kay reported to them that he was quite charming and good looking and had invited all of them to have cocktails that evening in his stateroom.

Jane arrived late, because she had to arrange for a babysitter. She found Mimi already in the hallway, knocking persistently. They walked through the unlocked door and found the room too dark and quiet for a cocktail party. Hearing some noise, they tiptoed through the suite and discovered Thompson, attired in his dressing gown, stretched out on his bed and obviously engrossed in piles of papers. Seeing their expressions of surprise and horror, which mirrored his own, he explained that he had indeed invited them to cocktails, but earlier that day, at noon, and in the bar. No one had shown up and he was slightly annoyed. After an awkward moment, Thompson suggested that they let him get dressed, and he would meet them in the bar for a drink.[42] Thompson took punctuality seriously and looked askance at those who did not. Once when he, as an ambassador, officiated at a marriage, the bride asked him what advice he could give her to ensure a happy marriage. "Never be late," he told her.

There are no details of what happened over the following few days, except that when Jane's introduced her daughter to him as "Uncle" Tommy, Andy remarked, "Oh no, not another uncle!" Somehow Thompson won Andy over, as well as her mother. By the time the ship reached Genoa in Italy, Tommy and Jane decided to get married, and he promised Andy that he would marry her, too. She was delighted and dubbed him "Gub-Gub," after the wise old pig in the *Doctor Doolittle* children's books. Years later, interrogated by their doubting daughters, neither parent could give a convincing explanation of how two people could know beyond any shadow of a doubt, in the space of just a few days, that they would spend the rest of their lives together. "We just knew" was the best they could do.

Jane and Tommy swore that they would burn "all their bridges" to their other relationships and marry at the end of the summer. Thompson got off the ship in Genoa, to proceed to Rome, and Jane continued on to Naples. His head was in the clouds. Thompson cabled her almost as soon as he had left the ship to tell her that in his absentmindedness, he had left his suit on board, which he asked Jane to hand over to the US consul in Naples, to be forwarded to him.

The Conference in Rome

Dunn opened the conference on June 14, 1948, by asking Thompson to provide the political background. Thompson acknowledged that most of the Balkan countries had not received as much attention from the State Department as they should have. With the rejection of the Marshall Plan by the Soviet satellite countries, economic inducements seemed a dead end for political reform there.[43] Thompson confirmed this after his tour of those missions. The United States, he said, did not intend to meet Soviet pressure with force. The American plan, therefore, was to build up Western Europe. He cautioned against pushing problems in the "curtain countries" too far before "substantial economic recovery [was] effected in Western Europe."[44]

The almost daily letters and cables from Thompson to Jane did not cease during the conference, or over the entire summer. Sometimes he would cable her twice a day, mostly asking why she hadn't written to him and if that meant anything. He also made numerous queries as to whether she had indeed "burnt her bridges," and he implored her to send him a photo of herself. Her answers were businesslike, with few details, but she did eventually send him a picture of herself, sitting on the beach, with a sullen expression on her face that was hard to decipher. There was no question that she was attractive—petite, brunette, with a sort of Lana Turner look to her—with large, mink brown eyes, but it must have

A studio portrait of Jane Monroe, Llewellyn Thompson Jr.'s future wife, circa 1947. Thompson Family Papers.

been obvious to him from the start that she was hardly the type to be either on time or discreet. Considering herself a free spirit, she pretty much said what was on her mind, whether it was diplomatic or not, but he adored her and nothing else mattered. As several of the embassy staff commented: "They were the perfect couple. He was quiet and serious and she was cheerful, talkative, and vivacious."[45] Another said: "The relationship between the two of them was always so special. We didn't really understand it. Perhaps they didn't either. He really enjoyed watching her operate. It was like going to the theater."[46] Many said she was an important part of Thompson's success in Moscow. "She lit up the place" with her entertainments of artists and intelligentsia.[47] Rada Khrushcheva would later say about her: "People trusted Jane because of her sincerity and spontaneity. Jane won over everyone, including my father. If that isn't the highest art of diplomacy!"[48] So perhaps Thompson did know what he was doing when they married.

Thompson kept Jane informed of his day-to-day activities in Rome: "If only I can control the times you creep into my thoughts, it would be alright, but you pop up when I least expect you. Today I had to ask the Ambassador to repeat a question he had put directly to me and he thought I was mad, which of course I am." When he didn't hear from her, he wrote, "My father told me never to write the girl I fell in love with or I would surely lose her," but even that did not deter him. Thompson continued writing to Jane after he left Rome for a tour of the US missions in the Iron Curtain countries.

He started out in Belgrade, a few days before the Soviets squeezed the door closed on Berlin, blockading all Western access by ground to that city, and a few days prior to the official Stalin-Tito split. Although conversation at the embassy concerned the increasing strain between the two Communist countries, he explained to Jane: "In Belgrade you signal which way you want to go by tooting your horn, one for left and two for right. Can you imagine what New York would be like in such a system?" Thompson's instructions were to persuade the chargé d'affaires in Belgrade, R. Borden Reams, and his subordinate, Charles Stefan, that they should retract a cable they had sent to the State Department, claiming there was trouble between Stalin and Tito. Whether Thompson's arguments were half-hearted or his state of mind not focused, Reams would not "see the light." The rumors, however, were not unfounded. Tito had summoned up the courage to defy Stalin, claiming that he (Tito) had come to power in his country through his own efforts, not through Stalin or the Red Army.[49]

Charles Stefan, who refused to change his mind about the situation in Yugoslavia, ended up driving Thompson to Budapest the next day, as a "placating gesture,"[50] where they learned that Stalin had thrown Tito out of the Cominform. Thompson shook Stefan's hand and said, "You were right and I was wrong." They all understood the event as "a break of the greatest significance."[51] Stalin eliminated anyone in the Communist bloc who showed signs of opposition to his treatment of Tito. This strategy helped Stalin consolidate his grip on the rest of the Iron Curtain countries, but it also gave the West new hope that the monolithic Soviet bloc had cracks. Tito took similar draconian measures: he purged or murdered those who professed loyalty to Stalin.

Thompson still had a few more stops before he could head home, including Vienna and Frankfurt, where he "cleaned up the Air Force, including General LeMay," at poker. By July 8, he had reached London and informed Jane that he had burnt his bridges, adding that he hoped she "had started some fires of her own."[52] By the time he returned to Washington, DC, in mid-July, the Berlin situation had worsened, the Soviet blockade of Berlin was in full force, and the Allied airlift to that city had just begun. He wrote to Jane that if he cabled her and used the words "insist you return," as opposed to "hope you return," it was a code to let her know the situation was increasingly serious and that she and Andy had better get out of Europe right away. He also told her that he was looking in the capital for a house with a grand piano for Andy.[53]

Meanwhile, his brother MWood wrote, "After waiting so long and looking the field over so carefully you should be getting someone extra special." MWood also had to ask Tommy to tell them *something* about Jane: how old was she, where did she come from, and maybe a photo? The news from Colorado was not happy, as Lula, their mother, was exhibiting signs of dementia, including repeatedly trying to contact the State Department. Worried about his mother, Thompson planned to go to Colorado later that summer to see his family and tell them about Jane in person. He returned to Las Animas at the end of August, to celebrate his father's eighty-fifth birthday. His family was excited to hear about Jane. Later, when she finally met her new father-in-law, he studied her over the rim of his glasses and said, "Well, you may be a 'grass widow,' but you come from mighty good stock."[54] Llewellyn Sr. had discovered that a well-known Baptist minister and writer, Elder Lemuel Potter, was Jane's great-grandfather.

Thompson could not stay long with his parents, since Berlin was still a problem. "The situation is very tense," he wrote to Jane in September. Jane finally arrived in New York

City on September 16, to find Thompson waiting for her "like a child waiting for Christmas." They had a few days together there before she left to arrange the wedding, and he went back to Washington, DC. As soon as he got there, he wrote: "I was so happy that I was frightened. All the love and affection I have held back all these years and would never give to anyone is now completely yours irretrievably."

On October 2, 1948, four months to the day after boarding the SS *Saturnia*, Jane and Thompson married and moved into the "strawberry box"—a tiny townhouse in Georgetown. Two years later, when Thompson was appointed minister at the embassy in Rome, they would make the same ocean crossing again, but this time with two children and a dog.

The Berlin Blockade

While the birth of US clandestine operations was underway, Stalin had moved another chess piece and began a postwar offensive against the city of Berlin. Thompson, as part of the Berlin Group at the State Department, was involved in drafting the formal note of protest to the Soviet Union. It warned that, unless ground traffic to Berlin was restored, the next obligatory step would be to submit the matter to the UN.[55] Thompson, as deputy director for EUR, knocked on the door of the Soviet Embassy in Washington, DC, on September 27, 1948, to personally deliver it. In an emblematic display of secretiveness and distrust, only a hand emerged from the door of the Soviet Embassy.[56]

The roots of the problem were planted as World War II wound down and the victors consolidated their positions in Europe. Germany and its capital, Berlin, were occupied, and both the city and the country were divided into four zones, all under the control of the Four Powers, also known as the Allied Control Council: the United States, the Soviet Union, France, and Britain. Any change to the status of either Germany or Berlin would require an agreement between all four.

Of the four zones of occupation in Berlin, three merged to become a Western stronghold and a showcase for the advances of capitalism—a situation Stalin feared. West Berlin, an island 100 kilometers inside the heart of Soviet-occupied eastern Germany, was like a keyhole through which the West could spy, a "hole in the control of the empire," and an escape route for thousands of East Germans and others in European satellite nations who were ready to forfeit ideology for the advantages of living in the West, especially once collectivization had begun in East Germany.[57] For both the West and the Soviet Union, their respective sectors of Germany and Berlin were the line drawn in the sand from which neither was willing to retreat or compromise.

Although General Lucius Clay, the military governor of occupied Germany, and General Dwight Eisenhower had not obtained written agreements guaranteeing land access to Berlin at the end of World War II,[58] there was a written agreement about air corridors into Berlin. To stop the Berlin airlift, Stalin would have to shoot down a plane, which would be an act of war. Stalin believed it was logistically impossible to supply the huge quantities of items, such as food and coal, the Berliners needed. He hoped his blockade would starve West Berlin, forcing it to join Communist East Berlin. It took a great deal of determination on the part of the Allies (in particular General Clay, in charge of the US zone in Germany), as well as the stamina of the Berliners, to make it a successful operation. For fifteen months, the Allies delivered 13,000 tons of food a day. At the height of the airlift, a plane reached Berlin every thirty seconds. In the meantime, the Western allies instituted a counterblockade, stopping all coal and steel shipments into the Soviet zone, crippling its industry. Contrary to Stalin's expectations, there was no sign that the airlift would stop, so he eventually backed down.

Thompson thought Stalin's choosing to cease the Soviet blockade did little to solve the problem of Berlin, since the pervious issues still existed there.[59] He later said that had "we submitted to the Soviet use of force we would have lost not only Berlin but probably Germany and possibly the whole of Europe."[60] Thompson believed that the airlift was a good example of military support of a political policy. He thought the Soviets agreed to lift their blockade, asking no price for doing so, for three distinct reasons: (1) to end the negative effects of the counterblockade, (2) to delay the formation of the West German government, and (3) to slow down the ratification of the North Atlantic Treaty and the creation of NATO.

Those sectors of Germany controlled by the United States, France, and the United Kingdom (known as the trizone), became the Federal Republic of Germany (FRG).[61] With its capital in Bonn, the FRG eventually obtained formal recognition as a nation, including by the Soviets. A few months later, on October 7, 1949, the Soviet zone became the German Democratic Republic (GDR), with its capital in East Berlin, but it did not receive formal recognition by the West. West Berlin's status returned to what it had been before the blockade.

Thompson would later say that perhaps "we should have made even greater effort than we did to prevent the creation of a Communist regime in East Germany and should have maintained Germany as a unit as was done in the case of Austria."[62] Stalin's German policy was a failure. For the duration of the Cold War, continuing pressure to get the Allies out of West Berlin would adversely affect all attempts at reaching any accommodation with the Soviets. Finally, in 1971, the Berlin Accords established a legal basis for unimpeded civilian access to West Berlin from West Germany.

10 ≋

Overseas Again

The military seemed to seek total security, which,
if it were ever achieved, would mean unacceptable
insecurity for the other side.
—LLEWELLYN THOMPSON, Policy Planning
    Staff meeting, December 1949

The Berlin blockade reinforced the belief that the Soviets had sinister goals. Thompson did not think the Soviet government was planning an armed action, but neither could he discard the possibility of war, since, in his opinion, the greatest danger was "from Soviet miscalculation."[1] The United States might underestimate the USSR's perception of a threat caused by American actions, or the Soviets might not fully recognize the Western nations' determination to safeguard what they considered important to their security.

In dealing with the Soviets, Thompson identified two principal problems. The negative one was the survival of democratic governments against the Soviet bloc's threat of Communist expansion. The positive problem was "maintaining and developing our own institutions, policies, and relationships to meet the strains of modern conditions."[2] Convinced that the Communist ideology was wrong and its goals unattainable, Thompson thought focusing on the second of the two problems was the better course. Throughout his life, Thompson's family heard him voice his conviction that Soviet Communism would be doomed if the United States shaped its society and government to exemplify its own professed virtues.

NATO

The Marshall Plan was not enough to dispel the fears that paralyzed Europe. Therefore, Thompson thought that the United States was correct in taking a lead in establishing the North Atlantic Treaty, which later became NATO.[3] He suggested that there were two objectives in its creation: (1) to win the Cold War using a political and diplomatic approach; and (2) to be prepared for a hot war, in the event it occurred. As he saw it, NATO was necessary to deter conflict, but it was not a first step toward an inevitable war.[4]

Kennan questioned the advisability of a broad military alliance like NATO, and the Hawks, such as Paul Nitze, had reservations about the military preparedness of the United States and its allies versus the Soviets and their satellites.[5] Nitze argued that a clear military advantage was essential to effect the policy of containment. When the Americans signed the NATO agreement in April 1949, it broke with that country's tradition of not tying itself to long-standing alliances. NATO committed the United States to ensuring Europe's security, thus enabling those nations to enjoy a period of political stability and economic growth. Like the Truman Doctrine, what was perhaps a logical and positive move at the time, as protection against Soviet aggression, became moot with the fall of the Soviet Union in 1991. By that time, however, NATO was an entrenched institution, with too many vested interests to simply disappear.

As the North Atlantic Treaty was being signed, Thompson received a letter from MWood, telling him that their Aunt Jenny was ill with liver cancer. She was sore, feverish, and weak, "just skin and bones," and those around her felt "pitiful and helpless." Meanwhile, Jane was pregnant, and the humid heat of Washington, DC, made her uncomfortable, so Thompson took her to a tiny place called Clark's Island, in the middle of Plymouth Bay in Massachusetts.[6] In preparation for fatherhood, and perhaps in keeping with the primitive state of the island, Thompson decided to grow a mustache like the one his father had worn, but he shaved it off again a year later, rather than take a new passport photo. The couple was there when they received news of Aunt Jenny's death one August night, and they decided that if their unborn child turned out to be a girl, which it did, they would name her Jenny. They were still on Clark's Island when Thompson, relaxing and reading on the porch, and half listening as his step-daughter Andy and her friend played nearby, suddenly pricked up his ears as the youngsters started screaming "Dean Acheson" at one another. McCarthyites had been accusing Acheson, despite his work on the Truman Doctrine, of being soft on Communists and, later, of having played a role in "losing China."[7] So when Thompson asked Andy what she and her playmate meant, she said, "Oh Daddy, that's just a dirty word we use." Thompson later told Acheson the story, and they both had a good laugh over it.

The State Department left Thompson off the promotion list yet again that summer. Thompson's boss, Hickerson, wrote to Ambassador Smith, "Frankly I do not know what else an officer would have to have in the way of ability and performance to merit promotion."[8] In his evaluation report, Hickerson called Thompson "one of our ablest Russian and Eastern European specialists," who would soon be ready "for one of the top jobs of the Service."[9] Thompson eventually got the promotion, but not until a year later.

The Communist Threat

The Soviets tested their first atomic bomb on August 19, 1949, and less than two months later, Mao Zedong took over China. There was a heightened sense of danger, now that the world's most populous nation had joined the Communist bloc. Perhaps for that reason, President Truman asked for a review of all the US strategic and military programs, in order to meet the new threats. Paul Nitze, heading the PPS, took an active role in Truman's call to action. Nitze was a very intense and methodical person. He did not come to conclusions based on intuition, or provide any analysis that was not backed by hard facts and watertight logic. He even smoked cigars with a vigor that left a chewed and mangled stump in the ashtray. Later, the Thompson girls were amazed that he could play tennis with men half his age and often win, even though he ended up drenched in sweat and dangerously red in the face. He seemed unfazed by inflicting an unnecessary torture on himself.

Nitze's work led to a top secret document known as NSC 68.[10] In March 1950, he gave the final draft to senior officials in the State Department, including Thompson, for comment. Nitze claimed the writing of that document was the most important act of his life.[11] NSC 68 was essentially a manifesto. In it, Nitze first characterized the struggle against Communism almost as a religious crusade: "The Soviet Union, unlike previous aspirants to hegemony, is animated by a new fanatic faith, antithetical to our own, and seeks to impose its absolute authority over the rest of the world. . . . The issues that face us are momentous, involving the fulfillment or destruction not only of this Republic but of civilization itself."[12] The Soviet state—or "slave state," as Nitze called it—stood against "the existence of freedom." The USSR was developing its military capacity for world domination. Second, he argued that any measure, "covert or overt, violent or non-violent, which served the purpose of frustrating the Kremlin design" was worth pursuing. In other words, the ends justified the means, whatever they might be.[13] Preemptive war was ruled out, but only because it was repugnant to most Americans. Third, the document recommended an unspecified but large increase in military spending.

Thompson read the draft but did not buy Nitze's argument and ignored his rhetoric. In his typical low-key fashion, Thompson said that the paper's conclusions "are not directly supported by the analysis."[14] He also suggested that the entire paper be reorganized. Thompson did not seem to think that new events had put the "free world" in more jeopardy than it had been before. Furthermore, he recommended that a "top-level board" examine the conclusions. He disagreed that increased military spending was necessary, instead arguing for a better allocation of resources. "The problem," he said once again, was to "create such political and economic conditions in the free world, backed by force sufficient to inhibit Soviet attack, that the Kremlin would accommodate itself to those conditions, gradually withdraw, and eventually change its policies drastically." Thompson's friend Bohlen also disagreed with the document. Bohlen did not think the Soviets were expansionist. Nor did he believe that they either anticipated or promoted the Communist takeover in China but, once it had occurred, Stalin "had no course except to help [China]."[15]

Nitze would never alter his perception of the Soviet threat or change his belief that it was America's duty to do whatever was necessary, even to the use of extreme measures, to ensure its own survival and security. In 1950, Nitze and his NSC 68 document inspired the creation of the Committee on the Present Danger (CPD). Nitze helped reestablish this organization in 1976, to lobby the US government to take action against Moscow. The CPD gave many of those later referred to as neoconservatives their launching pad and augmented their mindset. When the danger changed from Communism to terrorism in the twenty-first century, the CPD reappeared once again, its principles and its rhetoric remaining much the same.

The Korean War, which began in June 1950, seemed to vindicate those who had argued for the military brand of containment. One immediate consequence was a substantial increase in the US defense budget, for which NSC 68 had argued. It also gave a new sense of purpose and importance to NATO. It was no longer seen as a paper organization, but rather as a force capable of resisting a Soviet attack.[16] Few in those days would have accepted that the Korean War was not blatant, Soviet-inspired aggression. Several scholars, later reviewing newly available material, concluded instead that Stalin had not instigated that war, but had merely let it happen, hoping that it would strengthen the Soviet position in the Far East.[17] The Korean War lasted for three years and, after the armistice negotiations were concluded, left that country divided.

Rome

In 1950, Thompson was finally promoted to Foreign Service Officer (FSO) 1, with the rank of minister, and became the deputy chief of mission in the embassy in Rome—a position he was looking forward to. He already knew his new boss, Ambassador James Clement Dunn, well. It was also a good time to leave Washington, DC. Senator McCarthy was beginning to make accusations that Communists had infiltrated the State Department, the army, and many other American institutions. McCarthy accused Truman and the Democrats in his government of being "soft" on the Communists. Attitudes toward America's wartime ally had certainly changed in the nation's capital. McCarthy's zeal in ferreting out pro-Communist individuals would affect some of Thompson's closest friends and colleagues, such as Charles Thayer. Everyone was scrutinized. In one investigation, even Thompson's temporary Clark's Island mustache appeared as something possibly suspicious about him, since he had changed his appearance in so short a time. Thompson was suspect because he was thought to be a Truman appointee, but that line of inquiry was dropped when Thompson's aide told the investigators that Thompson had actually first been appointed by Calvin Coolidge.[18] Philip Mosely, however, who had gone on the fact-finding mission with Thompson in late 1945, was caught in McCarthy's crosshairs. Thompson wrote a letter testifying to Mosely's character, which Mosely later credited as helping him reestablish his security clearance.[19]

Yet all that seemed far behind as the Thompsons' ship pulled into port at Naples. He and Jane were back in Italy, a country they both loved, where a new era was starting for them. The debris in the harbor had been cleaned up, and the bottoms-up ships had disappeared. Instead of disembarking with only an attaché case and a raincoat, as had been his custom, Thompson had his eight-month-old baby in his arms. They were followed by his step-daughter Andy, with her boxer dog Bounce underfoot. Jane came last, balancing bags of baby supplies and formula while tottering in the very high heels she liked to wear. Thompson described traveling with young children as being "similar to that of going fifth class in Bulgaria."

The Thompsons had certainly not picked the best time to arrive in Rome. Mid-August in Italy includes Ferragosto, and the entire country was celebrating this public holiday.[20] All the shops were closed, and it was impossible to get anything done. Worse, all their household belongings were submerged in New York's harbor. The freighter carrying them had somehow collided with another ship, sending everything to the bottom of the sea. All of Thompson's notebooks on Buddhism and the family's mementoes, clothing, and furniture were lost. They would need to start from scratch. Still, Jane managed to settle everyone in, with help in the form of Ida Del Fiol, a hefty Italian woman from Udine. She had been sent by Fernanda, Jane's ex-mother-in-law, to look after Jenny and Andy while Jane learned the ropes of being a diplomat's wife. This meant lessons in Italian, as well as a long line of visits to make and callers to receive. Thompson only gave her one piece of advice, "Don't ever [take] anything or any attitude that comes your way in this business personally—either the good or the bad."

From the moment Ida stepped into the house, she not only took perfect control of the nursery, but she also tried to take over the entire household. She even changed the family's main language to Italian, and she caused endless conflicts with everyone from the chambermaid to the chef. It took a while for all those in the household to learn that the best tactic was just to ignore her. Ida was a remarkable-looking woman, hardly the kindly Mary Poppins Jane described her as, except perhaps for arriving with an umbrella under her arm. She was stern faced, always wore round spectacles, and tucked her mousy-gray hair inside a hairnet. Her large body was ensconced in a nurse's uniform, and dark elastic stockings— which matched her disposition—hid varicose veins.

That August, Jane sent Andy to visit her grandmother Fernanda and left Jenny in Ida's care. Thompson and Jane went to Venice, to meet with Ambassador Dunn and his wife, who were there on vacation with their grandchildren. When the Thompsons arrived at the Excelsior-Lido, they discovered that, with it being the high season, the only room available was at the back of the hotel, with a bathroom down the hall. It seemed as though they would have to take it, and then Jane discovered that she had forgotten her passport. Thompson, annoyed by this oversight on the part of his wife, awkwardly gave only his to the desk clerk and mumbled apologetically. After some time spent consulting in the back room, the clerk returned. To the couple's surprise, they were shown to the best seaside suite in the entire hotel. Apparently the desk clerk believed that the passport incident was a cover story and that the young lady accompanying the American minister was someone other than his wife. The clerk's Italian sense of romance would not permit him to put them in a back room.

Mary Dunn was an experienced hand at the business of diplomacy. She advised Jane that the most important part of her new role was to be herself, and to make sure to find the time to pursue her own interests. Jane's main interest at that moment was exploring Rome. "Not once did I meet an Italian who was not clever in one way or another," she wrote.[21] Postwar Italy was waking up, and it was a fantastic time to be an American there. They, and their dollars, were welcome anywhere they went, and it was difficult not to feel good, as well as important. As their big cars passed, the Italians would comment, "*Que bella machina*

(What a beautiful car)!" The Thompsons' social life was glamorous, and for Jane, a marvelous world was opening up.

Thompson hated tardiness. One day, Jane was running late to meet him at a reception at Ambassador Dunn's residence. A policeman, directing traffic around a demonstration over the Allied occupation of Trieste, forced her into a side street, much too small for her big yellow Chevy convertible. Making the turn, she ran into a Fiat 500. All traffic came to a halt as people began to gather to see this American woman in her fancy car. Soon two groups formed, one shouting that the accident was her fault, and the other coming to her defense, all this accompanied by the honking of backed-up traffic. Jane noticed that the Fiat's license plates belonged to the Ministry of Defense. She tapped on the window and an Army officer got out. "This is entirely my fault," she told him. "I am the wife of the US minister and a good friend of Defense Minister Piccardi. I will tell Minister Piccardi this was all my fault and pay for any damages." Hearing this, the officer kissed Jane's hand and told her most gallantly that she should not worry about a thing. With the hand kissing, silence descended on the crowd, and Jane drove home to don a gown for the party. To avoid using the convertible with its bashed-in fender, she got a ride on the back of the *portiere*'s Vespa motor scooter and made quite an entrance among the chauffeured limousines at the ambassador's residence.

In November 1951, the NATO council met in Rome. The US delegation was headed by General Eisenhower and Secretary of State Acheson. Acheson, remembering Thompson's story about Andy using his name as a dirty word, asked Thompson if he could meet his daughter for a stroll in the Villa Taverna gardens before lunch.[22] When they returned, Acheson was clearly smitten by this Alice in Wonderland–looking girl, and Jane was curious to find out what they had talked about. "My dear Jane, a gentleman does not reveal to one woman what he says to another," he told her.

Andy was the cause of several embarrassments. While Thompson attended NATO meetings, his wife escorted military personnel around Rome and hosted events for visiting dignitaries. These events included showings of American movies, one of them being a new film, *Harvey*, starring Jimmy Stewart, who had an invisible friend in the form of a six-foot rabbit. The Thompsons hosted a reception following the film. Andy had hidden her disproportionately large pet rabbit Angelo in the downstairs guest bathroom, and when one of the guests used the restroom, this enormous white creature jumped out from behind the shower curtain, giving her a dreadful fright. On another occasion, when a guest asked Jane for the secret to her delicious cocktail meatballs, Andy piped up, claiming that Octavio the cook rolled them on his stomach before plopping them into sizzling oil.

It was also a six-year-old Andy who, lounging on her parents' bed as they dressed for a party, commented that life was like a huge Gorgonzola cheese: the white part was good, but it was the dark green, moldy veins that gave it all its flavor. Andy was an early lover of classical music and played the piano well. She spoke Italian, French, and German fluently and wanted to become an opera singer more than anything. Yet her precocious beginnings brought her few rewards. Most unfortunately, she developed mental illness in her twenties, which tortured her for the rest of her life. It was as if the dark green, moldy part of life had completely absorbed her.

While his wife was busy with receptions and trying to keep their family in line, Thompson was occupied with managing a large embassy, consisting of a hundred Foreign Service and military positions, not including all the US consulates in Italy and not including the civilian personnel. Thompson remarked that the growth of the Foreign Service was one of the most striking developments in the State Department, noting that when he started in 1929, the entire department was smaller than the embassy in London in 1952. Nonetheless, although the Foreign Service was growing, it was actually engaged in a smaller percentage of foreign relations activities. This was due to an increasingly globalized world, which encouraged, for example, members of Congress to conduct their own tours abroad, something common today, but a new phenomenon then. When the Thompsons were there, the Rome embassy hosted fifty congressmen within three weeks. While it certainly put a strain on the US missions abroad to host, give tours to, and educate these "visiting firemen," Thompson thought it was mainly a positive development and cited the Marshall Plan as evidence of the benefits of a US Congress actively engaged in thinking about foreign policy.[23]

Work at the embassy was also affected by Truman's Campaign for Truth, which was underway at that time. This was an effort to make sure the "truth" was exposed, to counter Communist propaganda.[24] Much of the rhetoric in the Campaign for Truth was similar to that of NSC 68, and it may have been developed to counter McCarthy's accusation that the Truman administration was soft on Communism.[25] All the US embassies were supposed to implement the campaign in every way possible.

With Italy supposedly the European nation most vulnerable to Communist influence, the Rome embassy attracted all sorts of groups and individuals engaged in both overt and covert activities. On the overt side, there was an alphabet soup of public international organizations: the UN, UNESCO, ECOSC, the OECD, NATO, the EDC, the ILO, and the ECA.[26] It also included private organizations, such as the Red Cross; American business interests; and roughly 40,000 academic student exchanges. While many of these officials received instructions from the Secretary of State and some answered to him, more did not.[27] Directing the good intentions of these various interest groups was not a simple affair, especially when so many of them were new and still establishing their turf.

On the covert side, the main interest of the US government in Italy in the early 1950s was to limit, if not eliminate, Communist influences in that country's government, labor unions, and institutions. These results were less than satisfactory. The left-of-center parties had been virtually eliminated, and the more right-wing parties, although certainly anti-Communist, did not support social reforms that the Americans thought would counter Communist influences. The Christian Democrats, who were the most acceptable to the United States, were slow to get rid of the Communists in their party, having realized that keeping such a threat alive guaranteed them economic support and helped maintain their hold on power. How much Thompson knew about the covert activities that were going on at the time is not certain, but he must have been aware that something was in the wind as the Italians played one agency off against the other, including the US embassy.

Between the various competing interests and the dark McCarthy cloud, Thompson had walked into an embassy where morale was low, exacerbated by poor coordination and cumbersome inefficiencies. There were "problems of both [an] administration and personnel character" that needed attention. As one staff member wrote: "Mr. T. set about in a quiet, unassuming way to remedy the situation. By sheer dint of ability, industry, graciousness, and gentlemanly handling of situations arising from these problems, he has brought about better coordination, a more friendly spirit among the staff who feel they have a friend in him, and a general toning up of the entire organization."[28] It fell to Thompson to make all these disparate people feel and act like a team, including his growing harem: a wife, two daughters, a female dog, and a battle-axe nanny. He succeeded, and this was one of the reasons why Ambassador Dunn relied on him, as well as why, after Thompson had spent two years in Rome, Dunn recommended him to lead his own mission.

PART II

Negotiations

11 ≋

Chief of Mission

Austria is … the only place outside the United Nations
where we are regularly doing business with the Russians.
—LLEWELLYN THOMPSON, testimony
to US Congress, 1955

Three Friends, Three New Ambassadors

Thompson got his own mission when President Truman appointed him as the US high commissioner and ambassador to Austria in summer 1952. That country, although liberated from the Germans, was still occupied by the victors of World War II. Negotiations for a final settlement had been going on for nearly a decade, but no resolution was in sight. Nor were there indications that anything important was supposed to happen in Austria. Thompson was merely expected to hold things together and continue with those endless discussions.

It had been an election year in the United States and General Dwight D. Eisenhower was soon to replace Harry Truman as president. Given that the United States was "eyeball to eyeball" with the Soviets in Austria, someone with Russian experience was desirable to head the US embassy in Vienna, but the better known Moscow hands were tied up: Bohlen was the resident Soviet expert on Dean Acheson's staff, and Kennan had just accepted his first post as an ambassador, to the USSR.

Kennan's appointment had received a great deal of publicity, and he told reporters that if Stalin died while he was there, he was the ideal person to negotiate with the new rulers. Junior staff in the embassy hoped Kennan's fame and expertise would open doors in the Soviet Union, but they were disappointed. Kennan's time in the USSR ended badly—even brilliant scholars are not always successful at maneuvering in real-life situations. The Soviet government, which, by that time, had seen Kennan's "X Article" in the journal *Foreign Affairs*, responded by isolating him and keeping him under close surveillance. He slept a lot and, like Averell Harriman before him, spent most of his days at Spaso House. His wife, who was expecting a baby, had not accompanied him, and he felt alone. The situation became unbearable for Kennan. He had to take a break and leave Moscow temporarily. When

Kennan left, a reporter asked him what Moscow was like, and he answered that it was like being interred in a Nazi camp. The Soviets immediately declared Kennan persona non grata, precluding his return. People who saw Kennan in Switzerland shortly thereafter reported that he was shattered by the Soviets' decision.[1]

Bohlen then became an ambassador for the first time, replacing Kennan in the USSR. First, though, he had to pass through a difficult ordeal with Senator Joseph McCarthy, who opposed the appointment during Bohlen's confirmation hearing. McCarthy used Bohlen's closeness to Dean Acheson and his participation at the Yalta summit to question Bohlen's anti-Communist bona fides. McCarthy, however, went several steps too far, resulting in Bohlen's confirmation by a 74 to 13 vote in 1953. Some say this was the beginning of McCarthy's fall.[2] Two months after Bohlen arrived in Moscow as ambassador, Stalin died, and everything changed.

Austria Mission

Austria's struggle for sovereignty had started on November 1, 1943, when the United Kingdom, the Soviet Union, and the United States declared that, as a victim of Hitler's aggression, the country deserved to become free and independent again. The three occupying nations began to craft a state treaty to enact this declaration, but after more than four hundred meetings and countless draft versions, they failed to agree, and Austria remained in occupied limbo. When World War II ended in 1945, Austria was divided into four zones—British, French, American, and Soviet—with each sector run by a high commissioner. The symbol of the quadripartite, or Four Powers, was "four men in a jeep" (made famous by a movie of the same name)—although in reality it was a sedan. Like the city of Berlin in occupied Germany, Vienna was an island in the middle of the Soviet zone. Austrians and foreigners were allowed to move about Vienna freely, and only street signs indicated the borders of the sectors. Yet individuals did not feel as safe in the Soviet sector as they did in the others, because people had ways of "disappearing" mysteriously there from time to time.

The Soviet zone in Vienna was important for intelligence reasons. It was a perfect arena for the emerging field of covert-action propaganda. It also contributed to that cynical yet oddly romantic feeling about postwar Europe, captured in the 1949 film noir, *The Third Man*. Everyone was involved with gathering information. The Americans drew up whole strategies for making contact with the Soviets, in order to obtain as much personal information as possible. This would later be dutifully reported and entered into files.[3] The Soviets did the same. Austrians who worked in the Soviet industrial sector added to their salaries by reporting what they did and saw to the Americans.[4] Some operations backfired, and others were more successful.[5] One example of both aspects was the story of a CIA operative, who was bearing a letter from the US secretary of state to a declared Soviet defector in a bar and was met instead by NKVD agents, who photographed everything and were about to take the American away. Luckily for the CIA operative, a Four Powers patrol was passing by at that moment. Hearing the ruckus coming from the bar, an American patrol officer went in and rescued him.[6]

The Llewellyn Thompson Jr. family's arrival in Vienna, Austria, after his appointment as US ambassador / high commissioner to Austria, 1952. *From left to right*, Jenny, Llewellyn, Jane, and Fernanda ("Andy") Goelet, Jane's daughter from her previous marriage, accompanied by Andy's boxer dog, Bounce. Embassy staff photo.

At the time of his ambassadorial appointment to Austria, Thompson was forty-five years old and keen to run his own post. He and his family flew from Rome to Vienna on a US Air Force plane, a small propeller craft outfitted to carry cargo, not passengers. Jane recalled that the trip was not a smooth one. The Soviets had given permission for the plane to fly over their zone of occupation, but in a restricted corridor and at a specified altitude. Just as the plane entered the corridor, a terrible storm hit, jerking the plane in all directions. This made a sergeant on board worry that their aircraft might leave the corridor, so he kept looking out the window to see if they were being buzzed by Soviet planes. The Thompsons' Italian nanny started crossing herself and shouting at every bounce, their boxer dog persistently scratched at the door, and one of their children started crying, because of an earache. When it was revealed that they had been circling the Vienna airport for fifteen minutes, to allow time for the welcoming band to arrive, Thompson said enough was enough and instructed the pilot to land.

Once safely on the ground, they still had to endure welcome speeches and a troop review before the family was stuffed into a large black Cadillac and driven to the ambassador's residence on the Weidlichgasse, a street in the Hietzing district of Vienna. The Cadillac was equipped with flags, flashing lights, and sirens, and it was followed by an Austrian security car. This was not Thompson's style, and he quickly put an end to the show. He allowed the flags to be displayed on only one occasion during his stay in Austria: at the farewell reviewing of the troops for a general who was retiring. All the generals who had shown up for the ceremony had flags with stars on them, reflecting their rank. At the entrance to the field, Thompson's chauffeur asked for permission to put out two flags: the American flag and the ambassadorial flag, a blue one with thirteen stars in a circle. Thompson replied that on such an occasion, the chauffeur certainly could. A friend later told Thompson that some GIs sitting behind him in the stands were determining who was in each car by the number of stars on its flag. When the ambassador's long black Cadillac came onto the field, one of the soldiers remarked, "Who in the world do you suppose that is?" Another exclaimed, 'I don't know, but from the looks of the stars, it may be God himself!'"[7]

Occupied Vienna was a shabby and somber city, bearing the scars of war. The buildings hadn't been given the scrubbed look they now have. The opera house and a number of other grand, historic buildings were boarded up or under reconstruction. Driving past the Schönbrunn Palace gardens, the Thompson entourage noticed that the grounds were being used to cultivate vegetables, and the lawns were turned into hayfields—majesty subordinated to practicality. It was in stark contrast to the colorful existence that had already sprung back to life in postwar Italy.

Envoys to occupied Austria had dual roles: civilian ambassadors / high commissioners had replaced military commanders.[8] As ambassadors, they represented their respective countries, which gave Austria some semblance of being a sovereign nation, but as high commissioners, they formed the Allied Council, with an administrative authority superior to that of the Austrian government. The high commissioners switched places every month as head of the council, in what was called the Four-Powers turnover. This included a grand ceremony, with troops marching, bands playing, national flags changing places, and, finally, a buffet lunch. For some reason, the event couldn't be done without a meal. As US ambassador to Austria, Thompson lived in the American section of Vienna. The embassy residence, a modern-looking Bauhaus structure, was too small for many official functions. On the other hand, it generated a cozy feeling for the family, and its plainness (Jane called it "fascist-colonial") was offset by the beautiful gardens that surrounded and isolated it from the rest of the city. President John F. Kennedy's historic meeting with Nikita Khrushchev took place in this residence years later.

As high commissioner, Thompson had an additional residence in the American zone, at St. Wolfgang, an idyllic lakeside village on the Wolfgangsee, not far from Salzburg, where the family spent weekends and summers. Thompson had the privilege of having a train available to him, and he would commute by railcar from Vienna, through the Soviet sector, to the US zone on what was dubbed the Mozart Train. Since it was the high commissioner's exclusive train, it was exempt from some security restrictions. With rare exceptions, other people had to obtain a Soviet gray pass in order to go through the Soviet zone surrounding Vienna, adding to the apprehension of those travelers who ducked under that fringe of the Iron Curtain. Trains would stop at the Enns Bridge, Austria's version of Checkpoint Charlie. It consisted of a little wooden shack in the middle of a cornfield, manned by Soviet soldiers with rifles and bayonets. A friend who was coming to visit the Thompsons

had her pass inspected at that stop and was ordered to follow the soldier off the train. She feared the worst, having read true accounts of people who had disappeared in the Soviet sector. She was shown into the shack, where another Soviet official sat behind a desk. She couldn't understand anything he said. After inspecting her passport, the official opened his desk drawer. She fully expected him to pull out a gun. Instead, he brought out a bottle of vodka and two glasses and said, in heavily accented English, "Heppy Beerzdey!" It was indeed her birthday that day, and she nearly fainted with relief.

Jane and Llewellyn Thompson Jr. fishing at the Wolfgangsee, a lake by their secondary ambassadorial residence near Salzburg, Austria, 1956. USIS, © ÖNB/Wien.

The US embassy was anxious to use the Mozart Train as often as possible, to reinforce the agreement that it could pass through the Soviet zone unmolested. The only conditions were

Llewellyn Thompson Jr.'s step-daughter Fernanda ("Andy") Goelet (*right*) and Ottavio the chef (*left*), in the kitchen of the ambassador's residence in Rome, Italy, 1951. Thompson Family Papers.

that a list of passengers be submitted and that identification, matching the names on the list, be presented. No Soviet soldiers actually boarded the train, despite rumors that it carried Iron Curtain refugees from Vienna through the Soviet zone to Salzburg. When Thompson travelled on the Mozart Train, he had his own car, with a sitting room, two sleeping compartments, and elaborate bathrooms with peculiar plumbing fixtures. The last car on the train, but certainly not the least, was an archaic sleeping car that contained an oversized iron bed and plush Victorian furnishings. Paneled in beautiful mahogany, with inlays of the Austro-Hungarian double eagle above the bed, this car was rumored to have been used by Franz Joseph, the Emperor of Austria and King of Hungary.

In 1952, on the Thompsons' first trip out of Vienna, their chef Ottavio—sporting a Salvador Dali mustache—occupied that end car. The Thompsons only learned of its existence because, in the wee hours one morning, all did not go well at the Enns Bridge. It seemed that there was one more name on the passenger list than there were passports. Ida, the nanny, was hiding in Ottavio's bedroom in the last car on the train and had refused to relinquish her Italian passport from its hiding place in her ample bosom, for fear the Soviets would not return it and she would be stuck in the Soviet zone forever. The ensuing impasse caused the Thompsons to navigate through the train's cars in their pajamas. In the end car, they found the chef, with a hairnet on, reclining in Franz Joseph's bed, oblivious to the argument between Ida and the sergeant, as well as to Thompson's entrance, accompanied by several army soldiers. Finally, Ida's 98.6°F passport was violated with a Soviet stamp and returned to her.

The duties of ambassador / high commissioner demanded an occasionally elaborate social life in Vienna. In honor of a visiting US senator from Texas, Tom Connally,[9] Leopold Figl, Austria's foreign minister, hosted a dinner at a restaurant overlooking the city. The Danube River laced like a blue ribbon through the twinkling lights of Vienna, while the twilight and the distance screened off the scars of war. Figl, finishing his speech with a dramatic flourish, had the musicians strike up the nostalgic "Wien, Wien nur du Allein" [Vienna, Vienna, you alone]. The senator, with his back to the view, was arguing with his wife about his ability to see the lovely sight. She was insisting that he stand up and turn around, and he was maintaining that he could see it while still seated, by its reflection in the mirror. Busboys wiped condensation off the windows as the musicians struggled through a fifth rendition of the song to wait out the standoff between the American couple. Suddenly the strains of "The Eyes of Texas Are Upon You" took over, and Connally instinctively sprang to his feet. Thompson had borrowed one of the violins, and his action settled their dispute.

One Bastille Day, all the high commissioners and their wives were sitting at the same table at the French Embassy. The British high commissioner's wife and the Soviet high commissioner found themselves alone at the table when the band struck up a tune. "What's the matter, General, don't you dance?" she asked. He told her he was too old to do so. She chided him by saying: "But you are four years younger than my husband and look at him out there dancing with Jane Thompson. I know—you just don't know how to dance." The general, insulted, insisted: "No no no. Eyee am knowing how to dance. When eyee am young eyee can do waltz and eyee can do mazurka. Also eyee can fox fast and eyee can fox slow!" Perhaps the jab made an impression on him, or maybe he had to cable back to Moscow to get permission, but the following November, at a celebration of the Great October Revolution, the Soviet high commissioner asked Jane Thompson to dance. She accepted, and before long couple after couple left the dance floor to stand around in a circle, watching the Soviet high commissioner doing something unbelievable—dancing with the wife of the American high commissioner.

Jane had another curious run-in on a dance floor, this time with chargé d'affaires, Sergei Kudriavtsev,[10] at the Jaeger Ball, a formal occasion that called for everyone to be dressed in elegant Austrian folk clothing: dirndls and Jaeger suits. Jane found herself on the dance floor with the ex-spy, blocked from returning to their seats by a group of performers. Some friends at a nearby table gestured for her to join them, whereupon she took Mr. K. by the hand and led him there. As she introduced him, she realized that everyone at the table was a refugee from one of the Iron Curtain countries, and none of them wanted to socialize.

Unpleasant Visitors

In June 1953, Loy Henderson was the US ambassador to Iran. He and his wife were on their way back to his post in Tehran after consultations in Washington, DC, where he, among others, argued for the removal of the Iranian prime minister, Mohammad Mosaddegh, from power.[11] Mosaddegh had gained this leadership role on the strength of his argument that the country's oil fields should be in Iranian, not foreign (i.e., British) hands. He undermined the Shah, Mohammad Reza Pahlavi, by nationalizing the Anglo-Iranian Oil Company and used his popularity to begin enacting Socialist reforms. He also took formal control of the military, all of which frightened the United States and the United Kingdom. The CIA was responsible for Operation Ajax, a coup to depose Mosaddegh. It was run by Kermit Roosevelt, grandson of Teddy, who arrived in Tehran with $100,000 in cash for bribes. The operation went as planned,[12] thwarting the spread of Communism—according to the CIA's chief, Allen Dulles—and the Shah ruled Iran as a mostly faithful American ally for many years. An unintended consequence of this CIA success would be Iran's Islamic Revolution, which drove the Shah from the throne in 1979. This and other such operations validated Thompson's warnings, dating from the early days of the OPC, that employing covert efforts to effect regime change was a tactic that was likely to backfire in the long run. In an ironic footnote, it remains far from clear that Mosaddegh was actually a Communist.[13]

The State Department did not want Henderson to arrive in Iran until Operation Ajax was well underway, so he would not seem to be implicated in it, and suggested that he and his wife stay with the Thompsons until the time was right. Thompson and Jane were at their house near Salzburg, on the Wolfgangsee, and about to leave for Venice on a short holiday when they learned of their houseguests' impending arrival. Thompson was happy to accommodate an old colleague,[14] and he made their home available to the Hendersons. The staff was instructed to meet them at the train and put them in the guest quarters at the end of the second floor hall, past the children's wing.

When the Thompsons returned, they found the house in an uproar. The children and their nanny had moved from their wing, as Ida was afraid for the girls, explaining that Signora Henderson had the "evil eye." The cook was upset, because no matter what menu Mrs. Henderson had ordered the day before, it was changed in the middle of the night by a letter left in the kitchen, along with an untouched basket of fruit labeled "uneatable," "too ripe," or "not mature." Looking for her guests, Jane found Mrs. Henderson seated on the terrace overlooking the lake, facing five men lined up against the railing. Given the men's expressions, Jane feared her guest might be staging an execution. Mrs. Henderson unwittingly tried to dismiss her hostess by saying, in German: "You've come on the wrong day. I will interview the parlor maids tomorrow." After apologizing to Jane, Mrs. Henderson clarified that she was interviewing butlers for the ambassador's residence in Iran, because she had fired her butler Feredoon. She discovered that Feredoon had set up a very profitable laundry business by using the embassy washing machines. Since Mrs. Henderson supplied the soap, and the US government provided the overhead, she felt entitled to take a percentage of the profits, which Feredoon, it seems, felt was too high. To her dismay, Feredoon was caught spitting in her soup, and she couldn't "put up with such disrespect, even from a business partner."[15]

After the Hendersons left, summer was nearly over, and Thompson returned to the business of the stalled Austrian State Treaty. The quadripartite structure was a cumbersome way to govern, and it required deliberating everything from shipping to telecommunications to managing the post office. The Soviets and the Americans played a kind of gamesmanship that was a reflection of the intensifying Cold War. For example, under the occupation agreement, Austria could not maintain an army but was permitted a gendarmerie. There was constant tension about the size of this gendarmerie, which the Soviets claimed was a de facto army. The gendarmerie was clandestinely armed with caches of weapons supplied by the Western allies, and food was hidden in the countryside, in case of a Soviet attempt to take over by force. The Austrians were also not allowed to have an air force, but the Americans kept Austrian pilots ready to fly by establishing a sports club for gliding planes.

The Hendersons, however, weren't the only unpleasant visitors to the Vienna embassy. Senator McCarthy sent his minions out hunting in the various foreign missions, and they appeared in Vienna, in the form of the infamous Roy Cohn and G. David Shine, dubbed "junketeering gumshoes."[16] Their official task was to inspect all the US Information Agency (USIA) libraries, in order to root out subversive literature. When they asked Thompson what he thought of their library purge campaign, he replied, in typical Thompson fashion, "I have no way of judging its value, but I can tell you it has been of great assistance to the Communists and to the Soviets in Austria."[17]

One of the aims of the McCarthy purges was to eviscerate the State Department by severely reducing its budget and firing many of its officers. As a consequence, all home leaves that year were cancelled, because the department did not have enough money to bring the fired officers back to the United States and also pay for leaves for the ones who were still employed.[18] Secretary of State John Foster Dulles did little to repair the damage done to morale. Thompson recounted one story of how Dulles's personal aide told a group of Foreign Service officers that they should be "quite happy to sacrifice [themselves], because it was so important" that Dulles keep his job, which "didn't go down very well" with them.[19] Many officers resented the lack of support from their boss. His brother, Allen Dulles, the director of the CIA, was much better at protecting his own people. Bohlen's dislike for Secretary Dulles was well known. He joked that he was "Dull-Duller-Dulles," and this eventually got back to the secretary of state. When Bohlen was facing McCarthy's obstacles to his confirmation, Dulles did little to stand up for him or for Bohlen's brother-in-law, Charles Thayer, who was forced to resign.

Thompson agreed that John Foster Dulles should have supported his people in the State Department. Nevertheless, he developed a quiet sort of rapport with the secretary. Thompson thought Dulles likeable in person, and he wished Dulles would have brought more of his personal aspect into his public persona. Having grown up with a staunchly religious father probably helped Thompson tolerate the secretary of state better. Dulles used to carry around a book, a short history of the Communist Party, which he'd underlined and annotated, and that contributed to his becoming stuck on the opinion that working with the Soviets was impossible.[20] Thompson thought that Dulles did not take into account the changes that were occurring in the Soviet Union, especially after Stalin died in March 1953.

Spring 1953 was a difficult time for the Thompsons. Jane had a miscarriage, as a result of a skiing accident. They didn't know if they would be staying or leaving Austria under President Eisenhower. Thompson's home leave had been cancelled. Jane's parents had to sell their house and move into a small apartment, because of financial problems resulting from her father's mental illness and inability to work. Thompson's parents were not doing well, either. His ninety-year-old father was bedridden, remaining at MWood's house until he died in October 1953. Not only had the ranch's business matters fallen to MWood, but he was now responsible for their mother, who was suffering from advanced dementia. Thompson always felt some guilt over not being able to help MWood more with the family's affairs.

Thompson was finally confirmed as ambassador to Austria by the new Eisenhower administration, so he was able to remain in that country and continue working on the Austrian State Treaty—or, as Jane put it in one of her letters home, "keep knocking our heads on the old stone wall."[21] An important step toward unknotting the Austrian tangle came when Thompson was called upon to negotiate the Trieste settlement.

12 ≋

The Trieste Negotiations

A nation is a society united by a delusion about its ancestry
and by a common hatred of its neighbours.
—WILLIAM RALPH INGE, *The End of an Age*

At the end of World War II, the city of Trieste and the surrounding area were claimed by both the Yugoslavs and the Italians. It went to neither. Just as in Austria and Germany, Trieste fell hostage to failed negotiations. Thompson was not the State Department's first choice to lead the new attempt at negotiations about Trieste. Julius Holmes, who had worked on the Trieste issue for years, had topped the list, but the department rejected his candidacy because the Justice Department was investigating him for alleged financial wrongdoing.[1] Only a few knew about Holmes's problems, leaving Dulles to awkwardly rebuff advocates for Holmes, including Thompson's old friend from their Geneva days, James "Jimmie" Riddleberger, who was then the US ambassador to Belgrade. Even Thompson was surprised to find out at the very last minute that he would lead the negotiations. He was planning to attend the Big Four's conference of foreign ministers in Berlin in 1954, which, among other things, was to discuss the status of Germany and Austria. Out of all his achievements as a career diplomat, Thompson would later recall Trieste with the most satisfaction. His pride in his role in this effort may puzzle many, however, since the Trieste issue is little known today.

Background

The beautiful Venezia Giulia (the Julian March) was a natural crossroads between the Italian peninsula, the Balkans, and Central Europe.[2] It was where cultures met, as well as being an area of nearly continuous contention. At the end of World War I, with the defeat of Austro-Hungary, Italy annexed Trieste and a large area of ethnically Yugoslav coastal territory, an unacceptable outcome for the Yugoslavs, who had to make do with the less strategic hinterland area. Italians were in the minority in the Venezia Giulia region, and when Italy became Fascist under Benito Mussolini, the majority population of Slovenes in that part of the nation suffered badly. Since 1934, Yugoslavia had been governed through a regency, which ended in 1941 when the Yugoslav military installed the country's seventeen-year-old Prince Peter as head of state. This was done to reverse the alliance the regent, Peter's cousin Prince Paul, had made with Hitler's Axis. This forced Hitler to postpone his invasion of the Soviet Union by a fatal six weeks—until winter would be approaching—in order to take care of recalcitrant Yugoslavia. Hatreds, once unleashed, found justification for even the worst atrocities. King Peter II fled into exile.[3] This promoted a bloody genocidal civil war, with the Royalists under Draža Mijailović on one side, and the Communist Partisans under Josip Broz Tito on the other. Those escaping the Ustaše (the Croat Fascists), the Germans, and the Italian occupation—or whatever hatred prevailed in their area—were natural recruits for either side.

The Americans did not discriminate between the Royalists and Communists, as long as these groups resisted German occupation. Thanks to Allied support, the Yugoslav civil war had a built-in arms race until a British covert operations group convinced Winston Churchill that Tito and his Communist Partisans were more efficient in their opposition to the Germans, so the Allies then chose to support them.[4] The Partisans reclaimed the territory in Venezia Giulia from Italy and then made a quick advance against the German occupiers, in order to reach Trieste before the British and American troops. When the Allied military finally arrived in that city, Tito's forces effectively remained in control. Before Truman and Churchill reached a decision on what to do about this situation, thousands of anti-Communist Italians and some Slovenes (between 3,500 and 15,000) were shot as Fascists and dropped into crevasses, known as *foibe*, in the Karst mountain range.[5]

Truman finally decided to put a stop to all the "uncontrolled land grabbing" by presenting Tito with an ultimatum to vacate the city of Trieste. This had been the first concrete effort on Truman's part to contain Communist expansion. Stalin gave lip service to supporting Tito but would not provide military assistance. So Tito, swallowing his ego, had to leave Trieste. When the Stalin-Tito split occurred in June 1948, Tito's position vis-à-vis Trieste became considerably stronger, because the Allies wanted to encourage him to go forward on his "separate road to Socialism." Stalin's death made Tito even more important to the West. Fearing the Soviets might lure Tito back into the Communist bloc, the United States gave him military assistance and extensive economic aid.

The Free Territory of Trieste (created to facilitate the Italian peace treaty) divided the area into two temporary zones of occupation and administration. The more northern Zone A (including the city of Trieste) was administered by the United States and the United Kingdom, and Zone B, including the predominantly Italian coastal towns, by Yugoslavia. The Italians expected to get Trieste, and they made this an internal political issue. If the British and Americans didn't deliver Trieste to Italy, that country would lose national pride and its government would fall. The possibility of a win in that nation by the Communist Party was enough to keep the US ambassador to Italy fired up.

The newly elected president, Dwight ("Ike") Eisenhower, had appointed Clare Boothe Luce, wife of powerful publishing magnate Henry Luce, as ambassador to Italy.[6] She had access to Eisenhower and John Foster Dulles, which she did not hesitate to use when she thought the State Department did not share her passionate support of the Italian position on Trieste. She threatened Ike with the loss of Catholic and Italian US votes, which had just helped him win the 1952 presidential election. She was relentless. At one point she sent him her arguments in poetic form:

> For the want of Trieste an issue was lost.
> For the want of an issue the election was lost.
> For the want of an election, De Gasperi was lost.
> For the want of De Gasperi, his NATO policies were lost.
> For the want of his NATO policies, Italy was lost.
> For the want of Italy, Europe was lost.
> For the want of Europe, America . . .?
> For the want of a two-penny town.[7]

Innumerable attempts to sit the Italians and Yugoslavs down at the negotiating table proved to be fruitless. Ambassador Riddleberger supported Tito's position, so both of the State Department's ambassadors lobbied to resolve the issue in favor of their respective host countries. Tensions rose when Italian troop movements in late summer and fall 1953 suggested that Italy might occupy Zone A. Luce was able to persuade Eisenhower and the British to announce that they would give their section (Zone A), including the city of Trieste, to Italy if there was no resolution of the impasse by October 8. This became known as the October 8 Declaration. Luce believed that the Yugoslavs would be satisfied with hanging on to Zone B, but she was seriously mistaken. The withdrawal decision triggered a crisis. Troops gathered on both sides of the borderline between Zones A and B, ready to confront each other—with each side, ironically enough, militarily supplied by the United States.

The State Department's Bureau of European Affairs then suggested that the occupying allied forces—the United States, Britain, and Yugoslavia—could negotiate a solution trilaterally. The Italians, thinking that the United States and the United Kingdom would come down on their side, did not object, but the Yugoslavs were wary. They were anxious to meet with Italy at the conference table and worried that the British and American negotiators would favor their Italian NATO partners. Despite predictions of failure from Ambassador Riddleberger in Belgrade, the State Department chose to go forward with the plan for tripartite negotiations. Thompson was to represent the United States; Geoffrey W. Harrison, assistant undersecretary of state in the United Kingdom's Foreign Office, would lead the British; Vladimir Velebit would head the Yugoslav team; and, when the time came, the Italians would be represented by their ambassador in London, Manlio Brosio.[8]

The Negotiations

When Thompson accepted his assignment to go to London to work on the Trieste situation, he did not do so enthusiastically. His wife was about to give birth, and he was already more than fully occupied in Vienna. Lastly, there was no "great hope" that the talks would succeed.[9] Luckily, Thompson had a strong staff and a very able deputy chief of mission

(DCM), Charles Yost, whom he trusted completely to run things until he returned. The State Department later removed Yost during the Trieste talks without consulting Thompson, which upset Thompson considerably.

On Monday, January 18, 1954, while most of the US foreign policy personnel were fixed on the upcoming Four Powers meeting in Berlin, Thompson went home to break the news to his very pregnant wife that he would be spending most of the coming months on a secret mission in London. He found her in the library, rearranging the books by size, a sure sign that delivery was imminent. He asked her not to have the baby on the coming Friday, because he was due to depart then. Thompson left Vienna on January 22, two days after his daughter Sherry was born. He first went to Washington, DC, supposedly for briefings on Austria, and then on to London, ostensibly to buy clothes for himself. He went on "buying clothes" for nearly a year.

Thompson followed the weight gain of his new daughter, along with the weight loss of her mother, by mail. He wrote to Jane constantly, grumbling that she didn't write back often enough. His was a newly formed family, and it was a difficult time to be apart. In almost every other letter he talked about "winding things up in a week or two." He also wrote: "I wish I could tell you how important I think [Trieste] is. Perhaps that would help."[10] He found London to be expensive, and cold. He had a lot of homework to do, which he could only accomplish under the bedcovers, because it was so frigid in his little room at the then not-so-posh Connaught Hotel. It took a toll on him. When the talks finally concluded, this already lanky man had become almost skeletal, having lost twenty pounds since his departure from Vienna.

Thompson quickly came to respect and trust his British counterpart, Sir Geoffrey Harrison. He already knew his Yugoslav peer, Vladimir Velebit, as a colleague from their days in Rome. Velebit did not have a nice time during his appointment, having been shunned by the Italian government, and characterized his reception in Rome as "glacial."[11] Thompson had been friendly, and perhaps this helped to later melt some of that ice in London. The Yugoslav also came with baggage. Stalin had accused him of being a spy for the West and had told Tito to get rid of him, but Tito, in defiance, had kept Velebit on.

Prior to the first formal meeting, Harrison met with Thompson to talk about how they would approach the negotiations. Harrison put forth a strategy to get a general agreement on principles from the Yugoslavs and then leave the two opposing sides to work out the detailed bargaining. This might have enabled them to wrap up the US and UK involvement more quickly, but Thompson, looking at the long-term consequences, disagreed. If regional stability and cooperation were the goals, he did not want to leave room for bickering later on. He hoped to offer the Yugoslavs enough carrots to make their inevitable sacrifices on Trieste more palatable by including agreements on trade, fishing, and the use of Trieste's port. The stick was that the United States and Britain would implement the October 8 Declaration (giving everything to a very satisfied Italy), should they be unable to hammer out an agreement. Unfortunately, the State Department's instructions to Thompson called for a settlement that he characterized as "hopelessly lopsided in favor of Italy." The department felt that only their plan would convince the Italians to negotiate, but Thompson warned that if the Italians wanted modifications or concessions down the line, "a quid pro quo satisfactory to the Yugoslavs would be required." In a later cable, he pointed out that a direct appeal to Tito should be left aside until they were "closing the final gap."[12]

The State Department thought its plan seemed perfectly reasonable. Their instructions to Thompson were to give the entire coastal area of Yugoslav Zone B, where the majority of the population was Italian, to Italy. In exchange, a correspondingly larger area in the hinterland of the US-British Zone A, where the population was predominately Slovene, would go Yugoslavia. The proposal seemed reasonable enough, even simple, but that was its problem. The solution had been drawn up in Washington, DC, and did not take certain nuances into consideration. Tito feared that if he could not get a satisfactory deal, it would look like he capitulated to a Western diktat, damaging him in the eyes of his Communist Party members. On the other hand, the Italians had already been promised the entire Zone A in the October 8 Declaration, so they were understandably expecting to get *at least* that—and wanted more. Thus the negotiations would have to reallocate a finite territory, so it would appear that each side got more than it started with. This would take very fine tuning indeed.

In the background, the United States and the United Kingdom wanted Italy to ratify the European Defense Community (EDC) agreement.[13] The new Italian prime minister, Giuseppe Pella, suggested that a Trieste solution favorable to Italy would facilitate this aim. The Americans and the British were also urging Italy and Yugoslavia to resolve their differences because they needed both of the latter nations to cooperate, acting as a buffer against possible Soviet aggression.[14] Thompson sought to craft an agreement that would have incentives for each side to continue to honor it. Only this interdependency, he thought, would provide the West with the security it was looking for.[15]

Phase One: The Yugoslavs

On February 3, 1954, the three negotiators and their entourages of experts bustled indoors from London's unpleasant weather for the first official meeting, held in the imposing and somber-looking Lancaster House.[16] The first sessions were as formal as the building's façade and as showy as the coffered ceilings and gilded moldings of its interior. Thompson's heart must have sunk when Velebit argued that the *entire* Free Territory of Trieste, including the city of Trieste, should be turned over to Yugoslavia, although Velebit was aware that this would not happen. He knew Trieste city was lost to them forever when the Yugoslavs were forced out by Truman in 1945, but he had been told to make this opening gambit.[17] Tito felt that the outcome of the Trieste negotiations would either enhance or diminish his international standing. The West needed him on their side, and Stalin's recent death reopened a possible portal to the East. So, like a once-spurned lover who was now desired, Tito reacted with arrogance and played hard to get. Thompson reminded the Yugoslavs that Tito had been prepared to accept a less favorable territorial division in 1952, and that making an impossible stand "was not going to get us anywhere."[18] Velebit then hinted that a third, alternative territorial division could be found. He stressed safeguarding the ethnic rights of people who would find themselves in one or the other of the territories once the boundaries were drawn.

Thompson decided to concentrate on those points he could work with and wrote home, telling his wife he thought he could wrap things up quickly. He was wrong. As the days passed, there was much rhetoric on both sides—and little progress. By February 16, Thompson cabled the State Department that, though nothing else had been accomplished, they had at least convinced the Yugoslavs that "our interest in a settlement was due to wider issues at stake and not just some maneuver in an Italian game."[19] At this point, Thompson realized more than ever the need to seek flexibility in the lopsided instructions from the department, so he contacted Livingston "Livie" Merchant, the assistant secretary of state for European affairs, and asked if he could come to see him in Paris on Merchant's way home from Berlin.[20] Thompson flew to Paris on February 19 to discuss tactics on Trieste and get news about the Berlin conference.[21]

Thompson returned from Paris on February 23, to discover that there were leaks in Belgrade about Thompson's "secret talks." He was annoyed and later said, "Our greatest weakness in diplomacy in my opinion is our inability to keep our mouths shut." He implored the State Department to authorize his DCM, Yost, to let the Austrians know why he was in London, lest it compromise his position in Vienna. But what he got was a long telegram from EUR, reiterating in painful detail the same old lopsided directions. Thompson told his wife his work was "reaching a crisis," and that if he failed, he would probably be back in Vienna soon.[22] Then he caught a lucky break. A frank exchange of views during a friendly dinner between Thompson and Velebit changed the whole configuration and character of the talks. Thompson realized that he had to get rid of the audience, so he suggested to Harrison that the next meeting be just with the three primary negotiators. Thompson later claimed that they made more progress in those few hours than in the previous two weeks at the negotiating table.[23] Privacy made it possible to explore options and avoid taking public positions from which they could not retreat later on.[24] Thompson came to understand Velebit's short leash and the courage it would take to go beyond it, and Velebit came to appreciate Thompson's efforts to change the American starting position.

The private diplomacy between the three men was so effective that they dismissed their entire delegations. All three negotiators agreed that secrecy was decisive for their success, so they met at Velebit's apartment at 34 Harrington Gardens. Many of the meetings were between Thompson and Velebit alone, since, being in London, Harrison had to continue his full-time job at the Foreign Office. The two men sat together day after day, with Velebit constantly sucking on licorice tablets in an attempt to give up smoking, and hammered out the provisions of the settlement.[25]

Territory

Thompson knew that understanding the problems and tactics of the other side was fundamental to good negotiating, and he had remembered the importance of patience in dealing with the Communists from the Potsdam summit. Because of the rigidity of their system, it was never wise to spring a new move on them or expect immediate answers. For the

Communists, saving face was more important than achieving a mutually advantageous compromise.[26] Yet even though the private meetings allowed Velebit to be more forthright, he was still very discreet. Thompson and Velebit kept going over the territorial question again and again, but they could get nowhere. It puzzled Thompson that, although Yugoslavia would gain more territory in the hinterland than Italy would gain with the coastal strip, Velebit always dismissed this hinterland as not being of much value, even though it was agricultural and the people there were mostly Slovene. It became clear to Thompson that something else was at play. Looking at the maps, Thompson realized that the local Yugoslav fishermen in the coastal towns would have to defect to Italy to have access the sea and be able to continue plying their trade. It would be embarrassing for the Yugoslavs to have an "exodus of people going into Italy."[27]

Thompson decided to "reshuffle the proposals" and make a new deal that gave Yugoslavia a coastal area. The new proposal, however, would require the State Department to modify his instructions, something he had already attempted. On his repeated try, the department resisted this change at first but finally let it go forward."[28] Velebit confirmed Thompson's understanding by immediately saying, "I will recommend to my government that they accept this."[29] Shortly thereafter, Thompson saw a cable from Luce, suggesting they should take public advantage of Velebit's confidential remarks. Infuriated, Thompson wrote that this was a private talk, and besides, he had also made candid, private remarks that he wanted to be kept confidential.[30]

The new proposal went back to the basic division of Zones A and B proposed in the October 8 Declaration. The boundary, however, would be moved north to Punta Sottile, a small piece of land on the seashore, overlooking Trieste's port, thus giving Yugoslavia an additional mile and a half of coastline. In exchange, the Yugoslavs would give Italy a larger triangle of land, which the Western negotiators descriptively called the "rock pile," inside the Yugoslavs' Zone B. This small change would allow each side to claim that they had received more than what had been stipulated in the October 8 Declaration. The level of detail was such that surveyors had to go along the proposed border to deal with situations where individual properties and homes, and even one outhouse, were split in two by the new boundary. Thompson's deal also included solutions to difficulties over port access, minority rights, and reparations payments, all of which were structured in such a way as to create an interdependence that made long-term mutual cooperation profitable for both countries.

Port Access

Thompson discarded the idea of a corridor through Italian territory to give the Yugoslavs port access, because it would create a platform for further feuding. He thought the better solution was to develop a Yugoslav port in Zone B. The US embassy in Italy complained that a Yugoslav port could present competition for the Trieste port, but Thompson argued that Yugoslav traffic represented a small percentage of the port's activity.[31] Furthermore, a diversion of Yugoslav traffic from their small port farther south would increase the use of the Trieste repair facilities, which would benefit Italy and contribute to the interdependency Thompson was seeking.[32]

The Yugoslavs initially rejected the proposal, because a new port would entail a large capital expense. Thompson asked the State Department to provide fiscal help, which he eventually got in a roundabout way. These funds were embedded inconspicuously in a "package deal," where the Yugoslavs would be forgiven a payment to the United States for wheat shipments.[33] The Yugoslavs would then use that money to build port and rail projects. In the deal, the US government would give Yugoslavia $20 million in "economic assistance," and the British would provide £1 million.

Minority Rights

Velebit introduced claims against Italy for discrimination, and he made a compelling case. That led to safeguards for minority rights and movement in both territories. Thompson may have begun to feel hopeful, but not for long. He wrote to his wife: "I am beginning to despair of ever seeing you again. Each time I think that the next meeting will bring things to a head, but it never does. They are as bad as the Russians. Next week I shall really put on a floor show."[34] While he was trying to consolidate the package deal regarding Trieste, he received a disturbing letter in March from the US embassy in Belgrade, stating that they thought Thompson's proposals could never be accepted by Yugoslavia, and that Tito was especially "indignant, saying any child could see the offer they were making was worse than October 8." Thompson objected to the embassy's posture and worried that they were giving the Yugoslavs the impression that Thompson was "being tougher than the Department thought was justified."[35] On the contrary, Thompson felt he had bent over backward to make it possible to concede points to the Yugoslavs and rescind his original pro-Italian instructions. Fortunately, Thompson had the understanding and backing of the people in EUR, who could clearly see what he was trying to do. Thompson, Velebit, and Harrison were now very close to finalizing the package deal, and Thompson's hopes again began to rise.

At this point, he wished that he was in Vienna, so he could see his old friend Charlie Thayer, who had just come from Moscow, where he'd gone to shoot a bear and write a story about the trip for a sports magazine. Thompson's wife and eldest daughter, Andy, went to the train station to collect him. It was hard to tell where his fur coat started and his beard stopped. Jane only "realized that he belonged to us [because] he spoke English. He even had the combined odor of eau de cologne and cabbage that I had begun to associate with the Russians." Thompson was sorry he'd not been there, certainly to have had a chance to see Charlie, but also because his wife had innocently ransacked Thompson's wine cellar. Jane thought she was being frugal by telling the butler to serve whatever wine they had the most of in stock, but this turned out to be six cases of Romanée Conti and six of Montrachet, which Thompson had hoped to have sitting in the wine cellar during his months away and had looked forward to drinking on his return. Since Foreign Service officers had to supply the food and drink for their mission, and Thompson had prided himself on his wise wine purchase, this development was particularly painful. He tried not to think about it, and instead turned his attention to how to handle the Yugoslav demands for reparations.

Reparations

Yugoslavia claimed reparations for Italy's occupation of that country during World War II.[36] Thompson strongly argued against leaving the reparations settlement for later negotiations, as that could poison subsequent relations between the two countries. He even figured out a way to make the settlement become a positive incentive for both parties. The United States would give Italy aid, which Italy, in turn, would use to provide goods and services to Yugoslavia, in lieu of cash. The deliveries would be spread over several years, to act as a restraining influence on Yugoslavia. Moreover, it would develop trade contacts and a basis for continued economic cooperation between the two countries.[37] Eisenhower agreed, and by April 1954, EUR cabled Thompson that they would find a way to give this aid to Italy.[38]

The breakthrough in negotiations persuaded Thompson to think about taking the risk of booking rooms at the Broadmoor Hotel in Colorado for a long-overdue home leave that summer,[39] as he hadn't seen his siblings and other family after his father had died. In the end, however, his home leave would be postponed indefinitely. Moreover, Thompson and his wife had not seen each other since their daughter was born four months previously. The State Department—in a small gesture—allowed him to send for her, but not their children, who had to remain in Austria. The department offered a modest per diem of $12 but refused to pay for Jane's passage from Vienna to London. She arrived in that city in time for Easter and stayed for a month. As a consequence of her absence, however, their infant daughter became very sick from the too-rich formula provided by the American embassy's doctor.

The day after his wife returned to Vienna, Thompson sent a letter to a friend in Rome, declaring that "if they don't wind this up soon, I shall probably return in a box."[40] He also wrote to his wife, saying that some of the little love notes she'd hidden all around the room for him to find after her departure had not been discovered by him, but by the chambermaid. The maid thought Thompson had written them for her, causing some embarrassment.

Rumors, Leaks, and Betrayals

On May 9, the *New York Times* published an article by Cyrus Sulzberger that disclosed most of the details of the package deal. The *Times* also printed Sulzberger's interview with Tito.[41] Tito told Sulzberger about his plan for a Trieste settlement, which, the journalist pointed out, looked very much like the one being negotiated in London.[42] It appeared that Tito wanted to expose the deal before the Americans and British even approached the Italians, thus jeopardizing everything.[43] It remains a mystery where the original leak came from, but it could have been a deliberate ploy by the Yugoslavs. By letting the cat out of the bag, it would be more difficult for the Italians to make changes.

As the negotiations with the Yugoslavs were coming to an end, Velebit suggested not informing the Italians of his country's maximum bargaining position, saying that they would come back with a counterproposal. Although Thompson had also predicted the probability of this scenario in his cable to the State Department back in February, he argued that he could not make such a pact behind the Italians' backs, as this would be negotiating in bad faith and could backfire.[44] Velebit agreed to present his country's highest offer if the United States and the United Kingdom would impose this solution on Italy—something the Yugoslavs repeatedly insisted was their understanding of the situation—but Thompson refused to give the Yugoslav negotiator any assurance that what they had agreed to thus far would be forced on the Italians. Velebit accepted this, but he was not happy about it. The reasons for Velebit's stance only became clear much later, when Tito admitted that even though he knew he did not have such a commitment from the Americans and the British, he had assured the people in his party that he did.[45]

Despite these setbacks, an "Agreed Record of Positions Reached" was initialed in London between the US and UK representatives and the Yugoslavian ones on May 31, and it became known as the May 31 Line. After four months of discussions, the agreement that was reached differed from the State Department's suggested solution but was remarkably close to the October 8 Declaration. Italy and Yugoslavia would take over Zones A and B, respectively. Trieste city would go to Italy. Side agreements enabled the construction of a new port in Zone B for the Yugoslavs. Reciprocal guarantees would protect national minorities. Another side deal would resolve reparations claims, and measures would be taken to encourage cooperation between the two countries.

Thompson and Harrison now had to get ready for phase two, negotiations with the Italians, who were understandably upset when they read the Sulzberger interview. Thompson went to see the Italian representative in the discussions, Manlio Brosio, and asked the Italians not to react to the news story, because the negotiators were very close to being able to present them with a satisfactory settlement. Besides, the details in Sulzberger's story weren't *exactly* accurate.[46] After all, was it not more important to the Italians that they would get the city of Trieste?

Life Does Not Stop

On the personal side, Thompson's father-in-law's deteriorating mental state resulted in him sending ranting letters to State Department officials. Thompson was worried about how to take care of his in-laws and wrote to Jane, "I am very much afraid that within a year we will have a couple of additional dependents to worry about, but we will work it out somehow." The financial difficulties of working in the State Department, compounded by the worries of having a young family with three children, and knowing that his health had always been delicate, prompted Thompson to seriously consider changing jobs. In one missive to his wife, he stated that Princeton University had offered him a position as a scholar, but he didn't want to be an academic. He confided to Jane in a March letter that he hoped to stay in England, as he found London to be a wonderful city. Thompson would get several offers, but, in an August letter, he finally concluded that he and his family "should stay in the service at least two or three more years," to get the maximum pension amount. He ended this letter as he almost always did, with a small cry of despair and a dose of optimism: "I can't tell you how much I miss you all. I certainly can't stand much more of this but am sure it will be over now."[47]

While Jane waited for her husband to finish the tedious Trieste negotiations, she attended various functions back in Vienna. She was determined to be a good helpmate and keep the negotiations her husband was involved in a secret. For some reason, the French ambassador, Jean Payart, thought it was rather amusing to ask, whenever he saw her, "Où est [Where's] Tommy, Jane?" One evening, Yost was hosting a reception at the Thompson residence. Monsieur Payart came up to Jane and, for the hundredth time, asked her where Tommy was. She said: "In spite of being fond of the old boy, I was rather mean to him and tugged at his Smith Brothers' cough-drop beard and said, 'You know very well where he is. Please don't ask me that question again.' " Just then, some people were pulling the Austrian minister of the interior out of the bushes, and he confided to Jane that he'd overheard the conversation and been so surprised he'd fallen over. Then he thanked her for pulling the ambassador's beard so hard: "The Ministry of the Interior has often pondered the fact that the beard might not be a real beard and you have given me evidence that it is. I thank you. Now that subject can be dropped from the weekly Ministry meetings."[48]

Phase Two: Negotiating with the Italians

The second stage of the Trieste negotiations started in London on June 1, 1954, with Ambassador Brosio. Thompson was determined to keep it controlled: one man, one place, no negotiations in other capitals. Ambassador Luce tried to get some of her people from the Rome embassy to London, to "help." Brosio complained that Italy, as a NATO ally, was entitled to preferential consideration over Yugoslavia, a Communist regime.[49] The Italians asked for "small adjustments"—and Yugoslavia was simultaneously was asking for the same. By July 14, the Italian counterproposal was clear. They pretty much agreed to everything, except giving up Punta Sottile, claiming that a Yugoslav sniper stationed on that high ground could shoot downward to the Trieste port. The Yugoslavs flatly refused to let the Italians keep Punta Sottile, even though doing so would lead to reparation payments by the Italians of up to $30 million in goods and services, "the most profitable real estate deal ever heard of."[50] They were still insisting that the Italians be forced to accept the May 31 Line, with absolutely no adjustments. Thompson wrote to his wife that his spirits had never been so low, "On top of everything else, Jimmie Riddleberger [in Belgrade] sent a lot of excited and critical cables and, although the Dept. backed me up, it didn't help my morale."[51] Dulles supported Thompson's judgment and told Riddleberger to follow Thompson's line with the Yugoslavs.[52] Brosio later confirmed that Thompson had been right, stating that if the negotiators had come to the Italians with anything less than what they did, Italy would have refused to negotiate altogether.[53]

At this point, everyone's patience was at an end, and several carrot-and-stick attempts were made to crack the stalemate between the Yugoslavs and the Italians. The possibility of a visit to Belgrade by Secretary of State John Foster Dulles was put forward as a condition in reaching a settlement, but Thompson did not think that would work. First, if such a promise were made public, it would "have a dangerous effect on the Italians," who would perceive undue favoritism. Riddleberger thought a visit could be kept secret, but that seemed unlikely. Moreover, how could Tito mollify his people over a compromise on Trieste by using the prospect of a state visit if he couldn't tell anyone about it? In addition, it would put Dulles in Belgrade early on in the settlement's implementation, an unpredictable time that Thompson thought the secretary might best avoid. In the end, Dulles did not go.[54]

On August 23, Ambassador Clare Boothe Luce, who'd been in New York City an entire month for medical tests because she feared she was being poisoned, returned to Italy. Some speculated that she suffered mental illness as a result of accidentally ingesting lead paint chips that had fallen from the ceiling of her bedroom in Rome. In a later oral history, Luce gave a fanciful account of a mysterious man who telephoned the embassy and asked to see her. He told her a great secret: what the Trieste dispute was "really" about. Instead of reporting this to an intelligence service, he chose to tell her, because she ought to get the "first crack" at it, since she had worked so hard on the situation and was the only one who had. Luce felt the secret was such that she could not put it in a cable. So she decided to go to Washington, DC, and "tell the president."[55] Eisenhower was not in the capital at that time, and there is no record or recollection that Ambassador Luce spoke to anyone at the State Department or the White House about the "great secret." It will go down as one of the several mysteries surrounding the denouement of the Trieste settlement.

In the meantime, the British prime minister, Anthony Eden, met with Brosio, who picked up on an idea that Thompson had put forward the week before as a possible solution to the stalemate.[56] Brosio said that the Italians might consider a modest trade of the "rock pile" in return for Punta Sottile. Velebit was enthusiastic and said he would personally support it strongly with his government.[57] But not only did the Yugoslavs reject it, they raised the ante. They now wanted a lump-sum cash payment, instead of goods, as reparations. In his letters home, Thompson made it clear that he felt there was little more he could do.

Phase Three: The Murphy Trip

The last few days leading into September were near pandemonium. In view of the Yugoslav intransigence, there was a last-ditch effort made in Rome to convince the Italians that the May 31 Line *was* an improvement over the October 8 Declaration, because it included all sorts of deals over consulates, fishing rights, and the like. This did not soothe their national ego, however, and the Italians continued to refuse. The State Department told Thompson to prepare a joint US-UK proposal to present to the two countries in a take-it-or-leave-it manner, but this solution was fraught with perils and was sensibly rejected. Thompson observed that doing so could end up repeating the situation that led to the October 8 Declaration, in which neither side accepted the diktat. He stated that "the British believe we should remain neutral brokers."[58] The Italians had said "No" to the May 31 Line. The Yugoslavs had said "No" to giving up Punta Sottile. The British had said "No" to a forced settlement. Then, seemingly out of nowhere, on September 2, someone proposed that Deputy Undersecretary of

State Robert Murphy go to Belgrade and make a direct appeal to Tito to relinquish the small piece of land under contention. With this simple decision, the knots began to unravel.

Whose idea was it to send Murphy, and how did it come up? This is another mystery worth examining, because it shows the problems historians face in trying to recreate "fact." In the end, no matter how well something is investigated and documented, there remains the possibility that it wasn't that way at all, just like Clare Boothe Luce's mystery visitor. According to Luce, sometime between August 31 and September 1, she sat next to Murphy at a Pan American Union ball and realized that he was "just the man we need to bring Tito around."[59] Robert Murphy stated in his memoirs that "she told me she had an appointment with President Eisenhower the next morning and would suggest to him and to Secretary Dulles that I be sent to Yugoslavia."[60] The only problem with their recollections was that it was impossible for Luce to have had an appointment with the president, because he was in Denver, Colorado, and had been there since August 20. In all probability, Luce met with the assistant secretary of state for European affairs, Livingston Merchant.[61] On the evening of September 2, Merchant's deputy, Robert Knight, telephoned Luce to inform her of the decision to send Murphy to Belgrade.[62] Knight characterized Luce's role in Trieste as "minor." He did not remember his phone call to Luce, nor that it was her idea to send Murphy. It was possible, Knight granted, but he also thought it might have been Merchant's idea.[63] Leonard Unger, Thompson's assistant, asserted that Thompson, in a cable to Secretary of State Walter Bedell Smith, suggested sending Murphy.[64] Given the timing of these events, however, it may indeed have been Luce's idea to send Murphy to Belgrade, as she claimed.

A number of people had, at one time or another, suggested that the Trieste negotiations would inevitably end with a direct appeal from the United States' highest office to bridge the inexorable gap. Merchant even named Murphy as the probable envoy in a cable to Dulles in October of the previous year.[65] Thompson had said it in January 1954, at the start of the negotiations, and repeated it in his later cables to Merchant. Riddleberger suggested that some direct appeal was necessary when he endorsed the Dulles trip to Belgrade. Velebit also talked about a direct appeal to Tito,[66] as had Italian ambassador, Alberto Tarchiani, to the secretary of state in August 1954.[67] The idea was like a cloud of gas in the air, and it didn't take much to finally ignite it.

The following week was a scramble to arrange everything. The October 8 deadline, the sword of Damocles in the Trieste negotiations, was fast approaching. On September 3, cables were crossing each other over the Atlantic and hurtling between Washington, DC, and Denver. Eisenhower wanted something conclusive to happen on Trieste. Thompson recommended that Murphy's appeal to Tito be accompanied by a message from the president or, at the very least, from Secretary Dulles,[68] resulting in a letter from Eisenhower to Tito that Murphy took with him.[69] This direct appeal from President Eisenhower was crucial. The fact that the US president addressed Tito as an equal and asked for his assistance was enough to break through Tito's stubborn ego.

On September 12, Murphy arrived in London to meet with Thompson for a briefing. Thompson warned him that the Yugoslavs might use their leverage to open up other issues, and he asserted that Murphy should force them to stick to the territory in question: an exchange of "Punta Sottile for rock pile and nothing [else] which could open up other non-territorial issues."[70] Tito, the "expert intimidator,"[71] absented himself from Belgrade during Murphy's visit. If Murphy wanted to see Tito, he would have to go to Brioni, Tito's personal island. Murphy, now that he was in Belgrade, discovered that the Yugoslav wheat shortage was much bigger than previously thought. He did not like the arrogant attitude of the ministers he had to deal with, so he decided to hint at a wheat deal but not to discuss specifics.[72]

On September 17, Murphy and Riddleberger made the trek to Brioni for the fateful meeting. After lunch and other niceties, Murphy handed Tito the letter from Eisenhower, along with oral greetings from the president and Secretary Dulles. Tito took the letter into his study to read it alone. After a few minutes, he came out and the three men discussed the proposal. Tito agreed to it, but he said there would have to be some territorial compensation on the other end. Murphy asked Tito to indicate where he meant on the map. Tito "pointed to the rock pile. He did not say he insisted on ALL the rock pile area but generally contemplated an area reasonably proportionate to the concession he was making."[73] The conversation concluded with Tito making reference to his country's bad crop failure that year. There is no question that the Yugoslavs were desperate—the Soviets had refused to bail them out, and the collective farm system was a general failure. On this occasion, though, Murphy lived up to his reputation as a great diplomat and only stated his "regret over Yugoslavia's bad luck and confidence the US would have some good news for him regarding wheat." Murphy understood that Tito did not want to appear to have sold out any part of Trieste for wheat, so Murphy studiously avoided putting anything on the record that would indicate such a thing. In his memoirs later, Murphy was able to truthfully report that he did not mention the wheat deal in his conversation with Tito.[74] What Murphy did not officially recall was that in light of Tito's conciliatory attitude, he told the deputy foreign minister—in strictest confidence—that the United States would be willing to deliver 400,000 tons of wheat to Yugoslavia.[75]

There were also attempts at last-minute, slippery maneuvers. For instance, the Yugoslavs wanted to give up a smaller piece of Punta Sottile and forego the rock pile swap, and the Italians asked them for the *whole* Punta Sottile wedge and just a *small* part of the rock pile. Murphy told the Italians that he had only two choices to offer them: they could get a small section of Punta Sottile and keep the rock pile Tito had agreed to, or they could keep the larger Punta Sottile area and give up the entire rock pile. The final agreement allowed the Italians to claim they saved Punta Sottile, and the Yugoslavs were able to assert that they wrested more coastline than was proposed in the original split. The solution allowed Murphy to go home and report to Eisenhower that within a few days the Trieste Settlement could be signed.

After Thompson put Murphy on a plane to Washington, DC, on September 24, he was so relieved—or so tired—that he went off to dinner on his own and forgot to go to a reception at the Austrian embassy. Finally, and almost unbelievably, Thompson, Harrison, Velebit, and Brosio initialed the Trieste Memorandum of Understanding in London on October 5, only three days before their deadline. Sadly, this memorandum was not formally ratified until November 1975, in the Treaty of Osimo, and by then nobody who was involved, including Thompson, was alive. His duty done, Thompson immediately boarded a train for Vienna. A

few years later, when he was about to leave Austria for good, he recommended Riddleberger as a possible replacement. If he had ever resented Riddleberger's criticisms, he soon let them go.[76]

Perhaps Thompson's most important achievement in the negotiations was that he was able to convince both the Yugoslavs and the Italians that he *was indeed* an honest broker. Privacy helped with that. Dulles was

From left to right, Vladimir Velebit, Llewellyn Thompson Jr., Geoffrey W. Harrison, and Manlio Brosio, signing the Trieste Memorandum of Understanding, London, England, October 5, 1954. British Pathé Films.

so pleased with this method of secret and personal diplomacy that he thought the United States could use the formula with the Arabs and Israel.[77] Secrecy, empathy, and patience were the three real keys to success in Trieste. The whole set of difficulties over Trieste, which had been disputed for generations, is no longer remembered as a problem, which is a testimony to that success. Later, when Thompson was asked why he did not get more credit for the Trieste negotiations, he would reply that those who mattered knew what he had done, and that was enough for him. When it subsequently became time to negotiate the Austrian State Treaty, Dulles would back Thompson completely in a last-minute standoff with the Soviets.

13 ≣

The Austrian State Treaty Negotiations

For about two thousand years now there has been a
figure in mythology which symbolizes tragic futility...
Sisyphus.... Now, year after year has gone by, when we
have repeatedly been almost at the point of concluding an
Austrian State Treaty, and always some evil force manifests
itself and pushed the treaty back again. So we have to start
again from the bottom of the hill.
—JOHN FOSTER DULLES, Berlin conference,
   February 16, 1954

Each time the question of independence arose at one of the postwar conferences, Austrians hoped to see an end to their country's occupation, but one Soviet obstacle after another dashed their dreams. They were also frustrated by what they saw as equivocation by the Western allies and felt caught in a balance-of-power struggle between East and West.[1] Julius Raab, less pro-American than his predecessor as chancellor, Leopold Figl, won the Austrian elections in February 1953, perhaps reflecting this frustration. The Soviets, however, had not been equivocal. They had used every pretext to make matters more difficult for a treaty, ranging from objecting to the distribution of dried peas from Nazi warehouses to insisting that a conclusion on Austria could not be reached until after the issues of Trieste and and Germany were solved. The Trieste settlement removed one obstacle, at least.

On February 8, 1955, Foreign Minister Vyacheslav Molotov made a six-hour speech to the Supreme Soviet about international affairs. In the middle of it, he mentioned that the Soviet Union would be prepared to sign an Austrian State Treaty without waiting for a resolution on the German peace treaty.[2] By separating discussions on the German and Austrian treaties, Molotov set a heavy train in motion, loaded with years of negotiations and frustration. Part of it picked up speed on April 15, 1955, when Austria's leaders accepted a Soviet invitation to come to Moscow for negotiations on a bilateral agreement; accelerated sharply during the ensuing ambassadors' conference; almost derailed over a little-known incident close to its destination; but entered the station on May 15. There it was welcomed by a cheering nation that had been waiting for over a decade to regain its sovereignty and rid itself of the occupying nations' troops.

Home to Vienna

Once the Trieste negotiations finally ended in October 1954, Thompson finally returned to the embassy in Vienna, where his staff greeted an exhausted but exhilarated Thompson. They were as proud of their boss's accomplishment as he was of their ability to hold together such a sensitive post under difficult circumstances. But his thin countenance also dismayed them. He frightened his nine-month-old daughter Sherry, too, who reached out to the butler to be removed from this stranger's arms. Some on Thompson's staff, who had been with him in Vienna, recounted that he had a gift for delegating, doing so in a way that his subordinates interpreted as praise. They described the US embassy in Austria during that period as an unusually collegial and happy post. All were acutely aware they were making history, and that their work was creating a legacy, both for Austria and for the West.[3]

After Trieste, Thompson thought he would be able to take his family back to the United States for their long-postponed

A joyous crowd in front of the Belvedere Palace in Vienna, Austria, after that country had regained its independence with the signing of the Austrian State Treaty on May 15, 1955. USIS, © ÖNB/Wien.

Llewellyn Thompson Jr. skiing in Lech, Austria, on a brief vacation after the Trieste negotiations were completed, 1955. USIS Okamoto, © ÖNB/Wien.

home leave. Staff cuts, however, forced them to settle instead for a short skiing junket to Lech, in the Austrian Alps. It was during that February holiday when Molotov made his long speech. Thompson seized on the statement about Austria in the middle of Molotov's speech, seeing it as a signal that important things were imminent. His wife recalled that Thompson's ruminations about Molotov clouded their too-short reprieve.

Thirteen Days

The State Department also concluded that Molotov's speech was significant and asked for opinions from staff members. Thompson and Charles Bohlen, who was then the US ambassador to Moscow, discussed what may have motivated the change in the Soviets' attitude toward the Austrian State Treaty in a series of cables to the department.[4] Thompson thought the Soviets still hoped to influence the Germany question. But he also believed that, as a counter to NATO, the creation of the Warsaw Pact in May 1955 enabled Soviet troops to stay in Hungary and Rumania, making it less critical to keep troops in Austria.[5] Moreover, a united and neutral Austria would encourage the Germans to push for a similar settlement. Bohlen, on the other hand, was of the opinion that the Soviets now realized West Germany would certainly join NATO, precluding a neutral unified Germany. Therefore, the Soviets saw no point in keeping Austria as a playing card in that deal.[6]

There were other considerations, too. The Soviet sector in Austria, unlike its counterpart in Germany, was too small to make it a separate Socialist state, nor did the Austrians show any inclination of going in that direction. By 1955, the Soviets had already extracted most of the economic benefits from Austria that they could hope for. It was now clear to Thompson that the Soviets were going to offer the Austrians an expedited treaty in exchange for neutrality. But a Soviet propaganda campaign, blaming the Americans for blocking a treaty, fueled Austrian frustrations. During the subsequent Austrian State Treaty conference, Thompson fought his own "little Cold War," watched anxiously by the allies and the indignant Austrians alike.[7] These negative feelings even affected Thompson's ten-year-old stepdaughter. She was bullied by her Austrian classmates, who blamed Andy's father for the latest setback in negotiations. Thompson calmed Andy down and explained that for the Soviets to accept an Austrian treaty, it had to appear to be a Soviet victory. One way in which the Soviets could to do that was to say the Americans were against it. So Thompson saw this as a good sign, and he was sure there would be a treaty soon.

Austria Goes It Alone

A decisive step was taken when the Austrians accepted Molotov's invitation to participate in bilateral treaty discussions in Moscow on April 12–15, 1955. Alarms went off in both Washington, DC, and at the embassy in Vienna. The Austrian leadership was under great pressure to gain independence for their nation. Dulles feared that this pressure might make them vulnerable to Soviet maneuvers, and he instructed Thompson to make it very clear to Chancellor Raab that his delegation should not sign anything binding while in Moscow. Bohlen warned that the Soviets might try to include measures that could allow interference in the internal affairs of Austria or involve the right for the Soviets to reenter Austria.[8] Thompson reassured Dulles, stating that Raab had given his word that no commitments would be made in Moscow. Thompson believed that Foreign Minister Figl and Adolf Schärf, chairman of the Socialist Democratic Party—both part of the contingent going to Moscow—would keep the impetuous and less-predictable young Austrian undersecretary for foreign affairs, Bruno Kreisky, in line.

What Thompson did not know was that Kreisky had already met secretly with Figl, Schärf, and Raab, and they had agreed that, should the Soviets offer them a treaty in exchange for a declaration of neutrality, they simply could not turn it down. Raab knew this when he assured Thompson that nothing would be agreed to in Moscow. Perhaps this explains why the Austrian delegation, after their first meetings with the Soviets, were not forthcoming when they briefed the US, French, and British ambassadors in Moscow, and why they were reluctant to turn over the actual written agreement when the delegation returned to Vienna. The US embassy there had to press for it and only finally received a copy of what became known as the Moscow Memorandum a few days later.[9]

Thompson might have felt ill used by the members of the Austrian delegation, but he saw that the cards were now on the table, with the fate of Austria at stake. It was obvious to all players that if this opportunity was lost, another chance might not come.[10] After the signing of the Moscow Memorandum, the Soviets felt they could control the Austrians during the treaty negotiations, so the throttle was thrown wide open for the ambassadors' conference, which was to begin on May 2.

Los Angeles Times reporter Don Cook went to Vienna to cover the conference. He walked into Thompson's office, finding this "most cautious of diplomats in an unusually discursive mood." Thompson was relaxed, in anticipation of the conference. He was leaning back in his chair, with his long legs stretched out and his feet resting on an open desk drawer that contained all of the positions taken over the previous three years on every article in the Austrian treaty. He told Cook that those in Washington, DC, seemed shell-shocked and had given him no instructions, so he had proposed to Secretary Dulles that he be allowed to handle the American side of the negotiations. Thompson said: "If I understand the Soviets correctly, when they make a strategic decision like this to go ahead and conclude a treaty, then they are ready to give and will not hold things up over tactical details. So I'm going back in and ask for everything we've asked for [over] the last three years." Then he added, "I'm not going to have the Austrians saddled with a bad treaty simply because they are now in a hurry."[11]

All four foreign ministers had busy schedules. Harold Macmillan was running for Prime Minister. John Foster Dulles and Antoine Pinay, the French foreign minister, were at a NATO meeting in Paris. Vyacheslav Molotov could not arrive before May 14. So the onus was on the ambassadors to sort out the voluminous draft that had been haggled over for a decade. Events had conspired to align the train tracks for only a few seconds.[12] If the ambassadors' conference was not successful, Austria's future would remain uncertain. After Cook left, Thompson called in his staff and told them to be prepared for a grueling two weeks.

The Ambassadors' Conference

The conference took place in the Haus de Industrie on the Stalinplatz—which the Austrians rebelliously insisted on calling Schwarzenbergplatz—in Vienna's Soviet zone. A few feet away stood a Soviet tank and a row of international police sedans, with the flags of the United States, the United Kingdom, France, and the USSR on the front. The façade of the large, gray, solid-looking building was normally decked with the Soviet red star and portraits of Lenin and Stalin. During the conference, however, these were replaced by the shields of the four participating countries, along with their national flags and that of Austria. Thompson represented the Americans; Sir Geoffrey Wallinger, the British; Roger LaLouette, the French; and Ivan I. Ilyichev, the Soviets. Leopold Figl and Bruno Kreisky, representing the two major Austrian political parties at that time, were present at the meetings, but only Foreign Minister Figl intervened in the discussions.

Each Western ambassador had guidelines and regularly consulted his superiors, but they had the latitude to make on-the-spot decisions. Ilyichev, on the other hand, did not. Later in his life, when describing negotiating with the Communists, Thompson spoke of the importance of understanding the constraints under which they worked. He described how time consuming this was, because they were afraid to take any initiative—possibly fearing for their very lives. It was necessary, he said, to empathize with them and not paint them into untenable corners. As the conference went on, it became clear that Ilyichev's

standing order was to resist all Western attempts at modification, but it was also apparent to Thompson that these objections
were not to delay the signing of the treaty. Thompson used this
to his advantage, right up to the end.

Halvord Ekern (*left*) and Llewellyn
Thompson Jr. (*right*) arriving for the
Austrian State Treaty ambassadors'
conference in Vienna, Austria, May
1955. Courtesy of Halvord Ekern.

The main meetings took place in a large, ornate, high-ceilinged
hall, with tables arranged in a large pentagon. Each of the four
nations' representatives took turns chairing the meetings (the
Americans went first), and a team of stenographers recorded the minutes.[13] Instead of releasing these verbatim minutes, each meeting ended with the four ambassadors agreeing
on an official record and a report to the public. When the ambassadors went into restricted
sessions, they did so in the Allied Council Room on the other side of the hall, with just one
aide or interpreter each—in other words, only four eyes for each country. No one took
notes or minutes at these sessions, and Thompson's cables back to the State Department
gave only very brief summaries of the sequestered meetings.

The opening session, on May 2, was a ritual dance, with each ambassador uneasily trying to set the right tone and the right attitude. For that reason, it took over two hours just
to agree on procedure. Two articles of the utmost importance caused more-serious problems.[14] Unless they were changed, they could create undue hardship for the Austrians and
provide legal cover for the Soviets to reintroduce troops, even after officially leaving the
country. Thompson was determined to eradicate these loopholes from the treaty.

Article 16

Figl proposed the deletion of one of those articles—Article 16, which dealt with displaced persons (DPs)—toward the end of the first day. It permitted the forced repatriation of current or former Soviet citizens back to the USSR from Austria. The resolution of this article could literally mean life or death for thousands of people, and the Austrians and the Western delegates were keenly interested in removing it. There had already been a shameful postwar history of the Western allies allowing forced repatriation of Soviet prisoners of war and hapless civilians to the Soviet Union. The British had ordered their mission in Vienna to turn POWs over to the Soviets. The Americans in Vienna sidestepped the order by claiming that instructions had never arrived from Washington, DC, and they placed their freed prisoners in DP camps.[15]

In addition, as part of denazification—which the Soviets complained was never aggressive enough—all Austrians were required to fill out forms detailing their pasts. Fearing reprisal, many fudged on their forms, which the Soviets then used as an excuse to arrest them and put them in prison camps, where many died from exposure and starvation. The Soviets were not the only ones to inflict abuses, however. Nazis arrested in the Western occupied zones were also put in prison camps. Glasenbach, one such camp near Salzburg, was merely a vacant plot of land, surrounded by barbed wire. The prisoners had to dig pits in an effort to survive the harsh winter, and many died. One person who witnessed this said it would not have surprised him if those responsible for this atrocity were accused of war crimes, which they never were. Conditions in those DP camps in the Western zone of Austria, however, did improve later.[16] Nonetheless, it is easy to see how an emotionally charged Article 16 could cause the talks to become contentious.

Thompson claimed that Article 16 meant that Soviet repatriation teams could scour Austria, creating a basis for interference by them. Figl quickly added that anyone who wanted to leave Austria would be allowed to, and Austria's future status of neutrality was therefore not compatible with Article 16.[17] Ilyichev dismissed Figl's comments, accusing him of not knowing what was going on, since the DP camps were under American and British jurisdiction. Thompson retorted the United States had never stopped anyone who wanted to be repatriated from leaving the DP camps. Furthermore, since a Soviet repatriation mission had operated in the US zone for six years, surely they'd already identified anyone who wanted to return. By then it was already past 3:00 p.m., and Thompson proposed that they close the meeting. The wording on their joint communiqué, however, caused a further delay. After a long harangue, the participants finally issued a statement, and Thompson reminded them that what had taken place in the meeting was not to be discussed outside the room.

Ilyichev chaired the second meeting, on May 3. His opening remarks indicated that the Article 16 impasse was not going to be solved easily. Thompson then tried a little coercion. He stated that he was disappointed by the attitude of the Soviet ambassador. The world was watching what was happening in Vienna, and he reminded Ilyichev that Austria was a testing ground for the new line in foreign policy—the prelude to Nikita Khrushchev's strategy of peaceful coexistence—the Soviet Union was trying to show to the world.[18] Ilyichev, as usual, said he would consider it and return to this point later.

Behind the scenes, the Soviet spy and Jane's former dance partner, Sergei Kudriavtsev, contacted Swedish diplomat Sven Allard and told him that, as a friend of Thompson's, Allard should warn Thompson that pressing too much might jeopardize the entire treaty.[19] Thompson kept his cool, however, and reported in a cable to Dulles that the Soviets had "berated the Austrians" for having proposed so many revisions. Thompson described Ilyichev as openly and unmercifully twisting Figl's arm, demonstrating how much power the Soviets thought they had over the Austrians. He also noted in the same cable that this maneuver by Ilyichev so thoroughly cowed the Austrians that Thompson feared they would be willing to accept practically anything Ilyichev proposed, leaving "the entire burden of carrying the fight" to Thompson.[20] The Austrians were so desperate to get a treaty signed that they were even prepared to concede on forcibly returning refugees.[21]

Article 35

An even more serious stumbling block, which almost caused the conference to fail, was Article 35 (listed as Article 22 in the final treaty). This article dealt with the disposition of German assets in Austria. This is where the Soviets decided to draw the line, and where Thompson took his biggest gamble. Article 35 was discussed in open session from the second day of the conference (May 3) on, and it repeatedly drove the ambassadors into sequestered sessions from May 5 until the very end of the conference.

Thompson gave this article his most concentrated attention. He knew from Bohlen that they had come very close to an agreement on an Austrian treaty during the Berlin conference the year before, when Thompson was in London, working on the Trieste agreement. The great sticking point in Berlin had been that Moscow insisted on the right to reintroduce troops into Austria if the terms of the treaty were not observed.[22] Thompson saw that this was where he had to make a stand. Dulles sent him an encouraging cable, congratulating him for "all the skill and resourcefulness which you are devoting to this very difficult negotiation. Even so it must not be quite as hard as Trieste."[23]

At the end of World War II, the Soviets had taken over the Austrian oil fields, all located in the Soviet zone, which the Germans had previously seized and nationalized, and which therefore fell under the heading of German assets, according to the Potsdam conference. The Soviets also took over the refineries and the Danube Shipping Company, with all its docks, ports, and ships. Even small businesses fell under this provision.[24] The wording of Article 35 gave the Soviets the right to occupy and exploit all of these physical properties for thirty years. It also guaranteed the Soviet Union a cash payment of $150 million in reparations—with this coming *after* the Soviets had already picked their zone clean of anything that wasn't tied down, and even a few things that were, such as the miles of telephone cable they ripped out of the ground and sent back to the USSR.

When the Austrians were in Moscow in April 1955 to conclude their bilateral agreement, however, the Soviets, in a conciliatory gesture, had modified those terms. The Soviets agreed to return the oil fields and refineries to Austria in exchange for the delivery of 1 million tons of oil annually (one-third of the fields' total capacity) for a period of ten years. Furthermore, they agreed to return—or, more correctly, sell back to Austria—the Danube Shipping Company properties. The catch was that the agreement restricted Austria from transferring any of the returned property in the Soviet zone to *any foreigners*. Ostensibly, this was to prevent Germany from recouping anything it had lost in World War II. This bilateral agreement between the Soviets and Austrians was the Moscow Memorandum secured on that April trip.

This created a contradiction between Article 35 in the treaty and the new agreements that were reached in Moscow. Thompson therefore thought that the arrangements in the Moscow Memorandum had to be represented in the final treaty. The Soviets, however, did not want the memorandum included at all. They didn't even want it mentioned. Yet if the Moscow Memorandum was not somehow included in the treaty itself, Thompson believed that the Soviet Union could use Article 35 to legally repossess the oil fields and other properties. The Soviets could then reintroduce their troops into the country to protect those properties, a right that would be allowed by the Austrian State Treaty. Thompson wanted to make sure no such thing happened.

On the second day of the ambassadors' conference, Thompson explained the US position on this matter quite clearly: "Under the terms of Article 35 as they now stand, the Soviet Union has rights running for 30 years which offers a possibility of intervening in Austrian affairs. Suppose that the economic understandings reached at Moscow are not carried out, or for one reason or other the Soviet Union alleges that a violation has occurred, [then] the Soviet Union might, for example, reoccupy the oil fields. We would have no legal basis to object. That would give the Soviet Union a kind of right of economic reoccupation."[25]

Ilyichev's position was that the agreement reached in Moscow between the Austrians and Soviets concerned only them and no one else, and that the Soviet Union was entitled to dispose of its property in any way that it liked. During the ensuing back-and-forth discussions, Thompson threw out an idea that, in the end, would prove to be the solution to the stalemate. He offered a hypothetical situation in which the United States and Austria might also reach a bilateral agreement to not return similar properties in the Western zones to Germany. Would the Soviets not want *this* bilateral understanding to be included in the treaty? The French picked up on Thompson's hypothetical offer to restrict Austrians from turning over properties in *any* of the zones to the Germans, rather than just keeping returns in the Soviet zone from going to any foreigners. Thompson indicated that the Americans would not oppose such a proposal. This "irritated Adenauer and the Germans deeply," because it meant that Germany would be prevented from recovering property from any part of Austria.[26]

Ilyichev did not immediately understand the importance of this proposal and stuck to his position. He threatened that any reconsiderations of Article 35 now would delay the treaty, and he reminded the participants that they had all agreed on the first day of the conference that this should not happen. Thompson countered by saying that "there are no tricks to our proposal," and he urged the Soviet representative to seriously consider it. Then Ilyichev, almost out of the blue, offered a sort of package deal. He accepted the deletion of the much-argued and unresolved Article 16 on displaced persons, along with some other, minor articles, "in the interest of the speediest conclusion of the treaty."[27] In return, he "hoped" he would get the same consideration on Article 35.

At the end of the first week of the conference, the ambassadors issued their agreed-upon statement, which read that they would rest over the weekend but that progress was being made. No indication of the deadlock on Article 35 appeared. The following morning, Thompson packed his bags and left for Paris. He needed to consult with Dulles in person, not wanting their conversation to be recorded in telegrams. Jane had heard rumors that Thompson was being very tough in the negotiations and that there was even the possibility there would be no treaty. When she asked her husband if this was true, he told her, "Of course there will be a treaty, but we've got to see that the treaty the Austrians get is one that they can live with."[28]

At Thompson's meeting with the secretary of state and other State Department advisors, Dulles went around the table. Everybody was reluctantly in favor of conceding on this last article except Thompson, who said, "I disagree." Quietly but firmly he asserted, "I believe the Russians will concede," and he asked for instructions to go back to the negotiations and stand firm on this point.[29] "Dulles brooded and doodled on the pad of yellow paper which he always kept in front of him, and finally gave his grunting assent: 'Well, if you think so, alright.'" A friend of Thompson's asked him if he was sure about this stance. "Do you know how far your neck is out?" he asked Thompson, warning that Dulles "really wants this treaty and you are taking an awful chance if this goes wrong." Thompson then returned from Paris, in time for the next meeting, with an ace up his sleeve. While he would imply that Dulles would refuse to come to Vienna to sign the treaty unless it somehow reflected the Moscow Memorandum, Thompson would actually be bluffing. If the stalemate couldn't be broken, what he really thought was that Dulles should come to Vienna and make progress at the ministerial level, by appealing directly to Molotov.[30]

The ambassadors went into restricted session just after the conference reopened on May 9. At this meeting, Thompson pulled out his ace and informed the delegates that Dulles would not come to Vienna unless Article 35 was changed. Four hours later, there was still no agreement. During the tea break, Thompson tried to figure out what the stumbling block was. The Westerners had offered quite a nice compromise: they would extend the prohibition of not returning German assets to the whole of Austria, not just to the Soviet zone. He now wondered if the problem was the oil fields, which the Soviets wanted to make sure would not be handed over to their previous Western owners, since that might jeopardize the oil the Austrians had promised to provide to the USSR. Thompson told Ilyichev that the Austrians had already stated that they would not transfer the oil fields to the United States or anyone else, and if this was the problem, it could be made clear in some form. This *did* interest Ilyichev, but it would require consultations.

Thompson's stand on having the Moscow Memorandum included in Article 35 took place at the same time as negotiations for a bilateral agreement between the United States and Austria—the Vienna Memorandum—which Thompson described as being "long and vexatious." This side agreement, in part, was to codify the prohibition against Austria restoring its oil fields to Western ownership, and it included an Austrian agreement to compensate Western companies for losses because of this.[31] It stated that the relevant Western companies would relinquish all their claims on current oil fields and all their rights to future exploration. In return, they would be given "satisfaction" through part interest in an oil pipeline and in at least one refinery.[32] The details of what "satisfaction" meant, however, were to be worked out at a later date, by direct negotiations between these companies and the Austrian government. It was the Austrians who insisted on the term "satisfaction," instead of "compensation."[33] The oil companies did not consider Austrian oil per se to be all that important, but they thought the precedent was. Volatile events in Iraq, Iran, and Egypt represented a far greater potential threat than the loss of Austrian oil, and the affected companies wanted to be sure that they retained the ability to reclaim assets lost as a result of occupation or nationalization.

Since both the Moscow and Vienna Memorandums dealt with some of the same "assets," it would be understandable for those involved to simplify the issue and conclude that the Americans were stalling, due to pressure from the oil companies to obtain compensation.[34] Thompson warned the State Department that their stubbornness on Article 35 could be interpreted that way.[35] He urged them to make the American bilateral agreement with the Austrians public, to avoid such a conclusion. This would make it clear that oil was not the primary reason for holding up any agreement on Article 35, since the Vienna Memorandum ensured that the oil companies would get the "satisfaction" they wanted without an adjustment in Article 35.[36]

Thompson's stand at the ambassadors' conference, with Dulles's backing, was to prevent the Soviets from having any excuse to backtrack on their exit from Austria. It was a move in the Cold War chess game that Thompson had personally seen played badly before. By Wednesday, May 11, the only obstacle left was Article 35, but Thompson continued to hold out and Dulles was still not coming to Vienna. That day, the sequestered session lasted for four hours. Even though the Soviets now understood the offer to not transfer any oil fields to Western ownership would be included in the treaty, the conferees had not yet reached an agreement. Thompson then made a new proposal. Article 35 would contain two new paragraphs, 13 and 14:

- In paragraph 13, the Austrians would agree not to turn over German assets, in any zone, to any German national. They would further agree that Austria would not turn over specific, listed assets—including oil fields—to any foreign national, meaning Western oil companies. Because these changes affected both the Moscow Memorandum and the draft of Article 35, the memorandum would have to be mentioned in the treaty if the Soviets were to accept the deal.
- Paragraph 14 would make the treaty subject to Annex II, where the economic provisions of the Moscow Memorandum would be mentioned. Perhaps more importantly, Annex II specifically stated that, other than what was articulated in paragraph 13 of Article 35, the Austrian rights to these properties would be absolute. This eliminated any possibility of future claims of extraterritorial rights by the Soviets.[37]

Thus the bilateral nature of the Austro-Soviet Moscow Memorandum would be preserved, while still being incorporated into the treaty.

Ilyichev said that he needed to consult with Moscow and asked for a postponement of the next meeting, in order to allow time for a reply. No one objected. It was a good sign, but Thompson had every reason to be worried. There was literally no time left. According to his cables, after a "violent debate,"[38] the Austrian delegates had decided to withdraw their insistence on tying the Moscow Memorandum to the treaty and were practically pleading not to let Article 35 stop the signing. They were sure the Soviets would carry out the bilateral agreement in good faith.[39] Yet Thompson came home that evening so calm, it worried Jane. He practiced his violin, which he rarely found time for, made plans for their long-awaited home leave, and even putted on the lawn.

Thursday, May 12, was the last chance to finalize the outstanding dispute. It was now or never. The participants went into a sequestered session, expecting to wrap things up. Thompson, who was chairman again, called the meeting to order and asked Ilyichev what he had to say to Thompson's proposal of the previous day. Ilyichev called Thompson's bluff and said he could not accept it. It was as though a bomb had dropped. Thompson calmly asked if anyone else had anything to say, but everyone was too shocked. He then announced in a quiet, restrained manner that in that case, Dulles would not come and the United States would not sign the treaty. Figl's face blanched, and a deep silence shook the room.[40] Thompson quickly adjourned the session and announced that the official meeting would be reconvened at 4:45 p.m.[41] Thus the most important meeting of the ambassadors' conference had lasted just a few minutes. Thompson then took his aide, Hal Ekern, outside the room and told him to take the official limousine to the airport, get on the ambassador's plane, fly to Paris, tell Dulles about "what they had done there," and inform the secretary of state that he should not come to Vienna the next morning. Thompson told Ekern to hurry, not even stopping to collect his toothbrush, although this last instruction most likely was theatrical.[42]

The next hour was a manic scramble. The Austrians were desperate for a conclusion to the treaty discussions and were willing to give in. The British, too, were ready to drop the whole matter of Article 35 and sign the treaty as it then stood, provided that the three dissenting occupation countries—Britain, France, and the United States—signed a declaration strongly objecting to Article 35 on the grounds that it contradicted the Moscow Memorandum. The Soviets' old tactic of waiting the other side out, until the opposition was so anxious or so tired that it would agree to something vague (or worse), was having its effect. Thompson told the British he would sign the joint declaration for the record, but he also said that Dulles would still not come to Vienna, and the United States would still not sign the treaty. Thompson had understood that a kind of tipping point had been reached, and that the Soviets now *did* want the treaty. Once this was the case, he knew he could press the negotiators quite far. This experience had a deep effect on Thompson, and it would influence his thinking in 1962, during one of the most dangerous moments of the twentieth century.

Shortly thereafter, Ilyichev must have told Thompson that he was ready to accept the latter's proposal, because when the group reconvened at 4:45 p.m., Thompson, in an ef-

Signing the Austrian State Treaty, in the Belvedere Palace, Vienna, Austria, May 15, 1955. *From left to right, at the table*, Llewellyn Thompson Jr., John Foster Dulles (*standing*), Ivan I. llyechev, Vyacheslav Molotov, Leopold Figl, and Adolf Schärf. USIS photo, Vienna.

fort to retain secrecy—and knowing full well the potential embarrassment for Ilyichev—said that it was not necessary to give a report about what had happened, but to simply state that an agreement had been reached on all articles. He then added, "The price was rather high in that it may cost at least one ambassador [referring to himself] his job."[43] The meeting adjourned at 4:50 p.m.

In the meantime, Hal Ekern arrived in Paris. He was told that he didn't have to see Dulles, as everything had been worked out. Dulles, who had just cabled Eisenhower that he was not going to Vienna, had to send a second cable a few hours later to say that he was headed there, after all. Ekern came back on the secretary's plane the next day with a glittery entourage.[44]

The Ceremony

The signing ceremony took place in the Belvedere Palace, on a drizzly day. The interior setting was at least as grand as the occasion was auspicious. The room was a gilded Rococo affair, situated at the top of cherub-lined marble steps, with painted angels gazing down from the ceiling above. It contained an enormously long table, set up like that for the Last

Supper, with the ministers and ambassadors all seated on one side, surrounded by a standing throng of supporting actors and the press.[45]

All the ministers had agreed to limit their remarks during the ceremony to two minutes. Molotov, however, launched into an impassioned and lengthy speech, crediting the Soviet Union with nearly single-handedly delivering a treaty and securing political and economic prosperity for Austria. Thompson was obliged to interpret for Dulles, who was sitting next to him at the table.

Austria's foreign minister, Leopold Figl, displaying the Austrian State Treaty from the balcony of the Belvedere Palace in Vienna, Austria, where the signing had just taken place, May 15, 1955. USIS, © ÖNB/Wien.

Dulles, realizing that he had to improvise on his own short, courteous remarks, kept asking "What's he saying? What's he saying?" while Thompson stumbled through as best he could. He recalled having a very hard time of it, because of Molotov's stammer,[46] but he felt that Dulles did an effective job in answering Molotov.[47]

Thompson was adept at containing his own emotions, a comment made by most people who worked with him. This quality also made him a good poker player, as well as an effective negotiator. But on May 15, 1955, when the ambassadors, the ministers, and their entourages stood outside the signing room, on the balcony of the Belvedere Palace, there was emotion written all over his face. Figl held the treaty in his hands and waved it about, while the mass of people below and in the streets beyond waved their white handkerchiefs and cheered.

Conclusions

The protection of Austrian territorial rights drove Thompson to push for a modification of Article 35. Under no circumstances would he allow the Soviets any loopholes, such as the ones that were left by the Potsdam summit. In a remarkable reversal of their strident pledge not to give up an inch of soil, the Soviets were willing to withdraw their troops from a part of Europe they occupied after World War II. Sergei Khrushchev remembered that his father was proud of the Austrian State Treaty and spoke of it often. It represented a win for him over the hard-liners' Stalinist policy of no negotiations with the West. Molotov, a hard-liner himself, had not been in favor of Nikita Khrushchev's change in policy on Austria but, knowing his position in the Politburo was not secure, the foreign minister had followed the new Soviet line.

The important lesson to be gained from the Austrian treaty negotiations is that there was a strong will on all sides for diplomacy to succeed. It was evident when the Soviets reopened the issue of neutrality and, in a brilliant move, side-stepped the Western powers to deal directly with the Austrians and present the world with a fait accompli. It was also apparent when the Austrians were able to get the best possible terms for their country, both in Moscow and in Vienna.

At the ambassadors' conference itself, the negotiations worked because Thompson, who had learned about the nature of his adversary from the Potsdam summit and the deliberations on Trieste, recognized the importance of patience, secrecy, and direct and frank discussions among the negotiators. When Thompson was later asked to turn over his "notes," for the sake of history, he declined, just as he had done after both the Potsdam conference in 1945 and the development of the Truman Doctrine in 1947 and 1948. He also convinced the State Department not to release the unofficial verbatim minutes of the 1955 ambassadors' conference in Vienna.[48] What was important for history, he said, was the final agreement, not the steps that had been taken to get there.

One of the most symbolic events after Austria regained its freedom was the reopening of the Vienna State Opera (the Wiener Staatsoper) on November 5, 1955, with a performance of Beethoven's *Fidelio*.[49] It was a choice fraught with meaning, as this opera highlights the values of fidelity and freedom. John Foster Dulles and his wife came to Vienna for the event, a gesture the Austrians appreciated. Clare Boothe Luce and her husband Henry, and the US ambassador to Britain, Winthrop Aldrich, and his spouse also came. All three couples stayed with the Thompsons at the ambassadorial residence and met in the downstairs hall to board limousines to travel to the opera house. Jane recalled seeing a side of Dulles few ever did.[50] She described "the beautiful Clare Boothe Luce and Mrs. Winthrop Aldrich, both dressed in satin and adorned with emeralds and diamonds, [and] the Hon. Winthrop Aldrich, dressed in white tie and tail coat, adorned with decorations from various governments, which were so numerous they undid the craft of his London tailor and left one side of his tail coat two inches longer than the other." The three couples looked up as Dulles and his wife descended the staircase to join them in the hallway.

SECRETARY DULLES, *observing Aldrich's decorations*: "That is a rather handsome display you're wearing, Winthrop."

AMBASSADOR ALDRICH, *fingering his medals*: "Yes, yes, they are rather handsome, aren't they?"

MRS. DULLES: "Oh yes, Foster has that one. That must be a Dutch medal. Foster has that one, too, and he has that one. In fact, I don't see any that Foster hasn't got!"

SECRETARY DULLES, *patting his wife affectionately on her behind*: "Atta girl, atta girl Janet."

14 ≋

Open Skies, Closed Borders

President Eisenhower made a mistake in suddenly
putting forward his Open Skies proposal at the summit
conference in 1955.
—LLEWELLYN THOMPSON, speech,
    Foreign Service Institute, April 12, 1971

In summer 1955, finally able to get home leave, Thompson and his family boarded the
USS *Constitution*, traveled to New York City, and then went on to the Broadmoor Hotel
in Colorado Springs. While in Colorado, Thompson received a phone call telling him
to cut his vacation short and rush to Geneva to attend a summit with the Soviets. That
summit propelled Nikita Khrushchev onto the world stage.

Open Skies

When the Americans met with the Soviets in July 1955, they hoped to gain insight into the
policies and character of the post-Stalin government. The idea was to discuss disarmament
and lessen international tensions. They would also tackle the question of German reunification, with neutrality still being an option. The American delegation was headed by President Dwight Eisenhower, and it included Secretary of State John Foster Dulles and
Charles Bohlen.[1] Anthony Eden headed the British delegation, and Premier Edgar Faure,
the French. There were five in the Soviet delegation, one of whom was a little-known Nikita Khrushchev, but it was Nikolai Bulganin who nominally led it.[2] President Eisenhower
recalled that it took some time to figure out who was really in charge. Although Bulganin
did most of the talking initially, it soon became apparent that Khrushchev was the boss. It
was as if he was too insecure to officially head the delegation, but once he saw that he could
hold his own, he took over.[3] In his memoirs, Khrushchev let on that he was not sure he
should attend that meeting, since he did not head any ministry, but he wanted to meet the
heads of the Western powers personally and size them up. He left convinced that he had
"worthily represented his country." Regardless, the men representing the Western nations
at the summit were both amused by and underestimated this small, energetic man. Harold

US delegates Llewellyn Thompson Jr. (*left*) and Charles "Chip" Bohlen (*right*), with an unknown man (*center*), in Switzerland for the Geneva summit, July 1955. Hank Walker, *Life* Picture Collection / Getty Images (50347444).

Macmillan described him as a "fat vulgar man with pig eyes"; French Foreign Minister Antoine Pinay, as "a little man with fat paws", and Livingston Merchant, as a loquacious person with "extraordinary table manners."[4]

The summit opened on July 18, 1955. That evening Eisenhower hosted a dinner for the American and Soviet delegations. There, Thompson talked with Khrushchev for the first time. He also met Anatoly Dobrynin, later to become the Soviet ambassador to the United States, who was someone Thompson would ultimately befriend (at least as much as circumstances allowed).[5] Eisenhower's plan was to keep the Soviets on the defensive by meeting "Soviet generalities about their peaceful purposes with specific proposals." One such proposal, Open Skies, called for mutual aerial inspections of such things as troop movements and ground installations, giving each country evidence that the other was not preparing for war. Just as Eisenhower finished his presentation, a deafening thunderclap thrust the room into total darkness. There was complete silence, until Eisenhower remarked, "I had not dreamed I was so eloquent as to put the lights out." When the lights returned a few minutes later, Eden and Faure, who had already known about Open Skies, quickly agreed to it, but the Soviet delegation was taken off guard. Bulganin evaded the question by simply stating that it was a proposal that merited study.

When Eisenhower spoke with Khrushchev shortly after the meeting adjourned, Khrushchev told him Open Skies seemed to be an espionage plot against the USSR. Thompson would later cite Open Skies as an example of how not to negotiate with the Soviets. Suddenly injecting the proposal into the discussions put the Soviets "off balance and [they] almost *had* to take a negative view."[6] It was a good proposal, but it was badly handled. It did more harm, by raising Soviet suspicions, than it helped, in gaining propaganda points for the United States.

Khrushchev later brought up Open Skies at a Politburo session, claiming that Eisenhower was bluffing, and then suggested that the USSR accept the proposal and "watch the White House squirm in the propaganda spotlight." The Politburo, however, rejected it out of hand.[7] The Soviet military took Open Skies more seriously, but Khrushchev used this attitude against Marshal Georgy Zhukov when he later dismissed Soviet the minister of defense.[8] Dobrynin thought that there were a number of occasions when both the United States and the USSR missed great opportunities to slow down the armaments race, and this was an example.[9]

Yet Eisenhower probably had not been bluffing, at least not entirely. It was a no-lose proposition for the Americans. What most of the delegates did not know, but Ike did, was that a new high-altitude spy plane, the U-2, had finally completed its testing phase and was ready to be deployed. If the Soviets refused his Open Skies proposal, which was the outcome Ike may have preferred, the United States would be able to fly reconnaissance over the Soviet Union with little chance of detection, and thus have a both unilateral advantage and a sweet propaganda victory. Moreover, there was really no reason *not* to go ahead with Open Skies if the Soviets had accepted it. The Soviets could learn almost everything they needed from publicly available maps and publications, whereas the inherent secrecy of the Soviets made it a lot more difficult for the Americans to obtain the same kind of information.

Conversely, from the Soviet point of view, it was lose-lose proposition. Refusal would undercut their new "make nice" strategy, but acceptance would allow America to see how limited the Soviets actually were, both militarily and technologically. Their bluff, where they seemingly had many more missiles than they really possessed, enabled Hawks in the United States to claim that a "bomber gap"—and later a "missile gap"—existed in favor of the Soviets. Although there was a warranted fear of Soviet nuclear capability, US politicians in both parties took advantage of this myth for political gain, while the military used it to inflate its budget.

The Geneva summit did not accomplish anything immediately tangible. Open Skies went nowhere, and the delegations failed to settle the questions of Germany or disarmament. Moreover, the Soviets made it clear that they would not stand for any interference in their Eastern European sphere of influence. Bohlen described Geneva as "one of the most disappointing and discouraging of all the summit meetings."[10] Eisenhower left the summit with the impression that the Soviet leaders were implacable and unmovable. Yet despite its apparent failure, the discussions were conducted in an exceptional atmosphere of cordiality and good will, which became known as the "spirit of Geneva." Thompson thought one positive aspect of the summit was that the Soviet Union finally started to come out of its isolation by creating openings for cultural and scientific exchanges. For

Merchant, the most important thing was that it helped to reduce the "genuinely dangerous risk of Soviet action based on a miscalculation of our own intentions."[11] Khrushchev came away from the summit elated. He "realized that our enemies probably feared us as much as we feared them."[12] Khrushchev would consolidate his power in 1957, the same year Thompson became the US ambassador to Moscow.

Once the Geneva summit was over, Thompson picked up his wife in France, at Le Havre, in a large station wagon and drove with her and his golf clubs to Paris, where they joined Bohlen and his family. It was mid-August, and it seemed as though Paris belonged to them. During a luncheon where a number of State Department colleagues were present, someone brought up the Soviet proposal to guarantee the "security and territorial integrity of any country wanting to pursue a policy of neutrality and no participation in military blocs. Witness the example of Austria."[13] Thompson replied, "Well, to answer your question of how far I think they'd go toward pushing any neutrality policy adopted by a Western country, I think it would [be] pretty close to 100 percent, but they certainly don't entertain such ideas or support for any Eastern bloc county suggesting such an interest."

1956: Year of Choices

Big choices took place in 1956. It was an election year in the United States. Eisenhower was running for reelection against Adlai Stevenson, a Democrat, and in their campaign the Republicans emphasized their party's three foreign policy successes—the Trieste Agreement, the Austrian State Treaty, and improved relations with the Soviet Union—all of which had involved Thompson, although he would be quick to explain that he had no partisan role.[14] In the USSR, with Stalin gone, 1956 was the year Khrushchev took a risk and gained control of the Soviet empire, rather than continue in the shadows of the new collective leadership. The Austrian State Treaty and the "spirit of Geneva" were all part of his strategy to show that a new Soviet era had begun, one in which he was in control. Khrushchev introduced his policy of "peaceful coexistence" at the Twentieth Congress of the Soviet Communist Party in February 1956, and he went even further by making a shocking speech in which he exposed the crimes committed by Stalin. The text of it was leaked, allowing deep-seated resentments to surface.

Khrushchev's "Secret Speech" presented people in the USSR's satellite countries with choices, or so they thought. Undoubtedly encouraged by the treaty solution of neutrality for Austria and the subsequent withdrawal of Soviet troops, people in Eastern Europe interpreted Khrushchev's speech as a crack in the wall of Soviet domination. Riots broke out, first in Poland, and then more virulently in Hungary. It was a situation the architects of the rollback strategy and the constructors of US covert operations had been trying to create for years. In neither Poland nor Hungary could they take credit, however. The events of 1956 took everyone by surprise. It was a perfect storm, composed of passionate idealists who believed the free world would rally to their cause; a still-untested, post-Stalin Soviet Union backed into a corner; and a United States distracted and stymied by the self-interested actions of its allies over Egypt's move to nationalize the Suez Canal.

Hungary

Although the Austrian occupation had ended, the Western propaganda machine was still humming and plenty of "spooks" remained in Vienna.[15] There would be great debate as to how big a role, if any, these covert operations had in fomenting the Hungarian Revolt. On October 23, 1956, a protest taking place in the streets of Budapest, where students were agitating for more-liberal social and economic policies, soon escalated into a full-scale rebellion after security forces killed some of the demonstrators. Soviet troops and tanks entered Budapest, but instead of the situation calming down, the riots spread to the provinces. The extant Hungarian government fled from the capital, and a more moderate—but still Communist—reformer, Imre Nagy, took office as premier, with János Kádár as first secretary. Nagy managed to negotiate a cease-fire, as well as the withdrawal of Soviet troops to the outskirts of the capital city.

Thompson's contact with Hungarian refugees and their Austrian confidantes spurred him to write two long cables to Washington, DC, one at the end of October and another on November 11.[16] In the first, Thompson relayed Austrian concerns and perspectives. Then he offered his own "tentative personal views." He noted that the strength of the uprising was in its genuine populist nature, but he feared that the Hungarians might overplay their hand. Since it was unrealistic to expect the Soviets to accept free elections and their country's complete withdrawal from Hungary, he suggested that the Hungarians should contact the Soviets and concentrate on getting them to remove their troops. Thompson thought that if the "patriots," as he called them, could be influenced to accept the Nagy government—which some did not want to do, because it was still a Communist government—there was a chance that the Soviets would acquiesce to this and remove their military forces from Hungary.

Events then spun out of control as Nagy agreed to the demands of those leading the populist revolt. He declared that Hungary would introduce a multiparty system, with free elections, and it would withdraw from the Warsaw Pact. He then asked the UN to provide security for Hungary's declared neutrality. At this point the Soviets did not know what to do. Khrushchev said that he "vacillated" throughout the crisis, as did others.[17] In his long October 11 cable, Thompson also suggested that the US agree to recognize Hungarian neutrality in advance, hoping it would ease tensions, but this cable was written too late. Thompson said it was like watching a person drown, knowing he or she could never be reached or saved.

Simultaneously with these events, Tom Wailes, the minister-designate to the US legation in Hungary, was cooling his heels in Vienna, waiting for the State Department's permission to go to Budapest.[18] Thompson felt that his former colleague from the Truman Doctrine had to get into that country immediately, as his presence would mean US recognition of the Nagy regime and might strengthen Nagy's ability to take control of the situation—or at least stay the Soviet hand long enough for Wailes to do so.[19] Thompson and Wailes were unable to reach anyone in the State Department with sufficient authority to change the instructions. When Wailes was finally cleared to go, it was too late. Thompson would later cite this incident as an example of the breakdown of communications during the Hungarian situation.[20] When the crisis was over, he wrote to his friend Bohlen, noting that in these early days, those in the department were not making any real attempt to work out a policy, and the timing of the moves they *were* making was wrong.[21]

Some analysts say that the Hungarians went too far in their demands. Others maintain that Khrushchev came to his senses and realized that if Hungary left the fold, the Soviets would lose *all* the Eastern bloc countries, resulting in his own demise. Khrushchev eventually opted to crush the rebellion. He used Kádár, Nagy's number-two man, to provide legal cover by persuading Kádár to form a new pro–Warsaw Pact government and then formally ask for Soviet intervention.

On November 3, Dulles entered Walter Reed Army Hospital for an emergency operation. He had colon cancer. The next day, eleven days after the start of the revolt, the Soviet army, with new recruits from as far away as Central Asia, invaded Hungary and initiated air strikes. The Hungarian rebels made dramatic pleas over the radio for support, but none came. Communication with the American legation in Budapest was sporadic at best, with one officer frantically describing the situation on a teletype from under his desk, afraid that if he cut the link, he'd never get it going again. Hungarian refugees poured across the Austrian border, with a total of 190,000 managing to escape.[22] By November 10, the uprising had been defeated, and Nagy had taken refuge in the Yugoslav embassy.[23] A scared Tito turned him over to the Soviets, who shot him. In all, 20,000 Hungarians and 1,500 Soviet soldiers lost their lives.

The Hungarian refugees clamored for the US to do *something,* as did members of the Austrian government. Whenever Thompson asked them to make a concrete suggestion, all they could come up with was that the United States should give the Soviet Union an ultimatum, although everyone quickly backed away from this when he asked them to consider the implications. No one wanted another war. The only tool the United States had, short of a confrontation with the Soviets, was the UN, which was rendered ineffectual by the horrible timing of the another upheaval in October 1956, in Egypt.

Suez Crisis

When Dulles reneged on promised funds for the construction of Egypt's Aswan Dam, that country's president, Gamal Abdel Nasser, moved to nationalize the Suez Canal, precipitating a crisis. Britain and France then struck a secret deal with the Israelis to "take back" the canal. Israel would invade the Sinai Peninsula, giving the British and the French a pretext to intervene by demanding that the Israeli and Egyptian armies withdraw from their respective sides of the canal. They would be replaced by Anglo-French intervention troops, which would take control. In exchange for their secret role, Israel would be granted passage through the Suez Canal. The Egyptians resisted, however, and a shooting war broke out. Eisenhower was furious, and Dulles felt betrayed. The United States was forced to intercede, in order to effect a cease-fire and remove Israeli, French, and British troops. America even censured its own allies by speaking out at the UN.[24]

As a result of this misjudged adventure, Britain's Conservative government fell. By November 8, a thousand Egyptians and almost two hundred Israelis had died in the fight, and the Suez Canal was completely blocked by sunken ships. The British and the French tried to divert attention from their Middle East campaign by bringing the Hungarian problem to an emergency session of the UN General Assembly. The Americans, though, who wanted to end the fighting in Egypt, blocked this plan by delaying the UN resolution process concerning Hungary until November.[25]

The Suez crisis also took away any propaganda advantage the West might have accrued from what had occurred in Hungary. It was difficult for the United States to denounce the invasion of Hungary by Soviet troops when its British, French, and Israeli allies had, in effect, invaded Egypt. The contrived Israeli invasion of the area around the Suez Canal occurred just before Khrushchev made up his mind to invade Hungary. It may have removed whatever doubts this Soviet had about clamping down.

Covert Responsibility?

The Hungarian uprising spilled into the Thompson household in Vienna when a rundown bus parked in a spot reserved for the ambassador's car. Its occupants demanded that they be given the arms they believed the Americans had stashed in the basement of the embassy. A similar bus was parked in front of the British embassy, and it took a great deal of talking to convince the Hungarians that no arms cache existed. Their belief was partly the result of Radio Free Europe propaganda broadcasts, which had increased during the uprising.[26] Although a study after the fact concluded that these broadcasts had not *explicitly* caused the uprising, Thompson believed they did create false expectations.[27]

The Hungarian revolt touched Thompson personally for three reasons: the desperate appeals of the Hungarians and Austrians, his wife's personal experiences, and the anguish of his friend, Frank Wisner. Earlier that month, Wisner and his intelligence-agency colleagues debated about how an uprising in Eastern Europe might be supported. They concluded that outright intervention on the part of the United States—or using émigré armies that were no match for the Soviets—would be out of the question, but at least America could supply such forces with arms. Now that a rebellion had actually occurred and the Soviet troops began flooding in, every scenario they played out resulted in a complete showdown with the Soviets, which was unacceptable. There were practical considerations, too. CIA case officers in Vienna "knew too little, we had absolutely no picture at all of who needed weapons, when, what kind, or where."[28] Nor did the CIA send any personnel who spoke Hungarian to Vienna.

Wisner had spent much his life's work and energy trying to make just such a revolt occur. Now that it had happened, he was powerless to do anything and could only watch in horror as events unfolded. On the day the revolt started, Wisner was on a routine visit to CIA stations in Europe, which included Vienna. He was supposed to meet with the head of the US-British Joint Intelligence Committee, Sir Patrick Dean, in London, but Dean never showed up, because he was in Paris, plotting the Suez operation. It was embarrassing to Wisner to know nothing about the Suez machinations. Having worked closely with British intelligence, he felt personally betrayed.

Wisner arrived at Thompson's house on November 8 to set up his base camp, but there was little he could do besides watch as Hungarian refugees struggled to cross the border.

Wisner, whose anti-Communism had been sealed by witnessing Romanians being loaded into boxcars for what was certain to be their eventual slaughter during World War II, must have been struck to the quick to know that the carnage was being repeated in Hungary. It was, Jane thought, the beginning of Wisner's end. He suffered a nervous breakdown shortly thereafter and never fully recovered. Tragically, he committed suicide in 1965.

Jane and the Hungarian Refugees

Jane, too, wanted to do *something*. Although Americans could not help the Hungarian refugees directly, because of Austria's neutrality, they were permitted to assist the Austrians in aiding the refugees. Jane received an unusual number of calls from Austrian friends, wanting to find out if she had any plans to leave town. One friend finally explained the reason, "You see, all of us have a number of relatives or friends who are still stuck in Czechoslovakia or other places [where the Soviets had moved in after the war], simply because they didn't leave in time." Word had gotten out that Jane had cancelled an engagement in order to take the children to the PX (a retail store on a US Army base) in Munich for shoes, and some had feared that this was a cover story for her escape.[29]

Thousands of Hungarians hurried to cross the border before the Soviets could block the flow of refugees.[30] They trudged across fields and woods. Some even fashioned snorkels from hollow reeds and walked underwater across the river. If Article 16, on repatriation, had been left in the Austrian State Treaty, the Austrians would have been obliged to ship all of those refugees back to Hungary.[31] Jane joined the other foreigners, and many Austrians, who had flocked to help. She volunteered at the border, where several village buildings had been converted into hostels and a makeshift clinic. Since most of the crossing activity took place at night, the helpers' shift was from dawn to dusk. Jane wrote: "No one much felt like talking.... The eerie quiet [was] punctuated only by the hiss of a teakettle or the squeak of a rusty hinge. Then muffled voices and dark figures emerged through the thick ground mists at the edge of the field. As the first group came closer, they appeared to be pulling a ribbon of dark figures out of the mist behind them. As they approached, one after the other, hand in hand, I counted twenty-five."[32]

She was assigned to help an Austrian doctor, who explained that his greatest concern was for children who'd been drugged to keep them quiet. Jane noted that sometimes a child might be given a second sleeping draught if the group's crossing had been delayed. While the parents of such children were attended to by others, the Austrian doctor would give the youngsters a stimulant and then turn them over to a volunteer, who would try to awaken them, starting with sponging the child's face with cool water, and later even spanking or slapping them, if necessary. Crying was good, as it would stimulate the lungs. Once awake for an hour and a half, the child could be returned to his or her parents, if they hadn't already fallen asleep from exhaustion in the hay-bed dormitory. Jane had a hard time waking her first drugged child, a two-year-old boy. She finally resorted to spanking him, just as his mother arrived to protest this treatment and yank the child back. The doctor then took the boy and said: "You are too gentle. Let me show you." He shook him hard several times, turned him over his arm, and, after a couple of good stiff spanks on the child's bottom, the child began to cry. Then the doctor gave the wailing tot back to Jane, explaining: "This is what is needed. Keep him crying or that mother won't have a child to worry about." Back home, and unable to sleep from the haunting images, Jane resorted to her own sleeping draught. Thompson came home that evening to find her sobbing in her sleep.

The Hungarian Crisis Unravels

On November 11, after the Kádár government had been installed, Thompson sent his second cable to the State Department, containing another proposal to contact the Soviets.[33] His proximity to the events and to the refugees was reflected in the tone of his cable and showed how personally he had become involved. Thompson would later admit that his reports were "somewhat wild."[34] In this follow-up cable, he suggested offering neutrality and economic assistance to Hungary and other Soviet satellite countries, in exchange for the USSR withdrawing its troops. He felt strongly that the US position in the world would "suffer greatly if the Hungarian affair ended without some action on the part of the US of a nature different from anything we have done, or at least made public so far." Thompson also suggested that a confidential letter be sent to Nikolai Bulganin, chairman of the Council of Ministers of the Soviet Union, not for propaganda purposes, but to sincerely point out that the United States had no designs on the Eastern bloc satellites.[35]

The State Department was doubtful about a direct approach to the USSR, because they feared the Soviets might ask for a corresponding move in the Suez crisis. In Moscow, Bohlen was also doubtful, having concluded that the USSR was already committed to crushing the Hungarian revolt.[36] He was possibly also a bit annoyed at Thompson for offering advice about how to handle the Soviets. Being in Moscow, Bohlen felt that he was a better judge of Soviet intentions, although in his private correspondence with Thompson, he confessed that the Soviets probably would have welcomed such an approach, even if it didn't succeed.[37] Bohlen believed that, although the USSR had accepted Władysław Gomulka as the de facto leader in Poland, it was too late for Hungary to follow suit.[38] Thompson had been suggesting just such a scenario, with Nagy in a similar position to Gomulka's, although Thompson later conceded that his cable to the State Department was wrong in mixing how to make people feel better in light of their hopeless situation with "a clumsy attempt to do something about the problem itself."[39] Thompson told Bohlen that he would now "sign off on Hungary," except for matters that directly concerned him.[40]

Bohlen also opposed Thompson's proposal that the Soviets withdraw their troops from Hungary within six months to a year, in exchange for certain economic commitments. Bohlen thought this would give the Soviets time to install a puppet government and get rid of any anti-Communist residue that remained. Thompson did not agree and wrote: "I realize that by carrying their deportations and liquidations deep enough, they could create a Communist regime, but unless I am badly mistaken I do not believe that any pro-Soviet regime could exist after their troops were withdrawn. My judgment may be warped by the closeness to the situation but I believe this uprising is unique in that the whole people [with very few exceptions] are united in lasting hatred for the Soviets. The Hungarians seem almost bent on mass suicide and it is incredible that the youth and workers are still plastering up their demands on billboards under the mouths of Soviet tanks.... The Russians of course have the capability of deporting half the country but it seems to me they would have to go almost this far if they are going to create anything that will stick if the Soviet troops ever leave." He believed if the United States could find a formula that would allow the Soviets to disengage, there was a "slight possibility" they would take it, rather than face negative world opinion from "maintaining a completely repressive regime in Hungary."[41] Bohlen acknowledged that six months to a year "would probably not be sufficient to consolidate a Communist regime in Hungary, but it certainly would have given the boys an opportunity for a good college try."[42]

Bohlen and Thompson both believed that US policy toward the USSR's satellite countries should be reexamined. Thompson thought that past propaganda from the Truman and Eisenhower administrations and other rollback activities had led people to believe the United States would step in to help if they attempted to break free from Soviet tyranny. Since it was now obvious that this was not so, the Cold War in Eastern Europe had reached a stalemate. Therefore, the United States had a choice of intensifying the war by isolating these countries, or taking a compromise road and encouraging nationally oriented Communism in Eastern Europe.[43] Both Thompson and Bohlen preferred the latter choice, and Thompson remarked that he was happy to know Bohlen's opinion, because "much of the thinking at home ⌊was⌋ going the other way."[44]

As these events played out in history, the Hungarian opposition was eliminated, and the Soviets' domination of Hungary was complete and unequivocal for the remainder of the Cold War. Together with the United States' inability to nurture the smaller revolt in Poland, its inaction in Hungary was the "tell" that allowed the Soviets to call America's bluff.

The Aftermath of the Crisis

The care and feeding of refugees was more than Austria, which only recently had been relieved of its remaining World War II refugees, could handle. It was winter, so the Austrians housed the Hungarians in the still-existing DP camps. The Refugee Relief Act of 1953, which allowed the US embassy to issue visas, would expire in December 1956. Working long hours, including at night and over weekends, the embassy staff managed to process about 21,000 refugees before the deadline. Eisenhower, however, wanted to allow more of them to enter the United States. He sent Vice President Richard Nixon to Vienna, where Nixon, Thompson, and other embassy officials discussed ways to get congressional leadership to modify the existing US immigration rules.[45] As a result, a special "parole" program was set up for Hungarian refugees, allowing 35,000 more to enter the US.[46] The rest went to Canada, Australia, South America, and a small number to Western European countries. While the refugees were being processed, however, they needed to be taken care of and fed. The United States provided most of that food.[47]

The French, the Americans, and the Canadians all set up camps, and the Swiss inspected them. Gray clouds shielded the planes bringing in relief supplies, and their muffled noise gave the impression of a gigantic swarm of bees hanging above the city.[48] Refugees lined up to receive clothing to replace their tattered and soiled apparel. Undergarments were at a premium, so when volunteers found one German box marked "underwear," they pounced on it, only to find dozens of beautifully ironed pantaloons, made before buttons and elastic had been invented. They sent these undergarments over to the costume department of the Wiener Staatsoper.

Now the refugees needed immigration papers. The American and Canadian consulates, as well as various relief organizations, were located in the square behind Vienna's town hall. Refugees, fearing that the various country quotas would fill up, stood there—grouped in families or alone—for long hours in the cold December weather. Sometimes an ambulance took away someone who had fainted, thus forfeiting his place in line. As the weather got worse and worse, it was clear to Jane that the children were suffering the most, so she persuaded the mayor to allow a day nursery to be set up in a city-owned building on the square. The Americans rounded up clothing, toys, and food for the nursery, but they wanted Hungarian doctors to run it. A female Hungarian doctor named Holmos arrived, with "buckets and disinfectant and rags, soap, and two men, a Hungarian metallurgist and a theoretical mathematician. Before long the whole place had been scrubbed clean."[49] During one of her visits, Jane commented on what looked like a bruise on Dr. Holmos' arm. Holmos smiled disbelievingly and explained that she had been in a Nazi concentration camp. She and her mother were freed, but her brother and father, who were in another camp, disappeared. This time she had tragically been forced to leave her mother behind in Hungary, because she was "too frail for the crossing."

Jane realized that the women refugees were at a particular disadvantage, with many of them never having worked, and their future was unknown. She helped organize sewing circles, where they made and embroidered Hungarian jackets and coats, which were then sold. The garments were an immediate success, and the women made some money. Jane's involvement with the refugees was untiring, and she would look back on this as the most rewarding year of her career as an ambassador's wife.

In December 1956, when Vice President Nixon and his entourage came to stay at the Thompsons' home, he turned the residence into a sort of command headquarters, and every room was full of clicking typewriters. Then, in a flash, they and all the cars in the driveway disappeared. Jane found the private Nixon to be relaxed and witty, "not the ruthless politician who seemed to speak from both sides of his mouth at once."[50] She had the opportunity to view the public Nixon a few days later, when he gave out fountain pens to stunned refugees at the border. Nixon was impressed with Thompson and the work the embassy was doing. He praised Thompson in a meeting with the president on December 26, after Nixon's return to the United States, although this praise might have inadvertently caused trouble between Thompson and Bohlen, when their friendship was soon put to the test.[51]

Leaving Austria, and Trouble between Friends

Thompson had to make decisions and choices every day, including deciding what he had time to make decisions about. Charles Yost, removed from Vienna in the middle of the Trieste negotiations, had never been replaced, which made Thompson's days very long. A typical one would start with meeting a visiting US dignitary over breakfast and end after a late night of receptions with him back at the embassy, eating a sandwich and drinking a glass of milk for his ulcer, because dinner had escaped him somewhere along the line.[52] It was during those hectic days that Thompson had to make a very tough choice between his career and friendship.

Thompson's father's death, the consequent burden of the family ranch, his father-in-law's deteriorating mental state, and his concerns for his young family were all weighing on his mind as he gave serious consideration to leaving the Foreign Service. He loved the service but suffered from a premonition, perhaps planted by his sister's early death, that he would die young. Thompson had never been in the best of health, and he knew, given the age difference between him and his wife, that his death could leave her in a difficult situation. So when Ellsworth Bunker, president of the American Red Cross, wrote to him in August 1955, suggesting that Thompson replace Bunker, he was interested.[53]

Thompson had had career successes, he was in his early fifties, and he could withdraw proudly from the Foreign Service. Working for the Red Cross would mean more stability. The family could move back to Washington, DC, where he would have more time to be with them. He could introduce his daughters to the United States, and to what remained of his own family, without having to mount a huge campaign for home leave. More importantly, the Red Cross would keep him in public service, which was where his heart was. He accepted enthusiastically. "After reading the materials you sent me, my head is buzzing with ideas," he wrote to Bunker.[54] Thompson would ask the State Department for cash, in lieu of vacation time, to help him buy a house and settle his family in Washington, DC. He thought he could begin the job in spring 1956.[55]

Thompson then wrote to Dulles to tell him of his plans. After twenty-seven years in the State Department, "it was a most difficult decision to make. . . . In all justice to my family I have no alternative but to retire now, which should enable me to save my pension and part of the salary I can earn in other employment."[56] Yet coincidences lined up to enable Thompson to stay in the Foreign Service. Loy Henderson, having returned from Tehran to become the State Department's deputy undersecretary for administration, proposed a new pension scheme to Congress. Dulles wrote to Thompson that this change had just been approved, and the secretary of state doubted that the Red Cross could offer Thompson anything better. Dulles wanted Thompson to stay in the Foreign Service and promised him posts of "continuing responsibility and increasing public recognition."[57] He urged Thompson to come to Washington, DC, for consultations, to discuss his options in person.[58] Always the moralist, Dulles added, "There is also the fact that you have an unusual opportunity to serve your country this way." Without waiting to go to the capital, Thompson informed Bunker in mid-September that, given the changed financial situation, he could not resist the pressure to stay on in the Foreign Service.[59] Then he recommended Henderson as someone Bunker might consider for the job he was turning down. Jane fully supported her husband's decision. She said she knew he would never be happy doing anything else.

Thompson went back to Washington, DC, in October 1955 to find out the details of the new financial terms and see what Dulles had in mind for him. Dulles, unaware that

Thompson had already declined the Red Cross job, offered him a post as US ambassador to Moscow, to entice him to stay in the Foreign Service. Bohlen, Dulles explained, wanted to retire to write, and he had already served as ambassador to Moscow for three years, which was as about as long as anyone could stand in that place.[60] This was the only time Dulles spoke to Thompson about the Moscow post. Thompson then told Dulles that he thought Bohlen had special qualifications for the job and should stay on for as long as possible, which Dulles did not contradict. Thompson also informed Dulles that he would not be leaving the State Department after all.[61] Thompson did not make any specific reference to the Moscow post, but the secretary of state might have concluded that this was what had persuaded him to stay on.[62] It was not the case, however, as Thompson had his doubts about Moscow. As he explained to Henderson, it wasn't the best place to raise children, and, having spent four years there already, Thompson wasn't sure he wanted to spend another long period in the Soviet Union.[63] Nevertheless, the prospect of such a vital post was enticing.[64]

A complicated and painful series of misunderstandings involving Thompson, Bohlen, Dulles, and Henderson then took place. In essence, Dulles had decided to replace Bohlen with Thompson and wanted Bohlen out of Moscow considerably sooner than Bohlen had expected or desired. Bohlen understandably assumed that Thompson had some role in all this, and he ultimately wrote an agitated letter to Thompson in early January 1957, saying he would leave Moscow right away, but, given that he had told journalists that he did not want to leave, a public announcement might cause "controversy or recrimination. . . . In short, this matter seems to be quite a mess." Bohlen assured Thompson that he would not let "this mix up (if that is what it is)" hurt their friendship and, for that reason, would not argue the matter with Secretary Dulles. But, he added, a skiing trip Thompson and Bohlen had planned to take together was now out of the question.[65]

Bohlen's letter was "quite a shock" to Thompson. He had only talked to Dulles once, and if there had been any misunderstanding, his conversation with Henderson should have cleared that up. Thompson told Bohlen that, from a personal point of view, it would be a "great handicap to me starting out [in Moscow] if the impression prevails that you were shoved out to make room for me."[66] He also tried to talk Bohlen out of leaving the Foreign Service, citing the new pension plan and telling him something would surely be worked out if he stayed on a bit longer. The letter ended with Thompson hoping Bohlen would still consider the skiing vacation. Thompson was trying to deal with the situation practically, but he obviously missed the main point, which was that Bohlen was very upset because the whole thing had come about without anyone in the Foreign Service consulting him. He told Thompson so in a letter a few days later, accusing him of not questioning Dulles's interpretation and accepting the assignment without asking Bohlen what his views were.[67] Bohlen said he would not pretend he was leaving by his own choice. "Perhaps you and [Dulles] had better get together and work out a story," he advised.

This letter hit Thompson hard. Perhaps he was a pawn in some scuffle between Dulles and Bohlen. Perhaps it was just a genuine misunderstanding. It was the economics of continuing with a job in the Foreign Service, not the offer of the Moscow post, that had changed

Thompson's mind about resigning. He didn't know what Dulles's reasons were for telling Bohlen otherwise, but he could hardly come out and call the secretary a liar. One thing was obvious. He had assumed Henderson had cleared everything with Bohlen before contacting Thompson, but it was now evident that Henderson had not done so. Thompson wrote to Henderson, saying that "the last thing I wanted was to in any way be responsible for Chip's leaving Moscow . . . particularly as Chip is one of my best friends."[68] In looking back and trying to figure out what the whole mess was all about, Bohlen, in his memoirs, concluded that Dulles had simply made up the story that Bohlen wanted to retire to write as way to get him out of Moscow and ease him out of the State Department.[69]

Thompson, who was so careful not to cause ripples, let alone waves, was mortified that his friend could think he was trying to push him out of the Moscow position. Loyalty to his friend, to the secretary of state, to his family, and to the Foreign Service were all strained to the breaking point.[70] After difficult deliberations, Thompson informed Henderson that he was prepared either to remain in Vienna or accept another assignment (even though it could not be a Class 1 posting). Thompson also wrote a long letter to Bohlen, "imbued with the deepest personal feeling,"[71] telling Bohlen he would withdraw his name from the offer of the Moscow post. Bohlen considered it "a typically admirable gesture on Tommy's part," but he would not accept it.[72] Understanding both Thompson's dilemma and his sincerity, Bohlen reassured his friend and urged him to take the job, because Bohlen did not think anyone "could possibly be more eminently qualified."[73] Although this incident deeply marked both men, it also solidified their friendship. They would remain close for the rest of their lives.

Bohlen thought about resigning but finally consented to be "exiled" to the Philippines. Thompson stayed on in Vienna until that summer. When he finally began his new job, it couldn't have been at a more critical time to arrive in Moscow. The Anti-Party Group, led by Communist Party leaders Vyacheslav Molotov and Georgy Malenkov, had just failed in their attempt to oust Nikita Khrushchev, making reports from the State Department's Moscow mission more important than ever.[74]

PART III

Diplomacy

15 ≣

Khrushchev's Decade (1953–1964)

The Soviet political tradition does not dismiss
liberty as a trivial concept but it does put forth
the principle that today's liberty must be sacrificed
to ensure tomorrow's. The American system rejects
the assumption ... that the suppression of today's
liberty can be justified for whatever reason.
—LLEWELLYN THOMPSON, "The Soviet System
and Ours"

By the time Thompson arrived in Moscow in 1957, Khrushchev had reshuffled the cards of the Soviet government and come out on top, having successfully thwarted the Anti-Party Group. Thompson had never dismissed Khrushchev as an ungraceful peasant, the way some Western leaders had. He also recognized that Khrushchev was different from Stalin. Despite having a totally unpredictable character, Khrushchev was sharp and shrewd, and he wanted his nation to succeed. Khrushchev came by his Communist zeal honestly. He had grown up in paralyzing poverty, where food was not a certainty, shoes were not wasted on those who had not yet survived childhood, and education was a luxury. Communism changed all that, which helped justify Khrushchev's support of Stalin's ruthless rule. The basic tenets of Marxism had to succeed, lest the "fig leaf of ideology," as Kennan called it, be removed to expose the naked autocracy.

"The Soviet System and Ours"

Thompson felt that he gave more importance to the role of ideology in the Soviet regime's behavior than did most of his colleagues. He believed it was the underlying barrier to resolving the conflict between the Soviets and Americans, even if both countries were prepared, for reasons of expediency, to put it aside from time to time.[1] "One of the paradoxes that arises from comparing the Soviet system and ours," wrote Thompson, "is that Marx's theory of capitalist exploitation has come to apply much more to the Soviet Union than to the US."[2]

He noted that workers in the Soviet Union were deprived of the fruits of their labor, since many desired goods that were not available to them, and they were denied a role in political decision making, "which the American trade union movement, unforeseen by Marx, has guaranteed to the working man in this country. The [rising middle class and the] union of the managerial and working class[es] has made possible our economic growth and political liberty." Khrushchev believed that the Communist Soviet Union would overtake and "bury" the capitalist United States in an economic and social competition.[3] Thompson allowed that the Soviet system had the "virtue of being able to act swiftly, decisively, and efficiently," but he was convinced that it could never outweigh the tyranny it imposed on its citizens and the resulting inhibition of individual achievement and innovation.[4] Instead, collectivization destroyed initiative and ground the economy down.

The Soviet Union found itself in a contradictory situation. To prevail in an economic competition with the United States, the Soviet system needed to adapt. Yet it also had to remain the same, so as not to admit any mistakes in its ideology, thereby threatening the regime's control. What made Khrushchev remarkable was that despite this stringent curb, he chose to change anyhow. Not very much and not very fast, but his strategy of "peaceful coexistence" with the West, in order to allow the Soviet Union to regroup and catch up, was an extraordinary departure, fraught with risk. Thompson thought it important to encourage this move toward decision making based on national pragmatism, rather than strict ideology. He saw that one way to do this was to open a crack in the Iron Curtain. A Soviet Union that interacted with the rest of world was far less dangerous than one lost in its own isolation. Hence Thompson advised his government to leave channels open, even in moments of the greatest tension, when closing the door might have felt like the correct step.

Khrushchev believed it was inevitable that global economic systems would evolve from feudalism, through capitalism, to Communism, as his ideology demanded. Thompson felt equally certain that as long as the United States stayed true to its ideals, it would be an irresistible beacon of democratic freedom that would prevail in the long run. He did not see democracy as an end in itself, but "as a means to secure the rights of the individual."[5]

The Bluff

Khrushchev's ambitions to beat America in this peaceful competition faced enormous challenges: failing agricultural policies; the need to rebuild infrastructure still devastated by World War II; the expense of maintaining a large military force, both for supporting Warsaw Pact allies and propping up satellite states, like East Germany; and the formidable task of feeding the legitimate needs and wants of a massive, exhausted population.

Eisenhower, after being reelected by an overwhelming margin, reiterated his policy that the United States would now rely on nuclear rather than conventional forces to deter adversaries.[6] In late spring 1957, he had the National Security Council put it in writing.[7] Khrushchev also decided to use a nuclear threat as a deterrent, because, like Ike, he thought this would allow him to divert resources from a huge military budget into the domestic economy.[8] The problem was that, although the Soviets were ahead in space technology, they were far behind in nuclear arms production. So Khrushchev based his nuclear deterrent on bluff, which worked for a while. The United States estimated that the Soviets would have over a hundred intercontinental ballistic missiles (ICBMs) by 1960, although they actually had about ten.[9] In order to keep this secret, Khrushchev would go quite far in his brinksmanship efforts.

16 ≋

Moscow 2

Upon his arrival in Moscow, Ambassador Thompson had to plunge
into the icy waters of the Cold War. As is required of an ambassador,
he followed his government's policy. In my opinion, however, as a
person he was doing his best to keep peace, to improve the
relationship between our states, and to promote mutual understanding
between both common citizens and governments. And Jane was his
faithful ally. She was a true devotee of peaceful coexistence and mutual
understanding, as the politicians called it. And she followed it with all
of the passion in her heart.... The year was 1957. It had been 12 years
since the end of the Second World War. Yet the wounds it inflicted
were far from healed. The whirlwind of battle had burned Russia to the
ground. It left behind cities destroyed, factories and villages laying in
ashes, mines flooded, and millions dead.
—RADA KHRUSHCHEVA, Moscow, August 2010

Thompson wrote from Vienna to his soon-to-be deputy chief of mission, Edward
Freers: "I must say, I have mixed feelings about the job. It will be difficult to suc-
ceed Chip, particularly after all of the hullabaloo about it and we do hate to leave
Vienna. On the other hand, it should be an extremely interesting period."[1] And so it was.

Impressions of Moscow

Summer 1957 was beautiful in Vienna. The packing was finally done and the Thompson
family prepared to leave. The freight that was being shipped to Moscow included crates
and crates of food—powdered milk; cans of nectarines, tomatoes, and apricots; pasta;
eggs; and other items not available in the USSR—so the plane was sitting a bit low on the
tarmac at Schwechat airport. A large contingent of Hungarians, many of whom were ben-
eficiaries of the craft factories Jane had helped start, came to the airport to say goodbye
with music and song. Nervous about the future and sad to leave, the whole family knew
that things would never be the same.

On July 10, the flying cornucopia descended slowly through the high clouds, past shimmering birch forests, to land at Vnukovo airport, near Moscow. Their propeller plane taxied past Aeroflot's shiny new turbojet-powered Tupolev Tu-104s to the solid, square airport building.[2] Unlike the terrifying flight when they first arrived in Vienna, which concluded with a splendid welcome, replete with smiling faces and music, the flight of the fat, slower DC-7 was uneventful and ended with a greeting by Soviet soldiers, carrying rifles tipped with bayonets. The family piled into a long Cadillac and a black Ford station wagon for the trip into town. It was their first look at their new home. If Vienna had seemed to still be muted with the dust of war, compared with Rome, Moscow was positively bleak, even in the bright white summer light. Their first impression was of a city of cranes, like giant steel giraffes standing over the low-slung buildings. The streets were lined with old ladies who were sweeping and cleaning the streets and gutters, wearing padded jackets and light summer dresses and carrying brooms and pails and mops. Jane turned to Tommy and said something along the lines of: "Good grief, look at the refugee potential. Maybe we shouldn't be too quick to raise the curtain."

The car went around a little square, named after the domed Church of Salvation on the Sands, which sat at one end, and pulled into the driveway of Spaso House, at the other end. The building, familiar to Thompson, looked to Jane like a miniature (and slightly dingy) White House, stark and gray and badly in need of flowers. She would soon fill its central

A Soviet guard in front of Spaso House, the ambassadorial residence in Moscow, USSR, circa 1957. Howard Sochurek, *Life* Picture Collection / Getty Images (62577684).

portico with bright red geraniums. The driveway, with a small wooden guard shack where it met the street, followed along the right side of the house and through an arch by the main entrance. Here the cars stopped and the family piled out.

They walked through the entrance to the house to find twenty servants, in black-and-white suits and dresses with aprons, lined up waiting to be introduced. Jane found the house to be in poor condition, dirty and down at the heels, but it must have looked rather splendid, compared with Thompson's previous stay there, since there were no longer bomb holes in the roof or automobile outhouses in the yard. Thompson went straight off to the office to see his staff, while Jane began organizing the household. It was 11:30 p.m. by the time they were reunited. They stood on the balcony over the portico and watched the guards pace back and forth in the evening glow of the late summer twilight, since it was not quite the land of the midnight sun.

Jane, trying to sort out her first impressions, remembered Chip Bohlen forewarning her that trying to describe Russia to an outsider was like describing the act of love to a sixteen year old. Thompson was once again stepping into his friend's footprints, but Thompson's would look quite different to his staff. They anticipated his arrival positively, because Bohlen had said only good things about Thompson, and they all respected Bohlen.[3] Some would find the new ambassador a welcome change, and others less so. Where Bohlen was gregarious and jocular, Thompson was reserved, and his humor was as dry as his high-desert homeland. As he had in Vienna, Thompson made a formal effort to have his staff feel as though their work and opinions were important, but in this US embassy of 197 Americans and 92 foreigners, 47 military personnel, and 103 dependents, some missed the witty, easy-going Bohlen and thought Thompson came across as aloof or withdrawn.[4]

Thompson continued the tradition of Sunday night poker games that Bohlen had started. There were never more than sixteen players—diplomats, embassy officers, and journalists—with the seating spread over two tables.[5] Comparing the difference between Bohlen and Thompson at the poker table, a former colleague said: "Bohlen played poker to have fun. . . . Thompson wanted to win. Thompson was a more serious player who analyzed his prospects carefully. Both ambassadors were cheerful and friendly. . . . There was no awareness of rank distinctions."[6]

There were also differences between Thompson and his predecessors in how they ran the embassy. "Bohlen was social and charming and staff meetings were a free for all."[7] Bohlen was a teacher, and Thompson a role model, said Ted Eliot, who served in the embassy under both men and would later go on to become US ambassador to Afghanistan. "For example," wrote Eliot, "knowing [that] our counterparts in other embassies got information from their ambassadors on their [the ambassadors'] private talks, we put a colleague up to asking Thompson at a staff meeting if he would tell us about those conversations, too. Rather than replying, Thompson simply turned to the next person for a report. He was not about to break confidentiality. . . . He knew how to obtain the enduring confidence of presidents and secretaries of state and key people in Congress. He achieved this not only because of his knowledge and wisdom but because these people learned that he would never violate their trust and would not talk to the media without their permission and would not promote himself in any way, shape, or form."[8]

"In contrast to Kennan and Bohlen," recalled Richard Davies, who later served as US ambassador to Poland, "Thompson gave free reign to the political, economic, cultural, and agricultural sections to draft and send to the [State] Department messages embodying their own views of developments in their spheres of responsibility. If he disagreed with something or had something pertinent to add, he would send a subsequent message, plainly marked as [coming] from him, containing his own comments."[9] According to Davies, "Kennan pursued the opposite tack; he would send messages labeled from him and then ask officers to comment on them when it was too late to change."[10] Thompson's low-key personality and his equanimity were also reflected in how the embassy worked: smoothly, with no great dramas. "Everyone knew what they were supposed to do. Thompson did not have daily staff meetings. Rather, he walked around the chancellery, asked people into his office, and asked questions; he did not get involved in a lot of minutia. He relied a lot more on people doing their job. If there was a problem he wanted to know about it, but he wasn't on your back. He never stopped people reporting back [to the State Department] what they wanted."[11]

One of the key people in the embassy was Thompson's assistant, Constance Gagnon, who would, through thousands of cups of steaming hot coffee, offer unwavering loyalty and good humor. She became an indispensable part of Thompson's life. Connie would marvel at how Thompson read the lengthy and dry documents on things such as Soviet industrial output without losing his concentration, while the embassy office bustled about him.[12] Another key staff member, especially at a post as isolated and difficult as Moscow, was the administrative officer, Idar Rimestad, a large man with a personality to match. Rimestad was in charge of the well-being of all the staff at the embassy, and he showed a remarkable lack of sympathy for the difficulties they found when living in Moscow. All of the journalists and many of the embassy personnel resided in apartment blocks that were hastily built to alleviate the terrible housing shortage in Moscow—hence those giraffe-like cranes all over the city. These were depressing structures: dull, dark, rectangular affairs, without a single bit of architectural relief, that appeared to be functional, yet weren't. One of the buildings housing embassy staff was so poorly constructed that the elevators would not work, because the shafts were not quite vertical. Apartments with balconies had them taped off, because they could not hold the weight of a person. One officer's apartment was so small that his youngest daughter slept on the dining room table. Idar accused the complainers of expecting little white houses with picket fences. He flatly told them all that as far as he was concerned, the ambassador was first, he (Rimestad) ranked second, and everyone else came last.[13] Rimestad, like OPC's Carmel Offie long before him, was a fixer, but he only fixed things for those he thought could forward his career. It worked, too, because he rose quite high in the State Department.

The embassy staff found Jane to be very different from her husband: outgoing, talkative, and friendly. She did not put on airs and was understanding of the situation the embassy wives had to deal with in this difficult post. The Thompsons, together, thus made a good team and represented the face of the new Foreign Service.[14]

Beginning of a Relationship

Some early manifestations of Khrushchev's new policy of peaceful coexistence were taking place as the Thompson family arrived. One was Soviet participation in the International Geophysical Year, a series of activities for scientists from around the world. Another event was the Sixth Annual World Youth Festival, a bold move that opened up Moscow to 34,000 young people from 130 countries, something previously unheard of in the USSR and a most audacious departure from Stalinist behavior. American students were encouraged not to attend the festival, because the US government saw it as a Soviet "propaganda extravaganza."[15] But the West benefited from this mutual exposure. Soviets openly talked to foreigners. They danced in the streets. Young people did what young people do: they met each other, they made friends, and they sang the Russian hit "Moscow Nights" together. Thousands of young Western visitors had a profound effect on Soviet youth, introducing them not only to jazz, but also to blue jeans and the exuberant freedom of expression in rock 'n' roll. The Soviet establishment could dismiss this music as decadent and American culture as inferior, but young Soviets embraced it.

New Place, New World

Thompson sent a cable to the State Department only a few days after he arrived in Moscow, concluding that, although Khrushchev was firmly in the driver's seat, he could not implement a one-man rule the way Stalin had. The Central Committee was closely watching the outcome of Khrushchev's policies, and failure would probably result in his removal.[16] Two events, however, encouraged Khrushchev to take his first major gamble on the international scene.

The first was Sputnik. In August 1957, the Soviets launched their first ICBM delivery rocket, the Vostok. Two months later, they launched Sputnik, the first satellite to orbit the earth.[17] This feat captured the world's imagination and terrified many Americans.[18] Thompson anticipated that Sputnik would embolden Khrushchev, and he thought that the Soviets would be likely to exert pressure for big-power talks. Thompson pointed out that, for the first time, Sputnik brought US technological superiority into question, and this might incline uncommitted nations to seek Soviet help or trade links. It now seemed as though Khrushchev was leading from a "position of strength."[19]

The other event was the removal of World War II hero and Khrushchev's then defense minister, Georgy Konstantinovich Zhukov. Zhukov had supported Khrushchev at the time of the attempted Anti-Party Group coup, but now Khrushchev saw him as a threat. Zhukov disagreed with Khrushchev's new strategy of reducing conventional military forces in favor of a nuclear deterrent and, worse, Zhukov had attempted to interfere in foreign policy issues. Thompson concluded that Khrushchev turned on Zhukov because of the "rivalry between the Party and the armed forces as institutions, rather than a personal fear on the part of Khrushchev that his leadership of the Party was threatened."[20] A few years later, Khrushchev would tell Thompson it had taken all of his persuasive power to get the military to agree to troop reductions.[21] As it turned out, making missiles would prove to be more costly than Khrushchev had expected, and his scaling back of the military would create a quiet, underlying opposition.[22]

New Policy, New Year

One of Khrushchev's main goals was to settle the unstable situation in East Germany. When Yugoslavia recognized East Germany in October 1957, Thompson felt that "it might presage a more aggressive Soviet policy" toward Germany.[23] So on November 6, when Khrushchev made a speech at the Jubilee session of the Supreme Soviet, saying that he wanted further high-level negotiations on this issue, Thompson reported back that he thought it meant Khrushchev wanted a summit.[24] Dulles disagreed, and the White House was not interested. As Thompson had predicted, Khrushchev wanted to work out his new policy of coexistence directly with Eisenhower. There were several reasons for this. Eisenhower, especially as the Supreme Allied Commander in Europe during World War II, was much admired, and Khrushchev wanted to be seen as his equal. Since major decisions were made at the top in the Soviet government, Khrushchev assumed that this was also the case in the United States and that Eisenhower, surrounded by "imperialist industrialists and anti-Communists," would be the only one able to respond positively to Khrushchev's overtures. So he wanted to meet with Eisenhower face to face. Khrushchev had Bulganin send several requests for a meeting, but only received stony silence in reply. He decided to make yet another attempt at "peaceful coexistence" that New Year's Eve.

On December 31, at 11:00 a.m., Thompson received an invitation to a reception at the Kremlin for 11:00 p.m. that evening. New Year's in Soviet Russia was a big occasion, because all the secular traditions associated with Christmas (which, of course, Marxists were not supposed to celebrate) were moved to New Year's. This was a command appearance. Thompson invited his British and French counterparts to join them for an informal dinner beforehand at Spaso House. As they chatted, the French and British ambassadors mentioned that inflammatory speeches had made all of them walk out of the drab Soviet reception the previous New Year's Eve. This year they did not know what to expect. As Thompson and Jane headed up the fifty-eight steps of the impressive Red Stairway at the Kremlin, he instructed his wife to keep an eye on him and, if he walked out, not to ask why but to just get up and follow him.

The stairway opened up onto the largest room in the palace, the magnificent St. George's Hall, in all its imperial splendor. The parquet floor, made up of twenty different types of wood in an intricate, carpet-like pattern, was polished to a mirrorlike shine. Eighteen twisted columns and large, flat pillars supported the vaulted ceiling of the long hall. Each of the pillars listed the various kingdoms conquered by Russia, as well as the regiment responsible for each victory. The room, lit by six enormous bronze chandeliers, was truly resplendent. As Jane recalled, "It was obvious that this was not going to be a typical stand-up affair." A long table stretched across one side, with settings for the fourteen Presidium members. Tables seating at least a thousand guests radiated out like sunbeams from the head table. The diplomats were placed according to protocol, based on the date of their accreditation, so the Thompsons, being new arrivals, were some distance away from the Presidium table, although they could clearly see Khrushchev in the middle. They were just finishing the first course, a bouillon soup, when Khrushchev stood up to make a speech in front of a large microphone. Jane was new to the Russian language, so she only understood random words in what he said, such as "Eisenhower," "Hitler," "terrible," "USA," "unthinkable," and "Thompson." She could not see the expression on her husband's face, because he had slightly turned his back on her to see Khrushchev better, but she feared the worst, nice table settings or not, and made ready to storm out of the dinner.

Instead, Khrushchev had chosen this unusually lavish reception to make a very friendly speech, talking about Soviets' and Americans' wartime collaboration against Hitler. He went on to say that neither the Russians nor, he was sure, the Americans wanted a terrible war, and the first priority of the new year should be to work together to solve world issues. He ended up with a toast to Eisenhower, at which point Thompson stood up and crossed the room to clink glasses with Khrushchev, unaware that his wife was following him. Jane thought she and her husband were walking out of the hall and was worried that Thompson was going the wrong way. When they reached Khrushchev and she saw smiling faces all around, she realized her mistake, but it was too late to turn back. Anastas Mikoyan came to her rescue by handing her a glass, so she could follow her husband up and down the table, toasting the entire Presidium.[25] Jane would always remain on friendly terms with Mikoyan after that. The Western ambassadors all agreed that it had turned out to be the most successful party they had ever attended in the Kremlin.[26]

Peace and Friendship?

At that time, it was unusual for Soviet high officials to mix with the diplomatic corps. But that, too, changed under Khrushchev's new strategy. Khrushchev himself made an unexpected appearance at a national-day reception at one of the smaller NATO embassies. The Soviets stayed in a group to one side, and the Western diplomats huddled together on the other side of the room. The nervous host, not knowing how to handle the awkward situation, asked Thompson to break the ice. Thompson agreed to take the lead and walked up to Khrushchev, with his Western colleagues following a few steps behind. Khrushchev said to Thompson, as he came near, "I see you are leading a NATO attack on me!" Thompson replied: "Not at all. . . . The NATO ambassadors are just afraid that you and I will make a deal together at their expense." Khrushchev was amused.[27] It was that sort of bantering that would make the Thompson-Khrushchev relationship unique. Vladimir Toumanoff, who accompanied Thompson on many occasions when he went to see Khrushchev, noted that Khrushchev always treated Thompson with respect. Khrushchev, whose main conceptions about the world came from Communist Party schooling, would approach Thompson "on all kinds of topics that had nothing to do with Soviet relations . . . a sort of reality check."[28]

In January 1958, shortly after Eisenhower was inaugurated for his second term as president in the midst of a major recession, the United States and the USSR signed the Cultural Exchanges Agreement. It would begin with an exchange of national exhibitions on culture, technology, and science. The Soviet exhibition would take place in New York City, and the American one in Moscow. Thompson was fascinated with science. He had built his town's first radio as a boy, and he always had a copy of *Scientific American* on his bedside table, along with all the briefing papers and political books. He maintained a correspondence with the editors of the magazine and was very pleased when one of the Pugwash conferences on confronting the perils of nuclear weapons came to Moscow.[29]

Another result of the Cultural Exchange Agreement was that it brought dozens of American celebrities to Moscow, including Lana Turner, Elizabeth Taylor, and Leonard Bernstein. The most popular exchange events for Soviets were Holiday on Ice and the Harlem Globetrotters.[30] In April 1958, comedian Bob Hope came to film a show for American television, and, during his visit, he performed for Soviet audiences. Russians have a robust sense of humor, but some of Hope's jokes were aimed more for his home audience, with the Soviets being the brunt of them. Hope also gave a performance in the ballroom at Spaso House. The film of that event shows a camera-shy Thompson introducing him, and the giddy Thompson children receiving lots of hugs, even though they had no clue who Bob Hope was. Neither did Jane, apparently, since, in his biography, Hope recalled the ambassador's wife introducing herself with a big smile and exclaiming: "I do like your show Mr. Benny. Did you bring your violin?"[31] But her charm won Hope over, and he forgave her eventually.

In February, Khrushchev had made overtures about a possible visit to Moscow by Vice President Nixon and a conference at the highest level.[32] Despite the thaw in relations and the goodwill gestures from Khrushchev, the West still did not respond to his overtures. Thompson returned to Washington, DC, that same month for consultations, and he tried to convey that things were changing in the USSR and Eastern Europe.[33] He saw signs of weakness in the monolithic bloc and pointed to the young as the cause. They had challenged Communism in Hungary and Poland and were fleeing East Germany in ever greater numbers.

In April 1958, the same month as the Hope visit, Thompson was the first American official to appear on Soviet television. His speech began with a personal recognition of the Soviet sacrifices during World War II. He went on to lament that the collaboration of the war years did not continue afterward. He said that some of the differences between the United States and the Soviet Union were not unusual. Instead, they represented normal conflicts of interest between countries. Others, however, arose from misunderstandings and a lack of mutual knowledge, and Thompson was of the opinion that these differences should be the easiest to fix. He was "convinced that their removal can make a significant contribution to the solution of the bigger problems."[34] To that end, Thompson made Spaso House a destination for many American authors, artists, performers, scientists, businessmen, and politicians.

Sometimes these visits created problems. When Moscow hosted the 1958 US Olympic wrestling team, there was a grand reception, including all the coaches and the press, at

Jane Thompson and gardener in the greenhouse at Spaso House, the US ambassadorial residence in Moscow, USSR, 1968. © Elliott Erwitt / Magnum Photos (68-5-4 25A).

Spaso House. About half an hour after they all left, Thompson called the embassy's information officer, Hans N. "Tom" Tuch. Tuch had only been in Moscow for a week, so he was a bit shaken up, wondering what he might have done wrong. It turned out that most of a large collection of silver ashtrays were missing from the ambassador's residence. Thompson didn't want to make a formal complaint, so the coaches were simply told to return the ashtrays by mail. Tuch then started getting packages: ashtrays, cocktail glasses, all kinds of things, but never all of the ashtrays.[35] Twenty years later, Jane received an ashtray in the mail from someone who'd been harboring guilt all those years.

Jane also compiled some routine statistics. In 1959, they averaged 420 guests for cocktails per month, and 260 guests for meals. The meager entertainment stipend provided by the State Department never covered all of the expenses incurred from that steady stream of people coming through Moscow. She had no administrative help, so she personally had to keep the accounts, write all the invitations and place cards herself, and order and arrange for supplies to be bought in from abroad whenever the ambassador's plane made a trip outside the USSR. To save some money, she had a greenhouse built, where she grew vegetables and flowers. She created decorations for the official parties that took place in the huge ballroom. It wasn't unusual to discover one of the residence's bathtubs filled with flowers to be arranged in bouquets for some big event, and later to find Jane, in stocking feet, walking down the middle of the forty-foot table, arranging them and supervising the place settings.

Jane received and paid official calls whenever there was an addition to or a change in the diplomatic corps, gave orientation sessions for all the new spouses, intervened in disputes between members of the domestic staff, and learned Russian. According to her, Thompson was even more occupied. Allowing for seven hours of sleep, he averaged one hour and fifteen minutes of free time per day when he wasn't in the office, engaged on official business, eating, or dressing. On the weekends, he also worked six hours, on average, on both Saturdays and Sundays. The cocktail hour before dinner was the time the Thompson daughters were most likely to see their parents. A second good possibility was when Thompson and his wife were in their dressing room, getting ready to go out, with the children watching Jane do her hair, put on her makeup, and spray herself with ample amounts of Joy perfume before the couple disappeared into the black Cadillac and the Moscow night.

Another example of the new openness in the Soviet Union was when, in April 1958, the first Tchaikovsky International Piano Competition chose a young American from Texas, Harvey Lavan "Van" Cliburn as the winner. Cliburn stayed with the Thompsons at Spaso House and gave the family an impromptu recital. He charmed the whole family. Jane gave him the affectionate moniker "Brillo Top." Little Sherry was completely smitten when he took her in his lap as he played the Steinway piano in the residence's Great Hall, transport-

Van Cliburn (*center*) and Llewellyn Thompson Jr. (*right*), with (*in foreground*) Jenny Thompson (*left*) and Sherry Thompson (*right*), at Spaso House, the US ambassadorial residence in Moscow, USSR, July 1, 1960. Carl Mydans, *Life* Picture Collection / Getty Images (50662382).

ing them all to another planet. Cliburn made a terrific impression on the Soviets, too. Huge crowds appeared at his concerts, and a sort of mass hysteria ensued. It was Beatlemania, except with classical music. *Time* magazine called Cliburn the "American Sputnik."[36] On his tour, young women threw flowers at Cliburn, followed him everywhere, and stood for hours in front of his hotel, hoping to catch even a glimpse of him. The State Department had some concerns about this enthusiasm, so Thompson took the young pianist aside and had a chat with him. After their talk, Thompson reassured the department that they had nothing to fear.[37]

Things cooled off, however, in July 1958, when the United States sent troops to Lebanon to bolster the pro-Western Lebanese government of President Camille Chamoun against internal Muslim opposition and threats from Syria and Egypt.[38] In reaction, there were "spontaneous" anti-American demonstrations in Moscow. On the first day, about two or three hundred demonstrators showed up, but by the third day, their numbers were in the thousands, probably surprising their sponsors as much as the embassy staff. Many of the demonstrators were just curious to see what was happening. Nothing like a demonstration had occurred in the Soviet Union since the 1917 Revolution. The embassy staff's children were on an excursion to the country that day and could not return to the chancery, so they were rerouted to the ambassador's residence. The Thompson girls were delighted to have a house full of children. Jane was told to secure the gates to the residence, as the demonstrators were on their way over, but she could not find any chains with which to do so. A man from the Soviets' main state security agency, the KGB, greeted her in a friendly way and told her she needn't worry. Looking at his watch, he said, "The demonstration will be over in an hour and a half." Jane then had to persuade Ernesto the cook to climb down from the tree where he was perched, holding a water hose and ready to spray any potential intruder.

A week later, at the Polish national-day reception in that country's embassy, which the Thompsons attended, Khrushchev made an anti-American speech to protest the stationing of US troops in Lebanon. The Thompsons sat with other Western ambassadors and had their backs to Khrushchev, who was sitting with other members of the Presidium and Soviet satellite country representatives. The atmosphere was tense. Shortly after 8 p.m., just as the event should have been ending, Khrushchev made a point of approaching the Thompsons' table, with the neutral Indian ambassador in tow. Soon after that, Mikoyan and the Russians' interpreter showed up. The conversation at the Thompsons' table had stopped as all these men sat down. It was typical of Khrushchev to first apply pressure and then alternate it with friendly gestures. Thompson thought it best to avoid serious conversation and deliberately put his wife between himself and Khrushchev.

Jane, who was cross about the unkind things Khrushchev had said in his speech earlier during the reception, brusquely told him: "It is too bad, Mr. Chairman, that you've never been to the United States as you are badly informed about our country. You seem an honest man and if you had been to the States you couldn't have said some of things you said today." Instead of getting annoyed, Khrushchev replied that perhaps she was right. He then asked, "Do you think if I went disguised in a beard they would let me in?" Jane answered,

in Russian, that a wig would work better. The interpreter's face blanched, and Jane wondered for a moment if she had said something truly terrible, as her Russian was still at the beginners' level. Khrushchev rocked with laughter, and the atmosphere relaxed. Just at that moment, the background musicians were playing an old jazz tune, "Mean to me . . . why, baby, must you be mean to me?" Thompson translated the lyrics, and the entire table broke into laughter.[39]

A Polish national-day party at that country's embassy in Moscow, USSR, July 1958. *Seated*, Nikita Khrushchev (*back to camera*), Jane Thompson, Llewellyn Thompson Jr., and others. Howard Sochurek, *Life* Picture Collection / Getty Images (50349191).

Khrushchev then extended an invitation to the Thompsons to spend their vacation in the Crimea. (They did not take up his invitation until years later, however.) It was obvious that Khrushchev was trying to make amends for the attitude he portrayed in his speech. He expanded on the role of India as a go-between for the United States and the USSR, and again Jane entered the conversation, saying she did not understand why their respective countries couldn't just talk directly with each other. Khrushchev agreed that there was no valid reason for not doing so. Thompson reported that he endeavored to maintain as reserved an attitude as circumstances permitted and described the entire performance as eerie.

The whip-saw effects of Khrushchev's personality led Thompson to write the State Department in August that this man had an "exceedingly complex character . . . [and was] sensitive to real or imaged threats." Thompson speculated on the possibility that Khrushchev might not remain in power for long and worried that the Soviet leader's successors would not continue his policies or honor his agreements. Perhaps the idea of a Khrushchev visit to the United States germinated with Jane Thompson's comments. In any case, it was something Khrushchev would pursue, and it was a development that Thompson favored. Dulles, however, was against Khrushchev coming to the United States, and it would take almost a year before Eisenhower extended the invitation.

Adlai Stevenson, a former Democratic presidential candidate, was one of many official visitors to Moscow who supported the idea of a Khrushchev visit.[40] Stevenson reported that Khrushchev was interested in trade with the United States. Prior to Stevenson's visit, Thompson had responded to an inquiry from the State Department on developing trade with the Soviet Union.[41] Thompson expected an increase in Soviet invitations to US businesses and suggested that the State Department should tell them to contact the US embassy in Moscow, not only because it could be helpful to foreign relations between the two countries, but also because business people could open up new and different contacts within the USSR. In general, Thompson was in favor of a more positive trade policy with the Soviet Union. He conceded that as the Soviet economy developed, that country would be able to pursue an agenda toward underdeveloped nations which would be contrary to US interests. Thompson felt that this was a narrow point of view, however, and that the bigger objective was to encourage an evolution of the Soviet system in "such a manner that we will eventually be able to reach a reasonable settlement." To this end, he thought the United States, although "never losing sight of the necessity to maintain its own security," should examine its policies and determine whether they contributed to this essential evolution. Openness, Thompson believed, would lead to a softening of a Soviet policy that was dominated by ideology. If there was any hope of finding a working relationship between the Americans and the Soviets, though, it was Khrushchev himself who made this virtually impossible when he set his Berlin gamble into motion.

17

Khrushchev's First Gamble
Berlin Poker

A wrong decision at the top is clothed by the Soviet system
with the mantle of oracular infallibility, thus mistakes
sometimes reach cosmic proportions.
—LLEWELLYN THOMPSON, "The Soviet System
   and Ours"

For the Western allies, Berlin was either an active problem or one that lurked in the
background, ready to spring out and color all the major moves in the Cold War.
Thompson stepped into it soon after his arrival in Moscow. The division of Germany was an intractable problem that produced a series of crises collectively known in
the West as the "Berlin Crisis." For Khrushchev and the Soviets, it was an East German
problem, with the city of Berlin being either an impediment or a lever, depending on the
moment.

The first Berlin Crisis occurred in 1948, when Stalin had tried to cut off West Berlin
from Germany's western zones, until the allied airlift caused him to relent. The allies ended
their occupation of and established diplomatic relations with the Federal Republic of Germany, or West Germany, in 1955, and West Germany joined NATO that year. Although
West Germany was now considered a sovereign state, the German Democratic Republic,
or East Germany, was not, so its status remained uncertain.[1] Both the Western allies and
the Soviets publicly espoused the desire for a unified Germany, but the reality was that
there were two Germanys, and the danger perceived by both the Soviets and the West was
that either one of the two Germanys could eventually reach accommodation with the
other half, to their disadvantage. The French, and to a lesser extent the British, didn't really
want a united, and possibly threatening, Germany either, but they often differed in how to
deal with the crisis, complicating their collective ability to handle it.

Khrushchev was especially worried about losing East Germany to the West after the
East German uprising in 1953. If East Germany collapsed or was absorbed into West Germany, other satellite countries, such as Poland, Hungary, or Czechoslovakia, could fall like

dominoes. A formal recognition of East Germany as a sovereign state would place it firmly in the Soviet bloc. After all, reasoned Khrushchev, the Soviets recognized West Germany, so why couldn't the West recognize East Germany? Furthermore, Khrushchev's options for compromise were limited. In June 1953, while paving the way for his own rise to power, he had orchestrated the ambush that ousted Stalin's heir apparent, Lavrenti Beria. Among other things, colleagues accused Beria of being willing to forfeit a Socialist East Germany, in the wake of the uprisings there, in order to gain access to US aid.[2] Had Beria stayed in power, Walter Ulbricht, the political head of East Germany, would not have lasted long in power. Khrushchev did not fail to remind Ulbricht of this whenever the East German became impatient with him.

Could Germany realistically be reunified in a way acceptable to both the Soviets and the West? One possibility was neutrality, as had been the case with Austria. Yet if the choice was between a reunified neutral Germany, or a divided one with West Germany firmly tied to the West militarily and economically, the American government wanted the latter. The US military believed that without German manpower, it would be impossible to resist a Soviet invasion of Europe with conventional forces. West German Chancellor Konrad Adenauer had staked his political future on firmly allying West Germany with the West and would not hear of either neutrality or accepting formal recognition of the "other" Germany.

Thompson shared the allies' concerns, but he was also not in favor of formally accepting the status quo of a divided Germany. He felt the long-term consequences of this would be dangerous. Thompson observed, "Sooner or later a demagogue would yield to the temptation and exploit German nationalism for his own ends, and if then reunification was attempted by force . . . it would probably result in the revival of German militarism and a new German threat to Europe."[3] Thompson understood Khrushchev's strategy of forcing recognition of East Germany as a defensive move. Thompson concluded that the Soviets were so preoccupied with securing East Germany because West Germany had entered NATO, and with the "completion in a few years of German rearmament, including the stationing of atomic weapons there,[4] the position of the East German regime will be even more precarious and Khrushchev fears that West German intervention in an East German revolt under such circumstances might face the Soviet Union with the choice of almost certain world war or the loss of East Germany and subsequently most or all of his satellite Empire." Thompson also mentioned that the "strengthening of US bases surrounding Soviet territory" added to the Soviets' insecurity.

The situation was further complicated by Berlin, which was still a divided city. It was both what Khrushchev called "a bone in my throat" and an Achilles heel for the West.[5] East Berlin was the capital of East Germany. Khrushchev, however, did not want West Berlin, which was physically located in East Germany, tied politically to West Germany, because it could then become a NATO base within the East German borders. West Berlin had become an escape route for thousands of East Germans and other Soviet-satellite Europeans who were ready to forfeit ideology for the advantages of living in the West. It was also a springboard inside East Germany for Western spying, with the OPC's largest field office in West Berlin. The Eisenhower administration worried that if the allies let West Germany down over West Berlin, the impact could cause that nation to move toward neutrality and make alternative security arrangements with Moscow. Thus the West might lose West Germany and, with it, Europe. Berlin thus became the front-line position in the Cold War—a sort of "super-domino."[6] Khrushchev's moves in Berlin started a dangerous game. It was impossible to protect West Berlin by conventional forces, which left only a nuclear deterrent. It was a game of bluff in which neither side wanted to call the bet.

Less than a year into Thompson's Moscow appointment, Khrushchev decided to make recognition of East Germany a priority. He would use Berlin to prod the West. The first taste of his strategy came at Christmas. To prevent aerial spying, the Soviets required American planes landing in Moscow to first pick up a Soviet navigator in West Berlin, which meant flying over East German territory. In November 1957, the American Embassy was told that permission to fly over East Germany would now be handled by the East German government, no longer by the Soviets—meaning a de facto recognition of East Germany, which the United States was not prepared to do. As a result, the ambassador's plane, which was sitting on the Berlin tarmac, loaded down with office supplies, mail, and food for Thanksgiving and Christmas, did not arrive, putting a damper on the holidays. One package, though, had made it through a month before. Thompson's sisters-in-law had spent an entire year making a large box of doll clothes for the girls. All in all, it was one of the Thompson girls' most memorable Christmases.

On November 10, 1958, in a speech at the Sports Palace, as part of a friendship meeting with Polish leader Władysław Gomulka, Khrushchev played his next set of cards. He announced his intention to end the Potsdam Accords unilaterally and turn over all functions and access controls exercised by Soviet agencies to East Germany. This would require the West to deal with East Germany directly, thus forcing its recognition by those nations. Everyone, including Thompson, wondered why Khrushchev had chosen to shake up the world. In analyzing Khrushchev's speech, Thompson reported back to the State Department that it was a most dangerous move on the Soviet leader's part. Thompson concluded that Khrushchev was building up tensions to "an almost intolerable pitch," in order to bring about his long-coveted summit meeting. What Khrushchev wanted, Thompson said, was tacit recognition of the status quo in Europe.[7] Having failed to secure a summit by a "soft approach," he intended to force a meeting by causing a crisis.[8] Furthermore, Thompson reported that the incessant flow of East Germans using Berlin as an escape route was causing "a brain drain," not to mention embarrassment to the Communist cause, since so many of its citizens wanted to leave the Socialist paradise.[9]

Khrushchev wanted to secure the Communist empire before the rearmament of West Germany was complete. While the West saw this move to recognize East Germany without the consent of the other occupying powers as a severe provocation, Khrushchev saw it as necessary self-protection—another example of where, according to Thompson, "we both look at the same set of facts and see different things."[10] Thompson warned that all this made Khrushchev "a man in a hurry," adding that the Western powers "should prepare for a major showdown in the coming months."[11] Thompson concluded that, although Khrushchev's immediate concern was the removal of foreign troops in West Berlin, his long-range objective was to absorb West Berlin into East Germany.[12]

Thompson supposed that Khrushchev wanted to see what effect this heightened tension would have on Western cohesion, but he believed Khrushchev had miscalculated the Western nations' reaction, thinking he could "get away with it."[13] For that reason, Thompson recommended making it unmistakably clear that the West would defend its rights in Berlin, especially with respect to overland access to that city. He felt the worst policy would be one that showed uncertainty.[14] In dealing with the Soviets, Thompson thought one had to show firmness and resolve, on the one hand, and, on the other, one had to be careful not to appear threatening. It required a delicate touch to get exactly the right combination. If one exhibited signs of weakness, the Soviets would simply push further, but if they were threatened in the wrong way, they could be very dangerous.[15] Throughout the crisis, Thompson would have a difficult time trying to get this point across to his own government.

Khrushchev's Sports Palace speech drew a reaction from inside the Kremlin, too. Mikoyan did not agree with the move and thought there should have been a previous consultation with the Presidium.[16] At the next Presidium meeting, Mikoyan rallied the group to soften Khrushchev's unilateral proposal.[17] Yet they still needed to replace it with something that would demand a change in the status of West Berlin, in order to get Western troops out of the city, so they chose to demand negotiations with the other signatories of the Potsdam Accords to finalize the postwar status of East Germany.

On November 27, just as the Thompsons were celebrating Thanksgiving with American exchange students, Khrushchev held a press conference, where he informed the stunned reporters that he had delivered an ultimatum to the Western powers, demanding negotiations within six months, or else the Soviet Union would act unilaterally to sign a separate peace treaty with East Germany. West Berlin would become a demilitarized "free city," and access to that city would be handled by the East Germans. Khrushchev expected that this formula would satisfy the West's commitment to a non-Communist West Berlin and, at the same time, ensure that Western forces left the city. It was also a compromise between what Ulbricht wanted, which was total control of Berlin, and what Mikoyan proposed, since he was concerned that Khrushchev not take undue risks. The free-city idea was Khrushchev's alone, but free cities don't last, as postwar Trieste demonstrated.[18] One thing that has become clear in hindsight is that Khrushchev's decision to make this move was pretty much spontaneous. Any drafts of a possible peace treaty with East Germany weren't even written until over a month later.[19]

The British, in analyzing the threat, saw three possible alternatives: "(a) abandoning Berlin; (b) resorting to force; [or] (c) staying in Berlin but dealing with and, if necessary, ultimately recognizing GDR [East Germany]."[20] They estimated that they really had little choice, and that the West would have to let the East Germans control access to Berlin. Thompson was appalled. He wrote: "While I believe the Soviets would refrain from any action which they were convinced would cause us to use force, once they have turned [their] functions over to [East Germany], they would go very far and take great risks rather than back down.... Almost [the] only way out for them in such circumstances would be [a] demand for immediate top level meetings from which they could hope [to] obtain sufficient concessions from [the] Western side to save face." To prevent the Soviets from choosing this path, he thought it was necessary to convince them absolutely that the West would indeed use force, in the event that the Soviets did. This made the British waver dangerous.[21]

Before the dust had settled from Khrushchev's drastic step, Hubert Humphrey, then a US senator from Minnesota, made a visit to Moscow. Thompson had been taken ill and asked his aide, Ed Hurwitz, to pick Humphrey up at the airport. When Hurwitz reported to Thompson that Humphrey had let loose a tirade because the ambassador was not there, Thompson shrugged and said he'd receive the senator the next day, which Thompson did while still in his sickbed. Once recovered, Thompson went with Humphrey to meet Khrushchev on December 1, 1958, in a session that lasted well into the night.[22] During their meeting, Khrushchev again bolstered his nuclear bluff by famously bragging of having tested a five-megaton H-bomb and offering to "spare" Humphrey's hometown of Minneapolis.[23] But Humphrey felt that the purpose of the conversation was to impress upon him the importance that Khrushchev attached to the Berlin question.[24]

Khrushchev tried to convince the senator—as he would many others—that his motive was not to take over West Berlin. The Soviet Union already had enough inhabitants. Khrushchev pointed out that he went against Molotov and the Council of Ministers in withdrawing Soviet troops from Austria—thus removing a source of conflict with the West—because it only made sense to have those troops there if he meant to expand westward, which he didn't. He meant to do the same in Berlin, except West Berlin was surrounded by East Germany, and the best solution would be to make it a free city and remove all foreign troops. Moreover, he would support the presence of observers from the UN, to guarantee noninterference. Khrushchev said he would allow all countries to have equal access to West Berlin, and the Soviets would not try to impose a stranglehold on the city. He accused the West of using the "freedom of West Berliners as an excuse to keep troops there." What he did not mention was that the free-city concept he proposed was only for West Berlin and did not include East Berlin.

Thompson thought the most important issue for the Soviets was the exodus of skilled workers and intellectuals through West Berlin. As long as this escape route existed, it would be difficult to bring East Germany into line. Thompson referred to the refugee problem in almost every cable back to the State Department about Berlin, but there was no reaction to it. Thompson thought some solution to West Berlin might be found, but that any solution acceptable to the Soviets would have to include a way to cut off this exodus.

The way Khrushchev spoke to Humphrey and other diplomats showed Thompson that the Soviets were beginning to realize the danger of their posture. If the allies showed sufficient determination and unity, Khrushchev might accept a solution that was not entirely satisfactory to him, but would still allow him to get out of the dangerous situation into which he had put himself.[25] Thompson also noted that, although neither Khrushchev nor the Soviet government wanted war, a loss of prestige might make them reluctant to back down from their stance. Therefore, it was important to open some way for Khrushchev to retreat and yet still save face. There were some things that could be done that would not jeopardize West Berlin but would nonetheless be important to the Soviets, such as the cessation of overt Western propaganda and spying activities, and recognition of East Germany's eastern border at the Oder–Neisse line.

Mikoyan's Adventure

Having already seen Khrushchev in action on a number of occasions, Thompson predicted that pressure by him would, as usual, "alternate with friendly gestures and declarations of sweet reasonableness." In January 1959, Mikoyan went to the United States to soften the Soviet ultimatum. With sixteen-year-old Andy in boarding school in Maryland, Jane took her two younger daughters to Switzerland to go skiing in Gstaad. Thompson accompanied Mikoyan to America. Mikoyan's objective in the United States was to take a softer, gentler approach to Khrushchev's threat and mitigate the Western reaction to it. But, as was typical of Communist negotiating methods, Mikoyan went to America without the authority to make decisions.[26] Although he tried to soften the Soviet line, he couldn't really do anything concrete about it.[27]

Mikoyan argued that German reunification was unrealistic. The best they could hope for was some kind of confederation. As far as Berlin went, the Soviet's six-month deadline was not really an ultimatum, but an attempt to establish a timeframe for negotiations. Dulles said he was glad it wasn't an ultimatum, because otherwise, there could be no negotiations. Mikoyan did

Anastas Mikoyan's trip to the United States regarding the Berlin situation, 1959. In the White House, Washington, DC, *from left to right, front,* Dwight D. Eisenhower, Anastas Mikoyan, and John Foster Dulles; *standing,* Llewellyn Thompson Jr. and Mikhail A. Menshikov. Ed Clark, *Life* Picture Collection / Getty Images (50574558).

not understand the depth of Western resolve over West Berlin. He concluded matter-of-factly that because of its geographic location within the borders of East Germany, West Berlin would inevitably become part of it. It was another example of the Soviets seeing the whole crisis through one lens, that of East Germany, while the Americans saw it through another lens, as a Berlin problem. Mikoyan's messages were sufficiently mixed to cause Eisenhower's son John to later write that those who met with Mikoyan thought he had been deliberately sent to "muddy the waters."[28]

Mikoyan asked Dulles if he thought the Soviet Union wanted war.[29] Dulles said, "No," and then asked Mikoyan if he thought the United States wanted war. Mikoyan responded, "Not now, but you are setting up bases all around the Soviet Union so I cannot say the same for the future." Richard Nixon, who was also present at this meeting with Mikoyan, declared that the United States did not believe in the concept of preemptive war, and that "anyone who did should be in an insane asylum."[30]

Dulles then mentioned that China, Korea, Vietnam, and Germany were divided, and that any attempt at unifying them by force would surely lead to war. Mikoyan replied that the collective security agreements the United States had made with countries in Asia and the Middle East, as well as all the military bases that were being set up in those places, were a threat to peace. In them lay the danger of America being sucked into local conflicts. Dulles countered that US missiles had already made these bases obsolete. Then why, demanded Mikoyan, was the United States setting up bases in Turkey and arming them with atomic weapons? Dulles claimed that this was more psychological than practical. People in that country wanted to see something concrete, to counter the overwhelming power of the USSR, which was so close by. These missiles would later play a pivotal role in the 1962 Cuban Missile Crisis. Then Mikoyan brought up Hungary. The Soviet Union had to act whenever it saw that the West was actively trying to break up its bloc, as had happened during the Hungarian uprising—referring to Western leaflets and radio broadcasts in that country. What if a government hostile to the United States came to power in Mexico or Canada? Surely the United States would not stand for it.

In addition to his time in Washington, DC, Mikoyan—accompanied by Thompson—traveled to New York City, Chicago, and Los Angeles. In describing the trip to Jane, Thompson told her that a number of Russian refugees had filled their coat sleeves with eggs and gone to the Los Angeles airport, to throw them at Mikoyan as he left. The police learned about what was planned, so they vigorously frisked all the visitors in the departure area, breaking the eggs. When Mikoyan heard about the frisking, he thought the incident was very funny.

The skiing trip for Jane did not end well, since the nanny and both girls came down with the flu, and the whole group was held over in Frankfurt, where they had stopped to pick up supplies. When they reached Moscow, Jane was dismayed by how tired her husband looked after his US trip. She began insisting that they go cross-country skiing on Sundays, both to get fresh air and to help him disconnect. Jane had procured the latest in colorful snowsuits for her girls in Switzerland, and she had Sherry bundled up in one to play on the *ploschad*, or square, outside of Spaso House one afternoon. The Russian babushkas and mothers cluck-clucked in disapproval, and Jane asked them what was wrong. They pointed to Jane's and their furs and then to the nylon snowsuit, which looked to them like it was made of summer silk. Without enough Russian to explain advancements in synthetic materials, Jane unzipped Sherry's suit and gently guided the hand of one of the ladies onto the girl's warm tummy, to show that her daughter was suitably dressed. A few others poked their hands in, too. There were murmurs of amazement and, satisfied, the ladies decided that this crazy American woman was OK after all.

A few weeks after Mikoyan's return to the USSR, he chanced to see the Thompsons at a reception at the embassy of the United Arab Republic (UAR).[31] Jane asked Mikoyan about his impressions of the trip to America. He told her that it had been a pleasant and interesting time, and that he had been surprised to find the press and the police friendly to him. At this point Jane, remembering how the Los Angeles police had frisked demonstrators for eggs hidden in their sleeves, patted Mikoyan gently down both arms and said in her best Russian, "Ou vas Yaitsi yeste?" Jane thought this meant, "Have you got any eggs?" There was a brief pause, and then Mikoyan quickly changed the subject, talking about something trivial before heading out the door. When Jane told her husband about Mikoyan's reaction to her well-intended joke, he turned pale and informed her that she had just asked Mikoyan if he "had any balls." Jane decided this incident proved yet again that the dapper Mikoyan was indeed a gentleman. He hadn't batted an eye, and he understood at once that she had no clue as to what she was really saying.[32]

Macmillan Takes the Initiative

On February 16, 1959, the Western allies proposed a conference of foreign ministers (CFM) in Geneva to discuss the issue of Germany and suggested that advisors from both the FRG and the GDR should be present. Rather than maintaining a unified front, however, the allies each had different agendas and attitudes. West Germany's chancellor, Konrad Adenauer, was absolutely against anything that did not include complete reunification of Germany on Western terms, and he reacted violently even to internal discussions of alternatives. The French were against negotiating anything at all with the Soviets, because they were busy forging a Franco-German alliance for Europe that would put the French in a prominent position. Britain's prime minister, Harold Macmillan, on the other side of the coin, was prepared to recognize East Germany as a separate nation and wanted a summit with the Soviets as soon as possible.[33] Thompson, knowing a CFM meeting would not solve anything, because Khrushchev would never allow subordinates to negotiate something that important, urged Eisenhower to consider bilateral talks between the United States and the USSR instead, as a precursor to a Four-Powers summit. He believed any of the other allies would have done so, had they been in the same position as the United States.[34] While Eisenhower was mulling this over, Macmillan preempted him, deciding to go to Moscow and talk to Khrushchev himself. He, like Thompson, was of the opinion that Khrushchev's Berlin ultimatum was a defensive act, and believed he could influence a more flexible approach.[35] Eisenhower was not pleased.

Thompson voiced a concern that Khrushchev would try to exploit the prime minister's visit, because Macmillan, faced with elections in his country, would want things to end on a positive note. His visit was like being on a roller coaster. Just before Macmillan's arrival, the United States had responded negatively to a Soviet draft of a peace treaty for Germany, putting Khrushchev in a bad mood.[36] A debate between Khrushchev and Macmillan over Berlin then ensued, and it ended with Khrushchev shouting, "You have insulted me!"[37] A few days later, Khrushchev gave a speech in which he rejected the allied overture for a CFM meeting and made reference to a possible British-Soviet nonaggression pact, even before the two heads of government had discussed it.[38] Thompson thought that the greatest contribution Macmillan could make toward peace would be either to pack up and go home or to answer Khrushchev in kind.[39] Things got worse when Khrushchev declined to accompany Macmillan on a trip to Kiev, citing a "toothache" as an excuse. Macmillan put on his best British stiff upper lip and visited that city without Khrushchev. By the time Macmillan returned to Moscow, Khrushchev had gone from sour to sweet. The two leaders were actually able to discuss a nuclear test ban agreement, which Macmillan would keep pushing until a version of the ban succeeded in 1963. Khrushchev accepted the CFM meeting after all, and when Macmillan returned from his trip, the polls in Britain showed it had indeed enhanced his political standing.[40]

In a speech in Leipzig, East Germany, in early March, Khrushchev announced a six-month extension to his Berlin ultimatum.[41] The British told Thompson they believed Khrushchev's acceptance of the CFM meeting and the extension of the deadline were thanks to Macmillan's trip. The Americans thought the Soviets' latest roller coaster response was a tactic to try to get negotiating advantages, but Thompson agreed that, despite his initial concerns, the situation had improved as a result of Macmillan's visit.[42] Once more, Thompson suggested that the Americans issue an invitation to Khrushchev to visit the United States and hold bilateral talks.[43]

While Thompson was busy with the Macmillan visit, his older brother sent Jane hundreds of flower bulbs and seeds to start in her greenhouse, so everyone except Thompson was recruited for greenhouse duty to plant them. In addition to flowers for important occasions, Jane planted corn, arugula, and other vegetables, to get some greens into her family. She started making tentative plans for a home leave, which would not come until the summer. She was also coping with a wet spring, which caused a number of leaks in the old roof of the mansion, one of which brought an enormous chunk of plaster down into the ambassador's bathtub, revealing listening devices.

Thompson had been observing the Soviets under Khrushchev for some time, and he pondered long and hard about the crisis Khrushchev had begun over Berlin. In March, Thompson wrote a cable to the State Department, giving his thoughts about the Soviets' perspective on the matter.[44] He reiterated his contention that Khrushchev's moves in Berlin and East Germany were defensive. In his own way, Khrushchev was actually seeking to improve relations with the West.[45] The Soviet leaders, Thompson wrote, could not be understood as "rational" human beings, in the Western sense of that word, because they held their power on the basis of their ideology. Until such time as the Soviets' superior economics inevitably brought world Communism to pass, however, they were willing to deal with the capitalist West. Thompson thought this should be exploited.

Quite a lot had changed since Stalin's death, as a result of education and internal improvements in living standards. Many in the Soviet Union, including Party members, Thompson wrote, were no longer really interested in pursuing international Communism. Khrushchev had come quite a ways toward "normalizing" the Soviet Union. He had opened up the country to Western influence, introduced a steep reduction in its army troops, and advocated coexistence, rather than war, with the capitalist world. Although Thompson said it might seem "dreamy," there was a genuine possibility of achieving total disarmament, and this was one of the things Khrushchev might want to discuss at a summit.[46] Thompson believed Khrushchev wanted to talk, but the Soviet leader was getting a cold shoulder from the West.

Thompson believed the allies had to stand by their commitment to West Berlin, and he favored doing everything possible to prevent the Soviets from signing a separate treaty with East Germany. Recognition of East Germany could eventually drag the United States and the USSR into a major conflict in order to defend their respective Germanys, if one or the other attempted reunification by force. The only solution was to keep the situation flexible, either by a time-phased system or a confederation, which would mean more contacts between two the Germanys and would be advantageous for the West.

Lastly, Thompson noted that although Khrushchev did not want to risk a war over Berlin, the Soviet leader believed the West didn't either, so the danger lay where "both could drift into a situation that might get out of control."[47] Thompson argued that public opinion would hardly accept the risk of going war because the East Germans were stamping documents, once the Soviets had turned control over to them, even though it would mean a de facto recognition of East German sovereignty.

He ended his cable by stating, "I give more weight to internal developments in [the] Soviet Union than the vagaries of Soviet foreign policy since I believe the former are more lasting and in the long run hold greater promise of making peaceful existence with the Russian Bear." He maintained that détente with the Soviet Union would, on balance, be beneficial and in America's interest.[48] Thompson's stand was "courageous," but it was not shared by others in the Eisenhower administration and did not "noticeably affect policymakers."[49] Moreover, it damaged his standing in the eyes of many in the administration. Thompson, however, did not change course.

In April, Thompson again wrote to the State Department, emphasizing that there were areas to which not enough attention was being given, "probably due to difficulties of making a soup with so many cooks."[50] One was that the allied powers were only concerned with *their own* access to West Berlin and did not include West Germany's access in their discussions. Another was not paying attention to Khrushchev's Leipzig speech, because it explained "how Khrushchev ticked."[51] In it, Khrushchev set the field of battle on economic competition with the West, in which he predicted that the Soviets would excel while the West plunged into economic crisis. His more immediate aim—to force recognition of the status quo in Germany and Eastern Europe—was consequently a way to work toward military disengagement. Thompson ended his note by asserting that he did not see Khrushchev's primary goal as changing the status of Berlin for the moment, but, rather, that he would use Berlin to obtain high-level negotiations and achieve broader goals, such as disarmament and trade arrangements. Thompson did not think that Khrushchev wanted or anticipated war, but he felt that the Soviet leader would create maximum tension and use repeated threats of force during the Berlin Crisis to achieve his goals.[52]

Council of Foreign Ministers

Thompson predicted the Soviets would use the CFM meeting in Switzerland to sound out the US positions and produce just enough in the way of results to entice the Americans to a summit. Thompson reasoned that Khrushchev may have had second thoughts about his Berlin ultimatum, since he realized the East Germans could stir up incidents that would force the Soviets to honor their Warsaw Pact commitment.[53] In May, Jane accompanied Thompson to the CFM in Geneva, the city where he had spent so many of his early years in the Foreign Service. They stayed at the stately old Hotel Bergues, the city's first hotel, which was right on Lake Geneva. The couple dined with journalist Cyrus Sulzberger, and Thompson told Sulzberger he thought a deal on Berlin was possible, because Khrushchev needed a diplomatic success after the problems in Hungary, Yugoslavia, and the UAR. Moreover, Khrushchev was worried about China, and about diverting the USSR's military budget to meet civilian needs. Khrushchev, Thompson told Sulzberger, wants a "big deal at the summit."[54]

By including East Germany in the ministers' conference, the West had given it minor recognition. This, and concessions regarding the formation of an East German–West German committee, led the Soviets to the mistaken conclusion that they were on their way to getting the allies out of West Berlin.[55] The meeting in Geneva certainly indicated that the West was willing to consider concessions, but this was not enough for Ulbricht. He was disappointed and impatient, but Khrushchev explained to him that in the interim, it would give East Germany more time to strengthen herself economically. He added, "If you have thrown the adversary to the ground, you don't need to kneel on his chest."[56] Khrushchev then chided Ulbricht, noting that the USSR had had to wait at least sixteen years before the West recognized them—so East Germany should have to wait for at least seventeen.

The conference seemed to go on and on, and Jane began to feel guilty for leaving their two younger daughters in Moscow. With no real progress and no practical reason to stay, Thompson and his wife returned to that city in mid-June, just in time for Averell Harriman's visit. Nothing further came out of Geneva when the CFM meeting finally closed, nearly two months later.

Harriman Comes Back to Moscow

Khrushchev had concluded that hard-line methods were the best way to deal with the West, so it was important to maintain the perception of superior nuclear power, in order for these tactics to work. The Swiss ambassador told Thompson that Khrushchev had said to him: "If I go to a cathedral and pray for peace, nobody listens. But if I go with two bombs, they will." Harriman's visit played into Khrushchev's hard-line strategy. Khrushchev had a knack for appearing jovial and friendly while actually saying outrageous things. For example, he told Harriman that West German chancellor Konrad Adenauer did not represent the whole of Germany: "If you look at Adenauer naked from behind you can see Germany is divided, and if you look at him from the front he demonstrates that Germany cannot stand." Khrushchev then rattled off how many bombs he had targeted toward West Germany, France, England, Spain, and Italy.[57] He said they would liquidate Western rights in West Berlin, but, on the other hand, he wasn't interested in taking over West Berlin. The USSR didn't want 2 million more mouths to feed. "We would rather let you feed them!"

While Charles Thayer, who accompanied Harriman, described Khrushchev's remarks as tirades, Harriman and Thompson found the Soviet leader to be genial.[58] President Eisenhower apparently didn't think so, deploring Khrushchev's "threatening tone" in statements to the press. Journalist Joseph Alsop obtained leaked copies of Thompson's reports of the CFM meetings, which had been sent to the State Department. Harriman characterized Alsop's interpretation of those meetings as "rather hysterical."[59] The Soviet press, on the other hand, completely ignored Harriman's interview with Khrushchev. In a non sequitur, Khrushchev turned to Thayer and told him that he was angry at Thayer's brother-in-law, Charles Bohlen, because Bohlen had told people that Khrushchev was a drunk.[60] Bohlen wrote to Thompson that he had never said anything of the kind. Later, Thompson took the opportunity to correct this misunderstanding with Khrushchev, telling him that there were a "great many people who had an interest in bringing about bad relations between us and that this might account for the report."[61] Khrushchev agreed that this interpretation might indeed be true.

Thompson hosted a lunch for Harriman on June 25. At it, Khrushchev complained to Thompson that he knew the West was looking to have a united Germany as part of NATO. Thompson did not deny the statement, but he said it was a problem that could be dealt with. The Americans, Thompson stated, sought no military advantages from German reunification. The real problem, he continued, was that the Soviets seemed unwilling to ever allow a country that had gone Communist to change its mind and revert to a capitalist system, a contention that Khrushchev, in turn, did not dispute. Thompson itemized concessions that the West had made at the CFM meeting in Geneva, and Khrushchev conceded that a genuine effort to meet the Soviet point of view had been made.[62] In his own report back to the State Department, Harriman suggested that inviting Khrushchev to the United States might be a good thing, as it could help correct some of the Soviet leader's misperceptions.[63]

The Invitation that Wasn't

On March 14, 1959, Eisenhower discussed the idea of a Khrushchev visit to the United States with Dulles.[64] Secretary Dulles was against it, because he thought it would enhance Khrushchev's prestige. He could not think of any issue on which the two leaders might agree. His objection to a visit became moot, however, when Dulles, suffering from cancer, died that May and was replaced by Christian Herter.[65]

The next big event on the world agenda was the scheduled exchange of US and USSR national exhibitions, part of the cultural agreement signed the year before. The first was the Soviet exhibition in New York City in June 1959. Deputy Prime Minister Frol Romanovich Kozlov came to open it and then traveled around the United States. No incidents occurred, and Kozlov was well received. This may have bolstered Ike's inclination for a US visit by Khrushchev.

In early July, Khrushchev told a delegation of American governors visiting Moscow that he was interested in going to the United States. The press asked Eisenhower about this. Sensing that the media was favorable to the possibility, the following day Eisenhower called in his new secretary of state to discuss it. Ironically, that same morning Eisenhower gave in to CIA pressure to renew high-altitude U-2 spy plane flights over the Soviet Union, although Ike only approved a single mission. The intelligence community and the US Air Force were increasingly worried about a Soviet strategic missile advantage and wanted proof of the missile gap they believed existed. Eisenhower, however, wanted to show that it didn't exist.

During his meeting with Eisenhower, Herter suggested sending word to Khrushchev "very confidentially," through Kozlov, who was still in the United States. "If there were sufficient results at Geneva to warrant a summit meeting," Khrushchev could meet with Eisenhower for a few days at Camp David, the presidential retreat in the Maryland countryside, before Khrushchev's scheduled appearance at a UN General Assembly meeting. The president could then reciprocate by a visit to the USSR in October. Also present at the meeting with Herter were Undersecretary of State Douglas Dillon; his deputy, Robert Murphy; Livingston Merchant, assistant secretary of state for European affairs; and General Andrew Goodpaster. They discussed a draft invitation to Khrushchev, as well as a "talking paper" for Murphy to use. On July 11, the president initialed both the invitation and Murphy's talking paper, in which Khrushchev's meeting with Eisenhower was predicated on enough progress being made at the CFM meeting in Geneva to lead to a summit.[66]

Murphy went to see Kozlov at the Soviet mission's headquarters at 8 p.m., to relay Eisenhower's message. He told Kozlov that this matter was being kept "in the strictest confidence." Khrushchev accepted the invitation, happily postponing his scheduled trip to Scandinavia. He was convinced that his pressure on the Berlin situation had worked, and that the invitation for him to visit the United States was proof of this. Eisenhower wrote in his memoirs that when he received Khrushchev's letter of acceptance on July 21, he was very disturbed. It was clear that Khrushchev was under the impression he had received an "unqualified invitation."[67]

The president called in Murphy and the secretary of state, incredulous that Khrushchev could have missed the connection between the invitation and substantial progress occurring at the CFM meeting in Geneva. Eisenhower was even more disturbed when Murphy told him he had not understood the link and thus *did* deliver an unqualified invitation. Moreover, Dillon, much to Eisenhower's surprise, reminded the president that the letter and the talking points, both of which Ike had approved, did not imply the "same condition for a [one-on-one] meeting with Khrushchev as for the Four-Power summit meeting." Eisenhower answered back somewhat unreasonably that it obviously was so because he wanted it to be that way! Now Eisenhower would have to go through with a meeting he "despised," one that could be open to serious misinterpretation by the American public.

In his memoirs, Eisenhower wrote that he decided to write Khrushchev a second letter, on July 27, not revoking the invitation but putting a little twist on it by warning that he could not "order" a warm reception for Khrushchev in the United States if he "came as the person responsible for the breakdown in fruitful negotiations." The actual letter to Khrushchev, however, was quite watered down, compared with what the president said privately to Murphy and Dillon, as well as with what he wrote in his memoirs. In his letter, Ike simply agreed to Khrushchev's wish to come to the United States in September, when it was less hot, and added that he could not "stress how great an improvement there would be in public opinion if our meeting would take place in an improved environment resulting from progress in Geneva."[68] The foreign ministers still were not making any headway in the CFM meeting in Geneva, so the talks adjourned on August 5. If there was to be any progress, it would take place when the US and USSR heads of state met.

Khrushchev was not the only one running hot and cold. Eisenhower, perhaps to blunt accusations by his critics, wanted to appear tough. On the other hand, he also recognized that if the United States and the USSR were going to "wage peace," some kind of breakthrough was needed. It is hardly likely that an experienced diplomat like Murphy could have "misunderstood" Eisenhower's wishes. Goodpaster, who wrote up the memorandum on the meetings with Eisenhower, is frustratingly vague on certain points that might have actually explained what occurred.

Peace and Friendship

Eisenhower's invitation markedly improved the atmosphere in Moscow. The US embassy staff and American reporters found it easier to meet with Russians. The Thompsons had postponed their annual leave in order to be in Moscow for the opening of the American exhibition, which kept Jane and her husband very busy. Their two younger girls had a lot of time on their hands once school was over, and the grownups were too harried and anxious about the upcoming event to take them to the river to swim or to the dacha for weekends.

One hot afternoon, Thompson came home to find a distraught nanny, with her two charges in tow. She told the ambassador that the girls had disappeared, and she had been frantic until the policeman at the gate told her they were playing in the square. She had dutifully rushed out to bring his daughters back into the safety of the compound. The girls protested that they had already been taken out on the *ploschad* that winter, when they had more or less mastered the game of sliding on ice.[69] Now, in summer, although the site was dusty and hot, that drab square full of children looked far more appealing than the comforts of Spaso House. Hungry for companions their own age, they had encouraged each other to walk down the long driveway and continue past the Soviet guard stationed at the entrance. Going outside those gates felt like freedom. Thompson asked his daughters what they had done out in the square. They said they'd traded postcards and stamps with the Russian children for old pre-Revolution coins and notes and other trinkets, and they had skipped rope with the practically professional Russian girls. They were worried now, because they didn't quite know how he would take their escapade, and they asked him not to be cross. On the contrary, Thompson quite approved of their adventure. He told them that they could go out to play whenever they wanted, as long as they got permission first.

This was entirely in keeping with Thompson's diplomatic method. He strongly believed that contact between people was the best way to dispel the misconceptions they had about each other and soften tensions. His daughters should be no different in this respect. Thus they started going out to the square regularly, although they never did master the art of skipping rope. They even introduced a little capitalism into the scene on the square that summer. Having read stories about children with lemonade stands, the Thompson girls decided that they would set one up outside the walls of Spaso House. They did an incredible amount of business until their mother found out and shut the enterprise down. They apparently were not very good businesspeople, since they sold their product at twenty-five kopeks a glass, while the lemons, imported from Finland, cost vastly more than that.

18 ≋

Dueling Exhibitions

We have a very free and easy relationship.
He [Khrushchev] scolds me and I scold him.
—LLEWELLYN THOMPSON, *Time* magazine,
   August 3, 1962

The Thompsons, and everyone else in the embassy, prepared for Vice President Nixon's arrival. He was coming to open the American National Exhibition in Moscow, part of the Cultural Exchanges Agreement. Between the time when the invitation to Khrushchev to meet Eisenhower was proffered and when Khrushchev answered on July 21, Eisenhower had signed a congressional resolution making the third week of July Captive Nations Week, to raise public awareness of countries oppressed under Communism and other nondemocratic governments. This infuriated Khrushchev, who took it out on Nixon when he toured the Soviet Union and opened the exhibition in August 1959.[1]

Vice President Nixon's trip was important for reasons beyond this exhibition. One was because it was a trial run for Eisenhower's visit to the Soviet Union the following year. Another was that Nixon used it to jump start to his own presidential campaign. Nixon had not been pleased about Eisenhower's invitation to Khrushchev, as he thought it detracted from his own spotlight while he was in the USSR. The Soviets later complained that confidential conversations were leaked to the press in a way that was flattering to Nixon.[2] The vice president was convinced that he could handle Khrushchev, so Nixon was in a confident and feisty mood.[3] Ike, however, had sent his brother Milton along to give his own report—and possibly to serve as a check on Nixon.[4]

In the run-up to the American exhibition, Thompson encouraged the organizers to tone down the propaganda, as he thought it simply was not necessary. The exhibit would already have an explosive effect, as the Soviet public could plainly see that the "slight improvements projected in their standard of living are only a drop in the bucket of what they should have."[5] The idea was to open the curtain, not to pull it down. Thompson also urged care in exhibiting America's flaws. He agreed that these things should be addressed, but he pointed out that the Russians were not used to seeing negative things about their own country voluntarily exposed by their government. Therefore, they might take this part of the display as confirmation of Soviet anti-American propaganda.

In the family's household staff the previous fall, Ida had been replaced by a proper English nanny, Gillian "Gill" Bordeaux, who introduced the two younger Thompson girls to the joys and escapes of reading. Fed on Enyd Blyton books, they had spent a good part of the winter exploring the basement of Spaso House and having adventures there.[6] They discovered how to get into the food storage *sklad*, which was heavily fortified by the embassy's flamboyant cook. Jenny would push Sherry, who was small and skinny, through the tiny window, left open for ventilation, at the top of the door. Once inside, Sherry crawled down the shelf and opened the door, and the girls then helped themselves to treats. They also explored the basement, attic, and outdoor storage spaces. They made a number of interesting finds, including top secret documents from World War II that were in a dark, forgotten corner of the garage.

Before Nixon's arrival, an advance team of secret service agents came to Spaso House to check every nook and cranny of the enormous ambassadorial residence. The Thompson girls were told to stay out of the way and behave themselves. One day, the Thompsons invited the Secret Service men to share a family lunch. Their daughters arrived late, looking scruffy and smelling a bit musty, but in fine spirits, whispering and laughing at having discovered a new tunnel that morning. The tunnels under Spaso House were installed just before the 1917 revolution, as an escape route in the event an emergency exit would be needed during those troubled times.[7] One of the secret service men tried to make forced small talk with the girls and asked what they had been doing. When they explained that they had been following secret tunnels, which they thought must go at least as far as the Mongolian embassy on the other side of the square, the men did not wait to finish lunch and immediately had the girls lead them to these hidden passages. It was very disappointing to Jenny and Sherry to find that their tunnels had been bricked up the next day. The girls swore a solemn oath never to tell a grownup in a suit anything else ever again.

The security team also investigated the level of microwave radiation, coming from Soviet eavesdropping equipment, that was bombarding the residence. (The United States used similar equipment to listen to the Soviet embassy in Washington, DC.) The team detected a spike in the radiation level, creating some question as to whether the vice president should stay at Spaso House. The level was reduced after a protest was made to the Soviets, and the trip went as planned. No one seemed to care, however, if the radiation continued or not after Nixon left. Although a connection to microwave radiation was never proven, John Foster Dulles died of cancer after visiting Moscow. Three US ambassadors to Moscow would also die of cancer at a fairly young age.[8] It was enough of a concern that Johns Hopkins University received a $400 million grant to study the issue.[9] Both Thompson and his youngest daughter had bone marrow samples taken for the study, he as a person exposed for the longest time, and she as the youngest.

The Exhibit

Thompson and Khrushchev went out to the exhibition site together when it was still under construction. Thompson returned there when the embassy crew was doing last-minute painting and cleaning up, the night before it opened.[10] He was fascinated with the exhibit's geodesic dome, which followed designs by Buckminster Fuller. Thompson had come up with a number of inventions and experiments of his own. One idea was for an inflated dome, covered with a spray of cement, to serve as cheap, strong housing, which is why Fuller's dome so intrigued him.

When Nixon finally arrived in Moscow on July 23, 1959, aboard a US Air Force plane, the Thompsons received him at Vnukovo airport. Once in the embassy's Cadillac, heading toward the city, Mrs. Nixon amazed Jane by asking her why there were no people on the streets to meet and wave at them. Jane tried to explain the realities of Moscow life but was not sure the information had registered with her guest.

Nikita Khrushchev (*center, in light-colored coat and hard hat*), with Llewellyn Thompson Jr. (*standing, to the right of Khrushchev, with pocket handkerchief*) and others, in front of Buckminster Fuller's geodesic dome, American National Exhibition, Moscow, USSR, 1959. Staff photo.

Once in Spaso House, the Thompsons hosted a formal event for the Nixons in the Blue Room. The two Thompson girls escaped the dull affair and went to one of their hideouts, which happened to be the guest bathroom, little visited unless a reception was going on. When the girls entered, they discovered Mrs. Nixon sitting on one of the chairs, smoking. Seeing their surprise, she

had to let them in on her secret. She was not allowed to smoke in public, so the girls mustn't tell anyone what they had seen.[11] Her husband kept Pat Nixon on a short leash throughout the trip, preventing her from engaging in conversations during visits to a school or when seated next to Mikoyan at a dinner.[12] This may also have been because Pat's drinking problem was beginning to manifest itself. Jane said she felt sorry for Pat, who had told her: "You don't know what it is like to be a politician's wife. I've only voted once in my life and that was for Roosevelt."[13]

On his first day in Moscow, Nixon visited a local farmer's market, where he was approached for tickets to the American exhibition. Since he didn't have any on him, he made the unfortunate choice to hand out hundred-ruble notes, so people could buy them. The problem, however, had not been money, but the availability of the tickets. The Soviet press's spin on this gaffe made it seem as if Nixon were bribing people to go. Altogether, about 3.2 million Russians attended the exhibit during the next six weeks, not including a large number who dispensed with tickets by going over and under fences.[14]

Nixon went to see Khrushchev, accompanied by Thompson and Milton Eisenhower. Khrushchev was waiting for him, sitting at his desk and looking at a model of one of his rockets, just to remind the American vice president—after the successful Soviet launches of Sputnik I and Sputnik II, with its famous passenger, the dog Laika—of Soviet achievements.[15] Nixon never forgot the point. Knowing that Nixon's bellicose, anti-Soviet statements had preceded him, as well as how touchy Khrushchev was about them, Thompson counseled Nixon to tone down the rhetoric and even compliment the Soviets on Sputnik.

Front, from left to right, Vice President Richard Nixon and his wife Pat, Admiral Hyman G. Rickover, and Jane and Llewellyn Thompson Jr. at the airport opening of the 1959 American National Exhibition in Moscow, USSR. Staff photo.

Thompson couched his explanation in Nixon's own phraseology, saying that the Soviets were "suckers for flattery," given their inferiority complex.[16] Even so, Thompson knew that the niceties would not last long. Khrushchev was quick to show just how much the Captive Nations Resolution annoyed him. Nixon tried to explain that the resolution was a restatement of a well-known American position, but Khrushchev believed that an action by an authoritative body such as Congress must have a purpose.[17] "This resolution stinks," said Khrushchev, "like fresh horse shit and nothing smells worse than that." Not to be outdone, Nixon (who knew from intelligence briefings that Khrushchev had cleaned pigpens in his youth) said, "There is something that smells worse that horse shit and that is pig shit."[18]

At noon, they all drove out to the exhibit in Sokolniki Park. In his opening remarks, delivered on the set of RCA's color television studio, Khrushchev wished the organizers success on the exhibition and Nixon a good visit, adding that it would have been an excellent visit if it hadn't been for the Captive Nations proclamation: "You have churned the water yourselves. . . . Why this was necessary God only knows. What happened? Did a black cat cross your path and confuse you? But that is your affair; we do not interfere with your problems." Wrapping his arms around a Soviet workman, he added, "Does this look like a slave laborer?" Nixon, speaking next, returned only platitudes, saying the United States could learn from Soviet rocketry, and the Soviets could learn from the Americans about things like the state-of-the art color TV taping that was taking place.[19] But Khrushchev would have none of that, stating that the Soviets also had color television. He then wondered if his words would be translated, so Americans would know what he said. Both countries agreed to simultaneous broadcasts in both languages, but the United States broke this agreement and aired theirs first.

Khrushchev did not deny the advances made by the United States, but he added some pointed comments: "This is what America is capable of, and how long has she existed? Three hundred years? One hundred and fifty years of independence and this is her level? We haven't quite reached forty-two years, and in another seven years, we'll be at the level of America, and after that we'll go further. As we pass you by, we'll wave 'bye-bye' to you, and then if you want, we'll stop and say, 'Please come along behind us.' . . . If you want to live under capitalism, go ahead, that's your question, an internal matter, it doesn't concern us."

Although the exhibit contained displays featuring science, technology, agriculture, the social sciences, and research, it was American consumerism that took center stage. Just because the average Soviet wanted to see what American cars looked like, however, didn't mean that he was ready to revolt, as some American articles suggested. The famous kitchen debate took place in Whirlpool's "miracle kitchen." Correspondent William Safire, using a chain and a jeep, tore down a fence that stood between Nixon and Khrushchev and the exhibit's model suburban house. He then bade the two leaders over, like a carnival barker. When Safire also let in fairgoers, a pack of reporters followed them, so Khrushchev and Nixon were literally trapped. Nixon felt Khrushchev had "creamed" him in the RCA studio, and the vice president didn't do much better in the kitchen, but he did manage to get photos of himself poking his finger into the Soviet chairman's chest.

Thompson, who was standing in the corner of the crowded space with Milton Eisenhower, leaned over and whispered in Milton's ear, "Can't someone just pull the plug on this whole thing?"[20] Khrushchev, doubting that the average American housewife had such a kitchen, said: "Don't you have a machine that puts food into the mouth and pushes it down? Many things you've shown us are interesting but they are not needed in life." When Nixon maintained that even ordinary workers could afford this type of house, Khrushchev claimed that Soviets could, too. The difference was that American houses were built to last only twenty years, so builders could sell more new houses, whereas, Khrushchev asserted: "We build firmly. We build for our children and grandchildren." He then continued: "You think the Russian people will be dumbfounded to see these things, but the fact is that newly built Russian houses have all this equipment right now. Moreover, all you have to do to get a house is to be born in the Soviet Union. You are entitled to housing. I was born in the Soviet Union. So I have a right to a house. In America, if you don't have a dollar—you have the right to sleep on the pavement. Yet you say that we are slaves of Communism." The only thing Nixon and Khrushchev seemed to agree on was not liking jazz.

The reality in the Soviet Union, of which Khrushchev was well aware, was that most people lived in communal apartments, where two or three families had to share a kitchen and a toilet. Many of the apartments had no showers or baths. Instead, people had to use public baths or, if they were lucky, knew someone with a full bathroom who would make it available to friends and family. Those fortunate enough to be assigned to one of the new apartments in the suburbs lived in sad-looking high-rises, which tended to crumble and fall apart. Therefore, these buildings were surrounded by netting, to catch the pieces.[21] The American prefab house, built for the exhibit by the Gunnison Company, may or may not have lasted for twenty years, but it survived for at least ten, because it was still in use as the office for Sokolniki Park's caretaker when Thompson returned to Moscow in 1967.[22]

Khrushchev enjoyed taking jabs at Nixon, who would always hold a grudge against the Soviet leader for it. Nixon tried to brush off his evident discomfort during the entire debate with Khrushchev by joking to the Americans in the audience, making comments like, "If he were in the Senate we would call him a filibusterer." Khrushchev's show of not being impressed by the exhibits led Nixon to tell Eisenhower that the Soviet leader was "a man with a closed mind," who would be indifferent to what he saw in the United States.[23] Khrushchev was wrong if he really thought what was on display wouldn't impress his people, since the Soviets had to build a wall around the American exhibition to control access.[24] The Russians were clever enough to realize that few American housewives really had a "miracle kitchen," but they understood that Americans could buy items in the Sears Roebuck catalog. That catalog, as well as all the art books on display, had to be chained and bolted down to the stands, so they would not be taken. Toward the end of the exhibit, most of them disappeared.[25]

The evening after the opening, Thompson gave a buffet supper for a glittering, mostly American crowd of celebrities and VIPs.[26] The following night, Thompson hosted a formal dinner, which did include the Soviets. Khrushchev proposed a toast to the elimination of military bases in foreign lands. Nixon suggested that they drink to peace instead. After a few more toasts, Khrushchev impulsively suggested they all drive out to his dacha that very moment. The trip was postponed, however, until the next day, July 26. In the morning, Khrushchev, in his Ukrainian linen shirt and sandals, showed up, along with his entourage, to take Thompson and Nixon on a boat trip down the Moscow River. Mrs. Nixon and the wives of the three top Soviet leaders accompanied them. Stopping to ask bathers whether they were "captives" or "slaves," the Soviet leader poked Nixon, sweltering in his business suit, in the ribs and said, "See how our slaves live!"[27] They then drove out to the government dacha at Novo Ogaryovo for a five-hour lunch, where Khrushchev got into a long argument with Thompson and then apologized when it was over.[28]

The thorny topic of Berlin came up between *zakuski*. Comparing the benefits of solving this obstacle in US-Soviet relations to a thread in a garment that, once pulled, unravels all the other difficulties, Khrushchev claimed that the Soviet Union wanted no advantage for itself and had only proposed reasonable solutions, which the West refused to accept. The West, he said, had shaped West Germany without regard to Soviet interests and then had rearmed it. Moreover, while insisting on free elections in Germany, the West refused to countenance free elections in Vietnam. Nixon responded that this was because Ho Chi Minh would not allow the International Control Commission into his territory. Khrushchev said that he had come up with the free-city idea for Berlin to safeguard the prestige of the Western powers. It was the West, he said, that was prolonging the Cold War over Berlin and perhaps even turning it into a hot war. Nixon answered back that the present situation was all due to Soviet actions.

At this point, Thompson intervened. The Soviet Union did not want an indefinite prolongation of the occupation's regime in Berlin, Thompson said. The West, on the other hand, did not want to agree to a permanent division of Germany, which is what the Soviets proposed. Thompson argued that since the two sides were unable to find a solution, the best option was to leave things as they were. If the Soviets forced a crisis, it would not reconcile with their words about peace. Instead, Thompson suggested that they make headway in other areas, such as disarmament and atomic testing. Then other problems might become easier to deal with. At this, Khrushchev blew up and put on one of his "floor shows."[29] He said Thompson's use of the word "peace" sounded threatening. Taken aback, Thompson replied he had not meant any personal insult. What he meant was that forcing a crisis was not a step toward peace.

Khrushchev then accused Nixon of not having the courage to say these things to him directly and of putting Thompson up to it. Thompson was embarrassed. Nixon denied putting Thompson up to anything, but he saw no reason to disagree with what Thompson said. The argument went on for quite a while, but at the end of the evening, when they were getting into their cars, Khrushchev put his arm around Thompson and said, "I hope you are not mad at me." Thompson responded, "Well, *I* am not mad, but what about you?" "Oh," replied Khrushchev, "Let's just forget it!" Thompson concluded that there must have been a lot of discussion among Khrushchev's colleagues in the Presidium over his German policy, so Khrushchev's outburst was in large part for their benefit.[30]

The Tour

Nixon left Moscow to tour Leningrad, Novosibirsk, and Sverdlovsk, and the Thompsons accompanied him. Among Nixon's delegation were several intelligence officers, whose main target was to collect information on Soviet ICBMs.[31] When they were flying over Sverdlovsk, the Americans took photos of missile sites below that would intrigue the CIA's Richard M. Bissell Jr. and induce him to persuade Eisenhower to approve Gary Powers's ill-fated U-2 flight.[32] In Novosibirsk, the Americans went to see heavy machinery plants and a regional version of *Swan Lake*.[33]

On the last day of the trip, Thompson accompanied Khrushchev and the famous Soviet airplane engineer, Tupolev, on a tour of the Boeing 707 the vice president was using. Khrushchev was particularly jovial as he climbed on board and proceeded directly to the cockpit. Tupolev, even more corpulent than Khrushchev, had to endure the premier's teasing that there might not be enough room for both of them on the plane. Liking the way the plane was outfitted, he told Tupolev to take notes and make sketches, and then joked to Thompson that all plane designers steal from each other. Inspecting the bar, Khrushchev scoffed at the terrible vodka and asked Thompson what the other, darker-colored liquor was. He was told it was sour mash whiskey. Khrushchev then declared that since he was on American territory, he ought to drink whiskey. He made toasts to Eisenhower, Nixon, and Thompson. Then Thompson offered his own toast, observing that this was a retooled military plane and saying that he hoped a time would come when all military planes were converted to passenger use. Khrushchev exclaimed, "That's very good!" and then leaned over to tell Thompson a secret: the Soviets had already started converting their military planes, and they had a retrofitted a bomber that could reach the United States and come back to the USSR without refueling.

When Thompson returned to Spaso House, Nixon asked him to look over a draft of his speech for Soviet television. Thompson found it too belligerent and explained to the vice president that he understood Nixon had two audiences. This draft was too oriented toward internal American politics, and some statements would not be received well by his Soviet audience. He told Nixon: "You are the first American vice president to address the Soviet people. You've got to make sure that you are not the last." He then sat down with Nixon until the "wee small hours of the morning" to rewrite the speech.[34] Nixon subsequently acknowledged to journalist William H. Lawrence that Thompson had been a great help to him in understanding Khrushchev and the whole Communist problem, and that Thompson was the best adviser Eisenhower could get on those matters.[35]

Thompson had helped Nixon see things in a different light. When Nixon had said that the whole group of American visitors were depressed by Soviet drabness and uniformity, Thompson explained that in the not too far distant past, it had been a lot worse. Old repressions had eased considerably, he said, and noted that these changes in Soviet Russia, albeit subtle, were important. They did not include the abolition of labor camps or the establishment of trials by jury, but large numbers of people no longer were suddenly shipped off to

Llewellyn Thompson Jr.'s family arrives in New York City in August 1959, shortly before Nikita Khrushchev's US visit that September. *From left to right,* Jenny, Llewellyn, Jane, and Sherry. Morris Warman Estate, courtesy of Ronald and Richard Warman.

Siberia. The question was, how far should the United States should go to keep the door from being slammed shut again? Thompson went on to explain that Khrushchev was taking very real risks in coming to the United States and letting Ike visit the USSR, but that the Soviet leader was doing so in order to gain respect, which was why he was willing to let Nixon talk on TV. If these trends—more Soviets seeing the outside world, and a greater infiltration of ideas—continued, the more pressure there would be on Khrushchev and his regime to loosen up.

On his last night in Moscow, Nixon had a few drinks too many. He went over the important moments of the visit, glorifying his own performance and using inappropriate invectives and foul language. Besides leaving a bad impression on those present, it demonstrated the vice president's deep insecurity.[36] Nixon then left Moscow for Warsaw. He said it was like going from night to day, and Pat Nixon finally got her big welcome. The route from the airport was lined with cheering Poles, who tossed so many flowers that, at one point, the cars had to stop to remove them from their windshields, so the drivers could see.[37]

When Nixon returned to Washington, DC, to brief the president, Thompson's influence was obvious. Nixon told Eisenhower: "People who don't know better don't rebel. They have to know something better. This is why Poland is showing more resistance to Communism. People there are closer to the West and know it better."[38] The vice president stated that the only long-range answer to the Communist problem was a gradual opening of the door, through contacts. People were hungry for news of the outside world.[39] Thompson saw increased interactions as a way to find accommodation between the two countries. Nixon, however, interpreted them as a tool for undermining the Communist regime.

Mr. Khrushchev Goes to Washington, or I Want to Be in America!

When the American exhibition in Moscow was over, the Thompson family left in August for their long-postponed home leave. It was the first time five-year-old Sherry had been to America, and it had been too long since Thompson and Jane had seen their families. Thompson wanted to introduce his children to the America they'd only read about. They stayed at the fabled Broadmoor Hotel in Colorado Springs, near Thompson's mother's home, thanks to the largess of the hotel's owner, Thayer Tutt. It was like a fantasy come true for the children. They visited the "North Pole" at the top of the cog-rail line on Pike's Peak. That fall, their cousin Jeff, who went with them, would be rebuked by his teacher for fibbing when his "What I Did on My Summer Holiday" paper included going to the North Pole with his cousins from Russia. The girls bought Barbie dolls and Annie Oakley outfits and prospected for gold around the lake behind the grand hotel. While Thompson was able to pursue his favorite pastime of golf, the girls mostly swam and turned brown and discovered hamburgers and hot fudge sundaes—a nice change from potatoes and cabbage.

Meanwhile, Khrushchev was still greasing the path to his hoped-for summit conference. In a speech at Dnepropetrovsk, he announced his wish for a speedy resolution of the Berlin issue at the CFM meetings in Geneva. Shortly thereafter, the assembled foreign ministers announced their failure to agree on any item. Then, in a press conference, Khrushchev cited the need for a summit in addition to the planned exchange of leader visits to the United States and the USSR. He declared—to everyone's relief—that there would be no unilateral action taken on Berlin as long as talks would still be ongoing.[40]

19

The Russian Is Coming

Ike was . . . mystified by the puzzling, unpredictable, funny,
nasty, prickly, charming, insecure, obnoxious, frustrating
man he had accidentally invited to America.
—PETER CARLSON, *K Blows Top*

On September 12, 1959, something momentous happened—the Soviets launched the first manmade object to reach another celestial body, the moon. Almost as fantastic, two days later, the leader of the Soviet Socialist Republics landed in Washington, DC, for an official visit to the United States.

The Thompsons left their two younger daughters and the girls' nanny in the care of Carl Hummelsine at magical Colonial Williamsburg in Virginia, a huge stage set filled with costumed interpreters in the world's largest "living museum."[1] For children who had learned about America through books, to see its history come alive in this idyllic place was truly amazing. While their girls were getting to know the country through American kids in Williamsburg, the Thompsons were preparing to take a similar adventure with Khrushchev.

Khrushchev Arrives

At the military air base closest to Washington, DC, they joined a greeting party of 3,000 meeting the flying giant Tupolev Tu-114, too big to land on the runway at National Airport.[2] The plane taxied to the red carpet rolled out on the ground, and Khrushchev climbed down the stairs, which were specially constructed to reach the giant aircraft's door. Eisenhower greeted him in a cowboy hat. It was the first time Jane "had ever seen Mr. Khrushchev a little unsure of himself. He was constantly glancing at the president to follow suit as they reviewed the troops, and his quick and many short strides to the president's long ones made him appear even more unsure."[3] Khrushchev was convinced that the Americans would find some way to humiliate him, so he boned up on issues of protocol before the trip. He also worried needlessly that Camp David, in rural Maryland, was some kind of backwater outpost, and that receiving him there was a slight. Khrushchev's son, Sergei, would recall that this stuck in his father's mind as a testament to how little the Americans and Soviets knew each other.[4] Every move of the welcoming ceremony was detailed in a fifteen-page memo by the State Department's Protocol Office, down to the marks put on the tarmac so everyone would know where to stand. This was not the case, however, for the remainder of the trip. Unlike today, where security dictates every move of a visit of this magnitude, back then the schedule was often improvised, and the Soviet party had a lot of latitude, even though *they* would not think so.

After the ceremony, everyone headed for their assigned cars. Jane was in Rada Khrushcheva's car, and together they would cover "thousands of kilometers, side by side—in the car, on the train, and on the plane."[5] Rada later recalled: "A great many people, even children, holding American and Soviet paper flags had lined up on both sides of the road. There wasn't a sound—just dead silence. The motorcade moves slowly. The people silently peer into the windows, trying to discern what the Russians look like. This curious suspicion followed our delegation for the first two days."[6] Aleksei Adzhubei, Khrushchev's son-in-law and editor of the newspaper *Izvestia*, couldn't understand the silent treatment from the crowds, and he seemed to portray everything he saw in a negative way.[7] Mikhail A. "Smiling Mike" Menshikov, the Soviet ambassador, told them that the crowds were silent because their motorcade had been preceded by a car carrying a large banner, telling the crowd to show restraint and no emotion.[8]

That afternoon, Thompson was to meet with the president and vice president, along with Assistant Secretary of State Henry Cabot Lodge—who was to be Khrushchev's escort throughout the trip—and others in the Oval Office. Nixon was not there, however, most likely because Milton Eisenhower had disapproved of the vice president's comportment in Moscow and thought that putting him and the Soviet chairman in close proximity for two weeks would not be a good idea. Nixon, considering himself an expert on all things Khrushchev, told the president that the way to deal with the Soviet leader was to "argue or perish." He advised Eisenhower to instruct Lodge never to allow Khrushchev to make an anti-American statement without offering an immediate rebuttal. Lodge dutifully carried out that order—at least to a point. Khrushchev did not really object, saying he understood Lodge's need to "praise his country." Nonetheless, after speaking to Thompson, Lodge and the president decided to abandon that tack.[9] Eisenhower was determined to make "one great personal effort, before leaving office, to soften up the Soviet leader even a little bit. Except for the Austrian peace treaty, we haven't made a chip in the granite in seven years."[10]

Only a few hours after they landed, Khrushchev and his top-level deputies joined the Americans in the Oval Office. Khrushchev presented Eisenhower with a gift, a lovely wooden box that contained a model of the Soviet moon rocket. Ike thought rubbing his nose in the Soviets' space achievement was clumsy, but he accepted the gift with "interest and appreciation."[11] The two leaders discussed generalities about the agenda for the meetings at Camp David that would be the final stage of the trip. Both men wanted to talk about substantive issues, but both had allies who were suspicious of accommodations the Soviet and American leaders might make. The president talked about the need to discuss "points of irritation," such as Berlin. The Soviet leader asked if Ike would also agree to discuss disarmament, which was Khrushchev's principal issue, and Eisenhower consented.

Khrushchev declared that the Soviet government believed "you do not want war; and we assume that you also believe this about us," to which the president nodded. Khrushchev then stated that the main thing was to establish trust, and he described what Thompson had been saying repeatedly: each side tended to misinterpret the other. That was why the face-to-face talks were so important. When the ministers met, Khrushchev continued, each side understood what the other was saying but "immediately suspected that they were thinking otherwise. . . . If we approach each other with the expectation that the other's system will be overturned, then there will be no basis for understanding. Let us allow history to be the judge [of] which system is preferable and meanwhile live in peace as good neighbors."[12]

A seven-course dinner, resembling a Thanksgiving feast, at the White House was the first formal event of the trip, and it was a crucial one. Fortunately, the dinner was uneventful, with Khrushchev trading humorous but cordial quips with the likes of J. Edgar Hoover and CIA director Allen Dulles. The next morning began with a visit to a large agricultural research station in Beltsville, Maryland, where Khrushchev was subjected to endless lectures about the benefits of capitalism to agricultural progress. The irony was that Beltsville was an 11,000-acre government farm, employing 2,000 federal employees, not a private enterprise.[13] Passing the Jefferson Memorial on the trip out to the research station, Lodge and Khrushchev enjoyed debating the merits of the two nations' systems. Lodge was pleasantly surprised. Khrushchev gave him the impression, "which Ambassador Thompson has spoken of, of a man who has an open mind on some things." He was also "a good listener," Lodge observed.[14]

That day was a typically humid, sweltering, late summer day, and most of the participants were happy to be let loose from the unairconditioned lecture hall to go outside. Once in the fields, reporters asked Khrushchev's daughters, Rada and Julia, to identify themselves. They were so nervous that they declined, until Jane persuaded them to respond. The Khrushchev women were keenly aware of being observed and worried that the American reporters would portray them in the worst possible light. Rada, who soon warmly worked her way into Jane's heart, was so circumspect that she asked for permission to take a packet of matches from the White House for her mother's collection.[15] Khrushchev's daughters weren't the only ones who had a bit of paranoia. The Soviet chairman himself was reluctant to ride in the presidential helicopter for an aerial tour of Washington, DC, until he learned that Eisenhower would be on board, too.

The next morning dawned bright and sunny for the train ride to New York City. Thompson joined his wife and the Khrushchev siblings for breakfast on the train. Jane told him that after reading the American newspapers, Mrs. Khrushcheva became rather agitated, because she thought she saw a photograph of herself drinking from a mug and eating. She said that if she'd known they would take such a photo, she would not have come. Jane showed her that the caption indicated it was not a photo of her, which seemed to placate Nina Petrovna.[16] Khrushchev also read the American newspapers on the train, through an interpreter, who had what appeared to be a second interpreter looking over his shoulder as he read.

When they arrived deep underground in Pennsylvania Station in New York City, they wended their way to a freight elevator, got into their assigned cars, and departed for the Waldorf Astoria Hotel. As they left the dark station and emerged into the crystal-clear day, both Adzhubei and the minister of education exclaimed in Russian, "Now there's a real city!" But again the crowds were eerily silent, curiously staring as the group's cars went by. Adzhubei rolled down his window and glared back. Then he noticed a huge cross, commissioned by an anti-Communist Christian group, being created across the sky by smoke from skywriting planes.[17] The welcome luncheon was held at the Commodore Hotel, because a dentists' association had refused to relinquish their booking at the Waldorf Astoria for the leader of the Communist bloc. The mayor of New York greeted the guests with a speech promoting his fine city, followed by Lodge, who made a preemptive lecture on the progress made by the nation's Negroes [sic], in anticipation of Khrushchev's tour of Harlem.[18]

The next day, Rada and Adzhubei went window shopping before heading over to the UN building to listen to Khrushchev's address to the General Assembly. This time Yuri (or Yury) Georgy Aleksandrovich Zhukov,[19] the chairman of the Soviet Committee on Cultural Relations with Foreign Countries, was also in the car, laughing at the protesters across the street holding signs reading "Free Ukraine!" He remarked that the Soviets ought to start putting up posters about California and Mexico, whereupon Jane pointed out that Mexico was quite independent of the United States. Zhukov ignored her, and the car became as silent as the crowds it passed. Virtually every gathering on the tour had at least one wiseguy who tried to gain attention at Khrushchev's expense, metaphorically poking him in the chest like Nixon had physically done in the kitchen debate. Possibly the worst was the Washington Press Club luncheon, early in the tour, where the host told a crude joke about Khrushchev's "Secret Speech" in 1956. Khrushchev had taken a great risk in laying bare the truth of his country's history under Stalin, and he was rightly not amused.[20]

By the time the group flew to Los Angeles, they all seemed to be comfortable with each other, if not "cozy." On the plane, the men studied the American press's accounts of the trip, which ran the gamut from factual to appalling. If they thought the West Coast would provide a respite from the heat, however, they were mistaken. Hollywood was as hot and sticky as the Washington, DC, area. The president of the Motion Picture Association, Eric Johnston, and Spyros P. Skouras, the president of the Twentieth Century Fox motion picture studio, hosted a huge luncheon, replete with movie stars, at the Café de Paris. The head table was an all-male affair, seating the hosts, the mayor of Los Angeles, Khrushchev, Lodge, Thompson, and a few others. Jane sat at another table with Mrs. Khrushcheva, who was amused by her neighbor, Bob Hope.[21] They were joined by Glenn Ford, Tony Curtis, and David Niven.[22] Khrushchev and Skouras seemed happy and were friendly toward each other, sharing laughs after lunch.[23]

The meal was followed by a tour of the set for the movie Can-Can, to see the filming of a dance scene featuring Shirley MacLaine. It was not particularly racy, but just risqué enough to get some of the audience snickering. The American press and photographers attempted to set up a photo with Khrushchev between two of the dancers. At the time, Khrushchev seemed happy to have his picture taken, but he expressed his displeasure to Thompson afterward. He told Thompson that he could not understand how such good and hard-working people could indulge in such vulgar entertainment. Khrushchev attributed this to the extreme abundance of wealth in the United States. He also complained that reporters tried to make the dancers lift their skirts while being photographed with him. This, he thought, was in very poor taste.[24] The Los Angeles visit was further marred by a security alert that prevented an outing to Disneyland, which had opened four years previously. In the American version of this story, Khrushchev had been anticipating this trip and was horribly disappointed that it was cancelled. In the Soviet version, he didn't really know what Disneyland was, and he was simply irritated at once more being thwarted in an attempt in mingle with "ordinary" Americans. Whatever the reality, the remaining entourage, tired and feeling the heat, wasn't disappointed at all.

That evening, Jane sat next to Adzhubei and sensed a "turning point" in him. He questioned her about the "Free Ukraine" signs. To Jane's surprise, Adzhubei was puzzled, saying he could understand Hungarian protesters, but why Ukrainian ones? Jane tried to explain that small political groups in the United States all sought a voice and attention, but certainly not at the behest of the government. Then he asked her why there were so many police escorts, and why the Disneyland trip was cancelled. Jane explained, "We have a number of crackpots," to which Adzhubei replied, "We have crackpots, too, but they do not require that many police." She responded, "Maybe we have more crackpots than you do," making him laugh. Then they chatted about the Soviet Union, and he asked her, "Do you think you understand us?" Jane answered, "There is not any one of us who is living in Moscow in our group that is not trying desperately to understand the Soviet Union and trying to improve relations." She went on to observe, "So if we as a group [i.e., the State Department], your worst enemies, are trying, there is hope for the rest of the American people to try, too." Thompson also perceived that Adzhubei had changed over the course of the trip, softening his perspective and beginning to consider less-hostile interpretations.[25]

While Jane and Adzhubei were chatting, Ambassador Lodge was doing his best to forestall the mayor of Los Angeles, Norris Paulson, from delivering a provocative speech, full of "gross insults." Paulson resisted, because he had already distributed a draft of it to reporters. According to Chalmers Roberts of the *Washington Post*, Lodge did get some of the insults removed, but the speech was still negatively charged, and it referred to Khrushchev's "We will bury you" remark. Khrushchev explained in subsequent speeches to the UN, to the National Press Club, and to countless reception attendees that "bury" was used in metaphorical sense. The inevitable development of worldwide Communism would "bury" capitalism, but Khrushchev meant that it would do so economically, not militarily. Despite his clarification, it is this quote for which he is most remembered in the United States.

Jane remembered the mayor's speech as: "We won't bury you. You won't bury us. We will live together in friendship." And she did not notice any reaction from the Soviets standing around her, including Adzhubei and the minister of education. But Khrushchev responded with a furious tirade, threatening to leave. Jane turned to a nearby interpreter to confirm what she had heard. She asked why Khrushchev was so upset, and she noticed that Adzhubei and the minister were taking notes on her questions.[26] She was distressed, because she thought the mayor had been mistranslated. She later learned that the interpreter she questioned was American, not Soviet. Adzhubei and the minister reported that Jane was so frightened by Khrushchev's remarks that she was in tears over the prospect of imminent war. Khrushchev later cited this incident at a meeting of the Soviet Presidium, to demonstrate how scared the Americans were of the Soviet threat.[27]

According to Khrushchev and his son Sergei, they went back to their hotel room, where Khrushchev continued his tirade in an escalated mode, announcing his intentions to go home immediately. But as he did so, he gesticulated at the wide-eyed entourage, to indicate he was speaking for listening devices hidden in the ceiling, visualizing Ambassador Lodge hunkered over a speaker in his own room, hanging on to Khrushchev's every word. As it happened, Lodge was in his hotel room having a drink. Khrushchev sent Andrei Gromyko there to convey his anger at the constant jabbing and attempts to keep him from talking to ordinary people. Eventually, everyone calmed down, and the trip continued.[28]

The Soviets and the Americans took a train from Los Angeles to San Francisco, where a "cheerful and friendly attitude all around" prevailed. Wylie Buchanan, one of the State Department representatives, suggested that they could make the journey be like one on a campaign train, so the train stopped at various towns along the way, where Khrushchev got off and shook hands and kissed babies. He loved it. The crowds loved it. Even shy Rada got off at Santa Barbara and mingled with Americans "eager to shake hands with them and personally greet Khrushchev and the other Russians."[29] After that, the people who came out to gawk at the Communist leader either cheered or waved or booed, but they were no longer silent. At one point on the train, Khrushchev remarked that he was beginning to understand some of the problems that Eisenhower faced. The good mood lasted throughout their visit to the city by the bay. Toward the end of the train trip, Khrushchev even made a "startling" remark to Jane: "This is really a very rich country. You know, we do not have the economic basis you have. It will take us ten, fifteen, or maybe even twenty years to catch up to you." He said this end result was what he wanted for his people.[30]

San Francisco was a rousing success. The Soviets loved the city and its beauty, enjoying a boat tour at night. They visited the IBM plant. Its cafeteria, with plastic tabletops and a self-service setup, impressed them even more than its state-of-the-art computers. Khrushchev took notes on how much more efficient the eating arrangements were than having servers and tablecloths, and he determined to duplicate this in the Presidium cafeteria. On the group's last night in San Francisco, Lodge sent a very long telegram to Secretary of State Herter, describing Khrushchev's "good humor" and expressing the opinion that "the gains of this trip definitely outweigh the losses and I can document this in many different ways."[31]

The next stop on the tour was flying to the Roswell Garst farm in Coon Rapids, Iowa. Khrushchev, who saw himself as an agricultural expert, had been looking forward to this. Some years earlier, Khrushchev had sent a delegation to Iowa to learn more about growing hybrid seed corn, which he thought could help feed his huge country. Khrushchev became a fanatic about corn and a devotee of Garst and his methods. The Iowan had even toured Soviet farms, teaching modern farming methods, toasting "peace through corn," and selling quite a bit of seed corn in the bargain.[32] Garst was no Communist, nor was he shy about making some of his views known. During the tour of his company's facility, he encouraged

Khrushchev to allow disarmament inspections. He also questioned Khrushchev on "cases of compassion," which would give certain Soviet citizens permission to emigrate to the United States.[33] Khrushchev responded that he wanted to settle these cases, which Thompson followed up on later. Khrushchev did not mind Garst delving into politics. He respected the man on a number of levels, and he was impressed that Garst shared his "secrets" with the Communists. He also was impressed by Garst's frugality and noted that he would like to inspire the same attitude among the administrators of the collective farms back home.[34]

After the farm visit, they got back on the plane, landing late at night in Pittsburgh, center of the American steel industry, which, at that moment, was on strike. The situation could have been seen as a either bad thing or a good one, since it was a clear, if unintended, demonstration of the power of the American worker. Union leaders declined to meet with Khrushchev, however, which he interpreted to mean that they were lackeys of the state. Since the steel mills were shuttered by the strike, the group visited a factory owned by the machine-tool heiress and supersocialite Perle Mesta. What impressed Khrushchev was not the socialite, but her factory and the discipline of its workers. He noted that despite much of the machinery being very old, the plant was productive and profitable.[35] Perhaps this was why Khrushchev was so open to a proposal to have Soviet plant managers come to the United States for training.

As important as trade and exchanges were, they were not foremost in Khrushchev's mind. For him, the Camp David meeting with Eisenhower, above all, would be about disarmament and Germany. Khrushchev was interested in disarmament for two reasons. The first was to divert some of the Soviets' vast military investment to civilian uses. The second was to achieve parity by having the armaments stockpiles of both countries be at the same level. He wrote in his memoirs that as long as the United States had weapons superiority, it was easier for them to determine the most expedient moment to start a war. He thought that there were "enemies who believed conflict was inevitable and were in a hurry to finish us off before it was too late."[36] The problem was that his own reasoning (although correct) worked against him, in a catch-22. He could not accede to real inspections, a requirement the Americans insisted on if they were to disarm, for fear that the Soviets' inferiority would be discovered, so an accord on disarmament was always out of reach.

Shortly after their arrival in Washington, DC, and prior to heading to Camp David, Thompson, Lodge, and others attended a posttrip, preconference briefing with the president and his senior advisors, to exchange their impressions. Thompson observed that although Khrushchev relied on Gromyko for policy questions, the foreign minister did not help Khrushchev prepare his speeches, but the chairman's son-in-law, Adzhubei, did. Thompson said what impressed him the most was the change in Gromyko—a softening of his anti-American suspicions. Thompson described the Soviet ambassador, Menshikov, as "constantly feeding poison to Khrushchev throughout the trip," and Lodge confirmed this observation.[37] What Thompson found instructive was that this seemed to be obvious to Khrushchev, too. Thompson didn't think Menshikov would last long in his post. Shortly after this trip, the Soviets established a USA Institute, under Georgi Arbatov, to study and accurately report on events in the United States.[38] Arbatov said that Thompson's support—

and his affirmation that the institute was a serious enterprise, not just a propaganda machine—enabled it to gain access to respected American scholars.[39]

Thompson encouraged Eisenhower not to put a price on his reciprocal visit to the USSR. While the president said he would not do that, he did want Khrushchev to make some statement to reassure Ike that there wasn't going to be a "catastrophe over Berlin."[40] Eisenhower expressed the opinion that since the Americans had a treaty with West Germany, they could not keep Khrushchev from having one with East Germany. Secretary Herter quickly interjected that it was important to ensure Khrushchev knew that he could not terminate US rights in Berlin by concluding such a treaty. Thompson suggested that they begin by asking Khrushchev just what he thought the consequences of such a peace treaty would be.

The Summit at Camp David

Camp David is a large campus of semirustic cottages in a wooded, hilly setting. Originally built by the Works Projects Administration, the massive governmental jobs program of the 1930s, its selection for the president's first major meeting with the head of the Soviet Union represented a kind of nice irony, which probably did not occur to any of the participants. By now, Khrushchev understood that being received at Camp David was an honor, not an exile, as he'd feared at first. Eisenhower, Khrushchev, and their interpreters were in one helicopter, with Herter, Gromyko, Thompson, Adzhubei, and Menshikov in another. The rest of the entourage stayed in Washington, DC. Sergei went butterfly hunting, and Nina Petrovna and her daughter Rada were dragged through a tour of a dry cleaning business. September was still stifling in the capital, and Mrs. Khrushcheva declared that of the many things the Russians should adopt from the Americans, the first ones on her list were iced tea and air conditioning! It was a blessed relief for those at Camp David to have a cool fog settling in overnight.

There were many scheduled meetings at Camp David over the course of the two days the high-level entourage spent there, but there was also time for informal, relaxed exchanges, which allowed these men to directly observe each other. The evening they arrived, the movie that was screened for them was a western. (One wonders if Eisenhower knew that Khrushchev had been subjected to this genre of films, among others, by Stalin, who was a film buff, during some of his awful all-night movie marathons.) At breakfast the following morning, Thompson and others watched as the two leaders discussed World War II military strategy and their experiences.[41] It must have been satisfying for Khrushchev to be chatting with another former general, as one soldier to another.

The first serious meeting took place after breakfast, on September 26. Khrushchev's primary issue was disarmament, while Eisenhower's was convincing Khrushchev to rescind his threat to make a separate peace treaty with East Germany. Eisenhower opened the discussion with a statement that, in essence, said if you ease the tension on us in Berlin, we can make progress on disarmament. After all, the president noted, the United States did "not want to perpetuate the present situation in Berlin and keep [its] occupation troops there forever." Khrushchev expressed disbelief that his proposal for a free-city solution for West Berlin could threaten the security of the United States. Then Eisenhower, remarkably, said he "did not mind if the Soviets signed a treaty with the East Germans," as long as it did not affect Berlin. Khrushchev responded that this was an impossible condition. It would mean maintaining a part of West Germany within the borders of a sovereign East Germany. But, he went on, he was optimistic that something could be worked out to guarantee the people of West Berlin that their lives would not change.

According to notes of the conversation drafted by Thompson, the president said Americans "have the impression that we are in the shadow of some kind of—he did not want to say ultimatum—but at least some threat of unilateral action. This was a bad situation and the American people would not understand dealing with other problems if this were not resolved. It would be tragic if peaceful efforts foundered on this less important question." Khrushchev then offered the Soviet version of how they had reached this impasse. The United States operated from "positions of strength," creating an imbalance of power and leaving the Soviets always in the minority when disputes arose. Because the Soviets saw no prospect of an agreed-upon settlement, they decided to go ahead on their own.[42] Eisenhower admitted that the current state of affairs (akin to a state of war) in Berlin was—and here Thompson's memo of the conversation says "uneasy"— but it has also been reported that Ike said "abnormal."[43] He also conceded that German reunification was not probable, at least in the short term. Khrushchev retracted his ultimatum and left the topic of signing a treaty up in the air. Most importantly, both men pronounced their mutual desire to resolve the issue peacefully.

They reconvened at 1:00 p.m., so Khrushchev could go over Herter's draft summary of the morning's meeting, and the Soviet leader got somewhat excited, saying that it was an attempt to bully him into accepting an indefinite status quo in Germany. Khrushchev said the entire trip had been designed to impress him with America's power, in order to make him accede to its wishes. After Khrushchev had talked himself out, Eisenhower said that, in view of the fact that the United States did not want to perpetuate the occupation's regime and that the Soviet Union did not want to try to force the United States out of West Berlin, both sides would try to negotiate and see how soon the differences on this score could be resolved. If progress could be reached, "then other, broader areas could be broached."[44]

The American and Soviet entourages then joined them for a late lunch, during which Khrushchev continued his agitated remarks and attacked the "miracle kitchen" part of the American exhibition in Moscow in July. Thompson pointed out that the same exhibit had been shown all over the United States as merely a glimpse into the future, and that there was no intention whatsoever to mislead the Soviet public into thinking that all Americans had such kitchens. Khrushchev rejoined, in a rather irritated manner, that the Soviets had a high standard of living of their own, and that "any attempt to lure them toward capitalism would fail."[45]

Thompson skipped the next meeting, on trade issues, to nurse the terrible ulcers that had plagued him throughout the tour, severe enough to send him to bed on several occasions. He rejoined them for the meeting that was a discussion on disarmament. Here the president and Khrushchev started off on a more congenial note. They briefly discussed sharing information and cooperating on the topics of peaceful uses of atomic energy and research in nuclear physics. The president agreed that disarmament ought to be the first item in any agenda for future negotiations, because it was "the most important question."[46] Khrushchev then inquired what the US policy toward China might be in the future. This led to a long argument regarding Chiang Kai-shek's government in Taiwan and Mao Zedong's in mainland China.[47] Herter inserted himself into the conversation quite a few times. Conspicuously, Gromyko did not. Years later, when Khrushchev compared his meeting with President Kennedy and this one with Eisenhower, he would cluck that Eisenhower had to depend on Herter to tell him what to say.[48] Gromyko simply remembered it as Eisenhower stonewalling on disarmament.[49]

The two leaders then ended this part of the meeting and entered into a private discussion about possibly issuing a joint statement at the conclusion of the Camp David talks. They had accomplished little, except to agree that their communiqué would be general, since their respective positions had yet to be clarified, especially on disarmament. The two men discussed the president's reciprocal trip to the Soviet Union, which would happen late the next spring. Eisenhower allowed that now meetings at the highest level were possible, since the state of "duress" had been lifted. After a little tit for tat on the meaning of "duress," Khrushchev said that the Soviet government had never meant to "create a situation of duress."[50] Then they left it to their staffs to draft the actual language of the communiqué, which would name the discussions the "spirit of Camp David."

The draft communiqué read: "With respect to the specific question of Berlin, an understanding was reached, subject to the approval of the other parties directly concerned, that negotiations would be reopened with a view to achieving a solution which would be in accordance with the interests of all concerned and in the interest of the maintenance of peace. It was further agreed that these negotiations should not be prolonged indefinitely (but that there would be no fixed time limit on them)." Everyone felt a rush of accomplishment, but they were exhausted by the grueling schedule and the stress of the sessions. Then, in classic Soviet negotiating fashion, Khrushchev, after reading the draft, said the parenthetical language about "no fixed time limit" had to be removed. The Americans agreed to omit the entire sentence, as long as Khrushchev would not issue a denial if Eisenhower made a public statement that there was, in fact, to be no fixed time limit. The president was willing to say, in a separate press conference, that the leaders had agreed to reopen negotiations on Berlin, noting that these discussions would not be prolonged indefinitely nor would there be any time limit imposed on when they should take place. Khrushchev stated he would then publicly confirm "his agreement to the president's statement."[51]

Everyone then trooped back to Washington, DC, and were reunited with their families. That evening, they attended a ceremony where they made friendly promises to visit each other.[52] The Soviet entourage went back across the ocean without incident in the outsized, gleaming, but possibly cracking Tupolev Tu-114 plane, fully loaded with shopping trophies.[53] Thompson had to attend debriefings and consultations, so the girls stayed on in Williamsburg. Jane went down to join them with her mother, whom the children called "Grannie 'Roe." They stayed there for several weeks after the Camp David meetings and then went to New York City, leaving for Moscow in November. Although the girls missed quite a lot of school, their nanny's tutoring took care of that.[54]

Thompson's written observations about the tour concluded that Khrushchev was deeply impressed with the richness and strength of the United States, both in material and human terms: "He is a shrewd observer and unlike many Communists is objective in his judgments, whatever he may say in public. . . . The comparison between a small Iowa farm community and a similar community in the Soviet Union must have been very striking indeed. He obviously also observed weaknesses in our society and I think was particularly struck by the lack of discipline and the difficulties the president has to face in carrying out foreign policy."[55]

It was clear to Thompson that Khrushchev's basic motivation in forcing the Berlin issue was not the city itself. Presaging the inevitability of the Berlin Wall, or something like it, in the absence of a solution to the overall question of Germany, he wrote: "The Soviets could always deal with the refugee problem by unilateral action and the invidious comparison between East and West Berlin will probably decrease rapidly as the Soviets raise living standards in East Germany. Rather, Khrushchev's chief motive is to stabilize the situation in Eastern Europe generally and particularly the question of frontiers."[56] In other words, the Americans were concerned about Berlin, and the Soviets, about securing the current German borders.

While in Washington, DC, Thompson had greater access to his own government. He made a presentation to the leadership of the US Information Agency (USIA), and then to the staff of *Amerika* magazine, to persuade them to concentrate on "straight news reporting and avoid commentary which [a] Soviet audience dismisses anyway." He told them that things had changed a lot in the Soviet Union, particularly in the past few years, and that this liberalization had made the current government there quite popular, which was unprecedented. He pointed out that the American exhibit in Moscow contributed to the popularity of Khrushchev's government and made him even more "cocky." Thompson further thought that it was no longer likely for the Soviet government to revert to the brutality and reign of terror of the Stalin years. Thompson wanted the Americans' efforts to be more nuanced. The Russian people were very adept at reading between the lines—indeed, that was the only way they could discern what was really going on in their own country. It was unnecessary to overexplain.[57]

After the Camp David sessions, Thompson met twice with the president before heading back to Moscow. He was a bit alarmed at Eisenhower's suggestion that the United States "face the fact" that Germany was not going to be reunited any time soon and, in order to help progress on the Berlin problem move forward, officials should be clear about that "fact" in public statements. Thompson respectfully suggested that the president weigh carefully any statements on this matter with regard to public opinion, not just in the United States, but also in both East and West Germany.[58] Thompson reiterated his thoughts that resolving the East German border issue (the Oder–Neisse line) would lessen tensions over Berlin, and he hoped that Eisenhower could bring Adenauer around on this point.

Then the president asked for Thompson's judgment on the topic of disarmament.[59] Thompson told Eisenhower that he thought the Soviets had rejected the president's proposal on the cessation of atmospheric testing because they wanted a comprehensive ban, which included underground testing, in order to keep the Chinese and the Germans from acquiring atomic bombs. He stressed that China "loomed large" in the Soviets' planning. Thompson also told Ike that he was worried US efforts to achieve a nuclear test ban might be breaking down at the CFM conference in Geneva, and that this could be construed as a signal that the United States wasn't really serious about easing tensions.[60]

Both Eisenhower and Thompson thought informal top-level visits could continue by Lodge coming to Moscow as Thompson's guest. Thompson also anticipated that he himself would have a better opportunity to probe Khrushchev's thinking in less-structured, private conversations after the Soviet leader's US tour. Khrushchev was a "very sharp operator," though, and it would be easy to make errors of judgment. The president observed that an honest error of judgment was tolerable, and he thought such conversations were a good idea, so Thompson should pursue them.[61] For a while, at least, these talks proved to be fruitful.

While Thompson was stateside, a young American and former Marine, Lee Harvey Oswald, went missing in Moscow. Oswald had told the Soviets that he wanted to defect, but his application was rejected until he faked a suicide attempt, which placed him in a psychiatric ward for observation. One Saturday afternoon, he saw the consular officer at the US embassy, Richard E. Snyder, who took his passport but did not accept Oswald's renunciation of American citizenship, on the basis that the embassy was officially closed. Thompson received a briefing about this on his return to Moscow. Oswald stayed in the Soviet Union for a while, but, like quite a few Americans who also thought they wanted to become Soviet citizens, he would change his mind and return to the United States just prior to the end of Thompson's US tour.[62]

20 ≡

U-2
The End of Détente

An embarrassing political reversal (the U-2 incident)
served as a catalyst for the latent opposition to
Khrushchev.... Thus 1960 witnessed a serious blow to
Khrushchev's ambitions and forced him to accept some
sharing of power. His decline seems definitely to date
from this period.
—MICHEL TATU, *Power in the Kremlin*

When the Thompson family returned to Moscow in November 1959, they found the city captivated by a kind of "coexistence euphoria." The embassy staff was already busy preparing for the Four-Powers summit in Paris and President Eisenhower's visit to the USSR, now scheduled for June the following year, so if Thompson and Jane thought there'd be a little respite after their long and grueling trip through the United States, they were wrong—starting with another memorable New Year's Eve.

The formal event in the Kremlin's beautiful gilded rooms included dancing and lasted until 2:00 a.m. One noteworthy comment in Khrushchev's monologue was a hint at further Soviet troop reductions. As Thompson and Jane were leaving, Khrushchev invited them to join him in a side room, decorated in the Soviet modern style, with a fountain filled with colored plastic rocks gurgling away in the corner. As they walked in, Khrushchev extended a highly unusual invitation to Thompson and his family to spend the weekend at his dacha. The only others present that early New Year's morning were Frol Kozlov, Anastas Mikoyan, the Italian Communist Party representative, and the French ambassador and his wife.[1] The British and German representatives had already gone home. Khrushchev said he supposed the German hadn't liked his remarks at the reception. Thompson stated that he had also not liked some of Khrushchev's remarks, but the Soviet leader brushed this aside, saying that at least he and Thompson could still talk to and understand each other. Khrushchev offered the palliative that he'd been "exceedingly" pleased by his trip to the United States and that "President Eisenhower [had] overwhelmed him with his personality." Another round of toasts began, and in one, Khrushchev made a jab at Nixon, whom Thompson tried to defend but admitted that "by this time an alcoholic haze had settled over [the] entire company as result [of the] toasts and I did not get very far."

After repeatedly and "solemnly" asserting his desire for peace, Khrushchev enumerated the quantity of bombs the Soviets had earmarked for France, Britain, and Germany, whereupon Jane inquired, "And how many have you got for us?" Khrushchev winked and answered, "That is a secret." In what seemed like a non sequitur, Khrushchev told a cautionary tale about a Soviet soldier who had recently gone berserk, killing five fellow soldiers and himself, as an example of why the current situation in Berlin needed to be resolved, lest some nut start a war. He warned Thompson that if the West let Adenauer take things "down the wrong path," Khrushchev would surely be obliged to conclude a separate peace treaty with East Germany, ending Western rights in Berlin. Thompson asked if this meant that the Soviets would attempt to throw the allies out of Berlin. Khrushchev said no, but he added that the East Germans could deny them access and then the Soviet Union would be obliged to support that decision. When the subject came up for a third time, the French ambassador asked if this meant that the Soviets would block access to Berlin. Khrushchev "vehemently" stated that it did not and said that the Soviets would never attack the allies.

Kozlov and Thompson tried several times to break up the party, but the see-saw comments continued until dawn. In describing this boozy, rambling night, Thompson counseled that although Khrushchev's remarks could be construed, if taken literally, as a reversal to a pre–Camp David stance, he—Thompson—did not think this was Khrushchev's meaning, noting that the Soviet leader's bellicose remarks were interspersed with "protestations for his desire for peace and an accommodation."[2] Nor did Thompson think Khrushchev was probing to see how far he could go. He believed Khrushchev was sincerely trying to impress upon his company just how serious the German situation was to him. At the end of the conversation, Thompson told Khrushchev privately that he felt it his "duty as ambassador to be sure that he had no misunderstanding and that if they attempted to force us [the allies] out of Berlin, we would fulfill our responsibilities to [the] people of West Berlin." Khrushchev scoffed, repeating that Berlin was inconsequential and that he didn't understand why it was a sticking point for the Americans. Thompson knew Berlin was important to Khrushchev and pressed him to say why, but the Soviet leader only replied, "Because it was surrounded by East Germany." Khrushchev said that the Berlin question was one of geography, which he intended to make use of. West Berlin was both a thorn in his side and a useful poker with which to prod the West.

Only hours later, a hung-over, sleepy Thompson took his daughters to a Soviet New Year's Day ice follies performance, which was so saturated with political allegory that Thompson reported it to Washington, DC. In the performance, Father Frost gave one ice skate each to two children, one dressed as a Russian youngster and the other as Tom Sawyer, so the only way they could skate was to do it together, which they managed to accomplish, despite a nasty character dressed as Mars trying to make the children quarrel. The story revolved around a golden nut, which the children could only open through cooperation. Once that occurred, skaters dressed in the costumes of various nationalities came onto the ice. Red China was featured in only one brief number. In Thompson's estimation, it was significant that friendship with the United States was given such prominent play in front of a large number of Soviet children.

Two weeks later, Khrushchev announced the unilateral reduction in forces that he'd hinted at on New Year's Eve.[3] He coupled this announcement with a reminder that the Soviet Union's nuclear and ballistic missile strength compensated for the smaller number of soldiers. Despite Thompson's reports, this speech surprised and alarmed the CIA and worried the American military, who saw only the nuclear threat and not that Khrushchev was cutting his country's forces back to pre-1956 levels. We now know that the Soviet military protested Khrushchev's move.

The reduction was remarkable, because a week earlier, on January 7, the Americans had successfully launched a Polaris missile from Cape Canaveral, Florida.[4] Thompson believed that this challenged the Soviet military's expectations that they would beat the United States in missile capability, while Khrushchev knew the Soviets were behind in rocketry.[5] Shortly after this, Thompson, Jane, and the children visited Khrushchev at the state dacha, the Soviet equivalent of Camp David, for the weekend.[6] The Thompsons were joined by the Klosson family. Boris Klosson was the deputy chief of mission at that time, and his children were similar in age to the two Thompson girls. They drove out together on Saturday, January 16, and were greeted by the household staff and Mrs. Khrushcheva in the large, warm entry hall. Khrushchev, along with his children Sergei, Julia, and Rada, as well as his son-in-law Adzhubei and what appeared to be an endless supply of grandchildren, arrived the following morning. The American children were offered a buffet dinner with Russian delicacies, one of which looked like "mystery meat" in aspic and turned out to be bear meat. Jenny dutifully ate it, as the Thompson daughters were under strict orders to behave and be polite, but Sherry wouldn't. Luckily for them, the very pretty room they were to share that night was stocked with fizzy pink lemonade and a large box of Trufflie—dark lumps of chewy chocolate covered with a pale dusting of cocoa—simply the best chocolates ever made.

The next morning, the American children went out to the stables to watch the horses be harnessed to sleighs for a Russian fairy-tale ride. When they asked about a particularly beautiful horse, they discovered its name was Can-Can! Khrushchev just smiled. The sleigh ride through the countryside—horses trotting, sparkling snow flying from under the troika runners, and blue sky punctuated by a delicate pattern of birch branches—was magnificent. Khrushchev had Thompson ride in his sleigh, so they could speak privately. He asked Thompson what he thought of the military reductions, and Thompson replied that it was a sensible step.[7] Khrushchev then confided to Thompson that he had been "obliged to use all of his authority to persuade the Soviet military of this move." Additionally, Khrushchev would withdraw many soldiers from East Germany and Hungary, as part of modernizing the Soviet military. They also talked about some of Khrushchev's internal reshuffling of the Soviet government.

After the sleigh ride, the American and Soviet children were taken to an anteroom, while the adults entered a large banquet room for one of those famous meals that seemed to last forever. The children quickly finished eating and turned to racing and chasing, until the girls' tulle ribbons and little white socks slumped and the boys' crisp white shirts lost their gray flannel moorings. One of the girls in ribbons still remembers the day as being thoroughly enjoyable, noting that "although we did not speak really any English and you spoke hardly any Russian, we managed to communicate what we wanted to play."[8]

The banquet table for the adults was impressive, barely fitting into the room and glittering with crystal for the cognac, vodka, and wine glasses, one for each course. It is a tradition in Russia that when you drink a toast with vodka, you literally do "bottoms up," turning the glass upside down over your head to prove that you did your part to honor the toast. While everyone else was obliged to drink it up, Khrushchev had a secret weapon, courtesy of Jane Thompson. Rada Khrushcheva recalled: "In my personal collection is a secret shot glass. It holds just one sip, yet it appears to those at the table that you are drinking an impressive dose of spirits." The glass had a solid false bottom that left only a small space for liquid. It was this glass that Jane had brought out to the dacha as a hostess gift for the weekend, and it endeared her to the Khrushchev women. When she presented it, Jane said to Khrushchev: "You often have to toast and to drink when others toast. . . . With this glass you will be able to strategize a little bit, and therefore spare yourself."[9]

The atmosphere was relaxed, relatively speaking. Khrushchev abstained from speechifying, having given over the job of toastmaster to Mikoyan. Thompson was struck by the apparent good nature of the Khrushchev-Mikoyan relationship, with Mikoyan daring to stop Khrushchev from interrupting him, as well as making jokes. In contrast, Thompson noted that Adzhubei, who was clearly a "man on the rise," still seemed intimidated by his father-in-law.

At one of the breaks between courses, the children were herded into the banquet room, whereupon the Soviet children performed perfectly rehearsed songs extolling the virtues of friendship and harmony: let there be sun, let there be peace, and so forth. The adults applauded approvingly, and Khrushchev suggested that perhaps the American children could regale them with a ditty of their own. Panicked, the Thompson and Klosson children went back to the adjoining room for a quick huddle. Seeing the multiple bottles of booze and the stalwart but slightly slumping adults, they came up with a song to the tune of "Frère Jacques," which went: "I like vodka, I like vodka. Drink it up, drink it up. Mix it with martini, mix it with martini. Drink, drank, drunk. Drink, drank, drunk." Watching their parents' faces turn as white as the tablecloth, they realized that in their cleverness, they'd overstepped the bounds. Fortunately, after a moment of silence, Khrushchev roared with laughter. US-Soviet relations had not been destroyed. Khrushchev made a toast expressing great admiration and friendship for President Eisenhower and declared that if he could, he would vote for Ike. Thompson, on a more serious note, proposed his own toast to Khrushchev's work to improve relations between the two countries and said that he, Thompson, hoped they would "patiently continue their efforts despite reverses and obstacles that were certain to arise." He had no idea just how dramatic those reversals and obstacles would soon be.

Toward the end of that month, Thompson sent a long dispatch to the State Department in preparation for the upcoming Paris summit, scheduled to begin on May 16. This cable was a digest and an interpretation of how Thompson saw affairs were going in the Soviet Union, and, specifically, a review of the problems facing the Soviets at that time. He used it again to brief the Kennedy administration a year later. Thompson wanted to give those in Washington, DC, the context he felt was badly needed. He was concerned about the recent military reforms Khrushchev had initiated, but for very different reasons from those of the CIA. This move was popular with the general Soviet public, but not the military. It would put a lot of privileged military officers back into civilian life, bringing the total of "incipient Khrushchev opponents to an appreciable figure and could in future be a real cause of concern to him." Thompson perceived internal fissures developing between the country's Communist Party and the people. The inevitable failure of the "new Soviet man" to emerge could have possibly disastrous consequences for Khrushchev.[10] Moreover, there were the USSR's persistent economic and agricultural problems. Regarding external affairs, Thompson thought a complete break between the Soviet and Chinese Communists was a real possibility. A recent campaign to develop Khrushchev's cult of personality was further evidence of this, because, Thompson said, it had been mounted to counter Chinese attempts to discredit Khrushchev's promotion of peaceful coexistence. Thompson thought that if the United States pursued the peaceful coexistence Khrushchev was touting, it would make a split between the two Communist nations even more likely.[11] Thompson had the ability, as Robert McNamara would describe it decades later,[12] to empathize without sympathizing, and this cable was one attempt to get the people in Washington, DC, do the same: to see the issues from the Soviet (and Khrushchev's) perspective and thus better anticipate what the Soviet response to US policy might be.

Détente Continues

As planned, Henry Cabot Lodge came to Moscow to continue the Camp David discussions.[13] Meanwhile, the second Cultural Exchanges Agreement was signed in early 1960, but not without problems. With the exception of ballet and possibly classical music, there was the difficulty of an uneven demand. The United States only had so many movie theaters that wanted to show Soviet films, whereas everyone in the USSR wanted to see American films. With no private sector, the Soviet government underwrote its entire exchange program. The US side was funded by a combination of government support and private investment. American entrepreneurs, such as Sol Hurok, needed to make money on the exchanges, and that limited reciprocity, which was one of the cornerstones of the agreement. As for academic exchanges, the Soviets limited the foreigners' use of libraries and laboratories, thinking these students could be spies. Perhaps some were, but most weren't, and they saw no point in spending a semester in the USSR under those circumstances. The Soviet exchange students, in contrast, had freedom to travel and access to all American university facilities.

The Americans wanted to fix these issues in the new agreement, and it proved to be an arduous task. Thompson sat through a preamble by Yuri Zhukov, the chairman of the State Committee for Cultural Relations with Foreign Countries, in which Zhukov said terrible things about the United States and claimed that the only reason Americans wanted cultural exchanges was "to get more spies into the country." Thompson assured his cultural attaché, Hans Tuch, that he would answer Zhukov's harangue. Tuch anticipated that Thompson was now going to "let Zhukov have it." Instead, Thompson simply asked, "Are you quite through, sir?" Zhukov answered, "Yes." Then Thompson said, in a calm voice, "In that case, let's go on to the next point." "He discombobulated them," Tuch said, smiling as he remembered the scene.[14] Before the press conference, which was scheduled at the end of the negotiations, Thompson went over to Zhukov and said: "You have just made a very long and disagreeable comment. Now we can handle the press conference in two ways. You can continue on this course, or you could just say that we had a very interesting discussion and I would say thank you for your hospitality and that everything worked out fine. So you, Mr. Zhukov, decide which tack you want to take and I will follow." Zhukov got up and said the discussions had been interesting and useful.[15]

It is hard to measure, but also hard to overestimate, the importance of cultural exchanges. Thompson saw that with patience and exposure to each other as people, there could then come accommodation. After the signing of the second Cultural Exchanges Agreement, the United States sent a delegation of American composers—including two luminaries of contemporary classical music, Aaron Copland and Lukas Foss—to Moscow to perform and meet with Russian composers. By 1988, more than 50,000 Soviet scholars and students, scientists and engineers, writers and journalists, musicians and athletes, and government and Party leaders came to the United States, and tens of thousands traveled to countries in Western Europe. Of course, they were screened beforehand by the KGB, but come they did.[16]

Back in Washington, DC, for consultations in April 1960, Thompson met with Soviet ambassador Mikhail Menshikov. During their conversation, he hinted to Thompson that despite the recent successful test of the first French atomic bomb, progress on atomic testing and disarmament might be possible at the Paris summit.[17] Bohlen accompanied Thompson on his return to Moscow, and on the way they stopped in Paris, where they dined with journalist Cyrus Sulzberger. Thompson told Sulzberger that he was concerned about what would happen with the Berlin situation once President Eisenhower's visit to Moscow was over. The Soviets were letting things rest, Thompson thought, because Khrushchev wanted the trip to take place. Thompson also told his dinner companions that it would be a mistake to underestimate the seriousness of the trouble between the USSR and China.[18]

Thompson and Bohlen found time during Chip's stay to play a little poker and perform some music, Thompson on the violin and Bohlen on the Steinway grand piano in the Great Hall of Spaso House, with the dogs howling and the children raptly listening. In terms of diplomatic business, Bohlen accompanied Thompson on a courtesy call to the normally dour Soviet foreign minister, Andrei Gromyko. Gromyko expressed optimism for agreement on a test ban. Bohlen told Gromyko that he did not see much chance of progress on the Berlin issue unless the Soviets moved off their position. Gromyko did not offer that, but he did hint at hopes of an interim agreement.[19] In his follow-up cable after the meeting, Thompson wrote that Khrushchev would not sign a treaty with East Germany prior to hosting a visit from his "friend," Eisenhower.[20] But the "spirit of Camp David," the Four-Powers summit in Paris, and Eisenhower's proposed visit would all come plummeting down.

Détente Crashes

Since the use of espionage balloons in the early 1940s, the United States routinely organized reconnaissance (known as "ferret missions") that hugged the Soviet borders. The Soviets ran similar missions.[21] During the Cold War years, over forty American flights—not including the balloons—that breached Soviet borders were shot down.[22] Eisenhower was ambivalent about aerial reconnaissance. He wanted the intelligence information, but he feared the consequences and did not like the process, calling it a "dirty trick."[23] The record is murky on Eisenhower's specific authorization of these missions, but his frustration at their failures is clear, and he repeatedly had them stopped.[24] The reality of these flights was either denied, claimed to be accidental, or ignored altogether, unless it was necessary to recover a crew or equipment.

May Day Parade 1960

May 1, International Worker's Day, marked one of the most important Soviet holidays, with a week-long series of celebrations and meetings of the Supreme Soviet. It came at the start of a long-awaited spring, with its promise of new beginnings and liberation from the cold. In preparation, the Kremlin grounds were swept clean of the layers of soot and dirt exposed by the warming weather. That particular May Day, the third since Thompson's arrival as ambassador, was most unusual. Although Red Square sported the obligatory display of military firepower, this May Day was marked by banners promoting *druzba i mir* (friendship and peace). Schoolboys in red neckerchiefs and girls with white ribbons in their hair possibly outnumbered the tanks. The parade included floats of red-tipped, olive-green rockets and a three-story banner bearing Lenin's likeness. But it also included trucks festooned with huge silhouettes of peace doves, thousands of marchers carried pink-blossomed tree branches, and signs proclaiming the wish for a successful summit meeting in Paris.

Thompson and his family were in the crowd, as cheerful as the other ten thousand celebrants. After Khrushchev's trip to the United States, and with the prospect of the upcoming Paris summit, to be followed by Ike's trip to Moscow, everyone held some extra hope that maybe this was the spring when things would really improve. Jane said, "You wanted so much with all your heart and soul for there to be an understanding."[25]

In the middle of the festivities, Marshal Sergei Biryuzov, the head of Soviet air defenses, rushed up to the Presidium's reviewing box, perched atop the ziggurat-like tomb of Lenin, and said something in Khrushchev's ear. Khrushchev's mike was live, and the whole of Red Square heard him exclaim, "Well done!" Whereupon, Hans Tuch recalled: "They all climbed down from the tomb and disappeared. We were, of course, wondering: What . . . ?"[26] Thompson turned to his wife and said, "Jesus, I wonder what's happening now." He would soon find out that a U-2 spy plane, piloted by American Gary Powers, had been shot down.

The Flight of the U-2s

Eisenhower had the U-2 spy plane as an ace up his sleeve when he proposed Open Skies. The Skunk Works promised that their invention could peek into the Soviet Union without being caught.[27] Ike had seen photos from test flights over US cities and was amazed that he could even make out the lines for parking spaces.[28] The U-2s first made test forays out of Wiesbaden, to places around Eastern Europe. The success of these missions persuaded the president to permit a quick series of Soviet overflights. Because the planes flew out of West Germany, Eisenhower sent Richard Bissell, the special assistant to CIA Director Allen Dulles, to get Konrad Adenauer's approval, to which the Iron Chancellor enthusiastically agreed.[29] With permission in hand, Bissell sent a one-word coded message, authorizing the first U-2 flight over Soviet territory on July 4, 1956.

The camera for the spy plane was developed by Edwin Land, inventor of the Polaroid, and the film from it averaged 10 miles long. The photographic results from this initial U-2 flight over the USSR were rushed back to analysts, who read the strip of film in twenty-four hours.[30] The data from these early flights was highly useful, as they clearly disproved the "bomber gap" claimed by the US Air Force.

The spy planes, which could cruise at 65,000 feet, were thought to fly high enough to be unseen by Soviet radar. But right from the start, U-2 pilots knew the Soviets had detected them, because they recorded pings from radar and saw fighter planes from the USSR flying below, searching for them. The CIA, however, counted on Soviet aircraft and surface-to-air missiles (SAMs) not being able to reach the U-2's altitude. Once Eisenhower knew these spy planes were detected, he suspended the flights over the USSR. For the next three years, until 1959, it was an on-again, mostly off-again operation. Eisenhower argued that if the Soviets flew reconnaissance planes over the United States, the "reaction would be drastic," and he insisted that the development of the U-2 planes be a civilian operation, in order to keep it from being "legally an act of war."[31]

There were two currents flowing in Washington, DC, at the time: those who believed a large missile gap existed in favor of the Soviets, and those who thought this argument was overstated. Eisenhower and most in the intelligence community held the latter view, but neither could persuade the skeptics.[32] Bissell's U-2s were looking for ICBM sites that the US Air Force claimed were hidden around the 22 million square kilometers of Soviet territory. Ike may have hoped the U-2s would disprove the missile gap, or at least restrain those who wanted to raise the defense budget. That wish was pointless, however, as it is impossible to prove a negative. Even if the U-2s had not found any ICBMs, it would not have assuaged those who claimed the missiles existed someplace where the spy planes hadn't yet looked.[33] Moreover, an August 1959 report by the CIA estimated that the Soviets only had ten operational missiles—certainly not a missile gap in favor of the Soviets.

After a 1958 incident from an overflight of Soviet territory, CIA director Allen Dulles had told Thompson that such flights were being stopped.[34] Although Dulles, who favored human intelligence gathering, was less enthusiastic about the U-2 planes, he joined Bissell to plead with the president to restart the flights, and Ike finally authorized one in early spring 1960.[35] While Thompson was in Washington, DC, for summit preparations, a U-2 took off as planned on April 9. Soviet radar followed the plane turn for turn. It was only a fluke that the surface-to-air missile (SAM) site at Shari Shagan was not launch ready that day, and that plodding Soviet bureaucracy held up permission to use the top-secret Semi-palatinsk airfield until after the spy plane had passed. Khrushchev, not having been able to get the United States to even acknowledge his official complaints about earlier U-2 flights and hoping to avoid embarrassment because of the Soviet military's failure to deploy the SAMs, said nothing. He figured he wouldn't get anywhere until he could shoot one of them down.

US Air Force intelligence experts informed Bissell that the Soviet missiles could probably reach 70,000 feet, if the U-2s were detected in time.[36] The previous year, a Chinese-operated Soviet SA-2 missile brought down a Taiwanese-operated US reconnaissance aircraft, capable of flying at 65,000 feet. So Bissell clearly knew that the Soviets were able to take down one of his birds. Eisenhower worried that "if one of these aircraft were lost when we were engaged in apparently sincere deliberations, it could be put on display in Moscow and ruin my effectiveness."[37] Nevertheless, he approved one more flight, but it had to occur before April 25, to avoid risking an incident any closer to the upcoming Four-Powers summit, scheduled for mid-May.

Perhaps Eisenhower was emboldened by or misunderstood the fact that Khrushchev had not protested the April 9 flight. Or perhaps he was convinced by Bissell's assurances that the U-2 carried a self-destruct device, and that neither pilot nor plane could survive a crash from such an altitude. Neither was exactly true. The self-destruct mechanism was designed to render the camera inoperable, but it would not destroy the film, let alone the plane, and it had to be manually engaged.[38] The plane's large wingspan tended to make it go into a flat spin when control failed. This type of spin slowed its descent and lessened the eventual impact of a crash into the ground. Not only had the test planes not always disintegrated, but Skunk Works crews had actually salvaged parts from wrecked planes to build new ones.[39] As to the pilot's survival, those flying U-2s paradoxically carried both suicide and survival kits. Eisenhower's son John later complained, "They promised us the Russians would never get a U-2 pilot alive and then they gave the SOB a parachute!"[40]

The U-2s required good visibility to be effective, and the Strategic Air Command supplied weather forecasts for their operation. In the days prior to Ike's April 25 deadline for the cessation of Soviet overflights, the weather was reported to be bad: "Clouds and snowstorms concealed much of the route."[41] Allen Dulles and Bissell prevailed upon the president for an extension, in order to wait for the weather to clear. Eisenhower's trusted aide, Brigadier General Andrew Goodpaster, wrote in a memorandum for the record that Ike gave permission for an extension, but it had to take place *before* May 1. No flights were to take place *after* May 1,[42] leaving the date of May 1 in limbo—oddly ambiguous for something this important, especially considering the significance of May Day for the Soviets.

Historical weather data along the U-2 route, indicate that visibility and precipitation were actually better on a number of days between April 11 and May 1 than they were on April 9 (the date of the previous flight) or on May 1 (the date of Powers's flight).[43] Why did they not fly when the weather opened up? Was it because they didn't have accurate weather information? Was that information not accurately conveyed? And why couldn't they have waited until after the Four-Powers summit, such as sometime during June or July, the months that technicians had determined were the best for reconnaissance? The only apparent explanation is that the decision makers preferred to risk flying close to the date of the Paris summit rather than to that of Eisenhower's July trip to Moscow. At the very least, as Georgi Arbatov later put it, the whole incident of the disastrous U-2 flight and the way it was handled was "very revealing: the administration valued routine intelligence gathering higher than a chance to improve relations with the USSR."[44] Senator J. William Fulbright would later wonder: "Why, in the midst of those efforts by President Eisenhower and Khrushchev to come to some understanding, was the U-2 incident allowed to take place? No one will ever know whether that was accidental or intentional."[45]

Grand Slam

While waiting for the go-ahead for the U-2 flight, Francis Gary Powers cooled his heels in Peshawar, Pakistan. Pilots were assigned to different planes and, at the last minute, Powers' original plane was changed to a plane pejoratively called a "hangar queen."[46] It was the same plane that had made a belly landing in Japan's Atsugi base when Lee Harvey Oswald was a radar specialist for the U-2s there.[47] This was one of the oddities and coincidences that would later fuel conspiracy theories. There were also claims that Powers's plane was not equipped with the best camera. Enough questions lingered[48] that a few years later, President John F. Kennedy called Thompson into his office to ask him about the U-2 incident.

On the morning of May 1, at 6:20 a.m., Powers got permission for the flight. Because atmospheric interference made the prearranged secure channel unusable, the "go" signal was sent over open radio.[49] Though Richard Bissell had staked so much on this flight, he was on vacation in Europe, and it was Allen Dulles who gave the final OK. The flight was long, with a limited fuel load, so the route allowed for no deviations, and it was so tricky that some of Powers's colleagues devised bail-out plans.[50] It would have been highly unlikely for radar in the USSR not to notice Powers, since most of the Soviet airspace was clear on May Day. Indeed, the U-2 was picked up within fifteen miles of crossing the border.[51] After bungling the April 9 attempts to shoot down the plane, Soviet military personnel all knew it was hit this one or move permanently to Siberia, and clobber it they did. That's what Marshal Sergei Biryuzov was whispering in Khrushchev's ear as the brightly dressed boys and girls and the other marchers waving tree blossoms paraded by that May 1.

Aftermath

On May 3, the State Department issued the prearranged cover story for any lost U-2: a NASA research plane, on a joint NASA–US Air Force weather-service mission, had gone missing over Turkey after the pilot reported having trouble with his oxygen system. Two days later, when the weather had turned drizzly, Thompson and his political officer, Vladimir Toumanoff, sat side by side in the front row of the balcony overlooking the Supreme Soviet as Khrushchev addressed this key group. That seating protocol struck Toumanoff as unusual. Thompson, a relatively new member of the diplomatic corps, should have been placed farther back. Several hours into his speech on May 5, Khrushchev announced that the Americans had been "sending aircraft across our state frontiers and intruding upon the airspace of the Soviet Union." A sunbeam suddenly appeared through a skylight in the big building, spotlighting Khrushchev, the reflection making a halo on his bald head just at the moment when he shouted that the Americans had chosen to repeat their aggressive act "on the most festive day for the working peoples of all countries—May Day." He triumphantly proclaimed that the USSR had shot the spy plane down![52] Continuing his harangue, Khrushchev craned his head to look directly at Thompson and said, "So what was that, a May Day present?!" The Swedish ambassador, Rolf R. Sohlman, who was seated nearby, confirmed Thompson's complete surprise.[53]

Thompson went back to the chancellery, steaming mad. John Scanlan, one of the embassy's general services officers, recalled: "Thompson was furious. He was a very calm, quiet, very well-mannered person who rarely showed emotion. But I just happened to be in the elevator when he came back and he was obviously very upset. I wasn't in the meeting with him after that, but I was told that what upset him so much was the fact that Washington had not told him."[54] Thompson had been lied to about the U-2 program, and the Eisenhower administration had made a public relations mess of it. Thompson felt the flicker of hope he had allowed himself just days before sputter. He also told his diplomatic colleagues that he "had absolutely no information on the plane incident."[55] Thompson would speak of this betrayal with resentment, even decades later. He had received assurances from Secretary of State John Foster Dulles back in 1958 that there would be no further overflights of the Soviet Union without "specific authority of the president."[56]

That afternoon, after a meeting with his staff, Thompson sent a brief cable reporting on the revelation of the downed U-2 spy plane. He made a point of stating that Khrushchev avoided any mention of the fate of the pilot. Thompson thought this might be "a warning shot to us" and suggested "that he [the pilot] may have survived and be in Soviet hands," although the Soviets could also have been bluffing, without any knowledge about the condition of the pilot at that point.[57] Thompson left the office to attend one of those receptions that were going on all over town, this one hosted by the Ethiopian embassy at the Sovietskaya Hotel. It was clearly going to be uncomfortable, and he went without his wife, on the pretext that the children were ill. He hoped not to stay long.

Thompson did leave the reception early to write an analysis cable, but he sent a different one first. This one was labeled "MOST URGENT," warning those in Washington, DC, that the Soviets indeed had the U-2 pilot and, furthermore, that he was alive. Sohlman, the Swedish ambassador, had phoned Thompson to tell him that Soviet Deputy Foreign Minister Yakov Malik let it slip that the Soviets hadn't decided what article of the UN Charter they would use to protest the incursion by the US spy plane, because they hadn't finished questioning the pilot who had parachuted from it.[58] According to Sohlman, Malik also told the Indian ambassador that "the plane was flying at 60,000 feet and had been followed by radar all the way and was destroyed deep in Soviet territory."

Thompson's warning cable went out to Acting Secretary of State Douglas Dillon on May 5, stamped at 7:00 p.m. Moscow time, which was noon in Washington, DC.[59] His cable, however, was not logged in as received by the State Department until 1:34 p.m., making it four minutes too late to stop NASA's chief information officer from reading a second announcement, tying in with the agency's fabricated May 3 statement on the loss of its "research" plane near the Soviet border. How long it took cables from Moscow to reach the State Department varied wildly. A cable had to be typed into a coding machine at the embassy and then hand carried to the Soviet Telegraph Office in the Moscow Central Post Office for transmission.[60] What might have happened if Thompson's cable hadn't been waylaid for an hour and a half is anyone's guess. Officials in the administration did not yet have verification of the "rumor" that the U-2 pilot was alive, and Eisenhower may still have been convinced that the plane and its pilot could not have survived. If Thompson's cable had reached them earlier, those in the administration may have chosen to issue the NASA statement anyway, but they might not have woven the web quite so tightly around themselves.

After sending his alert cable, Thompson worked on one that dissected Khrushchev's speech to the Supreme Soviet.[61] He observed that Khrushchev had actually shown restraint, had squelched any hostile demonstrations by the audience, and had carefully considered his words, so as not to "slam any doors." As evidence of Khrushchev's careful approach, Thompson pointed out that the Soviets had moved toward the US position on underground testing and had confirmed Marshal Konstantin Vershinin's visit to the United States *after* the plane had been shot down. But no one in Washington, DC, would pick up on Thompson's suggestion that Khrushchev was trying to find a way to keep détente alive.[62]

That same evening, unaware of these developments, journalist Priscilla Johnson and Hans Tuch, the US embassy's information officer, went to a reception, hosted by the Union of Journalists at the Dom Zhurnalistov, celebrating Press Day.[63] This was the first time the union had ever invited Tuch to a Press Day affair. After Khrushchev's startling revelation at the Supreme Soviet, the Americans carefully observed the mood in town, trying to ascertain how deep the damage was. Johnson recalled that in the "morning we Americans were in good odor and treated with great cordiality." So when Adzhubei, the editor of the newspaper *Isvestia*, summoned Johnson to the head table, she passed through the smoke-filled, low-ceiling room without much concern. Once there, she was surprised to find Adzhubei surrounded by smiling Chinese faces, indicating that the mood had changed. Adzhubei took out his anger over the U-2 incident on her, throwing out obscenities. She was grateful for a sympathetic KGB official at her elbow, who promised to escort her from the premises if things got too rough. Johnson was expelled two months later because of the U-2 affair, one of the many times she would be sent out of the USSR and later readmitted. She racked up fourteen visas during her time in Moscow, and she credited Thompson with getting the Soviets to leave her alone after she confided to him that she was being harassed.[64]

Hans Tuch remembered: "When I arrived [at the press reception] I was immediately surrounded by a group of journalists, some of whom I knew, accusing the US of nefarious deeds, sending planes over Soviet territory. I responded, saying that it was an unfriendly act to shoot down a plane of a friendly country. One of the journalists whom I knew said, 'Gospodin Tuch,[65] what should we have done? The plane was flying over Sverdlovsk!' Incredulous, I said, 'Where did you say the plane was shot down?' Whereof the group abruptly faded away, leaving me standing there."[66]

Tuch immediately left the reception, reaching the ambassador's residence at around ten or eleven that evening, and found Thompson in his robe, nursing a glass of warm milk for his ulcer. Tuch hurriedly told Thompson that he knew the plane had been shot down over Sverdlovsk, one of the Soviet's nuclear test centers. Sverdlovsk was located just about in the center of that vast country, and it was the same city that intelligence officers on Nixon's plane had taken photos of prior to the opening of the American Exhibition (see chapter 18). Thompson told Tuch: "This is something Washington will want to know. Get over to the embassy, get hold of the communicator, and get an immediate message off to Washington within the hour." Supposedly, nobody in Washington knew where the U-2 had gone down, but it certainly wasn't in the area of Lake Van in Turkey, as NASA had claimed. In another mystery of timing, Tuch's cable with this critical news was not date stamped as having been sent until 6:00 p.m. the following day.[67]

Officials in Washington, DC, however, knew where the plane went down even before the Malik slip and Tuch's encounter, but they had inexplicably used the cover story anyhow. According to the CIA's paper on the chronology of the U-2 incident, on May 1, in the late afternoon, all key project personnel had assembled in the Agency's Control Center, along with officers from the air force, the press secretary from NASA, and Hugh Cumming, the State Department's director of intelligence and research. The CIA document clearly states that "on Sunday May 1 following the receipt of information that the U-2 was down in the Soviet Union *in the vicinity of Sverdlovsk*" [emphasis added], and goes on to say that "it was decided to issue a story from the base at Adana, Turkey, to the effect that a NASA high altitude weather plane was missing . . . in the vicinity of Lake Van."[68] Why, then, did they choose to go with a cover story that was so easily proven false? Journalist Michel Tatu speculated that if it hadn't been for the Americans' deliberately erroneous statements about the U-2, Khrushchev might have succeeded in "keeping things under control." It would have been possible to cloak a Paris summit failure under a "few reassuring generalities," giving Khrushchev a way out of his ultimatum on Germany.[69]

On May 7, Khrushchev closed the weeklong meeting of the Supreme Soviet with a bookend to his May 5 harangue—a long speech that presented concrete evidence of the U-2 flight. Thompson thought he should go to that session, despite knowing he would bear the brunt of more vitriol, because he thought it important not to hide. The State Department, however, advised him to stay home and send someone in his place that had the technical expertise to verify photos and other evidence.[70] Khrushchev confirmed that the plane's pilot was captured and gleefully presented images from the spy camera and photos of the wreckage of the U-2. When he divulged the poisoned suicide pin they found on Powers, the delegates erupted in chants of "Shame, shame!" Toward the end of his speech, Khrushchev left open a crack, saying that the affair was the fault of the "Pentagon and their monopolist allies," and that he was sure the "president knew nothing about the fact that such a plane was sent into the Soviet Union." The American technicians deemed the photos to be fake, and it was assumed that the Soviets didn't want to show just how accurate and detailed the real images were.[71]

After watching this speech on television, Thompson sent a series of cables back to the State Department. He described the mood of the Soviet citizens as one of "deep resentment—particularly [the] fact that [the] event occurred on May Day." He thought Khrushchev believed that this incident would put him "in [an] advantageous position at [the] summit. There is no doubt that we have suffered a major loss in Soviet public opinion and probably throughout the world."[72] Thompson speculated that "a more menacing interpretation" of Khrushchev's speech could be that certain recent events might have led Khrushchev to conclude that he would fail to gain ground at the Four-Powers summit and therefore was possibly exploiting the U-2 incident to mitigate negative world opinion were he to sign a treaty with East Germany.[73] Khrushchev was having some difficulties within his own government, and, although the evidence was slight, he might be using the U-2 as a "convenient diversion."[74] It was inevitable that all of Khrushchev's coexistence and cooperation rhetoric would pull the doctrinaire hard-line Communists out of the woodwork. Certainly the Chinese were quick to point out how "certain persons" had been misled by Eisenhower, and that Mao Zedong hoped this incident would make them wake up to reality.[75] Could these neo-Stalinists and the disgruntled personnel in the Soviet military now line up with the Chinese to cause Khrushchev real problems? This question, however, would not be answered until the Twenty-Second Congress of the Communist Party of the Soviet Union in October.[76] Secretary of State Christian Herter contributed to Khrushchev's difficulties when he made a very harsh speech on May 9, which was characterized as "turning the knife in the wound" by revealing that Soviet leaders had known about previous American surveillance flights.[77]

Thompson offered some "thoughts" in a cable to the State Department about how to handle the U-2 fallout.[78] It was no longer plausible to repudiate charges of a deliberate overflight. Eisenhower might deny actual knowledge of the mission, accompanied by some "drastic action" to prevent a recurrence without his knowledge. Thompson suggested that this would preserve the high regard the Soviets and other people had for the president. As Thompson also pointed out, the Soviet leader had described the dilemma he, Khrushchev, had put the president in. Eisenhower had to either admit his knowledge of the breach or deny it and be perceived as not having a firm grip on the nation's tiller.

Thompson also suggested issuing a statement affirming that both sides practiced espionage, and the Soviets had done so most successfully, due to their advantage in being able to "exploit the openness of our society." Because the Soviet Union had repeatedly boasted of its ability to destroy the United States and other nations, those responsible for America's defense felt it necessary to take every step to be able to ensure that protection. Importantly, Thompson stressed that any such statement be coupled with an admission of the impropriety of the U-2 overflight, and that it be accompanied by another one, asserting a continuing desire by the United States to achieve progress on political issues, particularly disarmament. He closed his cable with a recommendation that the Paris summit should not be called off, but that a final decision about the president's visit to the Soviet Union be delayed.

The department's statement used Thompson's rationale that spy flights were necessary, because of the closed nature of Soviet society, but those who crafted it did not follow Thompson's recommendation to acknowledge the impropriety of such a violation and America's desire to continue to seek agreement with the Soviets in other areas. Khrushchev interpreted this statement as indicating that the United States planned to continue the spy flights. Even after the Soviets shot the U-2 plane down and had its pilot in hand, not only were the Americans not contrite, but they simply ignored his proof and dismissed his outrage.

Two days later, Thompson and Khrushchev were both at an event at the Czech embassy. Khrushchev made a point of greeting Thompson warmly. He took the ambassador aside and assured him that he was certain Thompson knew nothing about the flight, which was true. Khrushchev also stated that he believed Thompson opposed such operations, which surely would have been true of this particular flight on May Day, so close to the start of the Four-Powers summit. Khrushchev then said he had something to tell Thompson "only personally." Thompson reported that Khrushchev divulged that he might cancel Ike's visit to the USSR over concerns that, after the U-2 incident, the president could be poorly received by the Soviet public.[79] Thompson, however, thought the opposite was true and that Khrushchev was worried that Eisenhower would be very well received, which would further embarrass the Soviet leader after having made such hay out of the U-2 affair.

Journalist Harrison Salisbury later wrote that Thompson told him about a private conversation between the ambassador and Khrushchev that evening. Khrushchev had confessed that shooting down the U-2 had put him in a "terrible spot," asking Thompson to help smooth things over, and Thompson promised to do what he could. When Khrushchev and Thompson rejoined the reception, several Soviet marshals "came up to Thompson . . . each with the same message . . . 'We don't want any war with the USA.'"[80]

In his public toast, Khrushchev repeated what he had already privately told Thompson—that he believed Thompson didn't know about the flight. He went on to say "with great force" that if the Soviet Union was obliged to conclude a separate treaty with East Germany and the West attempted, on the basis of that situation, "to use force, this would be met with force." Thompson said that although Khrushchev professed the contrary, the Soviet leader was adding fuel to the fire. After this belligerent toast, Khrushchev hounded the Norwegian and Pakistani ambassadors about their nations' roles in the U-2 flight. Thompson reported that the "whole performance shocked those of my colleagues who have not seen him put on this act before."[81]

At this point, preparations for Eisenhower's scheduled state visit in October were still on. The Americans had a beautiful fiberglass motorboat and trailer secretly flown in, with a brass plaque on the dashboard that commemorated the gift from Eisenhower to Khrushchev. On the Soviet side, it was rumored that Khrushchev took some golf lessons.[82] Could the Four-Powers summit still be saved?

"The Summit That Everyone Lost"

The Paris summit was originally planned for the end of 1959, but Charles de Gaulle stalled it until May 1960, to enable France to complete its own nuclear detonations before a possible accord on a test ban.[83] When Khrushchev visited France in late March for a pre-summit meeting,[84] the French president bluntly told him that there would be no agreement on Berlin. West German chancellor Konrad Adenauer didn't want a summit at all, because he was afraid that concessions would be made on Germany. Eisenhower, exasperated with this intransigence, seemed worn down by it all. Thompson was pessimistic about prospects for a resolution on the Berlin problem, but he was hopeful of some progress on disarmament. If the meeting produced a test ban and an agreement to continue working on the situation in Berlin, while forestalling a separate Soviet treaty with East Germany, then it would be a success.

Prior to the U-2 debacle, Khrushchev vacillated between optimism and worry about the summit's prospects. According to biographer William Taubman, in the "afterglow of Camp David, Khrushchev considered a summit agreement on Berlin almost a sure thing, and a test ban accord also likely."[85] Documents from British, East German, Russian, and American archives also indicate this.[86] When historian Kitty Newman compared those documents, she concluded: "Had the summit gone ahead, both sides might well have reached a compromise on Berlin. Thus the collapse of the summit was an even greater landmark in East-West relations than previously recognized." Because the failure of the Paris summit was a product of the consequences from Gary Powers's overflight, we would further assert that the U-2 incident is underappreciated as one of the seminal events in the Cold War.[87]

In the days prior to the Four-Powers summit, Khrushchev was stewing over what to do about the U-2 affair. On the one hand, he ordered the press not to print anything that might cause further tension. On the other hand, he was infuriated over what he saw as a personal betrayal. What stung Khrushchev was that he felt he had been fooled at Camp David and had never really been taken seriously. This perception would affect how he dealt with John F. Kennedy at a later summit. Khrushchev would not let himself be fooled again. Nevertheless, he still held out hope that he hadn't completely misjudged Eisenhower and that they might meet alone, before the formal summit, to work things out, so he arranged to be in Paris two days early.[88] Eisenhower, meanwhile, was also considering reaching out to his counterpart privately, to try to mitigate the damage, but Ike was talked out of it by Secretary of State Herter, who thought it might portray weakness on the part of the United States. Khrushchev never knew about Eisenhower's intentions in this regard, because an invitation for the two to meet in advance of the summit never came.

Khrushchev ruminated over what to do before he left for the Paris summit. He gave a bizarre performance at the end of a press conference, held where the wreckage of the U-2 was exhibited in Moscow's Gorky Park. Only a few correspondents had stayed on to witness Khrushchev standing on a chair, surrounded by the remains of the spy plane, and talking for over an hour. Priscilla Johnson said it was clear to her that Khrushchev had not made up his mind at that point. She remembered his performance as oddly surreal. Khrushchev went on as though he was debating out loud with himself about whether he should go to Paris. Michel Tatu, who was also present, wrote that it was the first time he detected "genuine embarrassment" on Khrushchev's part.[89]

Accounts differ as to whether Khrushchev's final decision was made at the Presidium meeting that took place a few days before his departure for Paris, or on the tarmac at Vnukovo airport, or even on the plane. Nonetheless, it seems evident that Khrushchev decided what to do at the last minute. He would demand a public and personal apology from Eisenhower, along with a commitment to stop any further "criminal" trespass of Soviet airspace and punish the perpetrators, as a prerequisite to the Soviet Union's participation in the Four-Powers summit. Eisenhower had already ordered the U-2 overflights to cease (mostly because the U-2 was soon to be replaced by satellite surveillance), but he hadn't made the decision public. So it was conceivable that a private pre-summit meeting with Khrushchev could have brought the two leaders to some kind of terms on this issue. But there was no way Eisenhower could accede to the other two demands.

On May 12, Thompson sent a cable from Paris, stating that Khrushchev might try to "extort maximum propaganda advantage from the summit rather than [make an] attempt at serious negotiation," which Thompson described as being a change in the Soviet leader's attitude.[90] He thought it likely that Khrushchev wanted to kill the summit meeting, because if it went badly and he got no concessions from the others, he'd be forced to take some kind of dramatic action on Berlin in order to save face. Failure to achieve anything in Paris could also jeopardize Khrushchev's position as leader of the Communist bloc. The Chinese were looking over his shoulder every step of the way. By the end of the summit conference, Thompson confided to Sulzberger that he was becoming skeptical of Khrushchev's odds for survival.[91]

On the morning of May 15, as Ike and his entourage were arriving in Paris, Khrushchev presented his demands in a meeting with de Gaulle and then left a written copy with the French president. Khrushchev reiterated those demands to Harold Macmillan later that afternoon. While the meeting between those two leaders was taking place, Eisenhower convened a roundtable session with the members of his group. Thompson thought that giving de Gaulle a printed version was direct evidence that Khrushchev was going to sabotage the summit.[92] Bohlen agreed. After all, Khrushchev must have understood that giving the French written proof of his demands eliminated any possibility of coming to a private understanding with President Eisenhower. The Americans wondered why Khrushchev had decided to come this far, only to break off the conference, and they tried to decide how to handle the situation publicly. Their rambling discussion shows that, if Khrushchev was improvising about whether to put the kibosh on the summit, the allies were winging it, too.[93]

The next morning, May 16, a communiqué came from Khrushchev, changing the format of the summit from private discussions between individual leaders to a more public forum, which would limit its potential. Herter cabled Washington, DC, saying evidence was mounting that the Soviets intended to "wreck the conference."[94] In Paris, Thompson worked out of an enormous office, under a US Marine guard, from which, British journalist Ed Crankshaw later wrote, he "modestly ruled the world."[95] Thompson was not at that day's 11:00 a.m. meeting, but he knew what to expect. When Khrushchev took the floor, he made his predictable tirade. Bohlen, who was taking notes, related in his memoirs that the longer Khrushchev spoke, the pinker Eisenhower's bald head became. Yet when it was the president's turn to speak, Eisenhower calmly stated what he had decided the week before: the aerial spying would be discontinued. He refused, however, to apologize for the flights. Khrushchev surprised Bohlen by asking the delegation to "please understand that our internal politics requires this, which is very important to us. It is a matter of honor."[96]

Testifying later before a congressional committee, Bohlen said it was the first time he'd ever heard a Soviet leader admit to internal pressures of that sort.[97] Khrushchev was stunned by the U-2 incident and its aftermath, because Camp David had convinced him that the Americans were ready "to talk." Georgi Zhukov told Sulzberger that the Soviets were appalled at the choice of May 1 for the flight and could not understand why Eisenhower had not reached out to meet with Khrushchev before the summit, in order to explain.[98] The Soviet leader had let himself believe that he shared in Eisenhower's trust, a trust that was now broken. For Khrushchev, the U-2 debacle not only was a political slight, it was also a profound personal slight. That evening, Thompson and some of the advisors had dinner with Eisenhower, after which there was a long, informal discussion. Most were pessimistic, saying that affairs were effectively at a stalemate. Neither side could retreat from its stated position. Someone suggested that Bohlen and Thompson visit with Gromyko to settle the dispute, but that idea was dismissed.[99]

On the morning of May 17, the heads of the three Western nations and a few individuals from their delegations assembled at the Élysée Palace to formally invite Khrushchev to the opening meeting of the summit at 3 p.m.[100] They reconvened at that time and waited, but Khrushchev did not show up. Macmillan was the most distraught—brought to tears—alarming the rest of the delegation.[101] He pleaded for the French president to make a personal appeal to Khrushchev, but de Gaulle dismissed the idea as being too byzantine. That finished it. After waiting for four hours, the three Western powers eventually agreed to a joint communiqué, stating that Khrushchev had not appeared and that the summit had, therefore, not taken place.[102]

Eisenhower went to the ambassador's residence to be checked out by his doctor, who feared that the week's events were straining his heart. The rest of the group went out for drinks. In a last blast before departing, Khrushchev held a multihour press conference, in which he shouted down hecklers and generally lost it.[103] The Parisian crowds booed and jeered him on his way out of the city. An odd sense of relief crept into the next day's meetings among the American delegation, where they strategized about Berlin and how to deal with the U-2 incident at the UN. Some, including Thompson, thought the Soviets had overplayed their hand and that the United States might not come out too badly in world opinion after all. Contrary to what Khrushchev might have schemed when he nabbed Gary Powers and caught US officials in a web of lies, the whole episode served to solidify the allies, hearten the Chinese, embolden Ulbricht (and his quest for an East German peace treaty), and anger pretty much everyone else.[104]

That evening, Thompson, his wife, and the Bohlens went to the American ambassador's residence for supper. Eisenhower sometimes relieved his stress by cooking, and he'd decided to have a barbeque in the small backyard. It is a testament to the ingenuity of Ambassador Houghton's wife, Laura, that she managed to find a barbeque grill and utensils in Paris for the president to make his famous steaks. Eating the steaks promptly as they came off the grill was essential, for Eisenhower took his cooking seriously.[105]

Summit Aftermaths

Eisenhower returned to the White House with a cheering crowd lining the route of his motorcade from the airport. Khrushchev also received an ovation from the crowd in East Germany, his next stop. Would he sign a treaty with Walter Ulbricht, the political head of East Germany? Thompson was so sure Khrushchev would not do it, unless further provoked, that he sent a cable from Paris back to the State Department, to try to forestall them from doing anything that might force Khrushchev's hand.[106]

Francis Gary Powers was tried and convicted on August 19, 1960, to ten years' confinement, but he was released in 1962 in exchange for a Soviet spy. Powers was ridiculed back home for not having committed suicide. Feeling betrayed by his country, he quietly settled in California, working as a helicopter pilot for a television station. He died in an accident when his helicopter ran out of fuel and crashed.[107]

In a tour-de-force of delusion, the Bureau of Intelligence and Research (INR) issued a postmortem report on the U-2 affair and the Paris summit, which ominously concluded that the Soviets doomed the summit in order to stop U-2 overflights from discovering that the Soviets were intensifying their ICBM construction.[108] The one good thing Eisenhower could have gotten out of the May 1 flight—clear evidence against the existence of a missile gap—was simply dismissed by the report's assertion that it just meant the Soviets were on the eve of an intense buildup. It appears that whatever the results of the overflights, they would have been made to fit the a priori conclusion that the Soviet Union was bristling with missiles. In reality, this observation better described the United States at that moment.

Conclusions

Khrushchev could not back down from his demand for an apology from the United States for the U-2 incident on May 1, once he made it public, and Eisenhower could not pretend that he did not authorize the flight. Khrushchev faced many foes in his overtures to the West. The Soviet military didn't like the possibility of détente any more than it liked Khrushchev's reliance on a nuclear arsenal, because it meant less funding for conventional weapons and troops. (The same could be said of Eisenhower and the US military.) The Chinese were pushing a hard line and mocking Khrushchev for not being a "true" Communist. Worse, hard-liners in his Soviet government agreed with them. To have the United States poking him in the eye just now was a severe embarrassment. Khrushchev couldn't ignore the insult, so he had no choice but to respond. His mistake was baiting the Americans and taking his comments to the point of provoking an equally strident response from them.

Eisenhower felt pressure from US Air Force officials, who insisted that the Soviets were producing new missiles by the day. He had conservative columnists, like Joseph Alsop, accusing him of being too soft on the Soviets, and he had political foes castigating him for being asleep at the wheel, playing golf instead of attending to business. Eisenhower's own strong military code of ethics said the buck stopped with him. Disavowing the decision to send the U-2 on a reconnaissance mission over the Soviet Union, thus making it seem as if he did not control his own government, was similarly not possible. He, too, had no choice. His mistake (besides agreeing to send the plane in the first place) was in not reaching out privately to Khrushchev when the latter had gone out of his way to offer the American president a way out. Khrushchev believed Eisenhower had been pressured to approve the U-2 overflight by dark forces around him. He even extended a private invitation to Eisenhower to visit the Soviet Union once the president left office, which Ike never accepted.

It is difficult to overstate the importance of the consequences of the U-2 affair. Khrushchev's decline in power seems "to date from this period."[109] If something concrete had come out of the Paris summit, it might have postponed Khrushchev's political demise and possibly changed the course of the Cold War. Khrushchev himself later claimed that the U-2 incident was the beginning of the end for him. In 1970, he said, "From the time Gary Powers was shot down in a U-2 over the Soviet Union, I was no longer in full control."[110] The spy plane contretemps increased Khrushchev's paranoia that the West was after him, and it buttressed the hard-liners in the Soviet government.[111] Although Khrushchev would later try to reset the relationship between his country and the United States when Kennedy became president, each step forward would have to clear the hurdle of the U-2 legacy.

21

Picking Up the Pieces

Do not include what you wished you had said
or leave out what you wished you hadn't said
in your reports to the Department.
—LLEWELLYN THOMPSON, speech,
 Foreign Service Institute, 1963

At the end of May, the Thompsons returned from Paris to Moscow to find the city looking particularly well—the trees on the boulevards had a shiny green tinge, and lilac bushes perfumed the air.[1] Even Spaso House had been transformed from a dull battleship gray to a happier yellow and white for Eisenhower's now-cancelled visit. Despite the pleasantness, the Americans in Moscow worried about how the failed summit would affect Khrushchev's "peaceful coexistence," as well as détente. Yet none of the embassy officers encountered hostility from their counterparts or from the public at large.[2] As Jane wrote home, "So far, the attitude of the locals toward us is about the same as always, and after our hectic stay in Paris, we find Moscow very relaxing." Thompson attended a dinner for Van Cliburn, where the Soviet cultural officials were courteous and avoided politics. He reported, "In general contacts remain friendly but anxious, hoping present tensions will disappear."[3] It seemed as though everyone wanted to get back to the pre–May Day atmosphere—everyone, that is, except Khrushchev.

Lest anyone think Khrushchev had forgotten what had happened that day, he put on an "outrageous performance" at a June press conference. He made statements like "A man doesn't go to dinner in a place he has fouled" to explain why he had to call off Eisenhower's visit, and he suggested that the American president would do well as a kindergarten teacher.[4] Khrushchev orchestrated 400 correspondents who were present to shout "Yes" to his question, "Am I being clear?" when he referred to a separate peace treaty with East Germany. Khrushchev could be crude, and he may have acted like "a woman scorned," but Thompson counseled the State Department not to take his performance at the press conference too seriously.[5] Khrushchev genuinely liked Eisenhower, Thompson noted, and his bravado probably stemmed from hurt pride. Thompson did, however, convey a worry that there *might* be more to it. Khrushchev's behavior toward the American ambassador was very different from their previous encounter at the Czech embassy, when he exculpated Thompson from knowing about Powers's U-2 flight. Khrushchev was, Thompson added, both impulsive and calculating. He might have been trying "to neutralize if not remove American bases around the Soviet Union." Or, with all the brouhaha, perhaps Khrushchev thought he could influence the upcoming American elections.

Thompson was concerned that, if Khrushchev continued attacking the president, it could become "virtually impossible" for Thompson to operate. He decided to pay a call on Leonid Brezhnev and Alexei Kosygin, to caution them about criticizing Eisenhower personally and to try to get the relationship between the two nations back on track. They talked about the current negotiations on disarmament and a ban on atomic tests, as well as about the cultural exchanges. Brezhnev replied that, given recent events, there should be a cooling-off period, but he saw bright prospects ahead in six to eight months, demonstrating the Soviets' willingness to leave the door open.[6] They were waiting until a new US president and his administration took over.

Khrushchev, as Thompson had reported, was furious, not only about the U-2 incident, but also because the Chinese were gloating that his peaceful coexistence policy was in tatters. This upset him as much as the overflight itself, and he lashed out. That summer, Khrushchev went on another tirade, this time "an anti-Chinese blitzkrieg," delivered at an unplanned visit to the Romanian Communist Party Congress on June 20.[7] In July, the Soviets announced that they would withdraw all their advisers from China. In addition, on June 27, Khrushchev pulled out of the Geneva disarmament talks, because no progress was being made. The Soviets' all-or-nothing position demonstrated that they were not serious about negotiations,[8] and the "missile gap" that John F. Kennedy kept citing in his campaign also hindered progress. The talks had degenerated into nothing but an exchange of propaganda.[9]

Moscow River outing, in the outskirts of Moscow, USSR, circa 1958. *From left to right,* the driver, Sonia Golofkina (head of the Bolshoi Ballet School), Nina Borisovna (*with cigarette*), an unidentified man (*wearing glasses*), and Jane Thompson. Thompson Family Papers.

Thompson left for the United States in mid-June, to participate in his first university graduation ceremony.[10] Harvard was awarding him an honorary doctorate. Jane stayed in Moscow, which was uncommonly hot that summer. Along with other Muscovites, she and the children spent afternoons at the Silver Forest, a park and recreational area by the Moscow River, dutifully followed by KGB escorts, who sweltered in their Volga cars while everyone else was splashing in the water. Feeling sorry for them, Jane offered the men watermelon, which they accepted gratefully. One particularly hot day, the KGB escorts couldn't stand it anymore and also went for a swim. They did not see the family packing up, and the ladies giggled as the men rushed to their car in their bathing trunks.[11]

Perhaps inspired by Eisenhower's cookout in Paris, Jane took to barbequing on the front veranda of the ambassador's residence. The smell of grilling steak and burning charcoal brought heads popping out of neighboring windows, as well as skeptical looks from the chef, but Jane carried on. Jane's Russian-language teacher was a large, stern-looking woman with a mustache hovering above lips overloaded with purple lipstick, which left smeary trails on glasses and cigarette stubs. Scampy, the Thompson's airedale terrier,[12] disliked the teacher. Despite precautions to lock him up when she was around, one day he managed to escape and bit her. Rather than risk any further mishaps, Scampy was banished to a stud kennel, where, by all accounts, he did very well. Since Thompson had said no to another dog, the girls collected several stray kittens and kept them in a huge birdcage they found in one of the basement storage rooms.

Yet Another Plane Goes Down

On July 1, 1960, a Boeing RB-47 reconnaissance plane, carrying six crew members, was shot down in the Barents Sea, off the Soviet coast. It was picking up signals just outside the Soviet borders. Soviet fishing boats rescued two Americans, navigator John R. McKone and pilot Freeman Olmstead, and recovered the body of another.[13] The other three crew members were never found. McKone and Olmstead were taken to the Lubyanka prison for interrogation, but the Soviets did not inform anyone of their capture for a week.

Not knowing about the downed plane, the Thompsons prepared for the American embassy's annual Fourth of July reception. Jane always did her best to put on a good show, and this year was no different. Van Cliburn, who had written to Thompson to congratulate him on his honorary Harvard University degree, was on a tour in the Soviet Union and promised to play at the event. After the U-2 crisis, no one was very sure of the state of US-USSR relations, so it was a pleasant surprise when top Soviet officials showed up, along with a near-record 300 other Soviets.[14] The party also included a busload of American tourists. So many people came that one lady wondered if Eisenhower hadn't arrived, after all. When Van Cliburn played Liszt's *Twelfth Rhapsody*, Mikoyan put a fatherly hand on Sherry's shoulder, and when Van Cliburn swung into some lively Russian songs, Mikoyan joined in the chorus. *Time* magazine wrote: "In Moscow, where parties are judged by the quantity and quality of Russian officials who attend, the US party was a smashing success. Some attributed it to the popularity of Ambassador Thompson, others felt it was another sign that coexistence is still Soviet policy in spite of Khrushchev's blustering. Said one Western observer: 'It was as if the U-2 incident and the summit collapse had never happened. The descent from the summit seems to have halted at the halfway mark.'"[15]

The Soviets allowed Thompson to make a second television appearance, on the occasion of the Fourth of July. He delivered a brief lesson on American civics, stressing the US government's system of checks and balances and the importance of a free press. He concluded by saying that he was encouraged by both countries' efforts to change the false impressions they had of each other: "We are quite aware that your country, no less than ours, is in a new stage of development and growth and that it would be just as much a mistake for us as it would be for you to rely upon stereotyped images of the past in evaluating national developments in the present."[16]

Once the US embassy learned of the imprisoned RB-47 flyers, it sent an official note to the Soviet Foreign Office every week, requesting the flyers' release. The embassy also asked for permission to visit them and sent along a care package of food, which the flyers never received.[17] While the interrogators tried to clarify exactly how the RB-47 had violated Soviet air space, Powers's trial was set to begin, and the Soviets made formal complaints about their ships being harassed.[18] In less than two months, US Air Force planes had buzzed Soviet merchant ships on twenty-three separate occasions, diving and frequently dropping objects.[19] Thompson later reported that he thought this had made the Soviet military "literally wild" and had played a role in their shooting down the RB-47. Setting the record straight, he added that it was not a one-sided affair, as the Soviets had also engaged in "improper practices."[20]

Respite

That August, Thompson concentrated on his family. He actually managed to spend several uninterrupted weeks with them on the island of Elba, off the western coast of Italy. While lying on the sunny rocks, the Thompsons talked about the upcoming presidential elections and what might change if John F. Kennedy won.[21] Thompson was extremely careful not to show a preference, but in Italy, everyone was relaxed, and the conversations took on a hopeful tone when Kennedy's name came up. He was young, energetic, and more likely than the Republican candidate, Richard Nixon, to try out a new attitude toward the Soviets.

The family's time on Elba was pure bliss—eating peaches the size of small melons, scrambling over rocks and diving into the sea, fishing, or walking to the nearby farmhouse/café where a communal TV kept all the neighbors entertained. After Elba, the Thompson women traveled farther south and stopped in Positano, along Italy's Amalfi Coast, to meet the young American girl taking Gill's place as the family's nanny.[22] Sally Chase was zaftig and chatty, with a southern drawl that fascinated her charges, accustomed as they were to the tall, lean Gill and her perfect, royal-sounding British English.[23]

While the family was away on their holiday, a few more cats mysteriously appeared in the birdcage. There were twelve altogether by the time the Thompsons returned. Then Jane noticed a strange marking on Sherry's arm, in the shape of a red circle. She had ringworm, a fungal infection transmitted by the cats. More cases followed, and the patients had to paint their rings with purple medicine, which was sort of fun if you were a kid, but Jane had to calm the hysterical Italian maid, who was certain her hair would fall out. The Thompsons finally decided that a dog was better than twelve cats. Jane took the train to Vienna, delivering Andy to her school in Florence, and returned with a playful boxer puppy, housed in a large orange crate with a mesh door.

When Thompson came back from the family's vacation on Elba, he wrote to Nixon, congratulating him on being nominated as the Republican Party's presidential candidate. He told Nixon that although several top Soviet officials were opposed to him, he had assured them Nixon was anti-Communist in the same way that they were anti-capitalists, and it did not mean that he was opposed to negotiations or agreements.[24] But Khrushchev just did not like the vice president, and Nixon felt the same way about him. Nixon wrote a note of appreciation for Thompson's comments on his acceptance speech as the Republican candidate and added: "It was almost as hard to prepare as the one we worked on together in Moscow until the wee hours of the morning! . . . We shall be looking forward to Khrushchev's visit [to the UN General Assembly] with interest. I was wondering if he might decide to take the trip in one of their rockets. He isn't, of course, a dog, but most people think he is a son of a ——!"[25] Nixon hoped to get Powers and the two RB-47 flyers released before the election,[26] but despite Thompson's attempts to show Nixon in a more palatable light, Khrushchev purposefully said "*Nyet.*" Khrushchev had, in effect, cast his vote for Kennedy.[27]

In late August, Thompson saw Foreign Minister Gromyko, in order to press for the flyers' release. After giving Gromyko some time to pass his request on to Khrushchev, Thompson approached the Soviet leader directly, at a Kremlin reception on September 7, to test the waters.[28] Khrushchev began to banter with him, in a loud voice, over the U-2 affair. Thompson, who was standing with the rest of the diplomatic corps, had no escape. All eyes were on him. "How was the Soviet Union supposed to capitulate in the face of such aggression?" he asked Thompson. As the entire diplomatic corps crowded around, Khrushchev said, "This is how Eisenhower should have handled his mistake." He proceeded to step on Thompson's toe and then said, "Excuse me!"[29] Thompson grimaced, not because Khrushchev had trod on him particularly hard, but because of a corn on his foot. Trying to suppress a painful expression, Thompson calmly replied that he did not think the reception was the place or the time to discuss such a matter. Khrushchev then linked the U-2 flight to the RB-47 one, to justify his indignation. Thompson asserted that the RB-47 had not violated Soviet airspace, and the Americans had evidence to support this contention. Khrushchev did concede that "these planes [fly] very high and it was easy for a pilot to make a mistake."[30]

Thompson and Khrushchev then traded examples of violations. A US submarine had entered the Gulf of Riga and got away. Soviet ships were constantly along US borders, and a Soviet plane overflew Alaska. At this point, Khrushchev changed the subject. Thompson looked at his watch and suggested that, since Khrushchev was the host, he, Thompson, had better leave first. Khrushchev insisted that they leave at the same time and agreed to receive Thompson the next day. As they began to walk out, the entire diplomatic corps followed closely behind, in case anything else happened before the two men parted.

The Conversation

Their private meeting the next morning lasted an hour and half without translation, the equivalent of what would otherwise have been a three-hour conversation.[31] Thompson played with his cigarette lighter, sliding it through his thumb and forefinger, flipping it over, and then repeating the action, while Khrushchev gesticulated wildly and made angry accusations. It was impossible to tell if Thompson's occasional wince was from his own cigarette smoke or Khrushchev's commentary.

Khrushchev claimed the RB-47 was evidence of a continued US policy to fly spy planes over Soviet territory. Thompson rejected this, since President Eisenhower had publicly stopped the U-2 flights. Khrushchev declared, "We don't care what type of plane it is." Thompson replied: "Well, actually there is a big difference between the two. The U-2 flight over Soviet territory was deliberate, whereas the RB-47 had strict orders *not* to fly over your territory."[32] Khrushchev reprimanded Thompson: "No, look, the United States should not act like this. This is not right."[33] He then threatened: "The Soviet Union is not just Afghanistan, a country that can only protest. . . . We can also defend our sovereignty through our own power." Thompson leaned in and gravely stated that he'd said what he was instructed to. Then he went on: "But now I would like to just make some personal remarks. As you know I have been trying in every way to facilitate relations between our two countries . . . [but] both sides act based on preexisting mistrust and concerns regarding each other. Each side is convinced that they are the one who wants peace and so both sides think that everything they do is defensive and therefore justified. At the same time, the other side considers those moves provocative and threatening. This is a vicious circle and, honestly, I don't see a way out of it."

"The United States could treat the Soviet Union as an equal," replied Khrushchev. "As things stand, the United States has only shown disrespect toward our country." Thompson sighed at this repetition of a theme: "I know there was never any intention to humiliate or discount Soviet power. On the contrary, it was the United States' fear of increased Soviet power that drove many US actions." Alluding to Berlin, Thompson added that the many difficult current situations, such as with the Congo and Cuba, made it important not to take any actions that could possibly hinder mutual understanding. But Khrushchev would not give up. After he had made positive statements "to the world" about his friendly conversation with Eisenhower, the United States had turned around and justified its right to fly over Soviet territory "by saying we were keeping secrets." "If the United States had not taken such action," Khrushchev went on, "there could have been a productive meeting in Paris and we could have received Eisenhower as a guest of honor. But if someone comes to visit you and you catch him redhanded throwing a dead cat over your fence, you could not respect yourself if you received him as an honored guest."[34] Khrushchev then instructed Thompson *not* to report what he was about to say, whereupon Thompson stopped taking notes.[35] Khrushchev liked and respected Eisenhower and had been criticized for it. He still believed that Eisenhower did not know about the U-2 flight on May 1. He conceded that Eisenhower was faced with an impossible choice: to admit he had not known what was going on, or acknowledge guilt. "What an absolute disgrace to prepare for a visit and at the same time to deceive the person you are going to visit. Well, we believe that a certain reconciliation will happen, but not while President Eisenhower is in office."

Warmed up now, Khrushchev went on to deliver an invective against the American electoral system. He stated that all the candidates lied, and that there was no difference between the parties, as both represented monopolistic capitalism, while noting that there was no labor party. He scoffed at American labor leaders, calling them sellouts and declaring, "One day the working class will have its say." He confessed that "certain Communists" accused him of being on "an imperialist leash." Then he refuted that there was any split in the Communist Party, claiming that everyone supported peaceful coexistence. He also denied that the USSR used war to force social change in other countries, but he admitted to using unrest "to the advantage of the working class. . . . They say we want to bury capitalism. It's not us who will do it. Capitalism is creating contradictions and it will bury itself."

He boasted of the meteoric increases in Soviet industrial output: "In 1970 our output per capita will have caught up with your country. How can you explain such fast growth? Certainly not because Uzbeks, Ukrainians, or Russian are smarter than Americans, but rather because we have a different social system." He leaned toward Thompson and said, "Having been ambassador here for three years, you can judge for yourself how far we have progressed." Thompson, outwardly patient and calm, rolled his lighter and nodded his head, saying, "That's true." Khrushchev then continued: "You often speak about freedom under your system, but surely you have seen the extent to which people here are free. You are free to go [he was about to say 'anywhere' and corrected it] where you like in and around Moscow."[36]

Thompson was about speak, but Khrushchev was on a roll. "He exuded confidence and it was impossible not to be convinced that he genuinely believed what he was saying," recalled Thompson.[37] "In the future," Khrushchev bragged, "mankind will recognize our system is the right one and then Communists will triumph. . . . You believe capitalism is everlasting—at least Rockefeller says so. But we believe it is just a transitory period and that in any case your grandchildren will live under Communism, so let's live in peace and resolve controversial issues amicably." Thompson listened until all the steam finally poured out of Khrushchev's long-winded monologue. When Khrushchev was done, Thompson replied: "I am glad that although you consider Communism the best system, you support . . . peaceful competition as opposed to a violent solution. Personally I don't agree yours is a better system and you have not convinced me." Khrushchev responded, "Well I am not going to waste my time trying to convince you." "No, and I won't try to change your mind either," said Thompson.

Nonetheless, Thompson did argue about the economic points Khrushchev made and offered to send him research articles comparing the US and Soviet systems, prepared for the Joint Economic Committee of the US Congress.[38] Thompson mentioned that the growth of US heavy industry was slower than that of the Soviets, because the United States did not need such accelerated growth. "You want to catch up with us in butter output," he said as an example, "but we have as much butter as we need to meet demands and so why would we want to out-produce you? Your rate of industrial production is higher than ours but our system is geared to produce what we need." "Yes, I see," Khrushchev nodded, and then added, "Yes, I would like to see those articles."

Thompson admitted that it was "painful" for him to talk about the U-2 incident, but he wanted to clear up any misunderstanding. Herter's statements about the affair were perhaps ambiguous, but Thompson noted that the secretary of state had not meant to say the flights would continue and alleged that Khrushchev was "blowing the situation out of proportion" for propaganda reasons. He also offered a reminder: as soon as Khrushchev had arrived in Paris, he had given de Gaulle a written demand for an apology from Eisenhower, which the Americans interpreted to mean that the Soviet Union was unwilling to reach an agreement at the summit meeting. Thompson continued: "I also think you have misjudged the president. I would admit, although I don't have all the facts with me, and this may be indiscreet for me to say, but the president definitely was not aware of the U-2 flight."[39] Khrushchev then touched Thompson on his arm, saying, "Please keep in mind I will never use these words against you." Thompson smiled wanly, as he would report the conversation himself to the State Department later that day.

Thompson then changed the subject and said he hoped nothing would be said during the US election process that might jeopardize settling disputes between America and the USSR. Khrushchev tried to get Thompson to admit that this meant he did not want the RB-47 flyers put on trial before the elections. "No," replied Thompson, "what I want is for them to be released in order to begin a new era of relations between our two countries." Khrushchev said that releasing the airmen without a trial would harm the Soviet Union's reputation, so he would postpone *any* action until after the elections. Thompson replied, "Well, my position is to have them released *before* the elections." Smiling, Khrushchev said: "You know, this is your first position . . . as they say, your 'maximum position.' But you see there is a 'minimum position' too, which perhaps should be taken." The two men then said goodbye, and Thompson wished Khrushchev a good, safe trip to New York City. Knowing the Soviet leader's upcoming visit to the UN would probably not go smoothly, Thompson told him to expect stormy seas, because of a recent hurricane near Puerto Rico. Khrushchev smiled, and jokingly asked Thompson to make sure there were no hurricanes.[40]

A year later, Senator Albert Arnold Gore Sr. reported to then-president Kennedy that a friend of his talked to Khrushchev about the downed RB-47. He claimed Khrushchev told him that "when Thompson came to see him about the release of the RB-47 flyers, he came with a proposition from the administration that if he [Khrushchev] would release the flyers, he would set himself in right with Mr. Nixon, the next president." Neither Thompson's nor the Soviets' reports of the same conversation, however, indicate that this happened.[41] A comparison of the two countries' reports shows that the accounts of these conversations were virtually the same.[42]

Emerging Nations

At the UN General Assembly meeting, Khrushchev was disappointed again. The Third World countries that had asked him for help did not vote in favor of his resolution to restructure the UN. He had hoped to have a troika of a Communist, a capitalist, and someone from an unaligned country replace the UN secretary-general, Dag Hammarskjöld, who he believed was meddling in the Congo. Some say that Khrushchev pounded the lectern with his shoe during this UN session, although there is no photographic evidence of this, and eyewitnesses do not concur.[43] In the midst of all the banging, whether with a shoe or a fist, Macmillan is reputed to have calmly asked, "Could somebody please translate that?"

Thompson worried that the American government's backing of colonial regimes and lack of a clear policy regarding emerging nations left those nascent governments vulnerable to the Communists' idealist propaganda. Although the forces resisting colonialism were, for the most part nationalistic, not Communistic, if the United States ignored them, they would have no alternative other than to reach out to the Soviets for backing, and some did just this. Khrushchev's diversion of resources to the Third World raised resentment toward the USSR among the other Communist bloc nations, especially when the aid went to countries not committed to Communism.

The year 1960 was the year of Africa. Seventeen countries became independent, one of which was the Congo. When it ceased to be a Belgian territory, on June 30, 1960, Joseph Kasavubu was elected president and Patrice Lumumba became prime minister. These two men were the leaders of rival political parties, and a power struggle soon ensued.[44] Hammarskjöld sent in peacekeeping troops to try to restore order. In the meantime, Joseph Mobutu, chief of staff of the Congolese army, staged a coup, with CIA help. In the struggle for power, Lumumba would be assassinated, and Hammarskjöld, while mediating the conflict, died in a plane crash.[45] The circumstances of the two deaths were never clarified, but many believe that Allen Dulles and the CIA were involved in the Lumumba affair.[46]

In summer 1960, the Eisenhower administration was developing a strategy for the removal of Fidel Castro, the prime minister of Cuba, who had shown undeniable signs of turning toward the Soviet bloc.[47] Moreover, trouble began brewing again in Southeast Asia. Laos, proclaimed a sovereign country by the Geneva Accords of 1954, was a complicated mess, with varying factions and members of the royal family vying for power.[48] Although Laos was supposed to be neutral, the Americans viewed the country's government with suspicion, because of its willingness to deal with the Communist Pathet Lao.[49]

Children's Détente

When the Thompson girls invited their Soviet friends from the *ploschad* to come into the Spaso House garden to play, some of the youngsters worried that the guard at the gate would arrest them. Other kids said that the Americans wanted to hurt the Soviet Union and did terrible things to their own people. If they came inside the embassy grounds with the American girls, something awful might happen to them, too. Finally, a small group decided that it was worth the risk to see what was behind the fence. The policeman at the gate, however, said "*Nyet*" when they tried to walk through. Being children, Jenny and Sherry put their minds to circumventing another incomprehensible adult attitude. They enveloped the new puppy's kennel with a sheet and put it on their little red wagon from Sears and Roebuck. It looked just like the covered wagons they'd seen in Colorado, except for the horse. Instead, they substituted a bicycle, hooked to the handle of the wagon. The girls went into the square, past the unsuspecting guard. Once around the corner, they squeezed two or three children into the kennel and took it back to the embassy, past the guard, and into the backyard, where they unloaded their booty onto the grassy lawn. They repeated this until the backyard was full of children.

Tung, the Chinese butler, seeing the activity through the pantry window, instinctively brought out juice and cookies on silver trays and passed the refreshments out to the astonished children, as if they were important foreign dignitaries. It was already dusk before any other adult realized what had happened. Jane, certain that the Russian children's parents must be worried, explained that it was time to go home, but the youngsters were now afraid to walk past the guard. One little girl cried and asked if she could just stay forever. Jane explained that this was not possible, but said that the child could come back whenever she wanted.[50] Jane then lined up the children. "Follow me," she ordered, and, with Sally at the far end of the procession and her daughters on either side, she led the group out past an open-mouthed guard, who scrambled into his little hut to make calls. By the time he came out again, everyone had disappeared.

The White House Changes Parties

John F. Kennedy (JFK) defeated Richard Nixon in November 1960 by a very small margin, and this lack of a substantive mandate would mark the start of his presidency. Reporters asked Thompson for his opinion of the outcome, and he answered that his job was to follow orders from whomever won. He declined to say whom he voted for, but his daughter Jenny did it for him, stating, "But daddy, we all know you were for Kennedy!" The embarrassed ambassador could only smile and avert his eyes. Khrushchev also said he knew Thompson was for JFK, even before the election, although it was not clear where he got this information—most likely from hidden microphones in Spaso House.[51]

Soon after, Walter Ulbricht visited Moscow to press the issue of a separate East German peace treaty with Khrushchev.[52] Two years had passed since Khrushchev's ultimatum, and nothing had happened regarding Berlin. Khrushchev had put the issue on hold, waiting for the new administration in the United States. Now it was time to plan strategy. Khrushchev did not want Ulbricht to take unilateral action in Berlin before a summit meeting with the new American president. Ulbricht wanted the treaty, but he was also afraid that it could hurt East Germany, should the West respond with a boycott. He groused that "if East Germany had gotten the kind of aid that West Germany had gotten from the United States in the first postwar decade, it would not have such serious economic problems."[53] Khrushchev suggested that they could gradually push the Western powers out of Berlin, but not by force. At the end of January, he wrote to Ulbricht that their probe to the president-elect indicated Kennedy needed time, until he "stakes out his position on the German question more clearly."[54] The probe Khrushchev was talking about was through Thompson, but also JFK's "back channel" at the Soviet embassy in Washington, DC, the journalist (and Soviet intelligence agent) Georgi Bolshakov. Kennedy, however, had no clear idea what he was going to do about Berlin, except to wipe the slate clean of everything that had been worked out under Eisenhower.

Sino-Soviet Split

At the same time that Ulbricht pressed Khrushchev, a meeting of 81 Communist parties took place in Moscow. Discussions centered on a dispute between the Soviets and the Chinese. The Soviets insisted on being the "vanguard of the Communist movement," while China wanted to call them the "leader of the Communist bloc," revealing the importance of language in Communist thinking. Thompson found this interesting, because leadership implied an obligation to help the more economically backward bloc countries.[55] This distinction would not be appealing to the Soviets, given that much of the Communist bloc was facing serious economic problems. As the vanguard, the Soviet Party would have greater freedom of action.

Thompson's ulcer flared up so badly that it kept him in bed for two weeks. He didn't make it to the New Year's reception at the Kremlin, so Jane went alone and sat next to Mrs. Khrushcheva. Khrushchev toasted, "We would like to believe . . . that with the coming of a new president, a fresh wind will blow."[56] As usual with Khrushchev, the winds would blow hot and cold.

22 ≋

Working for the New President

The most discouraging aspect of East-West negotiations is that
both sides look at the same set of facts and see different things.
—LLEWELLYN THOMPSON cable, February 1, 1961

The next year, 1961, started with bad news from Colorado. Thompson's mother had fallen and broken her hip. She was extremely frail, and her doctors doubted that she would recover well. The other bad news was Khrushchev's January 6 speech to a group of Communist Party ideologues. Jane called it "a real lulu."[1] The published version ran to more than forty-four pages, and the original was twice that.[2] Thompson reported that the speech was nothing out of the ordinary, and it was such a good example of Khrushchev as a Communist propagandist that he advised members of the new administration to read the entire speech. There were other sides to Khrushchev, Thompson added parenthetically. Perhaps he should have expounded on this, because JFK overreacted. If the president had read the speech as a propaganda act, he might have been better prepared to deal with Khrushchev-the-ideologue at their meeting in Vienna later that year.

In this speech, Khrushchev emphasized that he was against all wars—not only nuclear, but any wars that might involve the Big Powers. JFK and his advisors, with Thompson as a notable exception, focused instead on the part dealing with wars of liberation in the Third World. Struggles for national liberation and popular uprisings, Khrushchev stated, were indigenous and could not be prevented from the outside, but, he also added, these "sacred wars" had to be wholeheartedly supported. A year later, Khrushchev would clarify to the *New York Times*' Cyrus Sulzberger that he meant no nation had the right to wage war to liberate another, but that the Soviets recognized the right of people within a country to rise up and fight for their own liberation. Although Thompson would say some years later that the phrase "wars of national liberation" was simply a euphemism for subversion, he believed that, in this speech, Khrushchev meant he was shifting the Soviets' challenge to the West to anticolonial struggles, *instead of* East-West conflicts (even local ones).[3]

When Thompson discussed the speech with a young Foreign Service officer, Raymond Garthoff, they both agreed that Khrushchev was trying to back the core of the Communist ideology, as well as placate China's criticism of the Soviets, while also continuing détente

233

with the West. Soviet interlocutors later reported that Khrushchev was greatly disappointed that JFK didn't understand this, and he took Kennedy's reaction as a rebuff.[4] A few weeks later, JFK held a press conference where he expected to be questioned about Khrushchev's speech. That didn't happen. Instead, its focus was on the amazing announcement that the two imprisoned RB-47 flyers had been released.

The American Airmen Go Home

"You'll never guess who just called me," Thompson told his aide as he hung up the receiver. On Saturday, January 21, the day after JFK's inauguration, Khrushchev telephoned Thompson at the embassy and asked the ambassador to come see him. This was the first time Khrushchev had called directly or asked to see anyone during the weekend, so Thompson suspected good news. Khrushchev looked tired and sounded hoarse. He congratulated Thompson on the president's inauguration. Khrushchev said Kennedy's inaugural address contained some constructive elements, so he would have the full text published in the Soviet papers, humorously adding, "If they agree to do so." Khrushchev then came to the point. He wanted to release the RB-47 pilot and navigator as a goodwill gesture. Furthermore, the Soviets would not insist on discussing the "aggressive actions of the USA" (meaning the U-2 flights) at the next UN General Assembly. Instead, "let the bad past not interfere with our joint work in [the] name of [a] good future." To make the aviators' release happen, however, three conditions had to be met: (1) the announcement would be made simultaneously by both countries, (2) the United States would not generate a propaganda campaign against the USSR, and (3) the Americans would provide assurances of no more secret flights over Soviet territory.

Having finished with business, Khrushchev began another one of his long, rambling conversations with Thompson.[5] He said he was sympathetic to the difficulties Thompson had had as ambassador, because of the "uneven policy" of the American government. Thompson answered that, actually, he was convinced he had been a poor ambassador, as there were clearly wide misunderstandings on both sides, but particularly by the Soviets. Referring to Khrushchev's January 6 speech, Thompson said that the major difficulty was the Soviets' interpretation of everything through Marxist eyes, as a class struggle. Americans, on the other hand, were not concerned about Communism as an economic system. Many in the United States thought of the Soviet Union in terms of the worst days of Stalin, whereas the Soviets thought of capitalism in the West as it was in the days of Marx.[6] Both situations had changed.

What worried the West was that once a country became a member of the Communist bloc, the whole power of the bloc was used to make sure it remained Communist, regardless of the wishes of the people. Thompson cited Hungary as an example. Khrushchev retorted that the Soviets neither wanted to nor could dominate the world. Thompson read a quote from Khrushchev's January 6 speech, where the Soviet leader said he would do everything to "maintain [the] unity of [the] Socialist bloc." Thompson asked if this included using force. Khrushchev replied that he meant Communist countries had to make mutual concessions, in order to preserve the strength of the bloc. Thompson responded that it was impossible for him to believe that there would not still be a monolithic system until some country that had become Communist was allowed to change its system, stating, "I believed the Soviet people in general supported the system here, but this is not true of most other Communist countries."

Khrushchev observed that Hitler had counted on the people turning against the regime when he invaded the Soviet Union, but he had been wrong. Thompson corrected him and said that there had been serious disaffection in the early days, which even Molotov had been worried about. Hitler had helped the Soviets out by mistreating their country's population and calling the Germans a master race. Khrushchev retorted that Hitler was a fool, and that, "if he had been wise, he would not have been Hitler, but Stalin."

Khrushchev said there were "many problems for the new administration regarding the USSR, and . . . not everything could be done at once, but we could make [a] good beginning with [the] main subject" discussed that morning. Khrushchev then asked Thompson if he would remain as ambassador, but Thompson still did not know if this would happen. With a smile, Khrushchev said the Soviets would gladly give Thompson their vote, but he was not sure if that would be helpful. Thompson, smiling back, said he also had some doubts.[7]

Thompson advised his government to accept Khrushchev's conditions for the airmen's release. JFK's national security advisor, McGeorge Bundy, remembered that Kennedy regarded the offer with "a certain wariness" and wondered if there wasn't a trick sewn into the bargain. Nonetheless, JFK accepted and agreed to schedule the announcement for his press conference on Wednesday, January 25. Therefore, the two Americans had to be released by that day. Khrushchev was now out of town, but Thompson secured Soviet confirmation in the nick of time, at 9:30 p.m. on Tuesday. An American surgeon and an air attaché, plus their wives, had plane reservations for a KLM flight out of Moscow, and arrangements were made for the wives to give their seats to the released prisoners. This was done so that no one would find out what was happening before the joint public announcement in the United States and the USSR, although there was a buzz in the Moscow air.[8]

The RB-47 pilot and its navigator arrived at the US embassy in an ambulance on Wednesday morning. They were met by Thompson and then taken to the air attaché's apartment to wait until it was time to go to the airport. When they got there, the port authorities waved the four Americans onto the plane without checking passports. Just as the plane was ready to take off, both tires burst and all the passengers had to leave the aircraft. New tires had to be flown in from Vienna, which delayed the takeoff for four hours. It was past midnight Moscow time when the plane finally was airborne. In his press conference, JFK was able to announce that the two former prisoners were now en route home, and that American flights penetrating the air space of the Soviet Union would not be resumed. Given the importance Khrushchev had attached to the whole U-2 incident, releasing the RB-47 flyers suggested that he was ready to resume détente. Five days later, JFK gave Khrushchev an indication that he, Kennedy, was not.

Kennedy Comes Out Swinging

At the traditional transition meeting that Eisenhower and JFK had before the inauguration, Eisenhower focused on the Third World.[9] It was imperative, he told the young president-elect, to keep Laos out of the Communist bloc, lest still more dominoes tumble. If Laos fell, Thailand and other countries in the region would collapse. The other priority problem was Cuba. Eisenhower had already started plans to get rid of Castro, and Kennedy only had to follow through on them. Eisenhower didn't even mention Berlin or suggest that this was a point of difficulty with the Soviets. As a result, JFK made his position on the Third World clear right away, rather than be taken for a weak president—a preoccupation that would color many of his early foreign policy decisions.

In his State of the Union address on January 30, Kennedy said: "The first great obstacle is still our relations with the Soviet Union and Communist China. We must never be lulled into believing that either power has yielded its ambitions for world domination—ambitions which they forcefully restated only a short time ago [referring to Khrushchev's January 6 speech]. . . . To meet this array of challenges—to fulfill the role we cannot avoid on the world scene—we must reexamine and revise our whole arsenal of tools: military, economic, and political." He asked his secretary of defense, Robert McNamara, for a reappraisal of the entire US defense strategy and gave orders to accelerate America's submarine programs, as well as to bolster economic assistance programs for Third World countries. The president did not mention East Germany or Berlin even once. Khrushchev was disappointed. Not only had JFK ignored what mattered most to the Soviet leader, as well as misunderstood Khrushchev's intentions in the January 6 speech, but JFK seemed to be promising more trouble. Khrushchev's enthusiasm to find accommodation with the new president began to wane.

Starting Over

Perhaps sensing this, Thompson wrote a series of expository cables to the new administration in late January and early February. In one of the first, he suggested an early, informal meeting between JFK and Khrushchev, "before the president [is] in a position where he could be expected to take definitive positions on controversial issues."[10] The main reason for the two leaders to meet would be to enable JFK to "convince Khrushchev of his intention not to seek solutions by force and of his willingness to undertake serious negotiations."

Thompson stated his opinion, which was that US policy was affected by "grossly overestimating" the USSR's military strength. The Soviet attitude toward inspections was evidence that their nuclear program was not as strong as the United States had given it credit for.[11] A decade later, Khrushchev wrote in his memoirs, "[If] the US and its allies sent inspectors crisscrossing around the Soviet Union, they would have discovered that we were in a relatively weak position and that realization might have encouraged them to attack us."[12] The United States' overestimation of the USSR's military capability occurred, Thompson thought, because the American military tended to assess the enemy at maximum strength, and because the various branches of the US services competed for funds.[13] The Soviets did not consider a major war as an acceptable means of achieving their objectives. Yet Thompson recognized the need for America's armed forces to remain strong, stating, "We shall of course have to keep our powder dry and have plenty of it for obvious reasons."[14] Emphasizing the danger from the Soviet *military*, however, meant underestimating the seriousness of the Soviets' *political* threat, one that Thompson described as "lethal." Unless better methods were devised to meet it, he warned, "we will surely lose."

The Soviets "do not accept that our support for rightist or reactionary governments [is] motivated by our fear [of] their attempt [to] obtain world domination for power reasons, and instead see it in terms of exploiters banding together to maintain [the] exploited in subservience."[15] The Soviets would always take advantage of opportunities such as Laos, the Congo, and Cuba, although this did not mean that they had initiated difficulties there.[16] As part of a strategy to reduce US influence, Khrushchev brought students from these countries to Moscow's Lumumba University, giving them stipends and a living standard far exceeding that of Soviet students.[17] Thompson hoped JFK would see that America's failure to help newly emerging countries meet their challenges was dangerous, as it gave the Soviet leadership plenty of "evidence to justify to themselves their belief in class struggle."[18] The race, as Thompson saw it, was to alter the Soviet course before the USSR became economically strong enough to really influence the developing world. Even if only part of the budget in the Soviets' seven-year plan for foreign aid, subversion, and propaganda programs materialized, it evoked "awesome possibilities."

Thompson also tried to explain Khrushchev's inner struggle between his nationalism and his "religious faith" in Communism.[19] Khrushchev was a person with contradictory psychological layers, and "when he speaks of his desire . . . for peaceful solutions he is quite sincere and therefore effective." Yet the Soviet leader also said that if Communism did not demonstrate its superiority and prevail throughout the world, his life would have lost its meaning. Khrushchev, Thompson believed, was nevertheless the most pragmatic and least dogmatic of his peers. Ultimately, Thompson hoped, pragmatism would win out in the USSR, because economic realities would compel the Soviets to begin reforming their political system, particularly once a new generation took over.[20] As tensions relaxed and living standards improved, the "appetite would grow with the eating," he said.[21]

As far as the Chinese were concerned, Thompson thought a complete break with the Soviets was possible, and he referred back to his dispatch in early 1960, "Current Strains within the Soviet System."[22] Final decisions on how far the Soviets would go in making or breaking ties with the Chinese—and, therefore, pursuing or eschewing détente with the West—would most likely occur at the Twenty-Second Congress of the Communist Party of the Soviet Union, scheduled for October 1961.

Berlin Primer

In his cables, Thompson repeated his previous advice to Eisenhower: Soviet interests lay in the German problem as a whole, rather than merely in Berlin.[23] East Germany was "the Soviet's domino."[24] Khrushchev did not fully grasp the importance of Berlin to the West, which was their "super-domino."[25] He had miscalculated by threatening the status of that city. Once he had used the threat, however, Khrushchev was "out on a limb," and his prestige prevented him from backing down. Thompson reiterated that Khrushchev's motives in Berlin were really protective.[26] Even if the Berlin question could be solved, Thompson insisted, the problem of Germany would remain as a major issue between the East and the West. American military bases around the USSR aggravated this situation.

Khrushchev was under pressure from East Germany's political leader, Walter Ulbricht, to do something, because West Berlin, which served both as an escape route for those fleeing Communism and as a base for Western espionage and propaganda, threatened the stability of his regime. Thompson did not advocate going down the slippery slope of concessions on Berlin, and he believed it was essential to show a strong, united front against any attempt to change that city's status. If the Western powers could address some of the other Soviet concerns about Germany, however, it might allow the status quo to continue until a solution to the Berlin problem emerged. Thompson urged the new administration to take the initiative in finding interim steps, so they would not simply be in the position of always saying "No" to Soviet suggestions, but his advice fell pretty much on deaf ears.

The Hawks and the military believed that a showdown was still inevitable with the Soviet Union. For them, Khrushchev trying to remove the NATO allies from West Berlin was sufficient evidence to prepare for war, even a nuclear war.[27] Kempton Jenkins, second secretary and German specialist for the US embassy in Moscow, said: "We weren't worried about what the Russians might do, we were worried about what Washington might do. We all understood that the principal Soviet objective was to nail down their half of Germany, not Western Europe. [Thompson] had a broader view of this. I was more of a Berliner, but he saw it in the context of the Soviet-China dispute. He was always worried that we would drive them [Soviets] into a corner where they had no option except to lash out. He wanted to leave the back door open."[28]

Thompson Goes to Camelot

JFK called all the Soviet experts to Washington, DC, in February 1961. Thompson arrived in the middle of a snowstorm, grateful that his old friend Frank Wisner put him up at his large, comfortable Georgetown house on P Street. Wisner's wife, Polly, was one of Washington's grand ladies, hosting dinners and cocktail gatherings with a genuine knack for bringing the right people together, so Thompson had plenty of opportunity to catch up on news while he was there. He had to stay such a long time in the capital that he later moved to the Bohlens' home.[29]

JFK met with Thompson, Averell Harriman, George Kennan, and Charles Bohlen for over eight hours that February.[30] All of them welcomed his attention, a positive change from the way they had felt under Eisenhower and Dulles.[31] Thompson was impressed by how the president drew out everyone's thoughts without revealing his own, and by his exceptional capacity for grasping intricate subjects quickly.[32] This was going to be an interesting president to work for.

Thompson told JFK the Soviet government was strong, and its economic growth was a formidable reality.[33] The centralized nature of its regime made it possible to use resources in a showy way, such as constructing what was then the world's largest open-air heated swimming pool.[34] But agriculture was still a serious problem after three successive years of bad harvests in the USSR. The four Kremlinologists told the president that Germany and China were great worries for the Soviet Union. The Soviets' concern about West Germany acquiring atomic weapons was both a genuine fear and an excellent crowbar with which to pry at the seams of the NATO alliance. Because of the dual character of Soviet behavior, American policy had to be both rationally stated and demonstrably strong.

Thompson also had several long solo conversations with the president and found him knowledgeable about Soviet affairs. Bohlen thought the consultations Thompson had with JFK were unique and said that he, Bohlen, would have "given a good deal, while I was in that spot, to have had anything remotely approaching them."[35] Kennedy and Thompson discussed the

Llewellyn Thompson Jr. (*left*) briefing the newly elected president, John F. Kennedy (*right*), in the Oval Office of the White House, Washington, DC, 1961. Robert Knudsen / John F. Kennedy Library (KN-C20888).

latter's cables, with him advising JFK that the best course was to make the American system work, maintain the unity of the West, deal effectively with "the great forces of nationalism and anti-colonialism" and, finally, change the image of the United States so that it was "plain that we and not the Soviet Union stand for the future."[36] It would not do to just react in situations where the Soviets were gaining ground. The president informed Thompson that he was to stay on as the US ambassador in Moscow for the time being.[37] JFK did not quite trust the State Department, and Thompson would be his man on the inside.[38]

While in Washington, DC, Thompson testified in a two-hour session before the Senate Foreign Relations Committee. He told the committee members that he had a certain rapport with Khrushchev. Because he had always been straight with the Soviet leader, Khrushchev would accept most of what Thompson said, but, he added, "I am also anxious not to in any way spoil it." Thompson informed the senators that the Twenty-Second Congress of the Communist Party, scheduled for October, would be a key event, because it would set out the Soviets' operating plan for the next twenty years. Moreover, Thompson cautioned, there was not much time left for America to have any indirect influence on what took place, since Soviet policies presented at the Congress had to be prepared months in advance. Khrushchev was anxious to size up the new administration and find out what the possibilities were for negotiations on Germany. He needed to make up his mind if he was going to seek accommodation with the West, or with China. Thompson was trying to persuade his government not to close all the doors on possible approaches to Khrushchev for the sake of appearing tough, because that could adversely affect the next two decades of Soviet policy.[39]

To Summit or Not to Summit

Both Bohlen and Thompson were in favor of a meeting between JFK and Khrushchev.[40] Thompson felt that the many layers of Khrushchev's complex personality were impossible to convey secondhand.[41] Khrushchev tended to make decisions based on direct personal experience, so it was equally important for the Soviet leader to meet Kennedy.[42] The Khrushchev-Eisenhower meeting at Camp David had helped to convince Khrushchev that problems could be solved through diplomacy, not confrontation, and Thompson hoped a meeting with JFK might help pick up the shattered pieces of détente.[43] Kennedy's Kremlinologists recommended that the president show both a willingness to negotiate reasonably and great strength and firmness in any meeting with Khrushchev. JFK's statements should also be very clear, because it never helped in negotiating with the Soviets to use "ambiguous words or phrases" that might be understood in different ways by the two sides.[44] The president thought a face-to-face encounter was a good idea, because he was curious about Khrushchev and wanted to meet him. He, too, believed in his own personal judgment and the strength of his charisma, and he preferred to test his adversary face to face. "I'll have to sit down with him and let him see who he is dealing with," Kennedy told his aide, Kenneth O'Donnell.[45] JFK sent Thompson back to the Soviet Union with an invitation to Khrushchev for an informal meeting.

Thompson returned to Moscow on February 27, carrying JFK's invitation to the Soviet leader. In this letter, the president also wrote that Thompson enjoyed his "full confidence" and could "inform you of my thinking on a number of international issues."[46] When Thompson went to deliver JFK's message, he found that Khrushchev, whose initial gestures of reaching out to the new president seemed to have gone unnoticed, had left on an agricultural tour of the USSR. Things were not going the way Khrushchev wanted. Numerous problems with collective farms plagued his planned economic progress. In addition, perhaps Khrushchev had decided to play hard to get and was no longer in a hurry to find accommodation with the West.[47] Thompson insisted on getting JFK's message to Khrushchev and told Gromyko he could meet the Soviet leader wherever he was.

Jane was relieved to finally know their fate for the next year but wrote home that after one more winter, it would be time to go.[48] Her husband thought 1961 would be a critical year, "not the best time to change nags here, even though I feel most incompetent in the face of the enormous problems we have with these people."[49] It *was* an exciting and interesting time, but the Moscow winters tended to drain everyone and everything, including the Thompsons' car. Friends who were visiting from the United States had borrowed the ambassador's Cadillac to go out to Zagorsk, a historic town about thirty miles from Moscow, which was full of some of the most beautiful churches in the country. The worn and potholed road was too much for the fragile Cadillac, built primarily for better-paved American roads. On the trip to Zagorsk, it broke down for what seemed like the millionth time, necessitating a rescue mission. These friends told the Thompsons about the Checker Motors Corporation, a manufacturer of taxicabs and passenger cars that could withstand almost anything. Exasperated with the Cadillac, which required difficult-to-get high-octane gasoline, Thompson asked the department to buy a Checker car for Moscow. It lived up to its reputation.

Novosibirsk

Khrushchev knew Thompson had come back from Washington, DC, with a letter from JFK, but he was not pleased with the signals he had been receiving. Kennedy's tough State of the Union speech, an agreement between the United States and Turkey to place Jupiter missiles near the Soviet border, and Robert McNamara's declaration that there was no "missile gap" all worried Khrushchev. Had he taken the wrong road, as some of his critics claimed? Ten days after Thompson's return, he got word that Khrushchev would see him in Novosibirsk, a city 2,000 miles away that normally was closed to foreigners. On March 9, 1961, Thompson flew there on a Soviet passenger plane, accompanied by Boris Klosson, who was the embassy's political officer, and Anatoly Dobrynin, from the Soviet Foreign Office. They arrived late at night, and a driver took them along a large avenue to the only hotel in town. Thompson could not see much, as the car window had purposely been rubbed with soap. What he could make out was a gray and dimly lit city, with dirty snow and slush lining the streets. Novosibirsk was even less attractive than he remembered it from his train journey in the 1940s. Once at the hotel, he asked for some milk for his stomach ulcers but received kefir instead. This would be a long trip. Dobrynin asked Thompson for the president's letter to Khrushchev, so he could start on the translation and speed things up. Dobrynin promised he wouldn't show it to anyone and said that Thompson could review it the next morning. Thompson agreed.[50]

Khrushchev was staying at a dacha near the headquarters of the Siberian Academy of Sciences, and he was in a "foul mood."[51] When he received the Americans, Khrushchev looked "extremely tired and it even shocked the Soviets who accompanied me," Thompson reported. After exchanging niceties, which included Khrushchev saying he didn't have to offer the American president the usual wish for a long life, because he was young,[52] Thompson presented him with JFK's letter.[53]

Kennedy's advisors wanted to avoid having JFK and Khrushchev meet in the United States, so Thompson proposed to Khrushchev that the two leaders get together in a neutral capital, such as Vienna or Stockholm, stating that the president would be visiting heads of state in Europe and thus could avoid crossing the ocean twice. Khrushchev said he understood about transatlantic flights, and he preferred Vienna. In any case, he would think about the meeting but was inclined to say yes. A reason for a face-to-face discussion, however, had to be found. Thompson thought this comment was motivated by Khrushchev's need to offer an explanation for such a meeting to the Chinese. Dobrynin thought he was just referring to what kind of statement to give to the press.[54]

During lunch, Khrushchev remarked that the president had asked him to use diplomatic channels, so he proposed a toast to this method. It must also have pleased Khrushchev to read that JFK intended to do everything he could "toward developing a more harmonious relationship between our two countries."[55] Thompson chose this moment to confide to Khrushchev that the government would be lifting its ban on importing Russian crabmeat. To Thompson's surprise, Khrushchev received the news with considerable satisfaction, indicating how important trade was to him.

Khrushchev's enthusiasm dampened, however, when he realized that Thompson had no further news on Germany. Khrushchev did not know it, but Thompson had been instructed *not* to talk about Berlin.[56] If the topic came up, Thompson was to explain that it was better to leave things as they were while the recently installed administration consulted with its allies. JFK wanted to develop his own, new course of action. The problem was that Germany was *not* new for Khrushchev. The issue was something he had put on hold, first for the Camp David meeting with Eisenhower; then for the Paris summit that didn't happen; and, lastly, while awaiting the upcoming US elections and a change in American leadership. Furthermore, Khrushchev didn't have any more time to spare. The Twenty-Second Congress of the Communist Party was looming, and he needed to decide on his next moves.

Thompson then changed the subject to Laos and told Khrushchev that the United States was sincere in trying to secure it as a neutral country.[57] "We welcome a Laos that pursues a neutral policy on the model of Austria," Khrushchev responded. Thompson reported to the State Department that Khrushchev was keen on settling this problem, since the fighting there gave neither the United States nor the USSR any advantage and contributed to hurt relations between the Americans and the Soviets. Here, then, was something that JFK could use in a Vienna meeting with Khrushchev.

Thompson and the Soviet leader also discussed the Congo situation, but with less success.[58] They argued over the role of the UN, with Khrushchev accusing the international organization of bias. For him, the only solution to an impartial UN was his proposal for a troika—a three-man secretary-general—made up of representatives from a Communist, a capitalist, and a neutral country. Thompson said the problem with a troika was that the UN's secretariat did not make policy, it only executed it. So if the three parties in the secretary-generalship didn't agree, the UN would lose its effectiveness. Suppose the Secretariat was given a specific task, such as supervising the carrying out of an agreement on disarmament. If one side decided to cheat, it could block inspections. Khrushchev got the point but said that if there had been a three-person UN secretary-generalship, the Congo would perhaps have had a legally established government, and Lumumba might still be alive. The UN had become an instrument for inflaming passions, instead of maintaining peace. "You have your Belgian allies," the Soviet leader remarked, referring to the remnants of Belgian rule in the Congo.

When Thompson sounded Khrushchev out on a nuclear test agreement, a top Kennedy priority, he concluded that the Soviets were no longer interested.[59] Therefore, this was a proposal that could not be advanced in the Vienna meeting. JFK, however, ignored Thompson's warning and continued to press for a test ban, taking a shortcut around the advice of his own ambassador.

Khrushchev was forced to finally bring up the topic of Germany himself.[60] He told Thompson he wanted the United States and the USSR to be together on this question, just as they were during World War II, when they had shed blood together against Germany. He assured Thompson that West Berlin had "little importance" for the USSR, saying, "the annual Soviet population increase is 3.5 million and . . . the total population of West Berlin is 2 million—one night's work."[61] No one was encroaching on West Berlin, Khrushchev said, and added, "Let us work out together a status [for it]." Thompson replied that even if the USSR had no interest in it, Walter Ulbricht certainly did. Khrushchev brushed that remark aside, saying Ulbricht would also sign a commitment on West Berlin.[62] A "capitalist island" within East Germany might be possible, but if a treaty were not signed concerning East Germany itself, American and Soviet troops would confront one another. Holding out a carrot, Khrushchev said the treaty could even be implemented in installments, to allow an atmosphere of trust to develop. He wanted to make it clear to the president that, if an agreement were reached on Germany, it would "be a big success" for US-USSR relations.

On the plane back to Moscow, Thompson had a chance to talk to Dobrynin.[63] During their conversation, Dobrynin agreed with Khrushchev's premise that the USSR would overtake the United States economically. America was rich now, he told Thompson, and therefore less-developed countries looked to it for assistance, giving the United States influence, but in the future, those countries would turn to the Soviets. Thompson expressed his discouragement at ever reaching an agreement with the Soviets on major issues, in view of the disparity between their respective countries' perspectives. There was a twofold reason for this, he told Dobrynin. First, there were the Soviets' ideological interpretations of events. Second, there was a lack of objective information about particular situations, since the reports the Soviets received tended to only contain facts that supported the Soviet position.

Dobrynin, picking up on Thompson's insinuation, asked him for his opinion of Ambassador Menshikov. Thompson did not think him a successful ambassador and suggested that someone like Vassili Kuznetsov would be better. "A number of us in the Foreign Ministry would agree with you," Dobrynin said.[64] Khrushchev himself had been irritated by Menshikov during his American trip in 1959, confided Dobrynin. Thompson urged that any time there was doubt about the intentions of the United States or about American policies, they should speak frankly, rather than guess. Dobrynin acknowledged that there were frequent misunderstandings, and Thompson said that removing such misperceptions was one of the principal reasons for the president's invitation to Khrushchev for a Vienna meeting.

On March 17, CBS correspondent Daniel Schorr broadcast a detailed account of Thompson's conversation with Khrushchev in Novosibirsk, including unofficial comments.[65] Thompson was shocked, since his future conversations with Khrushchev would lose much of their value if the Soviet leader thought that even his chance remarks could be made public. Thompson suggested that the leak must have come from Washington, DC, or possibly Bonn, where he'd sent a copy of his report of the meeting. He asked the State Department to investigate, but the leak was never found.[66]

A week after the Novosibirsk meeting, Thompson once again alerted the Kennedy administration that Khrushchev would be likely to go forward with a separate East German treaty if there were no signs of negotiations, and he added that all his diplomatic colleagues agreed.[67] Thompson told JFK that Khrushchev would focus on this at their meeting in Vienna, and, depending on the outcome there, the Soviet leader would make a decision on his policy toward Germany, either at the same time or shortly thereafter. The president should be ready to say something to forestall a separate treaty between the Soviets and East Germany, which could lead to a subsequent crisis over the issue of Berlin. At least holding out the prospect of working toward a solution on Germany in general would help Khrushchev save face and thus defer a showdown.

The possibilities Thompson recommended included a declaration on German frontiers, as well as an interim Berlin solution, which would tone down the heat and give the West Germans a better basis for access to Berlin. At an absolute minimum, JFK could talk to Khrushchev about defusing the Berlin problem by unilateral actions on both sides, without coming to any formal agreement. For the Americans, he thought this might mean giving up on their propaganda machine and reducing covert actions in Berlin. He also offered a stark warning, declaring, "If we expect [the] Soviets to leave [the] Berlin problem as [it] is, then we must at least expect the East Germans to seal off [the] sector boundary in order to stop . . . [the] refugee flow."[68]

Thompson's cable also revealed his frustration with the West Germans' attitude. By putting off real negotiations, they were, in effect, indirectly choosing to allow a separate treaty between the USSR and East Germany. In that case, Thompson thought the West

German chancellor, Konrad Adenauer, should be asked what he would do once such a treaty was signed and the East Germans began to slowly harass and strangle West Berlin's economy, even if they didn't disturb the Western allies' access to that city. Thompson was one of the few people who stressed that West German access to Berlin was as essential as allied access. Also, he wanted Adenauer to be asked two other vital questions: (1) what would the West German reaction be if the "East Germans close [the] sector boundary," and (2) what would the West Germans do if the East Germans refused to deal with them on matters such as trade, "except on [a] formal governmental basis?" The latter would mean a de facto recognition of the East German government.[69]

Yet Thompson's efforts to get the Kennedy administration to study the problems regarding Germany did not go far. The president wanted to direct foreign policy himself, and in his own way. JFK assigned the development of his Berlin strategy to an adviser who was a former secretary of state under Truman, Dean Acheson. Acheson was Eurocentric, and a Hawk. Instead of defusing the Berlin situation, his solution was to not negotiate, but instead to build up forces for a possible showdown with the Soviets. The president was getting conflicting opinions on how to deal with Berlin, and he was not sure which tack to take.

Unbeknownst to Thompson, JFK, despite what he told Khrushchev about wanting to use diplomatic channels, was actually bypassing them to clinch an agreement on a test ban treaty as part of the Vienna meeting through his back channel, Georgi Bolshakov. Bolshakov, a journalist posted to the Soviet embassy in Washington, DC, was also member of GRU, the Soviet military intelligence agency.[70] Thompson thought this approach was an "error in judgment" and, when he discovered it, warned the president that using Bolshakov could cause misunderstandings. Thompson advised JFK that, at the very least, notes should be made of all the meetings with Bolshakov.[71] The president did not follow Thompson's advice, although he came to realize the pitfalls of this means of communication eventually. Robert F. Kennedy would later rue his failure to take notes during his meetings with the Soviet spy.[72] Khrushchev didn't care whether he communicated with the president through the American embassy or through Bolshakov. He left that decision up to JFK.[73] The president's choice, however, generated jealousy in Khrushchev's own foreign ministry.[74] Gromyko didn't like the Soviet defense ministry running this channel. Dobrynin thought it was precarious, because Bolshakov knew none of the details of USSR-US relations, in either the negotiations between the two countries or the Soviet position on those negotiations.[75]

23

Meeting in Vienna

Now, in the thermonuclear age, any misjudgment on either
side about the intentions of the other could rain more
devastation in several hours than has been wrought
in all the wars of human history.
—JOHN F. KENNEDY, radio and television address,
    July 25, 1961

JFK counted on getting a test ban agreement at the Vienna meeting, but Khrushchev
was not interested in freezing what was then America's lead in nuclear capability or in
opening up the Soviet Union to inspections. Thompson warned the president that a
test ban agreement was "extremely doubtful," and that the only point of agreement was
the neutrality of Laos.[1] Even JFK's back channel, Bolshakov, had passed the message to the
president that Germany was Khrushchev's focus for the meeting.[2]

Thompson met with Khrushchev on April 1, 1961, to pick up a position paper on Laos,
but again it turned into a long meeting that touched on many subjects.[3] Thompson told
Khrushchev that JFK was strengthening civilian control over military policy. The Soviet
leader agreed that this was important, confiding that he had once had problems with Marshal Georgy Zhukov, who had developed big ideas about his own role in government.
Touching on the Third World, Khrushchev declared that the Americans had made Patrice
Lumumba out to be a Communist. The Congolese leader had not been one, however, and
it was doubtful he would have become one. Turning to Cuba, Khrushchev said he did not
agree with American policy there, either, as bands of Cuban émigrés in the United States
had made threats against Fidel Castro's government. The Soviets had no base on Cuba, but
the Americans did. The United States also had bases circling the Soviet Union. America
sought special rights for itself everywhere. Khrushchev then asked, why didn't the United
States establish diplomatic relations with Cuba and resolve issues that way? Thompson
said the problem was that Cuba was trying to overthrow other Latin American governments, with Castro training Cuban pilots in Czechoslovakia. That was defensive, Khrushchev told him. The Americans, Thompson continued, had been prepared to accept the
Castro government until it had confiscated American assets without compensation.

On April 11, Thompson reported that Khrushchev had agreed to a June 4 date for a summit in Vienna.[4] The very next day, Yuri Alekseyevich Gagarin became the first man to travel to space. It was a great victory for Khrushchev, one he made full use of, sending Gagarin all around the world to show off this Soviet technological victory. It was also a confidence booster for his meeting with JFK.

Bay of Pigs

What Thompson did not know was that a few days later, on April 17, an event involving Richard Bissell—the same man who had organized the U-2 flight before the Paris summit—would interrupt plans for the Vienna meeting. Bissell was new to his position as the CIA's deputy director of plans.[5] Nonetheless, "ambitious as he was, he wanted to score with a spectacular operation."[6] This time he arranged an attack on Cuba, an action known today as the Bay of Pigs invasion. The plan was that anti-Castro émigrés, trained and armed by the United States, would invade the island, where, supposedly, discontented locals would join them. A provisional Cuban government could then ask for US intervention, if necessary. This was the operation that Eisenhower described to the president-elect in their transition meeting. JFK, being new to the job, decided that the political costs of not going through with the invasion were high, so he decided to carry out Eisenhower's plan, on the condition that it be done without US troops or air support and under a cover of plausible deniability.[7]

The operation was fraught with errors, not least being that Bissell counted on US military intervention if the chips were down, lest the mission fail. When it started going wrong, however, JFK did not back the émigrés. Over a thousand were taken prisoner and 140 were killed. In the end, the invasion made the president look indecisive and weak internally and furthered the Communist cause in Latin America, all of which put JFK at a disadvantage in his meeting with Khrushchev. The only positive outcome was that the president developed a healthy distrust toward his military and CIA advisors, and this experience affected the way he handled future crises. As a consequence, JFK removed Allen Dulles as the head of the CIA and replaced him with John McCone. He also replaced Bissell with Richard Helms as the CIA's new deputy director for plans.

On April 18, Gromyko handed Thompson a strong letter of protest from Khrushchev to JFK. The Soviet leader told the president he knew the United States was behind the invasion and brought up Kennedy's statement that America would not participate in military activities against Cuba. The Bay of Pigs invasion baffled Khrushchev, who wondered if hard-liners were now influencing the new president. Would Kennedy be able to stand up to them? Khrushchev's letter warned JFK that the Soviet Union would support Cuba against any armed attack. When Gromyko handed Thompson the letter, he softened the encounter by saying he hoped "the differences which have arisen recently would be resolved and the US-Soviet relations improved."[8]

The State Department and the White House reevaluated whether the Vienna summit should go forward. Thompson thought it should, because it would promote a more reasonable approach by the Soviets on matters such as Laos and disarmament, and it could still influence important decisions before the Twenty-Second Congress of the Communist Party occurred.[9] A meeting between Khrushchev and JFK would strengthen America's place in terms of world opinion, and it would put the United States in a better position to take a strong stand on Berlin. Lastly, despite the sharp exchanges, Thompson noted that Soviet policy had not changed since the Bay of Pigs invasion.[10] JFK agreed to the Vienna meeting, which was formally announced at the beginning of May.

On May 24, Thompson saw Khrushchev for the last time before the Vienna summit. Khrushchev took him and Jane aside during an American ice skating exhibition and told him he was "troubled by the problem of how to deal" with JFK on the question of Berlin.[11] The Soviet leader explained that he wanted to avoid discussions that might be "uncomfortable" when the two heads of government spoke in front of others, so he planned to use a different approach from the one he would now employ in private with the ambassador.[12] Nonetheless, Khrushchev expected Thompson to report their conversation to the president, which the ambassador did, word for word.

Khrushchev did not hold back. German reunification was out of the question, because neither de Gaulle, Macmillan, nor Adenauer wanted it. He added that de Gaulle had told him Germany should not only remain divided, but it would be even better if it were divided into three parts.[13] Khrushchev could no longer put off the issue of East Germany. His stand was even tougher than the one he'd taken in Novosibirsk. If he and JFK couldn't reach an agreement in Vienna, he would sign a separate peace treaty with East Germany that winter, probably right after the Communist Party congress. This time he did not show any signs of accommodation on Berlin, stating that allied access to West Berlin would require an agreement with the East Germans. "Your soldiers in Berlin may have to tighten their belts," he threatened. Thompson answered back sharply that Khrushchev could sign any peace treaty he wanted, but interference with allied access to Berlin would be met with force. Thompson's unequivocal delivery should have been a warning that this really was a line drawn in the sand. Perhaps sensing Jane's discomfort over the tone of the conversation, Khrushchev offered to take her to the Vienna meeting on his train. He reported to the Presidium that Thompson's wife had become frightened by the talk of war.[14] What had actually scared Jane, though, was seeing her normally calm husband exhibit such anger.

Using a mirror image of Khrushchev's own fears vis-à-vis East Germany and the Soviet satellite countries, Thompson explained to him that Western prestige was also on the line, and that the United States had to stand firm on Berlin, lest West Germany and Europe be lost. The two powers should agree to put things off for a few years, Thompson told him, but Khrushchev replied heatedly that he had waited thirty months—"long enough!"[15] Thompson responded: "We would rather deal with the Russians than leave it to the Germans to have responsibility for keeping peace in this area. I refuse to believe that your Germans are any better than ours."[16] Khrushchev laughed and shook Thompson's hand, and tensions relaxed somewhat.

Thompson offered that progress on disarmament could facilitate a solution to the German problem. But Khrushchev turned it around and told him that an agreement on disarmament would be impossible as long as the East German problem remained unsolved. With Vienna approaching, the failed Paris summit was on Khrushchev's mind. He referred back to it and said somewhat bitterly that if it hadn't been for the U-2 incident, some agreement might have been reached with Eisenhower. As he had with the U-2 affair, Khrushchev blamed "Allen Dulles's agents" for deliberately heating up the Berlin problem.

Thompson wrote another cable to the department on May 24, where he cautioned against allowing the East German problem to simply drift on.[17] The Soviets had succeeded in creating the impression that the allies were saying "No" to proposals aimed at avoiding war. Furthermore, Thompson continued, "we owe it to ourselves and to [the] world [to] make every possible effort to see if some way around [the] present impasse can be achieved." Thompson thought that suggesting something along the lines of the former Geneva proposals, spread out over time, could serve as an interim solution. This, coupled with some action on Germany's borders, could tempt Khrushchev. Such a proposal could also include a better assurance that West Germany would continue to have access to Berlin. Lastly, if there was any hope of arriving at a peaceful solution regarding the East German issues, it would have to involve face saving for both sides. This, Thompson suggested, JFK might explore with Khrushchev in private when they met. In a second May 24 cable, Thompson stated that Khrushchev was deadly serious about a separate Soviet treaty with East Germany, because he was firmly committed to having Walter Ulbricht achieve something within the year.[18] If not, Khrushchev would probably have to "change the East German regime if he [Khrushchev] is unable to carry out his commitment."

While Thompson urged finding a solution for the issues regarding Germany, to avoid a crisis, JFK was also getting advice from the "Achesonians."[19] They believed that the Soviets would try to forcefully drive the allies out of Berlin and destroy both the general European alliance and NATO. The American mission in Berlin, with approval from the US embassy in Bonn, also sent the president a briefing cable in May. Theirs urged JFK to take the opposite tack to Thompson's and be totally unbending.[20] Some staff members in the Bonn embassy and the Berlin mission, known by their self-designated nickname as the "Berlin Mafia," feared the "consequences of a particular carrot and stick approach for their constituents" and argued against any suggestion of an interim solution.[21] Thompson responded to the "Berlin Mafia" cable by stating that while he agreed that "the gradual erosion of our position by embarking on the slippery path of tempting compromise was something to avoid," taking the "completely negative stand suggested by Berlin and Bonn would probably lead to developments which had a 50-50 chance of the West having to make [an] ignominious retreat from its position or face war."[22]

Thompson understood that JFK had to be uncompromising on West Berlin, but he also wanted Khrushchev to get the message that the door had not been shut on negotiable measures regarding East Germany.[23] In Thompson's view, the president had the difficult task of convincing Khrushchev at the Vienna summit that, "on the one hand, we would fulfill American commitment to the people of [West] Berlin and on the other, that it is not our intention to saw off the limb on which he [Khrushchev] has crawled." The danger, as Thompson saw it, was that both sides were convinced the other was bluffing. The Soviets were sure the United States would not start a war if Khrushchev's contemplated treaty turned access to West Berlin over to the East Germans. The Americans were equally sure that Khrushchev would not create a situation that would require them to use force to uphold their access rights to West Berlin. But if each side carried out its declared intentions, at a certain point it would be virtually impossible for either to retreat without jeopardizing its credibility. Both sides were relying heavily on a nuclear position, which made the situation all that much more dangerous.

Just as Khrushchev hadn't decided to wreck the Paris summit until the last minute, it seemed as though he had not yet decided just how far he would go in Vienna.[24] The Soviet leader was unpredictable. On the one hand, he had been tough when he met with Thompson at the ice rink. On the other, he told Thompson that he hoped for a "pleasant" meeting with the president. Khrushchev said he would make proposals or take positions that would improve the atmosphere and relations between their two countries, although Thompson wrote to the State Department that he was at a loss "to imagine what this could be."[25]

Khrushchev had told Thompson that he wanted to avoid the thornier aspects of a separate Soviet–East German treaty at the Vienna meeting, that is, East German control of access to Berlin once the treaty came into effect. Khrushchev had tried during the meeting in Novosibirsk and on other occasions to dismiss Western concerns about Berlin, saying that Berlin was not important to the Soviets. So, at the end of another cable to the State Department, Thompson added that it was possible that, given their conversations, Khrushchev might try to "slide over the Berlin problem in [a] sweetness and light atmosphere." He then went on to say that "in this event, I believe the president should force the issue."[26] In other words, if Khrushchev avoided the Berlin issue or tried to slide over it in discussing a separate East German treaty, Thompson wanted to make sure that JFK brought it up, in order to make the importance of Berlin absolutely clear. The second part of this sentence, however, has been left out in several books that discuss the Berlin Crisis,[27] making it seem as though Thompson was telling JFK he had nothing to worry about in Vienna regarding Berlin. In fact, he was doing the opposite. The entire range of presidential advisors agreed on making the US position on Berlin unmistakably clear, but no one seemed to focus on what Thompson was suggesting, which was incremental steps toward a resolution of the problem regarding *East Germany*.

When the president read Thompson's May 24 cables and saw Khrushchev's harsh position on Berlin, it caused him to take a tougher line in his special message to Congress the next day.[28] He wanted Khrushchev to know that he was going to be tough, too. Ironically, his speech was reminiscent of Khrushchev's January 6 speech. JFK talked of supporting revolutions in emerging countries in Asia, Latin America, Africa, and the Middle East, in order to promote freedom and defeat Communism wherever it appeared.[29] If Khrushchev was still considering which of his impulses to follow in Vienna, he probably made up his mind after that speech.[30] Khrushchev called JFK a "son of a bitch" and told the Presidium that the new president could be made to concede on Berlin, especially after the Bay of Pigs invasion. Mikoyan warned Khrushchev against taking a hard line on Berlin in the Vienna meeting, but Khrushchev disregarded what he said.[31] Even so, no ultimatum had yet been planned when Khrushchev met with the Presidium on May 26.[32] Furthermore, the Soviet Foreign Ministry had not prepared very much for the Vienna meeting, either.[33] Everything and anything might happen.

On June 1, on the way to Vienna, JFK stopped in Paris to see French president Charles de Gaulle, who advised against bringing up the future status of East Germany with Khrushchev. The Soviet leader had been laying down deadlines for the past two and a half years.[34] West Germany's chancellor, Konrad Adenauer, was intransigent in his opposition to any negotiations between the United States and the Soviets on Germany, although he would send a secret message to Khrushchev through his ambassador, Hans Kroll, seeking direct bilateral negotiations.[35] Thompson also met with JFK in Paris the day before the Vienna summit began, but there is no record of their conversation.[36]

East Crosses West

The first meeting in Vienna took place at the US ambassador's residence, the same house where Thompson and his family had lived when he was high commissioner. When Khrushchev arrived, JFK was standing at the top on the stairs that led to the front portal. He descended partway down the steps and leaned forward to shake Khrushchev's hand as the Soviet leader emerged from the car. Later, reporters made much of the fact that Kennedy stood above Khrushchev during the handshake. As Khrushchev neared the top of the stairs, the president pointed Thompson out to him. Khrushchev smiled, pleased to see the ambassador, and greeted him. After the usual niceties, JFK and Khrushchev entered the music room and sat down next to each other on two identical chairs, separated by a coffee table, with their backs to the windows. Their respective advisors arrayed themselves around the room and waited for the action to begin.

The summit got off to a bad start. JFK did not heed Thompson's and Bohlen's advice to steer clear of ideology and ventured into a debate that involved Marxist theory, something Khrushchev excelled in and Kennedy had shallow knowledge of.[37] Thompson said later he had not known the meeting was going to begin like that, because a clear agenda had not been put out in advance. This first session was supposed to just be a "get to know each other" meeting.[38]

JFK expected Khrushchev to be more pragmatic and accept his proposal that neither side make trouble on each other's turf, but the Soviet leader pointed out that this was scarcely consistent with the Communist belief that Communism would inevitably and naturally develop throughout the world. Khrushchev said he could agree not to use force in solving disputes and not to interfere in the internal affairs of other nations, but he could not consent to a freeze on the conditions that prevailed in those countries.[39] Thompson did not think JFK fully appreciated Khrushchev's inability to concur with something contrary to Communist doctrine, even if he had wanted to.[40] For Bohlen and Thompson, Khrushchev's ideological rant in Vienna was "nothing new," so much so that Bohlen (drowsy from thyroid medication) fell asleep in the middle of the diatribe, and Thompson had to kick him in the ankle.[41] Kennedy seemed shocked that his logic and charm had so

Front: Llewellyn Thompson Jr. (*far left*) shaking hands with Nikita Khrushchev (*center*), while John F. Kennedy (*to right of Khrushchev*) looks on, just prior to the initial meeting of the summit in Vienna, Austria, 1961. Paul Schutzer, *Life* Picture Collection / Getty Images (50055083).

little effect on the Soviet chairman. According to his brother Robert, "It was the first time the President had come across somebody with whom he couldn't exchange ideas in a meaningful way, and have some point to it."[42]

At the White House briefings back in February, Bohlen and Thompson had been impressed by JFK's interest and his ability to grasp information. The young and intelligent president brought the promise of fresh air to a diplomatic stance that had seemed fairly stuck. Perhaps Thompson had not yet figured out JFK as well as he had Khrushchev. He had not anticipated that Kennedy could get himself so tied up in knots in the two leaders' initial interchange.[43] What was unknown at the time was that Kennedy was in a great deal of pain during the conference and probably taking painkillers.

On the second day, JFK did steer clear of ideology and got down to basics.[44] They agreed on a neutral Laos, but the discussion on nuclear testing went nowhere. Khrushchev said the only way he would accept inspections was if both the United States and the USSR agreed to disarm completely. The president suggested instead that they approach complete disarmament in stages. As Thompson had forewarned, Khrushchev would not bite.[45] Nor did the two leaders agree on Berlin or East Germany. Khrushchev tried to get JFK to accept an interim arrangement for Berlin, but Kennedy refused to consider it.[46]

Dobrynin said in his memoirs that he thought JFK was prepared to find a compromise, but that "Khrushchev was not patient enough and continued to press his own proposals."[47]

Perhaps it was another missed opportunity to solve a tricky problem. Khrushchev did manage to remain courteous at the summit, however, as he had told Thompson he would.[48] Theodore Sorensen, JFK's speechwriter and close advisor, was present at the meetings and found "no bullying or contempt. . . . Neither man retreated from his respective ideological views and national interests, [but] neither showed any disrespect or incivility for the other."[49] That is, until just about the end of the meetings. As he was about to leave, Khrushchev handed Kennedy an aide-mémoire, which bore the signs of haste. It amounted to a new six-month deadline on the USSR signing a separate treaty with East Germany. The decision was "firm and irrevocable." JFK ended the meeting on a sorrowful note, stating, "Then it will be a cold winter."[50]

In the Vienna summit, Khrushchev did not resolve the issues of East German recognition or Western rights in Berlin. Instead, things were postponed for another six months. But the Soviet leader did not leave empty handed. He had been tough and could go home feeling as if he was in the driver's seat. Now it was JFK who called Khrushchev a "son of a bitch."[51] Sorenson identified four sour myths that sprang up in the years after the Vienna meeting: (1) that the summit was a failure, a waste of time, or, worse, a show of US weakness that led to the construction of the Berlin Wall and the Cuban Missile Crisis;[52] (2) that Khrushchev had successfully bullied the young American president and thereby felt contempt for him; (3) that this experience convinced JFK that the meeting was a mistake and never to repeat it; and (4) that the continuation of the Cold War for approximately thirty years thereafter demonstrated the failure of Kennedy's hopes.

Thompson would have agreed with Sorenson that these conclusions were myths. Neither Thompson nor Bohlen had the impression that Khrushchev had bullied or tried to intimidate the president.[53] When Khrushchev later talked to Thompson about JFK, he told him that he envied Kennedy's youth and was impressed by his knowledge of the questions they had discussed.[54] Khrushchev had noticed that JFK did not need to consult his advisors the way Eisenhower had. He added that the new president was intelligent, seemed to have a "better grasp [than Eisenhower] of the idea of peaceful coexistence," and appeared committed to avoiding a hot war.[55] JFK asked Thompson if he thought Khrushchev had been tough on him in Vienna because of his failure in the Bay of Pigs affair, but Thompson said he did not think that event had much to do with it.[56] Khrushchev's prestige had already been committed on the topic of recognition of East Germany long before the Bay of Pigs invasion happened, and the Soviet leader would have made it an issue anyhow in Vienna. "Khrushchev knew he had us over a barrel on Berlin," he told the president.[57] JFK informed Thompson that, although the meeting had not gone very well, it had proved to be useful to him in getting to know Khrushchev and seeing what he was like.[58] As a result of their encounter, the two reached a "curious rapport."[59] Khrushchev would soon reach out to JFK in private correspondence—an attempt to defuse tensions in what would become known as the "pen-pal letters," a direct and secret communication between the two leaders.

Before JFK left Vienna, he asked *New York Times* correspondent James "Scotty" Reston to call on him. "How was it?" asked Reston. "Worst thing in my life," said Kennedy, adding, "He savaged me." He then told the *Times* reporter that now he had to figure out what to do about it. This meeting helped propagate the notion that JFK was so shaken up by Khrushchev that it turned him into a tougher and more resolute president in the following months. Ted Sorensen, however, claimed that Kennedy purposefully exaggerated his reaction in the "Scotty Reston interview in order to set the tone for a general mobilization, which was part of his plan to convince Congress to finance a military 'flexible response,' so as not to rely so much on nuclear weapons." This was something Maxwell Taylor, Kennedy's military advisor, had been advocating.[60] Though Arthur Schlesinger later quoted Thompson as thinking that JFK had overreacted, the ambassador denied this. He believed that Kennedy had reacted well to Khrushchev's threatening attitude over Berlin, which had an important effect on the Soviet leader. The main message Khrushchev got was that there would be no compromise on Western rights to access to West Berlin. This was a good thing, Thompson thought, as "otherwise it could have been very dangerous indeed."[61]

When the Vienna summit was over, Thompson wrote to his wife that it had gone "as expected."[62] Given that neither JFK nor Khrushchev had come prepared to solve the East German–Berlin question, and that Khrushchev had nothing to offer in the way of a test ban agreement, there was not much to expect out of the meeting beyond the two leaders getting an impression of each other and holding a discussion on the neutrality of Laos.[63] One decision made in Vienna was that JFK and Khrushchev would make reciprocal television appearances.[64] Kennedy also agreed to be interviewed by Aleksei Adzhubei, Mikhail Kharlamov, and Georgi Bolshakov, all of them reporters for *Izvestia*. After the interview, JFK met with Adzhubei in private. Impressed with the president's treatment of his son-in-law, Khrushchev decided that he would send Kennedy a personal message, although he would wait until September to do so.[65]

Thompson, exhausted after the Vienna meetings, arrived back in Washington, DC, for briefings. He played musical houses, staying with the Bohlens for a few days and then moving into the home of Paul Nitze, who was then the assistant secretary of defense. Thompson also flew out to Colorado to see his mother but was only able to stay for two days. He was back in the capital by mid-June and had a chance to talk to Secretary of State Dean Rusk about personal plans for himself. Rusk thought that the president desired him to stay on as ambassador in Moscow, but Thompson was not so sure he wanted to, telling Rusk that the place was beginning to get him down. He said he would stay until the following June, when school for his daughters was finished, but not longer.

Jenny had persuaded her parents not to send her to boarding school, but rather enroll her in the Soviet school next to the ambassador's residence. The Soviet authorities tried to convince Thompson to put her into one of the *spetzialni* schools, where exceptionally talented children and the children of high-ranking party members went, but Jenny wouldn't hear of it. Exceptionally talented children sounded like way too much work, and besides, she wanted to be where many of her playmates from the square outside Spaso House studied. Thompson wrote back, politely asking if there was anything wrong with the local school that prevented his daughter from going there. An answer immediately came back that there was nothing wrong, and that his daughter could start the following September. Jenny then took language classes to get her Russian up to an acceptable level for school.

Ultimatum: Now What?

After the Vienna summit, JFK spent most of his time and energy trying to figure out how to deal with Khrushchev's renewed ultimatum on East Germany. The Ambassadorial Group was revived, in order to coordinate policy among the Western allies, and Kennedy set up the Berlin Task Force to study the matter.[66] They met on June 16, with Thompson present. Dean Acheson—as the former secretary of state and, presently, a special consultant to the president—also came, to give the task force his views. Thompson and Acheson had developed a personal friendship, but Thompson did not agree with him now. Acheson did not think a political solution was possible. He saw the situation as essentially a test of wills, and America's prestige was at stake. The United States had to show that it was willing to go all the way, including in the use of nuclear weapons, to defend Berlin. If the European allies had serious inhibitions against such an action, it was best to find that out from the start: "We should proceed not by asking them if they would be afraid if we said 'boo!' We should, instead, say 'boo!' and see how far they jump."[67] Thompson, however, believed that it was absolutely necessary to initially get the allies on board. It was important that the Soviets not think the United States was isolated. It would perhaps be best, Thompson said, "not to say 'boo!' first before getting the British leaders with us."

To convince the Soviets that the possibility of a nuclear war was no empty threat, Acheson suggested military mobilization, as well as economic measures against the Communist bloc countries. A national state of emergency should be proclaimed. He wanted to prepare the American people by starting a civil defense program that included building air raid shelters. Knowing the dangers in this bulldozer approach, Thompson intervened. The difficulty he saw was that whatever the decision by the United States, it would manifestly have a bearing on Khrushchev's prestige. "We should leave room for him to back down," Thompson cautioned. He thought three time periods should be considered: (1) between then and the coming fall, when German elections and the Twenty-Second Congress of the Communist Party took place; (2) the time between those events and the possible signing of a separate peace treaty; and (3) the period thereafter. During the first time segment, Thompson felt the United States should take steps that exerted a maximum effect on the Soviets and a minimum effect on the allies, such as constructing air raid shelters and increasing the amount of military supplies sent to West Berlin. But declaring a national state of emergency would make America look hysterical and possibly provoke Khrushchev into a rash countermove.[68] Instead, Thompson advised, military preparations should be low key, but enough to be picked up on by Soviet intelligence agents. This would be more convincing to the Soviets.

Thompson wrote a memorandum to the secretary of state, with a copy sent to Acheson. In it, he stated that Khrushchev wanted to stabilize East Germany and prepare for its eventual recognition by other nations. Thompson dismissed the idea that Khrushchev's main motive was to damage America's prestige, because his free-city proposal essentially was a means for the West to save face.[69] He urged the Kennedy administration to come up with what would seem to be a reasonable alternative to the Soviets' free-city plan. One way to do this was to call for a referendum in West Berlin on whether to accept the free-city proposal or maintain the present situation, pending a reunification of Germany. Lastly, he suggested inviting Marshal Konstantin Vershinin, the commander of the Soviet Air Force, to the United States, in order to impress the Soviet military, through him, of the importance and strength of America's determination regarding the Berlin situation.

When Acheson presented his own report to JFK at the National Security Council meeting on June 28, 1961, he used Thompson's timeline and list of Khrushchev's objectives.[70] Acheson, however, called Khrushchev's moves a military threat, whereas Thompson thought they were essentially political. Berlin, Acheson said, was more than a problem over the fate of a city: "It has become an issue of resolution between the USA and the USSR, the outcome of which will go far to determine the confidence of Europe—indeed, of the world—in the United States. It is not too much to say that the whole position of the United States is in the balance." According to Acheson, Khrushchev's principal purpose in forcing the Berlin question was to humiliate the United States by making the country back down on a sacred commitment and, thus, shatter America's influence and position as a world power.

In Thompson's June 19 memo to Secretary of State Rusk, and later in a telegram from Moscow to Foy Kohler, the assistant secretary of state for European affairs, he offered four suggestions that, taken together, could lead toward a political solution for Berlin: (1) a postponement of German elections on reunification for seven to ten years; (2) a Western commitment to accept the current borders; (3) a NATO-Warsaw nonaggression pact; and (4) a ban on atomic arms for both East and West Germany.[71] "The Soviets might be tempted," he wrote, because "they could easily find [a] means of evading [German reunification] elections when the time came by accusing the West of violations." On the other hand, this would resolve the Berlin problem while Khrushchev was still in power and could provide assurance for better West German access to Berlin. Thompson thought Khrushchev "could paint such a settlement as a victory." For the West, it would avoid "a dangerous Berlin crisis" and actually strengthen "our position on self-determination."

There were two groups of advisors on Berlin, the "Hard-Liners" (Dean Acheson, Vice President Lyndon Johnson, and Assistant Secretary of Defense Paul Nitze), and the "Soft-Liners on Berlin," given the derisive acronym SLOBs by their detractors.[72] JFK thought that after the failed Bay of Pigs invasion and the Vienna summit, he needed to appear tough, so in some ways he leaned toward the Acheson group. Yet the possibility of having to face a nuclear confrontation over Berlin before attempting a negotiated settlement did not seem to be the right way to proceed. In the end JFK told Thompson, "I think we will go along with your plan for Berlin."[73]

Thompson sent another warning to the secretary of state on July 24, regarding the flow of refugees from East Germany into West Berlin. Any settlement would have to close the escape hatch. He concluded, "It would be better that the Communists bore the responsibility rather than us agreeing even indirectly to such a step."[74] Thompson pointed out that if the Communists decided to close the sector border in Berlin, any countermoves by the Western allies would be unlikely to succeed: "We should be careful not to initiate any measure which we might later have to abandon.... Both we and [the] West Germans consider it our long range advantage that potential refugees remain in East Germany. If Berlin developments go to the point of a separate treaty [between the USSR and East Germany], it is far better for us that the East Germans close the Berlin sector border than they attempt to interfere with our access by air."[75] Kennedy would later summarize this stance, saying, "A wall is a hell of a lot better than a war."

Despite Thompson's stark warnings, the US government made no contingency plans or preparations for a potential border closing in West Berlin. The intelligence community's failure to see this coming—in the face of Thompson's warnings and a later June statement by East Germany's Walter Ulbricht—would cause the president's Foreign Intelligence Advisory Board to question the competence of US intelligence agencies a few years later.[76]

Fourth of July

After the cold tone of the Vienna summit, there were those who thought the large annual Fourth of July celebrations at the US embassy in Moscow should be cancelled. The Thompsons, however, went ahead with the event as planned, and the top Soviet leadership members all showed up.[77] Khrushchev went through the reception line first, giving Jane an embrace and shaking hands with Thompson, after which Mikoyan followed suit. He was quite short, and his large mustache went straight into Jane's décolletage, which caused her to giggle and exclaim that it tickled. Khrushchev "just about rolled on to the floor, it was so funny."[78]

Khrushchev toured Jenny's vegetable patch in the garden. She was awarded a pat on the head by the Soviet leader, who called her *maladetz*.[79] Amazed at how high her corn plants were

Nikita Khrushchev (*front left*) and Llewellyn Thompson Jr. (*front right*), with Anastas Mikoyan (*center, with eyeglasses and mustache*) at a Fourth of July party, with them in the garden of Spaso House, the US ambassadorial residence in Moscow, USSR, 1961. Thompson Family Papers.

Jenny Thompson's corn patch in the garden at Spaso House, the US ambassadorial residence in Moscow, USSR, July 4, 1961. *Front, from left to right*, Jane Thompson, Nikita Khrushchev (*pointing*), and Jenny Thompson. Thompson Family Papers.

that early in the year, he asked if these came from special hybrid seeds. Jane proudly told him that she had grown the corn from seeds anyone could buy through the Burpee Seed Company's catalog. Khrushchev called over his agricultural minister and berated him for telling him corn could not be grown in the Moscow region. Dobrynin claims in his book that Thompson told him that day that the corn had been grown by the embassy's agricultural counselor, to surprise Khrushchev.[80] While the US ambassador may have said this, it definitely was not true. The Thompson family enjoyed corn on the cob for the entire summer. Jane even served it to the French ambassador at lunch one day. He, despite having said he had eaten this form of corn many times, obviously did not know what to do with the vegetable when it was given to him. He tried plucking out each kernel with a fork and knife, which gave Sherry an attack of the giggles.

Back in Washington, DC, JFK was still waiting for the State Department to draft an answer to Khrushchev's East Germany ultimatum from the Vienna summit. Since the allies had to be consulted, he knew it would take time, but after more than a month, Kennedy was impatient over the delay, reinforcing his disdain for what he perceived to be State Department plodding. Unfortunately, the president probably never knew the truth. The department had prepared the document fairly quickly, but it had been lost by someone at the

White House. When another draft was sent, it, too, was misplaced, accidently locked up in a safe by a White House aide before leaving on a two-week vacation.[81] Thompson finally delivered JFK's reply to Gromyko on July 17. Kennedy said the Soviet ultimatum "speaks of peace but threatens to disturb it." He rejected Khrushchev's idea of a free city, claiming it was a ploy to remove Berlin from Western protection and leave it subject to the will of a totalitarian regime.[82] Thompson assured Gromyko that, although the note was a firm statement of the American position, it did not slam the door on a discussion of the problem.[83]

In his July 25 address to Congress, JFK did not follow Acheson's advice to request a national state of emergency, but he did ask for an increase in military spending, a call-up of reserves in the armed forces, and the issuance of a threat to place economic sanctions on Warsaw Pact countries in the event of another blockade of Berlin.[84] The speech sounded tough, but there were also indications that the president was open to some sort of compromise. JFK said he was willing to remove "irritants," referring to espionage activities in Berlin, and would bear in mind the Soviet Union's historic security concerns in Central and Eastern Europe. Throughout his speech, Kennedy mentioned only *West* Berlin, leading the Soviets to understand that they could do whatever they wanted with *East* Berlin.[85]

Thompson was supposed to get a month's leave, but those plans were put on hold because John McCloy, a special advisor to the president on disarmament, came to Moscow to discuss possible arms talks. McCloy had barely started discussions with his counterparts when he was told that Khrushchev wanted him to fly down to the Black Sea to discuss JFK's public response to the Soviet leader's ultimatum on East Germany. Thompson and McCloy arrived at Khrushchev's dacha in Pitsunda, a Black Sea resort, on July 26, the day after Kennedy's speech. Khrushchev showed his displeasure over the president's statements with one of his typical outbursts. Given the nature of the ensuing discussion, McCloy decided that he had better leave the Soviet Union and return to Washington, DC, to report to JFK.

In his dispatch on the Pitsunda meeting, Thompson said that Khrushchev did display fits of temper but was mostly in good humor.[86] Nonetheless, "Khrushchev stated [the] president in effect had declared preliminary war on [the] Sov[iet]s because he had presented [the] Sov[iet]s with [an] ultimatum and had said if [the] ultimatum [was] not accepted that would mean war." Khrushchev seemed to forget, Thompson added, that he had been the one sending ultimatums since 1958. Khrushchev also said that he would not change Soviet policy regarding a separate peace treaty with East Germany. History would judge the two sides if a war occurred and would record who survived. Khrushchev was quite sure that it would be the Soviet Union.

After the bluster, Khrushchev then presented a softened posture. He pleaded for an understanding of the Soviet position and asked McCloy to convey his best wishes to JFK. The Soviet leader said he believed the president was displaying restraint and dignity in the Berlin matter. In Khrushchev's opinion, "True, he sometimes engages in polemics but always leaving door open for negotiations." If the United States had proposals, the Soviets would be happy to consider them and perhaps suggest counterproposals. Such an exchange might take place on a confidential basis. Khrushchev reaffirmed his willingness to guarantee the independence of West Berlin once a peace treaty with East Germany was signed and went so far as to say he thought "any Western proposal for such guarantees would be accepted."[87] The Soviet leader seemed as unsure as JFK about how to proceed on the Berlin question or the East German peace treaty. He was under constant pressure from Ulbricht to make good on his promise of a treaty between East Germany and the USSR or, at the very least, of closing the border between East and West Berlin. Unless something was done about the refugee flow, Ulbricht told Khrushchev's ambassador, collapse was inevitable.[88]

At the beginning of August, Khrushchev convened a meeting of the Warsaw Pact leaders to plan for implementation of a peace treaty with East Germany. At the end of the meeting, he gave a "secret speech" on Berlin. Thompson flew to Paris to meet Secretary of State Rusk and brief the European ambassadors on the Soviet leader's speech. Thompson told them Khrushchev had not shown any fundamental change in his position. The Twenty-Second Congress of the Communist Party was coming up, Thompson explained, and Khrushchev did not want his people to panic "into hoarding and [a state of] economic dislocation."[89] Khrushchev's speech, however, did cause more East German refugees to flee to West Berlin.

While Thompson was in Paris, his family prepared to take their vacation. They went to a US Army recreation center in Bavaria, instead of taking home leave, because, given recent events, Thompson needed to be near Moscow. His family expected him to join them, but he received a cable to go Washington, DC, directly from Paris. The Berlin Wall had begun going up on August 13, 1961.

Thompson arrived in the capital and met with JFK on Monday, August 14.[90] Kennedy's national security advisor, McGeorge Bundy, was also present. He told the president that the Berlin Wall was something "they were bound to do sooner or later."[91] This wall eased Ulbricht's pressure on Khrushchev. George Kennan, then the US ambassador to Yugoslavia, told JFK that it was Khrushchev's way of avoiding a confrontation, not causing it.[92] The West had grown accustomed to the Communists not letting their citizens travel outside their borders, so closing access to West Berlin almost made sense, except to the West Germans, who were extremely disappointed by the timid reaction of the rest of the world to this act. Willy Brandt, the mayor of West Berlin, was particularly critical of JFK's lack of response.[93] As general outrage grew, Kennedy realized that he had to do something, so he sent Vice President Lyndon Johnson, Charles Bohlen, and General Lucius Clay—the hero of the Berlin airlift in 1948—to Berlin, to show America's support. This did alleviate the worries of the West Berliners, although Clay's presence in that city would later cause trouble.

Thompson joined his family in Bavaria on August 25, a day after his birthday, but he hardly had time to play any golf, which he had been eagerly looking forward to. Thompson could clear his mind in the quiet of a golf course. Only five days later, the secretary of state sent him back to Moscow. JFK had decided to negotiate with the Soviets on Berlin and wanted Thompson to set up talks between Rusk and Gromyko to coincide with the opening of the UN General Assembly in September.[94] The Thompsons' servants at Spaso House were given a vacation break until September 7, and their nanny had written that family problems of her own kept her from returning. Jane used all her sources to try to hire a replacement, but it was impossible to find anyone willing to go to Moscow, due to the Berlin Crisis. Monica Henkle, a German nurse who was fluent in English, finally agreed to risk it.

From left to right: Jenny Thompson, Llewellyn Thompson Jr., and Sherry Thompson celebrating his belated birthday in the Blue Room at Spaso House, the US ambassadorial residence in Moscow, USSR, 1961. Carl Mydans, *Life* Picture Collection / Getty Images (622495154).

Once back in Moscow, Jane put Sherry into school after "a somewhat rebellious start."[95] Jenny, on the other hand, couldn't wait to start at her school and put on her new Soviet school uniform: a brown dress with a white collar, a black pinafore (a white pinafore was donned for special occasions), brown woolen stockings, and brown shoes. Jane walked her to school on September 11. Both were a bit nervous, but not as nervous as the headmistress, who was waiting for them at the entrance. Another American child from the embassy, Bruce Funkhouser, joined Jenny's class. School met for six days a week, from 8 a.m. to 1 p.m., and started with all the students lined up in front of their classrooms to do calisthenics. Red in the face from the effort but very much awake, they would then pile into their classes. Almost all of the students wore a red kerchief around their necks. This piece of clothing was a sign of belonging to the Pioneers, the Communist youth group, one of the rungs on a ladder leading to the top echelons of party membership.[96] Students who did not wear a red kerchief were generally ostracized. They were either very bad students or had displayed unacceptable behavior. When Jenny came home and asked her parents if she could wear a red kerchief, too, they had to patiently explain why it was not possible for the American ambassador's daughter to join a Communist youth group. Thompson and his wife attended parent-teacher meetings, where more than one teacher was at a loss for words

Jane Thompson's ballet class, with ballet master Misha, at Spaso House, the US ambassadorial residence in Moscow, USSR, circa 1959. Thompson Family Papers.

and just stared at the American couple. In time, everyone got used to the situation. Nonetheless, as Rada Khrushcheva said: "It is easy to sympathize with the teachers. Not long ago, communicating with foreigners was dangerous and even forbidden. Yet, at that time the American ambassador was able to send his children to a Russian school, and Russian teachers were able to accept this, even if it was a little bit unusual. I see this as an example of the US ambassador and Khrushchev, from opposite sides, simultaneously tearing a hole in the Iron Curtain that surrounded the USSR for so many years."[97]

Jane, obsessed with getting enough exercise, arranged for a former Bolshoi ballet master, affectionately known as Misha, to give classes in Spaso House to ladies from the entire diplomatic corps in the mornings, and to their children in the afternoons. It was a nice, informal way for people from the different nations' missions to come together. Sherry took a great liking to ballet and eventually became good enough to audition for famed choreographer George Balanchine. Jenny hated ballet classes and would try to hide behind the long drapes in the ballroom when the teacher wasn't looking. Years later, when Thompson was being investigated by the FBI as part of the confirmation process for his next appointment to Moscow, holding these very popular ballet classes would be cited as a sign of his being too pro-Soviet. They were stopped by his successor, Foy Kohler.

Talking to the Trees

Shortly after the Thompsons returned to Moscow, Cyrus Sulzberger was summoned from his vacation home on the Greek island of Spetsai to interview Khrushchev. On September 5, Sulzberger and Khrushchev met for over five hours.[98] The conversation ranged from the best way to hunt bear and cook pike to Berlin, thermonuclear war, and the differences in attitude between atheists and religious people toward death in war. Then Khrushchev became aggressive. He told Sulzberger that he would continue atmospheric nuclear testing. He stated that the Soviets had a 100-megaton bomb he was going to test and was planning to have many more of them fabricated, adding that although the USSR would never start a war, if there was to be one, it would definitely be nuclear. After building up this dire atmosphere, Khrushchev dropped a verbal bomb. All this nuclear confrontation could be avoided, he told Sulzberger. He wanted to start informal contacts with JFK to work something out. The correspondent told Khrushchev that if he wanted to send such a message to the president, then he should do it through Thompson. Khrushchev, however, said: "Thompson is very able but he is an ambassador. He would have to send such a message to Secretary Rusk. Rusk would tell Kennedy what's wrong with it before he told him what the message was. . . . Rusk is just a tool of the Rockefellers."[99]

Sulzberger showed Thompson his interview notes the next day, which gave the ambassador pause. Thompson knew that although Khrushchev's threatening tone was mostly bark and not much bite, it would stir up the more hawkish layers of American government. "This could mean war," he told Sulzberger. Perhaps the Soviets' microphones picked up their conversation, or Khrushchev himself may have realized that he had overdone things, for when Sulzberger took the draft of his article for Khrushchev to check, Khrushchev wanted to ease the tone of the interview. He did not want Sulzberger to mention detonating bombs, but instead say that Khrushchev would test a "device." The Soviet leader also wanted to remove the part about seeing "no use" in another meeting with JFK unless the president agreed to the "essentials of [German] settlement." Rather, Khrushchev wanted the interview to state that he would be willing to meet with JFK at any time to solve international problems.

The evening after this interview, Sulzberger suggested that he and Thompson take a stroll in the Spaso House garden. Sulzberger wrote in his diary that this was because "there was less chance of the trees being bugged."[100] Sulzberger revealed Khrushchev's personal message to JFK to Thompson, although he had specifically been asked not to tell the ambassador. Sulzberger went on to say that he intended to get the message off as soon as he got to Paris, and he noted that Thompson was "understanding and sympathetic to [his] quandary." There seems to be a discrepancy about what happened next. It is not clear if the message from Khrushchev to JFK was oral or written. In his own book, Sulzberger says he "wrote" it down himself and sent it to the president in a sealed envelope, through the American embassy in Paris.[101] We have found no evidence that Khrushchev ever wrote or signed a note, or any indication of just what the message was, so most likely it was verbal, as Sulzberger maintained. It's possible that Sulzberger did repeat this private communication to Thompson, "off the record," especially if it was an oral rather than a written message. The intent was to convey to JFK that he, Khrushchev, wanted to establish direct and secret contact with Kennedy, in order to find a means of settling the Berlin Crisis.

When Sulzberger went to the Paris embassy to send the message, the ambassador was away, so his deputy chief of mission, Cecil B. Lyons, took the envelope. It was not, however, sent to national security advisor Bundy, as Sulzberger claimed, but rather to Ted Sorensen, as special counsel to the president, on September 10, with a handwritten post-script from Lyons indicating that "Cy did not think the message so urgent as to require more rapid means of transportation."[102] Although it seems remarkable that this occurred, it explains why JFK did not receive Khrushchev's message until September 24, just before Kennedy's address to the UN General Assembly.

While JFK was wondering how to avoid a confrontation over Berlin, Khrushchev was wondering why he had no reply to his private message.[103] The Soviet leader wanted to make sure Kennedy did not make any waves before the Twenty-Second Congress of the Communist Party.[104] Khrushchev was worried that JFK might cause problems for him when the president addressed the UN General Assembly by giving another tough speech. So the Soviet leader sent someone to find out if JFK had received his message that "the storm in Berlin was over."[105] It was only when the Soviet press attaché, Mikhail Kharlamov, contacted Kennedy's press secretary, Pierre Salinger, and enquired about "the message" that anyone realized its importance. Salinger tracked it down.[106] When the president read it, he was pleased. It meant that Khrushchev was not going to sign a separate peace treaty with East Germany, at least not for the moment.

In the meantime, Thompson arranged the meeting between Soviet Minister of Foreign Affairs Andrei Gromyko and US Secretary of State Dean Rusk for mid-September, as JFK had asked him to. Rusk asked Thompson to write up his understanding of how the Soviets assessed the US-USSR power balance because there were, Rusk thought, "conflicting views within the [US] government." Thompson wrote back that the USSR's moves in Berlin had little to do with military factors, but that the Soviets believed the Berlin issue had effectively been exploited against them in the Cold War, destabilizing East Germany.[107] He went on to say that he thought the Soviets had a fairly accurate concept of America's military strength and most likely considered their position relative to the United States as having worsened. Thompson concluded that, in general, the Soviets were less fearful of the growing strength of the United States than they were about the increase in West Germany's military capabilities.

On September 10, Khrushchev made a speech where he said negotiations were "increasingly likely" and that "glimpses of new hope now have appeared." Yet the CIA document conveying this information also noted that "despite Khrushchev's asserted readiness for negotiations, he has adhered to the maximum position that negotiations should be directed toward a German treaty and the creation of a free city in West Berlin."[108]

The Rusk-Gromyko talks started on September 21 and did not result in anything new.[109] While it seemed as though the Soviets' public stance had not changed, something else had. Khrushchev sent the first pen-pal letter to JFK just as the Rusk-Gromyko talks were finishing up. This letter did not offer any alterations on the issues of Berlin and East Germany, but he suggested that Kennedy send someone to Moscow, or that he use Ambassador Thompson to continue the discussions.[110] One thing was clear. While the two sides talked, tensions were eased.

JFK kept his September UN General Assembly speech moderate. He reiterated the American position on Berlin, and spoke of disarmament; of a nuclear test ban "to halt the spread of these terrible weapons, to halt the contamination of the air, to halt the spiraling nuclear arms race";[111] and of colonialism. He concluded with words that indicated a willingness to reach international agreements on Germany and Berlin: "We are committed to no rigid formula. We seek no perfect solution. . . . We believe a peaceful agreement is possible."[112] The president saw Gromyko before the Soviet foreign minister headed back to Moscow on October 6, but he got nowhere. Gromyko did not budge an inch on Berlin, except to say that the Soviets would be willing to sign an agreement just on Berlin, provided the United States agreed to resolve other, larger issues separately. "You have offered to trade us an apple for an orchard," Kennedy objected.

24

The Twenty-Second Congress of the Communist Party

If Khrushchev were to be remembered in history for one
single reason, the word "destalinization" would suffice.
—MICHEL TATU, *Power in the Kremlin*

Jenny returned home one day from school to recount an unforgettable history class with a special guest teacher. The woman instructed the students to put their heads on the table and close their eyes and just concentrate on what she said. She described what life would be like once Communism reached its apogee. For now, she told her students, they had only reached the stage of Socialism, but one day true Communism would arrive. She told them what their day would be like from the moment they got up until they went to bed: "You will wake up in a well-lit apartment that is only for your family, no one to share with. You will have your own bed, and every apartment will have its own bathroom." She described what they would eat for breakfast, with plenty of food in the fridge that, once again, would not be shared. Everyone would work—not for too many hours, but enough. There would not be any need for money, because everything would be distributed equally and fairly. The afternoons and evenings would be dedicated to cultural activities and self-improvement. Finally, just before the bell rang for the class to finish, the teacher managed to get to the end of this marvelous day. When the students opened their eyes, they all looked happy. "I hope Communism comes soon, don't you?" one student asked her American friend. "Just think of it, a bathroom just for yourself, and everything you need. Won't it be wonderful?" "Well, yes," Jenny answered, "but, you know, I have that already, so I don't really have to wait for Communism to get here."

Thompson went to Washington, DC, briefly, where he talked to JFK, both about the Berlin situation and Cyrus Sulzberger's message from Khrushchev. He gave another briefing to the US Senate on the Soviet's leadership, calling Khrushchev the "best in sight." It would take years for any successor to him to establish the authority needed to reach agreements with the United States. Thompson then headed back to Moscow, to see what the Twenty-Second Congress of the Communist Party held in store.

Right at the start of the congress, Khrushchev announced that he would drop his ultimatum regarding East Germany, thus ending (once again) the Berlin Crisis. Peaceful coexistence with the West took precedence over conciliation with the Chinese. As Thompson had testified to the US Senate, this was a critical turning point, because each party congress laid out Communist bloc policies for decades, and it had not been certain which way things would go at this one. Khrushchev's decision was a bold one in the face of the ghosts that would come out of the Kremlin walls in the course of the meetings.

Khrushchev's biographer, William Taubman, described the event, called the Congress of the Builders of Communism, as triumphal.[1] "Builders of Communism" was an intentional label, signaling that the construction of Socialism was complete and the ideological advance to Communism would now begin, finally realizing the dream that Jenny had heard described at school. The metaphor of building was continued in the location for the event, the Palace of Soviets in the Kremlin, so new it still smelled of wood stain and fresh paint. It was a striking, modern, glass and marble building, surrounded by the walls and historical structures of the Kremlin. Jane thought it impressive—not the usual socialist-modernist construction that permeated the rest of the city.[2]

Khrushchev gave twin speeches that, together, lasted for ten hours, the first being a general report and the second an exposition of the Party Program,[3] which exaggerated the Soviets' (and Khrushchev's) accomplishments and potential. The speakers who followed outdid each other in heaping praise on Khrushchev, ratifying his dominance as the leader of the Communist world. But the congress was interrupted—and eclipsed, in the Western world by events in Germany.

Checkpoint Charlie

Walter Ulbricht, who still hoped the Twenty-Second Congress would bend toward strong, revolutionary Communist ideology, thus ensuring his long-sought peace treaty, took matters into his own hands by initiating various harassments of the allies in Berlin in the months prior to the Communist Party gathering.[4] General Lucius Clay, who was in the city after the construction of the Berlin Wall, was almost gleeful at this excuse to take action. He appealed for permission to respond to Ulbricht's harassments with "unpredictable" actions of his own, arguing that the risk of escalation ought to work "both ways." He ordered random "courtesy convoys" to drive back and forth on the Autobahn, daring the East Germans to harass them. He had tanks drive up to the perimeter of the wall and then turn around. The most provocative action he took was to set up a training exercise in the woods, where bulldozer tanks practiced tearing down a mock-up of a section of the Berlin Wall.[5] Soviet intelligence agents saw Clay's maneuvers, including his fake wall in the woods, and reasonably surmised that the Americans were going to tear down the actual wall.

This back-and-forth harassment would catalyze one of the great standoffs of the Cold War, right in the middle of Khrushchev's Communist Party congress. East German guards stringently demanded that the senior American diplomat in West Berlin, E. Allan Lightner Jr., and his wife produce documents at the Friedrichstrasse gate between East and

West Berlin, more commonly known as Checkpoint Charlie. Normally the guards just made a show of their demand, backing down in minutes, but this time Ulbricht wanted a real showdown, possibly to poke Khrushchev in the eye for having given up his East German ultimatum. Clay saw this as a continuation of the harassment. Marshal Ivan Konev, commander of the Soviet forces in East Germany, who'd been on the scene in Hungary during that revolt, called Khrushchev down from the conference podium. Irritated, Khrushchev asked him, "What's the meaning of this?" Konev told him that American tanks had put their guns into firing position at the Friedrichstrasse gate.[6] Khrushchev was appalled. He'd just removed the threat of a USSR–East German peace treaty, and now, right in the middle of his Communist Party Congress, where he was trying to subdue Chinese-led agitation, the Americans were provoking a crisis. Konev was sent back to Berlin to deal with the Americans. He was a mirror image of Clay, equally as hard line and as disappointed in the anti-Stalinist direction of the congress as Clay was in what the US general characterized as American appeasement.[7]

When Clay sent jeeps containing military personnel through the checkpoint, backed up by tanks and bulldozers, it corroborated Soviet intelligence data that the Americans planned to pull down the Berlin Wall. Three US jeeps flew past the gate, while the bulldozers and tanks stopped at the border. Meanwhile, the Soviets had already moved a battalion of men and a regiment of tanks nearby, on the East German side. Ten Soviet tanks went up to the gate, and ten American tanks pulled forward to face them. They sat nose to nose for several days, with American and Soviet soldiers occasionally getting out of their tanks to move around and ward off the cold.[8]

On October 27, Thompson went to see Gromyko to formally complain about the tensions in Berlin.[9] JFK then sent a message to Khrushchev via Robert F. Kennedy and Bolshakov. He implored Khrushchev to "establish a period of relative moderation and calm over the course of the next 4–6 weeks."[10] According to Sergei Khrushchev, the president reached out to Khrushchev to take the first step and assured him that the American tanks would withdraw within twenty minutes if the Soviet tanks made the first move, ending the standoff.[11] Khrushchev later told Thompson that realizing the United States would not or could not retreat, he ordered his tanks to redeploy behind some buildings, out of sight.[12] He also boasted to Thompson that Berlin was surrounded, and that the Soviets could have easily taken the city in a matter of hours. Thompson replied that the United States was aware that Berlin could be taken at any time and therefore did not think that Khrushchev could consider the number of Western troops in West Berlin as an aggressive force. Khrushchev retorted, "Well, this is true, but then why is it field troops and not a police force?"

Konev, who was sent to stop the crisis, was caught between Clay, who was itching for a showdown, and Ulbricht, who wanted his Berlin crisis, with or without Khrushchev. Clay and Ulbricht were each sure the other side would back down, and both were quite prepared to escalate the crisis to prove their bluff. Clay considered that he was vindicated, because he'd stood firm in front of Soviet aggression. The Americans thought that they had averted a crisis instigated by the East Germans, as proxies for the Soviets. The Soviets believed that they'd warded off a crucial state of affairs by standing resolute against an imminent attack by the Americans. The Soviets had made a show of force, blustered that they would win and "could take West Berlin in an afternoon," and the Americans had backed down. The two national perspectives are still being argued by historians today, but the more likely reality was exactly what Thompson feared the most: even small actions, instigated without taking different perceptions into account and carefully forecasting potential countermoves, can easily be misinterpreted and escalate out of hand.[13]

Legacy of a Congress

Khrushchev aimed to assert Moscow's primacy in the world Communist movement at the Twenty-Second Congress, but the bloc had not seen much growth toward world Communism under Khrushchev, with its only new member being the island of Cuba.[14] The "special attention" Cuba received from Moscow was not unequivocal. The State Department's Bureau of Intelligence and Research wrote, "Moscow places great hopes in the Communist foothold in Cuba . . . [but caution] was evident in their obvious reluctance to openly recognize Cuba's claims to being a Communist country."[15]

Early in the Twenty-Second Congress, Khrushchev once again delved into the darker side of Stalin's rule and followed this up by having Stalin's waxy corpse moved from the mausoleum in the dark of night and unceremoniously stuck in the Kremlin wall.[16] Unlike Khrushchev's "Secret Speech," which leaked out slowly across the USSR in the 1950s, these statements were public. Overnight, destalinization came out of the closet and onto the Soviet streets. The writer and dissident Alexandr Solzhenitsyn was so amazed by the congress that he decided to publicly release the books he had written in secret and make a comment that of all the Soviet leaders, Khrushchev, at least, had something human about him.[17]

Underneath all the handsome trappings of the Twenty-Second Congress, trouble brewed on domestic issues. Khrushchev decided it was time to finally purge the remainder of the Anti-Party Group.[18] Nonetheless, he did not fully succeed.[19] In the USSR, the perennial failure of agriculture, a sector that was personally overseen by Khrushchev, greatly troubled him. Thompson illustrated the inadequacy of the Soviets' agriculture infrastructure with a story about farmers who resorted to feeding price-subsidized bread to their hogs, rather than rely on their meager grain rations.[20] Yields from Khrushchev's Virgin Lands Production Program declined year after year, and the need to import wheat from capitalist countries had to be a particular pique.[21] The Soviet leader did not assume any blame, however, since "Khrushchev had concluded—in good faith it seems, if somewhat naively—that the whole trouble was due to the bad execution of a good policy."[22] His strategy to increase consumer goods at the expense of the country's military budget also met a significant roadblock that summer, in the period leading up to and during the congress. The Berlin Crisis required a greater military expenditure, so Khrushchev was forced to suspend his previous troop reductions from 1960 and significantly increase the Soviet defense budget.

Dacha Relief

The American embassy had a dacha in the country, outside of Moscow. It was a large, wooded property on the river. Huge crows, populating the tall pine and birch forest, spoke in harsh cries back and forth. A large, two-story stucco structure served most of the embassy personnel as a weekend retreat. But the Thompsons had use of a small, ramshackle wooden building a few hundred yards closer to the river. They would go there as a family to cross-country ski in winter and swim in summer. Jenny and Sherry loved it at the dacha, because they were free to wander the woods with the dogs and pick wild strawberries, or take the rowboat out on the river and explore, watching the families and the fat men and women sunning on its banks. They'd swim, too, although having to use cigarettes to burn off the leeches infesting the small river rather detracted from that pleasure.

That fall, after the Twenty-Second Congress, the Thompsons had one of their dacha parties, consisting sometimes of journalists, or other diplomats, or Soviets—who were often artists or writers—and sometimes a mix of all these groups. The parties were relaxed affairs, perhaps a cookout or a gathering around a roaring fire burning in the fireplace, replete with laughter, cigarettes, card games, and liquor, and perhaps with someone playing a guitar. This particular party was a picnic, and everyone talked about their amazement at the events of the congress. It was one thing to pass the text of a secret speech around, but it was quite another to have Khrushchev's address to the Twenty-Second Congress out in the open—including the struggles with the Anti-Party Group—and available to everyone, not just the intelligentsia. In a letter home, Jane described their friends' con-

Llewellyn Thompson Jr. in front of the US ambassador's private dacha in Tarasovka, USSR, with three unknown figures in the background, circa 1961. Thompson Family Papers.

Weekend at the US ambassador's private dacha in Tarasovka, USSR, circa 1958, with journalists (*clockwise, from bottom*) Boris Klosson, an unknown woman (*with beehive hairdo*), Carl Mydans, Harriet Klosson, 2 unknown women, Jane Thompson, Llewellyn Thompson Jr., Pierre Salinger, an unknown woman, and Preston Grover. Carl Mydans, *Life* Picture Collection / Getty Images (625738000).

versations as "fascinating, hair-raising, and at times unbelievable." She wrote that the effect on the locals, seeing for the first time their demigods as the rest of the world had seen them all these years, was staggering.[23]

These revelations were compounded by price hikes for foods (the cost of meat doubled) and a congruent reduction in wages or increase in working hours. The stress finally caused riots to break out in Novocherkassk.[24] Anastas Mikoyan, Frol Kozlov, and Marshal Issa A. Pliyev, an old-school Cossack cavalry officer, went to that city to put down the protest. Once Khrushchev gave an OK to quell the riot, Pliyev called in troops and then, when the demonstrators began climbing over the wall, some of his soldiers fired into the crowd. Many people were injured, and twenty-five were killed.[25] Sergei Khrushchev later wrote that the result was terrible for his father and haunted him.[26] Nonetheless, as a reward for the marshal's success in Novocherkassk, Khrushchev put Pliyev in charge of the missiles he was about to send to Cuba. The old-guard officer, with his command there, would very nearly bring the world, as he knew it, to an end.[27]

Khrushchev faced many problems at the end of the Twenty-Second Congress of the Communist Party. His Berlin policy had failed. The United States was still not giving the Soviet Union the respect it deserved. The USSR was surrounded by allied military bases, and nuclear missiles had just been placed in Turkey, Italy, and Britain. He was facing both internal and external opposition, with the latter from Albania and China, over destalinization. He had reasserted his authority, but it was still limited. His agricultural apparatus was failing, and his country's military was asserting itself. The result was deep-seated domestic unrest and pressure from all sides. So it's understandable that almost a year later, Operation Anadyr, in Cuba, seemed an irresistible opportunity to use missiles to solve all his problems.

Germany was still on Khrushchev's mind. He wrote to JFK, "We cannot turn our back on the facts and fail to see that until the existing borders of Germany are finally formalized, the sluice-gates which release the West German revanchist desires remain open." He claimed that "the followers of Hitler and his policy, who . . . still exist in no small numbers in the Federal Republic of Germany [i.e., West Germany]," were exploiting the lack of a postwar settlement to bring about a collision between the USSR and the United States. "I would think," he argued, "that the legal formalization of the State borders which have taken shape after World War Two equally meets the interests of both the USSR and the United States."[28]

Some More Equal than Others

In early December, Jane invited her daughter's Soviet classmates to come to Spaso House for Jenny's birthday. The school's headmistress was not sure how to respond at first, obviously having to check to see if such a thing was allowed. The answer came back that the Russian children could accept the invitation. The head teacher announced it in the class, but made it seem to be more of an obligation than a nice event. Only students who were Pioneers could go, however, and she instructed them to wear their school uniforms. Jenny raised her hand. The invitation, she insisted, was for everyone, not just for those who belonged to this Communist youth group. The embarrassed teacher tried to argue with her, but Jenny was firm. If only Pioneers were invited, she said, then she would not be able to go to her own party, and Bruce Funkhouser, the other American boy in the class, couldn't come either. Backed into a corner, with all the students looking at her, the teacher relented and said that everyone could go. The entire class was more than pleased, especially the non-Pioneer students. Jenny, however, would soon learn an important lesson. On the day of her party, everyone came—except those students who were not Pioneers. At that point, it was too late to protest. In the end, Jenny had lost, and it was even worse for the poor students she had tried to include. After the winter break, they disappeared from the class entirely. When Jenny asked what had happened to them, she was given evasive explanations.

At least her birthday party was a success. Jane piled the enormous table in the state dining room with party favors and food, which soon disappeared. Jane thought everyone would go home after the screening of Disney's cartoon film, *One Hundred and One Dalmatians*, but no one showed signs of being tired. One of the teachers started playing the piano, and the students sang and danced and played games. It turned out to be the longest party Jane had ever arranged and, she claimed, it possibly influenced détente more than any formal reception.

Jane wrote to her mother about the party and described going into the basement store-room to get her silver tree-shaped decorations.[29] Jenny, however, reminded her that she'd given them away to their Chinese butler Tung and his wife Natasha. "Don't you remember?" she described Jenny as stating, "[you said] they could have the trees as we certainly won't be here another Christmas." Jane then continued, "And when someone had asked for some other Christmas ornaments that I had, Tommy said, 'Oh, certainly you can have them. After all, we won't be here next year.' To which Jenny, eyes rolling, said 'Famous Yule messages at Spaso. Christmas 1960: We won't be here next year; Christmas 1961: We won't be here next year; Christmas 1962: We won't be here next year; etc. and etc., with her accent becoming more and more Russian, until by Christmas 1970: Is hundred perr cent sure Thompson family will be being in other town next year.' "

Jane began preparing for a family holiday trip to Bavaria for Christmas 1961, and she was feeling a tad guilty about not having the usual big party for the embassy staff. But the Thompsons never did get to Bavaria, and Jane ended up having a Christmas open house for 185 guests. She also danced with the dashing young Soviet cosmonaut, Yuri Gagarin, at the Soviet New Year's celebration at the Kremlin. When he invited Jane to go fly into space with him, she declined. When he persisted and asked, "Wouldn't you like to fly into space?" she replied, "No, I do not have a license to drive that kind of thing."[30] Neither she nor Thompson had had a license to drive anything for over a decade, something that they'd have to rectify once the family was back in America.

As 1961 came to a close, Thompson heard from a person he considered a "usually reliable source" that Anatoly Dobrynin, chief of the American Section of the Foreign Ministry, would be nominated as the USSR's ambassador to the United States, representing a blow to that country's hard-line faction. Thompson was pleased with this choice and thought Dobrynin was probably Gromyko's pick.[31] The Americans were happy to get rid of "Smiling Mike" Menshikov, but Khrushchev fumed at the January 8 Presidium meeting: "Thompson got hold of this information secretly even though it had not been announced to anyone at all. Who was the informant?[32] Thompson says he was told about it in confidence. This indicates that an informant does exist. This is treachery, this is treason."[33] Nonetheless, Dobrynin took up his Washington, DC, post that March.

At about this time, the State Department instructed Thompson to set up talks between himself and Gromyko on the continuing problem of Berlin. Although the Rusk-Gromyko talks that September had produced no change in the Soviet position on Berlin, the Twenty-Second Congress seemed to indicate that perhaps there now was a chance for something to happen. Each side felt that the other was just about to give in. It was Thompson's job to see "whether and in what area a basis for negotiations can be found."[34]

25 ≡

Up the Down Escalator
The Thompson-Gromyko Talks

Deception and lying are bad tactics. They catch up with you. So is
over-ingratiation. An Ambassador's job is to call the shots straight,
to interpret your country to the one in which you are stationed
and vice versa. You must have double vision, without losing your
own convictions. It's important, too, to keep up a certain form of
politeness and respect, whatever the provocation.
—LLEWELLYN THOMPSON, *Look* magazine, February 12, 1963

Thompson knew about his instructions before the State Department actually sent them, because the British Ambassador in Moscow had shown him a draft.[1] Thompson wrote to the department on December 21 to find out what was going on, and the official instructions came from an embarrassed State Department a week later.[2] Too many people were involved in the Thompson-Gromyko talks: the Ambassadorial Group from the Four-Powers summit in Paris, JFK's Berlin Task force, West German Chancellor Konrad Adenauer, the French (who opposed any kind of "talks"), the State Department, and the White House. All of them peered over Thompson's shoulder, leaving him very little room to maneuver. The Berlin Task Force drafted instructions which were approved by the Secretary of State, cleared with the president, and only then sent to Thompson. JFK wanted to be in the loop with everything involving the Soviets. After each meeting with Gromyko, Thompson sent long reports back to Washington, DC, which were carefully analyzed, in order to prepare detailed instructions for the following round. The first set of instructions from Dean Rusk informed Thompson that this was not "play acting" but was a real probe, and told him to stay "alert" to any leads the Soviets might give him.[3]

The Thompson-Gromyko Talks

On January 2, 1962, Thompson set off for the Soviet Foreign Office for the first meeting, accompanied by the US embassy's second secretary and German specialist, Kempton Jenkins.[4] There was so much expectation about these meetings that reporter Marvin Kalb and

Llewellyn Thompson Jr. in front of the Soviet Foreign Office, Moscow, USSR, April 1, 1958. *Life* Picture Collection / Getty Images (50401962).

many of the members of the press corps were standing in the parking area, "sort of waving bye-bye."[5] Gromyko was accompanied by his translator, Viktor Sukhodrev, and Soviet diplomat and former Austrian State Treaty negotiator Ivan Ilyichev, who was now head of the department that handled German and Austrian matters.[6]

The meeting lasted two and a half hours and was "cordial and businesslike."[7] Thompson presented the American position, which emphasized that the most important issue at stake was access to Berlin. Gromyko stated that the main issue was not Berlin, but the conclusion of a final treaty with East Germany. Overland access to West Berlin could be worked out later and appended to a final treaty, but it could not be dealt with in isolation. Gromyko was annoyed when Thompson brought up the "all-Berlin solution": "This question cannot be discussed. . . . East Berlin is completely integrated into GDR [East Germany]."[8] Thompson suggested establishing a corridor to West Berlin under an international authority, consisting of the United States, France, the United Kingdom, and the Soviet Union. East and West Germany would also be included as charter members, which would thus be a de facto recognition of East German sovereignty. This was the Western compromise: the East Germans would participate, in exchange for Soviet guarantees regarding West Berlin. Gromyko, however, had doubts, as his impression was that this could create a state within a state, but he did not reject the concept outright. It would require further "detailed study."

Thompson insisted, as he had been instructed to do, that the Americans were prepared to discuss questions other than access, but only once the nature of the access arrangements was clear. That was why the United States raised this issue first. By access, he meant the freedom for *anyone* to travel back and forth. Thompson told Gromyko that the Soviets' free-city proposal for West Berlin was not acceptable. Gromyko answered that if the status of Berlin was not going to change, what was the point of talking? Thompson replied, "To avoid a very dangerous situation."[9] Although they remained in the same spot on the treadmill of old arguments, Gromyko had shown some interest in the international access authority and the atmosphere had been cordial. It was not a bad beginning.

When Thompson and Jenkins left the Foreign Ministry, the press was still there waiting for them, but the only thing Thompson could say was that the talks would continue.[10] The *New York Times* concluded that the Soviet Union would take a positive attitude toward the talks, based on remarks Khrushchev made to *Izvestia*, stating, "people and States have only one choice, either peaceful coexistence and economic competition of capitalism and Socialism or mad, killing, rocket nuclear war."[11]

Thompson received his instructions for the second meeting a week later, on January 10.[12] The State Department was finally beginning to understand the dilemma in the negotiations, which was the "Western desire for an improved access arrangement with Berlin on [the] one hand, as against [the] Soviet desire for change in (1) status of West Berlin, and (2) other questions relating to Germany as a whole."[13] Nevertheless, the department told Thompson to concentrate on access to Berlin.

Reality was also beginning to dawn in the Kremlin. In a Presidium meeting just after the first Thompson-Gromyko talk, Khrushchev admitted that it would be impossible to get the kind of peace treaty the Soviets wanted against the will of the West.[14] Khrushchev told the Presidium, "I don't see any particular advantage they would give us by signing a treaty," noting that "we gained our advantage on 13 August," when the border between East and West Berlin was closed. He added, however, that any sort of intermediate agreement was worse than the current state of affairs.[15] At least now, everyone admitted that the situation was "abnormal." "What they want to do is to make this abnormality normal," Khrushchev said, adding that "this is like giving a Russian nesting doll to a fool, so that he returns thinking he got more than one present." Dean Rusk, for his part, referred to the Soviet proposals as "buying the same horse twice." Khrushchev told Gromyko off for even entertaining the possibility of an international access corridor to West Berlin and instructed him to "educate Thompson." A corridor would be a major concession, at the East Germans' expense, and it would be better to keep West Berlin as a source of contention.

"The situation will remain as it is," Khrushchev stated at the end of the Presidium meeting, with everyone approving.

The second meeting between Thompson and Gromyko lasted three hours, and this time, Ilyichev was not present.[16] Not only was there no forward progress, but it seemed like a step backward to Thompson. Gromyko, following Khrushchev's instructions, hardened his approach and did not want to even look at the paper by the State Department on the possibility of an international access authority.[17] Thompson thought the most likely reason Gromyko took a tough position was that, knowing what the West's minimum requirements were, the Soviets wanted the talks to break down, which would serve as an excuse to proceed with a separate peace treaty between the USSR and East Germany and would probably ensure, at least in the beginning, that allied access to Berlin was not interfered with.[18] He was half right. The Soviets were not prepared to do what it took for the talks to succeed, but they were not going to proceed with a separate treaty, either. There was no longer any imperative need. "When we closed the wall . . . we pulled out the bone . . . and now the bone is no longer working against us but in our favor," Khrushchev told the Presidium. So they would go on "talking" without agreeing to anything.

If Gromyko felt that he had still not been tough enough in the January 12 meeting, he corrected himself the next day, when he called Thompson back to the Foreign Ministry for an in-between meeting. Thompson and Jenkins arrived to find Gromyko "stony-faced." He began by attacking the United States and its allies for using West Berlin to incite unrest, and he went on in this vein for forty minutes. He warned that the USSR could not be threatened by the use of force, and that such things could lead to the incineration of New York City. As he spoke, Gromyko got more and more excited, pounding on the arms of the chair he was sitting on.[19] According to Jenkins, "Thompson sat quietly smoking until Gromyko blurted out, 'Well, Mr. Ambassador?' Then, in a quiet voice, Thompson rejected Gromyko's threatening language and said: 'I deeply regret you have been required to present such a performance. You know as well as I that if there were a nuclear exchange between our two great nations, the Soviet Union would disappear from the face of the earth.'" Then he got up and left with Jenkins.[20]

Thompson wrote to the State Department, saying that he found it difficult to recommend what to do next. He suggested calling the Soviets' bluff by informing Gromyko that, since their intention was "clearly to leave West Berlin to the mercy of the East Germans," their discussion should turn to what would happen when the Soviets signed a separate treaty with East Germany, in order to "avoid [a] highly dangerous situation."[21] JFK thought that perhaps it was time to open the discussion a little more: "There is a good deal in our own position that cannot be communicated if the British and Germans have to clear it first. . . . I begin to think we may be having the disadvantages of both types of talks at present: we are unable to talk frankly to the Russians and yet we cannot really pull our Allies into a position of responsible participation."[22]

JFK also considered whether Thompson might not be the right channel, or perhaps that instead he should be allowed more leeway. The president was not the only one to see that Thompson's hands were tied. Another was Henry Owen.[23] He thought one of the problems was that there was a lack of consensus on what the talks were about, since "some think it is a debating exercise, some are out to entice the French, and some view it as a prelude to a US-Soviet conference." Owen suggested that those in Washington, DC, get out of the "business of telling Thompson how to punctuate sentences, how to argue, in short how to deal with a wide variety of tactical issues that he is probably a lot better fitted to cope with than we are. I think the talks would be a lot more effectively conducted if he has a clear view of our purpose and of [the] allied attitude and then [is] left to plot his course . . . subject to our approval."[24]

Yet when Thompson got his instructions for the next round, none of these points had been taken into account. The third set of meetings took place on February 1 and 9.[25] The Soviets would not discuss access to West Berlin until the larger East German question was solved, and the West did not want to consider anything else until there was a solution to the access question. Thompson told Gromyko that he was perplexed by how the Soviets could believe they could dispose of their sector—East Berlin—according to their own will and then pretend to have rights in West Berlin. Gromyko responded that the existing situation regarding East Germany was the source of all the conflict. It was a stalemate. Yet for some reason the Soviets wanted to continue talking, although neither Thompson nor the State Department could fathom why. Adding to the frustration, as Thompson and Gromyko were meeting, the Soviets began buzzing civilian airlines in the Berlin air corridors, dropping chaff to confuse radar, and generally playing "chicken with airplanes." The harassment continued until March 29, as the Soviets wanted to demonstrate the fragility of the allied position.[26]

The fourth Thompson-Gromyko meeting took place on February 12. Thompson noticed that the Soviets put emphasis on the frontier between Germany and Poland, the Oder–Neisse line, which Thompson had suggested, early on in the game, could be used as a bargaining chip. He now wondered, however, how the talks could possibly continue much longer, unless some new element was introduced. Perhaps, Thompson speculated, they wanted "to put the onus for [the] break on us," should the talks disintegrate.[27]

On February 15, JFK sent Khrushchev a pen-pal letter.[28] The president complained that neither the talks between Thompson and Gromyko, nor the contacts through his brother RFK, had brought their positions any closer: "It would seem today that neither of us knows very much more about the prospects for accommodation than we knew many months ago. . . . Both of us, therefore, however differently we may view the issues, are confronted with the same basic question: how to deal with the present state of affairs in a manner which will (1) avoid any shift favorable to one side and detrimental to the other, and (2) ensure a greater degree of stability and tranquility in the entire German situation. I believe that if we take these two principles as a starting point, we might be able to see some light at the end of the tunnel." He also entreated Khrushchev to stop the harassment in the Berlin air corridors, stating, "As Ambassador Thompson has made clear, we view the recent acts . . . with very grave concern." JFK ended by saying that if the two leaders could find a *modus vivendi* on Berlin, they might be able to make progress on other issues, such as "the question of German frontiers, respect for the sovereignty of the GDR [East Germany], prohibition of nuclear weapons for both parts of Germany, and the conclusion of a pact of non-aggression between NATO and the Warsaw powers."

On March 2, 1962, the president delivered a major radio and television address on nuclear testing and disarmament.[29] The United States had "long urged an effective world-wide end to nuclear tests," JFK declared, and in 1958, America had joined the USSR in a nuclear test moratorium. The Soviet Union's breaking of that moratorium in September 1961, however, had prompted Kennedy's decision to resume underground tests and begin preparations for atmospheric tests, which would soon take place over the Pacific Ocean.[30] In late February, even though the Thompson-Gromyko talks were failing to progress, the White House consulted Thompson on preparations for the planned reciprocal television appearances by Kennedy and Khrushchev, agreed to at the Vienna summit between the two leaders in June 1961.[31] The Soviets, however, said "Nyet" to the TV broadcasts, because the Americans had resumed nuclear testing.

The next, and final, meeting between Thompson and Gromyko took place on March 6.[32] Thompson read out the points the State Department had instructed him to present.[33] No new element was introduced by either side. Perhaps it was on this day that Thompson tucked the cables containing the State Department's instructions next to where he was seated on his chair. When he got up to leave, he forgot he that had done so and left them there. Gromyko, seeing the cables, called his deputy, Georgi Kornienko, and told him not to show them to anyone in the Soviet Foreign Ministry, but to immediately get in touch with Thompson, "eye to eye," to give the ambassador back his papers, so that he would not be embarrassed by what had happened. According to Kornienko, this demonstrated Gromyko's respect for Thompson.[34]

Just as the talks between Thompson and Gromyko were petering out, Gerard Smith wrote a memo to the Secretary of State regarding an expository cable about the German issue that Thompson had sent to Eisenhower three years before and had re-sent to JFK early in his presidency.[35] The more he and the State Department's Policy Planning Staff studied Thompson's old cable, Smith wrote, the more "significant and provocative" they found it. In looking at the past ten years, maybe Thompson had been right, and Khrushchev really did believe that Communism could compete with other ideologies and win peacefully. Moreover, in 1959 a new generation of Soviets had already begun evolving, and their domestic fervor for Communism was waning.[36] Unfortunately, in the interim years, Khrushchev had become frustrated and belligerent. Thompson, too, was frustrated, enough so to consider a job offer from Princeton University.[37]

Rusk and Further Talks with the Soviets

In March 1962, the Berlin talks continued, but this time they were between Gromyko and Rusk, who were both in Geneva for a disarmament conference. Thompson was also in Geneva, off and on, in March and kept up with what was happening with regard to the Berlin situation.[38] JFK had instructed Rusk to develop his discussions on Berlin along the lines of a draft proposal for a *modus vivendi*, the goal being to keep things much the way they were.[39] Secretary Rusk wrote back to the State Department in early April to explain that, "in putting forward elements of possible *modus vivendi* to Gromyko, I have taken into consideration Ambassador Thompson's view that it would be tactically unwise at this stage to disclose categorically to Soviets that we would be prepared to accept GDR [East German] personnel at checkpoints." Rusk agreed with Thompson that this should not be done until there was more evidence of the Soviets' willingness to reach an agreement.[40]

At the conclusion of the Geneva disarmament talks, the US delegation drew up a five-point proposal for a *modus vivendi*, designed to give a fresh appearance to what was still the same American position: (1) the establishment of an international access authority for a corridor to West Berlin; (2) an agreement to deny nuclear weapons to both Germanys; (3) a nonaggression declaration between NATO and the Warsaw Pact countries; (4) committees composed of West and East Germans in equal numbers, to maintain "technical" contacts between them; and (5) a permanent conference of deputy foreign ministers of the Four Powers to meet regularly and review the Berlin situation.[41] They sent the proposal to West Germany, requesting that comments come back within two days, that is, by April 12. It was leaked to the press on April 13, most likely by people in the German government who resented getting such short notice in which to craft a reply, and who were afraid that the Americans were making some sort of deal behind their backs. The leak guaranteed that the proposal would fail.

The futile talks on Berlin continued in Washington, DC, now between Rusk and the new Soviet ambassador, Anatoly Dobrynin. Although Dobrynin was a fresh and welcomed interlocutor, the problem still had no resolution. Thompson, in the capital for consultations that April, briefed the Senate Foreign Relations Committee. He also met with JFK, to encourage him to consider working toward another meeting with Khrushchev, which was supposed to take place in November 1962.[42] This time, however, it would be the Soviets who would start a crisis, making it impossible for the two leaders to meet. Thompson also took time to have lunch with the new Soviet ambassador in Washington, DC.[43] The two would develop one of those strange diplomatic friendships, and their families would even spend a little time together at the Black Sea. Jane fondly remembered Dobrynin as being charming and a great teller of jokes that transcended both cultures.

Back in Moscow, Thompson wrote to the State Department with his thoughts on why the Soviets drifted along with talks that went nowhere.[44] Khrushchev, he speculated, was influenced by a missile gap in favor of the United States, as well as by East Germany's dependence on economic assistance from the USSR. Khrushchev did not want the Berlin situation to get to the point where interzonal trade would be affected, as this would exacerbate the Soviets' economic burden, as well as increase the risk of uprisings in East Germany and, possibly, war. On the other hand, Thompson went on, "Khrushchev was so deeply committed to [a] solution [to the] Berlin problem [that it is] difficult to see how he can allow it to drag on." While he believed that Khrushchev remained firmly in control, he had little doubt that there was disagreement within the higher reaches of the Soviet government on several of his policies. It was natural that Khrushchev would avoid initiatives that might aid anyone "inclined [to] question his leadership." His most serious problem was still agriculture, with his reforms having been stymied at the Twenty-Second Communist Party Congress.

Therefore, Thompson thought it would be rational to expect Khrushchev to pursue détente for at least a couple of years, stating that the "key to such détente, as K[hrushchev] himself has pointed out, is [the] Berlin problem." This indicated to Thompson that the Soviets *should* be ready to make concessions and seek compromises with the West. The problem with that analysis, however—as Thompson himself pointed out—was that the Soviets were "not always rational by our standards and [it is] always possible K[hrushchev] will conclude that to maintain his position at home and deal with [the] Chinese problem abroad he should make [a] radical change in policy." Thompson ended his cable by saying he didn't think Khrushchev would go that far, but neither was the Soviet leader likely to "pay our price for [a] real Berlin solution," so the most probable scenario was for the "present 'neither peace nor war' situation" to continue.

Little did Thompson know that, as he was sending his cable back to the State Department, Khrushchev was working on what he thought was a very good plan, which would take care of everything Thompson had mentioned, without the Soviet leader having to change his policies or spend very much money. It would also take care of another problem Thompson had not mentioned in his cable, but was one that worried Khrushchev—protecting Cuba. His plan was to secretly introduce missiles into Cuba and arm them with nuclear warheads. That would take care of the missile gap, the Chinese, and the dregs of the Anti-Party Group, as well as justify his troop reductions and eventually give him a better position in which to negotiate on Berlin. The only thing it didn't fix was the USSR's recalcitrant corn crop.

A Visit by Salinger

As Khrushchev was hatching his plan, the Thompsons were getting ready to leave Moscow. Jane began organizing the packing, an ordeal that lasted several weeks, with all their belongings spread out on tables in the grand hall. She also prepared for another house guest, Pierre Salinger, the White House press secretary.[45] His visit was supposed to be a private one, but he had really come to see about reviving reciprocal television appearances by JFK and Khrushchev.[46] Khrushchev, remembering how Kennedy had received the Soviet leader's journalist son-in-law, wanted to make Salinger's visit special, too. When Salinger arrived on May 11,[47] Thompson informed him of a change of plans. Instead of staying with the Americans, he was going directly to the Soviet government's dacha at Ogaryovo, some 20 miles outside of Moscow, to spend a few days with Khrushchev himself.[48]

The following day, Khrushchev appeared at about 11:30 a.m. and everyone, including Thompson, went for a motorboat ride on the Moscow River, followed by a long hike through the woods—all good opportunities for both small talk and serious talk. Although Salinger was not supposed to discuss "substantive matters," he revealed that he had a personal assignment from the president: to convey JFK's opinion on Soviet-American relations.[49]

On the Berlin question, Khrushchev restated the Soviet positions. The Soviets and the East Germans had practical control of access to West Berlin, and they could shut it off at any time. "So why," he asked, "should the Soviet Union and East Germany give away something they already have?" He and Salinger also touched on the issues of disarmament and a test ban. Khrushchev said that the Soviets sincerely wanted to achieve disarmament. Salinger told him that the president thought the greatest failure of his first year in office was not coming to an agreement on a test ban. Khrushchev said he was sorry to hear that, but the USSR would never tolerate inspection posts on its territory. Salinger also made reference to the previous use of Georgi Bolshakov as a back channel for communications between JFK and Khrushchev. Now he suggested going through Dobrynin instead, and Khrushchev agreed.

Khrushchev told Salinger that JFK "created the impression that he really was searching for the possibility of reaching agreement with us" in the Vienna summit, but added that such a result was not likely to be achieved, because Kennedy was guided by his predecessors' ideas.[50] Khrushchev had been stung by an article on "Kennedy's Grand Strategy," written by Stewart Alsop, in the *Saturday Evening Post*, in which the president admitted that America was not on the downside of a missile gap with the USSR and that, in some circumstances, the United States might have to take the initiative in a nuclear conflict.[51] A few days after the article appeared, Thompson had met with Dobrynin to mitigate damage from it.[52] Nevertheless, Khrushchev was still smarting.[53]

By talking so blatantly about US nuclear superiority, JFK had aggravated Khrushchev's internal problems and emboldened the Soviet military to ask for even more resources.[54] Salinger explained that the president had not meant a preemptive war, but instead was talking about retaliation to a Soviet attack, such as on Western Europe, by conventional forces. Khrushchev answered that if any Western troops crossed the border into East Germany, this would be met immediately by a nuclear attack. The Soviet leader said he was speaking of facts, whereas Salinger was speaking of a theoretical situation. Khrushchev told Salinger that, given the circumstances, "he would have to take [a] hard line and he preferred [to] wait until such time that both his and [the] president's TV speeches could be constructive."[55] Thompson had also talked to Khrushchev while the group was strolling through the woods that day. He came away with the impression that internal pressure on Khrushchev had very much brought to the Soviet leader's mind the difficult moments he had had with Stalin and the Anti-Party Group. Khrushchev even mentioned that Malenkov used to attack people in a backhanded way.[56]

Such thoughts, however, did not impede Khrushchev from enjoying himself and telling jokes during a three-hour lunch. One involved an American and a Russian arguing about which country was more democratic. The American said he could go the president and criticize everything he had been doing, and the president would receive him well and shake hands with him when he left. The Russian replied that they were equal on that score, because he could go to Stalin and criticize everything the US president had been doing, and Stalin would receive him well and shake hands when he left.[57] Gromyko then told another joke about FDR, Stalin, and Churchill. Roosevelt described a dream in which he had been made president of the world. Churchill said that was funny, because he had had the same dream, only he had been made prime minister of the world. Stalin said that was strange, because he didn't recall having appointed either of them to those positions.

In between the toasts and the multiple courses, Khrushchev teased Yuri Zhukov about leaving his ministerial post in the Soviet government to become a journalist. Zhukov said his deputy was very competent and that it was time to give young people their chance. Khrushchev shot back, "Look who he's saying this to—he wants to get me out!" and then added, "He's right, of course." Zhukov, visibly embarrassed, quickly changed the subject, saying that he understood Thompson was leaving Moscow soon, to take up another Foreign Service position in Washington, DC. Khrushchev smiled and said, "We have not yet agreed to this," which made everyone laugh. Thompson, for his part, remarked that John Foster Dulles had once asked him how Khrushchev kept himself so well informed while engaged in many activities. Khrushchev seemed pleased to hear this story and said that he had once asked his assistants to separate reports into two piles—one that they considered important, and the other that he need not bother with—but to give him both piles. The Soviet leader said he found, on examining them, that frequently the reports of greatest interest to him were in the pile designated as unimportant.[58]

Back to Laos

Before the party broke up, Thompson took Khrushchev aside to talk about Laos. Some headway had been made toward a neutral Laos, but then the Pathet Lao had attacked the Royal Laos Armed Forces.[59] Thompson was probing, hoping to get the Soviets to intervene, but Khrushchev told him the USSR could not make the Pathet Lao do anything. He said the important thing was for the Laotians to form a government, and Khrushchev repeated several times that he wished to maintain the agreement on neutrality for Laos that he had reached with JFK in their Vienna summit.[60]

As would happen again during the Vietnam War, the Americans believed that the Soviets were able to exert more influence on the Communists in Laos than they actually could. Thompson concluded that since neither Khrushchev nor Gromyko had mentioned the situation in Southeast Asia during the day, the Soviets did not intend to seriously oppose US operations in Laos, although they would undoubtedly criticize the Americans' actions.[61] Kennedy eventually decided to send a US military force through Thailand to the Laotian border, as a show of force. This was a bluff, but it helped to put pressure on the Pathet Lao to reconsider their stance. Talks between the various Laotian parties resumed, and the opposing factions formed a coalition government in June.[62]

26 ≡

Goodbye Moscow, Hello Washington

In conversation [Khrushchev] showed a great sensitivity to
what he considered threats and said the Soviet Union was a
great power, not a small country which could be threatened
with impunity.

—LLEWELLYN THOMPSON, cable to State Department,
    July 26, 1962

At the beginning of June 1962, Thompson traveled to Washington, DC, to meet
with JFK and discuss the new position he would hold at the State Department
after he left Moscow.[1] He also received an honorary doctorate from Columbia
University and learned that he would receive the President's Award for Distinguished Federal Civilian Service when he returned to the United States on August 7. He could now
reflect back on a career that had for so long looked like it was going nowhere and say that
he had made the right choice not to abandon it. He was pleased to learn that he would have
the honorary title of ambassador-at-large. He would also be named special advisor to the
president on Soviet affairs, the position Charles Bohlen had had. Bohlen was preparing to
go to France as the US ambassador, a post he badly wanted and was looking forward to.[2]

Between meetings in Washington, DC, Thompson looked for a house and a school for
his daughters. Georgetown was no longer the bohemian neighborhood it had been when
he and Jane were first married. It was now the most elegant part of the capital and too expensive for him. Instead, he found a nice townhouse off Connecticut Avenue, up the street
from the McNamaras. It needed work, but was near a school his daughters could walk to
(which was essential, because Thompson refused to own two cars), and it had a sort of
Georgetown look, which would please Jane.

Leaving Moscow

When he got back to Moscow, Thompson and Jane began their round of farewell parties.
It was sad to be leaving, but Jane and her daughters were excited about finally living in their
own home. For the girls, the possibility of living in their own country held promises of

extraordinary experiences to come. Jane was also a bit nervous. Thompson had an important position, and Washington, DC, was a tricky city in which to maneuver. Bohlen commented to Wisner that their wives would have to help Jane through the transition.

Unknown to Thompson, at the beginning of July, Raúl Castro, as head of Cuba's armed forces, visited Moscow and argued with Khrushchev about how to install Soviet nuclear missiles on the island. The Cuban government wanted the whole world to know, but Khrushchev thought it was better to put the missiles in place secretly and then reveal their presence as a fait accompli at the November 1962 Plenum, just before he went to the UN General Assembly meeting in New York City. Fidel Castro acquiesced. He understood that Khrushchev needed to equalize the "correlation of forces." In addition, he felt indebted for Khrushchev's support and obliged to help the Soviets.[3] There were also other reasons why Castro accepted the missile deployment. First, it would deter another American invasion of Cuba, which he was sure was in the planning stages, Second, it "had a visceral attraction." Fidel would no longer just be a bothersome dictator of a Caribbean island, but would be someone to contend with on the geopolitical plane.[4]

While Raúl Castro and the Soviets were putting the finishing touches on their agreement, the Thompsons held their annual July 4 celebrations at Spaso House. Many Soviets came to say goodbye. Khrushchev kissed the Thompson girls and hugged them, too. They were dressed in stiff organdy dresses that neither of them liked, especially Jenny, as her younger sister's frock was exactly the same as hers. Sherry just hated all dresses. Khrushchev was in a good mood. He talked and joked with Benny Goodman, even though he didn't like jazz. Mrs. Khrushcheva asked Jane why she and Thompson were leaving Moscow, and Jane told her that after five years, it was time to go. Jane was bewildered, however, by Mrs. Khrushcheva's next remark, "I would say that it is very important that you do not change ambassadors at this time." Jane could only answer that she hoped her husband could do more in Washington, DC, than in Moscow.[5] Khrushchev also invited the Thompsons to his personal dacha—not the official government one—for a private farewell. No other foreign ambassador had ever been invited to Khrushchev's private home, not even one from the Eastern bloc. It was an exceptional invitation. In the diplomatic corps, it was a sensation.[6]

At one farewell reception, though, Yuri Zhukov took Thompson aside. Relations between the two countries were particularly bad, especially after Alsop's interview with JFK, which had mentioned a preventive war. It left a bad impression, Zhukov said. Khrushchev "needed help and was faced with strong opposition to his policies."[7]

The Conversation

On July 25, Thompson went to the Kremlin to officially say goodbye to Khrushchev and met with him for about two hours. What they discussed is especially intriguing, in light of Khrushchev having just set the Cuban missile operation in motion.[8] Thompson came away from this conversation with an uneasy feeling. He was sure that Khrushchev was about to start another German crisis. Thompson had no idea that it would be a Cuban crisis instead, but there were small clues throughout their talk—hints that seem clear in retrospect.

The conversation started off with the usual chitchat: Thompson's departure plans and Khrushchev's vacation plans. Knowing Thompson would send back a complete report of their conversation, Khrushchev began talking about the trip he had recently taken to Murmansk, to inspect the Soviets' ocean-fishing fleet. Thompson observed that the USSR had plenty of freshwater fish, which Khrushchev acknowledged, but the Soviet leader said he wanted to explore fisheries beyond the Baltic Sea: "We are currently considering sending five fishing vessels to Cuban shores to explore the fishing prospects in that area. Provided we find plenty of fish there and Castro has no objections, our vessels will be based in Cuba."

The conversation then turned to technology, and Khrushchev said he was impressed with the American Telstar satellite. Thompson, chipping away at Khrushchev's obsession with secrecy, told him that technology made it impossible for people to live in isolation anymore, and for that reason both sides were wise to support an exchange program. Thompson said, yet again: "There are many misunderstandings between us and this can only be dispelled by greater knowledge through closer contact. Many of our problems are difficult enough to resolve, but they become even more difficult when each side starts with [a] different appraisal of facts."

Khrushchev, though, seemed more interested in talking about the capabilities of his submarines, which meant that his trip north had not been primarily to inspect the fishing fleet. He stated, "Well, I don't mean to scare you but when I saw our new military equipment, it is terrifying." He also told Thompson "a little secret." There had been military exercises in the area before Khrushchev's trip. According to the plans for that exercise, a make-believe "enemy submarine" was to enter a grid and be chased and bombed by dummy practice munitions. But when the "enemy submarine" left the exercise grid, another sub appeared, which was not in the plans. The first submarine turned out not to be the practice target, but instead had probably been American or British. That event, Thompson responded, reinforced the importance of reducing the risk of war from a mistake.

If Thompson's words had any effect on him, Khrushchev did not show it. Instead, he claimed that the Soviets were more sincere in finding an agreement on disarmament than the Americans, because, unlike the "US monopolies" making "fabulous profits" on weapons, no one in the USSR benefited from weapons production: "The Soviet Union is not facing any difficulties in its conversion to a peaceful economy. We cannot say that about our allies in disarmament." Khrushchev, however, was not entirely truthful here. He, too, was under pressure from his military.

Thompson answered: "According to a recent study, disarmament, introduced gradually, will not be harmful to the American economy. . . . By all means, monopolies have great influence, but they do not dictate our policy and they understand that if a war breaks out, it will not spare them either." Lack of trust, he concluded, was the basis for all these predicaments. Suspicion complicated matters. As the world got smaller and smaller, the Soviets' concerns with secrecy would grow less and less relevant.[9]

Khrushchev answered defensively that the Soviets took state secrets very seriously. When the other side tried to break through this barrier of secrecy, he said, it showed that this action was a priority for them, "so we are pushing back." "Well, obtaining information about military exercises in the US is not that difficult," Thompson answered. Khrushchev shot back, "It is unlikely that the Soviet Union knows more about the American military forces than the United States does about the Soviet Army." Thompson, lighting up another cigarette, responded: "That's just it. Americans don't know much about the Soviet Army. And this is the reason why they are worried more than is necessary. The military tends to assume the worst and expects the other side to own terrifying weapons."

At this point, Khrushchev—who always seemed to have the U-2 affair on his mind—set off on a long-winded dissertation about it: "American military cliques sent Powers's flight in order to find out Soviet military secrets. What should we call such an act? The flight was timed to coincide with the meeting of the [Soviet] heads of state." He then continued by saying that air surveillance was useless anyway, because things could be hidden from the air, and bases could be camouflaged in the same way as was done during World War II. Khrushchev indignantly exclaimed: "On top of that, President Eisenhower went as far as to say that, since the United States does not know much about what Russians are doing, that 'it has the right' to send in spy planes into Soviet airspace. This is robbery! This is a violation! Can you imagine what would happen if we sent in our planes to the American frontier? Such acts put us on high alert. As it turns out, we were looked upon as a colony, [viewed] from the [American] position of strength. We didn't even get an apology. De Gaulle and Macmillan tried to convince me, saying that the United Sates is a superpower and cannot apologize because this may tarnish its reputation. The Soviet Union is a superpower as well, and we are not going to tolerate insults. By the way, when we were talking about this, Eisenhower mentioned something about apologizing. Herter told him something, and Eisenhower fell silent. Kennedy, the new president, said he would have given an apology if he were Eisenhower. It is possible to find an appropriate way to do that."

Thompson ignored the fuming and tried to lead the conversation back to disarmament, saying he could not understand why the Soviets had not given serious consideration to the US plan for zonal inspections: "The Soviet Union has always insisted that inspections follow [complete] disarmament. The American plan provides for 30 percent disarmament and inspection of 30 percent of the areas disarmed, thus meeting the Soviet inspection requirements." Khrushchev replied that in order to know what a 30 percent reduction was, the United States would have to know what the USSR's total strength was.[10] Besides, he added, the American 30 percent reduction plan did not include provisions for overseas bases: "Americans point out that the Soviet Union is located near Europe, while the USA is far from it, and thus must keep their troops and bases there for defense purposes. On the other hand, if we destroy our intercontinental missiles, our planes will not be able to conduct nuclear delivery to the destination intended."

Khrushchev continued: "You should take into consideration our interests as well. Let us do the following: we destroy our missiles, and you destroy your bases and pull out your troops. If you don't treat us equally, there will be no disarmament. . . . The essence of the problem is that you may be willing to remove your long-range weapons which could hit us from the US, but only while preserving your overseas bases for use against us. . . . How can we agree to this?"[11] Thompson asserted that the US bases (such as the one in Italy and the one just being readied for nuclear warheads in Turkey) did not have much significance, but they were important for the Europeans' psychological well-being. Khrushchev responded: "Well, for the Soviet Union these bases carry physical and not psychological meaning. Thus it is impossible to accept unequal terms." In his subsequent cable to the State Department, Thompson concluded that given the nature of the conversation, there was little hope that a disarmament agreement could be reached in Geneva.[12]

The ambassador tried to bring the conversation to a close, saying that he knew Khrushchev had a lot of things to do, having just come back from his trip to Murmansk. Thompson thanked Khrushchev for his hospitality and hoped his successor as ambassador, Foy Kohler, would be treated in the same way. Then he asked Khrushchev for a signed photograph. Khrushchev said he appreciated Thompson's work, since "we have always felt nothing but deep respect for you and we hope you will continue to do your best promoting relations between both of our countries." He went on to lament that although ambassadors played an important role in international politics, they were often ignored.

When Thompson was about to leave, Khrushchev told him there was one other subject he wanted to discuss, although he disliked bringing up an unpleasant matter on the ambassador's last visit. It was clear that the Rusk-Gromyko talks in Geneva were going nowhere. Khrushchev would have no choice but to sign a separate treaty with East Germany, after which right of access to West Berlin would end: "We have told Gromyko to inform Rusk that the negotiations are at an end. We have said enough but apparently you want to keep your troops in West Berlin and maintain things as they are. We cannot agree to that. It has been seventeen years since the war ended but the occupational regime still remains. In history there are no examples of occupational regimes lasting that long. . . . The US wants to keep West Berlin as a NATO military base in case of a conflict, and it is the West Berliners who are stirring up this conflict." Khrushchev went through the old arguments and expressed disappointment that JFK had not furthered a solution to the Berlin question.

Thompson said that the US position was clear, and there was little he could add to it. He reminded Khrushchev that in 1959, the United States had endeavored to meet the Soviets' problem with the issue, but the American proposals were rejected. It was the Soviets who focused world attention on Berlin, to the point where the smallest thing became a test of intentions: "West Berlin has become a symbol for the people of western Europe. . . . Many hold the following opinion: if the West loses West Berlin, it will also lose Germany and all of Europe."[13] Thompson then went on: "You said that the troops in West Berlin carry no military significance. [The] Western powers have plenty of evidence as to what Ulbricht would do to West Berlin. East Berlin has already merged with East Germany, even though it was supposed to be under the control of the four states. The [allies'] troops remain in West Berlin with the sole purpose of appeasing its population and ensuring that [the] East Germans will not be able to occupy it. As for threats, stating that the treaty will be signed is a threat, because the [Western] troops will be cut off."

"Please try to understand our point of view," continued Thompson. "Provided we reach an agreement regarding this dispute, tensions will ease even without us signing the peace treaty. As for the troops, they remain stationed in West Berlin, in particular, to prevent their authorities from acting impulsively." Thompson ended this part of the conversation by telling Khrushchev that he should find a way to give the United States better alternatives. Apropos of these, Thompson told him an anecdote that he had heard in Washington, DC, (most likely from his friend Bohlen): "One man died and went to hell. The devil asks him where he would like to stay. The man asked to be shown his options. One room had sinners standing on burning coals. Another had people standing on sharp spikes. The third and the last room had people standing knee-high in manure drinking coffee. 'If this is all you have,' said the man, 'I will stay in this room.' When the devil left, the man heard someone say, 'The coffee break is over, get back to standing on your heads.'"

Khrushchev laughed and said that Russians did not want to stand on their heads, nor were they asking others to do so: "We are very particular regarding our international commitments. We have been on friendly terms with Afghanistan for forty-five years. Despite the total shared border line of 2,500 km, we have never had conflicts. Let us be wise and pull out this rusted splinter that is West Berlin. If Rusk and Gromyko do not reach an agreement, I don't even know what will happen." And then he added, "It would be really nice if they did."

As Thompson again tried to leave, Khrushchev said, as a by-the-way comment: "Would you also ask the president when American planes are going to stop pirating on the sea routes? They continue to conduct flights over our ships on the open sea, nosedive them and so on. The Soviet Union may come up with an appropriate response." Thompson told the Soviet leader confidentially that he had asked for these acts to be stopped, after which orders for the military aircraft had changed. There had been some improvement, until a Soviet ship was spotted not far from a US nuclear test site. Khrushchev replied that the Soviet ships being buzzed were commercial, not military, and that an American destroyer ordered a Soviet ship near Cuba to stop: "The captain of course . . . wouldn't have stopped even if the destroyer had opened fire. The ship could have been annihilated, but we would have found a way to retaliate, even though the United States owns more and bigger ships." He then ended this part of their discussions on an ominous note: "We ask you to take control of your overzealous military. You are not pleased with our good relations with Cuba and we are not pleased with your bases surrounding us. We have to put up with it. I was once considering writing President Kennedy regarding this matter, but changed my mind because we are not powerless either. Let us put a stop to this."

On July 31, Thompson reported that the Soviet leader heatedly asked him to speak directly to the president about these incidents.[14] Thompson had previously said that the American actions provoked reactions in the Soviet Union "out of all proportion to the nature of the incidents, due to Soviet pride and [their] inferiority complex." The Pentagon, however, claimed to have no knowledge of any incident, such as the one Khrushchev had described near Cuba.[15] Moreover, during their July 25 conversation, Khrushchev had puzzled the ambassador when he suggested that Thompson *personally* ask JFK—not through the State Department—if it would be better for Khrushchev to bring the Berlin question to a head before or after the US congressional elections, because, the Soviet leader said, he did not want to make things difficult for the president.[16] Thompson replied that he could not know how JFK might respond. Khrushchev then said he thought it would be better to do so after the elections. On the other hand, "if the Soviet Union and United States reached an agreement regarding Germany and Berlin and signed the treaty before the election, Americans would receive this well and it should favorably affect the president's campaign." "Yes, it would," Thompson agreed.[17]

Khrushchev's Dacha

That afternoon, after his long conversation with the Soviet leader, Thompson and his wife drove to Khrushchev's private dacha, about thirty kilometers from Moscow.[18] Khrushchev came out to meet them at the entrance. Wide-open territory surrounded the house. There were woods and fields, with a village and a church off in the distance. The Khrushchevs and the Thompsons strolled along a path through a meadow and then along the Moscow River—Khrushchev's favorite walk. They also stopped from time to time to talk. A Russian friend later lamented to us: "There are no more vast landscapes [like this] left. They have been fenced in and built up with pompous mansions of short-season rich men, the so-called 'new Russians.'"[19]

Nikita Khrushchev bids Llewellyn Thompson Jr. (*smelling rhubarb*) farewell at Khrushchev's private dacha in the USSR, 30 km from Moscow, 1962. Courtesy of Rada Khrushcheva.

They did not talk politics, and since Thompson spoke to Khrushchev in Russian, the translator, Viktor Sukhodrev, was able to film their walk with his new 8mm camera. The group walked through a field of plants that Jane had never seen before, and she asked what they were. Embarrassed, Sukhodrev was at a loss for the English word. Thompson bent down, pulled off a leaf,

and tasted it. "Why, it's rhubarb!" he said, adding, "My mother made the best rhubarb pie in the world." Years later, Sukhodrev stated that he would never forget that word.[20] Sukhodrev had been present on many occasions when Thompson and Khrushchev met, including the Vienna summit meeting with JFK. In recalling Thompson's relationship with Khrushchev, he said: "Thompson inspired in Khrushchev a feeling of profound respect. Khrushchev had the ability to have a feel for a person professionally. He thought Thompson was trying his best to bring USSR-US relations to normalcy, which is what Khrushchev wanted."[21]

Transition Period

When the Thompsons arrived back at Spaso House, the household goods had already been crated and taken to the airport, where a special US Air Force plane would take the family and their belongings to Copenhagen, Denmark. Unfortunately for Jane, this would be another one of those "exciting" flights. One of the four engines on the Fairchild C-119 "Flying Boxcar" died, and six fire trucks escorted the aircraft along the runway as it landed. The pilot wasn't worried, but Jane was ready to kiss the ground on disembarking. No American ocean liners were crossing at that time of year, so the State Department gave the Thompsons a special dispensation to take a Danish liner, the MS *Kungsholm*, to New York City.

The trip took nine days, and Thompson had looked forward to a shipboard break from telegrams.[22] Something, however, about Khrushchev's last talk with him bothered Thompson enough to send additional cables to the State Department when he got to Copenhagen. First, he wanted to calm the more hawkish currents swirling around JFK over the Berlin issue: "I am more convinced than ever that he [Khrushchev] does not intend to push the Berlin question to [the] point of [a] real risk of war. Much will depend, however, upon the attitude of his colleagues and allies as well as upon how we handle the matter."

Second, he understood Khrushchev's dilemma. The Soviet leader wanted to engage in disarmament, but his country's relative weakness would make it difficult for him to convince his own military, who knew perfectly well what their situation was. Thompson urged, "We must be extremely careful on the one hand to show we are serious in our determination to defend Berlin and on the other to avoid engaging their prestige, particularly in the military field as they are unbelievably sensitive about this." He suggested avoiding boasts about US military superiority and curtailing any action in Berlin that could be considered by the Soviets "as annoyance on our part. At the same time we should proceed vigorously with contingency planning which they will know about but without publicity." Thompson felt that Khrushchev's military disadvantage could drive him to do something risky, but he also worried that currents in the US government might lean toward risks, now that America's missile superiority was no longer questionable.

Eisenhower was also in Copenhagen, touring Europe with his grandson David. Prior to an embassy reception for the former president, Thompson talked to him about his farewell meeting with Khrushchev. Eisenhower told Thompson that when the ambassador wrote to Khrushchev to thank him for his farewell gifts, Thompson might mention the great impression the Soviet leader had made on Ike.[23] This shows that Eisenhower, too, must have felt sorry that his last meeting with Khrushchev had gone so badly.

David Eisenhower was a tall, confident, good-looking youth, several years older than the Thompson girls. On learning that Jenny had lived in the Soviet Union, David began a discussion about the horrors of Communism and how terrible the Russians were. Jenny, who unfortunately had her mother's lack of discretion, stopped him short and expounded a defense of the Russians that was probably too passionate for the occasion. Jenny was trying to correct what she considered to be a very limited view of what the Soviet Union was all about. David started to protest, but his grandfather gently told him that he should listen to what this young lady was saying. In recollecting the episode years later, David wrote to Jenny: "For the record, you won the argument. In fact, our exchange in Copenhagen caused me to read and interpret the news . . . and to see the Russians . . . differently, showing that there is no substitute for direct experience. At that point I had never encountered any American my age with experiences remotely resembling your experience in Moscow. That you were able to describe Russians and life in Moscow in 'human terms' made a big impression and it definitely influenced me, proving perhaps the value of 'people to people' exchanges in promoting international understanding."[24] This meeting also left an impression on Jenny. Somewhere in the recesses of her mind, she realized that the new country she was headed for harbored some of the same types of misunderstandings she had found in the Soviet Union.

The following day, the Thompsons boarded the MS *Kungsholm*. The girls walked their dog around and around the captain's deck, while their parents finally just relaxed. When the family arrived in New York City, they left immediately for Washington, DC, where Thompson received the President's Award for Distinguished Federal Civilian Service at an outdoor White House ceremony. Jane and the three girls all pleaded to meet the dashing young president, but Thompson did not want to interrupt "so many other distinguished people," he told an interviewer years later.[25] So the Thompson females stood aside on the lawn. Thompson was touched that Kennedy made a point of going over to his family to speak to them. Sherry, who'd been coached to say "How do you do, Mr. President" and curtsy, in the event they did meet JFK, instead boldly stuck out her hand and said, "Hello, Mr. Kennedy!"

The next day, Thompson met with President Kennedy alone for almost an hour.[26] JFK was curious about the U-2 incident and the breakup of the Paris summit conference in 1960 (see chapter 20). He wondered what would have happened if the incident had not occurred. Thompson said he thought they could have worked out some kind of *modus vivendi*, but he also commented: "I could never figure out why he [Khrushchev] surfaced the U-2. They knew about it before, and maybe they were afraid now that Russia's become so open that it would become known. There were too many military officers who knew it and too many civilians, but he could have sat on it." When Kennedy asked him if the "spirit of Camp David" was propaganda or real, Thompson said he thought Khrushchev felt it a lot, but added that the "Chinese angle" was very much on his mind. The Soviet leader wanted to show that his peaceful coexistence policy was bearing fruit and thus avoid criticism by Mao Zedong's Communists, but "the Chinese were saying that trying to build relations with the Americans was for the birds."[27]

JFK also wanted to know why Khrushchev had been so tough on him at their meeting in Vienna, and why the Soviet leader had later backed off from his ultimatum on East Germany. Thompson thought this also had to do with China. A faction in the Presidium wanted to heal the split between the two Communist nations, thinking it was too dangerous. The Soviets were having a dispute with the Chinese about whether they should exploit every opportunity, regardless of risk, or maintain the status quo, in order to mark time while dealing with their domestic problems. "Still," added Thompson, "I was glad you had the meeting." JFK replied, "Oh, it was educational for me, but, I don't know . . . it seemed . . . the fact of his, he was so sort of tough about Berlin." "Ah," said Thompson, "but he was impressed . . . by your determination—and that was important."

Llewellyn Thompson Jr. (*center*) receiving the President's Award for Distinguished Federal Civil Service from John F. Kennedy, White House south lawn, Washington, DC, August 7, 1962. Abbie Row / John F. Kennedy Library.

Then JFK asked him if the Bay of Pigs "thing"—and the fact that United States hadn't intervened militarily in Laos—might have given Khrushchev the impression that the president was going to give in on the Berlin situation, but Thompson did not think so.[28] Kennedy then turned to the possibility of Khrushchev bringing up the Berlin issue at the forthcoming UN General Assembly meeting. Kennedy thought that the United States' insistence on a presence in West Berlin could be justified, especially if put to a vote by the people living there, but he also was of the opinion that "if we refuse to recognize East Germany," it would be considered an unrealistic position in many parts of the world.[29]

After his conversation with JFK, Thompson and his family left for their long-awaited home leave in Colorado. It was not all pleasure, however. Both Jane and Thompson ended up in the hospital. She was there for a few days because of a gynecological problem, and he collapsed on the golf course, suffering from an acute kidney stone attack. While Thompson remained in Colorado for his operation, his wife and daughters left for Washington, DC, to get their new house ready.

Welcome to Washington, DC

The dwelling on Twenty-Third Street was the Thompsons' first since the newly married couple's "strawberry box" house in Georgetown. They were able to afford it, in part, because Thompson knew he was getting a $5,000 Rockefeller Public Service Award that December. It was a nice house, in a good neighborhood, but it needed painting and repairs. Having lived in well-equipped government housing for so long, the family had very little furniture. Andy was still in Vienna,[30] and Jane and her two other daughters would have to stay with friends, which could be an imposition, especially with a dog. The girls, however, were no trouble. They had just discovered American television. They stared for endless hours at this incredible box that opened an entirely new world to them. At Frank Wisner's request, Carmel Offie lent the Thompsons his house, since he would be away.

Jane soon decided that she could do very little living in someone else's home (and besides, they all found Mr. Offie's residence inexplicably menacing), so the family decided to move, whether their house was ready or not. Louisa, a young Italian girl who had entered the Thompson household in Moscow as a maid, had joined them by then, having decided to try her luck in the United States. Jane bought mattresses, and they all slept on the floor. They retrieved their belongings from storage and used a large cardboard box as a dining table. When Thompson returned from his hospital stay in Colorado Springs he found his new house in disarray. Jane was hard at it. Never one to shy away from a big project, she was reupholstering, fixing walls, putting up bookshelves, and painting every surface in sight. But what was happening with the children concerned him much more than the physical state of the house.

Their two younger daughters' entry into American life was not easy. They had loved their pilgrimage to Thompson's family in Colorado, where they discovered the romance of the West: covered wagons sitting outside low-slung restaurants, fancy cars, Indian teepees on display for tourists, fool's gold, and Annie Oakley costumes. It was all so exotic. The girls had played with their cousins, who seemed so free and welcoming, like they'd known each other all their lives. MWood and Aunt Enid tended to Thompson's mother, Lula, who was in the throes of dementia. Seeing Jenny—who was an uncanny duplicate of Thompson's deceased sister, Mary Virginia—set her off. Lula was transported back to her own childhood, and she insisted that the girls come and play dolls with her, which they did. It was painful for Thompson to finally introduce his wife and children to his mother, only to find her so ill.

Entering school life back in Washington, DC, however, was another story. Their reception at their neighborhood, second-tier, private girls' school—Holton-Arms—did not go well. Even though uniforms were required, somehow they both failed the fashion test miserably. Worse, when they passed the Soviet embassy's school (located in the Soviet Cultural Center, nearby) some American classmates also walking past shouted awful things up at the open windows. Jenny and Sherry felt compelled to shout out *"Privyet Druzia!"* ("Hi, friends") to compensate. Sherry was fortunate to have a companion, Cynthia "Cinny" Davis, who'd been in Moscow with her, and the two of them huddled together in the playground.[31] Jenny, however, was alone in facing the taunts and the strange looks she received for being so clueless about everything American. The final straw came when some girls teased her for the British table manners Gill had struggled so hard to perfect. Jenny put down the fork she had gingerly been squishing her peas on and walked out of the school.

Jane also found it difficult to adjust to life in Washington, DC, although she was reluctant to admit it. She went from being an ambassador's wife, where she ran a large household and staff, to being a normal housewife and mother. She was chauffeur to her husband and kids, handyman, gardener, and chef. Then she would scrub off potting soil or paint, dress up, and follow her husband to obligatory social functions. Jane tried to drown the smell of paint thinner with her signature Joy perfume—the result being a strange but not unpleasant smell. At the beginning, even going to the supermarket was an ordeal, simply because there was too much to choose from. As promised, Polly Wisner advised her on how to manage the city's social circuit. She sorted out Jane's evening dresses, which were not up to the standards in the capital, and even gave Jane some hand-me-downs. It helped a lot.

A New Job

His concerns notwithstanding, Thompson had to leave the house and the children to his wife and Louisa. The president was calling. JFK summoned Thompson and Bohlen to the White House on Saturday, September 29, before the latter's departure for Paris as the US ambassador to France. Kennedy wanted the two Soviet experts to help him interpret a letter he'd recently received from Khrushchev, through back channels.

Conservative Senator Kenneth Keating, a Republican, had sponsored a resolution giving carte blanche for the use of force against Cuba in the event that any "externally supported" military capability threatened the United States. He claimed the Soviets were building nuclear missile sites on the island of Cuba, but he did not furnish any evidence for this. Clare Boothe Luce, the US ambassador to Italy from the Trieste State Treaty days (see chapter 12), took credit for informing the senator. She'd been told about the missiles by a Cuban anti-Castro rebel, who'd come to thank her for a boat she had secretly financed.[32] Keating's resolution was seen as internal politicking, because nobody thought the Soviets would ever allow any part of their nuclear arsenal out of their hands.

Keating's Senate resolution, however, had incited Khrushchev's indignation (and, most likely, touched on his nerves), resulting in this harsh letter to JFK.[33] In it, the Soviet leader expressed his continued fury at the "abnormal situation in West Berlin" and, citing Keating's move, claimed he could conclude from it that the United States was prepared to unleash a nuclear war. The letter also inexplicably indicated that Khrushchev was agreeing to a proposed five-year moratorium on underground testing, using a new technology for off-site verification, none of which the Americans had proposed.

Moreover, it wasn't only the letter that bothered JFK. Secretary of the Interior Stuart Udall had just returned from a trip with poet laureate Robert Frost to visit the Soviet leader in Pitsunda. As they waded in the Black Sea, Khrushchev told Udall that soon he would force JFK to solve the Berlin problem. Udall tried to take it in stride, but the vitriol made an impression him.[34] Khrushchev also repeated what he'd told Thompson previously: although a move by the Soviets was coming, he would wait to make it until after America's November elections. The aging and bone-tired Frost told the press on his return that Khrushchev thought the United States and Europe did not have the will to fight, implying weakness and indecisiveness. Frost used the words "we modern liberals,"[35] and this was the last thing JFK needed. It reinforced a growing perception in Europe of this so-called weakness, recently repeated by de Gaulle. Kennedy was livid.

Thompson and Bohlen arrived for their 11:00 a.m. meeting and JFK began by questioning Khrushchev's assumption that the Americans had agreed to a five-year moratorium on testing.[36] It turned out that the president's brother, Robert F. Kennedy (RFK), had had a solo meeting with Soviet ambassador Anatoly Dobrynin on this subject. RFK had apparently said something that led Dobrynin to believe the Americans would accept this long-term moratorium while a comprehensive test ban treaty was being worked out, even though US policy prohibited preconditions for test ban negotiations. Since RFK did not make a record of the conversation, it was impossible to know, then or now, just what transpired.

Bohlen thought Khrushchev's letter provided an opportunity to refute the notion that America was weak-willed about Berlin. Thompson remarked that some response to the letter was required. Bohlen's preferred option was to answer Khrushchev's letter with "action," suggesting that the president declare West Berlin a *land* of West Germany, which, he said, would mean "complete recognition that you [JFK] are through with East Berlin." Thompson counseled that since the allies were currently holding the Soviets responsible for access to West Berlin, if the Americans simply declared it to be a part of West Germany, the Soviets could refuse to intercede should East German leader Ulbricht make mischief there. The president then asked Thompson and Bohlen why they thought the Soviets were building up forces in Cuba. Answering himself, JFK speculated that it might be because Khrushchev feared an American reprisal in Cuba, were Khrushchev to attack Berlin.

The three Americans struggled to understand what Khrushchev was after. The Soviet leader kept mentioning a top-level dialogue at the UN after the November elections in the United States. But if Khrushchev had put the kibosh on the Paris summit in the summer of 1960 because he couldn't get a settlement about Berlin and East Germany—as Thompson had suggested might be the case when he had met with JFK in August—what did Khrushchev think he could get now? They speculated on an answer. "Well," Kennedy concluded, going back to his original question, "why would they build up Cuba?" Didn't Khrushchev understand that all this movement in Cuba augured against his getting anything regarding Berlin?

Thompson was of the opinion that the Soviets were reluctant dance partners with Fidel Castro, pulled in because of their commitment to world Socialism and the pressures from China. Khrushchev's hand was forced when Castro announced publicly that he was going to join the Communist bloc.[37] Kennedy then speculated on what might have happened the previous year if the United States had actually invaded Cuba successfully after the Bay of Pigs affair, wondering if the Soviets would have just "grabbed West Berlin." Thompson said he didn't think the Soviets would "grab" West Berlin. Instead, they would be more likely to try to take hold of Iran. This seemed to surprise the president. Thompson's reasoning was that a Soviet retaliation in Iran would not directly engage US troops, thus making Khrushchev's point, but with less risk of a general war.[38] Nonetheless, despite the tenor of the letter, Thompson didn't think Khrushchev was about to provoke a war.

The three men went on to discuss the reunification of Germany, including that virtually no one wanted this to happen: certainly not de Gaulle, nor the Soviets, nor West Germany's Adenauer. "So what are we doing there, then?" questioned Kennedy. Thompson replied that even if other nations were against it, the Germans could never give up the idea that "eventually reunion will be the case." While Thompson, Bohlen, and JFK had had a frank discussion, they all left without a satisfactory conclusion.

A week later, on a bright Monday in October, Thompson, then fifty-eight years old, was quietly sworn in as an ambassador-at-large. At Thompson's own request, the only people present were the deputy chief of protocol, who administered the oath, and a lone State Department photographer.[39] After the brief ceremony, he settled into his new office and read a few letters of congratulation for a job well done in Moscow. One was from Thomas Watson Jr., the head of IBM, and another, which touched him deeply, was from Frances Perkins, who had contributed to his early letter-writing campaign to get out of an early and seemingly stagnant posting in Geneva (see chapter 2). She wrote, "How proud I am of you when I think how long I have known you and how wise you have become." She was prescient in adding that she was glad the strain on Thompson would now be less, but "you will undoubtedly be pushed into something else."[40]

A few days later, Thompson had lunch with Dobrynin. They discussed disarmament and nuclear testing, as well as, briefly, the Soviet military buildup in Cuba. Walter Lippmann would tell Dobrynin that he thought Thompson had come back from Moscow in a pessimistic frame of mind and was leaning toward Bohlen's point of view, which was that the Berlin problem was insoluble. Thompson, after the trying talks he had had with Gromyko in the early months of 1962, had indeed given up on the premise that the Soviets were serious about finding a solution to the Berlin question.[41] His strange farewell meeting with Khrushchev, and his attempt, in conjunction with Bohlen and JFK, to deconstruct the Soviet leader's seemingly nonsensical September 28 letter to the president, left him feeling that the Americans were getting the runaround. But why?

27 ≋

Thirteen Days in October

We should not think like hawks or like doves in debating
whether we got enough or too much, but we should think
like owls, who are always worried about the unintended
in history.

—JOSEPH S. NYE, in *Back to the Brink*

On October 14, 1962, an American U-2 spy plane flying high over western Cuba took the first photographs that proved Senator Keating's suspicions about the Soviets building nuclear missile sites on the island. In the wee hours of October 15, the chief of the State Department's Bureau of Intelligence and Research phoned Thompson's former aide, Vladimir Toumanoff, and told him their fears had come true. "That covers a lot of ground," Toumanoff groggily thought to himself, and asked for specifics. The INR chief simply told him to get to the office, ASAP. Toumanoff joined others in the National Photographic Interpretation Center, where film from the U-2 clearly showed Soviet medium-range ballistic missile components and Ilyushin IL-28 jet bomber planes being uncrated ninety miles from the mainland United States.[1]

CIA Deputy Director Ray Cline learned about it later that morning, just as Thompson was giving a speech about the Soviet Union to the National War College in Washington, DC. Secretary of State Dean Rusk learned of the results of the photo analysis in a chilling phone call that he took in the middle of a dinner for the German foreign minister. McGeorge Bundy, JFK's national security advisor, was interrupted by a similar call from Cline during a small going-away party for Charles and Avis Bohlen. Deciding that the president would need his rest before dealing with the information, Bundy chose not to tell him anything until the next day, October 16. At 9:00 a.m., Bundy broke the news to JFK. The president—who wanted to keep to his regular schedule, so as not to arouse any suspicion while the Cuba situation was still unfolding—saw Bohlen for their previously scheduled meeting, before the newly appointed US ambassador left for France. Kennedy told him the news and said that Bohlen could inform Thompson.[2] Everything Thompson had worried about—miscalculation, misunderstanding, pressure from hard-liners, national prestige dictating US actions, and events taking on their own trajectories—was about to be realized in both Washington, DC, and Moscow. The gathering storm would be known in the two capitals, respectively, as the Cuban Missile Crisis and the Caribbean Crisis.

JFK—along with Defense Secretary Robert McNamara; General Maxwell Taylor, the head of the Joint Chiefs of Staff; Secretary of State Dean Rusk; and others—met in the Cabinet Room for a briefing on the technical aspects of the U-2's photographs and what they meant. They tried to discern how long it would take to make the missile launchers operational, and if nuclear weapons were already in Cuba. Dean Rusk got to the essential point first and asked, how would the United States respond? Would it be a sudden strike, or something else? He was almost thinking out loud and made a kind of barrage of possible actions. Among them, he advised seeking help from the Organization of American States (OAS), which included a NATO-like defense agreement for Latin America. The OAS had recently removed Cuba from its membership.[3] Rusk closed by saying that the United States was "facing a situation that could well lead to general war."[4] Then he stated that he needed a few hours to think hard about the situation and consult with his colleagues in the State Department.

The remainder of the Cabinet Room meeting dealt mostly with assessing different attack scenarios, which would become options 1, 2, and 3: (1) an air strike on just the missile sites, (2) a more comprehensive strike, including on other installations, such as airfields, or (3) a strike, followed by a full-scale invasion. There was even some delusional notion that a strike might trigger a "nationwide uprising" against the Soviets and Fidel Castro.[5] JFK said they should reconvene at 6 p.m. to discuss the various options, but added that preparations should begin immediately for "what we're going to do anyway. We're certainly going to do [option] number 1. We're going to take out these missiles."[6] What the president and the other meeting participants did not know was that there were about 42,000 Soviet soldiers in Cuba, rather than the 10,000 estimated by the CIA.[7] These soldiers were armed with tactical nuclear weapons, which the Americans were unaware of until well after the crisis was over. The men in the Cabinet Room knew there were missiles on Cuba, but they had no idea how many there were, or that 98 nuclear warheads were also already on the island.[8]

After the meeting broke up, Rusk returned to the State Department and immediately called Thompson to his office. Bohlen joined them, and the three then met with the US ambassador to the UN, Adlai Stevenson, and others in the State Department to prepare a plan on how they could mitigate repercussions from the American public and the United States' European allies in the event of a strike against Cuba.[9]

The president decided not to convene the National Security Council, because he was unsure of the quality of advice he'd receive from that predetermined list of men, and even less certain that all of them could keep this secret. So he chose a group of fourteen men, including Thompson, who would form the National Security Council's Executive Committee (ExCom), a made-up name for the occasion. He wanted to keep these deliberations secret, to give the participants time to chart their course.[10] Therefore, like others tapped for the ExCom, Thompson had to attend his scheduled meetings as usual. In the middle of this day, still reeling from the enormity of the crisis he was encountering, he sat for an hour

Clockwise, from bottom left, General Maxwell Taylor, Douglas Dillon, Lyndon Johnson, Robert F. Kennedy, Llewellyn Thompson Jr., William C. Foster, Robert McNamara, and Roswell Gilpatric, at one of the National Security Council's Executive Committee meetings in the White House Cabinet Room during the Cuban Missile Crisis, October 1962. Cecil Stoughton / John F. Kennedy Library (ST-A26-20-62).

with Dorothy Ducas of Lobsenz and Company, the publicity firm for the Rockefeller Public Service Awards, to provide a "hometown" story for the press. Toumanoff and his colleagues in the INR had to work on the Cuban Missile Crisis during the night and then sit at their desks during the day, acting "as though nothing had happened."[11]

The ExCom convened at the White House at 6:30 p.m. on October 16. Edwin Martin, assistant secretary of state for Latin American affairs, suggested that they approach Fidel Castro, on the off chance that, given the situation he was in, he might break with Moscow. Rusk worried about possible retaliation against NATO allies. But this conversation was essentially disregarded in favor of the details of a strike. Taylor indicated that the JCS were unanimously against anything short of option 2—taking out all the missile sites, the airfields, and the military bases themselves— because otherwise, it would inevitably leave the Cubans with a retaliatory capability. More than once, someone mentioned that they could not be certain every launch site could be identified and destroyed, leaving at least one American city still vulnerable.

Defense Secretary McNamara outlined what he saw as his three options. The first was a political approach, such as Rusk had suggested that morning, which McNamara discounted. The second was a full blockade and open surveillance of the island, coupled with a threat of a direct attack on the Soviet Union if Cuba made a move against the United States. The third was any form of military strike against Cuba. Later in the conversation, he reflected that the ExCom group should, as a governmental body, consider "what kind of a world" they would have, depending on which action they chose to take.[12] This discussion set the tone for most of the ExCom meetings, which would later be either derided or applauded for their freewheeling nature. Indeed, the ExCom tapes show that the discussions often veered dramatically from one aspect of the situation to another and included vigorous debates.

The ExCom members all agreed that they would have to act before the coming weekend, since that was when analysts had estimated that the missiles could be operational. The president also wanted advice on how to handle an already-scheduled meeting with Gromyko on Thursday afternoon, October 18. JFK expressed frustration at not "knowing enough about the Soviet Union" and at not understanding why they made what he described as the biggest provocation since the Berlin blockade of 1948. Did the "great demonologists" have an explanation of "why the Russians are sticking it to us quite so?" The INR concluded that the Soviets thought their missile placement in Cuba was a low-risk operation and had bungled their way into it. Thompson disagreed, thinking the Soviets understood very well that they were taking a big chance.[13]

After JFK left, the group continued their discussion on an informal basis. They decided to prepare papers on McNamara's options and have them ready for the following morning. Secretary of State Rusk was not available that evening, having been stuck at a public dinner that would last until 11:00 p.m., but George Ball, U. Alexis Johnson, and Thompson met at the State Department. In discussing the defense secretary's three possibilities, some raised concerns (which would later be echoed by US congressmen) that a naval blockade was an even greater military action than a strike, and that the Soviets might implement a new blockade of Berlin. Thompson thought that if the United States made a surprise attack on Cuba, then the Soviets would retaliate somewhere, possibly in Berlin, particularly as Soviets troops would probably be killed in a Cuba attack, but he did not think they would impose a Berlin blockade in response to a *measured* blockade in Cuba. National security advisor McGeorge Bundy later wrote: "I clearly should have listened to Llewellyn Thompson and pressed him to develop further a judgment he put forward in our first week's discussions that the Soviet government would not react to the surprise of a blockade with a blockade of its own in Berlin. . . . The underlying reality is the same as the one that Thompson understood: the Soviet government in its pressure on Berlin might use nuclear threats, but it did not take nuclear risks."[14]

Later in the crisis, Khrushchev became "explosive," as Mikoyan recalled, when Deputy Foreign Minister Vassili Kuznetsov proposed action in Berlin in response to American pressure in Cuba. The Soviet leader told Kuznetsov that they were in the middle of one tangled adventure in Cuba, and now he wanted to start another in Berlin?[15] In the ExCom meeting, Pat Carter, the CIA's acting deputy director of intelligence, helped the argument in favor of a blockade by observing that it was a "series of unrelated acts, not [undertaken] by surprise," in contrast to a strike, which evoked the shadow of Pearl Harbor.[16] He went on to say that even if a strike was successful in taking out the missiles: "This isn't the end. This is the beginning."[17]

On Wednesday, October 17, Thompson started the day with Rusk, CIA Director John McCone, and others on the seventh floor of the State Department.[18] Thompson and Rusk spent many hours together during those tense days, often lasting from first thing in the morning until the end of the day.[19] Unlike many of the ExCom meetings, theirs were not recorded, but Rusk would later confirm McNamara's assessment of Thompson as the "unsung hero" of the Cuban Missile Crisis.[20] Rusk maintained that most of the important ideas coming forward during those days were developed in one-on-one talks outside the ExCom meetings, and that the "written record on the real story of the Cuban Missile Crisis is very scanty and will not reflect [Thompson's] contributions."[21] Thompson worked especially closely with Secretary of State Dean Rusk, Defense Secretary Robert McNamara, and Attorney General Robert F. Kennedy. Thompson was reticent by nature, and he understood his role as being subordinate to Rusk, so Rusk was the one to speak for the State Department unless Thompson was addressed directly, which happened more often as the crisis progressed. In order to draw out "subordinates like Russian expert Tommy Thompson, and Latin American expert Ed Martin," a significant number of the ExCom meetings were purposefully set up without the president being there.[22]

Both Bohlen and Thompson were quite certain that Khrushchev had a bigger picture in mind than just Cuba. In particular, they thought that the Cuban venture was meant to position Khrushchev for whatever move he had repeatedly warned he would take regarding Germany and Berlin after the November elections in America. The timing of that had now become obvious. Khrushchev wanted to postpone action in Berlin until the missiles in Cuba were operational, to force the United States to finally heed his desiderata. Although, as historian Svetlana Savranskaya pointed out, no Soviet documentary evidence exists that draws a connection between the missiles in Cuba and the dilemma Khrushchev faced over his East Germany–Berlin strategy, it was the elephant in the room. The Germany issue had been an obsession of Khrushchev's since 1958. Every attempt to find a compromise with the West had been brushed off. His patience, as he had told Thompson prior to the Vienna summit meeting with JFK, had run out. The missiles in Cuba would guarantee that the United States could no longer simply ignore him. It may not have been the primary reason behind the Cuban missile ploy, but it must have entered into Khrushchev's decision making. According to Rusk, a "top-ranking Russian" disclosed that the Soviets "wanted to get the missiles to Cuba secretly and quickly and then, after our November elections, use the Cuban missiles as additional leverage with us on Berlin."[23]

The ExCom group held some meetings at the State Department, rather than the White House, in order to not focus undue attention on what was taking place. It was during one such meeting, on October 17, that the currents between proponents of an immediate air strike and those in favor of a more measured response began to surface.[24] As these differences developed, Hawks—like Dean Acheson, Douglas Dillon, John McCone, Curtis LeMay, and others[25]—maintained that the launch sites and missiles needed to be removed immediately. Because the missile sites were unhardened—that is, not protected by thick concrete—and consequently vulnerable, the Hawks believed the missiles were meant for a first-strike use, not as defensive weapons.[26] Moreover, it showed that the missiles were not for Cuba's benefit, since it made the island a prime target for just the kind of preemptive military attack the United States was contemplating. Khrushchev had painted a big red target on Havana. The NATO missiles in Turkey were also unhardened and a "first-strike type,"[27] but no one among the American decision makers seemed to apply the same logic to conclude that those were not defensive, either.

There was a persistent faction in the United States who believed that since war with the Communists was inevitable, it would be better to begin it while the Americans still had a seventeen-to-one strategic missile advantage. The coldest of these currents flowed among members of the Joint Chiefs of Staff (most famously, General LeMay), who were adamant that just a limited strike was unacceptable, never mind a diplomatic or a political approach.

The other current, which included Thompson, Charles Bohlen, George Ball, Roswell Gilpatric, Ted Sorensen, and, at least at that point, RFK, struggled to bring the ExCom group over to the idea of a measured response, starting with a blockade. Thompson spoke strongly in favor of this approach, but only if it was coupled with a declaration of war. Without that, a blockade would be an act of war, initiated without warning. He was, however, also concerned that giving Khrushchev an ultimatum or opening diplomatic negotiations without taking some type of action, such as a blockade, could provide a cover for stalling by the Soviets, allowing the missiles to become operational. Thus Thompson favored a blockade, backed up by demands and real consequences if those demands were not met. He also "insisted" on some communication being made with Khrushchev, but his voice was mostly in the background at that point.[28]

Thompson was still a relative outsider in the Kennedy administration. The president was comfortable with Bohlen and knew him well. Yet JFK's resident Kremlinologist wasn't the one who guided him through this crisis. Bohlen decided that, in order to maintain secrecy, he would leave for his new ambassadorial post in Paris by ship on the morning of October 18, as planned, leaving Thompson as the "in-house Russian."[29]

That same morning, Sorensen summarized the difference between the suggestions Rusk and Bohlen had written up for JFK late the night before. Rusk was in favor of a strike without warning (although he would reverse this position later in the day). Bohlen thought that before the United States made a surprise strike, Khrushchev should be given a warning ultimatum, in case an attack could thus be avoided. At that point, it seemed as though the president was still considering an immediate strike as an inevitable part of the equation. This feeling was reinforced by news that the Soviet missiles were more lethal than was previously thought, since they could strike virtually any part of the continental United States except the extreme Pacific Northwest.[30] McNamara argued that the missiles in Cuba did not materially change the strategic balance of power. He reasoned: "[This is] not a military problem that we're facing. It's a political problem. It's a problem of holding the alliance together." To which JFK acknowledged that those "not under this gun" might consider a US attack on Cuba as a "mad act." How would our allies feel about America risking a Soviet retaliation in Europe over a situation Europe was living with—Soviet missiles already in place at their borders?

The ExCom members debated whether Khrushchev should be given a twenty-four-hour warning of an impending strike. They asked Thompson to help them understand communications with the Soviets and what the timing would be. Thompson gave an "if this, then that" answer. On the one hand, an unknown number of Soviet personnel would inevitably be killed in a first-strike scenario, especially if there was no warning, and that would force a severe Soviet reaction. On the other hand, giving Khrushchev prior notice could allow time for him to initiate some action against Turkey or Italy.[31] Mikoyan, according to his son Sergo, was convinced that even if the Soviets destroyed the NATO missiles in Turkey, it would not have been enough retaliation for the large number of Soviet soldiers that probably would have been killed in a US first strike on Cuba. Thus they would have been obliged to take action in West Berlin.[32]

JFK then asked Thompson to give his personal opinion, that is, his own preference between what were essentially the Rusk and Bohlen scenarios: a strike, with or without advance notice given to Khrushchev. Seizing the opportunity, Thompson chose neither. He recommended the course that would eventually be followed: a legal blockade, backed by the possibility of military action. Thompson doubted that the Soviets would resist a blockade of Cuba specifically targeting weapons that could be used for an attack. This kind of blockade, moreover, would be supported by world opinion. He further suggested that the United States demand the dismantling of the missiles that were already on the island, with a warning to the Soviets that if this did not occur, the Americans would threaten to take them out by force, "and then maybe do it." Thompson stated that this would most probably lead to the same thing—a strike and invasion—but that at least this way it would be done in "an entirely different posture and background and [with] much less danger of getting up into the big war." It was a more reasonable proposition, he argued, for America to declare war in order to prevent a threat to the nation from weapons in Cuba by stopping the delivery of additional armaments and supplies than for the United States to enter into a state of war by going in and destroying the missiles in a first strike.[33]

Thompson believed it was important that—if his idea was to have any chance of working—Khrushchev not feel directly threatened, but the Soviet leader had to be made aware the United States was "cranked up for an invasion," so he'd be convinced of America's resolve. Thompson later reflected that the key was "the combination of the two . . . our restraint, on the one hand, by using the blockade rather than the actual attack, combined with the fact that we were ready if need be."[34] He thought that a legal basis for any action was important to the Soviets. Because a formal declaration of war made a blockade legal, he did not think that the Soviets would run through it.[35]

Thompson had turned the contemplated American response on its head. Heretofore, the ExCom members had all operated under the assumption that the first order of business was to take out whatever missiles were already on the island with a strike: JFK's minimum option 1. Thompson's idea was to create a blockade to stop supplies and weapons still coming into Cuba and then to demand—under threat of attack—that the Soviets themselves take out the missiles that were already there. This was perhaps one of the places where Thompson made an important contribution to the eventual resolution of the crisis, because he introduced a new pattern of thought.

Then Thompson made a prediction about Khrushchev's response to a blockade. He said Khrushchev would deny that Soviet bases were on Cuban soil. The Soviet leader would maintain that sending missiles to that country was merely a defensive move, to provide Cuba with protection against members of an émigré community that "have attacked and are threatening attack."[36] Thompson also said Khrushchev would claim that American weapons in Turkey were more offensive in character than the Soviet ones in Cuba. Thompson cautioned that whatever steps the ExCom group decided to take, they should "make it as easy as possible for him [Khrushchev] to back down." Imbedded in all of this, Thompson thought, was Khrushchev's threat against Berlin, supposedly on hold until after the US elections. While Thompson believed the Soviet leader would be willing to cease current construction on the Cuban missile sites and agree to hold talks with the Americans, he did not think Khrushchev would "just back down."[37] The situation, however, would change and prove Thompson wrong about that aspect.

Later in the day, McNamara asked, "If there is a strike, how many Soviet citizens would be killed?" Even though Thompson had brought this point up several times before, it seemed to be an out-of-the-blue question. Thompson repeated that the killing of Soviet soldiers was the most compelling argument against a strike in Cuba by the United States. Thompson felt strongly about giving notice to Khrushchev of any action by the Americans. The Soviet leader would be compelled to show such a notice to others in his government, and they might persuade him to show restraint. Thompson recalled attempts by the Soviet military and others to pull Khrushchev from the brink of the Berlin Crisis after Gary Powers's U-2 spy plane was shot down, and perhaps those forces could be brought to bear again.

Sorensen said that the "messenger" delivering this notice would have to make it clear to Khrushchev that any response besides capitulation, such as an attempt at a delay or the offer of a counterproposal, would not be acceptable. But Thompson interjected that such an assumption "was worth a little bit of discussion," because negotiations with Khrushchev would inevitably include a broad complex of questions: "These other paths, it seems to me, [show] you're playing Russian roulette. You're flipping a coin as to whether you end up with world war or not." Nevertheless, the blockade idea seemed to be sinking as an option, since JFK brought the dialogue back to a strike versus a strike plus an invasion, with a possible prior notification sent to Khrushchev. Thompson summarized the advantages of letting Khrushchev know about any action by the Americans in advance. First, the United States might be able to retain support from some of its allies, were there to be Soviet reprisals in Europe. Second, it would give Khrushchev a chance to back down. Third, the United States and the USSR could at least enter into negotiations while the work in Cuba was stopped.

McNamara, who also favored a blockade, suggested several times that they form two discussion groups. One would be in favor of quick and severe military action, with or without notice to Khrushchev, and with or without an accompanying invasion of Cuba. The other would opt for political and limited military action, in the form of a blockade. Secretary of State Rusk and General Taylor thought the minimum response would be a blockade, followed by a strike. Then they took a kind of straw poll and asked, "Is anyone here in favor of a blockade without a strike?" Thompson, who must have been absolutely terrified at the trajectory of events, was the first one to speak up forcefully for a position now obviously against the president's own. He replied, "I am," followed only by Defense Secretary McNamara and RFK.

At about 2:30 p.m., Rusk summoned Leonard Meeker, the acting legal advisor for the State Department, filling in that day for his absent boss. Taking into account Thompson's remarks about the legality issue, Rusk asked Meeker to conceive of steps that the United States might take to get rid of the missile sites and weapons on Cuba—including a blockade of the island—that would still be legal under international law. The Secretary of State gave Meeker just four and a half hours to do the research and prepare a written memorandum.[38] Rusk and Thompson then left to join JFK for his previously scheduled meeting with Gromyko, at 5:00 p.m.[39]

The ExCom group and the president had speculated on the purpose of Gromyko's visit. They wondered whether the Soviet minister would divulge the existence of the missiles and pondered how much the Americans should reveal about what they knew, in turn. Thompson's advice was not to show Gromyko the U-2 pictures of the missiles in Cuba or to demand their removal. He argued that this would give Khrushchev the initiative, as the Americans' policy was still undecided: "It is rather like finding your wife [is] unfaithful. She may know [you know], but after you tell her, things are different. Then you had better be prepared, for things will begin to happen."[40] If the Cuban situation were to be brought up with Gromyko, JFK said the one thing he could think of to offer in exchange was to withdraw the nuclear missiles in Turkey. In fact, most of the men seemed to think that getting rid of the missiles in that country would be the smallest price they would have to pay for removal of the Cuban ones.

The president did not tell Gromyko that he knew about the Soviet missile sites in Cuba, nor did Gromyko inform JFK of their presence. Gromyko would later say this was because the topic hadn't been raised, but he couched his response to the question by saying he "hoped" he would have given a "proper" response if he had been asked.[41] His silence served to make the Americans even more suspicious. They took the secrecy of the weapons' deployment as ominous. JFK assured Gromyko twice during their meeting that the United States had no plans for an attack or invasion of Cuba, and he hinted he might be willing to assure the Soviets that the Americans *would not* attack.[42] Kennedy did this equivocally, by saying that the Soviet military buildup on the island changed the situation. Gromyko informed his government of these statements in his cable about the meeting with JFK, but the Kremlin failed either to see it or to act on it.[43] If the security of Cuba was the apogee of Soviet concerns at that point, surely they would have seized on this opening. Although it might become so, the defense of Cuba was clearly not Khrushchev's only purpose in secreting missiles there. Fidel Castro himself would point out, long after the fact, that the Soviets had many other ways of defending Cuba from an invasion without resorting to nuclear missiles.[44]

Between the meeting at the White House and the subsequent official dinner with Gromyko, Meeker presented his memorandum. He did not think the United States could use the 1948 Rio Treaty to justify a military move against missiles placed in Cuba, because there had been no attack yet.[45] He did believe, however, that another provision in the treaty, one calling for "consultation and recommendations" in the event of a "threat to the peace of America," could be used, and surely the installation of nuclear sites in Cuba was a threat not only to the United States, but also to other nations in the Americas. Therefore, the OAS council could, with a two-thirds vote, even recommend military measures to remove what might be characterized as a threat to the peace of the Americas. This would lend a legal basis for a strike or other direct action by the United States—if the OAS went along.

Meeker came up with the important idea that a blockade stopping only those items that contributed to the missile sites or were other forms of offensive weapons could be labeled a "defensive quarantine," and therefore would be legal, without a formal declaration of war. Thompson enthusiastically endorsed this idea, as it would remove the necessary—but disagreeable—step of declaring war before imposing a blockade. Without the legal cover that a quarantine provided, the Soviets might be able to "isolate the United States and mobilize world opinion against [it]," and that would affect the Soviets' judgment about "what they could and couldn't do" in response.[46]

JFK had Rusk and Thompson join him and Bundy in the Oval Office while he briefed Robert Lovett, his personal advisor and former secretary of defense under Truman. Lovett later recalled being in favor of the blockade and said that Thompson spoke at some length on that topic in the meeting. Bundy argued in favor of no action at all, for fear of possible consequences in Berlin and to the NATO alliance. Lovett, Rusk, and Thompson did not yet know that, even as the trend in their meetings was moving toward a blockade or a quarantine, Acheson had been invited to talk to JFK at lunchtime and had made a strong case for an air strike without notification given to Khrushchev. While Acheson had retired from formal governmental service at the end of the Truman administration, he served as an unofficial advisor to JFK. He had influenced the president by his statement that an air strike was the option least likely to cause an "extreme Soviet reaction."[47]

JFK did not attend the state dinner with Gromyko and left Rusk and Thompson to sit through the awkward affair. The two went back to the State Department shortly after midnight and met briefly with George Ball, U. Alexis Johnson, and others in the conference room, to catch up on the discussions.[48] The early hours of October 19 brought a general consensus, at least among that group, for a blockade or a quarantine.[49] Dean Rusk recalled that it was Thompson who was the final persuasive voice for the option of either the blockade or the quarantine.[50] Thompson and Rusk met for an hour or so later that morning, before the ExCom group convened in Ball's conference room at the State Department, which had become known as the "Think Tank."[51] But the tide had changed overnight. Bundy, the president's national security advisor, had gone from favoring doing nothing to supporting an air strike, and he called JFK to tell him so.

As the ExCom members prepared to gather at the State Department that morning, JFK met with the Joint Chiefs of Staff before leaving on a campaign trip. Among the JCS, General LeMay was the most outspoken proponent of an intensive air strike and invasion, but all of them felt it would be necessary to go all in.[52] Even General Taylor—who was selected as chairman of the JCS because he was more of a soldier-diplomat and thus might help ameliorate JFK's feeling of having been misled by that group over the Bay of Pigs affair—told the president that the JCS would prefer no strike to only a limited one.[53] Taylor warned of the near certainty that, no matter what the United States did in terms of an air strike, Cuba would retain some nuclear capability. The military could not guarantee to take out everything. JFK was again uncertain about what to do. He asked Bundy to make sure the strike option remained on the table while the president kept to his campaign speech schedule.

Between Bundy's change of heart and Acheson's and the JCS's conviction that aggressive action was needed, the mood once more swung back toward an air strike without advance notice. RFK pushed back against that option, equating a strike without warning to what had happened at Pearl Harbor. The group was at an impasse, with both sides pulling equally hard. At midday, Rusk declared that they could not make a decision for JFK and instead should develop "fully considered alternatives" for the president. So they split again into two working groups. Thompson joined Gilpatric, Nitze, Martin, and Meeker, under the leadership of U. Alexis Johnson, to develop the blockade alternative. Dillon, Acheson, and Taylor went with Bundy, to work up the air strike option.[54] Sorensen, the president's speechwriter and, in effect, his chief of staff, was to draft the two documents into the form of a radio address JFK would give to the American people. Sorensen began the drafts, but he confessed to being "unable" to write the strike speech, so he worked on the blockade one. That effort led to many questions, which the working group, including Thompson, reconvened to answer. Sorensen recalled that a significant reason why he had such a difficult time with the air strike speech was that he was present when scientists had come to brief JFK on what would happen in the event of a nuclear exchange. Those experts stated that the subsequent radioactive poisoning of the atmosphere would affect "every other dimension of the planet and would spread to the far reaches of the planet, until that planet was uninhabitable: no plant life, no animal, no human life."[55] Sorensen did compose a note for Khrushchev, to have on hand if JFK decided on an air strike with prior notification, and that draft became the basis for the "strike speech" someone else finished.[56]

The U. Alexis Johnson group debated and edited their positions on the blockade tack. Martin, the State Department's Latin American expert, expressed concern at being able to get the OAS to vote in time for the president's Monday speech. Thompson brought up a new point: the importance of allowing sufficient time between the announcement of a blockade or a quarantine and its enforcement.[57] Meeker, in his notes and his subsequent oral history said:

> Tommy Thompson had feted [*sic*] out the great necessity of giving the Soviets time, not only in which to reflect on what course they would follow in response to the president's speech and announcement, but also practical time within which to communicate new orders to ship captains, since various Soviet vessels were on [*sic*] route to Cuba at that time.
>
> He also had pointed out something else which seemed to me always of great importance. He said, "If the US were to begin enforcing the quarantine by actually

shooting at a Soviet vessel, and if the vessel were damaged, sunk, or personnel on board were killed or wounded, a whole new situation would arise, far more serious because, at that point, [it would be more than] simply a Soviet attempt to install nuclear missiles in the Western hemisphere, but actual armed conflict between the US and the USSR. The Soviets would consider that their prestige and honor were at stake. At that point, one could not predict what the Soviet response would be, or how the whole affair would end."

It always seemed to me that Thompson's advice was exceedingly sound. It was based on very long experience in the Soviet Union, knowledge of the Soviet government on how it works, understanding of the Russian mind, and that his counsel was very important in persuading President Kennedy to move with greatest care and to achieve his intended objectives with minimal risk.[58]

As it turned out, Khrushchev's first reaction to the blockade would be to respond in anger and defiance. The thirty-nine hours between the announcement of the blockade and its implementation allowed Khrushchev to calm down and rescind his order for Soviet ships to run the blockade.[59] Similarly, JFK would later say that if he, Kennedy, had not had the time to reflect and consider, he, too, would have made the "wrong" decision on how to react.[60]

The quarantine group spent two hours presenting its option, while Bundy's strike group used not much more than half an hour.[61] All of them were under tremendous pressure to make sure that something was done before the nuclear missiles in Cuba were operational, yet they wanted to consider every angle of the possible alternatives. McNamara made the point that the United States would have to pay a price to get the missiles removed, involving at least the US missiles in Turkey and Italy, and probably more. RFK steered back into the current that favored some kind of prompt action. Meeker quoted him as saying: "It would be better for our children and grandchildren if we decided to face the Soviet threat, stand up to it, and eliminate it, now. The circumstances for doing so at some future time are bound to be more unfavorable."[62] For anyone listening to the tapes and reading the transcripts of the ExCom meetings, RFK seemed to be all over the map in his positions. Thompson, in his later oral history, said that the president's brother played the role of devil's advocate throughout the ExCom sessions. In reply to a question about others finding the attorney general "irritating" during the discussions, Thompson explained that RFK would "deliberately bring out all the bugs in a given course of action, making sure that every possibility was looked at." He went on to say that "people who had formed strong opinions nevertheless wanted to be sure that facts contrary to their opinions had been understood."

By the time UN ambassador Adlai Stevenson came into the room at 6:30 p.m., the whole group had shifted to a course that Thompson had advanced the day before: a blockade, with the threat of—and, if necessary, the execution of—a subsequent strike, in the event the Soviets did not remove the missiles. Stevenson said he no longer needed to express his views, now that the discussion had taken this turn. The ExCom meeting broke up shortly after that.

On Saturday, October 20, JFK excused himself early from the campaign trail in Chicago, feigning a cold. Rusk, Thompson, and Martin drove together to the White House for an ExCom meeting with JFK, which was not recorded. There, a decision was tentatively taken to go forward with a "defensive quarantine" and seek support from the OAS to do so. The president, however, wanted to consult with air force officials at a meeting the next morning before committing to a blockade versus an air strike. Either way, the president would give one of the two speeches to the American people on Monday evening, October 22, followed by a resolution presented to the UN Security Council the next day.[63] Thompson and Rusk then spent the afternoon and evening together as the State Department apparatus laid out an action plan for securing the necessary two-thirds vote in the OAS.[64]

The next day, Sunday, October 21, Thompson opened the morning paper amid the family chaos of girls who wanted his attention and a dog who needed to be walked, to find a front-page article describing American military preparations in Florida and Puerto Rico and linking them to a "Cuban crisis." Thompson left his family to join the ExCom group and air force officials in the private family quarters of the White House, to conduct a final review of the two basic options. General Taylor made the argument for an air strike, and McNamara, for the quarantine. JFK asked each of the men who were present, one by one, to state his preference. Most favored the strike. In a 2002 essay, McNamara pointed out that the attack would have been massive, with nearly 1,100 sorties. (For comparison, the "shock and awe" offensive against Baghdad forty-one years later was 1,700 sorties.) The president then asked if they could be sure a strike would succeed. McNamara said he "could have kissed" General Walter Sweeney, who replied that while the US Air Force was the best in the world, there was no way to be certain that one or two nuclear missiles might not survive such an attack and be able to strike almost any American city.[65]

Stevenson and McNamara had advocated a blockade, followed by negotiations with Khrushchev. Rusk leaned toward a twist on the blockade-plus-negotiate version, suggesting that the United States ask only that work cease on the Cuban missile sites, followed by international inspections, rather than demand a removal of the nuclear weapons in the face of a certain US strike. Thompson, supported by McCone and Dillon, took a stand that was harsher than that of Rusk, asking for a blockade with a true threat of a strike if the Soviets didn't comply, as he'd said days before. Thompson differed from his boss in that he wanted to leave open the possibility of negotiations but preferred not to start there, because this could open the United States up to a typical Soviet talk-and-delay tactic, as well as risk the situation devolving into a missile-for-missile, plane-for-plane barter. He thought a quarantine would show America's resolve, ensuring that Khrushchev would believe unequivocally that Cuba would be attacked if work on the missile sites did not cease and the apparatus that was already on the island did not begin to be dismantled. JFK chose the middle route, the Thompson group's option of a blockade plus a threatened air strike, and took out the proposed language in Sorensen's draft speech inviting Khrushchev to a summit.[66] It may have been at the end of this meeting when JFK turned to Thompson, who was leaving the room, and said something to the effect of, "Well, Tommy, the lucky ones in there are the ones whose advice I *didn't* take."[67]

Thompson, greatly relieved, once again spent the afternoon with Secretary Rusk, ending his Sunday workday at 7:15 p.m.. He went home and told his wife, who was still organizing the house, that if he phoned her and told her to go to Paul Nitze's farm, she was to take the children and leave immediately, no questions asked. Nitze, the assistant secretary of defense, had built a bomb shelter on his tobacco farm in southern Maryland and had been kind enough to offer Thompson's family a place of refuge there, while the men would be spirited off to a government bunker in the Blue Ridge Mountains of West Virginia. Jane later complained to her husband that other wives had been told what was actually going on through "pillow talk" and did not get just a vague directive to "go" when told. Thompson, true to form, did not tell Jane any of the details about why the attorney general had sent his car to collect the ambassador-at-large in the midst of dinner or in the middle of the night until it was possible to do so, by virtue of the president's speech.

Monday morning, October 22, was one of the few times during the Cuban Missile Crisis that Thompson's day did not begin by meeting with Dean Rusk. Instead, he joined the secretary of state at the White House as part of the Berlin Group on Crisis Planning, set up to anticipate and deal with any repercussions in Germany.[68] Rusk also had Thompson look over Sorensen's draft of JFK's speech, which he did, making some adjustments to the first part.[69]

Shortly before the president's public address, Thompson and Rusk went back to the White House to take part in a briefing for congressional leaders, the first time any of them were officially told of the crisis. Congress was in recess, and many of the twenty senators and representatives were campaigning in their home states, so they had to rush back to Washington, DC, lending yet more drama to the event. JFK wanted Thompson there to help explain the rationale behind the proposed quarantine. CIA director John McCone and Arthur Lundahl, the director of the CIA's National Photographic Interpretation Center, started the intelligence briefing. Rusk recalled that one of the legislators "just groaned and fell over on the table with his head in his hands and stayed there for a while."[70] Once the nature of the crisis was clear, their questions began to shift to why. JFK called on Thompson, who described his last meeting with Khrushchev in the USSR and his belief that one of Khrushchev's purposes in the Soviets' nuclear missile buildup in Cuba was to help his position with respect to East Germany and the NATO alliance.

The president then informed the congressional leaders of his decision to implement a quarantine under the Rio Treaty. Their reaction to that was intense. Their initial thoughts, like those of JFK and most members of the ExCom group before them, was that nothing short of a massive first strike was conceivable. Richard B. Russell was a very influential senator, and his statement that settling for a quarantine would convince the world that the United States would not fight for Berlin had some effect on JFK. Senator J. William Fulbright was even more vocal, asserting that a blockade was the worst possible choice. These men would have to be brought along, in the span of one brief meeting, to a position that it had taken nearly a week for the president and the members of the ExCom to come to. The legislators raised many of the same arguments that had surfaced at various times in the working groups and the White House meetings. JFK invoked Thompson's strong opinion that the Soviets would regard any attack on the Cuban missile sites and the subsequent killing of thousands of Soviet citizens as a greater provocation than stopping or shooting at their ships.[71] Shortly thereafter, Kennedy left to make his speech to the American people.

The Cat Is Out of the Bag

At 7:00 p.m. on October 22, 1962, President Kennedy went on the air to tell Americans that the United States was on the brink of nuclear war.[72] The Soviets had installed military bases and offensive missiles in Cuba. "The purpose of these bases can be none other than to provide a nuclear strike capability against the Western Hemisphere" he told the nation, and this could not be tolerated. JFK announced that he would put a quarantine into place, and that any nuclear missile launched from Cuba against any nation in the Western Hemisphere would be considered to be an attack by the Soviet Union on the United States, requiring a full retaliatory response. He then called upon Khrushchev "to halt and eliminate this clandestine, reckless, and provocative threat to world peace," to abandon his "course of world domination, and to join in an historic effort to end the perilous arms race and to transform the history of man."

By 7:30 p.m., JFK was on the phone with Britain's prime minister, Harold Macmillan. He responded to Macmillan's questions with a statement reminiscent of Thompson's from a few days before. A quarantine was "the action we could take which would lessen the chance of an immediate escalation into war, though of course it could bring that result." In the course of the conversation, the president told Macmillan that he had "no plans to invade Cuba." The issue wasn't about Castro or the Communists; he just wanted to get the missiles out of Cuba.[73]

The Soviets and the Cubans, however, were convinced that the United States would invade sooner or later. The CIA's ongoing Operation Mongoose—covert operations to overthrow the Communist regime in Cuba, begun under Eisenhower in 1960—and the Bay of Pigs invasion made American intentions toward Cuba seem obvious.[74] The Kennedy administration had been fixated on removing Castro and the Communists from Cuba, and this occasionally still surfaced in the ExCom dialogues.[75] With Soviet missiles in Cuba, however, Castro was no longer the Americans' central concern.

Similarly, once Khrushchev's operation in Cuba was exposed, his priorities and motives changed, or at least that is what Thompson came to believe. No longer were the missiles a means to further Khrushchev's ambitions in Europe, or quiet the Chinese, or help with his domestic problems, or even make America understand how it felt to have missiles on the nation's doorstep. The USSR's defense of Cuba, their comrade revolutionary nation, from the neighboring imperialists would become the Soviets' central concern. Russian analysts claim this was always Khrushchev's motive. Doing nothing to prevent this newest Communist bloc member from being taken over by the Americans would put Khrushchev's role as leader of the bloc into question, not to mention the moral and ideological failure of letting the island fall to the capitalists.

Vice President Johnson joined the congressional leaders to watch JFK's speech. He reported that their attitude was much better than it had been at the briefing the day before, because, he thought, the president had improved his case. Thompson watched the president's speech with Rusk, U. Alexis Johnson, and others, and then went home to be with his family.[76] Now they waited. The country was in a state of subdued panic. What would Khrushchev do? What would happen in the waters off of Cuba? How far would this go?

As predicted, the next morning, October 23, Khrushchev made an assertive statement, warning the United States to renounce its actions. The weapons on Cuba were "destined exclusively for defensive purposes" and, according to the UN Charter and international norms, the United States had no right to inspect vessels bound for Cuba.[77] Meanwhile, low-altitude US reconnaissance flights over Cuba began, so low that one pilot claimed, "When you can see the writing on the side of the missiles then you really know what you've got."[78] Low-flying jets only reinforced the Cubans' certainty that the United States was going to invade their country. The citizens had no way of knowing whether the shrieking planes flying at tree-top level over their towns and villages were going to shoot photographs or ammunition.

At that morning's ExCom meeting, the men discussed how the Cuban quarantine should be implemented and what should happen if an American plane were shot down. Thompson listened until the discussion was mostly played out before once again raising his concern that the United States wait until the OAS had acted, and then *still* allow a day for the Soviets to respond before implementing a quarantine. He repeated that he felt the Soviets would be less likely to run a legal blockade, and that it would be better to wait before taking other actions.[79] He predicted that the USSR would probably try to test the quarantine by taking one ship through, but once it was clear that the Americans were not bluffing, the Soviets would pull any others back from the line.[80]

Thompson was about to go into a briefing for the Ambassadorial Group, and he asked what to tell them the US reaction would be to any Soviet action against Berlin.[81] He did not believe the USSR would implement a parallel blockade, but he thought the likely minimum response to the quarantine of Cuba would be ratcheting up inspections of US convoys into Berlin. JFK replied that he thought the United States ought to accept that. He didn't want to fight over truck inspections now. General Taylor submitted the idea that perhaps the US convoys should take a "time out" and not go through the checkpoints until the Soviets had had a chance to consider any such demand. Thompson agreed with Taylor and said, "Wouldn't it be better to stop the convoys for the next day or two?"[82] JFK worried that a temporary halt would make it harder to start the convoys up again, and he preferred simply to allow the inspections. The matter was dropped, but it suggests an uncertain president willing to capitulate on a long-standing position regarding access to Berlin.[83]

Bundy recommended that an interdepartmental group be formed to look at this particular issue and other possible repercussions in Berlin. He suggested that Paul Nitze was "the man to beat" for heading it up. Nitze convened a Berlin subcommittee, and they unanimously recommended against allowing any change in policy regarding the convoys.[84] This group, known as the Nitze Committee, would prove to be problematic later on by creating competing strategies on the Berlin issue.[85] One of the committee's tasks was to decide what to do should the Soviets seize Berlin. Nitze advocated an immediate military response, but, according to David Klein, who sat on the committee and was an assistant to Bundy on the National Security Council, Thompson totally disagreed, believing that an immediate response was careless and would unnecessarily broaden the crisis. The Nitze Committee never did provide a united report on what approach to take. "Thompson," Klein wrote, "believed that the Soviets did not want war [and] that the Cuban Crisis could be solved peacefully and fairly, which became President Kennedy's position."[86]

By midmorning on October 23, Rusk reported, to the great relief of those who were still in the room, that the OAS had unanimously adopted a resolution backing the quarantine and the removal of Soviet missiles from Cuba, thus clearing the way to begin its implementation. Then Rusk expressed what many felt by saying he was glad they were still there that morning. "We've passed the one contingency," he said, "an immediate, sudden, irrational strike [by the Soviets]." What he didn't say was that another contingency had also passed: an immediate strike by his own government.

The ExCom group reconvened that evening to work out what they would do in the event that a Soviet vessel did not stop. What if it was a shipment of baby food and the Americans fired on it? Or what if the ship didn't stop, but turned around and headed back? Amazingly, RFK pressed rather hard, arguing that the Americans should go after such vessels. The attorney general surmised that any ship that turned around was very likely to have weaponry on board, and he saw it as an opportunity to examine an aspect of Soviet technology. Bundy would later deduce that the quarantine had more power than they originally thought, because the Soviets were reluctant to have their secrets seen and thought that "we might have understood this advantage beforehand as indeed Thompson did."[87]

The quarantine went into effect on October 24, and much to everyone's relief during that morning's ExCom meeting, they received indications that at least some Soviet ships were stopping or turning back. Rusk was famously quoted as having said, "We are eyeball to eyeball and I think the other guy just blinked." It is not clear from the tapes of the ExCom meeting if Rusk actually said this, although there are some garbled moments in which it might have happened. But, whether myth or reality, the statement was put out there and quoted in articles, as well as in RFK's book on the Cuban Missile Crisis. While the crisis was still unfolding, Thompson implored Rusk to try to stop the "eyeball" quotation from spreading, and he offered some suggestions on how to manage what did come out.[88] Rusk later wrote in his memoirs that it was unfortunate how the remark got played up.

That evening, RFK went to see the Soviet ambassador, Dobrynin, and took the anomalous step of writing a memorandum of their conversation for the president. JFK wanted Thompson to be the interlocutor with Dobrynin, because they knew each other quite well. Thompson, however, suggested that RFK would be a better choice, because the Soviets would be more likely to believe the president's threat to invade Cuba should the quarantine be breached if it came directly from his brother Robert, rather than from a professional diplomat. A number of Soviet participants in later conferences verified that this was an accurate assessment.[89] Thompson helped prepare RFK for the upcoming encounters, but, unfortunately, RFK was animated and emotional at many of these meetings with the Soviet ambassador. Dobrynin later commented that it made the discussions "difficult."[90]

Also on the evening of October 24, a letter came in from Khrushchev, rejecting the authority of the OAS and informing JFK that "our instructions to Soviet mariners are to observe strictly the universally accepted norms of navigation in international waters and not to retreat one step from them."[91] In a broadcast that same day, the Soviet leader said he would do everything possible to keep war from breaking out and proposed a "top-level meeting" to figure out how to end the crisis. The United States, he said, should avoid "piratical threats," and the Soviet government would not accept them in any form. In other words, the Soviets would not abide by the quarantine. The consensus in the ExCom group was to reject a possible summit meeting between JFK and Khrushchev, because its members did not have a plan for what they would do if the Soviets threatened Berlin.[92] Thompson also did not think a top-level meeting was wise at this point, both because it could become a stalling tactic, and because Khrushchev would undoubtedly try to leverage it to gain an advantage on other issues.

October 25 was a tense day in both capitals. In Moscow, Khrushchev had already decided to resolve the conflict and remove the nuclear missiles that were already in Cuba, but he wanted something in return. In a Presidium meeting that day, Khrushchev instructed his Foreign Ministry to draft a letter to JFK offering to remove the missiles, but with the concurrent demand that the United States unilaterally withdraw *all* the NATO nuclear bases in Europe, including those in Turkey, Italy, and Britain, and do so under UN inspections.[93] At this point, Khrushchev realized the American reaction was greater than he had expected and that the situation was indeed dangerous. Roughly midway through the crisis, Soviet forces in East Germany had been sent to training areas, in preparation to support any major US move in Cuba, and Khrushchev now ordered them to return to barracks.[94]

In Washington, DC, the ExCom group followed the first intercept of the quarantine.[95] The Americans were allowing tankers and other harmless-seeming ships through to Cuba, but they followed the *Grozny*, a Soviet ship with hatches large enough to load missiles. Then they somehow lost the boat. This may seem surprising, in light of today's technology, but it was not so simple to track ships accurately in 1962. Those who were monitoring the movements could not be certain if a ship had stopped, turned back, or outmaneuvered the quarantine line.

That same day, in the UN Security Council, Adlai Stevenson challenged the Soviet ambassador to the UN, Valerian Zorin, to deny the existence of the Soviet missiles in Cuba and said he'd wait "until hell freezes over" for an answer. Then he presented the aerial photographs of the missile installations to the council.[96] Thompson thought the initial Soviet reaction was cautious, because it was the *Cubans* who complained about the quarantine in the UN Security Council, not the Soviets. But RFK was of the opinion that a harsher reply was forthcoming.

Moreover, the quarantine was only half of the issue. Even if it was working and no new materiel was coming into Cuba, missile site construction and preparations on the island were continuing unabated. On Friday morning, October 26, the ExCom members talked about how to verify that the nuclear missiles in Cuba were rendered "inoperable" and what role the UN might have in overseeing both the quarantine and the missile disassembly.

Thompson thought they'd have a better chance of success by requesting the Soviets to literally remove the missiles altogether, rather than asking them to accept UN inspections. The US ambassador to the UN, Adlai Stevenson, thought this international organization could verify that construction had stopped, followed by a round of negotiations that could begin to determine subsequent steps. Thompson disagreed, since stopping construction would not remove what was already there. Thompson did not think that removal of the missiles already in Cuba should be open to negotiation. Stevenson then took a telephone call from his deputy, Thompson's former colleague in Vienna, Charles Yost, who was in New York City and slated to meet with U Thant, the UN secretary-general, on Stevenson's behalf. JFK recorded the call, and it was apparent that Stevenson still thought his view of things would prevail.[97]

The president was clearly frustrated. He didn't agree with Stevenson's approach, but at least the UN ambassador had one. What was the United States going to do, besides continue the quarantine, if the Soviets continued constructing missile sites? So Thompson, Rusk, and others went back to the State Department, where they could brainstorm the next steps without JFK being present. The president was again pessimistic about the possibility that the crisis would be resolved without an air strike and a subsequent invasion. He'd reverted to the position he had held ten days previously, and time was running out, as the nuclear missiles in Cuba were close to operational.

Yost telephoned Rusk after his meeting with U Thant and told the secretary of state that the UN secretary-general thought the Soviets might withdraw the missiles in exchange for a noninvasion pledge. Rusk had also received word from Canadian officials that this was a possibility.[98] He phoned the president to inform him of the latest developments. JFK said he'd certainly agree to such a pledge, since the Americans hadn't planned to invade Cuba anyhow. He'd said as much to Gromyko a few days earlier.

Yet in another development on October 25, columnist Walter Lippmann had written: "The Soviet missile base in Cuba, like the US-NATO base in Turkey, is of little military value. The Soviet military base in Cuba is defenseless, and the base in Turkey is all but obsolete. The two bases could be dismantled without altering the world balance of power."[99] The existence of nuclear missiles in Turkey had represented significant psychological and political power for the NATO allies, but the idea of a missile trade was now out in the open. It was picked up by "British newspapers of all political shades,"[100] and even Austrian foreign minister Bruno Kreisky, speaking to a group from his Socialist party in Vienna, called for a trade.[101] Responses to the State Department's inquiries on possible reactions from Turkey and Italy, should the Americans have to offer up NATO missile bases there as a concession to end the crisis, began coming in. The US ambassador to Italy indicated that it would probably not be a problem.

On the other hand, Raymond Hare, the US ambassador to Turkey, reported that Turkey would be incensed if the missiles there were pulled out as part of a deal with the Soviets over Cuba. Appropriations for the base had only recently passed in the Turkish parliament, and the missiles had just become operational. To have to go back and say, in effect, "never mind" after convincing that country's parliament of the absolute necessity of the base would be politically embarrassing. In addition, the idea that the United States couldn't live with missiles near its borders but was perfectly willing to allow Europe and Turkey to do so received a very cold reaction. The Turks said they were "proud that, unlike the Cubans, they were not the stooge of a great power." Hare speculated that one solution might be to have a secret agreement with the Soviets, without telling the Turks, whereby the United States would promise to dismantle the missiles in Turkey.[102]

Mistakes and Misunderstandings

Over the next several days, conflicting information in both Washington, DC, and Moscow—coupled with mistakes on the ground, in the air, and under the sea—escalated tensions and uncertainty, all of which was already at a fever pitch. Simultaneously with the ExCom meetings, journalist John Scali opened an independent back channel through the KGB's station chief in Washington, DC, Alexandr Fomin, whose real name was Feklisov. One of the two men brought up the idea that the Soviets might remove their missiles in exchange for a US pledge not to invade Cuba. Who mentioned it first is disputed, but, in any case, neither man represented his government, and thus could not make an official offer.[103] Scali, however, characterized it to the US government as a legitimate back-channel offer from the Soviets, so it did play a role in the Americans' thinking. Scali's blunt and harsh demand that the Soviets remove the missiles that were already in Cuba also played some type of role in Moscow, although less so than in the United States.

On the evening of October 26, in his daily call with Harold Macmillan, JFK told the British prime minister that this idea of a noninvasion pledge only constituted "a couple of hints" and was by no means a concrete offer. It makes sense that the president would have been skeptical, since his same suggestion to Gromyko the week before had gone nowhere. Besides, the missile-removal exchange, which had been hanging in the air like cigarette smoke since the beginning of the crisis, was now being openly discussed by politicians and the media.[104]

Moscow was getting other disturbing signals from the US capital that evening, including an overheard conversation in a Washington, DC, watering hole, purporting that a *New York Herald Tribune* journalist was heading to Florida to "watch the invasion begin," and at least one message from Fidel Castro saying that, according to Cuban intelligence, they expected an invasion within a day.[105]

The Personal Letter

These dire indications prompted Khrushchev not to wait for the Soviet Foreign Ministry to finish drafting his letter to JFK, but to prepare one of his own. Perhaps a fear that the American military, especially hard-liners in the Pentagon, might use this opportunity to unleash war against the USSR—a possibility he had always considered plausible—prompted him to act now. Khrushchev consulted Gromyko and, most likely, Mikoyan, but he did not convene the Presidium to review his letter. It would not mention the NATO missiles. Khrushchev's advisors weren't too happy, but they did not openly disagree with the premier.[106]

At the American embassy in Moscow, at 4:43 p.m. Moscow time, political officer Richard Davies received Khrushchev's personal letter for transmission to Washington, DC. It wasn't unusual for the embassy to receive a letter from Khrushchev. Davies had received such letters before and would translate them, but this one was different. Two men had come over from the Soviets' Foreign Office with a letter in Khrushchev's own handwriting, containing margin notes in green ink. The men came off the rickety old elevator in the US embassy, panting and apologizing for delivering the letter without the usual Foreign Office seals, saying they simply did not have time for this formality. They'd come directly from the Kremlin. They were under "tremendous pressure" and were unusually polite and very nervous.[107] The letter from Khrushchev arrived in Washington, DC, in four parts, via teletype, at the State Department ten hours later, between 6 and 9 p.m.

It was a remarkable letter: rambling, personal, and passionate. In it, Khrushchev spoke of the need for peace, the calamity of war, and the requirement for statesmanlike wisdom. The Soviet leader proposed that he promise none of their ships bound for Cuba would carry any armaments, and that the United States should, in turn, declare that it would "not invade Cuba with its forces and [would] not support any sort of forces which might intend to carry out an invasion of Cuba. Then the necessity for the presence of our military specialists in Cuba would disappear."[108] It was peppered with accusations of "piratical actions" and of the Americans starting the whole business. Nonetheless, Khrushchev was making the hints of the day concrete: the crisis could end with the removal of the Soviet missiles in Cuba in exchange for a US pledge not to invade that country. A group composed of some ExCom members, including Thompson, reconvened at 10:00 p.m. to read Khrushchev's letter. They all would sleep better that night, planning to meet the next day to craft their reply.

Black Saturday, October 27, 1962

October 27 became known as Black Saturday. Nothing was certain that day. Khrushchev received mixed signals in rapid succession. Castro's messages seemed to go from frightening to lunatic, while new intelligence information contradicted reports from the day before of an imminent US invasion. That morning, the Americans had received another message from Khrushchev that conflicted with what he had written in his letter the night before, leaving the men at the ExCom meeting unsure of what to do. On top of this, that day included a series of incidents that came close to striking a match next to the powder keg.

Thompson started Black Saturday with Dean Rusk, joined by George Ball. They gathered at the State Department to discuss how the president should respond to Khrushchev's letter from the night before. They left together for the planned meeting of the ExCom group at 9:30 a.m. Khrushchev's second letter came to them in bits during that meeting, having been picked up from Radio Moscow.[109] JFK "commented that the statement was a very tough position and varied considerably from the tone of Khrushchev's personal letter to the President received last night." Those in the group weren't even sure the news was referring to the letter of the night before, which they'd somehow misread, or if it was a new one. The public letter the Americans received from Khrushchev was more formal and specifically asked for a trade in the removal of nuclear missiles—presumably Cuba's for Turkey's—but that was not yet absolutely clear. Perhaps he meant missiles in all the NATO bases. To make matters worse, this letter was public. The one from the previous night was private and was not broadcast. Whatever the Americans experienced the night before, they now felt blindsided by this seeming turnabout by Khrushchev. They did not know that the public letter was actually based on the draft that had been started by the Foreign Ministry, on Khrushchev's instructions, two days before.[110] They speculated on why Khrushchev changed the terms so abruptly, and Thompson hazarded that the first, "personal" letter the Americans received was written or dictated by Khrushchev himself, without input or editing by the Presidium. He then opined that the second letter, the "public" one mentioning the Turkish missiles, was sent because Khrushchev was pushed by his colleagues to do so, or possibly because he had been influenced by the mention of a trade in Lippmann's article or in Kreisky's speech.

Thompson was fairly accurate in his guess. Khrushchev had written the personal letter virtually by himself, and the public letter was prepared by the Foreign Ministry and approved by the Presidium before it was sent out. Khrushchev might have been influenced by the Lippmann article, but he had not been pushed by anyone to change his tune.[111] What Thompson could not know about were the other miscalculations going on in Moscow that led to Khrushchev's apparent flip-flop.

A Soviet diplomat reported that the same *Herald Tribune* reporter from the bar the night before was still in Washington, DC, and was in no hurry to witness an imminent invasion.[112] That morning, Khrushchev was given the Lippmann article, which proposed a trade, with the Soviets removing their missiles in Cuba in exchange for the Americans getting rid of the missiles in Turkey. So he asked Gromyko to finish the Foreign Ministry draft of October 25, but to change it slightly and only mention the missiles in Turkey, not the ones in Italy and Britain.

Khrushchev, in reading Gromyko's draft to the Presidium for its approval, ad-libbed, making it more cordial and noting the corrections in the margins.[113] When Gromyko suggested that it might be too late to preempt the personal letter to JFK, and that the Americans might already be crafting a reply to it (which they were), Khrushchev determined to take this new one to the radio station personally and have it read on air. His driver did not have the radio station's address, and they got lost en route, creating a delay. Once there, Khrushchev asked Yuri Levitan, the severe-voiced commentator of "This Is Moscow Speaking," to soften his delivery and not make what he said sound too aggressive. Khrushchev was doubtful that the Americans would respond to this public letter, and they indeed did not.[114]

To Trade or Not to Trade

After reading Khrushchev's public letter, JFK insisted that it would be difficult to turn down a Soviet proposal to trade the removal of missiles in Cuba for those in Turkey, because it would appear to be reasonable. But both Rusk and Bundy stepped in and agreed with Ball and Nitze that the Turkish missiles did not belong solely to the United States, but instead were NATO's, which was a different matter. The essence of this debate continued throughout the day.

The president spent the day trying to convince his advisors that they should just accept the Turkish missile trade, and the discussion became quite animated. Even though most of the men there had, at one point or another, assumed that the missiles in Turkey would be a casualty of resolving the crisis, they now gave reasons why they were opposed to it. CIA director John McCone was willing to have an outright trade of the Turkish missiles for the Cuban ones, and he grumbled to himself that everyone had thought it was a good idea— until Khrushchev himself had proposed it.[115]

There were several arguments against making an overt trade. One, the Americans didn't own the missiles, only the warheads for them. Two, the missiles had been installed under the auspices of NATO and could not be taken out without due process by that organization. Three, Turkey had now made its intense objections clear. Four, US foreign policy was based in large measure on the importance of credibility, particularly with respect to Berlin. To relinquish NATO missiles protecting Europe from a Soviet nuclear threat, in order to remove a similar threat to the United States, would certainly undermine that credibility. Five, the missile-removal trade would undermine attempts at nuclear nonproliferation. America was willing to provide nuclear protection for NATO, in order to stop individual NATO members from going nuclear themselves. France's assumption that the resolution of the Cuban crisis had been a trade of European security for that of the United States would become one reason why it would later pull out of NATO and develop its own nuclear capacity.

Thompson, who was also against the missile trade, had an additional argument. He said that the only way to justify a unilateral decision to take the nuclear missiles out of Turkey—over that country's protestations—was if it could be seen to be in Turkey's best interest. Yet such an action could only be construed in that way if Turkey was a retaliatory target in the event of an imminent US attack on Cuba. Therefore, according to Thompson's logic, choosing to remove the Turkish missiles could push the United States into an invasion course, when it was not yet clear that this was the direction to take.[116] Thompson further calculated that Khrushchev had upped the ante in this public letter, because the wording implied a tit-for-tat, plane-for-plane, missile-for-missile trade. Such a salami tactic (see chapter 5) could lead to dismantling the US military presence in Turkey entirely, not just removing the obsolete missiles, thus compromising NATO's strategic position.[117]

More Close Calls

Events were swiftly evolving, with rapid-fire mistakes. Reconnaissance images showed that construction on the launch sites in Cuba had not only continued, but had sped up, leading some of the Americans to speculate that the Soviets were just stalling. Then Soviet commanders on the ground in Cuba, carried away by the Cubans' revolutionary fervor and their own conviction of an imminent American attack, authorized antiaircraft SAM sites to shoot down U-2 planes. They could not let a U-2 return and give away the position of their rockets or any other reconnaissance information it had gathered for a potential attack by the Americans. For the Cubans and the Soviets on the ground, this would not be a crazy act, but a military decision that made sense, given their narrow perspective.

One of the U-2 planes flying over Cuba *was* shot down, killing its American pilot, which put the ExCom group into its own tailspin, reigniting the call for an immediate strike. Had the Cubans gone rogue and taken over the SAM installations?[118] If it was the Soviets who had given the order, was this a signal that they were going for an all-out confrontation? Even Thompson considered taking out the specific SAM site that killed the American pilot, who was the first casualty of the crisis. At this point, Khrushchev still did not know that one of his own commanders had ordered the U-2 plane to be shot down. Thinking it was a unilateral action by the Cubans, this was perhaps the moment when Khrushchev realized that events were slipping out of his control.

On the other side of the world, another American U-2 spy plane wandered off course, accidentally penetrating Soviet airspace. The Soviet military took this aircraft to be the advance scout for a nuclear attack on their country. Thankfully, cooler heads prevailed, and the Soviets did not take action before verifying that the U-2 pilot had made a mistake. Only in 2013 did it come out, through newly declassified JFK recordings, that another critical incident almost took place during the Cuban Missile Crisis: an insubordinate US admiral threatened to contravene the president's quarantine orders and sink a Soviet ship.[119]

If these near-calamitous events were not enough, the Americans also ordered their ships to drop depth charges at a shallow level, in order to harass a Soviet submarine that had not responded to a signal to surface, unaware that the sub was equipped with nuclear-tipped torpedoes. To avoid being forcibly surfaced and boarded by US forces, the Soviet sailors took the submarine down to a level where it was unable to receive any communications. The submarine's interior reached a nearly impossible temperature of over 122°F, and it was only because the captain refused to authorize a launch of his torpedoes that a disastrous mistake was prevented.[120]

The Americans were still following the Soviet ship *Grozny* when they realized that they hadn't explicitly told the Soviets exactly where the quarantine line was.[121] They hurriedly issued a clarifying communiqué, but the *Grozny* continued steaming toward the line, testing the United States' resolve. Then, as Thompson had predicted, the ship went precisely up to the line but did not go through it.[122]

Further Discussions about a Trade

The focus in the ExCom meetings continued to be on the two letters from Khrushchev and how to reply to them. Thompson had suggested in sidebar meetings, which included at least Rusk and McNamara, that the Americans simply ignore the demands of the public letter and respond to Khrushchev's offer in the personal letter— an idea the attorney general later voiced in the ExCom meeting.[123] But JFK was adamant. This second letter was a public statement, and the Americans could not ignore it. Thompson was absolutely convinced that a trade in removing missiles was unnecessary, given that Khrushchev, only the night before, had been willing to accept a US pledge not to invade Cuba.[124] At one point during the day, the president said: "We're not going to get these weapons out of Cuba, probably . . . by negotiation. We're going to have to take our weapons out of Turkey." To his colleagues' surprise, Thompson openly contradicted JFK and replied: "I don't agree,

Mr. President. I think we can still get this line going," meaning the Soviets taking their nuclear missiles out of Cuba in return for a US pledge not to invade that country.[125] When JFK pressed and asked how Khrushchev could take the missiles out of Cuba without getting something in return in Turkey, Thompson said that Khrushchev's position, "even in this public statement, is [that] this all started by our threat to Cuba. Now he's [able to say he] removed that threat."[126] David Klein stated that "in his quiet and inimitable way, he [Thompson] told the president why he believed the president may be on the wrong track if he followed the group's consensus."[127] After the crisis was over, this idea to reply to the personal letter and ignore the public letter became known as the Trollope ploy,[128] a most unfortunate appellation that implied some sort of subterfuge and, like the "eyeball" quote, took on a life of its own. It possibly was fed by a public relations machine that kicked into high gear when RFK ran for president. That, in turn, made the "ploy" a lightning rod for historians when information about a potential deal with the Soviets regarding the missiles in Turkey became declassified. Sadly, this tarnished Thompson's basic premise of giving everyone a way out by answering only Khrushchev's personal letter and ignoring his more belligerent one.

RFK was to deliver a paper copy of a reply letter from the United States to Dobrynin, at an appointment set for 7:45 that evening. The main ExCom group was at an impasse, however. The president returned to the meeting, where the mood drifted back to a more strident military solution, which then degenerated into gallows humor as the participants broke for a meal shortly after 7:30 p.m. The NATO allies received cables warning them that, although Khrushchev's personal message "seemed to offer real hope," the United States might have to take military action soon. The cables were accompanied by an oral message from the respective American ambassadors to these countries that any such events could "result in some Soviet moves against NATO."[129]

While the other ExCom members were eating or were busy drafting cables, JFK convened a small group of men in the Oval Office, including Rusk, RFK, and Thompson.[130] There is no written account, or at least not a declassified one, as to what happened in the Oval Office that night. Kennedy had made a decision that the missiles in Turkey would be sacrificed, despite having agreed in the larger ExCom meeting to only answer Khrushchev's personal letter. Dean Rusk and others recalled that the secretary of state suggested something similar to what Ambassador Hare in Turkey had posited in his cable. They could send RFK to Dobrynin with a written reply to Khrushchev's personal letter, agreeing to a noninvasion pledge in exchange for the removal of the missiles in Cuba. The president's letter, however, could also be accompanied by an oral assurance that the nuclear missiles in Turkey would be removed within a certain timeframe, but this information would have to be kept secret, and the removals had to occur through a NATO process.

RFK was to impress upon Dobrynin that, if the president's letter was not immediately accepted, with a reply received by the next day (Sunday), the Soviet ambassador was to tell Khrushchev that JFK was under enormous pressure from the US military and others in his government, and an American attack would be certain. RFK was to add that such a move was already planned for Monday (it actually was to occur on Tuesday). Khrushchev's intelligence sources would verify that preparations for an attack were underway, and that the US military's alert status was increasing to defense-readiness condition (DEFCON) 2, just below the highest level.[131] It would have been in character for Thompson to have advised RFK to make it clear to Dobrynin that the letter was not an ultimatum, but only that the United States needed an answer by the next day, because all parties were running out of time. Obviously it was a de facto ultimatum, but Thompson understood that if it was presented as a diktat, Dobrynin could not accept it.[132]

RFK went to his office in the Justice Department for his appointment with Dobrynin, while Thompson and Rusk drove back to the State Department together, just before 8:00 p.m.[133] RFK was about fifteen minutes late for the meeting, and Dobrynin was already waiting for him. As soon as Thompson and Rusk reached Rusk's office, the secretary of state phoned RFK, to remind him that the oral part of his message was not to be presented as an outright quid pro quo, but rather that he was just "informing" the Soviet ambassador that the United States would be taking its missiles out of Turkey as part of a previously accepted plan that had not yet been carried out.[134] Perhaps Rusk made this telephone call because he was unsure of how far RFK would go in letting the Soviets think they had a deal, albeit a secret one.[135] When Rusk got through to RFK, the attorney general told him that Dobrynin was already in his office and that he (RFK) had "already said what he was going to on the subject."[136] It is surprising that Rusk would think to phone RFK with these instructions within minutes after the Oval Office meeting in which the whole plan had supposedly been decided on. Perhaps it was because the instructions given to RFK in the Oval Office weren't specific enough, or because the secretary of state didn't trust RFK's emotionality. Rusk "detested" RFK and thought him inexperienced and untested.[137]

Dobrynin wrote a cable to Moscow describing his meeting with RFK, who had delivered the president's message: if the Soviets agreed to "halt further work on the construction of missile bases in Cuba and take measures under international control that would make it impossible to use these weapons," the United States would "give assurances that there will not be any invasion of Cuba and that other countries of the Western Hemisphere are ready to give the same assurances."[138] He also mentioned that RFK had said an answer was needed by the very next day. Dobrynin reported that RFK was more nervous than he'd ever seen him. The cable to Moscow stated that, on his own initiative, the Soviet ambassador demanded to know why the United States was "always referring to the security of the US, the security of the US? Why did they deny such a right to think about security to us [the USSR] and to Cuba?" He used as an example the nuclear missiles in Turkey, questioning "how come," if these missiles on the Soviet border were OK, "you raise such a racket about missiles in Cuba?" RFK, according to Dobrynin's summary, noted the ambassador's interest in the Turkish missiles and told him that JFK was ready to consider them and examine the question "favorably." It was at this point that Rusk's phone call came in—a little too late. RFK left his office to take the call, which Dobrynin incorrectly supposed had been from his brother, the president.[139]

Sorensen edited RFK's official memoirs of the Cuban Missile Crisis to reflect a meeting that went more along the lines of Rusk's phone call: RFK told Dobrynin the president had decided the missiles in Turkey were going to come out, that their removal would have to go through a NATO process that might take four or five months, and that this information would have to be kept secret. Sorensen later confessed that RFK's original diary indicated that he'd been more explicit about the Turkish missile trade in his meeting with Dobrynin than the version Sorensen edited for *Thirteen Days*.[140] RFK's original recollections are still classified as of this writing, so we only have Dobrynin's account as a counterpoint. Dobrynin's cable about the conversation can be interpreted either way, making the meeting another example of looking at the same event and drawing different conclusions. RFK may have felt he was conveying information about the Turkish missiles that was not couched as a quid pro quo, yet this *was* taken as an explicit offer of a trade by the Soviets.[141] This difference in understanding was borne out when Dobrynin handed RFK a letter that attempted to get the promise to remove the missiles in Turkey written down on paper.[142] Rusk's call to RFK in the middle of his talk with Dobrynin also indicates that Rusk (and possibly Thompson) had serious doubts about whether RFK had really understood or agreed to the way he was to approach the missile removal issue with Dobrynin.[143]

As RFK returned from the meeting with Dobrynin for an informal supper with his brother, Rusk and Thompson headed back to the Cabinet Room, where the ExCom group met again at around 9 p.m. Preparations had to be continued for an attack on the Cuban missile sites and an invasion of that country, as well as a possible general war, in the event that Khrushchev did not respond favorably—and soon.

Havana

While the ExCom members had been debating about how to deal with Khrushchev's two perplexing letters, Fidel Castro sent a new communiqué to Moscow. He had become increasingly convinced that an American attack would occur within hours and had removed himself to a bunker, where he wrote a letter to Khrushchev in the dead of night that became known as the Armageddon letter. Castro later maintained that Khrushchev misinterpreted what he wrote, which may be the case, but the message Moscow got was that the fiery Cuban leader was so certain of an American invasion that he was willing to sacrifice his own people and nation by suggesting—or so Khrushchev interpreted the letter's contents—that he would not object if the Soviets made a preemptive nuclear strike against the United States.[144]

Day 13

Sunday in Moscow

While RFK and Dobrynin were meeting, it was already the early hours of Sunday, October 28, in Moscow. Khrushchev had repaired to his dacha with his closest aides, so no one would see lights on all night in the Kremlin and think it was a sign of apprehension.[145] That morning, at the dacha, he convened eighteen members of the Presidium. The previous day's events had created a mood so intense that, as Khrushchev sat beneath a large map with flags showing the location of Soviet ships and subs surrounding the United States, he didn't even notice when someone came in the room.[146] Khrushchev was ruminating about Castro's Armageddon letter. The Presidium members had copies of both JFK's letter and the Armageddon letter in front of them.[147] The president's letter, responding to Khrushchev's personal letter, was a way out for the Soviets.[148] So they began working on an answer, accepting Kennedy's terms.[149]

Forty-five minutes into the meeting, Moscow received the official KGB report on the U-2 downed over Cuba.[150] Moscow had not been consulted on the authorization to shoot down the spy plane, and Khrushchev was horrified when he learned it was a Soviet general who had actually given the order.[151] Khrushchev well understood the implications this action had, because the Soviet tactical launchers (Lunas) were armed with nuclear warheads. Knowing just how emotional and worked up his men on the ground had become, the Soviet leader might well have wondered into whose hands he'd entrusted those weapons. Mikoyan later speculated that if the Americans had invaded Cuba, the Soviets on the ground would probably have deployed the Lunas, regardless of whether they had received an order from Moscow to do so. Indeed, they probably would have used all the arms they had at their disposal.[152]

Dobrynin's cable describing his conversation with RFK had just been received at the Central Committee offices by Gromyko's chief of staff, who now phoned the dacha. Oleg Troyanovsky, an advisor to Khrushchev, took the call. Dobrynin had reported RFK's assurances that the missiles in Turkey were going to be removed in due course, but he noted that this was to be a secret deal. The Soviet ambassador's report on RFK's obvious nervousness and the urgent pressure the American president was under — which Khrushchev interpreted as being a risk of JFK losing control to what the Soviet leader called the "Pentagon forces"—disturbed the men at the dacha.[153] According to Troyanovsky, the concerns the cable raised confirmed Khrushchev's "decision to accept Kennedy's terms to guarantee that there would be no attack on Cuba, but that the Soviet Union should withdraw all offensive weapons from Cuba."[154]

Khrushchev had already decided to take the missiles out of Cuba when the call came from Gromyko's office regarding Dobrynin's cable. Khrushchev was very happy to get at least part of what he'd wanted. Despite knowing that the Turkish missile deal had to be kept secret—and thus would be of limited use to him politically—he cabled Dobrynin to contact RFK and tell him that a positive reply to the Americans' proposal would be forthcoming.[155]

Just then, General Seymon Ivanov (General Taylor's Soviet counterpart) mistakenly informed Khrushchev that JFK was scheduled to broadcast an address to all Americans within the hour. They speculated that this could be the president's announcement of an air strike on Cuba.[156] While it turned out to be a rebroadcast of Kennedy's speech to the nation on October 22, this was not known at the time. Khrushchev therefore decided not to wait for Dobrynin to pass along his latest response to JFK, but to broadcast it immediately, before the president could make *his* announcement. Khrushchev's reply did not mention anything about the missiles in Turkey and accepted JFK's agreement to Khrushchev's first proposal on October 26, the one in the Soviet leader's personal letter to the president.

Early in the afternoon, a secretary from the Central Committee was summoned to the dacha to drive Khrushchev's public reply to Radio Moscow. He sped down the narrow road through the pines and birches toward town, all the while worrying that the fate of the world hung in the balance should he get into an accident on the way.[157]

And in Washington, DC

Sunday morning, October 28, dawned in Washington, DC, with Thompson and his colleagues comforted by still being alive, but remaining wary. It was an unusually warm and bright fall day, with the gift of an extra hour of sunshine, thanks to daylight savings time. At 10:00 a.m. in Washington, DC, (now late afternoon in Moscow), just as Thompson walked into Rusk's office, an announcement of Khrushchev's communiqué—the one broadcast over Radio Moscow—came over the teletype, followed by its text. "The Soviet Government, in addition to earlier instructions on the discontinuation of further work on weapons construction sites, has given a new order to dismantle the arms which you described as *offensive* [italics ours, as this would prove to be important later on], and to crate and return them to the Soviet Union." Khrushchev stated that would do this because he understood from JFK's message of October 27, 1962, "that there would be no attack, no invasion of Cuba."[158]

Not everyone sighed with relief, however. In the American capital, cold currents still ran, as General LeMay and others on the JCS, who had met to review attack plans that morning, thought it was all a trick and advocated for the United States to go ahead with the strike on Cuba anyhow.[159] Furthermore, there was perilous and delicate work ahead in negotiating this vague agreement and overseeing its application.

The ExCom group convened at 11:00 a.m., without RFK, who was with Dobrynin. The Soviet ambassador handed RFK a letter documenting their secret understanding. The attorney general took the letter, but he returned it the next day, telling the ambassador that he didn't want something that might turn out to hurt him, should he make a bid for the presidency himself.[160] It's quite remarkable that not one of the men who were privy to the secret arrangement for the removal of nuclear missiles in Turkey ever revealed it, and perhaps even more remarkable that its terms were upheld by both parties. Khrushchev later stated that he was assured of JFK's honor from their summit meeting in Vienna.[161]

It's tempting to deduce that this secret deal was the ultimate key to resolving the crisis (which is the latest myth regarding the Cuban Missile Crisis), but that would be wrong. First of all, Khrushchev had already determined to take the Soviet missiles out of Cuba even before he heard the text of Dobrynin's cable, containing the offer to remove the missiles in Turkey. Khrushchev hadn't fully believed, but he had hoped, that the Americans would go for the trade.[162] The land-based missiles in Turkey could—and would—be replaced by Polaris submarines, which were capable of launching nuclear warheads, so simply getting the missiles out of Turkey did not provide a significant strategic advantage for the Soviets. Thus they had no reason to press the matter too hard. Khrushchev intended to keep the deal a secret, so it offered very little overt political advantage to him. He could tell his close associates, which might be useful in the Presidium, but he could not publicize the trade, so it didn't help him in terms of world opinion. Sergei Khrushchev agreed that his father's prime motive was to ensure that Cuba was not invaded. The missiles in Turkey and Italy were "in the air, like Berlin. They were not important. [Khrushchev] kept it secret because it was more important to keep Kennedy's trust for future negotiations."[163] That's why the Turkish missiles weren't a prime subject of conversation among Khrushchev and his colleagues at the dacha that Sunday. They just weren't that important to the Soviets. What really mattered, as Thompson kept saying, was that Khrushchev could say he'd saved Cuba. Bundy called the missiles a "sweetener" for Khrushchev. They were not what "made things happen."[164] The deal represented a psychological reassurance that Khrushchev and JFK were partners, and it showed that their relationship didn't just involve empty words. As Sergei Khrushchev put it, the crisis and its resolution weren't about a balance of strategic power—in his words, "counting missiles"—but about a balance of respect.

Several years later, when Thompson's teenage daughter confronted him with a claim a Cuban émigré friend of hers had made—that the Cuban Missile Crisis was solved not because the president and his advisors stayed the course, but because they had "capitulated" and given up on the presence of missiles in Turkey—Thompson was upset. His explanation of the missiles' obsolescence, and his statement that their removal was coincidental to the crisis, sounded questionable to his daughter. Thompson must have realized, with a sinking heart, that, as he had feared, the decision about the removal of missiles in Turkey would open the door for many interpretations.

Post–Thirteen Days

Sunday, October 28, ended the official thirteen days of the Cuban Missile Crisis. That date was marked on the small wood and silver Tiffany calendar the president gave Thompson and the other ExCom members, to commemorate their intense time together.[165] The crisis was far from over, however, at least for Thompson and the rest of the ExCom group, and certainly for Castro, who accused Khrushchev of lacking *cojones*. JFK made a point of cautioning his men not to appear to gloat over a diplomatic victory.

Berlin Again

There was no time for gloating—or for rest—since the very next day, Monday, October 29, was when the internal politics began. The possibility that the Soviets might take some action in Berlin had been present during the Cuban Missile Crisis, so the familiar drumbeat of what to do about Berlin continued, only now with more focus. Thompson had tried to stop a proposal to continue Nitze's Berlin subcommittee (formed during the early days of the crisis over Cuba), on the grounds that the group was too large, which raised a security problem. On October 23, Walter "Walt" Whitman Rostow took over the group, renamed it the Advance Planning Subcommittee, and made it much smaller.[166]

In early November, this subcommittee, which included Thompson, came up with two alternative strategies for Berlin: Track A, which was essentially more of the same, and Track B, which was described as "more radical."[167] Track B was fairly vague, offering either an all-Berlin solution or a more-secure access to West Berlin, as well as a change in the status of the Western troops there. It offered an agreement of a "7–10 year stretch-out of the Western Peace Plan" and virtually no other quid pro quo to the Soviets. Thompson, in a form of dissent, offered a supplement to this report, which called for a possible package deal. In a typical move to influence its interpretation, Rostow sent it out with a cover memo, characterizing Thompson's proposal as "virtually the same" as Track B, without the seven- to ten-year extension.

Thompson, however, had not written the supplement just to restate things in his own words; he thought there were important differences between it and what the committee was proposing. Primarily it was a matter of process. Thompson had been negotiating with the Soviets for years at that point, and he had some idea of how to proceed. He understood that it was unwise to force an issue or be sneaky, but neither was it smart to succumb to salami tactics. He therefore suggested a tit-for-tat posture, where concessions from both sides would be identified. These could cancel each other out in terms of the overall balance, and they could be taken up incrementally, giving the United States and its allies what they wanted, while simultaneously giving Khrushchev what he needed to leave Berlin alone for a while. Thompson also pointed out that neither Track A nor B prevented Khrushchev from signing a separate peace treaty with East Germany, since this was not mentioned in either track.

Thompson's supplement listed possible concessions from the Soviets that were not included in either Track A or B. One, the Soviets would reciprocate on a Western offer to ban nuclear weapons, espionage, and radio propaganda in their respective parts of Germany (the Rostow committee was prepared for the Western allies to do this unilaterally). Two, these measures would be instituted only until Germany was reunified, thus keeping at least the idea of a single German nation alive. Three, they would agree to "a relatively secure access authority" to West Berlin.[168] His supplement also included concessions on the Western side. One, an agreement by the allies to withdraw their military presence in East Berlin, although they would maintain it in West Berlin. Two, a ceiling on the number of Western forces in West Berlin and a revision of their name, calling them "military police, but without any major change" in their equipment. Three, a prohibition on incorporating West Berlin into West Germany for the duration of the agreement.[169] He really thought the key was to make these concessions reciprocal, so as to keep a balance of prestige.

Khrushchev and JFK had developed some empathy for each other's positions. Cuba, as Khrushchev's son Sergei later observed, was now the Soviet leader's equivalent to what Berlin was for the president. It made Khrushchev appreciate the box the Americans were in there. The credibility and prestige of the United States really was at stake. The Western allies' insistence that they could not give Berlin up to East Germany was not merely propaganda.[170]

Unfortunately, time ran out before these ideas could be tested. The assassination of John F. Kennedy in November 1963 and Khrushchev's ouster in October 1964 interrupted attempts to resolve the Berlin issue. When Willy Brandt became chancellor of West Germany in 1969, he pursued a policy of Ostpolitik, establishing formal relations with East Germany, and eventually ended the problems over the status of Berlin in 1972.

Cleaning Up the Crisis

Thompson checked himself into the hospital October 30 for a day, to follow up on his recent kidney operation. When he got out, he met Yuri Zhukov for lunch, where they talked about the two letters from Khrushchev and the possibility of a test ban. Zhukov probed about the issue of a potential meeting between the president and Khrushchev, which Thompson deflected. They also discussed Mikoyan's upcoming stopover in New York City. He was going to Cuba to deal with the aftermath of the recent crisis there and negotiate with Fidel Castro about how to implement Khrushchev's agreement with JFK. The lunch partners agreed that they did not envy Mikoyan that task.[171]

Many of the remaining Cuban Missile Crisis negotiations took place in New York City, through Adlai Stevenson and Charles Yost. They included setting international controls in place for dismantling offensive weapons in Cuba and—more difficult still—agreeing to just what constituted *offensive* weapons. One concern was the IL-28 jet bombers, because they were capable of carrying nuclear weapons. Although the Americans did not *know* that a significant number of tactical warheads were already in Cuba, Thompson and others cautioned that they had to *assume* nuclear weapons were there. JFK had instructed Stevenson and presidential advisor John McCloy,[172] when greeting Mikoyan's plane, to give him a list of "offensive weapons" that were to be removed from Cuba and to stress to the Soviet emissary that it included the IL-28s. Unfortunately, Stevenson and McCloy forgot to give Mikoyan the list. Thompson pressed very hard for IL-28s to be included as offensive weapons and reminded JFK of the importance of doing so. Stevenson handed the list to Mikoyan the next day, as the Soviet official was getting into a taxi to go to the airport. Mikoyan was furious.[173] Nonetheless, the removal of the IL-28 bombers was politically as well as practically important to the Americans, because they had been mentioned in the president's speech to the nation on October 22. McGeorge Bundy later wrote: "Llewellyn Thompson proved to be right in his belief that the Soviet government, having agreed to remove the missiles, would not in the end refuse to remove the elderly light bombers as well. In return for this further concession, Kennedy removed the quarantine."[174] Mikoyan's son quoted Thompson as having said, "having swallowed a camel, he [Khrushchev] would also swallow a fly."[175]

Fidel Castro, however, was hopping mad. His expletives to describe Khrushchev rivaled the Soviet leader's own language when describing Castro's unreasonableness. In the Cuban prime minister's mind, Khrushchev had sold him out to the imperialists and hadn't even had the courtesy of informing him, never mind consulting him. Khrushchev, for his part, saw how risky it was to put a piece of the Soviet nuclear arsenal under the influence of a fiery, emotional leader. He sent Mikoyan, who had a close and personal relationship with Castro, and probably was the closest thing to a "Cold War Owl" in the Soviet government, to talk to the Cuban and smooth things out.

Mikoyan made a speech in New York City featuring Castro's demands for compliance with the agreement between the USSR and the United States, which proved to be a wise move on the Soviet official's part. Castro had not yet decided if he was going to even see the Soviet envoy, but after reading the speech, he changed his mind and received Mikoyan shortly after his arrival. Two hours into this first meeting, Mikoyan learned that his wife had died. Understanding how serious the situation was, especially with tactical nuclear weapons still in place in Cuba, he remained in that country and sent his son Sergo back to Moscow for the funeral. Like many of his colleagues who'd been there, Mikoyan had a great affinity for the Cuban revolution and could empathize with Castro's indignation. Yet he also recognized that it was prudent to get the IL-28s, with their tactical nuclear weapons, well out of his reach. The Soviet envoy used his prodigious diplomatic skill to bring the Soviet-Cuban part of the crisis to its conclusion. In order to convince the Cubans, he suggested that Khrushchev tell them there was a secret Soviet law that required the tactical weapons to be removed from Cuba.[176]

On November 18, in the midst of the aftermath to the Cuban Missile Crisis, Thompson received word from his brother MWood that their mother Lula had died. He mentioned to RFK in one of the ExCom meetings that he was sorry, but he would have to leave early to catch a flight to Colorado for her funeral. Shortly thereafter, one of JFK's aides leaned over Thompson's shoulder and told him a military jet had been arranged to take him there. Thompson never forgot that gesture of kindness from the Kennedy brothers.[177] In Denver, Thompson's nephew, Bob, received a call from the White House to make arrangements for Thompson's arrival, going into such minutia as how the ambassador liked his coffee. Bob's wife, Jeanne, was worried because one of her children had a fever, so she wasn't planning to go to Las Animas for the funeral. Thompson, who did not want to be treated like a celebrity by his own family, insisted they not make a fuss and told Jeanne she should stay home to take care of her son. Thompson and Bob made the eight-hour round trip drive from Denver to his mother's service at the Presbyterian Church of Las Animas (her hardshell Baptist husband having never succeeded in converting her). Then Thompson was back in Washington, DC, after an eye-popping two hour and forty-five minute flight.

Mikoyan, on his way back from Havana to New York City, stopped in Washington, DC, to meet with JFK. The day before, however, at Khrushchev's suggestion, Mikoyan asked to see Thompson at Thompson's home, even though Dobrynin had informed him that Thompson was still in the process of painting it.[178] Mikoyan, Dobrynin, and his wife arrived at 1:00 p.m. for brunch. What did they talk about? And why did the meeting have to be at Thompson's home? It's not known. Nonetheless, memoranda of conversation do exist for the meetings Mikoyan had later with JFK and Rusk, both of which included Thompson. With the secretary of state, Mikoyan spoke about a ban on nuclear tests and and how to monitor it. With the president, there was political posturing, but both men agreed that, to maintain peace and avoid lurching from one near disaster to another, the United States and the Soviet Union must each develop a better understanding of the other. "Once the Cuban crisis is resolved" said Mikoyan, "the next steps might well be a nonaggression pact between Warsaw Pact [members] and NATO, the cessation of nuclear tests, disarmament, and Berlin."

Within the following two weeks, the Soviet missiles were on their way home, uncovered and clearly displayed on the decks of ships, for the entire world to see. The tactical nukes came out secretly, due to Mikoyan's initiative with Castro. The Cuban Missile Crisis was officially over at the end of November, when JFK was satisfied and finally removed the quarantine, although Cuba never did get a formal noninvasion declaration from the United States.[179]

Conclusions

Before and during the Cuban Missile Crisis, the Americans and the Soviets each connected their dots and came up with different patterns of thought—different conclusions that almost led to a world-wide nuclear confrontation. Khrushchev linked Operation Mongoose, the Bay of Pigs, and agitated Cuban émigré activities to plans for an American invasion of Cuba, although the United States envisioned no such thing, at least at that moment.[180] On the other hand, Khrushchev's constant poking on Berlin and activities by the USSR in the Third World made the Americans see patterns of Soviet aggression that needed to be stopped, because they assumed the Soviets were orchestrating them all, although—in many cases, including Cuba—they weren't. Both the United States and the USSR saw the other country as the predator.

Weakness was another misperception. JFK thought Khrushchev made his move in Cuba because he considered the president to be weak, after his failure in the Bay of Pigs affair. JFK's poor performance in the Vienna summit perpetuated the thought pattern among some Americans that Kennedy had indeed been weak, and that Khrushchev had the upper hand.[181] Contrary to these American beliefs, Khrushchev thought JFK would have to take a strong stand to redress the Bay of Pigs failure and thus would be more likely to mount an all-out attack—this time not going halfway. The Soviet leader's military advisors told him that the Americans could take over Cuba in just a few days if they engaged in a full-blown offensive.[182]

Khrushchev and the Americans made completely different connections regarding a strategic balance of force. The Soviet leader's insecurity was reinforced by America's public declarations of US military and nuclear superiority, as well as by the establishment of NATO bases in Europe and Turkey. This imbalance, he felt, left the Soviet Union in a precarious situation and allowed the United States to ignore all his "reasonable" proposals. The Americans believed that openly revealing their nuclear superiority would act as a check on the Soviets, keeping them from initiating dangerous maneuvers, whereas this most likely helped push Khrushchev in the opposite direction. Feeling that he was regarded somewhat like Hans Christian Andersen's emperor who had no clothes, Khrushchev opted for a move to strengthen himself and his country again. Missiles in Cuba would shore up the Soviets' strategic imbalance with the United States and ease the Soviet's current seventeen-to-one nuclear missile disadvantage. The missiles would show him to be a protector of Cuba and reassert his position as the leader of the Communist camp, thus quieting Chinese dissent and releasing funds for critical domestic needs.

The Americans were stymied by trying to apply their own patterns of thinking when scrutinizing Khrushchev's adventure. Some analysts even blamed their own failure to predict the Cuban Missile Crisis on the Soviet leader, because the events were so completely "unreasonable." Khrushchev had probably just acted on a gut feeling, as was his character, and had connected his dots with a lot of wishful thinking. The American belief was that after the United States had prevailed in Cuba, the Soviets would become more manageable. The immediate prospects of going beyond the brink into a nuclear war did help to moderate both US and Soviet hyperbole, but the Soviets became even more sensitive to humiliation in the aftermath of Cuba, which actually hindered progress in some areas.[183]

Khrushchev underestimated the Americans' reaction when he thought they'd accept the presence of missiles in Cuba. The Soviet perspective, one most likely still held by Russia today, was that the Cuban Missile Crisis was created through overreaction by the United States. Sergei Khrushchev construed Sputnik, the Cuban Missile Crisis, and, later, 9/11, as examples of how Americans, who had come to take their security for granted, reacted to suddenly realizing that they could be attacked, as opposed to Russians or Europeans, who had lived under such conditions for a very long time.[184]

Thompson made several important contributions to the resolution of the crisis. Probably the one of greatest significant was changing the thought patterns of those most closely involved: shifting their ideas away from how to get rid of the missiles in Cuba with an air strike and toward how to persuade Khrushchev to remove them. When the president asked Thompson what *his* opinion was on the two strike alternatives, Thompson chose neither. Thompson pointed out the importance the Soviets placed on legality, which helped lead JFK and the ExCom group to the quarantine solution. Just as Thompson had done when he held firm during the last tense moments of the Austrian State Treaty, once he was certain that a noninvasion pledge had become Khrushchev's central concern during the missile crisis, Thompson strongly resisted an open trade of the missiles in Cuba for those in Turkey, going so far as to openly "disagree" with the president. He convinced JFK to answer Khrushchev's personal letter, not the public one.[185] In the end, JFK "answered Khrushchev's private letter publicly and his public letter privately."[186] Then, once the immediate crisis was over, Thompson was "an important voice on insisting that the IL-28 light bombers should be withdrawn."[187] Like the Soviets, he was worried about the damage Castro could do with them.

Years later, Dean Rusk said that an apocalyptic war could happen "if a man or group of men and women find themselves driven into a corner from which they can see no escape and lose all stake in the future. In that situation they might elect to play the role of Samson and pull the temple down around themselves and everyone else at the same time. [Thompson] provided crucial help to President Kennedy in understanding this aspect of the crisis. . . . Kennedy instinctively knew that he must not drive Khrushchev into such a corner. . . . [Thompson's] advice in this connection was critical to the way in which

President Kennedy handled the crisis." Thompson felt as though his batting average was running pretty high during the Cuban Missile Crisis.[188] His confidence gave the rest of the ExCom group the assurance they needed in making crucial decisions, especially as his predictions about Soviet moves proved to be correct. David Klein later recalled that Thompson's views "became the president's views, and from there on, at each of these meetings, Tommy more often than not had the last word because he had the president's ear."[189] Stewart Alsop, in a *Saturday Evening Post* editorial about the Foreign Service, wrote that "after the crisis President Kennedy confided that his soundest advice came from Llewellyn Thompson."[190]

It was luck that saved the world from a nuclear tragedy during the Cuban Missile Crisis—luck that the right people were in the room. As author Michael Dobbs observed, "The real good fortune is that men as sane and level-headed as John Fitzgerald Kennedy and Nikita Sergeyevich Khrushchev occupied the White House and the Kremlin in October 1962."[191]

28 ≋

Limited Test Ban

The early arms control and reduction initiatives, while not
always successful, did indicate the beginnings of a fresh way
of thinking. This new thinking, thought by many to be
naïve, was instead quite realistic, given the context of the
cold war, a war in which nuclear weapons were being
amassed in "overkill" numbers in a surreal arms race.
—WILLIAM J. PERRY, *My Journey at the Nuclear Brink*

After the Cuban Missile Crisis, the Washington, DC, rumor network held that
Thompson had a lot to do with things turning out right. Thompson and his wife's
social life quickly became more demanding. JFK and Thompson had connected
during the crisis, and the president began to consult him more frequently. This included
calling him at home after hours and on weekends. Thompson, a firm observer of protocol,
asked Secretary of State Rusk for permission to give JFK his advice on the spot, before
clearing it with Rusk, who told him to go ahead.[1]

Paul Nitze offered the Thompsons a house on his farm in Bel Alton, Maryland, to get
away from the capital on weekends and holidays. Everyone who was anyone in Washington,
DC, had a "farm" where the chosen few accepted weekend invitations—making connections, exchanging opinions, and creating impressions. The farms were a vestige of the old
British tradition of country estates. Jane, who loved the countryside and had always envisioned herself living on a "gentleman's farm," toyed with the idea of buying a property, and
she even managed to drag her husband and daughters to see some houses in Virginia. But
the family budget could not bear the cost, so Nitze's offer seemed like a good compromise.
Sherry rode horses, Jenny practiced her driving on the farm roads, and they all swam, except Thompson, who sat on the porch reading his papers. They spent hours at the Nitzes'
main house—filled with bridge, long lunches, and dinner parties where Nitze would hold
court with young protégés, often after leaving them breathless on the tennis courts. There
were magical Fourth of July celebrations, with fireworks that brought the whole town out to
sit on the lawn above acres of corn and tobacco. Once, when Nitze brought a Soviet digni-

tary to the farm, he pointed Thompson out, saying, "You see, there is no class separation in America, where even a rich man like me can be friends with a poor man like Thompson." Everyone laughed, sort of.

The Thompsons also found themselves invited to both of the Alsop brothers' homes. Jenny became friends with Joe and Susan Mary's daughter, Ann. Jenny spent more and more time at the Alsop house, where Joe would periodically give the two girls long, drawn-out lectures about Vietnam and the possibilities of Soviet general Andrei Grechko staging a military coup, charging Jenny with telling her father so. Alarmed, she conveyed the news, but Thompson reassured her that was not going to happen and advised her to take whatever Joe said with large grains of salt. The great thing about being at the Alsop table was that children were not excluded from the conversation. Susan Mary would listen as attentively to their adolescent drivel as she did to Henry Kissinger.

In November 1962, the president and his advisors met to see if anything positive could come out of the Cuban Missile Crisis. The common experience of having stood at the brink and the shared secret of the Turkish missiles aligned JFK and Khrushchev. Both sides recognized that the timing was right for a shift in policy. The question was, how? There were two possible areas of mutual interest where they could move forward. One was Berlin, and the other was nuclear disarmament. Thompson's was an important voice in the debate about which tack to pursue.[2]

From left to right, Frank Wisner, Charles Bohlen, Llewellyn Thompson Jr., and Donald E. Graham at Graham's Glen Welby farm, Marshall, Virginia, 1961–62. Photo taken by Kay Graham, courtesy of Ellis Wisner.

Time and again, Thompson had explained that Khrushchev's obsession with securing recognition of East Germany was a product of fear, not a quest for Communist expansion. Nonetheless, at the beginning of 1963, he noted a change in the Soviets' attitude toward East Germany in one of Khrushchev's speeches.[3] He surmised that the Soviets would no longer bail the East Germans out economically. He therefore predicted that although finding a solution to the Berlin–East Germany problem would remain part of the Soviets' declared policy, it was no longer as urgent, and they would not bring it to a head at this time.[4] Moreover, after the Cuban Missile Crisis, Khrushchev was not in a position to suggest any concessions on Berlin. When the Soviets proposed starting talks on the Germany problem in March 1963, Thompson concluded that their purpose was to maintain Khrushchev's commitment to Walter Ulbricht, the political head of East Germany, but it would not result in another ultimatum.[5] Thompson said any possible agreement with the Soviets would come on matters such as disarmament or nuclear testing.[6]

The Road to a Nuclear Test Ban

Both sides wanted a comprehensive test ban (CTB), but neither side was willing to either allow inspections (the USSR) or forego them (the United States). In one last effort before he left Moscow, Thompson tried to convince Khrushchev that the Soviet obsession with secrecy had lost its value and was a "shrinking asset," due to advanced technologies. Thompson said it was a natural human trait to fear the unknown, and in the end it did not work out to the Soviets' advantage, because it caused the American military to prepare for threats which might not even exist.[7] Six months later, Khrushchev finally accepted inspections—but only three of them.

The military and the more hawkish elements in the US government insisted on a larger number of inspections—a minimum of 8 to 12—to be absolutely sure the Soviets could not cheat. The problem, Thompson thought, was that the members of the JCS did not consider the other side in the equation: "If we are to attempt realistically to negotiate with the Soviet Union, this preoccupation [with not allowing inspections on Soviet soil] must be taken into account. I wonder if it might be worthwhile to ask the Joint Chiefs to put themselves in the place of the Soviet Joint Chiefs of Staff and draw up a similar list of criteria from the Soviet point of view, and then attempt to see whether they could arrive at a list that would cover the major preoccupations of both sides. It seems to me that any other approach will clearly result in a non-negotiable position."[8] He went on: "I can well sympathize with the Joint Chiefs in wanting to have an arrangement as foolproof as possible. On the other hand, it seems to me important to realize and recognize that Soviet military authorities have similar considerations in mind. Any disarmament arrangement that is completely free from risk for one side is bound to contain enormous risks for the other side and it would seem to me that what we should try to arrive at is an arrangement which reduces to a minimum, so far as practicable, the risks for both sides."

Besides overcoming the problem of inspections, both sides had to consider their allies: the Americans in placating both West Germany and France's aspiration to nuclear capabilities, and the Soviets in curbing China's atomic program. After a few bumpy months in late spring and early summer 1963, however, the two sides were able to come up with a limited version of the test ban treaty (LTB), which, thankfully, did not require onsite inspections.

Background

The door to a test ban opened when public protests reached "unprecedented heights" after the United States exploded a hydrogen bomb in 1954 at Bikini Atoll on the Marshall Islands, in the South Pacific.[9] It generated such widespread nuclear contamination that it poisoned not only sea life, but also, in a more directly threatening fashion, fishermen in the area. There were 231 atmospheric tests between 1953 and 1958, which may have caused more than 11,000 extra US deaths from cancer.[10] Public concern prompted Adlai Stevenson to propose an atmospheric test ban as part of his presidential campaign in 1956. Unfortunately for Stevenson, the Soviets praised his initiative, possibly contributing to his losing the election. An LTB would pop up again and again, like a bouncing ball, for the next seven years—alternating with attempts at a CTB—until it finally fit into the right hole during the Kennedy administration.

Eisenhower and British Prime Minister Harold Macmillan had made one serious attempt at an LTB in 1959, while Thompson was the US ambassador in Moscow. They wrote to Khrushchev to propose a partial ban: stopping atmospheric tests, but without onsite inspections.[11] Khrushchev put off responding until the Camp David meeting, where he and Eisenhower agreed to put disarmament on the agenda for the Paris summit, but, after the U-2 incident, that top-level gathering never took place.

Kennedy and the Limited Test Ban

JFK very much desired to have a ban on nuclear testing and a disarmament agreement be a part of his legacy, and he had wanted to talk to Khrushchev about a ban when they met in Vienna. Having been ignored on Berlin, however, Khrushchev was not in the mood to consider what interested Kennedy.[12] In Vienna, both leaders acknowledged that they were under pressure to resume nuclear testing. Both would succumb to that pressure, with Khrushchev doing so first.

After the Vienna summit, Thompson recommended that the United States (in consultation with the British and possibly the French) renew the Eisenhower-Macmillan 1959 LTB proposal. He said this would have a twofold result. First, "there is the slight possibility that the Soviets would actually accept a ban on atmospheric and undersea tests." If they didn't, they would be put in the position of turning down a reasonable proposal. Second, if the Soviets began testing, "the onus would fall on [them] and they could have the pleasure of dealing with organized demonstrations in Britain and elsewhere."[13]

Bundy and Schlesinger liked Thompson's idea and presented it to the president.[14] JFK decided to make one last effort toward an agreement before resuming nuclear testing.[15] He told Arthur Dean, chairman of the US delegation at the UN-sponsored Eighteen-Nation Disarmament Committee (ENDC) conference in Geneva, to go for a CTB and, if that didn't work out, to present Thompson's suggestion of an LTB.[16] If nothing came of his efforts, the president would make a major speech during the UN General Assembly meeting on disarmament and perhaps "put forward the Thompson proposal."[17] JFK also discussed this possibility in a letter to Macmillan.[18] Arthur Dean, however, feared that any retreat from a CTB would be a weakening of the US position, so he recommended saying only that the 1959 offer still stood, but without explicitly proposing a partial test ban, without inspections.[19] As a result, the Soviets passed over the offer and took a hard-line position. On August 13, 1961, the Berlin Wall began going up, and on September 1, the Soviets resumed atomic testing. Of all the Soviet provocations, this is what most disappointed JFK.[20] "Bitched again," Kennedy said to his advisors, with a profound look of discouragement on his face.[21] Now the whole world waited to see the president's response. A Gallup poll showed that the American public was decidedly in favor of resuming testing, and Congress was ready with its approval and the necessary appropriations. Still, JFK held out.[22]

On September 25, 1961, the president made his big disarmament speech at the UN: "Today, every inhabitant of this planet must contemplate the day when this planet may no longer be habitable. Every man, woman, and child lives under a nuclear sword of Damocles, hanging by the slenderest of threads, capable of being cut at any moment by accident or miscalculation or by madness. . . . The logical place to begin is a treaty assuring the end of nuclear tests of all kinds, in every environment, under workable controls." Then he mentioned the LTB: "We also proposed a mutual ban on atmospheric testing, without inspection or controls, in order to save the human race from the poison of radioactive fallout. We regret that the offer has not been accepted."[23]

In the now-familiar game of hot and cold, at the end of October, the Soviets exploded a 50-megaton bomb, the most powerful bomb yet. Then, in November, they turned around. The Soviets now said they wanted to renew the Geneva negotiations and were, at last, willing to accept an LTB, but with the condition of a moratorium on underground testing. This time it was the American administration that said "No."[24] JFK began atmospheric testing on April 15, 1962.

At the beginning of August 1962, just after his farewell talk with Khrushchev, Thompson met with JFK and resurrected the idea of an LTB. He told the president there was no way that the Soviets, especially after the U-2 affair, would accept inspections on their territory. He did think, however, that they might go for an LTB and a nonproliferation agreement.[25] JFK was of the same mind, so, at the end of August, the Americans decided to present two draft treaties for the ENDC in Geneva: one was a CTB with enforced controls and inspections, and the other was an LTB, without inspections.[26] At first the Soviets rejected both treaties, but then Khrushchev changed his mind and sent JFK a pen-pal letter, saying that although he really wanted a CTB, they could start with an LTB.[27]

Shortly after this, American and Soviet scientists at a Pugwash conference concluded that unmanned monitoring stations could verify the difference between earthquakes and underground nuclear tests.[28] Presidential Science Advisor Jerome Wiesner had said at a meeting with JFK, Thompson, and Bohlen on September 29, 1962, that such a distinction could be made. Weisner then added something unusual, "Suppose you start with the assumption that they are not going to cheat?" The Soviets always *could* cheat by claiming one test was an earthquake, but not a whole series of tests, which were necessary to be militarily or scientifically useful. He even said that he could see how the Soviets could "have some basis for suspicion" as to the US motives for demanding onsite inspections.[29] This was during Bohlen's farewell meeting, just before the Cuban Missile Crisis. Even at the peak of the crisis, when the American reconnaissance plane strayed into Soviet air space, Kennedy wrote to Khrushchev to apologize and used the incident to again stress the need for disarmament and a test ban.[30] Khrushchev replied that conditions were "ripe" for banning tests in the atmosphere, in outer space, and underwater, adding that "we are ready to sign an agreement."[31]

Then, out of the blue, Khrushchev sent JFK an upbeat pen-pal letter inadvertently derailing the LTB, in which he wrote that in order to conclude a *comprehensive* test ban he would accept *three* inspections.[32] That, he wrote, ought to satisfy America's internal needs, so the treaty could be ratified. The president was delighted. Khrushchev had acknowledged onsite inspections in principle, something he had always resisted, but Kennedy did not understand how he had come up with the number for three inspections. An investigation exposed that Dean, in an informal, private conversation, gave Soviet Deputy Foreign Minister Vassili Kuznetsov the impression that the United States would accept three or four inspections.[33] The Soviets assumed Dean's comment represented official policy, since it was inconceivable for a Soviet official to make such a statement without governmental sanction. Khrushchev's letter with the three inspections offer resulted in the Americans and the Soviets agreeing to send representatives to New York City to discuss the matter.[34]

Dobrynin called Thompson on Saturday, January 19, 1963, asking to see him urgently, so Thompson invited him to come by his home. Dobrynin told him that the Soviets were thinking of publishing three pen-pal letters, because US press accounts made it seem as though the Americans had taken the initiative to further a test ban, when the letters showed the opposite was true.[35] Thompson was alarmed, not because of losing the propaganda advantage, but because it was important for this channel to remain private.[36] It had not been easy for Khrushchev to convince the Presidium to go along with *any* inspections. Dobrynin later explained that the Americans did not appreciate how difficult it was for Moscow to accept "even a few foreign observers onto Soviet territory. Many Presidium members were far from agreement."[37] JFK, though, was sure that an agreement with less than eight inspections would never get approval from the US Senate. The president wrote back to Khrushchev, trying to explain the "misunderstanding" about the three inspections, but Khrushchev was furious and thought he had been double crossed.[38] Thompson himself had felt that three inspections would be adequate, because he did not think the Soviets would run the risk of being caught cheating. And he could see how the Soviets believed they had been misled into thinking a very limited number of inspections would be accepted.[39]

At one point, JFK and his advisors debated whether to inform the Soviets that the United States could pinpoint Soviet ICBMs. Thompson was against revealing this information, even though it might prove to the Soviet military that secrecy was fruitless. Playing that card was dangerous, because it suggested a first-strike incentive for the United States, which would be best kept in reserve for a time of crisis. For example, if the Soviets contemplated shutting off Western access to Berlin, on the assumption that the United States would not use nuclear weapons in response, this information might make the Soviets reconsider.[40]

In the end, the CTB went nowhere. The Soviets would not budge from three inspections and walked out of the discussions in New York City at the end of the month. Expectations on both sides had been ill-founded. Khrushchev thought the Americans would take up his offer and move forward with a CTB. The Americans, on the other hand, thought the Soviets could be drawn into accepting more inspections.[41] All of this miscommunication put both a CTB and an LTB in limbo once more.

Cuba Again

In a meeting with the full National Security Council on January 22, 1963, JFK stated: "The time will probably come when we will have to act again on Cuba. Cuba might be our response in some future situation—the same way the Russians have used Berlin. . . . We should be prepared to move on Cuba if it should be in our national interest . . . We can use Cuba to limit their actions just as they have had Berlin to limit our actions."[42] On January 25, in one of the last ExCom meetings that wound down the Cuban Missile Crisis, Thompson voiced concerns over a paper that was presented the day before. The Cuba paper recommended renewing covert operations and enlarging a ban on US goods.[43] Thompson said the paper looked only at Cuba and did not consider worldwide objectives. It was an imprudent risk, he said, particularly at this moment, when "we are seeking to negotiate a nuclear test ban treaty and when we do not yet know what will flow from the split between the Chinese Communists and the USSR."[44] The paper's recommendations, however, were approved by the president, despite Thompson's dissent. Cuba was still the bone in *Kennedy's* throat.

In March, Thompson sent a memo to Rusk explaining that Khrushchev faced a lot of problems, both abroad and at home.[45] He had taken a number of bold actions, which, although popular, had adversely affected influential segments of the regime, which represented a "formidable" opposition to Khrushchev. Further, his ability to maintain his leadership position would depend on how well he dealt with ongoing agricultural problems. Thompson also told Rusk that the Soviets were genuinely interested in disarmament but did not "consider the time propitious, or the West sufficiently interested to make meaningful agreement possible."[46]

Macmillan Tries for Another Summit

With the CTB negotiations stuck in the doldrums, Harold Macmillan tried to blow wind back into the sails. A long-time advocate of a test ban, his time was running out as prime minister of Britain. Being the first one to sign a nuclear arms control deal would be a fine legacy.[47] Macmillan penned an emotional appeal to JFK to jump-start efforts toward a CTB.[48] His plan was to call Khrushchev to a summit meeting, and he offered to write to

Khrushchev himself. As an alternative, Macmillan suggested that the president send an emissary, such as Averell Harriman or even RFK, to clear up the inspection misunderstanding.

Carl Kaysen, the assistant to McGeorge Bundy, JFK's advisor for national security affairs, called Undersecretary of State George Ball.[49] "Have you read the bombshell I sent over?" he asked.[50] "Our friend [Macmillan] is pushing us to a summit." Kaysen then suggested that some alternative means be found for dealing with the "pressure" and getting "our friend under control." He recommended having Thompson review the letter. When Thompson did so, he expressed concern.[51] Knowing that the Americans wanted to be in control of test ban negotiations, and perhaps recalling how Macmillan had upstaged Eisenhower back in 1959 when he preempted Ike's summit meeting with Khrushchev (see chapter 17), Thompson wrote, "Although Macmillan does not actually suggest he go to Moscow himself, it seems to me that the letter is designed to bring this possibility to the president's mind."

Macmillan may have been proposing a meeting just on a CTB, but Thompson knew the prime minister had to be aware of the effect such a summit meeting would have on French president Charles de Gaulle and West German chancellor Konrad Adenauer, who were consistently afraid that a deal with the Soviets might be made behind their backs. A summit meeting might clear up misunderstandings with the Soviets, but there was little assurance that anything concrete would come of it. Khrushchev's primary interest in a test ban was to prevent China and West Germany from acquiring any nuclear capabilities. Since the Soviets' split with China was imminent, and since West Germany was, at least in Khrushchev's mind, about to get access to atomic weapons, there was little reason for him to pay the price of inspections for something that would not meet his objectives.[52] Bearing in mind the strain such a meeting would have on the Western alliance, Thompson concluded that it would be unwise. He suggested the president reply that the timing was wrong.

JFK answered Macmillan along the lines Thompson recommended, saying that he did not think a summit propitious if it was simply to settle the onsite inspection quota.[53] On the other hand, if all other issues but the number of inspections could be resolved, or if a discussion of other important issues with Khrushchev was promising, then Kennedy would be prepared to consider such a meeting. In the meantime, the two leaders should send Khrushchev a joint letter to test the waters.

Tandem Tracks

Between April and the beginning of June 1963, there were two separate lines of contact with Khrushchev. One was a joint JFK-Macmillan effort to get an agreement for a CTB, and the other was a set of secret communications between Kennedy and Khrushchev on broader issues. Thompson usually drafted these pen-pal letters and gave them to Dobrynin for delivery. Thompson and Dobrynin had replaced the RFK-Bolshakov back channel, and this new set of participants would continue into the Johnson administration. Both lines of communication crisscrossed each other. The joint JFK-Macmillan letters to Khrushchev led to an American-Anglo mission going to Moscow to push for a CTB treaty.[54] The pen-pal letters prompted the president's decision to send Rusk on a different mission: to see Khrushchev, in order to both clear up misunderstandings and find points for agreement.

This aspect started when JFK was sent a pen-pal letter from Khrushchev (the first such letter since the mix-up over the number of inspections), this one so harsh and "insulting" that RFK refused to accept it.[55] Khrushchev, mad that the president had backed away from his offer to allow three inspections, chastised him for not being willing to put his prestige on the line and make the necessary effort to get congressional ratification for a CTB. If Kennedy were not so concerned about the Rockefellers and war-profiteering capitalists, he would take this step toward world peace. But what was most on Khrushchev's mind was US overflights of Cuba and raids against Soviet ships there. Spy planes crossing Cuba would meet the same fate as Gary Powers and the U-2. Thompson warned Rusk and Ball of his concern that the Soviets might be tempted to take some drastic action, such as shooting down a plane. He reasoned that the Soviet military was frustrated over a series of humiliations that included the forced withdrawal of their country's missiles on Cuba and overflights of the island.[56]

Thompson and Rusk, just back from a two-day military inspection tour in the western part of United States, met with the president, RFK, and Bundy on April 5 to talk about the letter the attorney general had refused to accept. They worried that Khrushchev might act on his threat. RFK described the letter as "poisonous" and said it was "as if by yelling that would make us equal again."[57] Thompson wanted to know if Khrushchev had mentioned testing before going into the Cuba diatribe and RFK said he had. The attorney general concluded that somehow Khrushchev didn't understand "what we are trying to do." It was as if he lived on Mars, RFK said. Rusk agreed that Khrushchev had misunderstood. The Cuba overflights were not intended to build up tensions, but to keep things under control. Khrushchev did not seem to appreciate that JFK had been battling against Republican accusations of being soft on Cuba in the aftermath of the missile crisis. Kennedy's televised briefing on Cuba, which included showing sensitive surveillance photographs, was not meant to threaten Moscow, but to prove that the administration was not hiding anything and knew what was happening in Cuba.

Communication had broken down, and RFK concluded that Khrushchev wasn't getting the right information. "If you are always hearing one side of it . . . it is pretty tough to get back and get acclimated to [the idea that] there is anything good about the other fellow . . . other than he is trying to give you the shaft right up to your gullet." RFK stated that in order to "get some improvement," it was best to send someone to talk to Khrushchev face to face. JFK asked, "What's your opinion, Tommy?" Thompson thought direct contact with Khrushchev could show there was an alternative to taking the hard line the Soviets were considering.

The participants then debated about who should meet with Khrushchev and if sufficient cover could be provided, so as not to provoke expectations or anxieties either at home or with the Western allies. RFK was anxious to make the trip. Finally, JFK turned to Thompson and asked, "Tommy, who do you think should go?" Thompson said it depended on the timing. He noted that a full discussion on Cuba would certainly arise, because it was mainly what was on Khrushchev's mind at that point. It was important to make clear—but with very careful language—that "if he shoots down a plane, this will be quite an issue." Nonetheless, this should only be mentioned once, he cautioned. Messages with references to these U-2 overflights created difficulty for Khrushchev. Thompson recommended that whoever brought the issue up with the Soviet leader should "try to do this in a general way so it doesn't rub it in that he is agreeing to these [flights].... Being pressed as he [Khrushchev] is on every side, he is concerned we are going to knock Castro off one way or another at a time he cannot afford it. If he loses Cuba at this time on top of everything else, he is going to have to go." Thompson maintained that regardless of who was sent, it held a "terrific disadvantage as far as the allies [were] concerned. The [West] Germans are so suspicious with the Berlin talks started. No matter what you say or [what] the arrangements are, they will be worried." The important point, they decided, was that these plans be kept secret. Only the five people in the room would know.

They also decided at that meeting to use the pen-pal channel, to give Khrushchev a way of letting off steam. As a first step, Thompson would get together with Dobrynin the next day to describe their general concerns and suggest that someone should meet with Khrushchev. The choice of that person was left up in the air.[58] In a memo to Rusk the same day, Thompson summed up his thoughts. Khrushchev's letter could have been a reaction to pressure from his military or from Communist Party colleagues to take some forceful action. The military was still smarting over the blockade of Cuba and the rejection of three inspections the Soviets had reluctantly agreed to. There were those in Khrushchev's inner circle who were in favor of saving the situation with the Chinese by taking a more aggressive stand toward the West.[59]

The next day, April 6, Thompson contacted Dobrynin, indicating that he wanted to confer with the Soviet ambassador on a personal basis and get some advice.[60] It seemed clear, Thompson said, that misunderstandings between the United States and the USSR had increased and were quite serious. For that reason, he had been thinking that some high-level official who had the president's complete confidence should see Khrushchev for informal talks. Dobrynin was all for it and wondered who Thompson had in mind. Pressed to give a name, Thompson mentioned the three that had come up the day before: Rusk, RFK, or Harriman. After consulting with Moscow, Dobrynin let Thompson know they preferred Rusk.

Thompson reported back, and JFK wrote Khrushchev a pen-pal letter on April 11, to calm the atmosphere. The president stated that he continued to believe a nuclear agreement was in both of their interests and reiterated that there had been an "honest misunderstanding" about the three inspections. Kennedy also touched on a sore point, Cuba. He asserted: "We are also aware of the tensions unduly created by recent private attacks on your ships in Caribbean waters; and we are taking action to halt those attacks, which are in violation of our laws. . . . In particular, I have neither the intention nor the desire to invade Cuba; I consider that it is for the Cuban people themselves to decide their destiny."[61] JFK concluded his letter by noting that it might be helpful if he sent a personal representative to discuss this and other matters personally with Khrushchev. The objective would not be formal negotiations, but a full, frank exchange of views, arranged in such a way as to receive as little attention as possible.

Unaware of this pen-pal correspondence, Macmillan replied to Kennedy's March 28 letter and insisted that although it was true that Khrushchev was "preoccupied with his Chinese problem," the British and the Americans should still send high-level representatives to deliver their joint letter to Khrushchev. This would convey the seriousness of attempting to solve the CTB impasse.[62]

At about this time, journalist and peace advocate Norman Cousins returned to the Soviet Union to meet with Khrushchev in the Caucasus. JFK asked Cousins to try to conciliate the Soviet leader over the three-inspections debacle. Soviet friends warned Cousins that he would find Khrushchev embittered, and that some of the Soviet leader's advisors were saying it was about time for him to make noises like a Marxist.[63] Cousins did find Khrushchev to be smarting. He told Cousins he had put his whole prestige into persuading the Council of Ministers to accept three inspections, and then he was slapped and humiliated. Cousins tried to explain that the US Senate would never ratify a treaty with only three inspections. Khrushchev said that he was constantly asked to understand JFK's difficulties, so why couldn't the president understand his? If the Americans could change from three inspections to eight, he could shift from three to zero.[64] He also told Cousins that the Soviet military was pressing him for more tests, and that the next move was up to JFK.[65] On his personal initiative, Cousins hinted that the two leaders might meet to straighten out the mix-up, but Khrushchev brushed the idea off. In the meantime, he told Cousins that he was "hatching an idea," and a "big egg was coming up."[66]

Thompson concluded from the Cousins interview that the egg Khrushchev was hatching was probably a resumption of nuclear testing. The Soviet leader was unlikely, therefore, to move on a CTB for the time being. Also, both a CTB and a meeting with JFK would be provocative to the Chinese. Thompson opined, "I suspect this in itself would not bother Khrushchev, but [instead] that it is important to him at this juncture not to do anything which exposes him to further Chinese attack, both for internal reasons and in connection with the struggle for control of other Communist parties."[67] The Soviet leader's egg, however, was a change of tactics in dealing with the West. Khrushchev met with the Presidium to get approval for an LTB with the West, in the event a CTB without inspections proved to be impossible.[68]

Kennedy and Macmillan finally agreed on a joint draft letter and wrote to Khrushchev on April 15.[69] They asked him for suggestions on how to break the impasse, noting that the number of inspections was not the only problem. They suggested that Britain and the United States each send a high-level representative to Khrushchev, with those individuals empowered to work out all the problems related to a CTB. Then they waited for a reply.

Laos resurfaced in April, too. It seemed as though the neutrality set in motion by the JFK-Khrushchev summit in Vienna was about to break down. Kennedy called for a National Security Council meeting and asked that Thompson also attend, so he had to be called back from San Francisco, where he was giving a series of lectures.[70] In the NSC gathering, Rusk suggested that Averell Harriman, who was already scheduled to make a trip to Europe, continue on to Moscow to discuss the situation in Laos.[71] Thompson recommended that Harriman go to Moscow alone, rather than being accompanied by a British representative. JFK commented that if Khrushchev did not make a move to stop the deteriorating situation in Laos, the United States "might be in a position to act against Cuba." Thompson interjected that a "US bombing raid on the [Communist] Pathet Lao forces in Laos would be easier for Khrushchev to accept than US action against Cuba."

On April 26, Harriman went to Moscow to discuss the situation in Laos and, on behalf of JFK and Macmillan, to prod Khrushchev on a CTB.[72] In regard to a test ban, Khrushchev, with a disparaging gesture, said, "We'll sign one right away, but," and he struck the table with his forefinger, "with no espionage inspections, ever." Three inspections had gone back to zero.[73]

On April 29, Dobrynin handed Thompson Khrushchev's pen-pal reply to JFK's April 11 letter.[74] Khrushchev complained again about "tensions around Cuba." Dobrynin told Thompson that the Soviets had agreed to have the president's representative come to discuss the issues that remained between the the United States and the USSR, and, further, that Rusk was the person they wanted for this mission.[75] Thompson feared someone might think he had arranged matters that way, but it was definitely Dobrynin's idea.[76] Rusk, accompanied by Thompson, would finally meet Khrushchev that August.

Khrushchev invited Castro to celebrate May Day in Moscow, hoping to try to patch things up after the way he had handled the Cuban Missile Crisis. The Soviet leader could now prove to Castro, from his exchanges with JFK, that he was doing everything he could to protect Cuba. Castro did attend the May 1 celebrations and stood on the mausoleum next to Khrushchev, to show that all hard feelings between the two men were over.

Just at a time when JFK was trying to tilt Khrushchev back toward accommodation with the West, Ambassador Foy Kohler in Moscow started what became known as the "May Day flap." Kohler decided to boycott the May Day parade because of Castro's presence. Thompson thought it an unwise and disproportionate move. It was not about being nice to Khrushchev, Thompson said, but about not making "a thing of it." Kohler, however, had already told the press he was not going to be present and thus could not backtrack, so the affair made headlines, annoying the president.[77] Somehow Thompson's disagreement with Kohler was leaked to the press, causing even more trouble.

It was not until May 8 that Khrushchev formally answered JFK and Macmillan's joint letter about a CTB. He stated that the USSR had always been in favor of a test ban, but not at the expense of Soviet security. Khrushchev's offer of three inspections was not because he accepted them in principle, but rather to help the president get the treaty ratified. Instead, the Western powers began haggling on the number. He surmised that JFK and Macmillan's letter now simply wanted to continue this horse trading on a higher level.[78] Khrushchev agreed to meet their representatives, but only if they could negotiate without "spying inspections."[79]

Now JFK and Macmillan needed negotiators for these CTB talks. Rusk suggested Averell Harriman, although the secretary of state later had second thoughts.[80] When Harriman returned from his Moscow trip on the topic of Laos, he agreed to head the test-ban talks in mid-June. Macmillan chose Lord Quinton Hailsham, his minister of science, as his negotiator. Thus by May, Khrushchev had one British and two American representatives lined up to see him—Harriman and Hailsham to discuss a CTB, and Rusk to clarify general misunderstandings. As Thompson put it, the "mountain was coming to Mohammed."[81]

The Stage Is Set

At this point, there had been *no* mention of an LTB—not by Cousins, Harriman, JFK, or Macmillan.[82] The only thing that had been agreed to was that Macmillan and Kennedy would each send someone to talk with Khrushchev. Given the Soviet leader's stubborn attitude on inspections, it was difficult to see what they were going to talk about. Then a break came. On May 16, before returning to Moscow to attend the Central Committee meeting, Dobrynin invited Thompson to dinner alone. Mostly they rehashed subjects, such as a CTB, nonproliferation, and disarmament. Dobrynin told Thompson that the Soviet Union could not point to a single accomplishment as a result of its policy of peaceful coexistence. All of this was ammunition for the Chinese. Thompson pressed him hard on why the Soviets had not taken up a US offer of a cessation of three types of thermonuclear tests: in the air, under water, and in space. It seemed as though this was of mutual interest to both nations, yet the Soviets, despite favorable comments by Khrushchev in various pen-pal letters to JFK, apparently had never seriously considered it.[83] Now it was Thompson's turn to say that the Soviet government had not seemed to appreciate what a bold step it was on the part of the Kennedy administration to make this offer. Furthermore, Thompson said, it would be "virtually impossible for any country that did not already possess atomic weapons to achieve a capability just through underground test[ing]."

Dobrynin agreed, but added that the Americans had an advantage, since they had more experience with underground tests and could afford the high costs associated with them. Thompson said the most sensible thing to do was to go ahead with an LTB while the United States and the USSR continued to seek an agreement on underground tests. Dobrynin then asked a crucial question. Did Thompson think such an agreement would be ratified by the US Senate? Thompson said it would not be easy, but it could be done if the president put his full weight behind it, which he was sure JFK would do. Thompson recognized from Dobrynin's question that this proposal had a chance of obtaining serious consideration by the Soviets, so he encouraged Rusk to pursue it in his meeting with Dobrynin two days hence.

On May 18, Thompson joined Rusk and Dobrynin on the Potomac River aboard the presidential yacht, the *Patrick J.*[84] They discussed a number of topics for two hours, but the main purpose was to convey the seriousness of the Kennedy administration's interest in an LTB.[85] The Soviets knew that Thompson was not someone who gave assurances about the president's commitment without any foundation to them, and having the idea of an LTB reiterated by Rusk meant that this possibility had a real chance of succeeding. There is no way of knowing if Dobrynin was aware that Khrushchev himself had been hatching the

LTB approach, and if the conversation between Thompson and Dobrynin was merely co-incidental. It was just one of those things that happened at the right time and in the right place.

"A Strategy of Peace"

While Dobrynin was back in Moscow, another important event took place. President Kennedy decided to give a "peace speech" for the commencement ceremony at the American University in Washington, DC. Ted Sorensen, his speechwriter, sent around a memorandum asking for ideas.[86] He said that "Thompson had an indirect influence on me and the president in the thinking of that speech."[87] Sorensen wrote the text "during one long night." JFK instructed Sorensen to have the speech checked by several people—including the secretary of defense and the undersecretary of defense, who had not seen it yet—and to inform the chairman of the Atomic Energy Commission about it, "but not get his views."[88] Sorenson was, however, to have a conversation with the head of the JCS, General Maxwell Taylor, in case he wanted to make any suggestions. Taylor thought that he shouldn't do so, as the speech's contents were a political decision. He also noted that it was unnecessary—and perhaps unwise—to show it to the other joint chiefs, as their comments were predictable and no useful purpose could be served. Lastly, Sorensen ran it by Thompson, who had returned to San Francisco to continue the lectures that had been interrupted by the recent Laos crisis. Thompson recalled that he "heartily supported the idea of the speech." He made one or two minor suggestions over the phone and "agreed fully" with the tone of its contents.[89]

JFK gave this speech at the American University on June 10, 1963.[90] The peace he envisioned was "not a Pax Americana enforced on the world by American weapons of war. Not the peace of the grave or the security of the slave. I am talking about genuine peace, the kind of peace that makes life on earth worth living." He called for a reexamination of attitudes toward the Soviet Union, recognizing that there was a gulf between the two nations: "No government or social system is so evil that its people must be considered as lacking in virtue. As Americans, we find Communism profoundly repugnant as a negation of personal freedom and dignity. But we can still hail the Russian people for their many achievements." He continued by stating that among the many traits the two countries had in common, "none is stronger than our mutual abhorrence of war. Almost unique among the major world powers, we have never been at war with each other. And no nation in the history of battle ever suffered more than the Soviet Union in the course of the Second World War. At least 20 million lost their lives. Countless millions of homes and families were burned or sacked. A third of the nation's territory, including nearly two-thirds of its industrial base, was turned into a wasteland—a loss equivalent to the destruction of this country east of Chicago." He noted that "we are both caught up in a vicious and dangerous cycle in which suspicion on one side breeds suspicion on the other, and new weapons beget counterweapons." Instead, it was time to concentrate on those common issues which would "make the world safe for diversity," for, "in the final analysis, our most basic common link is that we all inhabit this small planet. We all breathe the same air. We all cherish our children's future. And we are all mortal."

The president ended by making two important announcements. One, that he, Macmillan, and Khrushchev had agreed to high-level talks in Moscow to seek a CTB. Two, he made a unilateral offer to "declare that the United States does not propose to conduct nuclear tests in the atmosphere so long as other states do not do so. We will not be the first to resume. Such a declaration is no substitute for a formal binding treaty, but I hope it will help us achieve one. Nor would such a treaty be a substitute for disarmament, but I hope it will help us achieve it." Although this speech did not make ripples in the United States, Khrushchev would later tell Harriman that it was the best by any American president since FDR, and that it had taken courage for JFK to make it. It impressed him enough to publish the speech in its entirety in the Soviet press and stop jamming Western broadcasts.[91]

President Kennedy then left for a European tour, where he gave his famous "Ich Bin ein Berliner" (I am a Berliner) speech and saw Macmillan in London.[92] He returned to Washington, DC, on July 3. Khrushchev had made his own speech in East Berlin, reciprocating JFK's American University speech.[93] He emphasized the Soviets' preference for a comprehensive agreement with no inspections and stated that, "since the Western Powers are impeding the conclusion of such a treaty, the Soviet Government is ready to reach an agreement on the cessation of nuclear tests in the atmosphere, in outer space, and under water."[94] This time there was no mention of a moratorium on underground testing, a former Soviet prerequisite for an LTB.

At least now Harriman and Hailsham had something to talk about with Khrushchev. Before Harriman left for Moscow, Thompson told him he was absolutely sure that Harriman would get an agreement on an LTB. His conviction had grown out of his conversation with Dobrynin, who had assured him that the Soviets were serious.[95] Harriman, however, had his doubts. The idea was still to try for a comprehensive test ban, but if that didn't work, to accept a limited version. The JCS members were not happy about either one, and JFK concluded that if the Soviets accepted a treaty, his administration would have to fight for it in Congress.[96]

Limited Test Ban Negotiations

Thompson left the end of June for a month's vacation on Cape Cod. He told Ball that he would return if the president needed him.[97] Harriman left for Moscow on July 14, and Thompson was called back to Washington, DC.[98] JFK wanted him involved in monitoring the discussions going on in Moscow.[99] Communications between the Harriman mission and the American capital were kept on an extremely limited basis. Messages coming from Harriman automatically went to the White House. Only the secretary of state and three other people, including Thompson, received copies. Outgoing messages from Washington, DC, to Harriman followed the same system.[100] JFK was in contact with Harriman three or four times a day, essentially controlling the negotiations.[101] No one wrote memos about these discussions, however.

It was immediately clear that there was no chance for a CTB. Khrushchev presented two draft treaties on the first day: one for an LTB, and the other for a nonaggression pact. Harriman dropped the CTB right away, and they agreed to postpone discussions on the pact. Two sticking points almost put a spoke into the wheel of what were otherwise smooth talks. One allowed peaceful underground nuclear detonations, and the other provided for a withdrawal from the treaty. Khrushchev was against both. Once tensions had relaxed, he said, peaceful uses would be more acceptable to the public in general.[102] Apparently, Khrushchev counted on détente to continue beyond an LTB. The withdrawal provision seemed so self-evident to the Soviets as to be unnecessary.[103] The Americans, however, felt that it would make ratification by the Senate easier. In the final compromise, the treaty included a withdrawal clause, but no peaceful nuclear use clause.

JFK spent most summer weekends at his residence near Hyannisport, Massachusetts, and the LTB negotiations did not interfere with that. On Friday, July 19, Thompson flew up on the president's plane to join Jane and the girls, who were still vacationing nearby. JFK needed Thompson at Hyannisport that weekend, and he suggested that Thompson bring his family along, since the Kennedys were hosting a big clambake after the christening of the president's nephew.[104] Maxwell Taylor was there that same weekend, and they may have discussed the defense budget, as Thompson intimated in his oral history,[105] but more than likely, they focused on the LTB negotiations that were in progress in Moscow and how to get JCS support for them.

The negotiators ironed out the last few glitches in language and protocol, after which, on July 25, 1963, the treaty was ready to be initialed. The next night, JFK addressed the nation. He would have to gather public support, because many powerful forces opposed ratification of an LTB treaty.[106] Eisenhower was one of them. Although he had been in favor of a treaty in 1959, this was at a point when America had superiority in nuclear technology.[107] In JFK's address on national television, he explained that the treaty could "be a step toward reduced world tension and broader areas of agreement."[108] The president also hailed the treaty as a step toward stopping the spread of nuclear weapons to other nations, because, as Khrushchev had warned the Chinese Communists, in less than sixty minutes, a detonation could leave the survivors envying the dead. JFK ended by saying: "According to a Chinese proverb, a journey of a thousand miles must begin with a single step. My fellow Americans, let us take that first step."

Harriman Returns

Undersecretary of State Ball telephoned Thompson and asked for his help on a delicate matter. Rusk needed "a little push" to make it up to Hyannisport to meet with Harriman when the latter arrived back from the LTB negotiations in Moscow. Relations between the two men were strained, and Ball feared things "might get out of focus." Thompson said he would talk to the secretary of state. Since Rusk was about to go see Khrushchev on the mission that had developed from the pen-pal letters, it would be good if he was present in the photos of those receiving Harriman.[109] So Thompson again flew up to Hyannisport with the president and watched the whole reception discreetly, remaining in the background.

The Test Ban Treaty was finally signed in Moscow on August 5, 1963, by Secretary of State Rusk. JFK cleverly pressed six Senators from both political parties to make up the US delegation, as a show of support. The original drafters were not invited, which perhaps was a mistake, but UN ambassador Adlai Stevenson, who had first proposed an LTB back in 1956, was included.[110] Thompson was also part of the delegation, and Jane joined him after parking her daughters with friends on Martha's Vineyard. After the ceremonies, Rusk and Thompson (and their wives) went to Pitsunda to visit Khrushchev.

They flew down with Gromyko, who attempted to avoid serious conversation.[111] The Soviets spent most of the flight playing "parlor games with the ladies," but they did touch on some important topics: a civil air agreement (allowing for the exchange of civilian flights); a consular convention (establishing consulates in non-capital cities in both the United States and the USSR); new embassy buildings in both Washington, DC, and Moscow; a better communications system for the US embassy in Moscow (through a leased teletype hotline to Western Europe); and the eternal problem of Germany. Once at the Black Sea resort, Khrushchev played the part of an "affable grandfather."[112] He did not bristle over thorny subjects like Germany or Cuba and seemed to have other things on his mind than issues with the West. The tensions of the previous spring had disappeared. The group had lunch on the veranda overlooking the sea, where small talk and jokes predominated. Jane raised her glass to the absent Mikoyan, who was in the hospital with a kidney ailment. Khrushchev re-

August 1963 trip to Pitsunda, a Soviet Black Sea resort south of Sochi, USSR, to "clear up misunderstandings." *From left to right*, Rada Khrushcheva, Dean Rusk, Mrs. Kohler, Mrs. Rusk, Foy Kohler, Nikita Khrushchev, Mrs. Gromyko, Llewellyn Thompson Jr., Andrei Gromyko, Jane Thompson, and Anatoly Dobrynin. Thompson Family Papers.

plied that when he called Mikoyan later, he would tell his compatriot about the toast and was sure he would recover quickly.[113]

When Thompson reported to JFK, he said: "One of the things he [Khrushchev] hit hardest was trade. . . . He made clear he wanted [commercial] credits."[114] The president asked, "If they have all this legendary store of gold, what advantage are the credits to them?" Thompson replied: "We think they have a real balance of payments problem—the whole bloc. . . . We don't know what their gold stocks are but we don't think they're all that big and they've been drawing down on them undoubtedly. . . . So I think they are hurting." As far as détente went, Thompson said: "I certainly don't think this [LTB] indicates a great big turning to the West in a big way. . . . If we do go ahead now it's going to be small steps."

Near the close of the conversation, Thompson offered some observations on Khrushchev: "I think there are two things about Khrushchev. . . . The main thing about him is his interest in production and economics. This comes out in every way. . . . And the other thing is the German thing. He's really stuck with this." Thompson continued: "Almost every move he makes is related to one of these two things. He's utterly convinced he can beat us [unintelligible] production . . . [and] he certainly doesn't want to put all his money down the drain for arms that he doesn't have any need for." Thompson commented further that the Soviets' defense system was all tied to missiles and that Khrushchev would probably reduce the number of his troops.

While Thompson and Rusk were at the Black Sea, JFK put his all his efforts toward getting Senate ratification of the LTB, as Thompson had assured Dobrynin the president would.[115] He talked to all the Joint Chiefs of Staff individually, as well as to the head of the JCS, Maxwell Taylor, and appealed to them to make an effort to support the treaty, which, in the end, they did.[116]

First Steps in Détente

On August 26, Dobrynin, who was just back from Moscow, met with JFK and Thompson and handed the president a pen-pal letter from Khrushchev. The Soviet leader was pleased with the LTB treaty and his "useful" talk with Rusk.[117] He hoped they would continue to work on the issues between them in a calm and unhurried but consistent way. JFK told Dobrynin that the test ban had indeed been a useful first step.

No one else in the room knew it, but the president had learned that very morning that, in his absence, Roger Hilsman, NSC member Michael Forrestal, and Averell Harriman had sent a cable to Ambassador Henry Cabot Lodge Jr. in Vietnam that effectively gave seditious Vietnamese generals a green light to remove South Vietnamese president Ngo Dinh Diem from power.[118] JFK, although upset about the cable, did not revoke it or try to stop the coup. This was the first step into "the quagmire" that would impede many of the initiatives that had been so promising in spring and summer 1963.

On that August 26, Dobrynin, oblivious to the trouble that was coming, pressed JFK on trying to find areas of accord between their two countries.[119] The Civil Air Agreement and an opening up of trade looked promising to Dobrynin, but the president wanted these issues postponed until after the US elections. In the meantime, JFK would set Thompson to work on the outstanding Lend-Lease debt and the sale of wheat to the Soviets. JFK and Dobrynin also discussed the danger of Germany or China drawing the superpowers into conflict. Regarding Germany, Dobrynin reminded him about the Checkpoint Charlie confrontation (see chapter 24), to illustrate how a small incident could become something important. Just such an incident would occur several weeks later, on the Autobahn leading to Berlin.

Thompson had been wary of the Civil Air Agreement, because it could compromise America's ability to contain Soviet civil aviation in other parts of the world. Nonetheless, he was willing to accept it as a condition of a major improvement in US-Soviet relations, citing the potential conclusion of a CTB agreement as an example.[120] In his later meeting with Gromyko in October, Rusk tried to link the air agreement with one regarding a teletype line that would give the US embassy in Moscow direct links with Washington, DC, rather than relying on telegrams.[121] Thompson suggested that the president, in his upcoming meeting with Gromyko, hold the air agreement out in exchange for improving "communications on a reciprocal basis."[122]

After numerous meetings between Thompson and Dobrynin, Kennedy approved the sale of wheat to the Soviets as another initiative toward normalizing trade relations. There was also an agreement not to orbit weapons of mass destruction. The "hotline" between the superpowers, agreed to after the Cuban Missile Crisis, was set up on August 30, 1963.[123] Thompson and Dobrynin discussed mutual troop reductions, and RFK approached Dobrynin about the possibility of the president and Khrushchev exchanging visits.[124] Step by step, they were moving toward détente.

The Tailgate Crisis and Kennedy-Gromyko Discussions

The last time Thompson saw JFK was over a small incident that almost became a big issue, known as the Tailgate Crisis: the procedure to clear US convoys going into and out of Berlin.[125] The Americans generally moved their convoys back and forth through a checkpoint by simply lowering the trucks' tailgates, so the soldiers inside the vehicles could be counted without needing to dismount. On August 19, 1961, an American officer instead had his troops alight from the trucks, to have the head count go faster, and it soon became a common practice.[126] When top-level US authorities found out, they ordered this practice to stop. Then, on October 10, 1963, the situation came to a head. The Soviets held up an American convoy at the Marienborn checkpoint, because the US troops refused to get out of their trucks.[127]

By coincidence, on the same day when the convoys were stuck at the checkpoint, Gromyko arrived at the White House to talk with JFK as a follow-up on the Rusk-Khrushchev meeting, while the "spirit of Moscow" still prevailed.[128] Before the appointment with the president, Thompson and Rusk had lunch with Gromyko and told him about the convoy incidents, which the Soviet foreign minister had known nothing about.[129] During their own meeting, JFK complained to Gromyko that if there was going to be trouble over Berlin, it shouldn't be over how many men were sitting in a truck.

When Gromyko inquired about future US policy toward the USSR, JFK replied that his American University speech had already reflected this policy. Gromyko then asked, why not just sign the Civil Air Agreement now? "It's political," explained Kennedy, adding, "We have just had the Test Ban and the wheat deal and . . ." "Too much understanding?" Gromyko teased.[130] Cuba, the thorniest issue, was last. Gromyko reassured JFK that there were no Soviet troops remaining there, just some specialists who had stayed on.[131] When pressed for a withdrawal date, Gromyko said, "It is delicate for Khrushchev to talk about withdrawal." For his part, Gromyko talked of US provocations, bombs being dropped, and raids. Although the president had previously (on January 25) endorsed the paper that called for continued covert programs to destabilize Cuba, he told Gromyko that he had tried to stop such things, claiming that "they were not done with our agreement."

Gromyko and Dobrynin left the meeting still puzzled and upset over the tailgate incident. It was incomprehensible how this could have happened, Dobrynin told Thompson.[132] Thompson saw Dobrynin that evening, to press for the convoy's release. To convince the Soviet foreign minister that all of this was arbitrary, he gave Dobrynin a list of the dates when convoys of similar size had been let through East German checkpoints. This list seemed to provide the rationale Dobrynin needed, and the convoys were released.[133]

In a meeting with his advisors the next day, JFK wondered if the tailgate crisis was "a significant test of our intentions."[134] Thompson spoke at length (although the written record does not convey this). He did not think it was a "deliberate attempt at the top to cause trouble." He noted that the convoy dismount rules were never established and that the Soviet military in Berlin may have brought this issue to a head, to try to figure them out. Thompson transmitted the formal US convoy procedures to Dobrynin,[135] who forwarded them to the Soviets in East Germany. Kennedy had initially wanted the message to be sent at a higher governmental level, considering it to be a political measure, but the allies wanted to do it at the military level. Thompson, with the stance of allies in mind and cognizant of the need to act quickly, persuaded the president to follow the allies' preferred course. This subsequently caused some trouble, and, in his oral history, Thompson recognized that Kennedy had been right.[136]

Kennedy Assassinated

John F. Kennedy was shot in Dallas, Texas, on November 22, 1963. The assassination shook the very foundations of the country and left many unanswered questions.[137] When Thompson went to see Dobrynin the next day, Dobrynin found him to be very depressed. JFK's death was a severe blow to the confidential connection between the two heads of state. Thompson, Dobrynin said, had no idea how things would turn out.[138] That same day, Thompson wrote to a friend:" Yesterday was really a tragic day for the whole world and I feel it personally more than I can say. It was such fun to work with a man who really knew what the score was so far as my clients are concerned. I imagine that the burden on the [State] Department and the [Foreign] Service will now be heavier than ever."[139]

Thompson appeared before the Warren Commission, established by President Lyndon Johnson to investigate JFK's assassination, because he'd been ambassador to Moscow when Lee Harvey Oswald tried to defect to the USSR. Thompson, however, had little to say. He had been on vacation and was not in Moscow when Oswald first came to the US embassy to renounce his citizenship, and he had not seen the later dispatches dealing with Oswald's departure from the Soviet Union. All that did take place had followed standard procedures. Thompson had firsthand knowledge of the sad fate of people who had ended up in the Soviet Union for one reason or another, and he would have been sympathetic to anyone who wanted to leave. The only unusual thing he noted was that Lee Harvey's Soviet wife, Marina Oswald, was granted a Soviet exit visa with relatively few hitches, which was unusual, but that could have been because the Soviets were glad to get rid of Oswald.[140]

When Thompson met with Dobrynin on November 23, he recommended that the Soviets pass along any documentation they had on Oswald. The Soviets believed that JFK's assassination had to do in part with his trying to improve Soviet-American relations.[141] When Mikoyan attended Kennedy's funeral, Thompson advised him that this was not the time for propaganda battles and asked him to downplay any rhetoric in the press about the Soviets' theories on who was responsible. Thompson was convinced that the Soviets had played no part in JFK's assassination, and he did not want any backlash.

Thompson told Dobrynin that he didn't expect US foreign policy to change under President Lyndon Baines Johnson (LBJ): "I pointed out how closely the new President had followed these matters and been kept informed by President Kennedy. I expressed the opinion that, in general, President Johnson would continue the broad policies established by President Kennedy, and drew his attention to the fact that President Johnson had assisted in the formulation of these policies."[142] Thompson believed that Johnson would concentrate more on domestic policies. Dobrynin wanted to know if LBJ knew about the private communications between Khrushchev and JFK. Thompson was not sure that the new president had seen all of the pen-pal letters, but thought that, if they had a bearing on current events, he would be informed of them. Dobrynin wrote in his memoirs that Thompson told him LBJ had not been privy to the agreement on the removal of nuclear missiles in Turkey.[143] Since Thompson's memo of his conversation with Dobrynin that day was for the record, however, he would not have mentioned the secret deal regarding Turkey in it.[144] During a luncheon with the Soviet ambassador in mid-December 1963, McGeorge Bundy told Dobrynin that private communications between Khrushchev and President Johnson should still go through Thompson, so this back channel would continue.[145]

PART IV

Policy

29 ≋

The Lyndon Johnson Years

The trouble with Americans is that we see everything in
black or white, but there's a lot of gray in diplomacy. Foreign
relations is a very fluid business—the heads of Britain,
Germany, Italy, and the U.S. have all changed within the last
few weeks—and this is upsetting to Americans who like to
maintain fixed positions. We must remember that the
sandbars as well as the currents are constantly shifting.
—LLEWELLYN THOMPSON, *Seattle Post-Intelligencer*,
   December 9, 1963

Lyndon Baines Johnson was a crude man—outspoken, direct, and blustery, with a
cowboy manner and a Texas drawl. He enjoyed making his presence felt, to the point
of discomfort, by leaving no space between him and the person he was speaking to
and poking his finger in the other guy's chest. When asked if LBJ listened, one of his aides
said, "He listens so hard it's deafening—it's like being at the bottom of a lake, the pressure's
so high."[1] Thompson thought that "Johnson could turn on his people in a ruthless way,"
adding that "this made them less frank."[2]

In many ways, LBJ resembled Khrushchev, and in other aspects, he was similar to
Thompson's older brother. Eldridge was also a Texas type—large and strong physically,
sure of himself, and imposing—so these traits were familiar to Thompson. For his part, the
new president, who did not feel at home with the East Coast, Ivy League set, would feel
"very, very comfortable" with Thompson and soon came to trust his judgment.[3] The issues
LBJ grappled with as president were immensely complicated and intertwined, and they all
seemed to happen at once. Thompson's role as an advisor expanded dramatically during
the Johnson administration, into areas other than Soviet relations. Johnson was thrust
from the periphery of power to its center when JFK was assassinated, but this shrewd politician was painfully aware that he was a placeholder, not elected to the job by the American people.

LBJ's first order of business in late 1963 was to hold together a grief-stricken nation by assuring everyone that he would continue JFK's course for the United States—even maintaining the late president's staff. His second pressing concern was to make sure he won a decisive victory in the next election. To do that, he needed a vision for the country. LBJ saw that geographic, racial, and class-based segments of America had been left out of the post–World War II economic boom, and he devised his Great Society both to correct this wrong and to serve as a legacy—a new New Deal.[4] These Great Society reforms were incredibly broad, and the opportunity to put them into place had to be seized while the country was prosperous and Americans were feeling generous.

Yet LBJ's desire to avoid major changes or crises while he pursued these goals had a perverse effect on US foreign and economic policies. It caused the president to hide the truth about the United States' deepening involvement in Vietnam from Congress, the American people, and possibly himself. His advisors, with their eyes exclusively focused forward, led him along, one step at a time, until they realized that they were all deep in the jungle, with no path out.

The president's plan to keep things quiet would be challenged by events. He had to deal with a potential global economic crisis, precipitated by a balance of payments problem within the international trading system, which both influenced and was affected by virtually everything else that would vex his years in office. One of the most irritating issues was President de Gaulle's ambition to resurrect French nationalism and wrest independence from the United States (and therefore from NATO). Next was West Germany's ambivalence about its own dependence on the United States and its perceived second-class status. Then there was the United Kingdom, with its own trade problems and balance of payments deficit (i.e., more money was being sent abroad than was earned through exports or otherwise was coming back to the country). This, in turn, caused it to want to withdraw its military commitment to West Germany, putting more pressure on US forces there.

All these things pitted Johnson against congressional pressure to reduce US troop levels in Europe and work on America's own balance of payments deficit, with its threat of inflation. Thanks to the Bretton Woods accords—which were an effort to help establish global economic stability and foster trade after World War II, in part by creating an international monetary reserve with fixed exchange rates for currency transactions among nations, based on the US dollar—the value of the dollar was pegged to a set price for gold of $35 per ounce. The fixed value of the dollar left the president with few options for handling America's balance of payments deficit, something that would worsen over the ensuing decade. US currency became increasingly overvalued, to the point where there was a possibility of a run on the dollar—with other countries acquiring more dollars and then converting the dollars they held into gold—which would result in a higher demand than the United States had a sufficient gold supply to cover. Johnson, seeking to avoid a crisis but against confronting the problem openly, kicked the economic can down the road with a series of interim measures, until his successor, Richard Nixon, would take the drastic step of scuttling the Bretton Woods accords and unlinking the dollar from the price of gold.

Threatened Alliances

At this point, the Sino-Soviet split was on Moscow's mind, and the potential fragmentation of NATO was of serious concern to American policy makers. The gravitational pull of the stronger United States on its allies was beginning to weaken as their mutual fear of Soviet expansion lessened and their economies recovered.[5] International monetary problems, such as balance of payments issues, also strained relations. LBJ had to stop the forces pulling the Western alliance apart if he was going to achieve his goal: to maintain some manner of stasis until he'd won affirmation as president through a national election and could secure his legacy.

After the Cuban Missile Crisis, the balance of opinion—with the exception perhaps of the JCS and those still committed to the cold currents—tipped toward Thompson's view: unless some foolish mistake occurred, there was virtually no chance of an unprovoked Soviet attack on Western Europe. Nevertheless, the United States' commitment to deter such an attack with either conventional or nuclear forces now appeared less certain. The former was in some doubt because of America's balance of payments problem, and the latter arose because the advent of long-range ballistic missiles meant that Soviet retaliation to a nuclear counterattack would be against American cities, not European ones. This uncertainty led to a tendency on the part of the NATO allies to desire less US involvement and, in the case of General de Gaulle, to chafe against it.

Thompson recognized that apart from de Gaulle's own desire for "grandeur for France and himself personally," he was moved by his resentment of US domination in Europe, distrust of Britain, and a desire to control adverse developments in Germany. Thompson calculated that de Gaulle needed to tie Germany to himself, through a French nuclear capability, if he was to realize his nation's "hegemony over Europe."[6] France indeed did decide to pursue an independent nuclear program, remove its forces from under NATO's command, and insist on complete withdrawal of all US and NATO forces from French soil, creating a fissure in the Atlantic alliance.[7] De Gaulle could have his cake and eat it, too, by virtue of geography. To get to France, Soviet troops or planes would have to cross at least one alliance country, triggering NATO defenses anyhow and making NATO ground troops in France unnecessary, because NATO would never let the Soviets get that far.

De Gaulle made life so difficult that a powerful faction in the State Department emerged, one that wanted to draw a line to try to stop this "bad behavior" and put France in its place. Thus began a "crash effort within the bureaucracy to inventory all the ways the US could do injury to French interests."[8] But not everyone in the department wanted revenge. Thompson certainly did not agree with this approach. He thought the Germans ought to be allowed to consider their own fate. Nor was he totally opposed to eventual French leadership in Europe, writing that de Gaulle's "preparations today for his vision of the future ... [are] probably sound, although the timing is wrong."[9] As much as Thompson disliked the idea of America becoming enmeshed in European pecking-order quarrels, he thought that "if any one country were to dominate Europe, it would be in our interest [for] that country be France, rather than Germany." Charles Bohlen later wrote that "there was not the slightest possibility that we could persuade or force de Gaulle to alter his course." So Bohlen strongly urged LBJ to get US troops and bases out of France, and to do so politely. Contrary to French expectations that the United States would "behave in a bitchy fashion . . . we behaved with dignity, acted with efficiency, and got out of France on schedule; the French were astounded."[10]

Were de Gaulle's vision to come about, it would surely mean the end of NATO, an alliance Thompson had strongly supported at its creation. Thompson could see, however, that the elements making the existence of NATO essential had changed "radically." Looking back, he observed that NATO had been formed when Europe had virtually no defense against Soviet expansion, and when the United States did not have a nuclear deterrent capable of being delivered from the United States.[11] "Perhaps even more important," he wrote, NATO had been "necessary to give hope to the peoples of Europe that they would not succumb to Communist aggression."

Nevertheless, Thompson did not believe 1963 was the time to remove all US forces in Europe, mostly because he did not think the Europeans were ready to increase their own conventional forces to replace NATO's, and it would be better to rely on conventional forces than a nuclear "trip-wire."[12] There was a push, and Thompson was part of it, to try to get the allies to take on their "fair share" of the burden of European defense and assistance to the developing world, which had as much to do with America's balance of payments deficit as it did with the political and military realities in Europe.[13] In early 1964, Thompson wrote to Senator J. William Fulbright that the Marshall Plan to help Europe came at the "expense of Latin America and Africa." Now that Europe was awash in dollars, he argued, they ought to contribute more to the efforts in those places.[14]

In May, news from Moscow about the discovery of more than forty microphones in the American embassy caused quite a stir.[15] Thompson didn't think all that much of it. He recalled that part of the ceiling had dropped into his bathtub when the family had lived at Spaso House and microphones fell out (see chapter 17), so it wasn't a surprise. He even thought it was useful, in a way, because, if nothing else, the Soviets would realize that what was being told to them was the same as what those in the US embassy discussed amongst themselves. Thompson did, however, have Tom Hughes at INR do a study to see if the microphones' presence had created any observable shifts in Soviet foreign policy, but no such correlation was found.

In June 1964, Thompson returned to Vienna to give a speech encouraging European responsibility. It was an emotional trip for Thompson, and a happy one for Jane, who got to go along. Perhaps this is why he expanded on what he intended to say in his official speech—about the changes since Stalin and the need for European help—and wrote one that was much more universal and personal.[16] Thompson said that the single most important characteristic of the period they were living in was "the acceleration of the rate of change throughout the world." He talked about the emergence of developing nations and the importance of not being complacent. Conflicts had been between East and West, but economics pointed to the rise of North-South frictions in the future. Thompson, continually excited by advances in science, nonetheless told his audience that sometimes he found the monthly scientific briefings he attended with Rusk "troubling." He worried about the unintended consequences of technology and challenged his listeners to consider, for example, the effects of cheap synthetic cocoa or coffee on Africa and Latin America. Thompson predicted that computer technology (then in its infancy) would bring a revolution in production, as well as in other fields, but he worried about what that would do to labor. He cautioned that the increasing rate of technological change would also augment the vulnerability of any nation without flexibility or diversity. He said, "The energy and resources the world has devoted to the arms race have obscured the extent [to which] technology will be able to provide developed nations [with] the ability to bring the masses a level of living standard only [the] very rich had only a few years ago."

Yet, he added, "despite all this accomplishment in the material field [there] is little progress we have made in changing the nature of man." He expressed hope that the world was entering an era of disarmament and "recognition of the brotherhood of man." The United States, he observed, had not sought the world-wide responsibilities it had acquired and did not proselytize: "We recognize the advantages of a world of diversity and realize there are many places where our pattern of democracy, free enterprise, and systems of laws would be impractical. We do advocate self-determination." His formula for the success of a government in a rapidly changing world was "adherence to certain sound basic principles and a willingness to adapt institutions and practices to meet changing conditions."

It was an unusual and poignant speech for Thompson, in that he revealed a perspective on the world and his place in it just a month before his "second job" started. It must have been a rude awakening to be confronted, in that position, with the reality of what his government was actually doing. Paralleling what he had expounded in his long-ago treatise on the workings of Stalin's Soviet Union (see chapter 5), the United States' *professed* and *actual* foreign policies had become quite different.

The Second Job

Thompson's life would change drastically under LBJ. In July 1964, in addition to continuing as ambassador-at-large, he took on the position of acting deputy undersecretary of state for political affairs, the highest nonpolitical post in the State Department. U. Alexis Johnson, who had previously held that job, was sent on a temporary assignment to Vietnam as "deputy ambassador," and he remained in that invented position until September 1965. Thompson did not know he would be required to last that long in this secondary appointment when he agreed to replace U. Alexis Johnson.

Jenny remembers wondering why her father didn't seem all that pleased with his extra duties. The undersecretary of state for political affairs usually was the State Department's representative on a secret committee, initially known as Special Group 5412.[17] The Special Group, whose existence had been exposed in a book, was then quickly renamed the 303 Committee.[18] The 303 Committee's mandate was to provide oversight and an authorization mechanism for covert activities that either had reached a budgetary threshold or were deemed to be politically sensitive.[19] It essentially became a cover against accusations that the CIA had acted independently, while protecting the president from having to admit direct knowledge of these operations. The committee met every Thursday and took "agreed" minutes, virtually all of which are so super-secret that they do not even reside in the National Archives, but are rumored to be locked in a safe within the State Department.[20]

Experts in particular fields and countries were invited to participate in 303 Committee deliberations. Thompson had appeared as an outside expert for the 303 Committee before, but now he would be asked to pass judgment on topics outside of the expertise he brought to Soviet affairs. Because almost all of the committee's minutes are classified, it is impossible to tell exactly which activities Thompson participated in discussions on or what most of his decisions were. Available documents show that the committee deliberated about various kinds of activities, ranging from the benign, such as promoting democratic involvement in the World Youth Festival, to the questionable, such as looking at missions into North Vietnam. In the minutes that are available, Thompson tended to play a moderating role.[21] Perhaps later historians will be able to verify if this was true in the main, or only in these documents. Thompson tried not to get more involved than necessary, successfully deflecting a suggestion from Averell Harriman to chair the subcommittee on training for counterinsurgency.[22] It would have been impossible, however—despite what Dean Rusk asserted in his memoirs—for Thompson not to know about some of the more distasteful activities of his country's government, and it is possible that this was one reason why he actively sought ways to get out of government during this period. Nonetheless, Thompson became very much a part of the Johnson administration when he took on this "second job," as he sometimes unhappily called it. It wasn't just the 303 Committee meetings that made his assignment challenging. He once complained to a colleague that he was finding it difficult to keep up with all the details of Soviet affairs, since now he was deeply involved in the whole world. Moreover, so much of what he was now doing was secret.

This affected Jane and his family, too. In Moscow, he and Jane had been a real team, but he could not talk to her about his work during the Cuban Missile Crisis, and the distance this imposed between them applied even more after he took on his second job. On top of that, Jane's father, "Papa 'Roe," died in the first days of 1964. He was a tragic figure: a brilliant scientist who fell into the black pit of schizophrenia, from which he never fully emerged. In Washington, DC, Jane was no longer the hostess for grand events, but just a guest. She did not have a huge household staff to run; she *was* the staff. Polly Wisner, seeing that Jane needed to be involved in something, got her on the gifts committee for the newly named Kennedy Center, and she took pride in helping to secure the dramatic chandeliers for the Great Hall.

Jane also took a part-time job, working for Shirley and Stanley Woodward. He had been a political appointee, as ambassador to Canada, under President Truman. Woodward and his wife planned to create a collection of American art for exhibition in the public reception rooms of American ambassadors' residences overseas. They donated their personal collection and, with the help of Museum of Modern Art curator Henry Geldzhaler,

they purchased additional works by the best emerging post–
World War II artists, such as Helen Frankenthaler, Morris Louis,
Mark Rothko, Frank Stella, and Jasper Johns. The Woodwards
hired Jane to work with Geldzhaler. Jane thrived in the exciting
world of small galleries and artists' studios. Never one to go in
for the landscapes and portraits of the artistic academies, she
was a perfect candidate for the job.[23] When the Thompsons later
went back to Moscow, Jane took full advantage of the Woodward
collection for Spaso House. The exciting large canvases she chose
completely transformed its grand reception halls, and Spaso

The Kennedy Center, Washington,
DC, under construction, probably in
1971. *From left to right*, Polly Wisner,
Llewellyn Thompson Jr., Ethel
Garrett (an original trustee of the
Kennedy Center), Mr. and Mrs.
Charles Bohlen, and Jane Thompson.
Thompson Family Papers.

House became the most sought-after art gallery in Moscow. Soviet artists would do what
they could to get an invitation to receptions at the US ambassador's residence, just to see
the paintings. Jane took care to make sure the invitations from one occasion to the next all
looked exactly the same, after one artist told her they saved their invitations to give to
friends, who hoped to use them to gain entry to future events at Spaso House.

In 1964, however, Jane was still in Washington, DC, with Thompson busier than ever
and no more nannies for her two younger daughters. Instead, Jane was stuck dealing by
herself with difficult incipient teenagers. Thompson did not understand the situation at
all, as he thought the family could be run like an embassy. There, everyone knew what they
were supposed to do, so he assumed that each of them—Jane and the girls—just ought to
be left to it. That turned out to be a bad idea.

Ominous October

More than the color of the leaves changed in autumn 1964. A significant shift in Europe, as well as two major events in the Communist bloc, sent shock waves throughout the world. The election of Labour Party leader Harold Wilson on October 15 brought the thirteen-year Conservative Party government in Britain to an end. Nikita S. Khrushchev was removed from office on the same day. Then, on October 16, China detonated an atomic bomb.

Thompson was called to the Cabinet Room the morning of October 16 for a meeting of a small group within the NSC, to discuss Johnson's presidential campaign and the previous day's developments.[24] The Soviet news agency TASS had announced that Khrushchev was retiring, for reasons of health, but it was evident that he'd been forced out. The consensus within the NSC group's analysis, which Thompson agreed with, was that Khrushchev had been pushed out because of his adventurism and resentment from the Soviet military. Thompson had previously warned that Khrushchev was vulnerable. A little over a year before, he had written that, in the event Khrushchev was replaced, the rivalry for succession would most likely mean the Soviets' leadership would be split between a head of state and a head of the Communist Party. He had predicted that Alexei Kosygin would be a possibility to lead the government.[25] As it turned out, a split did occur, with Kosygin as head of state and Leonid Brezhnev as the Party's chief.

One thing intriguing Thompson was that each man represented one of the two important divisions in the Soviet Union and in the Party: with Kosygin, the "Leningraders," and the government bureaucrats as one faction; and Brezhnev, representing the Ukrainians and the Communist Party professionals, as the other. Thompson expected this duo to be rather cautious, and, while he thought they were both "very able administrators," neither was a "strong" or a charismatic leader in the Khrushchev mold. This was both good and bad: good, because they weren't likely to launch any impulsive ventures, such as Khrushchev had done in Cuba and Berlin; and bad, because they would be more orthodox in their ideology and less flexible on issues related to foreign affairs.[26] Thompson and Rusk emphasized that the United States ought to maintain attitudes of calm and of readiness "to cooperate with Moscow."[27]

Immediately after the NSC group's meeting, Dobrynin called on the president and Thompson, in order to read a formal statement regarding Khrushchev's "resignation" and to assure LBJ that the Soviets' basic peaceful coexistence policy would not change.[28] Thompson reported that Dobrynin obviously had no instructions beyond his statement, so all the Soviet did thereafter was to listen. The president, in turn, spoke at length of his commitment to peace and how winning the election would encourage progress "along the lines he had indicated."

Wins by a Landslide

LBJ was so successful in turning JFK's Camelot into his very own Oz—in that he had thus far kept the woes of the world well concealed from the US general public's view—that his win over Barry Goldwater was one of the biggest election victories in American history, one unsurpassed to this day.[29] Vietnam was the biggest problem that Johnson managed to hide from the spotlight. During his 1964 presidential election campaign, he told Americans that the Vietnam War had to be fought by the Vietnamese, although the United States would continue to provide what was euphemistically referred to as "advisory support." Compared with the more alarming rhetoric coming from Goldwater, who was his Republican opponent, LBJ's position on Vietnam sounded reasonable and safe. America would keep South Vietnam from turning Communist, without the danger of being drawn into an all-out war with the Communist bloc.

As LBJ escalated and americanized the Vietnam War, Thompson, although he did his best to stay out of it, would be dragged into the Vietnam nightmare. The president, however, also took timid steps to continue the détente efforts with the Soviets begun under JFK, and he relied on Thompson to pursue them. As an advisor to LBJ recalled in an interview with journalist David Halberstam: "Thompson had credibility because he had been right during the Cuban Missile Crisis. He had called it correctly."[30] This would lead LBJ to seek Thompson's counsel on Vietnam.

30 ≡

Strand One
Vietnam (1962–1967)

It is possible that the violence and inconclusiveness
of the war have raised doubts in many minds abroad
as to whether it is not worse to be saved than to be
abandoned by the US.

—J. WILLIAM FULBRIGHT, *Arrogance of Power*

The tragic dilemma of Vietnam was that there was no acceptable solution.[1] Once the United States had a presence in South Vietnam, Cold War logic maintained that withdrawal meant losing. Countries in Asia would fall like dominoes as Communism advanced, jeopardizing America's global strategy.[2] The United States would be seen as the paper tiger China claimed it was. Furthering the war was the sole means of protecting America's global credibility, as well as the Johnson administration, from accusations of "losing Vietnam to Communism." The United States could only accept defeat, argued presidential advisor McGeorge Bundy, after having done everything it possibly could and, in the process, having suffered a high cost.[3] Defeat did indeed come at a high cost. Over 58,000 Americans and 3 million Vietnamese died.[4] Losing a war for the first time traumatized the US populace and left them agonizing over what went wrong. Even today, most Americans want to keep the Vietnam War buried in the quicksand of the past, but its memory haunts the nation. It is questionable whether the United States ever learned the true lessons of that terrible experience.

Why?

The argument that the war was lost because the US military was constrained by a political agenda does not hold up to scrutiny. LBJ gave in to their demands at almost every turn, at least as far as he could without declaring war, which he could not do without congressional approval. He almost certainly would not get that. Thus the United States was fighting a war that technically wasn't a war. Moreover, if the American military had loosed enough bombs (possibly some with nuclear warheads) on the whole of North Vietnam to begin "winning," it would, without question, have pulled the Soviets and the Chinese into the conflict. Neither of those nations wanted to be involved in the war, but they could not stand by and watch a stronger United States invade and drive their ideological soul mate back into the Stone Age. Since the United States could neither lose nor truly win, the Vietnam War became an endurance contest. The idea was that, once the North Vietnamese and the Communist Viet Cong in South Vietnam had suffered enough losses, they would be forced to the negotiating table on US terms. Though they did suffer enormous losses, they didn't give up. It was the American losses—despite the most strenuous efforts of the US military—that became unbearable.[5]

Richard Nixon ran his presidential campaign on ending the war, but when he became president in 1969, he, too, thought he could beat the "raggedy-ass, little fourth-rate country," as LBJ had called Vietnam. Half of the American deaths in Vietnam happened under Nixon.[6] During secret negotiations between Nixon's national security advisor, Henry Kissinger, and North Vietnamese general and politician Le Duc Tho, both finally made enough concessions to bring about a cease-fire. In 1973, they jointly received the Nobel Peace Prize, but Le Duc Tho declined it. He did not consider that true peace had come to Vietnam yet. The cease-fire did not last, and two years later, North Vietnam overran and annexed South Vietnam. Television viewers worldwide witnessed the storming of the American embassy compound and a helicopter lifting out the last Americans, while frantic South Vietnamese scrambled over the compound's barbed wire fence with outstretched arms and tried to get on board.

After the Americans were gone, Vietnam was unified under a Communist regime, but no other dominoes fell. All of those Cold War ghosts vanished with that last US helicopter. The tragedy of Vietnam was not over, however. About 2 million of its citizens fled their country, many in flimsy boats. About 100,000 Vietnamese, mostly associated with the former South Vietnamese government, were executed, and another million were sent to "reeducation camps" or resettled in remote rural areas. The consequences of the American pullout are something no one did—or really still does—want to talk about.

Toward the end of his life, LBJ's secretary of defense, Robert McNamara, confessed in his memoirs: "We were wrong, terribly wrong. We owe it to future generations to explain why."[7] President Johnson and many of his advisors fundamentally misunderstood the Vietnam War. They believed they were fighting to stop an expansion of the Communist bloc, which they saw as being propelled by the Chinese and the Soviets. They would not accept that the South Vietnamese were fighting a *civil war* to remove the remnants of colonial power and foreign occupation. McNamara later claimed that there were no senior officials in the Pentagon or the State Department with a comparable knowledge of Southeast Asia to advise them the way "Tommy Thompson" had been able to do during the Cuban Missile Crisis.[8] But there *were* people who understood the war and who tried to explain. Their voices simply fell on deaf ears. The Cold War mindset sucked up all energy and ideas like a black hole.

LBJ will always be known as the Vietnam War president, because he began the serious escalation of the war and he americanized it. It was not LBJ, however, who took the first steps. As McNamara put it, "He inherited a god-awful mess."[9]

How It Started

Although America professed to be against colonialism after World War II, it found itself siding with the colonial interests of its allies. Even when they "gave" freedom to their colonies, the allies still wanted to maintain enough control to partake of their former territories' natural resources. Thus the United States supported Belgian interests in the Congo, French interests in Southeast Asia, British interests in Iran, and American business interests in South America. All nationalist aspirations appeared to be Communist inspired. Even "neutral" was a dirty word. As John Foster Dulles said, "You must be on one side or the other."[10] Instead of evolving and adapting to global changes, the United States used old prescriptions for new situations.

In the case of Vietnam, the 1954 Geneva Accords ended the long French colonial occupation and divided the country in two: a Communist north and a non-Communist south.[11] The accords stipulated that general elections would decide who would run a reunified Vietnam. Those elections, however, were never held.[12] Eisenhower, in his memoirs, said, "I have never talked or corresponded with a person knowledgeable in Indochinese affairs who did not agree that had elections been held as of the time of the fighting, possibly eighty percent of the population would have voted for the Communist Ho Chi Minh as their leader." But in Cold War dynamics, such an outcome was unacceptable. Thus the Republic of South Vietnam was born, with Ngo Dinh Diem installed as its president and America its guardian. When Eisenhower began sending advisors and military equipment to Diem, many in South Vietnam saw the Americans as simply replacing the French as occupiers, and Diem as a colonial stooge.

According to the domino theory, if South Vietnam fell, all of Asia could go. Eisenhower, JFK, LBJ, and Nixon all believed in this theory. No one really questioned it, even though studies were already available that argued it might not be true. When JFK became president, Eisenhower told him that the most important issue in foreign affairs was Laos, the first domino. Despite JFK's and Khrushchev's agreement at the Vienna summit to make Laos neutral, its neutrality remained shaky. The US perception was that Southeast Asia was dangerously close to falling to the Communists, so JFK continued to offer Diem support.[13] The president increased the number of military advisors: from 900 at the end of 1961 to 16,000 by 1963. Like Eisenhower, JFK made the preservation of South Vietnam a question of national security. As Khrushchev had predicted to Thompson at the time: "In South Vietnam, the US has stumbled into a bog. It will be mired there for a long time."[14]

It was President Kennedy who sealed the fate of both South Vietnam and the United States when he did not prevent the removal of Diem. Although Diem was fiercely anti-Communist, he was also nationalistic, and he often disagreed with his US patrons on how to run the country, making him increasingly difficult to deal with. The problem was, no one considered the consequences. Who would replace Diem? Duong Van Minh led a US-backed military coup against Diem on November 2, 1963. Twenty days later, when JFK was assassinated, Madame Nhu—whose husband was killed, along with Diem—said, "The chickens have come home to roost."[15] In her condolence letter to Jackie Kennedy, she compared JFK's assassination to that of Diem and her husband, saying, "I understand fully how you should feel before that ordeal which God has bestowed on you."[16]

This was the situation that LBJ inherited. South Vietnam was a politically unstable country, one that was at the mercy of a number of coups and countercoups. These followed in fairly rapid succession as different political and military characters took advantage of the vacuum left by Diem's removal and vied for control.[17] The result was a demoralized South Vietnamese army that had poor results against the Communist Viet Cong, the military arm of South Vietnam's pro-Communist National Liberation Front. What had started out as support for the brave South Vietnamese fending off Communist insurrection soon became an American war fought by US soldiers against an extremely determined, well-organized, motivated, and tough revolutionary force who needed little to survive, knew the jungle well, and received both arms and "volunteers" from North Vietnam.

Perhaps the biggest obstacle to finding a way out of Vietnam was that American presidents could not accept that the United States might not prevail. William Bundy, a foreign affairs advisor to both JFK and LBJ, wrote to Jane, "Obviously it wasn't [Thompson] who was wrong on Vietnam, but the rest of us for getting into what he called once to me, without a trace of rancor, "your piss-ant war."[18] Bundy said that the war blocked a lot of what Thompson worked toward, namely, disarmament and détente with the Soviets. Thompson, however, admitted to journalist David Halberstam that he had a "haunting feeling that he should have opposed it [the war] more forcefully at the time, somehow weighed in more."[19]

31 ≋

Thompson's Vietnam

The human understanding when it has once adopted an
opinion (either as being the received opinion or as being
agreeable to itself) draws all things else to support and
agree with it.

—FRANCIS BACON, *Novum Organum Scientarium*

Between 1964 and 1967, Thompson played key roles in the earlier stages of the Vietnam War. His first was to prevent actions that might induce China or the USSR to enter the war. His second was to strike a cautionary note against the americanization of the war in 1965. His third was to limit the bombing of North Vietnam. And his fourth was to promote an inclusive approach to peace negotiations.

In late July 1964, Thompson once again attempted to combine work with a family vacation, this time in Colorado, where he was speaking at the Aspen Institute, but he suddenly had to return to Washington, DC, to deal with an unexpected issue.[1] The USS *Maddox*, an American destroyer, was a part of a DESOTO patrol,[2] a program whose purpose was to gather intelligence and then pass it on to South Vietnamese forces. On August 2, the *Maddox* reported that it had come under fire by the North Vietnamese, in what would become known as the Gulf of Tonkin incident. This was the first time the North Vietnamese appeared to have directly attacked US forces.

The 303 Committee reviewed covert CIA programs like these. Military leaders, though, were the decision makers on operational details, such as dates and timing. In one of the first committee meetings Thompson attended, they approved a program that was known as Operation Plan 34-A. It consisted of covert operations in North Vietnam, planned by the US military, using US equipment, but carried out by the South Vietnamese. These activities ranged from simply dropping propaganda leaflets to naval sabotage, the insertion of agents, and offshore bombardments.[3] The USS *Maddox* arrived in the Gulf of Tonkin just a day after 34-A operations had been conducted there, which may have led the North Vietnamese to think the destroyer was coming to do more damage. They sent three torpedo boats to stop it. In the sea battle that ensued, four North Vietnamese sailors were killed and six wounded. There were no American casualties.

According to an official Department of Defense (DOD) chronology of the incident, the 303 Committee approved the *Maddox* operation in the Gulf of Tonkin on July 15.[4] But it couldn't have, because the 303 Committee did not meet that day, and its standing Thursday meeting on July 16 most likely never took place.[5] Perhaps the chronology was invented after the fact, accounting for the wrong date. Or perhaps sending the USS *Maddox* right after the 34-A operations was just botched planning. Nonetheless, it led to speculation that the *Maddox* was a provocation to create an excuse for US retaliation.[6]

From left to right, Llewellyn Thompson Jr., Lyndon Johnson, and Walt Rostow in the Oval Office of the White House, Washington, DC, September 21, 1967. Lyndon Baines Johnson Library, A4810-14, photo by Yoichi Okamoto.

When the USS *Maddox* returned to the Gulf of Tonkin two days later, reports came in of a second, similar attack. It was later shown that this supposed second incident by the North Vietnamese never happened.[7] Notwithstanding doubts about the reports, the United States authorized retaliatory strikes against North Vietnamese boats and a major petroleum storage facility on August 5. In the heat of the moment, by claiming US ships were under attack by the North Vietnamese, Congress passed the Gulf of Tonkin Resolution.[8] According to the US Constitution, Congress must authorize a declaration of war, but this resolution gave LBJ preapproval for broad military actions against North Vietnam without directly consulting Congress. In other words, it enabled him to increase US involvement in Vietnam while leaving the American public in the dark. It was not until US causalities increased substantially that the veil lifted.

Just after the second Gulf of Tonkin incident, George Ball, the undersecretary of state for economic and agricultural affairs, phoned Thompson in Aspen and told him that a military jet was being sent to bring him to Washington, DC. Thompson arrived on August 4 at 7:30 p.m., too late to take part in the NSC meeting regarding air strikes and the Gulf of Tonkin Resolution.[9] He did, however, participate in a series of meetings with Rusk and others before flying back to Aspen four days later.

As 1964 drew to a close, Thompson was thinking more about the détente with the USSR that JFK had started, hoping it might continue under the new president. In his State of the Union address on January 4, 1965, LBJ clearly hinted that he wanted to meet the new Soviet leadership. That hint became a proposal in a follow-up meeting between Dobrynin, Bundy, and Thompson, and nine days later the president sent a letter formally suggesting a meeting in the United States. On Dobrynin's advice to Thompson, the letter was not addressed personally to either Kosygin or Brezhnev, but instead to the Soviet government in general, because it was not yet clear which of the two men held the reins of power. When Dobrynin got back to Thompson, he proposed that LBJ also visit the Soviet Union, and on February 3, Johnson accepted.[10] It looked like Thompson would again be in the middle of a serious summit. Then, on February 6, the United States bombed North Vietnam, in retaliation for an attack at Pleiku in South Vietnam. On February 9, Dobrynin told Thompson the summit was off.

1965: Pleiku Sets Off the Escalation

LBJ set up a Vietnam Working Group, headed by McGeorge Bundy's brother, William Bundy, who was the assistant secretary of state for East Asia and Pacific affairs. The group never presented an option to withdraw from Vietnam, but instead concluded that the only way the president could get out of that country and still keep his promise to not "lose" Southeast Asia to Communism, as China had been lost, was to get deeper into the conflict.[11] As LBJ explained in a news conference: "We did not choose to be the guardians at the gate, but there is no one else. Nor would surrender in Viet-Nam bring peace, because we learned from Hitler at Munich that success only feeds the appetite of aggression."[12]

Ever since Diem's overthrow, South Vietnam had been mired in social and political turmoil, causing more and more South Vietnamese to side with the insurgent Viet Cong (VC).[13] Instead of confronting the problems in South Vietnam, the working group looked for a culprit, which to them was North Vietnam. To win in South Vietnam, the working group members believed the United States had to stop the infiltration of men and supplies from North Vietnam by bombing that country. LBJ, however, did not want his decision—to go from supporting South Vietnam's struggle against the Viet Cong to bombing North Vietnam—to be seen as a change in policy, although that is exactly what it was. Therefore, the Vietnam Working Group recommended that the United States begin by taking advantage of provocations made by the other side. Then these retaliatory measures could slowly intensify into a sustained bombing campaign. The president sent his national security advisor, McGeorge Bundy, to South Vietnam to brief the military on this plan.

Thompson and Ball apparently disagreed with the Vietnam Working Group's recommendations, because on February 3, Ball told William Bundy that Thompson "was [in agreement] with him" and that together, the two of them would try to put the brakes on the bombings.[14] Bombing North Vietnam meant attacking another country, which could draw the Chinese and then the Soviets into the war. Seeking Thompson's particular expertise, Ball collaborated with him on a number of memos to the president.[15]

Little time had passed since LBJ's decision to change the tenor of the US actions in Vietnam before the Americans were presented with a provocation. On the night of February 6, 1965, the Viet Cong attacked an American air base at Pleiku, resulting in the death of nine Americans and many more of them wounded.[16] It so happened that McGeorge Bundy and Alexei Kosygin were visiting their respective Vietnams at the time. Bundy was briefing the US military, and Kosygin was in Hanoi to talk about Soviet military aid, as well as to try to forestall actions that could further entangle the Soviets there.[17]

That same evening, the NSC met to discuss the Pleiku attack.[18] Ball brought Thompson with him. Everyone, including Thompson, agreed that some retaliation was necessary. On the phone from Saigon, McGeorge Bundy recommended the immediate bombing of North Vietnam, even though Kosygin was still there.[19] The only dissenting voice came from Senator Mike Mansfield, who argued that the proposed bombing would take American involvement to a new level. He warned that the attack itself showed that the "local populace in South Vietnam is not behind us." LBJ disregarded Mansfield and ordered strikes, justifying them under the cover of the Gulf of Tonkin Resolution.[20] This maneuver, called Operation Flaming Dart, was a reprisal against the *North Vietnamese* for an offence committed by the *South Vietnamese* Viet Cong.

Due to bad weather, the bombings by the Americans only hit one of the targets. At 8:00 a.m. the next morning, February 7, LBJ recalled his advisors to discuss whether to now strike the missed targets. Maxwell Taylor, the current US ambassador to Saigon, was in favor of this action, while Ball and Thompson were against it. Thompson argued: "Another attack cannot be called reprisal. The punishment should fit the crime. No additional air strikes should be made now."[21] The president accepted his recommendation.

As soon as the NSC meeting was over, Thompson called Dobrynin and asked the Soviet ambassador to meet him at his home.[22] Knowing that the Soviets would be upset that the bombing occurred while Kosygin was still in North Vietnam, Thompson tried to soften the news by telling Dobrynin that the Americans had called off a number of missions, so as not to embarrass Kosygin. The nature of the Pleiku attacks while Bundy was in Saigon, however, required a response. "We believe that our failure to act would have been misunderstood," Thompson stated. There had been previous attacks, and the United States had not reacted to them. If they once again refrained after what happened at Pleiku, the North Vietnamese—and China—would be able to "say that they had demonstrated that the United States was a paper tiger." Thompson also told him that the Americans thought the attack was a deliberate attempt by Hanoi to "mousetrap" Kosygin into expanding Soviet support for the North Vietnamese. Dobrynin said he would inform his government, but bombing another country was a deliberate provocation. Johnson was pleased with the way Thompson had handled the conversation.[23] Nonetheless, in the end both the Soviets and the Americans were mousetrapped, because the Americans were sucked deeper into the

Vietnam War, and the Soviets were persuaded to deliver SAM missiles to North Vietnam, which they had been reluctant to do.

Bundy, deeply affected by his experience in South Vietnam, returned to Washington, DC, around 10:00 p.m. that evening with a report in hand, urging that a sustained bombing of North Vietnam begin immediately.[24] LBJ still had reservations, but Bundy argued that it was worth doing, even if the bombing "fails to turn the tide." At the very least, such an action would show that the United States was doing all it possibly could to stop Communist "aggression in the South."[25] Mansfield took the opposite stand. He recommended that the president negotiate, but LBJ "brusquely" dismissed him: "I just don't think you can stand still and take this kind of thing, you just can't do it."[26] Mansfield, in addition to meetings in which he "endeavored to make [his] position clear on the situation as it has developed and may develop in Vietnam," wrote the president a letter on February 8, arguing against further involvement.[27] Disagreeing with Thompson's analysis—that Soviets' reaction to the reprisal bombing would be limited—Mansfield thought the action would "bring about a closer degree of cooperation by the Soviet Union and the Chinese" right away.

Members of the Johnson administration were slowly dividing into those who were for and those who were against the bombing. Perhaps the new zeal Bundy brought back from Saigon triggered Thompson to argue for caution at the next NSC meeting, which took place on Monday, February 8.[28] He urged that nothing be done for a couple of days, "until we see what signals come out of Moscow." CIA Director John McCone, who was taking notes at the meeting, complained, saying Thompson was implying "that our whole South Vietnamese policy must be governed by what the Soviets say. . . . Throughout the morning he [Thompson] seemed to be raising issues designed to stop action rather than move." LBJ had waxed and waned on the decision to ratchet up US attacks in North Vietnam. "The president's coyote-caution, his fear of commitment explains much that otherwise seems mysterious about his conduct of the war in Vietnam," one of his aides explained.[29] McGeorge Bundy's urging led the president to finally decide to go ahead with the escalation, but without announcing this change in US policy.[30] What began as reprisal bombings for specific actions would now become a bombing campaign.[31] At this point, it became a question of when to begin.

The next day, February 9, 1965, Dobrynin met with Thompson and delivered his government's reaction.[32] It was not logical to subject a country to bombing because of an armed attack perpetrated on the territory of another state, the communiqué stated. The Soviet reaction had not been very strong, but it was obvious that Cold War détente would go back into the freezer.

Soon thereafter, the Viet Cong set off a bomb in a hotel in Qui Nhon where US soldiers were housed. Twenty-three Americans were killed. The president immediately called his advisors to the Cabinet Room to plan retaliation. Thompson and Ball questioned the systematic bombing and tried, in Ball's words, a "filibustering tactic."[33] No one, including Thompson and Ball, challenged the need for a response. The issue was simply the timing of it. These two men argued against retaliation until Kosygin had left Hanoi, and Vice President Hubert Humphrey sided with them. Thompson also explained that Kosygin was on his way to North

Korea to seek support for a Communist Party meeting that the Chinese were against. Getting such backing from the North Koreans would widen the Sino-Soviet schism. An immediate attack on North Vietnam by the United States, however, might give the Chinese an upper hand in this argument.

In that afternoon's NSC meeting, McGeorge Bundy protested that the Soviets should not be able to control US actions by moving their diplomats "from one place to another," again bringing up the paper tiger argument.[34] Thompson asserted that if the Chinese Air Force were to become involved as a result of US attacks, the Soviets would come under "very heavy pressure to come to the aid of the [North] Vietnamese." He also favored issuing a warning before the attacks. Hanoi, Peking, and Moscow should be made aware that unless Hanoi changed its tactics, the United States "would end the safe haven they now have in North Vietnam." If they did not comply, then "graduated military pressures" should be applied. Thompson's objections were vetoed, and Operation Flaming Dart II followed twelve hours later.

During the next few days, Ball and Thompson worked together to prepare a memo for LBJ.[35] If they could not stop the bombing, they hoped to at least focus it toward achieving a negotiated withdrawal from Vietnam. They asked Tom Hughes from INR to provide intelligence to support their arguments.[36] Ball and Thompson spent one full afternoon going over their memo with the secretary of defense and LBJ's special assistant for national security affairs, but McNamara and Bundy would not support it. Ball outlined for the president what he saw as the major differences between the McNamara-Bundy position and the one he and Thompson held.[37] The first pair advocated increasing military pressure until Hanoi agreed to stop infiltrating South Vietnam and called off their insurgency efforts there.[38] They were willing to accept considerable risks, including the possibility of ground warfare with China. Ball and Thompson, however, felt that "short of a crushing military defeat," North Vietnam would not abandon its aggression. To stop the infiltration and withdraw "their volunteers" from South Vietnam was like asking them to accept an unconditional surrender, something China would not allow.

Like the nursery rhyme about an old woman who swallowed a fly and then swallowed increasingly larger creatures to catch the one before, if the bombing of North Vietnam continued, the Chinese air force would eventually become involved. That would cause the United States to strike air bases in China and, possibly, Chinese nuclear installations. If Chinese bases were hit, China would probably then introduce massive ground forces into the conflict, which would compel the Americans to do the same. If China came under attack, the Soviet Union would be obligated to join in, due to their Sino-Soviet Friendship Treaty. If the USSR became involved, that might lead to Soviet harassment of US interests elsewhere in the world. The eventual result would be a general war. To avoid this, Ball and Thompson recommended that, at the very least, any bombing be limited to south of the nineteenth parallel, the border between the two Vietnams. They concluded that the most the Americans could realistically hope for was to get the North Vietnamese to reduce their infiltration, so the United States could, in turn, reduce its forces. Then both sides could head toward negotiations. They advised a clear declaration of war aims, something LBJ was trying to avoid. LBJ met with Ball, Thompson, and Bundy and read their memo as they waited. The president then handed it back to Ball, without a word.[39]

Ball and Thompson then approached Tom Hughes, who had worked closely with Hubert Humphrey, to solicit the vice president's help. Hughes gave Humphrey all the documents he had, and on February 17, Humphrey wrote a personal memo to LBJ. He argued that escalation would result in political opposition from congressmen whose support the president needed to pass his Great Society programs.[40] LBJ was now not only irritated, but furious. He told Humphrey to stay out of issues on Vietnam. A year later, Humphrey, having been virtually exiled as a result of his intervention, came "crawling back" in support of the war.[41]

Understanding that LBJ's mind was made up, Ball started to moderate his position, in order to maintain any influence at all.[42] McGeorge Bundy, when reflecting on his own decisions during the bombing escalation, said that the big choice had already been made, and he was just working to carry it out.[43] Thompson also backed off. He told his daughters that he did not become deeply involved in the Vietnam mess because it was outside his field. He never tried to stop their participation in antiwar protests, but he did observe that the protesters failed to offer solutions.[44] He also said that being against the establishment was one thing, but if one worked from within, changes could happen. In this regard, Ball and Thompson's efforts did have somewhat of a restraining effect, since LBJ became sensitive to the danger from certain actions that might get China or the USSR directly involved in the war.

Yet Thompson could not disengage from the Vietnam discussion completely, because he was the main interlocutor with Dobrynin. Shortly after the Ball memo, the two ambassadors met again.[45] Dobrynin complained to Thompson that bombing North Vietnam while Kosygin was still there had been deliberate and humiliating. He asked Thompson to explain exactly what the American objectives were in Vietnam. Thompson told Dobrynin the truth—"to get out of South Vietnam"—but he added that this goal was impossible while Hanoi supported Viet Cong activities. The United States assumed that Hanoi was controlled by Peking, since the recent escalation in attacks by the North Vietnamese could only be in China's interest. Dobrynin could not understand why America had intervened to put down a strong, indigenous movement in Vietnam. Even if one accepted the argument that there were infiltrations from the north, the South Vietnamese had over 300,000 men, in addition to the sizeable American forces in that country, yet the rebellion was still strong. What would the Americans do, he asked, if the North Vietnamese agreed to stop their intervention and the incidents continued to occur? Thompson's reply was not very convincing. He said that if this happened, the United States would know about it and the situation would stabilize. Thompson pointed out that the Americans considered their actions to be defensive. It was the North Vietnamese trying to take over South Vietnam, not the other way around. Dobrynin finished by saying that the Soviet Union did not want to worsen relations with the United States, but those relations would be adversely affected if the present US policy continued.

Operation Rolling Thunder

On February 23, 1965, LBJ met with Rusk, McNamara, William Bundy, Ball, and Thompson in the Cabinet Room to discuss the situation in Vietnam. No record of this conversation has been found, but Rusk had prepared a paper, which he read during the meeting.[46] In it, he said: "I am convinced that there is no single miracle-working approach which can get the job done. I am convinced that it would be disastrous for the United States and the free world to permit Southeast Asia to be overrun by the Communist North. I am also convinced that everything possible should be done to throw back the Hanoi–Viet Cong aggression without a major war if possible. We cannot accomplish this result without the risk of major escalation; but the other side, too, must face and worry about the same risk." That seemed to finally settle the issue.[47] On March 2, 1965, Operation Rolling Thunder, the sustained aerial bombing campaign against North Vietnam, began.[48] When Rolling Thunder started, LBJ thought that it was not going to be a short war—it might take as long as six months.[49] Instead, it would last for eight more years.

Thompson knew that this escalation in Vietnam would worsen relations between the Soviets and the Americans, and he brought the subject up in the next NSC meeting, on March 26.[50] The Soviets could not dissociate themselves from the fate of a Socialist country, and this compelled them to give Hanoi assistance. Moreover, American actions in North Vietnam obstructed disarmament talks. Rusk commented, "The Soviets are paralyzed by US bombing and, as long as it continues, they cannot take any political action without exposing themselves to the criticism that they are not defending a socialist country." He then added, "We do not know what they will do, however, if the bombing is stopped."

Until now, US ground personnel in Vietnam were limited to "trainers and advisors," but a logical result of Rolling Thunder was the need for American troops to defend US airfields. So the first ground troops, 3,500 marines, landed in Danang Bay on March 8, 1965. At the beginning of April, LBJ took the irrevocable step of approving an increase of 20,000 more troops, and he changed their mission from base security to active offensive combat against the Viet Cong insurgency, using the "enclave strategy." This involved US troops clearing areas controlled by the Viet Cong and then protecting those sites, sometimes forcing the villagers to relocate. The tactic, however, served to alienate South Vietnam's rural population, who resented the Americans' presence. Once again, the US strategy in Vietnam had changed, without any public acknowledgement of it.[51] One of LBJ's aides said: "The White House kept insisting that there had been 'no change' in the American military mission in Vietnam. Thus the president seemed to be tricking the United States into a ground war in Asia by a process of 'little steps for little feet.' In fact, Lyndon Johnson was not trying to fool the country. He was trying to fool himself. As soon as the first platoon of combat troops dug in around Danang, the US was inextricably committed, and the president, who is anything but a fool, knew it in his bones. But for months Lyndon Johnson, with his horror of being fenced in, refused to admit it even to himself."[52]

Rolling Thunder had not stopped the infiltrations; it actually increased them. The North Vietnamese later insisted that the bombing strengthened their resolve.[53] The Viet Cong in South Vietnam, too, seemed more confident than ever. So when it became apparent that Rolling Thunder was not working, top-level discussions in the United States ran along the lines of whether to escalate the bombing further or introduce more troops on the ground. Thompson thought if the choice was between a wider area being bombed in North Vietnam or a greater US involvement in South Vietnam, he preferred the latter. Troop escalation in the non-Communist south would not affect the Soviets, whereas quick, intensified bombing strikes in the north would.[54] He believed that any solution to Vietnam would have to be figured out in the south.

At the same time, public voices for negotiation became louder, both at home and abroad.[55] "US policy is all stick and no carrot," Walter Lippmann complained in an article.[56] To subdue the voices calling for peace initiatives, on April 7, 1965, LBJ made a speech at Johns Hopkins University, where he professed that he was ready for unconditional discussions. To encourage negotiations, he offered a billion-dollar investment to help develop Southeast Asia and hoped North Vietnam would participate. Having fought first the French and now the Americans, Hanoi was not going to be bought off with a development program. North Vietnam rejected the president's offer and put forward its own conditions in a four-point peace formula. These were (1) the withdrawal of Americans from South Vietnam; (2) the implementation of the Geneva Accords of 1954; (3) self-determination for South Vietnam, in "accordance with the program of the Viet Cong"; and (4) peaceful reunification brought about with no foreign intervention. Three of the four points could be accepted by the Americans, but not the one about adopting the Viet Cong's self-determination program for South Vietnam.[57]

On April 21, Ball again spoke up, suggesting that since Rolling Thunder was not working, the United States should try to reach a settlement in Vietnam. LBJ told him that if Ball could "pull a rabbit out of a hat," he was all for it.[58] Ball then prepared another memorandum, but this one did not convince the president, either. According to McNamara, Ball had failed to show how to achieve his objectives. There is no direct evidence that Thompson collaborated on Ball's memo, although it is conceivable that their discussions continued, since they met quite frequently in those days.[59]

Pause and Rewind

Growing criticism both at home and abroad finally led LBJ to pause the bombing and test Hanoi's interest in negotiations. The president agreed to this strategy in part because, should the North Vietnamese not respond and show reciprocity, it would provide an excuse for the already-planned US troop increases. A short, unpublicized bombing-halt, code named Mayflower, went into effect on May 13, 1965.[60] Thompson had been one of the voices calling for a halt, but he criticized the way it had been done.[61] He believed a bombing halt should be clearly defined, with adequate diplomatic preparations. Instead, this one was implemented almost on the spur of the moment. Very few people within the governments of the United States and its allies were to be made aware of the cessation, and the North Vietnamese and the Soviets were the only ones officially informed of it.[62]

The bombing halt in North Vietnam, however, still allowed the United States to continue its military operations in South Vietnam—sort of akin to "trading a horse for a rabbit."[63] The pause—too short, unplanned, and unannounced—proved to be a predictable failure. The bombings resumed on May 18, five days later. Dobrynin told Thompson the pause was so limited it was "insulting."[64] George Ball called it a "hiccup," not a pause.[65]

It was at about this time that Rusk proposed a joint US-USSR effort to Dobrynin for reaching a settlement in Vietnam.[66] Thompson, Rusk, and Gromyko attended the anniversary celebrations of the Austrian State Treaty, which is where Rusk discussed this possibility with Gromyko, perhaps with the idea of solving the Vietnam problem along the same lines that were used for the Austrian treaty. Gromyko told the secretary of state that the Soviets did not want to negotiate for Vietnam. Two years later, Gromyko would ask Thompson for clarification of Rusk's overture, but Rusk asked Thompson to convey that the secretary of state had had no "particular proposal in mind for reaching a bilateral agreement in Asia."[67]

On June 5, 1965, General Taylor cabled Washington, DC, with grim news. The situation in South Vietnam was near collapse politically. Desertions from the South Vietnamese army were increasing, and he saw no other option but to commit more American ground forces to action.[68] Rusk, the Bundy brothers, Thompson, and Ball were in Rusk's office to discuss the cable when LBJ joined them unexpectedly.[69] "Lady Bird is away, I was all alone, and I heard you fellas were getting together, so I thought I'd come over," he said. Greatly troubled by Taylor's assessment, the president asked: "How do we ever expect to win? How do you expect to wind this thing up?" No one present could answer. Two days later, General William Westmoreland cabled LBJ, saying he needed more ground troops "to convince the VC they cannot win."[70] That increase went from 82,000 to 175,000 American soldiers.

By the end of June, the president decided, once again, that he needed to show he was searching for a negotiated settlement, even though the US bombing campaign against North Vietnam was intensifying and more American troops were entering South Vietnam. Ball again spoke out against sending more troops, but to no avail. In a multipronged approach, LBJ sent McNamara to Saigon to discuss troop needs with Westmoreland, Harriman to the USSR to engage the Soviets' help, and Ball to Paris to try to open direct contact with North Vietnamese representatives.[71] In an effort to encourage negotiations and forestall more bombing, Thompson sent William Bundy a memo, suggesting that the United States let Hanoi know the Chinese had indicated they would not enter the war unless America bombed China. In it, Thompson argued, "If Hanoi realizes that Peking considers them expendable, it might help in getting negotiations started."[72] LBJ convened a meeting of the "Wise Men" to get all the input he could.[73] Thompson sat on a subpanel of this group, which met on July 8.[74] Thompson wrote in his diary that it was an all-day affair. The panel agreed that withdrawing from South Vietnam would have repercussions and could validate de Gaulle's assertion that the United States "could not be counted on to defend Europe." They agreed that whatever combat force increase was necessary should be met, and some felt US actions had "perhaps been too restrained" up to that point. Thompson cautioned that blocking or mining Haiphong harbor would increase dependence on overland transport from China, thus increasing Chinese influence in North Vietnam. Moreover, it could lead to the sinking of Soviet ships.[75]

There was another important meeting of LBJ's advisors on July 21, where Ball spoke out against the large-scale addition of US combat troops in Vietnam. Although he declared that "if the decision is to go ahead, I'm committed," he did not believe the Americans could "win under these conditions." Ball warned that if the United States got bogged down, the costs would be substantially higher than defeat. He advised accepting the losses, letting the South Vietnamese government fall, and negotiating a withdrawal, even if it meant that South Vietnam would be taken over by Communists. As far as credibility was concerned, Ball asserted that "we'll suffer the worst blow to our credibility when it is shown that the mightiest power on earth can't defeat a handful of miserable guerrillas."[76]

This is exactly what LBJ could not fathom. How was it that the mightiest nation in the world could not defeat a backward Third World country? There had to be a way of beating them. The president asked at that meeting: "Have we wrung every single soldier out of every country we can? Who else can help? Are we the sole defenders of freedom in the world?"[77] He even sent a letter to Spain's dictator, General Francisco Franco, to solicit his public support for South Vietnam. Though a staunch anti-Communist, Franco advised LBJ to get out of that country.[78] Franco stated that the US mission was impossible: "Although subversion in Vietnam may at first glance seem to be a military problem, it really is, in my opinion, a profound political problem. . . . Even assuming that the strength of the Vietcong could be broken, the sporadic attack of the guerrillas would continue for a long time and would therefore demand a prolonged military occupation of a country where you would always be regarded as foreigners." He added: "Things are as they really are and not the way we would like them to be. We must work with the realities of the world and not with [a] chimera." The Spaniard concluded that Ho Chi Minh, "without doubt," was the man Vietnam needed.

On the evening of July 26, LBJ gathered his advisors, and a decision was made to destroy Soviet-supplied SAM sites. In a memo to Ball a couple of months earlier, Thompson had been critical of wiping them out.[79] The SAM sites, he argued, were defensive, intended to protect Hanoi and Haiphong. Attacks on these sites would signal an escalation of hostilities on the part of the United States, and demolishing North Vietnamese air defenses would pressure both the Soviets and the Chinese to provide air cover from Chinese air bases.[80] Thompson changed his mind, however, after American planes were brought down by SAMs.[81] At the July 26 meeting, he said that as long as it was obvious the SAM sites were targeted, and not Hanoi, "I think their [the Soviets'] reaction will be mild. We should not say they are manned by Soviets. . . . It would be good if we can tie it in with something else."[82] Another person in the meeting said, "If [the] Soviets put their men and material into a situation that knocks down American planes, they must expect retaliation." Thompson acquiesced, "On balance, I support the recommendation." The next day, July 27, the SAM sites and nearby barracks were hit with napalm and cluster bombs. The Soviet Union did not respond openly, but Moscow secretly accelerated its shipment of more SAMs to North Vietnam.

Thompson did not change his mind about not attacking North Vietnamese airfields, though.[83] On July 27, while American planes were hitting the SAM sites, LBJ called an NSC meeting to discuss the deployment of more troops. Thompson was present, but he did not intervene with on-the-record comments. Another participant was Averell Harriman, whose trip to the Soviet Union in July had proven to be fruitless. The Soviets, he said, did not want to get involved in the Vietnam problem, and they suggested that the United States come up with a counterproposal for the North Vietnamese four-points peace formula. By the end of the meeting, LBJ had made his decision. He would give the US commanders the number of men they felt they needed to do the job. He asked if anyone present opposed this plan, but no one did.[84] By 1966, US troops in Vietnam would increase by over 200,000 soldiers.

In the fall, Thompson tried to summarize his understanding of the Vietnam situation in a draft paper:[85] The Chinese, he guessed, wanted to weaken the position of both the United States and the USSR in Southeast Asia, while also avoiding large-scale troop involvements. They would try to hold down the amount of Soviet aid to North Vietnam, unless it was at least balanced by their own contribution. Hanoi, meanwhile, seemed to have hopes of maintaining its independence from China by playing that country off against the Soviets. Hanoi would probably accept a negotiated settlement, provided the Viet Cong could participate in a South Vietnamese government. The Viet Cong also wanted to avoid Chinese domination, but they probably would only accept a negotiated settlement when it became clear that they could not win. They were less interested in reunification than they were in obtaining a US withdrawal from South Vietnam and in forming part of that country's government.

In a speech Thompson gave in Washington, DC, in August 1965, he said that the US policy of containment had basically worked as far as overt aggression was concerned, but the problem was with "the wars of national liberation," for which Vietnam was a case in point. "This insidious method of subversion and penetration in support of guerrilla movements," he continued, "is a far harder problem to deal with and one [to] which we do not yet have a clear answer." He argued that the United States could not merely revert to isolationism, nor "just simply go around bombing everybody that got in our road because of the danger that this eventually would lead to an atomic conflict and that of course, is something in which there are only losers."[86]

In fall 1965, the CIA's Board of National Intelligence Estimates prepared a report that said a "hardening attitude" of the North Vietnamese—since, contrary to expectations, the bombing was not bringing the North Vietnamese to the table—meant that the bombing was not "rough enough."[87] McNamara asked the president to authorize a special group to study the reasons for this hardening attitude, and LBJ agreed. He appointed Thompson, Maxwell Taylor, John McNaughton, and William Bundy to what became known as the "Thompson Group,"[88] who presented their findings on October 11, 1965.[89] They advised against "a step-up in bombing," concluding that the war could last a lot longer than they had thought. They recommended a long bombing pause, to test Hanoi's interest in negotiating. The proposed bombing pause was initially received "coolly within the government," but its advocates kept up their pressure.[90]

In addition to what was stated in this paper, Thompson wrote a memo to McGeorge Bundy, outlining the advantages of an extended pause.[91] It would have both international support and, with American casualties increasing, domestic support. A pause would make it harder for Hanoi and Peking to pressure the Soviets into escalating their assistance to North Vietnam, and it would stimulate further dissension between Moscow, Peking, Hanoi, and the Viet Cong. If the pause did not produce results, a resumption of the bombing, with an increase in the number of American troops, would remove any doubt from the other side of the United States' determination to "stay the course." He also predicted that the Communists would demand participation by the Viet Cong in negotiations, which would have considerable global support. The best counter to this demand would be to preempt it by stating America's willingness for representatives of the Viet Cong be included in Hanoi's delegation.[92]

Another LBJ advisor, Walt Rostow, had the opposite reaction to North Vietnam's hardening attitude. He urged the president to expand the bombing to "the oil-refining and storage capacity and electric power facilities in North Vietnam."[93] Rostow was the director of the State Department's Policy Planning Council at the time and would soon replace McGeorge Bundy as LBJ's national security advisor. He was convinced that the Vietnam War could be won through bombing, and he would exercise more and more influence on the president's thinking.

At this point, demonstrations in the United States against the war intensified. On November 2, as a protest, a Quaker, Norman Morrison, burned himself to death outside McNamara's Pentagon window. McNamara later admitted that this event had a deep impact on him.[94] It also became clear to him that the choice was either to get out of Vietnam diplomatically or give General Westmoreland the additional troops he wanted. If the latter course were to be pursued, the United States could expect a substantial increase in American casualties, with the added aggravation that troop increases "will not guarantee success."[95] Perhaps this was the point at which McNamara's previous view of the war began to unravel.

In a December 4 memo, McGeorge Bundy told LBJ: "The opinion in favor of a pause continues to grow here. This morning there seems to be a favorable consensus among Rusk, McNamara, Vance, Ball, McNaughton, the Bundy brothers, and Tommy Thompson. We think this is the best single way of keeping it clear that Johnson is for peace, while Ho is for war. . . . It has advantages with all third [world] countries, and perhaps particularly with the Soviet Union. Thompson points out that a pause would greatly strengthen the Russian resolve to stand clear of our fighting in Vietnam."[96]

Rusk and Thompson both came away from a meeting with Dobrynin on December 8 with the impression that the Soviets would try to help if there were a pause in the bombing of North Vietnam.[97] Dobrynin told them he could not understand the US argument that a pause would be an admission of weakness, and he repeated that the Americans were trying to force the Viet Cong to admit that "they were only tools or stooges of Hanoi," which was not the case. The United States did not recognize that its troops were actually fighting local South Vietnamese. The North Vietnamese were being asked to ignore the

Viet Cong and accept the US position that only Hanoi was involved. Dobrynin asked if the Americans "were at war with Hanoi." Rusk answered back with certainty that "there were very few [Viet Cong units] that Hanoi did not control." Thompson also met with Dobrynin alone, to sound him out about how far the Soviets would go if there were to be a bombing pause, but Dobrynin was noncommittal.[98] He "did not rise to the bait," Thompson reported.

Although skeptical, LBJ agreed to extend a Christmas cease-fire into a pause for an undisclosed period of time, but bombing could resume at any time if the Communists "compelled such a move."[99] It was unlikely that the North Vietnamese would come to the negotiating table during this pause, which would give the president credibility for what he was actually planning. The pause would be "preparatory to knocking the hell out of 'em."[100]

Four days after the pause went into effect, the president inquired what reaction the world had to it. There was none. Rusk phoned McGeorge Bundy on December 27 to say Thompson, U. Alexis Johnson, and William Bundy all felt that if any diplomatic leverage was to be found, the bombing should be resumed at once, with a real pause developed after that. This pause should be longer, with advance notice given to the Soviets, as this group had suggested the week before.[101] Their suggestions, however, fell on deaf ears. On December 28, Thompson was sent to inform Dobrynin that the cease-fire had actually become a pause, although how long it would last would depend on reciprocation by the other side.[102] In the end, the pause lasted thirty-seven days, during which time LBJ launched a peace offensive.[103] The president's "fandangle diplomacy" came up with nothing, and it was precisely during this so-called peace offensive that the US dramatically increased the number of its troops.[104] Ho Chi Minh wrote an open letter to Socialist countries, calling it a "sham peace trick" designed solely to conceal a US "scheme for intensifying the war of aggression."[105]

Perhaps the undefined pause had sent the "wrong signal to Hanoi [and] China."[106] Thompson was in favor of resuming bombing "at some appropriate time." Disruptive debates in the nation at large and in Congress were becoming harmful. He also saw mounting pressure on the president to end the pause because of increasing US casualties. The bombing of North Vietnam resumed on January 31. LBJ said: "We've done all this diplomacy, now let's get on with it. Let's do the job."[107] The failure of the bombing pause undercut those who had supported it, such as William Bundy, McNamara, and Thompson, and bolstered those who had been against it, like Rostow. It also made the president skeptical of trying this again.[108]

1966: Changing of the Guard

At the beginning of 1966, McGeorge Bundy left his position as LBJ's national security advisor to take a job with the Ford Foundation. McNamara speculated that it was his frustration with the Vietnam War that led to his resignation.[109] Rostow, who replaced Bundy, had no doubts about the purpose or the merits of the war, and he would be a constant voice in Johnson's ear. Rostow became LBJ's most pro-war advisor and shielded the president from rising criticism of the war.[110] For Rostow, victory was always close at hand. One of his aides described him as being "like Rasputin to a tsar under siege."[111] Another called him a "fanatic in sheep's clothing."[112] Among his other ideas, Rostow even suggested a ground invasion into North Vietnam.[113]

Walt Rostow's brother Eugene became undersecretary of state for political affairs, and he also supported LBJ's policy in Vietnam.[114] McGeorge Bundy was not the only one to leave. Nicholas Katzenbach replaced George Ball in September 1966, and Bill Moyers, the president's press secretary and a war "doubter," also left. McNamara's reservations about the war forced the president to remove him the following year. LBJ could not put up with doubters. Thompson himself would leave Washington, DC, that winter. McNamara and McGeorge Bundy often take the blame for the americanization of the Vietnam War, because of their key positions at the time, but even dissenters like George Ball and Senator Mansfield weighed in behind the president when it was clear that LBJ had made his decision. Thompson did, too.

Despite an escalation of US troops and more bombings in the 1966–1967 period, the United States was not beating the Communists. Westmoreland's strategy became a strategy of attrition, where body counts measured the success of each mission. The aim was to inflict enough casualties on the Viet Cong and the North Vietnamese to make them come to the negotiating table. Westmoreland later faced accusations of having fudged the numbers, to make it look as though the United States was making headway.[115] A crucial point is that LBJ and his advisors, including Thompson, believed Westmoreland's accounts. As Thompson wrote to his friend Bohlen, "I think it will be very difficult for them [the North Vietnamese] to continue to take casualties at the present rate."[116]

The Soviets viewed the situation in Vietnam in a similar way, but they came to the opposite conclusion. Though US forces might not be defeated on the battlefield, the Soviets hoped war-weariness and dissatisfaction with the Saigon government would finally induce the United States to pull out. Thompson warned that Moscow's commitment to Hanoi was politically binding. Whatever fate awaited the South Vietnamese, the Soviets could not countenance a US military occupation and defeat of North Vietnam.[117] Therefore, even at this point it was clear, at least to Thompson, that beating the North Vietnamese militarily was not even a desirable option. Both sides were waiting for the other to give up. The Soviets did not want to get more involved. Neither did the Chinese, who were immersed in their Cultural Revolution. So in 1966, the war was at a stalemate, although no side wanted to admit it.

Bohlen wrote to Thompson: "What bothers me is the possibility that there are some people in the US government who believe that [the] bombing of North Vietnam will induce Hanoi to the conference table. I feel this is a very fallacious argument since it seems to me that all Communist history shows that they will never yield to external pressure of this kind." Thompson's response, on February 4, 1966, was, "I think there are very few people here who believe that [the] bombing of North Vietnam will force Hanoi to the conference table."[118] Rather, he said, it was a combination of bombing and operations in South Vietnam that might bring about some result. Ball had always been opposed to the bombing, and Thompson himself had "long argued for" a bombing pause lasting as long as possible. He then added, "I should think another pause will be necessary before we will have much hope of getting negotiations along." Thompson exhibited Bohlen's letter to Rusk and Ball, who suggested that it be shown to the president, as an example of another voice that doubted the effects of the bombings.

Thompson worried about Rostow's suggestion that the United States should start bombing petroleum, oil, and lubricants (POL) sites in North Vietnam.[119] Citing his World War II experiences, Rostow thought this kind of bombing would bring the North Vietnamese to the bargaining table faster.[120] Although Thompson suspected "we can get away with" bombing the POLs, he warned his government against it.[121] It would make the North Vietnamese dependent on imports by sea, pressuring the United States to offset this with a blockade or by mining the harbors. Such actions would put the Soviets in a very difficult situation. The long-term effect would be to harden the Soviet position toward the United States.

When POL bombing came up in an NSC meeting in June 1966, however, Rusk merely conveyed Thompson's assessment that there was no danger from the Soviet Union if the action was carried out, failing to say that Thompson was against doing so.[122] Thompson would again warn against bombing POL sites in September.[123] Most likely what troubled him was the same thing that worried Britain's prime minister, Harold Wilson, who told LBJ, "If you and the South Vietnamese government had a declared war [against North Vietnam], this operation would be clearly necessary and right, but since you have made it abundantly clear that your purpose is to reach a negotiated settlement and not striving for total military victory, bombing these targets without producing [a] decisive military advantage may only increase the difficulty of reaching an eventual settlement."[124]

Back in February 1966, Thompson had written to Bohlen that if the North Vietnamese airfields were taken out, this would pressure the Chinese to let the North Vietnamese use theirs, which would take the conflict onto Chinese territory.[125] He had made the same argument to LBJ a few weeks earlier.[126] Nonetheless, just as the cherry blossoms in Washington, DC, began to bud, Rostow renewed his pressure to bomb North Vietnamese POLs. Action along these lines was initially put off, in part because of opposition from the State Department, but by summer, the president changed his mind. After meeting with the NSC twice (Thompson was not present), LBJ decided to go ahead. The POL bombings began on June 29, 1966.[127]

When Thompson and Dobrynin met a short time later, Dobrynin protested that bombing POL storage facilities near Hanoi and Haiphong had set everything back, and he stated that there was "little disposition in Moscow or any other Socialist country to do anything under the present circumstances."[128] Moreover, a "substantial number of civilians" were killed—which did not correspond with information Thompson had been given—and this had an adverse effect on any inclination Hanoi might have had to change its attitude. Dobrynin also complained that the bombing pause seemed like a time bomb that could go off at any minute and, therefore, was a threat to force the other side to negotiate. In addition, Dobrynin told Thompson that the Soviet Union was very careful to deal with the Viet Cong directly, not through Hanoi, as the VC were, in many ways, quite independent. Unfortunately, Thompson gave Dobrynin the Americans' party line that it was North Vietnam's intervention in South Vietnam that had brought the United States into military operations in Vietnam.

Thompson wrote a long memo to LBJ on July 15, 1966, summarizing how the Soviets saw the situation in Vietnam.

> The Soviet leadership is suffering from a deep sense of frustration faced, as they are, with a number of intractable [internal] problems. . . . After all of their sacrifices to establish Communism in their own country and spread it abroad, they find themselves locked in a bitter struggle for leadership of the Communist world with Communist China and engaged in a two-front cold war. . . . Against this background, the Viet-Namese affair is particularly galling to the Soviet leadership. They stand to lose by it in almost any outcome and they want neither the United States nor China to come out on top. With their ideological background, their view is the reverse of ours. They are concerned that if we win we will be encouraged to use force to suppress what they consider popular movements wherever they develop. This would undermine their conviction that Communism is an inevitable phase of history. . . . In Viet-Nam, however, they point to the mere numbers of the Viet Cong and the staunchness of their struggle as evidence that we are, in effect, helping to crush a popular movement. Although this would in any event give them a serious problem they make a great distinction between what we do in North Viet-Nam and what we do in the South. I believe that we can take almost any action in the South without serious risk of Soviet involvement. I doubt that they will take any radical action as a result of our bombing of the POL. . . . I believe, however, that any dramatic step-up in our action against North Viet-Nam could bring us into an area of real danger. This would be particularly true of action to blockade or mine North Viet-Namese harbors because of the parallel with Cuba and the direct confrontation which this would involve.[129]

He hoped that the president would keep what he said in mind when considering escalation.

By August, it was clear that the Americans had failed to stop North Vietnamese infiltrations, lessen the Viet Cong attacks, or damage the North Vietnamese war effort. The POL attacks were halted in September 1966, after US intelligence admitted that there was "no evidence yet of any shortages of POL in North Vietnam."[130]

Peace Initiatives

In July 1966, the president had appointed Averell Harriman as his "peace czar," to seek a negotiated settlement. Harriman set up a Negotiations Committee and asked Thompson to join.[131] It met every week to seek options for negotiations.[132] One of their first tasks was to come up with America's own negotiating points, since the United States still did not have an official position.[133]

One option for negotiations that the committee examined, which Thompson was in favor of, was to include the National Liberation Front (NLF), also known by the name of its military arm, the Viet Cong. Thompson stated his position in a memo to Leonard Unger, the deputy assistant secretary of state for Far Eastern affairs:

> I doubt that Hanoi will ever agree to negotiations until the Viet Cong are in favor of a settlement. If the VC should decide they have had enough, it seems to me that there might be great advantage in negotiating with them . . . rather than with Hanoi. . . . I do not believe that we can get away with trading a cessation of bombing against a cessation of infiltration, and [I] believe it would be unwise to put such a position forward even as an initial bargaining position because of the damage we would suffer in a retreat from such a position. I believe that we would have to agree to trade a cessation of reinforcements for a cessation of infiltration and agree that so long as the provisions of such an agreement were observed we would not bomb North Viet-Nam. . . . I doubt very much that the North Viet-Namese will ever admit that they have sent in regular units and this is why I believe that our negotiations should be with the NLF or VC. The NLF would be representing Hanoi rather than the other way around."[134]

Both the US embassy in Saigon and the South Vietnamese government were against allowing the Viet Cong to participate in any negotiations. Thompson suggested that one way the idea "might be sold [was] on the basis that it offered the possibility of sowing dissension in the ranks of the enemy and peeling off non communist elements from the NLF."[135] The arguments were there, but nothing was done to implement them.

On September 15, 1966, the Negotiations Committee met to discuss the president's upcoming meeting with Gromyko, who was coming to the UN General Assembly. By this time, Harriman was convinced that the Soviets were the key to getting the North Vietnamese to the negotiating table, and Gromyko's willingness to meet with LBJ about Vietnam meant that they were now ready to pitch in and help.[136] Thompson, however, doubted that the Soviets were prepared to "talk seriously" about Vietnam. He even questioned whether Gromyko had acted on instructions from Moscow.[137] In reply to Thompson's reservations, Harriman said, "We should not snuff it out by being excessively negative about the possibilities." The committee supported Harriman and wrote to LBJ that "the only real chance to induce Hanoi to negotiate a settlement depends on the influence Moscow is willing to exert." Dobrynin said in his memoirs that while America believed the Soviets could do something to resolve the Vietnam situation, they really could do little.[138]

Both Thompson and Harriman sent LBJ briefing papers for his meeting with Gromyko, to which Rostow attached a note.[139] His summary for the president stated that Thompson was "too defensive on Vietnam." In his brief, Thompson advised LBJ to demonstrate that, despite Vietnam, the United States wanted to ease tensions, as well as to underline that the president was taking every step possible toward negotiations. Thompson told him to say, "We will be *grateful* for anything the Soviets may be able to do to enable us to reach a peaceful settlement of this problem" [emphasis added]. Harriman's briefing paper stated that LBJ should tell Gromyko the Soviets had "an *obligation* to work for the end of the hostilities," because of the USSR's position as the co-chairman of the Geneva Accords. Rostow's note said Harriman's brief had "a much more positive flavor." In a draft of his paper, Thompson warned that Gromyko might accuse America of continuing its military buildup in South Vietnam during each bombing pause.[140] He advised the president to answer that the United States would consider not only a bombing pause, but also "suspending reinforcements in return for [the] North Vietnamese stopping [their] infiltrations." This part, however, was not included in the final paper.

In his meeting with Rusk in New York City on September 24, Gromyko had said that in various statements, the United States claimed it was seeking a peaceful solution in Vietnam, but its actions led to the opposite conclusion.[141] LBJ referred to that meeting when he and Gromyko met in Washington, DC, on October 10, 1966.[142] The president used Harriman's point that "as co-Chairman [of the Geneva Accords], the Soviet Union should exert its leadership in trying to bring about a negotiation." He said the United States had expressed its willingness for unconditional negotiations and hoped the Soviet Union could exert an important influence on North Vietnam. LBJ claimed that he had no desire to destroy North Vietnam or change its government, but he did have an obligation to South Vietnam. He went on to complain that he had arranged a pause in the bombing, against the recommendation of his military, in the hope that Hanoi would send some message, but "when we called, the other side hung up the telephone."

Gromyko answered that the United States "had not taken any real steps to end the war. Statements made by the United States, both by the president personally and on behalf of the United States government at the United Nations had been accompanied by conditions known to be unacceptable to the other side." Gromyko then asked, what would happen if America continued on the same course? Other countries, including the Soviet Union, would give further aid to Vietnam. In that case, the USSR and the United States would find themselves drawn in. "Can it be that history has sealed our fate like this?" he wondered.[143] Gromyko stressed to LBJ that he could not oblige the North Vietnamese to do anything, but he did admit that he could exert some influence. The key, Gromyko said, was in the hands of the United States, and the first step was to stop the bombing.

The president ended their meeting by hoping that they might resurrect the idea of an exchange of visits, which they had talked about when he first took office.[144] When LBJ later relayed his impressions of what had been discussed to Senator J. William Fulbright, he painted it in optimistic terms. Asking the senator to keep what he was about to say between the two of them, the president commented: "My judgment is that he [Gromyko] moved very strongly in the direction of helping to find a solution. Now he didn't say that. . . . He didn't imply that. I just looked at him and if I know anything about human nature, I guess that, and I think Thompson got the same impression. There were no arguments, no quarrelling, very jolly, put his arm on my shoulder."[145] LBJ saw what he wanted to see.

Despite the president's sweet talk to Gromyko, he escalated the bombing shortly after their October 10 meeting. On November 4, Thompson wrote Rusk a memo in which he pointed out that Gromyko had indicated "a Soviet willingness to bring pressure on Hanoi"—if the bombing stopped—and that all the Eastern European governments had called for an end to the bombing, too.[146] Thompson then went on to say: "If our answer to this is an escalation of the bombing, I am afraid the Soviets would conclude that anything other than a hard line on their part merely encourages us to think we can safely go for an all-out military victory. The tragedy of this, it seems to me, is that such increased bombing would have only a marginal effect on military operations in the South and judging from past experience, is unlikely to dispose the North to be any more inclined toward a settlement."

Flowers for Peace

Another task of Harriman's Negotiations Committee was to follow up on peace leads. One came as early as 1964, when UN Secretary-General U Thant tried to mediate a settlement.[147] Dobrynin would tell Rusk in 1967 that a U Thant contact with Hanoi *through Moscow* had never happened.[148] Other initiatives included one brokered by the Hungarians, which Thompson did not think was serious, and a Canadian lead, when retired Canadian diplomat Chester Ronning brought a message back from Hanoi that talks could start if the bombing stopped.[149] This, too, was not considered to be of consequence. There was also an attempt by Jean Sainteny, a member of de Gaulle's cabinet who had been sent to Hanoi to explore peace negotiations,[150] which also went nowhere. There was an Asian Summit Conference in Manila in October 1966,[151] but this was more of a cheerleading event for the war than a peace-seeking effort. McNamara, in his memoirs, later said that as one diplomatic initiative after another fizzled out, his "frustration, disenchantment and anguish deepened."[152] How many peace initiatives were really serious, and how many were, as Rostow had cynically said, people "bucking for a Nobel Peace prize"?[153] How many were ruined by a lack of coordination between military and diplomatic tactics? It is difficult to say.

If peace was a priority, military actions might be expected to be subordinated to these efforts, but they weren't. This certainly was the case in one of the more promising peace feelers, which began in 1966.[154] Ball had informed Rusk that McNamara, Rostow, Thompson, U. Alexis Johnson, and he had recommended approval for Operation Marigold.[155] This was an attempt by a Polish diplomat, Januscz Lewandowski, and Giovanni D'Orlandi, the Italian ambassador in South Vietnam, who, together with the US ambassador Henry Cabot Lodge, tried to set up negotiations with the North Vietnamese. Thompson and others spent considerable effort writing up a US position.[156] Things looked promising as they drew up a new formula for negotiations: the Phase A–Phase B formula, where, if A happens, then B will take place. What this amounted to was that if the North Vietnamese gave private assurances of doing more than just talking, then the United States would stop the bombing, after which the North Vietnamese would reduce their infiltrations and military operations in South Vietnam. It seemed like a face-saver for everyone. Lewandowski claimed that on this basis, the North Vietnamese were willing to meet for discussions in Warsaw in early December.

As the Marigold meetings seemed to gain traction, Dobrynin returned to Moscow with a pen-pal letter from LBJ to Alexei Kosygin, the Soviet premier, making his plug for peace.[157] In it, the president said, "It is clear that we both agree on the most important objective—that the fighting should be brought to an end as quickly as possible." It is therefore doubly incredible that LBJ went ahead with new bombing raids on Hanoi on December 13–14. Marigold shriveled when those bombing raids began. McNamara, Thompson, and Katzenbach all urged the president to postpone the raids, but he rejected their suggestion. McNamara later said it was because LBJ was still influenced by the aftereffects of the previous bombing pause,[158] but if there was a chance to get the North Vietnamese to talk, it seems as though it would have been worth the risk. In addition to military causalities, the bombings also caused numerous civilian deaths. The North Vietnamese broke off all contacts with the Poles, and that was the end of Marigold.[159] On July 10, 1967, Rusk wrote to LBJ that he had learned, through Japanese sources, that Hanoi had said "No" to the Poles at the very beginning of the resumed bombing exercise.[160] Therefore, had Marigold truly been a lost opportunity, or had it been another mishap?[161]

When Dobrynin came back from Moscow in late December 1966, he told Harriman that the bombing of Hanoi put the kibosh on any possible meeting between the United States and North Vietnam.[162] When Dobrynin met with Thompson on December 30, he said that the Americans would have liked the Soviets' draft reply to Johnson's pen-pal letter, but the bombing of Hanoi had changed their minds, and a letter of "quite a different character" had been started.[163] To aggravate things, Dobrynin told Thompson that there was no doubt in Soviet minds that US bombs had fallen on Hanoi itself. Although Thompson and other senior advisors had argued strongly against those bombings, Thompson's response to the Soviet ambassador towed the US party line: "It was not our intention to bomb the civilian areas of Hanoi and we were sure that some SAMs had fallen on the city. . . . One of the targets was so situated that our planes came over the city after dropping their bombs and it was always possible that one of the bombs had been hung up and [was] subject to a delayed release."

Dobrynin said his government was "frankly baffled" and did not know how to judge the US policy in Vietnam. He wondered whether some in the US military were deliberately trying to frustrate negotiations, or if the Americans' policy was really one of military victory. Thompson assured him that there was genuine US interest in negotiations and said that, although there were some who felt even stronger actions should be taken, this was not a question of military officers disobeying orders. The raids, however, also put a damper on another initiative Thompson had been working on: arms control.

32 ≋

Strand Two
Nonproliferation (1962–1967)

Though men and women have now learned how to throw
thunder bolts, no external force commands that they be
thrown. We have thus preserved the values and the burdens
of free will but we have not yet shown that we have either the
will or wisdom to exercise that free will wisely.
—GEORGE BALL, speech, Oregon State University,
　October 9, 1985

Arms control in the 1960s was something everyone wanted in theory, but in practice
it was a balloon filled with problems—squeeze one end, and new problems poked
out the other.[1] There were two underlying currents at play in both the United States
and the USSR. One supported taking risks that could make the world safer. The other focused on gaining an edge over the adversary, in the belief that making any concessions on
arms control would jeopardize national security. Nuclear arms control consisted of three
connected issues—testing, disarmament, and nonproliferation—each with its own complex set of interconnected problems. In America, it also involved multitudes of agencies,
departments within agencies, and intergovernmental as well as international committees.[2]
It's no wonder that one of the main obstacles to arms control in the United States was the
inability of its government to agree internally. For purposes of clarity, nonproliferation and
disarmament will be dealt with separately in this book, although it must be kept in mind
that they advanced simultaneously, affected each other along the way, and occurred in the
shadow of the Vietnam War.

Thompson, in his post–Cuban Missile Crisis speeches, worked to convince his audiences that the threat of a Soviet attack was not the current problem. Rather, the greater
danger was the potential of ten to twenty countries acquiring nuclear weapons within the
next decade or two. The United States, the Soviet Union, Britain, and France had joined the
nuclear club, and more and more countries were anxious to be admitted. Germany was one
of those asking to be let in, which no one wanted to have happen. Recognizing the strong

attraction nuclear weapons were exerting on other nations, Thompson encouraged Rusk to press for disarmament and nonproliferation.[3]

Skybolt

Rewinding to 1962, Thompson—who had barely unpacked from a trip to Paris for a NATO meeting—accompanied McNamara and Ball to Nassau, in the Bahamas, for President Kennedy's meeting with Prime Minister Macmillan, in order to settle the Skybolt Crisis. Skybolt was an early attempt, under Eisenhower, to create a nuclear deterrent for the United Kingdom, and Macmillan was not happy that the Americans were abandoning the project after years of development.[4] Unfortunately, the Nassau agreement complicated nonproliferation by exacerbating French President Charles de Gaulle's suspicions of US favoritism toward the United Kingdom. Two weeks later, de Gaulle announced his refusal to admit Britain into the European Economic Community.[5] Thompson maintained that the Nassau agreement also played a part in de Gaulle's decision to further strain NATO by pursuing a Franco-German alliance.[6] Squeeze the United Kingdom problem, and out it pops in France.

Enter LBJ

The interests of the Soviets and the Americans in nonproliferation were aligned when LBJ became president, yet an agreement took a long time and was hard to achieve. On a cold, clear weekend in mid-December 1963, Thompson attended a two-day meeting to develop US positions on arms control that would be embodied in the new president's first message to the Eighteen-Nation Disarmament Committee, reconvening in Geneva. The weekend group came up with four points on nonproliferation: (1) that nuclear weapons not be transferred into the *national control* of states that did not have them;[7] (2) that nuclear states accept (over time) the same controls non–nuclear weapons states were subject to; (3) that all eighteen states adhere to a set of principles for nuclear-free zones; and (4) that a comprehensive test ban be developed. The point about a nuclear-free zone was removed from the president's message, as the JCS objected to it.[8] LBJ, having been a very vocal fan of Eisenhower's Open Skies initiative, made a strong address to the ENDC. It looked as though he would be a champion of arms control, but his support—at least in the beginning—proved to be more oratorical than substantive.

Multilateral Force

There was no reason to think Germany could not produce an in-house nuclear program, especially with the West German economy in full recovery. To assuage a growing appetite for national nuclear forces by West Germany and other allies, the State Department revived an idea that had been in discussion since 1960: a multilateral force (MLF). The MLF would consist of American-supplied nuclear missiles on surface ships and submarines.

These would be nationally owned and collectively manned by an international crew, with the United States retaining a veto authority on deployment.[9] A number of the MLF's strong champions were good friends of Thompson's, but Thompson was not among those in favor of an MLF. Nonetheless, he did not see an obvious alternative to alleviate West Germany's ambitions to have an equal seat at the nuclear table.[10]

The argument for an MLF was that its multinational character might forestall a dismemberment of NATO by easing nationalistic stirrings through a contrived interdependence. It might also mitigate urges in individual nations to have nuclear deterrents, thus serving the cause of nonproliferation. To Thompson, these arguments for an MLF implied a reaction to immediate developments in Europe, rather than a strategy based on a long-term appraisal of broad US interests there. He maintained: "A multilateral force would add little to strengthen the balance of power in [America's] favor, would be extremely costly to the countries participating [in it], and would be divisive as a result of any arrangements foreseeable for its control. Its chief advantage is in dealing with the problem of giving [West] Germans a sense of participation without actually having national control of strategic atomic weapons."[11]

By the time LBJ took office, the enthusiasm for an MLF had waned, both among its prospective members and most individuals in the Johnson administration. Yet Rusk allowed his pro-MLF subordinates to pursue it—with perhaps exaggerated vigor—and he even arranged an audience with the president.[12] LBJ, either persuaded by the MLF's stalwarts or because, like Thompson, he didn't see another option to the Germany problem, publicly endorsed an MLF in 1964, thus reenergizing its boosters, who then tried to pressure the Europeans to accept it.

Resistance to an MLF did not vanish after this presidential endorsement. An MLF was a solution to a political problem, but it was militarily inelegant. The idea of a crew that did not speak the same language, were confined on a submarine for long periods of time, and were in charge of nuclear weapons, did not seem prudent. Britain did not want to join, preferring to have the Polaris missiles promised to them at the Nassau conference, and West Germany was even beginning to waffle, in the face of an assiduous courtship by France. None of the allies liked having to start paying for their security, either.

Trying to get Europe to accept an MLF caused an even bigger problem with the Soviets. The USSR saw it as a bald-faced loophole to give West Germany access to nuclear weapons.[13] At a dinner with Dobrynin, Thompson tried to dispel his fears that an MLF would simply open the door to further West German demands.[14] Dobrynin cautioned that if an MLF were to be developed within NATO, the Soviets would be obliged to do the same with their allies, and these would not necessarily be limited to the Warsaw Pact nations. What baffled the Soviets, Dobrynin confided to Thompson, was that it seemed as though the pressure for an MLF was coming from the Americans, not the Europeans. Thompson did his best to persuade Dobrynin that the MLF was meant to prevent proliferation, but Dobrynin averred that, even if this were its intent, there was no guarantee that at some future time the MLF force would not be turned over to NATO completely, or that the US would loosen its controls. Indeed, since France would never accept an American veto of a plan for deployment, MLF advocates hinted that the United States might eventually step back from its overall control, once European unity was realized.[15] Because the Soviets would never buy the US rationale for an MLF, the MLF would hold the Non-Proliferation Treaty (NPT) hostage for some years.

Nonproliferation

The nonproliferation "regime" was a mixture of competing agendas. The JCS did not object to nonproliferation in general, as long as an agreement didn't contain any language that might inhibit future strategic developments or partnerships, no matter how remote.[16] At the other end of the continuum, the Arms Control and Disarmament Agency (ACDA) felt that nonproliferation was *the* paramount issue, and that it should take precedence over political considerations. In between were the State Department, the White House, the US Atomic Energy Commission, and the CIA. Thompson wanted to stop proliferation, but he did not think the idea should be pursued in a vacuum. Rather, he believed the possible consequences of any nonproliferation proposal ought to be carefully considered—thinking about where else the balloon might poke out before actually squeezing it.

Adrian "Butch" Fisher was the boots-on-the-ground man at the ACDA. He valiantly churned out draft after draft of disarmament and nonproliferation measures to present to the ENDC, but without US internal agreement, meaningful progress was limited. The JCS squashed his proposals, and MLF proponents eliminated any language that might prevent the formation of an MLF. While Thompson was not one of these MLF advocates, he was concerned about the timing of folding that political poker hand.[17] He also cautioned Adrian Fisher not to fall victim to a "standard Soviet tactic; that is, that we put forward sound proposals which they reject and, after a time, we abandon them and scratch around to find something else upon which we can agree. This often results in a serious weakening of our position."[18]

Thompson's eyes and ears into the rest of the arms control establishment was in the person of Raymond Garthoff, a tall, young, energetic Soviet scholar in the State Department. He was also an arms control specialist who had been a student of Frederick Barghoorn, Thompson's old roommate from his World War II days in Moscow. Garthoff was in the unique position of being the only person who sat in on virtually all the committees and the agency meetings dealing with both disarmament and nonproliferation, including those with the Defense Department. He and Thompson were compatible and in agreement on most things. They met frequently, and, on occasion, Thompson would ask Garthoff to draft commentaries for him on ACDA proposals.[19] In one such set of remarks, Thompson praised the ACDA for coming a long way from their one-size-fits-all ideas and leaning instead toward his view that any situation likely to trigger proliferation would be dependent on local conditions and, therefore, needed "case-by-case consideration."[20]

It was not unusual for Thompson to agree with the *basis* for some proposed move, but to oppose an *aspect* of it that he felt had not been fully considered. For example, Thompson accepted that China—which was racing toward its own nuclear capability—was unlikely to ever sign a nonproliferation treaty. He took issue, however, with the ACDA's suggestion to drop a condition for Chinese participation in the NPT, not only because he was adamantly opposed to prematurely revealing the US position, but also because a move that was designed to make an NPT easier to obtain could end up having the opposite effect. Thompson reasoned that such a change in America's policy would inevitably leak out, causing the allies to chafe at US pressure on *them* to participate in nonproliferation agreements while giving their collective adversary, China, an easy pass. India was estimated to be one of the top risks for nuclear proliferation, and that country felt particularly threatened by China. Thus, Thompson calculated, it would feel even greater pressure to move forward with its own nuclear weapons program as a result of such a policy.[21]

Another example was Thompson's reaction to a 1964 ACDA suggestion to accommodate the Soviets by inserting language that would prevent any European (i.e., German) control of nuclear weapons in the future. Thompson certainly did not think the United States would ever want to relinquish its veto on MLF launch decisions. Yet he also said changing the language at that time would be a serious mistake.[22] He argued that it would be improper to make an issue between America and its allies the subject of negotiations between the United States and the USSR. Moreover, it wouldn't mollify the Soviets enough to reach an *early* agreement.[23]

The Thompson Committee

Toward the end of August 1964, William Foster, the head of the ACDA, suggested that Thompson chair a group to look at nonproliferation on a local or a regional basis, as Thompson had been advocating. The Thompson Committee would be made up of the deputies of each of the member groups on the ACDA's Committee of Principals, so the obvious choice to head the new committee was Foster's deputy, Adrian Fisher.[24] Fisher, however, was seen by some as being too vested in nonproliferation to be objective. So Thompson was chosen, because Rusk and LBJ felt that he could be more effective in bringing about consensus. Thus the new Committee on Nuclear Weapons Capabilities became informally known as the Thompson Committee. In working to reconcile the opposing strategies of various governmental stakeholders, this committee played an important role in developing internal support for an eventual nonproliferation treaty.[25]

The committee looked carefully at national and regional pressures. Besides Asia, and particularly India, whose main concern was China, they looked at "near-nuclear" states. The primary concerns in Europe were Switzerland and Sweden; in South America, Brazil; and in the Middle East, Israel and the UAR.[26] Israel would prove to be difficult to dissuade, despite efforts going back to the Kennedy administration, which had pressured Israeli Prime Minister Levi Eshkol into allowing inspections of the Dimona reactor (given to Israel by the French in 1956) to make sure it was not being used for weapons production. Under LBJ, the Israelis eventually gave in, but they would only allow *Americans* to carry out inspections. These were halfhearted, and produced ambiguous results.[27] To eliminate its need for nuclear weapons, Israel persuaded the United States to provide incentives:

everything from tanks to favors for pro-Israeli nongovernmental organizations. That the Israelis had an advanced nuclear weapons program became common knowledge, but its existence was never really admitted.[28] Trying to restrain the propagation of atomic weapons must have seemed like trying to hold back a sandstorm.[29]

Each squeeze of the nonproliferation balloon had the potential for unintended consequences. For example, a strong reaction against China's nuclear weapons program made it harder to convince protonuclear states that nuclear weapons had little military or political utility. The use of a US nuclear deterrent to protect Europe (the MLF) argued that nuclear weapons were better than conventional ones. Acquiescence to the non–nuclear weapons states' demand that a nonproliferation treaty be accompanied by nuclear arms reductions could weaken the credibility of a US strategic force serving as a protective deterrent for its allies. Most of these circular positions had no real answer, but they gained urgency in the Johnson administration through the prospect of Communist China having a nuclear capability.

China Joins the Club

In September 1964, Thompson and Dobrynin had a long conversation when the Soviet ambassador returned from Moscow. They talked about personal issues, retirement, and career prospects. Dobrynin asked Thompson about his role as deputy undersecretary of state for political affairs, noting that there was no equivalent position in the Soviet Union. They discussed China, including the prognosis for the Chinese to test an atomic weapon. Dobrynin stated without hesitation that this could happen "at any time."[30] Indeed, the first Chinese test detonation happened in the following month. If the October ouster of Khrushchev had the arms control people wondering about the future of Soviet policy toward their work, China's nuclear test reinvigorated their resolve.

Inevitably, accusations surfaced that the Soviets "gave" the Chinese their nuclear weapon, but Thompson never thought the USSR had done so, "even in their days of closest collaboration."[31] Moreover, the United States and the Soviet Union had been sharing intelligence information on the Chinese program. Even with one or two bombs, it would be some time before China advanced from a "soft" delivery capability to any sort of military threat, but the opportunities for China to exert political pressure were worrisome. JFK had put out feelers to the Soviets to make a cooperative preemptive strike on China's nuclear program, but Thompson had not thought the Soviets would discuss ganging up on the Chinese, despite the grief China was causing in Moscow then.[32] The idea of a preemptive strike was resuscitated for study in both the Thompson and soon-to-be-formed Gilpatric Committees. It was later rejected, although a faction in the US government thought a nuclear-armed China was serious enough to warrant such a preventive military action.[33]

China was quick to try to defuse reactions to its nuclear test by declaring that it would not be the first to use an atomic weapon, and that its program was meant for deterrence only. This did little to calm those who attached more weight to Mao Zedong's prior statements that nuclear war with the United States was not all bad, because even if half of the human population were wiped out in such a war, the remainder would be Socialist.[34]

The Chinese test detonation had the effect of focusing US discussions on how to keep Asian countries that were vulnerable to Chinese intimidation from trying to get their own nuclear bombs. According to the INR's chief, Tom Hughes, the Pakistanis were "cozying up" to the Chinese, so American interests lurched toward India. Secret installations were opened up in that country, as well as U-2 bases for overflights of China.[35] Hughes also recalled that "following the Chinese test, efforts to hamper or delay the Indians lost steam, since any Indian nuclear development would have been regarded in many quarters as an appropriate, if regrettable balance." Regardless, the Thompson Committee continued to work hard on the Indian dilemma. One option was to offer India US protection. Thompson did not think this was a good idea, however, because the United States had not yet figured out what it would do in the not entirely unlikely event that two countries under US protection (a nonaligned India and a US ally, Pakistan) decided to face off.

The Gilpatric Committee

LBJ decided to assign a second committee to look at nonproliferation, headed by Roswell Gilpatric, a former deputy secretary of defense.[36] The Task Force on Nuclear Proliferation was established on November 1, 1964, but, like the Thompson Committee, it was eponymously known as the Gilpatric Committee. Thompson was kept informed of this committee's progress, but he was not active in it.[37] The Gilpatric Committee differed from the Thompson Committee in that it was not trying to work out intramural disputes within the US government. Instead, it was a blue-ribbon panel composed of business leaders, scientists, and current and former government officials. They were asked to examine nonproliferation issues from scratch, considering every possibility, no matter how radical.

In December 1964, Dean Rusk had Thompson present a scheme Rusk was interested in to the Gilpatric Committee. The idea was to stock, or bank, nuclear weapons in Europe and to raise the subject of making exceptions to nonproliferation, allowing certain countries to acquire nuclear bombs.[38] According to Raymond Garthoff, Rusk saw that nuclear-armed India and Japan could offset China's nuclear capability. Garthoff did not think Thompson agreed with this position, but he then qualified this statement by saying that, in cases where proliferation was unavoidable, Thompson believed that the political consequences needed to be considered.[39]

The Gilpatric Committee submitted its report to LBJ in January 1965, the day after his formal inauguration.[40] With his campaign platform as a "peace president" and his subsequent landslide victory over Senator Barry Goldwater, Johnson had plenty of latitude to publicly reveal the committee's recommendation and make nonproliferation his top priority. Instead, the president sealed the committee's report, and it did not see the light of day for thirty years. LBJ's decision to bury the Gilpatric Report might have been because Secretary Rusk, whom the president greatly respected, called it as "explosive as a nuclear weapon." Or it could have been, as some have suggested, because LBJ's political rival, RFK, pre-empted him in a speech to the US Senate that used near word-for-word excerpts from that report to demand swift action against proliferation.[41] The president even thought that Gilpatric himself had leaked his report. Although LBJ suppressed the report, over the next four years he went a long way toward implementing much of the spirit, if not the details, of its recommendations.

Thompson took issue with many of the Gilpatric Committee's conclusions, too.[42] Curbing proliferation was a desirable goal in general, but Thompson believed that to actually implement this process, one had to take the details into account. He did not think that other geopolitical considerations could or should be left out of the equation. "For example," he wrote, "to threaten withdrawal from Europe as a means to dissuade [West] Germany from acquiring a larger nuclear role would be the [surest] way to stimulate belief that the US could not be counted on and that a German or European nuclear force was needed." To threaten to cut off all economic aid to India "could persuade the Indians that they had no choice but to align themselves more with the Soviets . . . and we [would] lose all restraint on India over Kashmir."

Thompson did not think guarantees of protection would really work either, remarking, "It is doubtful that a country which feels really threatened and is capable of building nuclear weapons will indefinitely refrain from doing so."[43] Nuclear-free zones, advocated in the Gilpatric report, would be largely a feel-good measure, with little real effect. The Gilpatric Committee defined proliferation to include the deployment of US weapons overseas. While America's ability to launch weapons into Soviet territory without stationing them abroad was nearly complete, it was not yet total, and Thompson thought the decision to ban such deployments ought to be made more carefully. The devil really was in the details.

Thompson knew he was good at gauging the Soviets' readiness to enter into an agreement. He used this to his advantage in the Austrian State Treaty negotiations and with the limited test ban ones. He did not think the Soviets were really ready for a nonproliferation treaty in early 1965. The USSR had a continuum of interests, just as the United States did, and he supposed that the Soviets were at least as interested in "causing trouble" for NATO as they were in the treaty. Their primary interest in nonproliferation pertained to West Germany. Thompson pointed out that the USSR didn't make threats when Switzerland and Sweden were making motions toward nuclear development. As he wrote in a memo for Rusk: "I do not regard [proliferation] as an 'all-or-nothing' problem. . . . By paying close heed to the needs of each of the main potential nuclear powers, we might succeed in nine cases even if we fail in one. In addition, there are stages of nuclear weapons developments, and not all states which embark on this course will necessarily persist in it."[44]

By February 1965, the MLF was in its death throes, with or without a nonproliferation treaty. Britain was against it, and McNamara came up with an alternative option. He concluded that what was really needed was closer consultation on nuclear programs in the

NATO alliance, "rather than a hardware solutions like ships with multinational crews."[45] This proposal was not well received at first, but it gained traction by the end of the year. An MLF was doomed, but it would not be removed from the nonproliferation treaty's language for almost a year.

Thompson was now more embroiled in America's Vietnam policy, as well as in other issues relating to his "second job." In May 1965, he was disappointed to have to give up a planned trip to visit Bohlen and bemoaned the fact that there was no news on his replacement. The "two or three days" mentioned by the secretary of state when asking Thompson to sit at "that desk" had now stretched into eleven months.[46] He was sufficiently fed up by being the acting deputy undersecretary of state for political affairs that he again began pursuing the creation of a policy advisory group under either a private or an academic institution. He talked about this with McNamara and Cyrus Vance, and he approached the Brookings Institution, to see if this plan could be set in motion. In July, he wrote to Bohlen, because he had always seen the policy group as a two-man operation and had hoped that the other guy would be Bohlen. Bohlen was interested, but the timing was tricky. It would depend on the length of his appointment as US ambassador in Paris.[47]

As these letters were going back and forth to Bohlen, Frank Wisner's mental health deteriorated, worrying both Jane and Thompson. That fall, "Wiz" tragically took his own life at the family's Galina, Maryland, farm, where he had raised vegetables and hounds, and had entertained countless happy children and adults, including the Thompsons.

In summer 1965, the US government infused renewed energy into discussions on nonproliferation, and Thompson seized this moment to write up a review of the efforts that had already been made. In sum, America had been unable "to devise a program which offers high promise of preventing proliferation." On the other hand, US officials were able to reject a number of options, and he was pleased with a "vigorous program for strengthening safeguards." The best measure to avert proliferation might be a comprehensive test ban. Thompson went so far as to say that the United States should rethink its inspection requirements, and perhaps even consider if the advantages "might be so great as to warrant the assumption of the risks (and controversy) in giving up on-site inspections altogether." Lastly, he reviewed other promising nonproliferation options, such as choking off the supply of fissionable material.[48]

In January 1966, LBJ sent a "strongly worded message" to the ENDC, effectively telling them that he wanted the NPT, and that the MLF provision should not stand in its way.[49] Unfortunately, even after removal of the MLF language, the Soviets found other reasons not to like the treaty. Their next main point of contention was the clause on safeguards, which held up forward movement on the treaty until January 1968.[50] There was also a protracted squabble around who would enforce which safeguard standards.[51] Another issue involved inspections, to verify that those standards were being followed. The Soviets didn't want any inspections on their territory, and the non–nuclear weapons states thought that if they had to abide by inspections, the United States and the USSR should do so, too. The Soviets preferred a treaty that was silent on the matter, which is eventually what they got.[52]

Leaving Washington, DC

Dissatisfactions and Job Changes

In 1966, Arthur Schlesinger Jr. published his book on the Kennedy administration, *A Thousand Days*, which sent Thompson and Bohlen up the wall. They both thought that, while Schlesinger had been complimentary toward them personally, he'd missed the mark on his characterization of the State Department and of Rusk in particular. There was not much to be done about it, however, since the book had already been published. Still, they vented to each other by mail. Thompson wrote to Bohlen that the Brookings Institution deal seemed to be stalled, but the Woodrow Wilson Center at Princeton University had expressed interest in Thompson's idea of a two-man policy group, and he was still hopeful. Thompson loved the Foreign Service, but it was different now. He, too, had changed, because of the often unpleasant revelations of his "second job." His health was never the best, and it was not helped by all the stress he was under. He was ready to get out.

In late September, LBJ initiated a series of conversations about a reshuffle of diplomatic appointments, a circumstance that would stop Thompson's plans for leaving the government. The president had decided that Henry Cabot Lodge had served his purpose in Vietnam. LBJ called Rusk on Friday, September 16, to unveil his plan.[53] The president wanted General William Westmoreland to replace Lodge as US ambassador to South Vietnam, but he couldn't easily tell the influential Lodge that he didn't want him anymore. So LBJ planned to offer Lodge the prize ambassadorial slot in Paris. That would mean asking Charles Bohlen to move to Moscow, since the president also wanted a change there. He could give Foy Kohler, the current ambassador in Moscow, a good administrative job at the State Department, as the number-four man, right under Thompson. LBJ's plan was to tell Lodge he needed a breakthrough with de Gaulle, so he wanted Lodge in Paris, because he could "handle his French good."[54] The president would tell Bohlen that he needed him in Moscow, to direct the US strategy on Vietnam, since he required "the ablest, strongest man we can get." The only problem was that Bohlen said, "*Merci, non.*"

Bohlen, who was in the United States at that point, had been summoned from the countryside to Washington, DC, where Rusk made him the offer.[55] But Bohlen argued—presciently—that it was a "mistake to send envoys back to a post like Moscow for a second tour. . . . Eventually the excitement wears off, hope dissipates, and boredom and monotony sets in." When the topic came up again, Bohlen told the secretary of state that his reassignment to Moscow could be seen as an insult by the French, who could take it as a signal that the US government thought Moscow was more important than Paris. That night, Bohlen and Thompson worked on a list of recommendations for the Moscow post over dinner.

LBJ managed to get Lodge back to Washington, DC, as ambassador-at-large without insulting him, but by the time that happened, Ellsworth Bunker had been promised the ambassadorial post in Saigon. Kohler had already been informed that he was being called back from Moscow. Now the president had to have someone else there. Robert McNamara pulled Jane aside at a party and told her how much LBJ needed Thompson in Moscow, asking if they would even consider going back. She replied that her husband was a patriotic man and that if the president asked him to serve, of course he would. McNamara took that information to LBJ and pushed the president quite hard for Thompson to be picked for the Moscow ambassadorial post.[56] The president was hesitant because, as he told McNamara, he wanted Thompson as his Soviet advisor in Washington, DC, and wondered if there were other people who were good enough to advise him "on things like Haiphong." McNamara, knowing about Thompson's policy advisory group scheme, revealed to LBJ that the president would lose Thompson anyhow, because financial and health issues were pushing him out of government. That sealed it for LBJ. He had the State Department's chief administrator, William Crockett, work it up.[57] The president wanted to give both Kohler and Thompson financial rewards: Thompson through a raise, and Kohler by way of helping him with relocation expenses.

When he heard about the Moscow position, Thompson—who did not know about all of these machinations—wondered if someone wanted him out of Washington, DC. Before accepting the post, he needed to hear from LBJ directly that the president *really* wanted him there. LBJ waited to meet with Thompson until the latter had been greenlighted by the Soviets, primarily because the president was worried about leaks. "If you know it and I know it," he told Crockett, "then by God, George Ball'll know it and then it'll be in the papers."[58] LBJ fit Thompson in on Monday morning's schedule (October 3), to assure him his president indeed needed him. LBJ then made the formal announcement that afternoon. Looking back on it, this was probably the one time that Thompson's luck at being in the right place at the right time failed him. He and his family would have been much better off if he'd followed Bohlen's lead and said "*Spasibo, nyet.*"

McGeorge Bundy, who by then had moved on to the Ford Foundation, wrote to Thompson, ostensibly to congratulate him on the Moscow posting, but really to let him know that he was interested in Thompson's policy advisory group idea, and that they would approach the State Department together about it when Thompson returned.[59]

Nonproliferation

Thompson and Bohlen had a conversation-by-mail that fall about Soviet motives and concerns, as well as prospects for agreements. The two Kremlinologists agreed that a split with China was a continuing preoccupation for the USSR, but with the Chinese having isolated themselves in the Communist bloc, the Soviets were less concerned about Chinese attacks on Soviet policy, which, in turn, improved prospects for agreements with the United States. Thompson, however, was still much less optimistic than his colleagues about a quick resolution on a nonproliferation agreement.[60] One thing he believed could influence the USSR's attitude toward arms control was the Soviets' ongoing internal economic problem, especially in agriculture. Therefore, statements indicating a new openness to trade with the USSR might "have helped cause them to take a less hostile attitude toward us." Thompson surmised that the Soviets would, for the moment, continue to take tiny steps in reaching agreements, but any fundamental change was unlikely, at least as long as Vietnam was hanging over them. In keeping with this supposition, several small agreements would be concluded shortly, including the Outer Space Treaty and the Civil Air Accord.[61]

Thompson's professed pessimism about the nonproliferation treaty did not mean he thought it ought not to be pursued vigorously. Because the Soviets were using nonproliferation as a litmus test of US intentions, he worried that they would misinterpret inaction by the United States, so he urged the ACDA's head, William Foster, to proceed with discussions for a draft treaty.[62] This effort was hampered somewhat by Walt Rostow, LBJ's special assistant, who had a much more hands-on approach to managing the president's information than his predecessor, McGeorge Bundy. Rostow had a habit of putting little notes on top of other people's letters or memos to LBJ. These additions would often editorialize, highlight, or summarize the memos in such a way as to promote Rostow's particular point of view. Thus the president missed an opportunity in early October 1966 to advance nonproliferation with Soviet Foreign Minister Gromyko, who was in an uncharacteristically affable mood. LBJ had apparently not read the talking-points memoranda from his advisors, including those by Thompson and Harriman, but had only looked at Rostow's cover note, which suggested not discussing nonproliferation.[63]

There would not be a nonproliferation treaty, or even the near prospect of one, before Thompson left for Moscow. He was right in believing that the Soviets wanted a treaty, but they didn't want it badly enough—yet. In March 1967, during a meeting in Moscow, Thompson noted that Dobrynin told him "the Soviet Union was prepared to meet the 'legitimate interests' of the nonnuclear powers; but it was not prepared to pay a 'high price' for a treaty because they believed it was as much in our interest as theirs, and they would manage to get along somehow if the NPT failed."

The NPT was a perfect example of how difficult it was to gain an agreement between two parties who were suspicious of each other—to the point of near blindness—even on something that was beneficial to both. Eventually the United States and the USSR would come to terms, and the Nuclear Non-Proliferation Treaty was finally ready for signatures in 1968. The USSR agreed to certain things the non–nuclear weapons states desired, and the United States, in turn, accommodated nearly all of the points the Soviets wanted. The treaty had an escape clause—allowing any nation that signed it to simply remove itself from the treaty with a minimum amount of written notice and no penalties—which North Korea eventually used. India claimed that its nuclear detonation in 1974 was for "peaceful purposes." Israel has, but does not formally acknowledge, a nuclear weapons program. Both Iraq and Iran signed the treaty in 1968, but these nations have been the focus of proliferation worries in the twenty-first century. Even today, the NPT is not permanent, requiring "review conferences" every five years to reexamine and possibly emend the treaty.[64]

Thompson supposed that the most effective answer to nonproliferation could have been a truly comprehensive test ban. He may have been right, but that was not to be. The CTB did not happen until 1996, after the dissolution of the USSR. The United States still has not ratified it, although, as of this writing, 166 other nations have done so.[65] The NPT remains the main bulwark against proliferation. It may be weaker than many would prefer, but it has resulted in continued talks. Whether or not the NPT was responsible, Thompson's worry that as many as twenty states could go nuclear by 1980 was not realized.

The FBI

When Thompson's Moscow appointment became known publicly, he received stacks of letters offering either congratulations or condolences, depending on how much the sender understood about it. Being in the news, he and Jane were invited to New York City to attend Truman Capote's Black and White masquerade ball, "A Night to Remember," held in honor of *Washington Post* publisher Katharine Graham.[66] This amused Thompson and thrilled Jane. The other side of the coin was a new background investigation.[67] Though the FBI did not worry about whether Thompson had grown a mustache this time (see chapter 10), and though most of the responses to their questions were full of admiration for Thompson, not all were.

The bureau checked up on family and interviewed friends, colleagues, and subordinates, going back to the late 1930s. One of the young military attachés who had been in Moscow in 1939 under Ambassador Laurence Steinhardt had grown into an old hardliner. Colonel Ivan D. Yeaton said that he could not recommend Thompson, because he would pursue a "course of appeasement" with the Soviets. He called Thompson a "playboy type" and went on to accuse him of having compromised the United States by consorting with Russian girls who may have worked with the NKVD. This spurred the FBI to interview others from that period, who told them that of course Thompson had dated Russian girls—they all did. Thompson wasn't married at the time, so blackmail wasn't an issue. Besides, everyone knew the girls had to report to the secret police, so the Americans were circumspect in what they said.

Another individual who disagreed with Thompson's views on the Soviet Union said he'd rather see someone in the Moscow ambassadorial post who "would get indignant with a foreign government when the prestige of the US was at stake." Two accusations came from people who had known Thompson in Moscow in the 1940s and again in the early 1960s. Both are unidentified, since their names have been redacted in the documents. They reported that they were troubled to see Nina Borisovna and Volodya Alexandrov, Thompson's old friends from his World War II days, at social functions in Spaso House when he was previously the US ambassador in Moscow. They surmised that these Russians were reporting to the KGB. Obviously they were, but so were the butler, the chauffeur, the telephone operator, and nearly every other Soviet who set foot in the building. That Nina was only invited to functions when Jane was present meant that there was nothing between Thompson and his old flame except friendship. One of these unnamed accusers reported that Volodya had once made a pass at him. The upshot was even more investigations, including into Thompson's friendship with Charles Thayer, since Thayer had been accused of homosexuality during the McCarthy period. No evidence against Thompson was found, and the FBI finally cleared him for duty.

33 ≡

Strand Three
The Road to SALT (1962–1967)

The important thing is not to give up because no answer
to the problem is at hand, but to maintain communications
so that if a change does occur you will recognize it and
act upon it.
—LLEWELLYN THOMPSON, *Family Weekly*,
    Jan 20, 1963

I n the years from 1962 to 1966, disarmament seemed like tilting at windmills, and it
paralleled the efforts toward nonproliferation in many ways. Adrian Fisher at the Arms
Control and Disarmament Agency put out proposals for his boss, William Foster, to
present to the Eighteen-Nation Disarmament Committee. But the United States could not
agree internally, so many of these drafts never saw the light of day at the ENDC meetings
in Geneva. It seemed as though every time a consensus draft would emerge, the Joint
Chiefs of Staff would have the last look and find a reason to squash it, giving the impression that they were opposed to arms control in principle.[1] The United States kept pitching
proposals that would seal its advantage, and the Soviets would mostly ignore them, but the
Soviets did the same thing when they put forward their own proposals. For example, the
Americans wanted reductions in intercontinental ballistic missiles by their overall number, and the Soviets by a percentage, because the United States still had more ICBMs than
the USSR did.

Neither side wound up seeming truly serious about disarmament throughout this period. Nonetheless, they were still talking, and that was the important point. Despite all the
uncertainty with the new leaderships in the United States and the USSR, the fragility of
both the Communist bloc and the Atlantic alliance, the general economic problems that
were brewing, and the Vietnam War, there were no major showdowns between the two
superpowers during this period.[2] By the time LBJ settled into the Oval Office, some form
of disarmament—or at least a slowing or stopping of the arms race—was desirable to both
countries. Non–nuclear weapons states were insisting that if they had to give up their nu-

clear programs, the weapons states needed to at least reduce their arsenals. Moreover, the arms race was obscenely expensive and, by then, redundant, since both the United States and the USSR had enough weapons for deterrence. The Soviets still needed the money for domestic and agricultural reforms, and LBJ needed it for the Vietnam War and his Great Society programs.

These parallel situations did not make for smooth sailing, however. The two nations' arsenals were not equal in quality or quantity. The Americans had a greater number of smaller and more-mobile missiles. Though fewer in number, the "aesthetically contemptible" Soviet ICBMs were hardened and had huge payloads.[3] Each of these countries tried using mutual reductions in their respective defense budgets as a means of curbing the arms race. The difficulty, as Adrian Fisher liked to say, was that the less-revealing Soviet military budget was "some 16 words and one sum." When the United States announced a unilateral reduction in its military budget, the Soviets seized on it and reciprocated, with some fanfare. This move backfired, however, because escalations in Vietnam caused the US military budget to spike shortly thereafter, and the Soviets took the increase as a sign of bad faith.[4]

Two big technological breakthroughs occurring in the 1960s further complicated arms control: an antiballistic missile (ABM) system and multiple independent reentry vehicle (MIRV) systems, with a MIRV being a single missile with multiple warheads. In one of his early post–Cuban Missile Crisis speeches, Thompson made his usual remarks about how both sides had the capacity to destroy most of the world, but he also said that he believed the Soviets were seeking a breakthrough to redress the balance of power. He noted that if there were to be a scientific breakthrough, such as an antimissile missile, it would result in a "whole new arms race."[5] It was a fool's errand to think that any breakthrough would not engender an equal reaction from the other side.

The Soviets included components of an ABM system in their 1964 May Day parade. Their plan to deploy a small system around Moscow, called Galosh, reverberated throughout Washington, DC. The US military had also been working on an ABM system, dubbed Nike, but it was still on the drawing board and was not yet funded.[6] Many believed that ABM technology would be destabilizing, especially in the way the Soviets were planning to deploy it— around a city. The logic was counterintuitive, but it went like this: nuclear weapons are deterrents only if they are able to deliver an "unacceptable" retaliatory strike in the event of an attack. Therefore, anything that reduced that second strike's effectiveness was dangerous. If an ABM system protected a nation's citizens from a second strike, that country might be more prone to launch a first strike. The American approach was to place ABMs around its Minutemen missiles. The reasoning was that if an ABM protected retaliatory missiles instead of people, it would actually discourage a first strike by an opponent, because a second strike would be guaranteed, thus maintaining the deterrent. Convincing the Soviets of this, however, was not easy, as they kept asserting that their system was purely defensive, and that protecting their citizens should not be construed as an offensive move.

Another wrinkle in the ABM issue was that the Soviets had a sophisticated and extensive array of radar sites, strung up across the country like a curtain, which the United States called the Tallinn air defense system.[7] These were designed to detect aircraft, as an early warning of an attack, which was an element in the Soviets' obsession with overflights. Because radar was a primary component of an ABM system, however, the US military was convinced that this was a huge ABM system in the works and used its existence to argue for developing an equally large American ABM system.

The US response to both the Soviet ABMs and the rapidly expanding, hulking Soviet ICBMs was MIRVs.[8] MIRVs were like magic-bullet missiles, using a technology that could turn each single Minuteman missile into many, at a relatively low cost. This system had two benefits. First, having a single missile deliver not only multiple warheads, but multiple warheads that each had a different target, would be able to foil almost any ABM system, since there was no way to track the warheads until the very last seconds. Second, there was no way the Soviets could produce enough ICBMs to catch up with MIRV'd Minutemen, even if they were churning them out "like sausages."[9] So by the end of 1966, the arms race was poised like a racehorse in the starting gate, driven by technology and doomed to escalate without some way to rein it in.

Arms Control

The search for a means to slow the arms race was earnestly pursued, certainly by 1964, when Bundy wrote that "the way to begin is to begin."[10] Thompson became more deeply drawn into arms control because of his position as deputy undersecretary of state for political affairs. Ever watchful of the Soviet penchant for using legal loopholes, he looked hard at the language that was used and at how it could be interpreted. Raymond Garthoff— who served as a special assistant to Thompson and to his predecessor, U. Alexis Johnson— was again a conduit for information on the ups and downs of the various proposals.

Thompson objected to a number of ACDA's draft proposals, for various reasons: some were bound to fail internally; others could negatively provoke the Soviets; a particular proposal might be opening a door that ought to remain shut; and, for still others, the timing felt wrong. Thompson again tried to bring a broader geopolitical perspective to these ideas than the arms control people, who were one-issue oriented. It is a testament to their professionalism that Thompson's critical reading of the drafts did not inspire acrimony between him and Adrian Fisher or NSC staffer Spurgeon Keeney Jr., and they retained their respect for one another.[11]

A good example of Thompson's critique of one of these drafts is a long memorandum written in November 1964, shortly after Khrushchev's ouster. In it, Keeney complained to Bundy that "Ambassador Thompson essentially comes out against all of the arms control initiatives that [the] ACDA has recommended for discussion with the Soviets."[12] Given that Khrushchev had just been removed from the government, Thompson did not think this was a good time to push disarmament with the Soviets. The ACDA staff, however, was impatient to move things along.[13] Notwithstanding Thompson's advice not to "scratch around to find something else" when the Soviets stonewalled, William Foster urged the Committee of Principals to consider some kind of initiative to offer to the USSR and wanted permission to approach his Soviet counterpart. Thompson thought they should instead continue to write "sound" proposals and be patient.[14] When Thompson spoke of the requirement for patience in negotiating with the Soviets, he was thinking on an entirely different timescale than the men writing the drafts.

Besides the timing, he objected to other points in that particular ACDA proposal, some of which were broad and others were matters of language.[15] First, it was important to qualify nuclear delivery vehicles as *strategic* nuclear delivery vehicles, lest the Soviets apply the term to freight-type vehicles. This latter interpretation would be more problematic for the American force, which was more mobile, as opposed to the Soviet force, which was oriented more toward large, hardened launch facilities. Second he reminded them that the Soviets had not refused *all* onsite inspections, as the ACDA had written. Rather, they had agreed to three inspections during the comprehensive test ban negotiations. Thompson argued that the Soviets would resent reading such a statement in a formal US proposal presented to an international body, and they probably would assign malicious motives to its inclusion. Third, he observed that if the ACDA openly proposed relying on unilateral intelligence collection to solve the problem of inspections, it would reveal that the United States could detect ICBMs in the Soviet Union. The Soviets, in turn, would then want to know, if the Americans could do that, why did they still have to overfly Cuba?

The ACDA proposal also contained a tacit agreement to freeze the construction of ICBMs, without onsite inspections. Thompson thought this offer held the most promise for Soviet acceptance, although their government was unlikely to do so, since it would halt the USSR's efforts to catch up. He was good at foreseeing the unintended consequences of an idea. For instance, freezing ICBM construction could prompt the Soviets to increase their submarine-based launchers (SLBMs), which were more difficult for the United States to deal with. According to Thompson, a freeze on offensive systems (i.e., ICBMs) should also include one on defensive systems (i.e., ABMs), because it was the ABMs that could trigger a new arms race. He was ambivalent on this issue, however, because the Americans were still considering ABMs to protect Minutemen missiles, and he worried that it might "tie our hand[s]" on developing a small ABM system to defend against a Chinese bomb.

In June 1965, the ACDA recommended that a freeze proposal include a provision for extensive arms reductions, making it more acceptable to the Soviets. On June 16, Thompson wrote to Foster that that the State Department agreed with this suggestion.[16] Thompson still didn't think the Soviets would accept it, but it could have some utility in "undercutting the Soviet line that our freeze proposal involved verification without disarmament." This particular ACDA proposal, however, only offered to "explore the possibility" of reductions. Thompson also pointed out that before presenting such a proposal to the Soviets, the ACDA had to clarify what the reductions would be, in order to get a buy-in from within the US government and deal with the allies' concerns. He recommended soliciting the DOD's reaction to the proposal. The JCS members gave their review comments shortly thereafter, which were completely negative. They did not think the United States should negotiate with the USSR on any aspect of the ACDA proposal.[17]

In an effort to persuade the Soviets to resume the ENDC talks in Geneva, Foster pre-pared a speech offering a freeze and possible arm reductions, but he never gave it. Rusk warned Foster not to do so, because LBJ planned to announce an escalation of US forces in Vietnam the next day. Rusk and Thompson disliked the juxtaposition for different rea-sons: Thompson, because the Soviets already believed that the United States deliberately made peace moves in order to obscure escalations in Vietnam; and Rusk, because it would be hard to sell an arms cutback just as LBJ announced that America was in for "a hell of a job" in Vietnam.[18]

By the start of 1966, there was still no substantial progress on arms control. The ACDA urged the president to call for a moratorium on all ballistic missiles in his January State of the Union address. The ACDA circulated its draft, which received favorable replies from the White House, the State Department, and the Atomic Energy Commission, but it was rejected by the JCS. They advocated exploratory, private feelers to the Soviets on general ideas before making any public statements. This was quite the opposite of what Thompson had recommended, which was that the Americans approach the Soviets with specific pro-posals in hand. The ACDA finally completed its draft in April 1966 and sent a "guidance cable" to Geneva, authorizing general, private talks with the Soviets.

Fisher sent a memo to LBJ in May, along with a suggested draft letter to Kosygin, res-urrecting an offer of an eighteen-month moratorium, this time on both ICBM and ABM launchers.[19] Thompson wrote a memo opposing both the proposal and the letter.[20] He did not think the Soviets would go for anything quickly, because too much was in America's favor. One, it would freeze the US advantage in ICBMSs while holding back the Soviets' deployment of the Galosh ABMs. Two, it would have a bad effect on US allies at a time when NATO was already in disarray. Three, if a freeze was accepted, the Soviets might want to extend it indefinitely, which could not be easily refused. An indefinite morato-rium, with no inspections, would make it much harder to include inspections in a perma-nent agreement later. The president did not even grant the ACDA a meeting to discuss their idea.[21]

In June 1966, in a short break from arms control issues, Thompson and Jane went to West Germany at its government's invitation. It was a good interlude for the couple. Thomp-son could see first-hand the depth of that country's concerns over its place in a nuclear world and its incipient steps to reach out to the East Germans, the beginning of Ostpolitik. The West Germans, as always, wanted to talk about the prospects for reunification. Thomp-son replied that such a move could only realistically occur if it did not represent a defeat for the Soviet Union.[22]

In a subsequent debriefing to a group of German specialists in the State Department,[23] Thompson confessed that he was tempted, when asked if West Germany should recognize the Oder–Neisse Line, to simply say "Yes." Instead, he noted that if the West Germans waited until the very end of any reunification negotiations, the Oder–Neisse issue would no longer have any bargaining power. For some time, it had seemed to Thompson that the border concession was an unused chip, something that was very important to the Soviets, but which came at a relatively low cost to the West. Unfortunately the couple's trip was interrupted for an unexpected operation on Thompson's thumb. He did not get into East Berlin, but Jane did. She was impressed that this sector seemed more attractive and lively than it had been, with nicer things in the stores. Overall, the trip reinforced her feeling that the United States had better work to "keep these highly industrious people on our side."

In fall 1966, at the ENDC meeting, the Soviets offered a no-first-use agreement as an answer to the US freeze proposal on nuclear weapons. Since both the United States and the USSR were moving forward on their ABM systems, calling a halt to them did not look promising. Thompson conceded, however, that these new weapons systems might actually facilitate an agreement, because the threat—and cost—of a potential new arms race could spur both parties to action.[24] He now discerned that the Soviets might be serious.

The Breakthrough

December 1966 had started out as bitter cold and humid in Washington, DC, the kind of weather that goes into your bones, but Tuesday, December 6, was clear and warmer. Thompson had had an appointment at his daughters' school that day, to work out arrangements for them to enter its boarding department once he and Jane left for Moscow. Instead, he cancelled that engagement to have a long lunch at the Soviet embassy with Ambassador Dobrynin, who was heading back to Moscow for consultations. The two men discussed Dobrynin's imminent trip and the possibility that he might not remain as the Soviet ambassador to the United States.

The most important thing they talked about was ABMs. When Thompson brought the subject up, Dobrynin immediately stated that the US government had never replied to a Soviet overture to consider an agreement on ABMs.[25] Dobrynin qualified this by indicating that any ABM agreement ought to be jointly considered with one for ICBM systems. Thompson recognized that this represented a potential eleventh-hour breakthrough. Secretary of Defense McNamara was headed to Austin, Texas, to work with the president on his budget proposal to Congress. Great pressure was being applied to fund the Nike-X ABM system.[26] If the government's defense budget included Nike-X, it would be impossible to put that item back in the box. Dobrynin's imminent departure and his uncertainty about being removed from his ambassadorial post in Washington, DC, added to the tension and urgency. Thompson went back to his office, called Foster at the ACDA to verify Dobrynin's account, cancelled his afternoon meetings, and had a memo on his and Dobrynin's ABM conversation typed up and sent to McNamara, Rusk, the White House, and Foster.[27]

While all this was going on in Washington, DC, McNamara made his way to Austin. The president helicoptered in from his ranch and met for half an hour with McNamara, Walt Rostow, and the Joint Chiefs of Staff.[28] They gathered in LBJ's office on the top floor of the J. J. Pickle Federal Office Building downtown, a corrugated cement rectangle that reflected the severe, almost Soviet architecture of the public buildings in that city. The meeting was temporarily halted by a Medal of Honor ceremony in the plaza outside. After another interruption, LBJ rejoined his advisors and gave them ceremonial medals as souvenirs, joking that these weren't the real thing and would need some "shinin' from time to time."

During this fractured, distracted day, the president and McNamara arrived at the figures for the defense budget for the following year: roughly $235 billion dollars.[29] The Secretary of Defense reported, and the JCS concurred, that they had agreed on everything except five outstanding issues, which included the Nike-X ABMs. The joint chiefs and McNamara made their respective cases for and against this Nike system.[30] LBJ had questions about the cost and congressional perspectives. He then directly asked what determined the difference in judgment between the secretary of defense and the JCS. McNamara conceded that this disparity was more "emotional" in nature than one of "rational calculation." Both McNamara and the JCS did agree on one thing: the urgency of the situation. They needed a decision right away.

LBJ split the difference and suggested moving ahead with Nike-X, but on a limited basis, while also seeing what might be negotiated with the Soviets. The JCS argued that the Soviets were already moving forward with their ABM system, and the United States had to do something. The joint chiefs warned: "We are dealing with the descendants of Genghis Khan. They only understand force." McNamara said that was why the United States needed to maintain its second-strike capability at all costs. Although it has been widely accepted that the fate of America's ABM system was sealed by taking this program out of the defense budget that day in Austin, the minutes of the meeting do not reflect a hard-and-fast decision, other than LBJ's suggestion that they move to develop a *limited* ABM program while *still seeking negotiations with the Soviets*. At this point, neither the president nor the secretary of defense knew about Thompson's nearly simultaneous conversation with Dobrynin.

McNamara and Deputy Secretary of Defense Cyrus Vance flew back to Washington, DC, on December 7. Since Dean Rusk was in Asia, they asked Nicholas Katzenbach, the undersecretary of state, to gather the president's top advisors, including Thompson, for an urgent meeting that day. McNamara showed these men a "long and thorough memorandum" he'd given to LBJ in Austin, listing the pros and cons of production and deployment of the Nike-X system. McNamara said that after the president read the memorandum, he asked that his advisors "prepare, individually, memoranda describing what [they] each thought [the] Soviet reaction would be" to a "light" system, covering twenty-five large cities, and a "heavier" version, covering fifty cities.[31] It seems evident that when McNamara returned from Austin, LBJ had not yet made up his mind, but had instead simply asked for feedback from his top advisors.

Thompson then told those present at the December 7 meeting about his conversation with Dobrynin the previous day. Understanding the importance of what Thompson was telling them, McNamara phoned the president, who was still at the LBJ ranch, to get authorization for Thompson to pursue this opening with Dobrynin. McNamara later recalled that it was Katzenbach and Thompson who "insisted" on verifying that LBJ supported "such a dramatic new initiative" to reach out to the Soviets.[32] McNamara's version of his meeting with the president, however, conflicts with the draft minutes.[33] In McNamara's account, he says that the fate of the ABM system in the federal budget was decided at the meeting in Austin, and that it was he who "forcefully" put forward the formula to limit the budget amount for the ABM system "with the *initiation of discussions with the Soviet Union*" [emphasis McNamara's]. The draft minutes instead give LBJ that role.

In his fateful phone call with the president, McNamara did most of the talking. He asked for LBJ's permission to "do something." He told the president about Thompson's meeting with Dobrynin the day before and said that Thompson had another appointment to see Dobrynin in an hour to deliver a letter from the president to Kosygin about a routine matter.[34] They wanted authorization for Thompson to tell the Soviet ambassador that the Americans were interested in talks on limiting ABMs and ICBMs. LBJ replied: "Sure. Yes. I raised that question yesterday. . . . Go ahead."[35]

Thompson went back to the Soviet embassy for his 4:30 p.m. meeting with Dobrynin.[36] He told his counterpart that the Americans realized that an agreement would have to include both ICBMs and ABMs. Thompson stated that the United States also wished to avoid the cost of deploying this system, and added that "if we both spend these enormous sums, we would probably both end up still able to inflict terrible damage on the other . . . when we both had many other uses for our resources." Then he asked Dobrynin for the Soviet Union's ideas on how they might proceed to arrange discussions, and when these might take place. Dobrynin mentioned that he, personally, thought it would be possible to come to a formal agreement but, even without that, both nations could begin with a "tacit understanding" to refrain from being the first one to deploy their system. Thompson stressed that the situation was urgent, because the federal government's defense budget was scheduled to be sent to Congress the next month. Dobrynin replied that as soon as he returned to the USSR, he would immediately take it up with Brezhnev and Kosygin. Thus began the very long road to strategic arms limitation talks (SALT).

The next day, December 8, Thompson wrote a personal letter to Rusk, "since it might bear on conversations you will be having in Paris."[37] Thompson sent it in care of Ambassador Bohlen in Paris and instructed his friend that it ought to be opened only by the secretary of state when he arrived in France, en route back to Washington, DC. In his letter, Thompson described his meetings: first with Dobrynin, and then with McNamara. There were two urgencies in the matter that caused McNamara and company to act before contacting Rusk. One was the pending US defense budget. The other was to try to head off any decision by the Supreme Soviet, which would be approving its own plan for 1967. Thompson told Rusk that his guess was that the Soviets would take the United States up on this, but that they would be preoccupied with a meeting of the Central Committee, for which Dobrynin was returning to Moscow.

Why did the situation turn around in late 1966? Was it McNamara's trip to Austin to try to convince the president not to fund the Nike-X ABM system? Or was it Dobrynin's meeting with Thompson, when he told Thompson that the Soviets would get serious about disarmament talks? Raymond Garthoff, one of the closest observers of SALT and its long prelude, credited Thompson and Dobrynin with starting the SALT process, once it was clear that their governments were in earnest about doing something.[38]

At the end of 1966, the Soviets were closing the technological and numbers gaps in their weapons systems, which made maintaining a clear US superiority seem more and more futile. The prospect of a new and hugely expensive round in the ongoing arms race loomed at a time when the leaders in both countries had other pressing and costly agendas: in the United States, LBJ's Great Society programs and the escalating war in Vietnam; in the USSR, agricultural reforms, improved living standards, and Soviet commitments to the developing world. Meanwhile, the global economy was changing, and the United States no longer sat in its comfortable postwar bubble. An arms control agreement had finally become an important issue, in part because the two sides had kept talking throughout the long and frustrating years leading up to an accord, as well as because the men involved recognized that the landscape had shifted and then acted on it.

Trade Agreements

In one of Thompson's meetings with Dobrynin in Washington, DC, the Soviet ambassador brought up settlement of the USSR's Lend-Lease debts. Thompson thought that the first step in making this happen needed to be a congressional bill conferring most-favored-nation (MFN) status to the Soviet Union.[39] The Soviets, he said, had a "strong argument in saying that they cannot consider any settlement while the lack of MFN treatment makes it impossible to service a debt settlement." One idea surfaced in the Senate Foreign Relations Committee, chaired by J. William Fulbright, which proposed that the disputed Lend-Lease amount be committed to a common development fund, an idea the Soviets indicated held some interest for them. A cooperative venture between the USSR and the United States to contribute aid to developing nations became part of the platform that Thompson talked to the president about in agreeing to accept another "sentence" and return as US ambassador to Moscow.

Vietnam

In his very last meeting with Dobrynin before Thompson left Washington, DC—the December 30 one in which Dobrynin had said the Soviets had been baffled by America's Vietnam policy (see chapter 31)—the conversation closed with a suggestion.[40] Dobrynin hoped Thompson would contact a "certain Ambassador" when he got to Moscow, meaning the North Vietnamese ambassador. This short-lived initiative, with the code name Sunflower, turned out to be a failure. Sunflower consisted of a direct approach through the North Vietnamese embassy in Moscow, where Thompson was about to take up his post as ambassador, a personal letter from LBJ to Ho Chi Minh, and a week-long effort between Kosygin and Britain's Prime Minister Wilson. The latter caused an embarrassing misunderstanding and ruffled US-UK relations.[41]

34

Moscow 3

The idea of the two superpowers running the world has great
appeal to the Soviets, but I question this as U.S. policy.
—LLEWELLYN THOMPSON to Dean Rusk,
 April 7, 1967

I n early January 1967, Thompson took up his third posting to Moscow. He hoped he
could make some contribution, but he wondered if modern communications hadn't
made the role of ambassador less important than it used to be. Later, when he said
something to that effect to Kosygin, the Soviet leader disagreed, because, "in addition to
his chair and his telegram wire, an Ambassador has a head; if the head is good, people at
the other end of [the] wire listen to it."[1]

Thompson sold the family's house in Washington, DC, to one of the Rostow brothers
and arranged for his own brother, MWood, to take responsibility for his daughters in the
event something happened to him and Jane. If that didn't work out, Paul and Phyllis Nitze
agreed to do so. The two younger Thompson girls would arrive in Moscow the next summer, after finishing the academic year in boarding school in America. Thompson, Jane, her
daughter Andy, and their boxer dog Valli left the capital by train from Union Station, where
Ambassador Dobrynin was among those who saw them off. They boarded the SS *United
States* in New York City, bound for the German port of Bremen, where they then caught a
flight to Moscow. It was a long trip, but the final leg was an hour shorter, thanks to a huge
tailwind, perhaps a good omen for a posting Thompson had mixed feelings about.

The temperature was below 0°F and the sky was spitting snow and ice pellets when
they unloaded their belongings under the portico at Spaso House. The Kohlers had reno-
vated the ambassadorial residence with fresh paint and pretty new bathrooms. It was almost luxurious in comparison to when the Thompsons left in 1962. What a treat to find
Shura the phone operator and Tung the butler, and even Tung's surly wife, Natasha, still
there to greet them! Sadly, Chin, the other half of the "Chin and Tonic" pair of housemen,
had died only a few months before, and Tung was still quite shaken up about it.

The new ambassador's aide was Jonathan Rickert, a tall, good-looking, proper young
man in penny loafers. He would go on to head a Foreign Service post of his own, but at that

stage in life, he was still a young FSO, assigned to live in Spaso House and be at Thompson's beck and call (as well as Jane's, when she could get away with it, which was most of the time.) The staff was headed by a round-faced Italian, Clemente Pandin, who ruled with an iron fist and had an unhealthy entrepreneurial bent. Some suspected that he was involved in black market businesses, but he maintained a firm hand over the household and was careful, so he got away with it. Some years after Thompson's tenure he was murdered in Moscow under questionable circumstances.

In contrast to Spaso House, Moscow—if it was even possible—had become bleaker in the intervening time. Charles Bohlen, when he came to visit the following year, described it in his memoirs as a city "lacking in hope."[2] The vibrant intelligentsia had been restrained, the lively art and political talk was gone, and there was virtually no contact with the country's leadership. Perhaps the people were a tiny bit better dressed, and there were shiny new buildings on the Arbat behind the Spaso House garden, where their inhabitants could see the Thompson family play croquet, barbeque, and, even more strangely, watch Thompson hitting golf balls into a big net. The rapid, positive change Thompson had seen in his previous ambassadorial tour was no longer evident.[3] Rather, he found the Soviet press more critical and distorted than he'd realized from his desk in Washington, DC—not just about Vietnam, but with overt misrepresentations of American life and policies in general. Jane, on the other hand, had a more positive reaction. She liked the new "valuta" stores—shops that took hard currency—where she could actually buy oranges and lemons without literally going to Finland. Although about half the food for Spaso House was still being imported, it was a vast improvement in the family's quality of life. Jane also noted the new, tall buildings constructed with steel girders. Perhaps now the balconies wouldn't fall off.

Thompson had a good staff waiting for him. John Guthrie was the deputy chief of mission, having filled in as chargé d'affaires between Kohler's departure and Thompson's arrival. David Klein, who had worked with Thompson at the State Department during the Cuban Missile Crisis, was the political counselor. Klein proved to be a valuable officer, despite having disagreed with Thompson over a German reunification policy back in Washington, DC.[4] Many of the men who worked in that small but highly talented group would go on to head embassies of their own. Everyone on the staff was deeply committed to the post and wanted to be there in Moscow, with the possible exception of Thompson himself.[5] The ambassador did, however, have a couple of friends in the diplomatic corps who were still in the city. He respected Canadian ambassador Robert Ford, and Sir Geoffrey Harrison, his former partner from the Trieste negotiations, was the British envoy.

Thompson's Agenda

Before his departure from Washington, DC, Thompson had met with LBJ to confirm his assignment. The president was most concerned with having the ambassador work some magic on the question of Vietnam, while Thompson was interested in the possibility of pursuing common-ground ideas that had been percolating from his observations of the Soviet Union since the Khrushchev days. He'd talked about these in his speeches for years.

Thompson knew the Soviets still had desperate troubles with their economy, a population weary of sacrifice, an inadequate agricultural infrastructure, and an ever-larger portfolio of developing nations clamoring for help. Moreover, the USSR was the leader of a bloc that, like NATO, was showing fissures. In addition, the nation was in the starting gate of an expensive new leg of the arms race.

Thompson hoped the Soviets' difficulties would create an opportunity for détente, which LBJ had professed he wanted. Thompson knew the president was concerned about Soviet advances in the developing world, so he believed LBJ when the president said he supported an agenda of cooperation with the Soviets on aid to the developing world.[6] In addition, both men were eager to pursue arms control. Thompson had said that the best chance for early success lay in taking small steps, but he also thought his December 1966 talks with Dobrynin on reining in ABMs had real potential. A consular agreement to open respective offices in San Francisco and Leningrad (now St. Petersburg) had been negotiated, but it was scuttled at the last moment by J. Edgar Hoover, the notorious and powerful director of the FBI.[7]

Thompson's lack of personal contact with the Soviet leadership was frustrating. He was required to present his credentials, not to Kosygin, the chairman of the Council of Ministers, or to Communist Party leader Brezhnev, but to the chairman of the Supreme Soviet, Nikolay Podgorny, in a brief ceremony at the Kremlin on January 23. Ambassador-at-Large Averell Harriman was irate that Thompson acquiesced to doing so with Podgorny, because Harriman was anxious for Thompson to deliver a new pen-pal letter from LBJ to Kosygin. He believed this letter could open the Sunflower initiative's channel to North Vietnam and blamed Thompson for allowing a delay in its delivery.[8]

Thompson said nothing about Vietnam in his credentials speech. Instead, he talked about steps toward easing arms expenditures, and the underlying fears and suspicions that stood in the way; cooperative programs to build up industry in the underdeveloped world; and efforts to restrain the swift global population growth and increase food production. Podgorny, in his remarks, went on almost exclusively about Vietnam. Jane was annoyed, because no women were allowed at the ceremony. At its end, she was finally let into the room for a glass of champagne.[9]

A few days later, Thompson finally managed to deliver the pen-pal letter to Kosygin, not in a private meeting, but on the occasion of the signing ceremony for the Outer Space Treaty. Kosygin complained to Thompson that the latest news from Vietnam was not good. The United States had continued to escalate the war, and now there was talk of the Americans bombing airfields. When Thompson said that LBJ was earnestly trying to end the Vietnam conflict, Kosygin replied tartly, "Then [the United States] should act differently."[10] The ambassador quietly proposed that he and Kosygin secretly continue the talks on arms control that had started with Thompson and Dobrynin, but he got no response.[11] In Washington, DC, Garthoff and a select group from the arms control bureaucracy began drafting a US position to include limitations on both offensive and defensive nuclear weapons, but no more than a dozen people were aware that this was happening.[12]

Kosygin responded to Thompson's suggestion of arms control talks by boasting about how easily the Galosh ABM system around Moscow could knock out US missiles. In a statement that showed he did not understand—or perhaps did not care—about the potential destabilizing effect of such systems, Kosygin said that even if an ABM system was more expensive than an offensive system, "it is not the cause of the arms race but designed instead to prevent the death of people."[13] Thankfully, five days later *Pravda* published a clarification, stating that the Soviets were ready to avert the arms race in both offensive and defensive weapons. Still, nothing concrete was stated on when they would start talking.

A month into his most recent Moscow posting, Thompson, in a cable to the State Department, took stock of what he saw.[14] He thought the new Soviet leadership "appeared weak." While Brezhnev was "clearly number one, the Politburo is in fact operating collectively. A Soviet acquaintance from the old days groused to Thompson that previously, if you wanted to get a proposal through, you only had to convince Khrushchev, whereas now you had to "convince nearly every member of the Politburo, since almost any one of them could block it." On the other hand, the Soviet leadership had improved the nation's disastrous agricultural system by implementing a more "business-like" approach, although they could not quite give up the principle of collectivity, which still hampered bold initiatives. The standard of living in the USSR had improved, but only marginally. People were more open, but only in private conversation, while the intellectuals were "straining at the limits set on their activities." The Chinese harangues resulted in a resurgence of the importance of ideology in the Soviets' policies and propaganda. The USSR appeared to focus more on "internal problems" than foreign policy, although Thompson's limited contact with the country's leadership made it hard for him to interpret the motives for some of their policies.[15]

Sunflower[16]

In December 1966, there were competing currents in North Vietnam, too. The hard-liners were on the rise, and bombing close to Hanoi had helped their cause. Rostow, who had championed the air strikes, maintained that this bombing would not interfere with negotiations, while McNamara and Thompson disagreed.[17] Rostow won, and that was a mistake. As a result, North Vietnam had pulled the plug on the Marigold peace initiative. On December 23, 1966, LBJ tried to resurrect Marigold. Unfortunately, the president's statement had the perverse effect of boosting the North Vietnamese hard-liners by making it look as though their tough reaction to the American bombing raids was having a positive effect.[18] *New York Times* journalist Harrison Salisbury was in Hanoi at about this time, and he published a scathing exposé of the American bombing campaign.[19] It had indeed killed civilians, despite US assurances that it hadn't. Moreover, the bombing was not making any difference in the front lines of the war effort, and it was solidifying the North Vietnamese people's resolve. Salisbury told Dean Rusk that he was convinced Ho Chi Minh wanted to negotiate but didn't know how to arrange it without the political risk of going public. He further stated that Hanoi had now dropped a precondition to negotiations, left over from 1965, to which the Americans had objected.[20]

Rostow and Rusk recommended that LBJ make the first move by writing a personal letter to Ho Chi Minh, proposing secret bilateral talks. The letter wasn't drafted until February 1967, and by the time Thompson knew about it, he had several objections. He believed that personally addressing Ho might actually weaken the North Vietnamese leader's internal position. Moreover, possibly recalling the Trieste negotiations, Thompson thought that a letter from the president ought to be held in reserve, in the event of an impasse, not as a first move.[21] For his part, LBJ wanted to discern if Salisbury's impressions were correct before sending any letter. Were these feelers through Salisbury real? Just before Thompson's arrival in Moscow, John Guthrie, filling in as the chargé d'affaires, was instructed to deliver a message to his North Vietnamese counterpart, Le Chang, inviting the North Vietnamese government to begin "secure" bilateral communications. Chang, concerned with secrecy, responded that his government wanted clarification on just what "completely secure" meant and what kind of settlement the Americans had in mind.[22] Perhaps Salisbury had gotten the right impression after all.

This began a series of back-and-forth communications to try to feel out the chance for talks with the North Vietnamese, brokered through Moscow, which became known as the Sunflower peace initiative.[23] The State Department asked Thompson for his assessment of North Vietnam's readiness to talk and for suggestions on how to continue. Thompson cabled the department that, in his opinion, Chang's response to Guthrie sounded like the "first round in Oriental rug trading,"[24] this being a good sign. Thompson also warned the department that it was a mistake not to tell the Soviets about these communications.[25] He advised Guthrie to ask Chang outright if the Americans could tell the Soviets about these attempted feelers toward a peace negotiation. As it turned out, the North Vietnamese had kept the Soviets fully apprised of what was happening.[26] As for advice on how to continue the process, Thompson proposed four alternatives, depending on how serious LBJ was about talking with the North Vietnamese. These ranged from a halt in the US bombing of North Vietnam, in exchange for prompt talks and mutual deescalation, to a propaganda response that would put the United States in a favorable light, should the North Vietnamese make the talks public—which was a distinct possibility in Thompson's mind.

A cease-fire during the Vietnamese Tet holiday, which had already been agreed to, was fast approaching. Thompson, among others, thought this cease-fire could be extended unilaterally, as a means of stopping the bombing without making it *publicly* tied to an expectation of talks. To take advantage of this option during Tet, however, a decision had to be made in short order. In his next meeting with Chang, Guthrie delivered a written statement suggesting that the United States might be willing to stop the bombing on a unilateral basis if North Vietnam *privately* assured the Americans of equivalent "subsequent steps." When Chang asked him what that meant, Guthrie replied, "equitable and reciprocal" steps. At the same time, LBJ was holding a press conference in Washington, DC. In answering a question about what steps the North Vietnamese might take to show they were serious about negotiations, the president replied, "Just almost any step." When asked directly if it would be enough to for North Vietnam to agree to talk, in return for a halt of bombing, LBJ said the United States was waiting for an offer.[27]

In early February 1967, another part of Sunflower was germinating in London between Kosygin and Britain's Harold Wilson, with assistance from the American ambassador in London, David K. E. Bruce, and Chester Cooper, the assistant to Ambassador-at-Large

Averell Harriman. Over the span of about a week, they rode a roller coaster of hopeful possibilities and disheartening difficulties. Over dinner, Kosygin told Wilson that if the US bombing stopped, Hanoi would definitely enter into talks, which Wilson found promising. The prime minister cabled LBJ late that night with a recap of his dinner meeting.[28] Wilson and Kosygin had arrived at a proposed text to send to Hanoi. Its premises were that the United States would stop all bombing of North Vietnam, with the understanding that the North Vietnamese would enter into secret talks. For their part, the North Vietnamese would cease their infiltration of men and materiel into South Vietnam, at the same time that the United States would stop sending more troops there. Wilson asked the Americans to verify his communiqué with a similar one, as well as to tell Hanoi that, if there were differences in the text, the British text was authoritative.[29] This would be an important distinction, because a difference *did* surface.

Wilson was hopeful that a breakthrough was within reach. Kosygin jubilantly phoned Brezhnev in Moscow: "There's a great possibility of achieving the aim, if the Vietnamese will understand the present situation that we have passed them. They will have to decide."[30] The meetings being held in Washington, DC, while Wilson's were taking place in London, had a very different atmosphere. Secretary of Defense Robert McNamara and John McNaughton, the assistant secretary of defense for international security affairs, wanted to push for talks and seemed willing to forgo additional US bombing, but Rostow and the head of the JCS, General Earl Wheeler, insisted that the bombing was "indispensable," because, from what they saw, it was reducing infiltration from North Vietnam. Rusk simply said that it was time Hanoi made the next concession. It was like a bad game of telephone,[31] with completely different realities ending up on each side of the Atlantic.[32]

LBJ sent a personal letter to Ho Chi Minh, which was delivered on February 8, and the game of telephone got worse. The president and his advisors changed the draft language in the president's communiqué from future to past tense.[33] Wilson and Kosygin's version said that the Americans would stop the bombing of North Vietnam if the North Vietnamese promised to talk and *would* stop their infiltration at the same time as the Americans ended any additional troop deployment. The president's letter to Ho stipulated that the US would stop all bombing of North Vietnam once the North Vietnamese *had* stopped their infiltration, and *then* the US would ease its troop deployment. The next day, when those in Washington, DC, received the British text, Rostow phoned Prime Minister Wilson immediately with the important change in tense. The new proposed text was retyped and presented to Kosygin at 1:00 am, as he was boarding the night train to Scotland. The rationale the United States gave for insisting on this change was that North Vietnam had three divisions on the border of the demilitarized zone (DMZ), and the Americans were afraid the North Vietnamese would take advantage of the window between the bombing halt and the proposed halt of their infiltrations to pour more "volunteers" into South Vietnam.[34]

While this bartering was going on, Rostow pushed to end the Tet cease-fire and restart the bombing of Hanoi and Haiphong, beginning on February 11.[35] Harold Wilson had proclaimed that to undo the cease-fire's creation of a safe haven in Hanoi and Haiphong while Kosygin was in London, acting in good faith, would be a disaster, and it was only through intense pressure that the reescalation was temporarily called off. It is also possible that the president had mixed feelings about the effort, but LBJ was being told by Rostow that Wilson's chances of success hung at about five percent.

On February 12, the State Department cabled Thompson to inform him of the London efforts, on the assumption that Kosygin would be likely to call for him "for follow-up dealings with the Soviets," as well as to warn Thompson of the changed language in the proposal and Wilson's displeasure at the resultant situation. That same day, Wilson made one last attempt to broker some kind of agreement. He proposed that the North Vietnamese promise to keep their divisions above the South Vietnamese border, in exchange for a continuance of the Tet cease-fire through February 17. Rostow and the military disagreed with Rusk and McNamara over this latest proposal, too. In the end, their compromise was to approve the idea, but to demand that North Vietnam accept by 10:00 a.m. the next morning. This ultimatum was delivered to Kosygin in the wee hours of the morning, leaving no time to implement it.[36] Needless to say it, Sunflower, like Marigold, also failed.

The State Department wanted Thompson to take over from Guthrie, his deputy chief of mission, as the messenger to the North Vietnamese. The ambassador objected, saying that this activity would surely get out publicly and therefore give too much attention to what he believed was a supposedly secret, very long shot. So on February 15, it was Guthrie who received Ho's response to LBJ's February 8 letter, which amounted to a recapitulation of Ho's grievances, with Chang informing Guthrie that he could no longer meet with him.[37] In March, Hanoi made both Johnson's pen-pal letter and Ho's reply public.

Even if the Americans' expectations for these feelers were low, and LBJ was ambivalent about them, the failed attempt created residual harm. It was a blow to Harold Wilson, but it was an even bigger wallop to Kosygin. According to Dobrynin's memoirs, Brezhnev was unhappy that Kosygin had gotten involved. Kosygin would be quoted as saying that his intervention in London provoked "fury" in Peking, and that the Chinese had been the winners in the end, when his efforts failed.[38] Thompson had thought that the best opportunity for reaching an understanding in Vietnam would be with Kosygin.[39] The indication that the United States would accept "almost any step" by the North Vietnamese, and Harold Wilson's overtures presenting an American Phase A–Phase B approach, had persuaded Kosygin to put his neck out and act as a broker for peace. Kosygin could easily have seen the whole affair—miscommunication with Wilson, the switch in the proposal's text, and the ludicrous 10 a.m. deadline for a response by the North Vietnamese—as a set-up. On February 17, Thompson attended an event during which Kosygin's interpreter quipped, "That was quite a switch you pulled on us in the text of your proposal."[40] So this was Kosygin's mood when Thompson finally met with him on February 18.

An Audience with Kosygin

Thompson's meeting with Kosygin lasted for two hours. He found the Soviet to be businesslike and "vaguely positive," but unfortunately Thompson himself got off on the wrong foot. It had been nearly three months after a breakthrough with Dobrynin on the prospect of the United States and the USSR limiting their nuclear weapons. Kosygin had indicated that the Soviets were interested in talks, yet the Americans had been unable to pin him down to a date. Thompson opened the meeting by stating that his government hoped to forestall a renewed arms race in ABMs and ICBM delivery vehicles.[41] He said if the United States had to install an ABM system, it surely could, but that if both of their countries installed ABM systems, they'd "be where they had started from in terms of their security." The Americans had developed a good system, but they wanted to avoid installing it, believing it to be destabilizing. Kosygin misinterpreted Thompson's statement as being competitive, and he declared that any serious discussions to curb such expenditures would have to be "without any comparison of [our] respective systems." Thompson tried to explain that he had not intended to do so; after all, he had no detailed knowledge of the Soviet system. He merely wished to make sure that the Soviets knew that the United States was not proposing an agreement simply because it was not capable of installing its own ABM system. Kosygin finally agreed, but added that Thompson's "tone" smelled of an ultimatum. The ambassador then apologized for giving him the wrong impression. To Thompson's relief, this seemed to satisfy Kosygin, who said that if he and Thompson were to pursue this issue, the discussion could go far. Kosygin wished to assure LBJ that any delay in responding to the president's message was not due to the Soviets "underestimating" the proposal, but rather to a need for enough time to consider it seriously.

When the London talks on Vietnam came up, Thompson could not mention what he had written to the State Department, which was that he found it difficult to explain why concerns over troop movements across the border didn't apply to both sides. Instead, he noted that the change in the US formula in London was due to stepped-up North Vietnamese infiltrations during the Tet holiday cease-fire.[42] Thompson could not have known that these claims were dubious at best and were never confirmed by the Pentagon.[43] He expressed the Johnson administration's disappointment that US offers to negotiate at "any place, any time" had been rejected by North Vietnam. Kosygin explained he could not represent Vietnam and could only offer his personal view, which he did at some length.[44] The Vietnamese, he began, had, *for the first time*, stated plainly that they were ready to negotiate if the bombings stopped, a position Kosygin had supported publicly when he was in London. Yet the Americans persisted in increasing the number of their troops and the bombing of North Vietnam. The Americans complained of "infiltration" and outside interference in South Vietnam, yet what were they doing but interfering in a sovereign state? And on it went.

Thompson conveyed the president's sincere desire to solve problems between the United States and the USSR. He reported back to Washington that he told Kosygin, "I did not wish to be immodest and I did not know how much I could contribute to this objective, but I had come here in hope that I could make some contribution." Kosygin closed the meeting by saying that was exactly how Soviets had understood Thompson's appointment. They regarded it as a serious step by LBJ, reflecting his desire for improved relations.[45] Thompson breathed a sigh of relief as he stepped out into the freezing Moscow air. Returning to the chancellery on Tchaikovsky Street, Thompson wrote three cables about his meeting with Kosygin and sent them, plus a cover note, to Rostow.[46] He remarked in one of his cables that any escalation of the US bombing would make it more difficult for Kosygin to get support for pressing Hanoi to a political settlement. He also noted the British ambassador's view that Kosygin had probably gone beyond what was expected, and that may have caused the Soviet to have "trouble with his colleagues." Thompson went on to advocate for a continuation of the moratorium on bombing Hanoi and, especially, Haiphong. He warned those in Washington, DC, that this would result in a hardening of the Soviets' position and lead them to think the US was "prepared to throw the North Vietnamese into Chinese arms with all that would imply."[47] Rostow took the memos to LBJ, with his own summary on top. He characterized Kosygin's long invective on Vietnam simply as "Kosygin moves us not an inch forward," but at least Rostow did suggest that the president read Thompson's account from the point of view of revealing the "Soviet mind." There's no way of knowing, however, if LBJ did so.

Thompson was not aware that the day before his meeting with Kosygin, Rostow had prepared a paper for the president advocating a strategy of mining the North Vietnamese harbors and bombing the rail line between Hanoi and China, among other things, as a means of "narrowing the top of the funnel" for supplies into South Vietnam.[48] Rostow went so far as to claim it "might force an early negotiated end to the war by creating a crisis so severe for everyone on the other end that they would have to decide either to end the war or to undertake extremely risky or undesirable courses of action."

Thompson had already been on record as opposing Rostow's conclusions.[49] He wrote repeatedly in his memos to the secretary and the undersecretary of state that mining Haiphong harbor—since those mines could hit a Soviet ship—and bombing the area around Hanoi were bad ideas. North Vietnam had kept China at arm's length, but, Thompson said, if the United States succeeded in destroying North Vietnam's airfields and harbor, the North Vietnamese would be forced to turn to China for assistance. This would give China much greater influence, and—since it appeared to be in that country's interest to keep the Vietnam War going—such actions, he concluded, would actually reduce the chances of a settlement. Sunflower's failure ushered in a new era of violence in Vietnam, including such "firsts" as firing across the DMZ into North Vietnam; shelling supply routes, using warships, without restriction; mining North Vietnamese rivers; and bombing major industrial plants.[50]

Arms Talks

True to his word, Kosygin answered the president's pen-pal letter on the possibility of arms talks ten days after his meeting with Thompson. Early on Tuesday morning, February 28, Gromyko handed Thompson Kosygin's written reply. Gromyko also made an oral statement, in which he went on at some length to challenge what, as the Soviets saw it, was the US approach to arms negotiations, which was based on a premise of preserving the current "most stable" strategic position.[51] Thompson expressed this, in one of his cables that same day, as the unwillingness of the Soviets to freeze their inferior position, "which we [the United States] have publicly boasted is in our favor." Gromyko then lamented that such "stability" creates a practice where each party is compelled to react to one side by trying to strengthen its defensive capacity with an increase in offensive capability, which in turn spurs the other side to move up in the spiral of the arms race. The way out of this "vicious circle" would be to seek equal security for each side, not to try to solidify some advantage.

Thompson, in his interpretation of the meeting, wrote to Rusk that he thought the Soviets' statement was an effort to establish a negotiating position, not an attempt to avoid serious discussions. He then offered some solutions on how to equalize the two very different nuclear arsenals, such as allowing the Soviets to keep their limited ABM Galosh system, while the United States maintained a larger number of hardened ICBM sites. Both countries could also continue to improve the quality of their missiles. This premise would not preclude the development of MIRVS, which would appeal to the JCS, while allowing the Soviets to finish construction of the missiles in their pipeline, which would appeal to them. He concluded by saying the best way to expedite any agreement would be to present a concrete proposal. Thompson's analysis of his meeting with Gromyko was not included in Rostow's package for the president. It is not known if this was because Rusk didn't include it, or because Rostow withheld it.

Kosygin's formal written reply to LBJ agreed to an exchange of views on limiting strategic arms, possibly followed by bilateral talks, but only if the discussions included both offensive and defensive weapons. He qualified this further by noting that the "world situation" (and in this he cited specifically Vietnam) was not conducive to productive talks, and he pointedly challenged LBJ to put his actions where his words were in terms of returning "peace to the planet." This last part was ignored in Rostow's summary, which simply stated that "they are willing to talk; but leave the ball in our court for the first move." Thompson was a little annoyed at what he recognized as a typical Soviet attempt, when negotiating, to put a counterpart on the defensive. Kosygin knew full well that the United States was prepared to discuss both offensive and defensive weapons. Thompson suspected that Kosygin's "churlishness" was because he was being forced to acknowledge America's strategic superiority, and that any agreement with the United States would put Kosygin in disagreement with his military.[52]

Thompson was selected to be the chairman of the US delegation for the talks, which were slated to begin in Moscow, with expert support sent there as needed. Raymond Garthoff was chosen to represent the State Department, and by this time, the JCS and the full arms control bureaucracy were in the loop.[53] The Soviets would continue to resist being pinned down to specific dates. The Americans were not prepared to talk, either, because there was still no consensus among them as to a "hoped-for outcome."[54] Thompson's queries about when talks could start were mostly ignored or responded to with excuses. More time was needed to "study so complex a problem." At the same time, the Soviets made it clear that US actions in Vietnam were making the possibility of arms talks more difficult.

Other Complexities

As if the road to an arms control agreement wasn't arduous enough, at this point Svetlana Alliluyeva, Stalin's daughter—with a book manuscript in hand—defected to the United

States. The gleeful American press could not get enough of her. Thompson wrote to Rusk that the "more we can disengage from this operation the better." He also sent a letter to Bohlen, observing that "Uncle Joe must be stirring in his can to think that he had produced a religious, non-Communist, pro-Indian."[55]

Then there was Richard Nixon's forthcoming visit. Nixon decided to stop in Moscow in late March 1967, on his way to Saigon. He was planning to run for president and was visiting as a private citizen. He had hoped to meet with the Soviet leadership, but the Soviets snubbed him, no doubt because of his itinerary, as well as his past anti-Soviet rhetoric. Nonetheless, Nixon was undeterred. He even hatched a plan try to see Khrushchev again, since he had not succeeded in seeing the deposed Soviet leader during a 1965 trip.[56] Thompson thought this was a terrible idea and did his best to dissuade the former vice president. As part of that effort, he kept Nixon occupied with tourist trips to other Soviet cities, press conferences, and receptions.[57]

After the Nixon visit, Thompson left for West Germany, for a meeting in Bonn, while Jane took houseguests to Leningrad. She wrote to her mother that "Vietnam has put a damper on things at the moment," and that she was looking forward to her two younger children coming to Moscow soon.[58] Back in Washington, DC, the girls had their own difficulties. They were running out of money, what with vaccines and visas and Jenny's college application fees. Jane joined Thompson in Paris after their respective trips, in order to visit the Bohlens. Returning to Moscow's dreary conditions was painful after having enjoyed spring in Paris. In Moscow the detritus of winter was emerging layer by layer, while in Paris the flowers and the lovers were already out of hibernation.

Attempts to Resurrect Sunflower

LBJ tried—but failed—to renew the Sunflower peace initiative that spring. He asked Thompson to see the North Vietnamese ambassador, but Thompson was told that they did not want to communicate with him. In early April, the president sent a new letter to Ho Chi Minh, through Thompson. The letter was delivered, but it was returned the next day, opened but unanswered, with the original envelope bearing the words "*Non Conforme! Retour à l'Expéditeur*" (Faulty! Return to Sender). Officials in Washington, DC, then instructed Thompson to seek out Gromyko and try to renew the Soviets' intermediary role, but Gromyko declined and said the Americans should address themselves directly to the North Vietnamese.[59]

Thompson advised LBJ against sending a pen-pal letter to Kosygin on the subject.[60] His analysis was that the North Vietnamese position had hardened. They were less concerned with China's instability during its Cultural Revolution than they had been in January.[61] Thompson warned that the one new proposal in LBJ's letter, a joint US-USSR guarantee of stability in Vietnam after a peace settlement, was extremely risky. "The idea of the two superpowers jointly running the world has great appeal to the Soviets, but I question it as US policy." Thompson found it "appalling" that, "if we ever get out of this mess," the United States might risk being sucked back into the morass in Vietnam by promising to guarantee its peace.

Even if the Soviets agreed to get involved, which he doubted, they would insist on a concrete proposal for settlement before relaying it to Hanoi, and the Americans did not yet have a clear position on the crucial role of the Viet Cong. Thompson argued that approaching the Soviets at the present time could jeopardize later, timelier (and potentially fruitful) attempts, because an inflexible Soviet response now would, therefore, already be on the record. He seemed angry about the letter's content, but possibly he was even more incensed because it was scheduled to be delivered just prior to another planned acceleration of US actions in Vietnam. The Soviets, wrote Thompson, were half convinced that the American peace moves were a cover for escalation, and, "by coincidence," they had a fairly impressive case. An increase in the bombing of North Vietnam, coinciding or following shortly after the proposed pen-pal letter to Kosygin, would only serve to "complete the job."

The Johnson administration tried to revive Sunflower a third time, using the upcoming visit of George Brown, the British secretary of state for foreign affairs, to Moscow. In reaction, on April 19, Thompson sent an impassioned cable back to Washington, DC, in which he urged (nearly pleaded) that the United States consider suspending peace moves that had little chance of success, especially those involving the Soviets, as this was "positively harmful."[62] A revival of Sunflower was primarily aimed at the president's domestic political agenda, which would not bear enough fruit to warrant the risks. The USSR and the United States already knew each other's respective positions, and such attempts only added to the Soviets' suspicions of the Americans' sincerity. The North Vietnamese could not withdraw as long as the Viet Cong in South Vietnam were still resolute. Continued US bombing of North Vietnam did nothing to change that. Thompson closed with, "*It is against the foregoing background* [emphasis added] that I would suggest that rather than have George Brown make peace noises when he comes to Moscow, he should convey to [the] Soviets a sense of our determination to see this affair through." His tone was professional, but his frustration was evident.

Thompson wrote to Bohlen: "Our combining every peace move with an escalation of the bombing has pretty well convinced these people that we are determined upon a military victory. What action, if any, they will take, I cannot predict, but I feel uneasy."[63] He could not know that his entire argument to the State Department was neutralized by one of Rostow's little cover notes, which simply stated: "This telegram from Tommy Thompson will interest you, notably the last paragraph [advising Brown to convey a US determination to see the war through]. You were one jump ahead of your reigning Soviet expert."[64] In late April, Dobrynin visited Spaso House and assured Thompson the Soviets were still considering arms talks, but this possibility was adversely affected by US escalations in Vietnam.[65]

Eugene Rostow Enters the Mix

In May 1967, Thompson had a disagreement with the other Rostow brother, Undersecretary of State for Political Affairs Eugene Rostow. Although they agreed that the war in Vietnam posed a threat to US-Soviet relations, Gene Rostow believed that the Americans should follow a course he claimed had solved all postwar problems thus far.[66] According to him, the beginning of the end in the Korean War started with a warning issued by George Kennan to his Soviet counterpart at that time. Rostow believed that the United States ought to warn the Soviets that the present course could "get out of hand" and then offer to jointly bring the affair to an end, revealing the notion that the two superpowers could and should be in control.

Thompson was friendly enough with Gene Rostow and wrote back immediately.[67] He pointed out differences between the situations in Korea and Vietnam, including their respective relationships with China and the Soviet Union. The Soviet objective, Thompson surmised, was a North and a South Vietnam that were not dominated by China. When American peace moves coincided with escalations, the Soviet inferred that one of the US motives was to aggravate the Soviets' quarrel with China.

As to the idea of serving up a warning followed by an offer, Thompson took up the latter part first. The United States did not have anything new to offer that, "God knows," the Soviets weren't already aware of, except perhaps the idea to jointly guarantee a peace settlement. He did not call the scheme "appalling," as he had in his letter to Rusk, but he did say that the Soviets would not believe the Americans. Besides, the whole proposal posed great difficulties for both countries. For the Soviets, it meant joining with the United States in a move largely directed against China. As for the United States, why should it risk being brought back into the quagmire? Moreover, how could they enforce a peace settlement, when any violation would be very difficult to prove? In Thompson's mind, Rostow was suggesting that the United States agree a priori to guarantee a settlement when it did not yet know what it could contain: "I cringe to think what our position would be on the role of the Viet Cong. Without bringing them into the Government in some way, I think we would be even worse off in world opinion than we are now." He also pointed out the weakness of the current South Vietnamese government, which did not augur well for a long-lasting peace. Furthermore, Thompson was at a loss to come up with an effective formula for a warning that would not be taken as a threat by Moscow. "If there is one thing I have learned about this place," he noted, "it is that they react badly to threats."

Thompson went on, although not in direct response to Rostow, to say that he thought the "most dangerous period will be when we really begin to win." That was when the North Vietnamese would have to decide to come to the table sincerely or "cash the blank check" given to them by the Communist bloc and call for "volunteers." They had not already done so, Thompson asserted, because North Vietnam did not want to be overrun by Chinese volunteers who might not leave voluntarily later. If the rest of the Communist countries came in to help at the same time, however, the North Vietnamese might accept this. Thompson thought the continued increase in bombing had turned the North Vietnamese against any form of negotiating.

Thompson did not believe that either the Soviets or the North Vietnamese held the key to the situation. The definitive factor in achieving peace in Vietnam lay in South Vietnam, with the Viet Cong. He closed his letter with regret that the United States had not ended—or at least eased—its bombing of North Vietnam "some time ago," and with the lament that he wished he could be "more optimistic."

After his debate with Gene Rostow, Thompson wrote to Bohlen that he was leaving on June 1 for consultations in Washington, DC, and would use that trip bring his daughters back to Moscow in mid-June. He hoped to stop in Paris along the way, for some R&R with his friend. Jenny would be attending Moscow University for her senior year in high school, and he'd pulled some strings to get Sherry into the Bolshoi Ballet School for the year. He mentioned that Dobrynin had been back in Moscow for a high-level review of US-Soviet relations and expressed apprehension about which way the Soviets might jump. "Both Averell and Gene Rostow," wrote Thompson, "think this place [Moscow] is the key to the solution of the Vietnam problem," but he doubted it.[68] What worried him most was that he had seen "no indication that we have made up our minds what our position on negotiations would be."

Continuing the Bombing

Late in the evening of May 18, a cable arrived from William Bundy, Walt Rostow, and McNamara that seemed to suggest at first that perhaps those in Washington, DC, were listening.[69] The Johnson administration was considering confining the bombing of North Vietnam to supply routes south of the twentieth parallel. They wondered if Thompson might disclose this new bombing protocol privately to the Soviets. Perhaps, "not too far in the future," the Soviets could act on this knowledge. They wondered if Thompson might take this possibility to Gromyko, or perhaps directly to Kosygin. But no, they hadn't really heard Thompson after all. The cable went on to say that there would be a major strike against the main Hanoi power station prior to this new bombing regimen going into effect, and that it could be carried out that very night. They also wanted to include "some loophole in terms of possible continuing attacks to the north." Would Thompson give it his immediate attention and thought? The next day, Thompson lunched with Dobrynin, who said he heard that there was another raid on Hanoi. Kosygin's statements in London to the effect that Hanoi would come to the negotiating table if the United States stopped its bombing were "not made out of thin air," insisted Dobrynin, who was astonished that the United States had resumed its bombing above the twentieth parallel in North Vietnam.[70]

On May 19, the collective at the State Department, the White House, and the DOD sent a draft for a new pen-pal letter from LBJ to Kosygin via Thompson in Moscow.[71] Thompson must have been crestfallen by the rebuking tone of the letter. It did not say anything about new bombing protocols, but it contained a litany of grievances about North Vietnam and again challenged Kosygin, as co-chairman of the Geneva Accords, to bring about an end to the conflict. The letter went on to complain about the Middle East, calling on Kosygin to restrain Syria, and bemoaned Cuban interference in Latin America. It then declared that "there are two areas of opportunity where I deeply believe it is our common interest and common duty to humanity," which were to schedule ABM and ICBM talks and to negotiate a nonproliferation treaty. In that telegram, they also alerted Thompson that at least one more strike was planned for the Hanoi power plant.

Thompson answered the State Department on May 20 with great restraint.[72] He asked, "Could we not at least add a sentence to [the paragraph on Vietnam] that might read, 'for our part, we are currently giving urgent consideration to what steps we could take unilaterally to reduce the danger of widening the conflict and hopefully to initiate a reciprocal reduction of violence'?" Although Thompson never liked sending a suggestion of a peace move under the cloud of an impending new strike on Hanoi, he commented that if the latest pen-pal letter had to be delivered, it should contain some glimmer of a promise. He ended his very short response by proposing that the State Department not refer to Gromyko as "Mister" but as Foreign Minister.

The White House group didn't like the use of the word "unilateral," even though they had included it themselves in their earlier instructions to Guthrie. Rostow maintained in his cover note to Thompson's reply that they *had* in fact hinted "between the lines" that the Americans were preparing for an "interval of diminished bombing in Hanoi-Haiphong."[73] Moreover, he alleged, a "careful reading" of the letter by Gromyko would reveal this. This secret code, so to speak, was to be delivered via a sentence that read, "We have been disappointed in this lack of response [to the previous bombing restraint] and will try to probe the possibility further," and by an oral statement Thompson was instructed to deliver, saying that his "government is currently giving further consideration to steps which we might take to reduce the danger of widening the conflict," without the word "unilateral" appearing in either this statement or in the letter itself.

In the middle of all this, the CIA came out with two intelligence reports plainly stating that the US bombing campaign in North Vietnam was not having a deterrent effect, and that enlarging the scope of the bombing was unlikely to "weaken the military establishment [of North Vietnam] seriously or to prevent Hanoi from continuing its aggression in the south."[74]

Johnson's letter to Kosygin was delivered to the Soviet embassy in Washington, DC, late on Saturday, May 27, along with a message asking that it be transmitted to Moscow that night. This would diminish the oral statement about the change in bombing protocol that Thompson was to deliver to Gromyko the next morning. Thompson presumably carried out his instructions to deliver this letter, but there is no record that he ever saw Gromyko that Sunday.

A cable from Saigon (copied to the US embassy in Moscow) suggested that some signal for deescalation had been made by the Vietnamese. Thompson thought it was worth making a gesture to reduce the violence, to see if the signal was real.[75] So he sent one last cable from Moscow to that effect before heading to Washington, DC. Events in the Middle East were intensifying, and Thompson thought they would need the Soviets' cooperation to keep a crisis from igniting. Progress in Vietnam might help. Although it was surprisingly cool in the capital in early June 1967, the situation in the Middle East had heated up and was about to interrupt everything.

35

The Six-Day War
Hotline Diplomacy

Powerful as the United States is, it can't quite dictate to the
rest of the planet. Other countries guard their sovereignty
as jealously as we do, rarely see completely eye to eye with
us, and try to go their own way as far as they can or dare,
which is sometimes pretty far from what we would like.
—EDWARD P. MORGAN, radio address,
  January 12, 1967

Thompson planned to be in Washington, DC, for two weeks to review the United
States' Vietnam policy and US-USSR relations. Instead, he found himself embroiled
in another crisis, the Six-Day War between Israel and the United Arab Republic,
which broke out just as he reached the capital.[1] He spent the better part of the next week in
the Situation Room, a "bleak beige" room in the basement of the White House, "furnished
simply with an oval conference table and an assortment of comfortable chairs."[2]

Clashes between Israeli troops and Palestinian and Arab forces in both Jordan and Syria
were increasing.[3] One such incident turned into a major battle, with the Israelis shooting
down six Syrian MIG fighters over the Golan Heights, on the border between Israel and
Syria.[4] The Soviets, who had strong ties to the new left-wing regime in Damascus, suspected
that this was part of a Western plan to undermine Moscow's position in the region.

On May 13, 1967, the Soviets sent the UAR's president, Gamal Abdel Nasser, false secret information that Israel had amassed troops on the Syrian border. As the Soviets had
hoped, this intelligence induced Nasser to make a security pledge to Syria, as well as to
concentrate his own forces in the Sinai Peninsula and expel the UN peacekeeping forces
there. The Kremlin thought that Israel could not cope with a war on two fronts and hoped
that this move would keep Israel in line. The problem with meddling by superpowers,
though, is that they cannot control every event. The Soviets did not anticipate that Nasser
would close the Straits of Tiran, preventing Israeli shipping from reaching or leaving their
port of Eilat, on the southernmost tip of the country, and giving Israel a casus belli. On

May 21, diplomatic tensions were extreme. Not wanting to get into another armed conflict, LBJ condemned the UAR blockade but encouraged that country to solve the conflict diplomatically. On May 30, Jordan also signed a mutual defense treaty with the UAR, further complicating the situation.

Before arriving in Washington, DC, Thompson had written an assessment of the Soviet position in the Middle East crisis, stating that even if the Israelis should clobber their Arab neighbors, the Soviets might calculate that the hatred this would engender for the West would enable them [the Soviets] to reestablish their position in the Arab world."[5] He was convinced, however, the Soviets "did not want to become militarily physically involved in a Middle East war." Although they were probably not against the UAR action that had stirred up trouble in the region, he doubted that it included wanting to see the Straits of Tiran closed.

Nevertheless, events propelled the USSR into a dangerous role in the conflict. The situation was made even more uneasy by the presence of both American and Soviet fleets in the Mediterranean Sea. The hotline between the two powers kept both apprised of the maneuvers of their respective fleets.[6] Dobrynin said in his memoirs that the hotline played an "invaluable role," "preventing each side's perception of the other's intentions from becoming dangerously uncertain to a point that might precipitate rash acts."[7]

LBJ met with Israeli Foreign Minister Abba Eban in Washington, DC, in late May, urging him not to take action against UAR forces with a preemptive strike, but the United States could not control events, either. On June 5, 1967, Israel attacked.[8] By June 11, Israel

The Situation Room in the White House, Washington, DC, during the Six-Day War, 1967. *From left to right*, Robert McNamara, Nicholas Katzenbach, Llewellyn Thompson Jr., Walt Rostow, Hubert Humphrey, Dean Rusk (*seated*), Lyndon Johnson, and McGeorge Bundy. Lyndon Baines Johnson Library, A4235-9, photo by Yoichi Okamoto.

controlled the Sinai Peninsula, the Golan Heights, the West Bank, the Gaza Strip, and Jerusalem. Their rapid victory shocked the Soviets as much as the Arabs.[9]

The Hotline

After the Cuban Missile Crisis, the United States and the USSR implemented a hotline, which the Republican Party had criticized during the 1964 presidential campaign for being too accommodating to the Soviets. Contrary to popular impressions, the hotline was not a red telephone, but twin teletype machines, located in the Pentagon and under Kosygin's office in the Kremlin.[10] Thompson recalled that in its first trial run in 1963, US officers used the old typing-test sentence, "the quick brown fox jumps over the lazy dog," because it employs every letter of the English alphabet, but when it arrived at the Moscow end, it caused consternation. The Soviet operator, who had never heard the expression, wondered who was the dog and who was the fox. Was the Soviet Union being called a dog?[11]

At 4:30 a.m. on June 5, LBJ received a phone call from Walt Rostow with the news that the Middle East had erupted in a hot war. The president rounded up other advisors, including Thompson and Rusk.[12] After conferring with LBJ and his colleagues, Rusk sent a presidential statement to Gromyko. The secretary of state wrote that LBJ was "distressed about the outbreak of the fighting," and that "a very high-level delegation" was due in Washington, DC, that Wednesday. He also said, "We had assurances from the Israelis that they would not initiate hostilities pending further diplomatic efforts."[13]

About three hours later, Kosygin sent a message on the hotline, the first time it was officially used by the Soviets. The Soviet teletype operators were so alarmed at seeing Kosygin, Gromyko, and the head of the Soviet Communist Party, Yuri Andropov, in the transmission room that their hands were shaking as they typed.[14] At the Pentagon, the duty officer phoned his boss, Defense Secretary McNamara. McNamara, who did not know the hotline actually terminated in the Pentagon, asked, "Why are you calling me?" He remembered telling the caller, " 'General we are spending'—at that time I think it was about forty billion dollars a year. 'Can't you take a few thousand of those dollars and get these goddamn lines patched across the river to the White House? You call the Situation Room and I'll call the president and we'll decide what to do.' "[15]

Kosygin's message was brief and to the point.[16] The Soviet government, he said, was convinced that "the duty of all great powers is to secure the immediate cessation of the military conflict" between Israel and the UAR. Kosygin wanted to know "whether President Johnson is standing by the [transmitting] machine." Since LBJ was not there, they asked the Soviets to wait until he arrived. When the president got to the Situation Room, he dictated his own reply to Kosygin, via telephone, to the Pentagon teletypes. LBJ reiterated what Rusk had transmitted to Gromyko and added that he would "strongly support" any action in the UN Security Council to end the hostilities. He also noted, "We are pleased to learn from your message that you are doing the same."

After the president's message was given to the teletype operators, Thompson asked them to bring back the text exactly as it had gone out. To his astonishment, it was addressed to "Comrade Kosygin."[17] It turned out that during a testing period, one of the American operators had asked his Soviet counterpart on the other end of the line how to address the Chairman of the Council of Ministers. He had replied, "Comrade Kosygin," so that is how the first message was addressed. Dobrynin, on the Moscow end of the line, admitted to Thompson that he was startled by the greeting, and some had wondered if the president was making fun of them in some way. Fortunately, Dobrynin guessed what had happened.

It was still dark the next morning when Thompson was called back to the Situation Room. The place was already buzzing with phone calls. While the US contingent met, Kosygin and the entire Politburo remained in session.[18] At around 5:30 a.m. on June 6, Kosygin was on the hotline again. The Soviets had actually wanted to send the message even earlier, until Dobrynin pointed out what the hour was in the Washington, DC. Thompson later suggested to Dobrynin that perhaps they "might keep this time differential in mind" the next time they called.[19] Alarmed by the rate at which Israel was gaining ground in the war, Kosygin's new message insisted that both the United States and the USSR issue Israel a "decisive demand" to withdraw its troops to prewar armistice lines. He also implored that "everything possible should be done" to ensure that the Security Council took "a positive decision" when it met that day.[20]

LBJ went over this letter with the men in the Situation Room. In his reply, the president reminded Kosygin of Eisenhower's 1957 commitment to maintain international access through the Straits of Tiran and said he hoped that the resolution submitted by both the US ambassador to the UN, Arthur Goldberg, and the Soviets' UN ambassador, Nikolai Federenko, would be supported in the Security Council. The key passage, LBJ said, was that the resolution called "for an immediate cease-fire and prompt withdrawal . . . behind the Armistice Lines."[21] Kosygin did not reply to this message for more than eight hours, during which time a very important development took place.

Soviet Slipup

When Goldberg and Federenko met privately at the UN on June 6, they discussed the wording of the resolution, with Federenko wanting certain clarifications. Israel was "frigid" toward the wording. They just wanted a simple cease-fire. In the ensuing meetings between the various representatives, Federenko, perhaps by mistake, agreed to a simple cease-fire, not a cease-fire *and* a withdrawal. The men in the Situation Room, Thompson recalled, were "surprised" and "elated" by what Federenko had done.[22] They discussed whether they should take advantage of his mistake or stick to the message sent in the morning, which included a withdrawal. Everybody agreed to "take advantage of what had happened in New York."

When Kosygin's response arrived that evening, Thompson was in the Situation Room. The message stated that "we have issued the necessary instructions to the Soviet Representative in the Security Council," and Kosygin hoped LBJ would give his UN ambassador "corresponding instructions" to support the resolution for a cease-fire and a withdrawal of troops.[23] Kosygin was trying to undo what Federenko had done and introduce withdrawal back into the resolution. But the die had been cast, and LBJ wrote back: "Our two ambassadors . . . agreed to a very short resolution calling for a cease-fire as a first step. We authorized our representative to agree on behalf of the United States Government. The Security Council has just adopted this resolution unanimously."[24]

The next day, June 7, the fighting went on, despite the cease-fire agreement, and Israel continued to gain ground. This time, Kosygin used the hotline to complain that "Israel is ignoring" the UN resolution. LBJ assured him that the United States was taking steps to see that all sides implemented the resolution, and he agreed to another meeting of the Security Council.[25]

USS Liberty

A further complication occurred the following day. The Israelis torpedoed and strafed an American ship, the USS *Liberty*, which was collecting radio-signal intelligence off the Sinai coast of the UAR. Thirty-four Americans were killed and 171 wounded. There was total confusion and, at first, no one really knew who had attacked the *Liberty*. The crew believed it was an attack by the UAR, and LBJ thought it was the Soviets. Clarification came in a few hours. It had been a "mistaken" attack by Israel. Johnson sent a hotline message to alert Kosygin that he was sending an aircraft carrier from the US Navy's Sixth Fleet to investigate, as well as to rescue the American crew members. Had the hotline not been used, the Soviets might have thought the Americans were getting directly involved in the war. Thompson thought "we were using it [the hotline] in the right way, to prevent a danger of war arising out of misunderstanding." He also said the use of the hotline had made a "big impression" on the Soviets.[26]

Many, including Rusk, did not believe the attack had been an error, but the president, for political reasons, did not want to make an issue of it and accepted the Israeli apologies.[27] Garthoff recalled that all of the senior intelligence and US Navy personnel concluded that it was a deliberate attack.[28] He speculated that the *Liberty* had intercepted faked communications by Israel, to make it appear as though the UAR was encouraging Jordan to enter the war. It would not look good for Israelis if they were revealed as the ones trying to enlarge the war by involving the Jordanians.[29] There are other theories as to why the attack on the USS *Liberty* occurred, and, although both the United States and Israel conducted investigations, many questions still remain.[30]

Conflict Turns to Crisis

Friday, June 9, was the only day out of the six with no hotline communiqués, although there were plenty of events going on. One problem arose when thousands of Palestinian refugees fled from the West Bank to the East Bank in Jordan. In addition, Israel did not seem to be supporting the UN effort for a cease-fire on the Syrian front.[31]

Thompson recalled that the tensest day of the crisis was June 10, "a time of great concern and utmost gravity."[32] He was in the Situation Room, along with other LBJ advisors, and the president was having breakfast when another message from Kosygin arrived over the hotline. Israel, he said, was still ignoring the resolution for a cease-fire, and "a very crucial moment" had arrived.[33] If military action against Syria did not stop in the next few hours, Kosygin warned, independent actions could bring about a clash between the two superpowers, which would lead to "a grave catastrophe." The message ended by saying that "necessary actions will be taken, including military," if Israel did not stop its advance into Syria.[34] Alarmed, Thompson checked the Russian wording in the original Soviet transmission and confirmed that it really used the word "military."[35]

Katzenbach departed for the Israeli embassy to exert US pressure for a cease-fire, while those who remained in the Situation Room tried to find out what was actually happening in Syria.[36] Since both Syria and UAR had severed diplomatic relations with the United States, their information was limited. CIA chief Richard Helms was asked to verify whether it was true that the Israelis were "smashing ahead," as the Soviets claimed. The feeling in the situation room was that they were. Helms tried to reach friendly diplomatic missions that were still open in Damascus to find out what was happening. Thompson voiced a concern that the Soviets might suspect that America intended "to knock off the Syrian government" and remarked that he was impressed how much greater the Soviets' sensitivity was to the plight of the Syrians than to that of those in the UAR. After the crisis ended, Thompson said some US officials had speculated that they should have let the Israelis move on to Damascus, since "it was clear the Israelis could have done so," although he added that this was "strictly a post mortem" comment.

The situation was clearly dangerous, since the Soviets were willing to use force in support of their Syrian allies if Israel did not stop its advance. LBJ pushed his breakfast aside and left the room. Thompson, McNamara, and Helms remained seated around the table. The tension in the room was as "taut as a violin string," and their voices "were so low we might have been talking in whispers."[37] "There was something uniquely awesome about the moment a fateful decision is made," Helms recalled. McNamara suggested that they could send the Sixth Fleet closer to the war areas, and Thompson agreed. Moscow would understand this decision signaled that the United States would not back down in the face of Soviet threats, and the unpublicized movements would allow Kosygin to lower tensions without embarrassment to the Soviets. When the president returned, he agreed to their plan, and McNamara phoned the Pentagon.[38]

Those in the Situation Room speculated about whether Kosygin was just testing US resolve with his threat of military action. If the Americans' reply was too polite, it might make the United States seem weak. Thompson, trying to deflect a strident reply, declared that the president was a man who did not answer threats with threats, but who "kept his cool."[39] In the end, LBJ sent Kosygin a "calm and reasoned message." Israel had assured the United States that it "fully intended to achieve [an] actual cease-fire" with Syria, and that the Israelis had told Walworth Barbour, the US ambassador in Israel, that they believed the firing had just stopped.[40]

Kosygin answered back almost immediately, stating that this was not so. Israel was "employing all types of weapons"—aviation, artillery, and tanks—in their military offensive toward Damascus.[41] It was imperative that the president do everything in his power to stop it, as "the matter cannot be postponed." LBJ hotlined back that the United States had "categorical assurances from Israel that there is no Israeli advance on Damascus."[42] Fortunately, just at that time, the Israelis began to respect the cease-fire, and the crisis ended.[43]

Related Events

June 10 was also the day when the Soviets broke diplomatic relations with Israel.[44] Dobrynin recalled that "it was an emotional step," and, in the long run, was a mistake, as it practically excluded the Soviets from any role in a Middle East settlement.[45]

On June 13, with the immediate crisis over, Thompson and LBJ managed to talk for twenty minutes, discussing US-USSR relations. LBJ had told Thompson to join him for the president's regular Tuesday lunch (where LBJ reputedly got most of his actual business done). After lunch, Thompson held a press conference, where he managed to avoid saying much except that if the Vietnam situation were resolved, it would be easier to have bilateral relations with the Soviets. He also mentioned that no specific date had been set for the ABM talks. Thompson told the reporters he was leaving for Moscow as planned, taking his children with him, but that was not to be. The Soviets had called for an emergency meeting of the UN General Assembly to discuss the Middle East crisis.[46]

36 ≡

Glassboro
The Summit That Wasn't (June 23–25, 1967)

I wouldn't want to be quoted on this—but … it turns out,
our guesses were way off. We were doing things we didn't
need to do. We were building things we didn't need to
build. We were harboring fears we didn't need to harbor.
—LYNDON B. JOHNSON, remarks, Nashville, 1967

The Soviets called an Emergency Special Session of the UN General Assembly to deal with the worsening crisis in the Middle East. Kosygin would head the Soviet delegation, opening the possibility of a summit between him and LBJ, which Thompson explored in several meetings with Dobrynin.[1] Thompson was in favor of the meeting. His assessment of Kosygin was that, although a hard-boiled Communist, he was more intelligent and flexible than most of his colleagues, and he would be more inclined than his rivals to support policies favorable to the United States. He had stuck his neck out in London when he met with British Prime Minister Harold Wilson over the Sunflower peace initiative during the Vietnam War (see chapter 34). Thompson thought his initiating a special session at the UN, which was unlikely to succeed, was "probably a gamble on his part that shows considerable courage."[2]

The summit proved to be difficult to arrange because neither LBJ nor Kosygin wished to look like he was the one who wanted it, when both actually did. Thompson was in the middle. "This has been most strenuous," he wrote to his wife, adding that "I work till nine or eleven every night."[3] He went on to tell her that he wouldn't be bringing their two younger daughters back with him, as planned. Frank Wisner's widow, still a close friend, would drive the girls to the airport. They would meet their mother and their older sister Andy in Frankfurt, West Germany, and take the ambassador's plane to Moscow.

Dining alone with Dobrynin on June 19, 1967, Thompson suggested that if Kosygin accepted an invitation to meet with the Senate Foreign Relations Committee, it would be easy for the president to see him. Dobrynin replied that Kosygin had not planned to go to Washington, DC.[4] Thompson noted that their two nations were constantly involved in quarrels between small countries, and it seemed important that they cooperate more closely to maintain the peace. To draw Dobrynin out, Thompson said he was "troubled" in his own mind about a meeting of the two heads of state. Dobrynin stated that he was very much in favor of such a meeting, because it was of the "highest importance" that the two leaders get to know each other personally. Thompson, recalling the Vienna summit between Khrushchev and JFK, confessed that Kennedy used to tease him for having urged him to the summit, as it had not solved any problems. Nonetheless, Thompson said, JFK had always added that it had been useful for him to have met Khrushchev.

McNamara, McGeorge Bundy, Zbigniew Brzezinski, and Walt Rostow all encouraged LBJ to meet Kosygin, and they advised him on what to say and how to say it.[5] McNamara even suggested that one of the pluses of the meeting would be "to improve Thompson's value to [LBJ] and to the United States by emphasizing directly to Kosygin his confidence in him."[6] Thompson suggested that a meeting would be an opportunity to redress the false impression the Soviets had of the president and his policies. He told LBJ that the Soviets assumed the United States was using Israel to take down the Syrian government, and the USSR put Syria in the same category as Vietnam. It was, from their perspective, US expansionism, so they were committed to providing whatever the Arabs needed to bring about an Israeli withdrawal, "either by threat or actual conflict." The world, on the other hand, expected the president to have taken every step possible to prevent another crisis.[7]

Meetings in New Jersey

What no one seemed able to agree on was where the two leaders should meet. Kosygin would not come to Washington, DC, because the Arabs and Chinese would accuse him of using the special UN session in New York City as a pretext for making deals with LBJ behind their backs. The president did not want to go to New York, because he was afraid of encountering antiwar demonstrations, as well as not wanting it to look as if he was the suitor in a meeting with the Soviets. Kosygin would not contemplate going either to Camp David, because Khrushchev had been there, or to McGuire Air Force Base in New Jersey, because of its military nature.[8] He suggested they meet somewhere else, perhaps in a farmer's house.

They settled on a historical mansion, Hollybush, home to the president of Glassboro State College, about equidistant from Washington, DC, and New York City. The stone country cottage, with screened porches framed in white gingerbread trim, was a "simple Victorian residence," but it was transformed overnight to include air conditioning and a massive communications network.[9] The extra furniture was hastily removed and the fridge was restocked. Security arrangements were made, and a nearby gymnasium was turned into a press room. A taping system was not set up, however, so a White House secretary had to eavesdrop to take notes.

On the morning of Friday, June 23, Thompson and other presidential advisors had breakfast with LBJ, after which they boarded a helicopter on the South Lawn of the White House. Thompson, Rusk, McNamara, and Rostow were seated across from the president. LBJ told McNamara to keep former president Eisenhower informed, whereupon they decided that Thompson should go to Ike's home in Gettysburg, Pennsylvania, after the meeting to brief Eisenhower in person.[10]

When the helicopter landed at National Airport (across the Potomac River from downtown Washington, DC), they all transferred to the president's thirteen-passenger Jetstar for the half-hour flight to Philadelphia, where they transferred to yet another helicopter to take them to Glassboro—a complicated trip for such a short distance. The helicopter landed in the athletic field of the college, and everyone followed LBJ off the aircraft. The governor of New Jersey and the college's president, whose house they had turned upside down, met them. A motorcade brought the presidential party through the quiet, tree-lined streets to their Hollybush destination. An enthusiastic crowd was waiting there, cheering when the entourage arrived, although neither they, nor the 850 accredited members of the press who were also there, were really sure what was supposed to happen, except that in some way history was being made.[11]

LBJ waited for Kosygin on the front porch. The president stood chatting with Thompson, keeping his glasses off because the television reporters were covering his every move. Thompson could see LBJ clenching his hands into a fist behind his back and then releasing them again, unsure of just how this hurriedly put together meeting might go. The muggy day did little to lighten everyone's spirits as they waited. McGeorge Bundy joined Thompson and LBJ on the porch, to tell them that the Soviets were stuck in traffic.[12] The president took the time to shake hands with some of those in the crowd before retreating into the house for some antacid pills.

Kosygin finally arrived at 11:22 a.m. The president went out to greet him, and the crowd again applauded enthusiastically as photos were taken. People were not reticent, as they had been when Khrushchev first visited, and they gave Kosygin a warm welcome. De Gaulle had described Kosygin as a "worried looking man," but that day LBJ, too, had a serious mien as both men entered the house. One news account reported that the Soviets visibly relaxed somewhat when they spotted Thompson in the group, and they made a point of warmly "pumping his hand."[13] The two delegations stood around in the conference room for a few minutes and made some preliminary small talk. "How long did it take you to drive here?" "Did you get to see some of the country?" Kosygin mentioned the pollution in New York City, to which the president quipped, "That's why Ambassador Thompson chose to live in Moscow." With the niceties now out of the way, the two men and their respective interpreters adjourned to a private study to meet alone.

Nothing concrete developed, however. The president had hoped to center on what interested him: arms control and Vietnam. Kosygin's trip had been hurriedly arranged, and he had no mandate from the Presidium to make decisions or even take positions on anything—other than the Middle East. During that conversation, LBJ and Kosygin praised each other's ambassadors, and they talked about their families and their yearnings for a more peaceful world. Perhaps this was the best that could come out of that first meeting, with each man making it clear to the other that he had no desire to look for conflict.

The problem, Kosygin said, was that, although both he and LBJ agreed on issues at the global level, problems arose when they discussed practical solutions to specific issues.[14]

Summit conference, Glassboro, New Jersey, June 1967. *From left to right,* Dean Rusk, William Kremer (interpreter), Llewellyn Thompson Jr., Lyndon Johnson, Andrei Gromyko, Alexei Kosygin, and Anatoly Dobrynin. Lyndon Baines Johnson Library, photo by Yoichi Okamoto.

For example, Kosygin, in referring to the Federenko blunder—when the Soviet ambassador had agreed to only a cease-fire in the Arab-Israeli Six-Day War—complained that the Americans and the Soviets had agreed on one thing and then, a few hours later, the wording had shifted radically. The president claimed nothing had changed, and that he still believed in the territorial integrity of all countries.[15] Both stood just shy of accusing the other of not having done enough to prevent the conflict in the first place, but they agreed that the hotline helped to end the immediate crisis. LBJ offered that one way of keeping hostilities down was to disclose weapons shipments to the Middle East, and another was to agree not to furnish arms to either side. Kosygin said he did not think this was realistic at that time.

Kosygin described the Israelis as lined up on one side of the Suez Canal and the Arabs on the other. If Israel did not withdraw, hostilities would surely break out again, as "the Arabs were an explosive people." If they had no weapons, they would "fight with their bare hands" and eventually find someone who would sell them weapons. The Middle East, he said, was in "a state of uproar." In his speech at the UN Special Assembly, he had been careful to make it clear that the Soviet Union had no desire to hurt Israel, but it was unrealistic to think the Arabs would talk to the Israelis until Israel withdrew. LBJ said that mentioning withdrawal immediately raised questions of security for Israel.

The president then tried to steer the discussion to arms limitation talks. He was under pressure, he told Kosygin, to spend over $40 billion to develop an ABM system. He "had not taken a decision as yet" and wanted "to explore all possibilities of avoiding such a[n arms] race with the Soviet Union."

The small group left the study at 1:30 p. m., to join the rest of their respective delegations for lunch. Kosygin sat on the president's right, and Dobrynin on his left. Rusk sat opposite LBJ, with Gromyko and Thompson. They began by drinking vodka and made small talk. A few days before Glassboro, McNamara had approached Dobrynin with the idea that he, McNamara, could use military and scientific data to demonstrate the "futility of the ABM system."[16] McNamara gave Dobrynin a preview, and Dobrynin suggested that McNamara should give his presentation during Kosygin's private meeting with LBJ. Kosygin agreed to listen to what McNamara had to say, but the president never requested the defense secretary to join them in the study. Instead, McNamara was forced to make his pitch during lunch. He had prepared a private talk, not one to be heard by people who did not have security clearance for the confidential information he planned to use to bolster his case.[17] Nevertheless, this was his chance, and he went ahead without allowing anyone else to get a word in edgewise.[18] It seemed to bother the Soviets that LBJ's personal secretary was taking notes, so they closed the door. She went round and hid on the back stairs to continue, but the noise from the kitchen and the waiters made it difficult to get it all down. Therefore, McNamara's presentation was only partially recorded.[19]

Essentially, McNamara tried to make the point that each side reacted to the other, which meant that the United States and the USSR were engaged in an arms race beyond limit.[20] "What an insane road we are both following," he said. "How well you speak," replied Kosygin. McNamara argued that if the Soviets deployed an ABM system around its cities, America would have to counter it by expanding its offensive force. Kosygin declared that such a response was immoral. The Soviets were just trying to protect civilians with their Galosh ABM system around Moscow. Frustrated that Kosygin did not understand his point—that ensuring civilians could survive a second strike was actually provocative to the opposing side—McNamara pressed for the discussions to continue through Thompson, in Moscow, noting that "it is a complex subject and we can't complete our views in this meeting." Dobrynin described the presentation as "disjointed and uninteresting," and therefore not convincing. He confided to Thompson that McNamara's exposé to him privately had been much more compelling. Thompson told Dobrynin that McNamara had not even been able to finish before the luncheon party broke up. In his memoirs, Dobrynin admitted that the Soviets were not really prepared to start ABM talks, because they first wanted achieve parity in strategic offensive weapons. What happened—or, rather, *didn't* happen—over lunch at Glassboro was, Dobrynin said, a lost opportunity.

The lunch ended with a congenial toast, and the two groups retired to different rooms to confer for a half hour before the next meeting. This time the conversation turned to Vietnam. Kosygin told the president that he had contacted Hanoi before coming to the United States, to see if there was anything that could be done to stop the war. He had just received a reply while they were having lunch: "Stop the bombing and they [Hanoi] would immediately go to the conference table." Kosygin said he thought, very strongly, that LBJ should follow this proposal.[21]

The president answered with the usual argument that North Vietnam had divisions deployed immediately north of the DMZ. If LBJ stopped the bombing and those divisions moved south, he would be "crucified in this country" for having made that decision. He pressed Kosygin to play some kind of guarantor role, but the Soviet would not promise anything except to pass the president's answer along to Hanoi. They agreed to meet again on Sunday, June 25, with LBJ still hoping to talk more then about arms control. Kosygin ended by saying that Vietnam had damaged the developing détente between the USSR and the United States, giving China a chance to raise its head, "a great danger for the peace of the entire world." If it was a question of prestige, he reminded the president that de Gaulle had fought in Algiers for seven years and then had to withdraw, but his prestige had not decreased at all. Kosygin reiterated to LBJ that there were "forces in the world that were interested in causing a clash between the United States and the USSR."

After making statements to the press, the president escorted Kosygin to his car. As it reached the corner, Kosygin, responding to the cheers of the crowd, got out to shake hands. LBJ went back inside the house with Rusk, Thompson, Rostow, and Bundy.[22] After a brief meeting, they all headed back by helicopter to the Philadelphia airport. Thompson, however, did not continue on to Washington, DC. He went to Eisenhower's Gettysburg farm, as planned.

LBJ wanted to keep Eisenhower happy because, since Ike was a "determined must-win hawk," the five-star general exercised great influence on many senators.[23] There is no memorandum of conversation from the meeting between the former president and Thompson on record, but part of it ties in with the transcript of a call between Eisenhower and Lewis Strauss, the former chairman of the Atomic Energy Commission, in preparation for Thompson's visit, in which they discussed the Jordan River and desalinization plants in the Middle East.[24]

Eisenhower had come up with a scheme. As he saw it, there were two problems in the Middle East: water and refugees. He suggested that, to solve the water problem, the United States could set up a world corporation to build three large salt purification plants in the eastern Mediterranean and sell the stock to bankers all around the world, with the Americans buying up 51 percent. It would be so attractive that the Arabs and the Israelis would almost be compelled by their people to accept it, and this could create an atmosphere where both sides could do something beneficial.[25] Thompson listened to Eisenhower's plan, then sounded him out on Vietnam, probably hoping for public support if things went forward with Kosygin's efforts toward a peace initiative, but Eisenhower did not seem interested.[26]

Thompson spent Saturday in New York City, helping McNamara and Rusk prepare an answer to Hanoi.[27] LBJ would agree to stop the bombing if talks began immediately. He would further promise that allied forces in the northern part of South Vietnam would not advance farther north if the North Vietnamese forces would not advance toward the south. This was actually quite a big step for the president to take.

When LBJ's message was presented to Kosygin during their meeting on Sunday, June 25, the Soviet said that "it would be transmitted today and that any reaction would be conveyed to the US as soon as received," but nothing came of it.[28] The president, in both his discussions with Kosygin and his separate message, had demonstrated his willingness to stop the bombing and allow elections to be held in South Vietnam, but either Kosygin had less influence on Hanoi than he had led the Americans to suppose, or delays in transmitting LBJ's communiqué and the continued US escalation made Hanoi distrust the message enough to reject it. Dobrynin wrote in his memoirs that Kosygin was not confident Hanoi was prepared to negotiate, even if the Americans stopped their bombing, as the North Vietnamese leaders played their own game and seldom let the Soviets know their real views. Except for, yet again, raising false hopes, the Glassboro discussion on Vietnam proved to be fruitless.

LBJ had left Glassboro after the Friday meeting to go to a fundraising dinner in Los Angeles and then returned to his ranch in Texas to see his new grandson, but he traveled back to Glassboro for his Sunday meeting with Kosygin. In the day between the two Glassboro meetings, Kosygin, along with his daughter and fifty other colleagues, flew to Niagara Falls in the president's private aircraft.[29]

Alexander Akalovsky, first secretary in the American embassy in Moscow, flew in to be LBJ's expert interpreter for the second day of the Glassboro summit. After the long flight, it was incredible that he managed to translate everything so well. Thompson flew back from New York City to Washington, DC, on Saturday afternoon, in order to return to Glassboro the next morning and be there when LBJ arrived.[30] This time the president came with his wife and his daughter Linda, who took Kosygin's daughter off to the beach for the day. After photos were taken, Kosygin, his delegation, and the Americans entered the house to sit down to lunch. Thompson was again seated next to Gromyko. Kosygin announced in his luncheon toast that the Soviets were now ready to agree on the Non-Proliferation Treaty, which indicated some progress might be made at Glassboro.[31]

Thompson, Rusk, Dobrynin, and Gromyko met separately, to try to deal with the issue of electromagnetic signals that were constantly being directed against the US embassy in Moscow.[32] Gromyko was skeptical, but Thompson said there was "no doubt whatsoever about it" and added that it had been going on for years. He drew a rough diagram to indicate where the signal was coming from and where it was directed. Ambassador Dobrynin said there was similar activity directed against both the Soviet mission in New York City and the Soviet embassy in Washington, DC. It seemed as though each side was using the same tactics to spy on the other, and the discussion on this topic at Glassboro did nothing to stop it.

The two leaders emerged from their Sunday meeting at 6 p.m., looking calmer and happier than when they had first arrived. Heavy rains had not dissuaded the waiting crowds. Five helicopters were on standby: two took the Soviet delegation back to New York City, and the rest were for the president's party. During the flight, Thompson, McNamara, and Harriman helped LBJ prepare his statement for television that night.

Depending on how you look at it, the Glassboro summit was and was not successful. On the one hand, there was real communication between LBJ and Kosygin over Vietnam, even if nothing eventually came of it. There was also genuine progress made in paving the way for the Non-Proliferation Treaty. Moreover, just as had happened in the 1961 Vienna summit with JFK and Khrushchev, the escalating mistrust between the two countries was tempered to more realistic levels. This became the "spirit of Glassboro."

Continuing Arab-Israeli Problems

The situation in the Middle East was still up in the air as Thompson headed back to Moscow. Over the summer, the Soviets and the Americans had tried to work out a resolution both Israel and the Arabs would accept. The Soviets, Thompson said, were trying to find a compromise, probably related to their desire to reduce Arab pressure on them for massive amounts of military and economic aid.[33] The Six-Day War had left the Arabs humiliated, the Israelis euphoric, and thousands of Arab refugees uprooted. The question of East Jerusalem was also a major issue to be resolved. Israel, which had wrested it from Jordan during the war, now controlled the entire city. Shamed by their defeat, the Arabs were in no mind to make compromises. The Israelis, feeling self-confident, were not, either. Yet, given Israel's position of strength, if it had taken a first step at that point, might things have turned out differently?

David Klein, then the political counselor at the US embassy in Moscow, recalled that Thompson did a "memorable" analysis on the Arab-Israeli conflict at one of the embassy meetings and wrote an advisory cable to the State Department on how to deal with the complicated issue at that particular point: "Thompson was of the view that this was a propitious moment for Israel to give the West Bank back to the Jordanians. He felt strongly that this gesture would ultimately be appropriate, and that the Jordanians would respond in kind. I have since spent a lot of time pondering that proposition, and remain more convinced than ever that, had the Israelis done what [Thompson] proposed, the elements of the Arab-Israeli conflict at this juncture would be very different and more helpful to the Western side."[34] He also added that some Israelis were aware of the risks they ran in the long term if they attempted to digest all of the occupied territory, especially in light of the rapidly reproducing Arab population.

The only cable in the National Archives that dealt somewhat with this issue was written by Thompson on October 18, 1967. In it, he said that unless agreement with the Soviets on a settlement in the Middle East was found, the situation would become "increasingly difficult, if not impossible. . . . The Israelis will hold on to what they have and preparations for the next round will begin."[35] "The present situation," Thompson went on in his cable, "has the US as the spokesperson for the Israelis and the Soviets for the Arabs," which Thompson deemed "highly disadvantageous" for the United States. To avoid that, he suggested appointing a UN representative to carry on the discussions. In November 1967, Gunnar Jarring became the special envoy to the UN, to undertake just such a task.

Thompson said that although no optimum solution to the Arab-Israeli issue was in sight, some face-saving arrangement would have to be found to move the situation off dead center. He felt that it was crucial to do so as soon as possible, leaving the development of a general settlement to be worked out later. In that regard, he saw several possibilities. It was in the basic interests of both the Israelis and the UAR that a settlement be reached, and the major issue preventing an agreement with the Soviets was freedom of passage through the Suez Canal for Israeli ships. Even if this provision was of little real value to Israeli shipping, the Israelis insisted that the issue be settled, because allowing ships flying *their* flag through the canal meant a de facto recognition of Israel.

The UAR needed the revenue from the Suez Canal, and other Arab states would undoubtedly begin to put pressure on that country to reopen it. One possibility would be for the UAR to announce its intention to reopen the canal to Israeli shipping, in return for an Israeli commitment to withdraw halfway across the Sinai Peninsula, a territory Israel was not particularly interested in. An alternative compromise proffered by Thompson was for the UAR to accept the UN resolution and reopen the canal, giving Israel a legal right to use it, but to also state that the refugees from the Arab-Israeli war had the right either to return to their homes or resettle elsewhere. These two problems, Thompson felt, should be taken care of together.

On Jerusalem, Thompson suggested that Jordan, in order to get the West Bank back, might agree that the problem regarding the eastern section of Jerusalem could be resolved in connection with that of the refugees. Thompson thought that if Jordan could be persuaded to make a direct settlement with Israel, this would make it easier for the UAR to eventually do the same. Whatever approach was used, Thompson felt strongly that *any* opportunity had to be seized, before it slipped away. McGeorge Bundy had come to a similar conclusion, stating that "I think there is substantial agreement within the Executive Branch that Israel's own long-run interests would be served by a truly generous settlement with [King] Hussein [of Jordan]."[36] The US never pressed the issue, however, and no such settlement was ever made.

In November 22, 1967, all sides finally agreed to the wording of UN Security Council Resolution 242. It called for the "withdrawal of Israel[i] armed forces from the territories occupied in the recent conflict" and the "termination of all claims or states of belligerency and respect for and acknowledgment of the sovereignty, territorial integrity, and political independence of every State in the area and their right to live in peace within secure and recognized boundaries free from threats or acts of force."[37] Under this resolution, the Arabs and the Israelis were to return captured territories in exchange for an acknowledgment of sovereignty: the "land for peace" formula. It all sounded good, but how was this to be implemented? US Special Envoy Gunnar Jarring tried to find a way, but the Jarring mission had little success. In 1971, he presented his report and submitted a UAR-Israel peace plan. The UAR said it would be ready to enter into a peace agreement with Israel if the latter country withdrew from the occupied territories and arrived at a just settlement for the refugee problem, but Israel would not go back to the pre–June 5, 1967, lines.[38]

Post-Glassboro

As much as Thompson had wanted to finally reunite with his family in Moscow, he was glad to make a stop in Paris after the tensions of the Arab-Israeli crisis and the Glassboro summit. It gave him a chance to review these recent events with Bohlen. They discussed the State Department, prospects for better relations with the Soviets, and what, if any, possibilities there were for a place to house their proposed two-man think tank. Their conclusions on US-Soviet relations were grim, but there was still some hope for arms control, and maybe some accommodation could be reached in the Middle East. Thompson described how he'd been in the White House Situation Room for most days and many nights during the crisis, which earned him a ribbing from Bohlen, who chided him that it "was hardly in keeping with the sales talk they gave you when they sold you the position [as ambassador to Moscow]."[39]

The North Vietnamese had not replied to the message LBJ handed to Kosygin during the Glassboro meetings. Their negative answer would finally come to Thompson in August 1967, through Georgi Kornienko, chief of the American department in the Soviet Foreign Ministry.[40] The reason given was that US troop increases, bombing escalations, and McNamara's meetings with the American command in South Vietnam all signaled an expansion of the war, not a slowing down. Kornienko ended his message by saying, "One can only express regret with this turn of events."

The rest of 1967 was relatively quiet in the Moscow embassy. Attempts to coerce the Soviets into settling the Vietnam situation had come to naught, and Thompson rarely saw the Kremlin leadership, putting him in what he later called "a holding operation."[41] He was busy with ceremonial duties, a good portion of which were aimed at the stream of American VIPs and performing artists who came to the USSR once the Cultural Exchanges Agreement was finally renewed. Each one was entertained at Spaso House. The long list included politically luminary guests. Impresario Sol Hurok kept the flow of celebrities steady, too. These ranged from Lillian Hellman to Dinah Shore, and from Isaac Stern to the Charles Lloyd Quintet. Jane couldn't help but think about the soviet minister of culture telling her a decade earlier that the Soviets would only allow jazz bands "over his dead body."[42] At lunch during one of his visits to Spaso House, Hurok humorously characterized the cultural exchanges, where "the Soviets send us their Jewish violinists from Odessa, and we reciprocate by sending them our Jewish violinists from Odessa."[43]

Thompson's aide, Jonathan Rickert, described the ambassador as always polite and correct, but not above an occasional put-on.[44] Thompson was terribly pleased with having found a good Italian wine for thirty-nine cents a bottle, which he bought by the crate to serve at Spaso House functions, since the embassy budget never covered these expenses. It was good wine, although it was shipped from Italy in bulk and bottled in Sweden, to keep the cost down. Thompson asked Hurok—as he did for other unsuspecting wine

connoisseurs—what he thought of the wine, and then took great delight in revealing what it actually cost.

Anatoly Dobrynin (*right*) in the Blue Room at Spaso House, the US ambassadorial residence in Moscow, USSR, with the Llewellyn Thompson Jr. family: (*from left to right*) Jane, Llewellyn, Sherry, and Jenny, 1968. © Elliott Erwitt / Magnum Photos (68-5-14 12A).

It was good for Thompson to have his family in one place again—they all felt that way. On one of his first evenings back, the girls ran the film projector, and the American and Soviet guests viewed *The Russians Are Coming*, a comedy about a Soviet submarine that runs aground off the New England coast. The Soviets who came for the screening loved it, and for a while there was joy and laughter in Spaso House.

Although the stress of crisis eased, the tedious ceremonial duties and diplomatic dinners took their own sort of toll, rendered more boring this time around because the whole diplomatic corps had little contact with the Soviet leadership, and "such as there is, is not generally rewarding," leaving little of substance to discuss at these affairs.[45] At least on the ambassador's previous tour of Moscow, key Soviets were present at diplomatic functions, so real business could take place. He much preferred small gatherings with Soviet guests, either at Spaso House or at the ambassadorial dacha.[46]

Thompson had become a kind of celebrity among young Foreign Service officers, and they wanted his attention.[47] Rickert said that if Thompson had a fault as chief of mission, it was that his staff wanted to hear his opinions more often. William Pryce remembered Thompson telling them: "We had to be ready for a confrontation, we had to be strong, but that there was probably not going to be a confrontation, and that in the end we would survive; not only survive but our system would prevail. . . . There would be a gradual evo-lution within the Communist system which would force it to become less despotic." Ed Hurwitz recalled that Thompson was "not a hard taskmaster with embassy officers, but he [Thompson] certainly knew who was boss." Some even emulated his mannerisms. Hur-witz picked up one of Thompson's traits: "[The ambassador would be] standing at recep-tions talking to people holding his drink, not with his arm bent at the elbow, but with his arm straight down and his fingers grasping the glass from the top. The total effect was laid back and debonair." Another habit of Thompson's was "sitting back in his chair with his wrists on the top of his head, one hand grasping the other's wrist, while [he was] carrying on a conversation."

Many more friends came to visit during this tour of duty, and that helped to ease the burden of the post a bit. Washington, DC, socialite Marion "Oatsie" Leiter came through Moscow and, when asked by her guide if she was rich, Thompson was amused as she re-plied, "Very." When the Soviets asked her how she treated her workers, she said, "Well, I beat them, of course!" Just as the household was starting to recover from a visit by Jack Valenti, a former White House aide who'd recently become head of the Motion Picture Association of America, and his entourage of "prima donnas," *Washington Post* publisher Katharine Graham and journalist Joseph Alsop arrived. They all went down Moscow's Volga Canal to Yaroslavl for the weekend, reminisced, and had picnic lunches at the am-bassadorial dacha.[48] At first it was such fun to have them all in Moscow, but after a while Jane complained to Thompson that he seemed to enjoy talking to Kay Graham more than he did to her. She was probably right. He couldn't really talk to Jane about his work with-out bumping into the invisible wall of national security, but the boundaries were clearer with the publisher of the *Washington Post*, and Graham would respect them, without any explanation needed. Moreover, as Thompson confessed to Bohlen, he was depressed about the outlook in Moscow.[49] "These boys [the Soviet leadership]," he wrote, "are on a tough spot and can't agree what to do about it." He then added, in reference to the French president's ongoing disruptions of political and economic US-European relations, "Your boy [Charles de Gaulle] has gone completely off the deep end."

There was still no word on when the Soviets would agree to arms talks, or where, and now the USSR was beginning tests on Multiple Reentry Vehicles (MRVs), which carried several warheads that could be deployed in a pattern against a single target. These were not multiple independently targeted reentry vehicles (MIRVs), like the US missiles, with war-heads that could reach more than one target, but it was only a matter of time before that development happened. Once MIRV'd, the huge, cumbersome Soviet SS-9s could be stuffed until they were bristling with nuclear warheads and thereby gain an advantage.[50] Members of the Johnson administration would later lament a missed opportunity to keep the MIRV genie from escaping its bottle.[51]

Dobrynin was back in Moscow that August, and Thompson sounded him out on a date for arms talks between the Americans and the Soviets.[52] Thompson told him Kosygin was wrong in believing that the United States was only interested in limiting ABMs, not offensive weapons. Both countries were "in the same boat" with regard to the threat of a nuclear-armed

Communist China, a point that Dobrynin conceded. The Soviet ambassador then added that it was difficult for him, as a diplomat, to argue over technical points on arms control, which Thompson took to mean having discussions with military experts. Dobrynin went on to disclose that an extended debate was going on within the Soviet government on the problem. No date was offered for arms control talks, but Thompson wrote to Rusk (a personal letter, outside the usual cable channel) that he hoped to get into it further with Dobrynin later that month, at the Black Sea.

Going South

In August, the Thompsons headed out on a road trip to the Sanatori Parus, on the Black Sea. The embassy's fragile Cadillac limousine (which the pot-holed roads damaged with some frequency) preceded the second vehicle, a sturdier Ford station wagon.[53] The Russians along the road and in the little villages gawked at the unlikely convoy and inspected the automobiles every time they stopped. The family picnicked by the side of the road and drank Tang, an orange-flavored powdered drink used by US astronauts. None of this, however, was as impressive to the Soviets as the family's Polaroid camera. In today's world of digital photography, it's hard to understand how extraordinary an "instant" photo was.

The group eventually arrived at the Sanatori Parus on the southern Crimean coast, perched next to the cliffs for which it was named. As a reward for their labors through the year, certain Soviet citizens were assigned to various sanatoria for a vacation, based on their occupations. Parus was one of the jewels, reserved for important workers, although the Thompsons could never figure out just what sort of jobs they had.

The Black Sea area was a delight. There were palm trees and tropical-like flowers in the Soviet Union! The building itself was one of the more attractive Soviet cement-block structures they had seen. Each of the rooms was clean and spacious, with a balcony open to the fresh air, and fluffy down comforters encased in starched white duvets. As soon as the Thompson family arrived, the women in the group rushed down the steps to the small dock, to take in the view of the water, only to be dismayed at the swarm of small jellyfish and the odd lack of a sea smell.[54] It was a good vacation, one of the few uninterrupted ones as a complete family. The next day the jellyfish were gone, and the beach beckoned. Andy spent her days at one of the many chess tables that were set up in the shaded cement portal, routinely beating the Soviet men who played there—much to their consternation, and Thompson's pride.

Sergei, their chauffeur, sporting newly dyed hair in a color uncomfortably reminiscent of the Tang instant beverage, kept an eye on both the family and the bathing beauties. Thompson, ever uncomfortable at the beach, would sit nearby in a lounge chair, with piles of papers and newspapers. A highlight of their stay was an outing to the neighboring sanatorium, one for nuclear physicists, to see a Sophia Loren film. They all hoped no one got into too much trouble for having arranged that. The trip back to Moscow, with all of them sunburnt and full of fresh food, did not seem as adventurous, except for the Cadillac having several flat tires, mostly because Sergei was bringing back watermelons for his family. Each

(*Above*) Montage of a road trip to the Soviet Sanatori Parus, on the Black Sea, USSR, August 1967. *Top left image*, driver Alexei (*left*) and driver Sergei (*right*) changing a tire on the embassy's Cadillac. *Center top image*, Llewellyn Thompson Jr., pausing for refreshment. *Top right image*, driver Sergei filling up the Cadillac from mobile fuel truck. *Bottom image* (*front*), Jane, Llewellyn, and Sherry Thompson, and (*back*), driver Alexei, Llewellyn's step-daughter Fernanda ("Andy") Goelet, and driver Sergei. Courtesy of Jenny Thompson.

(*Right*) Jane Thompson's daughter from her previous marriage, Fernanda ("Andy") Goelet (*center, kneeling next to pole*), playing chess with a Soviet man, while two other men look on, at the Soviet Sanatori Parus, on the Black Sea, USSR, August 1967. Thompson Family Papers.

time the tire was fixed, the cache of watermelons had to be unloaded and reloaded. What really got Jane's dander up was that she hadn't thought of bringing fruit back for themselves.

In September, Sherry and her classmates inaugurated the modern new building for the Bolshoi Ballet School. Jenny drove to her classes at Moscow University in a tiny, tinny Moskvich car that Thompson had procured for her.[55] She had been driving herself to school in the United States, and Thompson saw no reason why she should not do so in Moscow. Although brand new, the gearshift did not work, and the car had to go back to the factory to be replaced, an event that was not unusual in Soviet Russia. A teenage girl driving her own car in Moscow, however, was.

Like many her age, Jenny found friendship and love at the university. When Thompson learned that his daughter had a Soviet boyfriend, he called her into the embassy and took her to the bubble room, where conversations could not be overheard. He would have to inform his government of what his daughter was up to, but she showed little concern over that. Thompson then did as he always did, and let reason dictate his next move. He told Jenny to bring the young man to the house to have a talk with him. Thompson told the two of them that if they were determined to carry on their relationship, he would not prevent it, but it was not what he wanted for his daughter. First, they had to finish their education, in order to have a means of support. If, after that, they still wanted to get married, he would accept it. From his own experience, Thompson knew that a lot could happen to one's heart in four years. Jenny's relationship came to a natural end a few years later.

Going MAD

With no date set for arms control talks, work would proceed on an American ABM system. Thompson did not want new approaches on arms limitations talks to be made to the Soviets, unless "we can tell them frankly" that an announcement on the ABMs was forthcoming.[56] Otherwise, he thought, "they will have a good case for charging bad faith." In his opinion, the announcement ought to be made promptly, along with a statement that the United States still wanted arms talks. He argued for putting forward some type of concrete proposal right away, to stave off the Soviet military, who could "conjure up all kinds of pitfalls in arguing against [arms control] talks." The State Department had asked Thompson how he thought the Soviets might react to using the threat of a nuclear-armed Communist China as the excuse for the Americans' deployment of an ABM system, and he replied that, from a Soviet point of view, it had "both pros and cons." He thought it best to avoid taking a formal position that was based on China.

McNamara's September 18, 1967, speech in San Francisco became known as the mutual deterrence speech.[57] The acronym MAD—for Mutual Assured Destruction—was later coined in a comedic critique of the term "mutual deterrence." The secretary of defense articulated the United States' strategic nuclear policy as the ability for each side to preserve a second-strike capability, in order to dissuade either side from launching a first strike. There were pro–mutual deterrence people, who saw the benefit to this practical parity, and those opposed, who wanted to push ahead and "win" the arms race.

McNamara tried to walk a fine line between the two ideas and announced a small, "thin" ABM system to protect certain population centers, being careful to preserve the option of a larger system, should circumstances change. He did use the Chinese Communists as a foil, and he went against advice from Garthoff not to make "categorical statements" about America's strategic superiority.[58] Nonetheless, there wasn't much Soviet reaction. Mostly the speech simply confused everyone. After the Glassboro meetings, it had seemed as though the United States was committed *not* to deploy an ABM system, so McNamara's speech would have appeared to be a reversal to the Soviets—and to the general public. McNamara could have argued for a very limited ABM system around the Americans' Minutemen missiles, but instead he announced something that could easily be converted into a "full-fledged 'counter-value' defense system."[59]

Jubilee

That fall, however, Moscow was preoccupied less with arms talks than with the upcoming jubilee, the fiftieth anniversary of the October Revolution. Thompson didn't think very much would happen until after the celebrations, but he was of the opinion that the Johnson administration should come to a consensus on its position on arms control, in order to move quickly once the jubilee was over. He was disturbed by a pattern of increasing vitriol against the United States in Soviet propaganda in the run-up to the jubilee. Looking back, he thought this hostility had started after the resumption of the US bombing of North Vietnam that spring, and that it became louder with the publication of Stalin's daughter's memoirs.[60]

One could argue that 1967 was a Soviet high point. The USSR was approaching parity with the US on nuclear forces. One nemesis was bogged down in a shockingly unpopular war in Southeast Asia, and the other in a misguided and also unpopular Cultural Revolution. Moreover, several recent Soviet agricultural harvests were good.

The huge jubilee parade took place on November 7, 1967, a clear, freezing day. Thompson's daughter Jenny, with her new Soviet friends and thousands of other Muscovites, climbed to the rooftops along the parade route to watch the spectacle. It was at least as big as a May Day parade. The teenagers looked down to follow the parade as it wended its way out of Red Square and through the canyon of streets between huge new Soviet buildings, with construction cranes still perched on top. Thompson speculated about the effect that "Kosygin Week"—the Sunflower negotiations in London with Prime Minister Wilson (see chapter 34)—had on weakening the authority of the chairman of the Soviet Council of Ministers. The fact that only Communist Party Secretary Leonid Brezhnev appeared in the official Soviet propaganda film of the festivities was a clear indicator of Brezhnev's ascendancy and Kosygin's decline.

37 ≋

1968
A Year of Frustrated Promise

Prague Spring in 1968 ... exhibited some of the same
effervescence that overtook Paris in May—a sense that it
might really be possible to escape the ruts of history and
create something truly new. Was this utopian impulse ... a
naïve and dangerous dream? It did not aim at human
perfectibility but only at imagining that life could really be
different and a whole lot better. In any case, the utopian
impulse is no longer much in evidence.
—PETER STEINFELS, *New York Times*, May 1, 2008

A kind of worldwide existential shift occurred in 1968. Young people, especially,
seemed to question the ways of the world, and these feelings were translated into
the way they dressed, the music they listened to, and the drugs they took to free
themselves from outmoded social constraints. They seriously questioned the values of the
older generation and often rejected them, in part or completely. The hippie movement and
other societal dropouts were à la mode. Greenwich Village and San Francisco's Haight-
Ashbury district became meccas for the counterculture movement. The year 1968 was not
just about a seemingly frivolous generational rebellion, however. This was also the year of
the Paris uprisings, where students and workers joined forces to question what had previously been unthinkable to the French—Charles de Gaulle's leadership. In the United
States, civil rights protests intensified with the assassination of Martin Luther King Jr. on
April 4, 1968. Anti–Vietnam War protests also took a serious turn when draft dodgers
burnt their draft cards or moved to Canada in open defiance of conscription into the US
military. Student protests took place in other European capitals, too—in London, Rome,
and Berlin. It was an unsettling time.

Thompson was frustrated by events. On January 4, 1968, exactly as he had forewarned,
a Soviet ship in Haiphong harbor was bombed by accident, creating a backlash by the
USSR.[1] Rusk assured Dobrynin that it had been a mistake and pressed for the Soviets to

mediate in Vietnam. In his memoirs, Dobrynin wrote, "How could I possibly tell him that the Vietnamese would not accept our mediation or anybody else's?" The North Vietnamese were caught in the middle of the Sino-Soviet dispute. While the Soviets were encouraging them to negotiate, the Chinese were telling them to do the opposite. So Dobrynin just gave Rusk the usual line about any resolution having to be between the Americans and the North Vietnamese.

Thompson also wrote to the State Department at the beginning of January, recapping his year in Moscow: "Today being the first anniversary of my current sentence to Moscow, . . . I can take little personal satisfaction from a record of no hits, no runs, and I hope no errors. The limbo in which we have been placed by the Vietnam affair as well as the style and methods of the present leadership has reduced my function here largely to a holding operation."[2] He then explained what he saw as the most important issues for the Soviets. One, the Communist Party had not been able to adapt its ideology or methods to modern conditions. Two, the gap between it and various elements in Soviet society, particularly the youth and intellectuals, was widening. Three, the rising influence of the military and the KGB was "clearly regressive." He more pointedly wrote to Bohlen that the "goons were taking over."[3] Four, reforms in agriculture were unlikely to solve basic problems, as too much of the USSR's resources was being invested in the military. Five, even if Vietnam were settled, he predicted that Communist ideological imperatives would perpetuate the Soviets' rivalry with the United States.

As far as foreign policy went, he thought the USSR currently had a greater influence in the Middle East than it had had a few years previously. In Southeast Asia, the Soviets wanted to see a political settlement but were unlikely to do anything to help bring it about. Concerning East Germany, sooner or later the USSR would make a strong play for some kind of deal with West Germany. In another of his points, Thompson noted that cultural and scientific exchanges, tourism, and commerce were among the few means of influence the United States possessed vis-à-vis the USSR, and he again recommended that trade barriers with that country be removed.

In Thompson's overall opinion: "The highly competitive nature of the Russians combined with the compulsions of Communist ideology will insure continued rivalry with the United States. I continue to believe, however, that our interests lie in doing whatever we can to stimulate the liberal trends in this country [the USSR] in the hope of reaching a situation in which real coexistence is possible. . . . But as long as policy making is in the hands of what is generally a narrow-minded group of party officials who see the world through thick Marxist lenses, progress in accommodation with the West and liberalization internally will be slow."

Eastern Europe

Vietnam was impeding détente with the USSR, the Soviets were still mum on arms control talks, and the NATO alliance was in danger of degrading. To put equivalent entropic pressure on the Warsaw Pact countries by encouraging more-liberal forms of Communism, and to distract from issues regarding Vietnam, LBJ decided to expand his bridge building to Eastern Europe. Some people in the Johnson administration, particularly Foy Kohler, saw the potential for nondoctrinaire Communism to spread like a virus and thought that it might lead to a Communist defeat in the Cold War.[4] This was a distortion of Thompson's position, which was that a *modus vivendi* could emerge as pragmatic interests superseded Communist ideology.

The pull to have alternate forms of Communism among the Eastern bloc states had been felt in Czechoslovakia. On January 5, 1968, a fifty-year-old, attractive, up-and-coming Communist politician named Alexander Dubček had unseated the Moscow-supported Antonín Novotný as first secretary of the Communist Party, taking the USSR's top men by surprise. Even though the act of picking an alternate leader to the "chosen one" was a daring poke at Moscow, at first the Soviets were not too concerned, because Dubček was a long-time Party politician. Those in Washington, DC, thought, or hoped, that the lessons of the Hungarian uprising in 1956 would constrain Dubček's reforms enough to avoid triggering Soviet reprisals, and they took pains not to lead the Czechs into thinking the United States would step in. Dubček was careful to make sure his foreign policy was in line with Moscow, and he limited his reforms to internal matters. Politicians often underestimate the force of a people unleashed, however, and by spring 1968, Dubček would be on a runaway train.

Tet

Thompson sent Rusk a personal letter at the end of January 1968. "Dear Boss," he began, "Dobrynin told me that . . . Averell had told him he thought it would be a good time for [Averell] to visit Moscow—I presume in connection with the Vietnam problem."[5] Dobrynin said the Soviets would not invite Harriman, however, unless the president wanted them to do so. "If there are real negotiations to be carried out on Vietnam, I would be delighted to see Averell handle them," Thompson continued, "but I would not like to see him come here simply on a grandstand fishing trip. The publicity would make it more difficult for the Soviets to do anything to help us." Thompson said he wanted Rusk to know the situation, in the event Harriman implied it was the Soviets who wanted him to come.

Two days after this letter was sent, the Viet Cong pulled off a set of well-coordinated surprise attacks against a large number of military and civilian objectives, which collectively became known as the Tet Offensive. More than 80,000 troops were involved in attacks on over a hundred villages and cities.[6] The VC even got close to the American embassy in Saigon. Although the end result was hailed as an American victory, because the Viet Cong and North Vietnamese forces were pushed back, they were far from capitulating to the American troops, and the psychological advantage they gained in this attack was enormous.

The Tet Offensive demonstrated that the United States was not in control in South Vietnam. Nevertheless, there was no substantial discussion in Washington, DC, about a change in the US strategy.[7] At this point, Clark Clifford had replaced Robert McNamara as secretary of defense.[8] He was the hard-liner substitute for a man who was seen as having gone wobbly about the war. Yet it would only take Clifford about two months before he, too, would conclude that the Johnson administration's policy in Vietnam was headed for disaster. LBJ met with his Senior Advisory Group on Vietnam in late March 1968, only to find that many of those who had supported escalation of the war a few years earlier had now changed their minds.[9] The Vietnam War was doing more harm to the country than good, both economically and socially. This group now accepted that previous studies had been right, and bombing did not work. Despite terrible losses by the North Vietnamese, their effective manpower had barely been reduced, making the strategy of attrition a resolute failure. After his meeting with his "wise men," the president understood that something drastic had to happen.

To make matters worse for LBJ, Senator Eugene McCarthy of Minnesota had received 42 percent of the vote in the New Hampshire presidential primary, and Johnson's old adversary, Robert F. Kennedy, announced that he, too, would run against LBJ for the Democratic Party nomination in the next presidential election, on an antiwar platform. Johnson called Thompson back to Washington, DC, at the end of March. With the failure of his Vietnam policy exposed, LBJ had decided to make a dramatic appeal for peace by announcing that he would not be running for president in the next elections, and that he would stop bombing North Vietnam above the twentieth parallel. Thompson called LBJ's move "a bombshell."[10] The contents of the president's nationally televised March 31 "withdrawal speech" became a personal bombshell for Thompson, because in it, LBJ named Harriman and Thompson as the men he wanted to send to negotiate with the North Vietnamese.[11]

Even before making his public announcement, the president met with Thompson, Harriman, Rostow, and Dobrynin, to inform the Soviet ambassador of his decision.[12] He told Dobrynin it was now up to Kosygin to make it possible for negotiations with North Vietnam to start, citing the Glassboro meetings, where the Kosygin had shown a willingness to be helpful.[13] LBJ could not, however, stop bombing the routes below the twentieth parallel in Vietnam, for fear that this would cause too many American casualties.[14]

The day after his public announcement, LBJ called Senator J. William Fulbright.[15] The president was sure the Vietnamese would enter into talks, saying "Now is the time to let Tommy Thompson and Averell go over there and start something." LBJ explained that he and his advisors had talked about who could handle the talks, and that Rusk, Bohlen, and Harriman were mentioned. Harriman was chosen because, as head of the Negotiations Committee (see chapter 31), he had been handling all the talks with other countries. "But," LBJ told the senator, "we needed a professional, and so we decided—everybody thought Tommy Thompson was respected and if we had to get the Soviets, he would be the best one with them to use. I hope you think that's all right." "Yes, he's a good man," Fulbright answered. LBJ said he had not talked to Thompson yet—although by this date, Thompson knew, either through the president or Secretary of State Rusk, that he was supposed to be one of the negotiators—and told Fulbright that it was Clifford who had suggested the ambassador. Thompson's been "a good deal of help," LBJ went on, "and I wish you'd spend whatever time you can with him, because he respects you and likes you and I think that we can bring the government a little closer together in these days ahead when we all need to be that way." Fulbright responded: "Yes, Thompson is a good fellow. I like him. . . . I'll do what I can."

On the same day when LBJ and Fulbright were talking, however, Thompson wrote to his wife: "I don't think [Johnson's decision not to run for reelection] will change my plans unless by some remote chance the North Vietnamese should agree to come to Geneva. Otherwise I shall be back as planned on the 17th." Thompson had not seen LBJ or Rusk yet, but he told Jane he would do his best "to get unhooked from this operation. It makes no sense for me to be involved."

Surprisingly, the North Vietnamese immediately accepted Johnson's call for talks. LBJ and his advisors met to discuss the course of action for Thompson's and Harriman's negotiations.[16] The president warned everyone about not getting their hopes up too soon: "Let's listen to old hands. That's why I have Tommy and Averell and Max Taylor. Let's look and think and get collective wisdom. Let's look at it carefully. [The] time to keep your head is when everybody else loses theirs." Thompson asked what the objective of the talks would be, but he did not get an answer. Bundy pointed out: "Contacts are one thing. Substantive talks are another. Talks are [a] whole different area of sensitivity." The first thing, Thompson thought, was to clarify what was meant in LBJ's "San Antonio formula."[17] The impression left by the tape and the transcript of this conversation is that LBJ's advisors were not of one mind. They seemed more concerned about avoiding a situation where the bombing would have to halt altogether.

Thompson was finally able to meet with LBJ alone that evening, and he told the president that he did not want to be involved in the talks. Thompson argued that in light of the pending arms control discussions, it would not be a good time for him to be absent from Moscow. LBJ agreed, and picked Cyrus Vance to replace him.[18]

Despite the president having said that he would go anywhere in order to start talks with the North Vietnamese, it took over a month of fussing before all parties agreed on Paris. Every detail—including whether the discussion table should be round or square—slowed things down. Moreover, the objective of the talks remained unclear. Was it to negotiate a compromise political solution, on the grounds that a military victory was clearly not possible? Or was it to put off any solution, in the hopes that with enough time, a military solution might still prevail and force negotiations to go the way the United States wanted? In the meantime, the bombing continued, and so did the war. Moreover, the Paris Peace Talks quickly bogged down, with each side throwing the same stale arguments at each other. Thompson met with Gromyko on June 5 to discuss the stalled talks. The Soviet foreign minister claimed that they were stuck because the bombings had been reduced but not stopped. If the United States unconditionally stopped all bombing, it would create a more favorable situation.

Prague Spring

Meanwhile, the rebellion in Prague took on a life of its own that spring. Thompson worried that it could trigger a possible Soviet invasion of Czechoslovakia, but his ideas did not align with those of the CIA or, at that time, of the US ambassador in Prague, Thompson's long-time friend (and godfather to Jenny), Jacob Beam. The CIA and Beam did not think the USSR would resort to military intervention, and both parties believed that the Czechs and the Soviets could reach some kind of a deal.[19] By mid-August, however, Beam was sure that danger loomed for the Czechs.

SALT

On May 20, 1968, Thompson was recovering from an inner ear infection when Moscow finally signaled that it was ready to get serious about strategic arms limitation talks. The talks were to begin that autumn, followed by a summit in Leningrad with LBJ and Kosygin. Gromyko confirmed the timing that June. Tom Hughes at the INR felt that the Soviets finally agreed to SALT, despite the ongoing US escalation in Vietnam, because doing so with LBJ as a lame-duck president would make him prone to concessions, and such talks might insulate a moderate US position from a possible election victory by Richard Nixon.[20] More likely, though, it was because the Soviets had finally manufactured enough ballistic missiles in their "sausage factory," as Khrushchev would have said, to consider that the playing field was now level, and because they saw the folly of incurring a crushing military expense that would not change the strategic balance between the two nations.

Thompson left Moscow a few days later, to be on hand as the Non-Proliferation Treaty went for a vote before the UN General Assembly. In an ugly, ironic twist, on April 26, the very day the NPT had opened for debate at the UN, the United States made its most powerful hydrogen bomb explosion in Nevada, in spite of eccentric billionaire Howard Hughes' attempts to bribe the government to test it elsewhere.[21] Thankfully, the test did not change the outcome of the UN vote. Thompson was present when it was signed by the Soviet Union in Moscow at a July 1 ceremony, in which the date for the August SALT talks was publicly announced.

Stop the Bombing

Just prior to going back to the United States, Thompson had an hour-long meeting with Gromyko. The Soviet foreign minister again told him that the North Vietnamese would negotiate if the United States fully stopped its bombing. As Thompson and Gromyko were in the midst of their discussion, information was just coming in about an attempt on presidential candidate Robert Kennedy's life by Palestinian Sirhan Sirhan, who later said this act was motivated by RFK's support of Israel in the 1967 Arab-Israeli War and his subsequent speech in favor of the sale of fifty fighter jets to Israel.[22] When Thompson returned to the chancery, he learned that RFK had died. Thompson walked into David Klein's office to tell him the news, and they both cried.[23]

On June 9, 1968, Thompson attended a cabinet meeting with the president and his advisors, including Bohlen. An unexpected letter on Vietnam had arrived from Kosygin.[24] It was unusual because Kosygin—not LBJ—had initiated the correspondence, and he referred not just to himself, but to himself and his colleagues. In his letter, Kosygin restated what Gromyko had told Thompson in Moscow: a complete stop to the bombing would lead to a breakthrough in the talks between North Vietnam and the United States in Paris. He also assured the president that if LBJ did this, it would not have negative consequences for either the security or the prestige of the United States. The cabinet session brought up the usual comments that had been made in endless other meetings.[25] Clarification was needed. What exactly would North Vietnam do if the Americans ceased bombing? How much damage could the enemy do if they continued to carry on with the war after the bombing did stop? Thompson and Bohlen both urged the president to halt the bombing and argued that "if you took a step and they didn't react, you could go back to all [the] bombing." LBJ was still wary, though. A halt would raise hopes, and there would be excuses to wait again. "I got burned on it before," he told his advisors. "I am not willing to take their assurance . . . on face value. We have softened. They have done nothing."

Thompson and Bohlen later lamented that Kosygin's suggestions were not picked up on. Dobrynin told both of them that the offer had been a serious one, and that the Soviets had all been disappointed by Johnson's reply. We now know from documents that have only recently come to light that even if the Americans did not have a set strategy, the North Vietnamese did: "Talk-Fight." In 1965, the North Vietnamese Communist Party leadership had decided that it would not enter into any negotiations "until it had first won a major military victory (to strengthen its hand in negotiations) and until it had 'crushed the American imperialist will to commit aggression.'"[26] Had LBJ stopped the bombing immediately, perhaps it would have called the North Vietnamese's bluff and would have compelled them to act. In his memoirs, Dobrynin said that Hanoi was not serious and had misled Moscow into thinking that they would become more flexible if the president had stopped the bombing. Nevertheless, LBJ's reply put a final end to Moscow's attempts to mediate.[27] Kosygin would pay a price in his own government for his efforts to broker a peace initiative between the United States and North Vietnam.[28]

The Thompsons' Last Summer in the USSR

While Thompson was in Washington, DC, after the UN meeting on the NPT and for consultations on Vietnam, Jane complained about thousands of "boring" receptions. She decided to do something new and different for the US embassy's annual Fourth of July festivities. All Americans in the Soviet Union, the entire diplomatic corps in Moscow, and Soviet dignitaries and officials were invited as usual, but instead of a huge ballroom setup, with the typical offerings of finger sandwiches and formal champagne toasts, she set the party in the backyard of Spaso House and arranged it like a state fair, with red- white-and-blue booths serving hot dogs, fried chicken legs, ice cream in Dixie cups, popsicles, and brownies, as well as sodas, beer, and gin and tonics. It was a raging success. She actually had fun preparing it, and Thompson, who had returned to Moscow by then, had fun hosting it.

It was only a one-day pleasurable interlude, however, as Thompson's worries about the situation in Czechoslovakia increased. He wrote to the State Department on July 11 that there was "a growing concern not only over [the] danger of contamination of other [Eastern European countries] . . . but also over possible reverberations in [the] USSR itself." He cited the delay in the departure of Soviet troops after Warsaw Pact exercises; grim letters to the Czech Communist Party from other Communist bloc parties; and the intensified public campaign in the USSR, condemning the "'anti-socialist' elements in Czechoslovakia."[29]

Another aspect that convinced Thompson he should worry about pending developments came from his daughter Jenny, who told him that all her friends at Moscow University had been called up to the reserves.[30] He concluded that the "Soviets probably do not hope [to] be able to turn [the] clock back in Czechoslovakia, but they clearly [are] making every effort [to] stop it."[31] The USSR tried to do that through bilateral negotiations with Dubček in the Czech border town of Čierna.

Later in July, Bohlen came to Moscow one last time, as the head of the American delegation on Pan Am's inaugural flight from New York City to Moscow. The reciprocal Aeroflot flight to New York City almost ended in catastrophe, however, because the Soviet pilots did not speak English well enough to follow instructions from the control tower.[32] Bohlen stayed with the Thompsons at Spaso House, where the two men had time for long talks. They also entertained the family, with Thompson on the violin and Bohlen at the piano.[33]

Now that the end of the Moscow tunnel was in sight, Jane decided that she should show her daughters parts of the Soviet Union and Asia, which they might never again have the opportunity to see. They went to Kizhi, a small island in the middle of Lake Onega, far north into the land of the midnight sun. The Soviets had moved a number of historic Russian Orthodox wooden churches, built without nails and complete with their characteristic onion domes, onto the island as an open-air museum, in order to preserve them. Then she took her girls on the midnight train to Leningrad, 270 kilometers away. Later that summer, they took an appallingly rickety boat going from the city of Baku (soaked with and smelling of oil) in Azerbaijan and across the Caspian Sea to Iran. They drove across that country from the coast, stopping first in Tehran to visit friends at the US embassy there. They then traveled south to Isfahan, gawking at the magnificent architecture and wandering in the city's huge bazaar. They ended the trip in Shiraz, the beautiful "city of roses." Along the way, they came upon an encampment of the nomadic Qashqai tribe, where they met astonishingly beautiful young women who'd gone blind from the very fine rug weaving they did, using their tiny fingers when they were girls. Stopping in a rural village to see a small mosque, they were accompanied to it by the van driver. The American women, who'd worn scarves on their heads but had on short sleeves in the scorching heat, were heckled by a small group of men, a couple of them even throwing stones in the ladies' direction to express their disapproval. All of this travel occurred before their real summer holiday in Italy, before boarding a ship for their last Atlantic crossing.

The trip to the Italian beach resort of Punta Alta didn't start out well. It was a long, slow flight, which included the plane that they were traveling on losing a motor, as well as suffering through a lengthy layover in Vienna while waiting for a substitute plane to arrive from Frankfurt. Then there was yet another connecting flight, followed by a train ride to get to what they all agreed was a too new, antiseptic high-rise hotel—luxurious, perhaps, but not what they had expected from Italy.

The family had left for Italy without Thompson, because he wanted to prepare for the upcoming SALT talks in August, which he thought were likely to be held in a phase one–phase two configuration. Even more importantly, he needed to be on hand to monitor the outcome of the Čierna talks as the situation in Czechoslovakia worsened. Since Thompson had originally expected to join his family for their vacation, all the Spaso House staff had left, except for Alexei the chauffeur, who wanted to stay. Thompson insisted that Alexei go on leave, too, but instead he went out to the Moscow River and caught a four-and-a-half pound catfish, which he brought back to Spaso House for

Charles "Chip" Bohlen (*right, at piano*) and Llewellyn Thompson Jr. (*left, on violin*), in the Great Hall at Spaso House, the US ambassadorial residence in Moscow, USSR, when Bohlen was visiting on the occasion of the first US commercial flight to Moscow, July 1968. Thompson Family Papers.

the two of them to eat. It was a sweet gesture, but Thompson was still lonely in the big, empty building, made worse because he was stuck there waiting, with no word out of Čierna as to what was happening with that situation.

In letters reminiscent of those he had sent from Trieste all those years ago, he kept hoping he'd be sprung in a "few days" and wrote that he hoped Jane and the girls "missed the old dictator a little but [would] have some fun just the same."[34] His wife and younger daughters had driven to Rome, in order to visit family friends Lawrence and Isabelle Roberts at the magnificent Villa Aurelia,[35] when one of Thompson's letters arrived, telling them that he expected to be in Rome that Wednesday. Jane decided to stay in Rome, and she sent Jenny and Sherry back to Punta Ala to collect their sister Andy, as well as to extricate all of them from the disappointing hotel there.[36] The three girls then drove back to

Rome, stopping on the way to visit Andy's grandmother and namesake. It was a rather sad interlude, as the once-magnificent Fernanda Goelet had become frail and small and was living out her life in a less-than-grandiose geriatric residence. Her exciting life had been reduced to complaining about the food, and her formerly ample jewelry collection had dwindled to a few thin chains around her neck.

Yet Thompson would not go on vacation then, either. Instead, he would need to tend to his "old friend," his ulcer, and prepare for a very confidential visit from Senator Mike Mansfield. Thompson was trying to figure out how—between SALT talks beginning in Geneva at the end of August and, probably, consultations prior to that; the onslaught of VIPs and "big shots" in Moscow; and the aftermath of the Czech summit in Čierna—he could find a week or two to be with his family, who were now in Venice and due to leave for the United States from Genoa, Italy, on August 21.

The Čierna meeting devolved into a debate between Dubček and Brezhnev, with neither moving from their positions, even when speaking in private in Brezhnev's personal railroad car. Brezhnev presented a number of demands, including purging key reformers from the Dubček government and reining in the media. Dubček made no promises.[37] Although Ambassador Beam was pleased with how the Dubček regime had been "staring down the Soviet threat of force" and "saving its skin" at Čierna, and Rusk thought the Czechs might still "keep the Russians off their backs,"[38] by the time of Senator Mansfield's trip, Thompson didn't think so.

On August 2, 1968, he sent the State Department a cable that he titled "Czechoslovakia-Soviet relations: the long range view."[39] He wrote: "So far as the Soviet leaders are concerned, undoubtedly one, if not their most important, concern is the preservation of their own power. No one gets to the top in this system without an unhealthy interest in power, and they can excuse their pursuit of it by rationalizing that they and they alone can preserve the gains and advance the aims of Communism." He went on to say that "the introduction of democratic processes in Czechoslovakia, even if confined to the party, would threaten to undermine the whole system." If "freedom of the press and other forms of expression" were added, he said, other Communist bloc countries could "catch the infection," and this eventually could spread to the Soviet Union itself. Thompson did not see "how the Soviet leaders can fail to consider it a serious threat to their hold on power." He also cited the strategically important location of Czechoslovakia; the threat of a loss of classified information, should Prague turn "friendly to the West"; the direct challenge to the Marxist ideology of a natural global evolution toward Communism, should any state abandon it; and, lastly, the Soviets' fear of "opening the skeletons in the closet to public view." Thompson surmised that the situation was untenable. He did not think Czechoslovakia would be able to walk this tightrope, and it would eventually have to end up on one side of the Iron Curtain or the other. The Soviets would use whatever levers they had to "restore an orthodox order" in Prague. If that failed, the Soviets' options would be "reduced to either direct military action or tacit acceptance of the new Czechoslovakia with the consequences that will flow therefrom."

Ports Unknown

Thompson finally met his family for a few days in Venice and accompanied them to Genoa, where Jane and their daughters boarded the SS *Constitution*. He, however, was to return to Moscow. On the morning of August 21, as the Thompson clan prepared to depart from the US consul's breezy and gracious old residence in that Italian port city, which was filled with the mosquito-like hum of Vespas, the news came in: Soviet tanks had rolled into Prague at nearly midnight the night before. Dubček was arrested and sent to Moscow. So instead of flying into Moscow, Thompson flew to Washington, DC, to help deal with the shrapnel from this explosive event. He concluded that Moscow had intervened because, as he had feared, "Dubček couldn't retain control of the Czech reform elements," and "largely because the Czech leaders were committing the heresy of giving the people real, rather than theoretical, power to make political decisions."[40] He did not think it was a deliberate rejection of either détente or arms control, however. Nonetheless, the timing of the Soviets' incursion into Czechoslovakia occurred on the day when the US Congress began the process to ratify the Non-Proliferation Treaty. The Soviet action delayed its passage, and the SALT talks, until 1969.

As Jane and the girls stood at the railing of the huge ocean liner, huddled around their transistor radio to catch the last bits of news, confetti flew and horns blew as the ship prepared to depart, and it seemed to Jane as though the whole world was oblivious, just as it had appeared to be during the Hungarian uprising in 1956. Just then one of the other passengers, a rather large American lady, turned to her friend and said, "Dubček, Dubček, isn't that the place we went last week?" For Jane, it confirmed that somehow America had changed in the short number of years she had been peering at it from afar, through the pages of *Look* and *Life* magazines. She had written to her mother earlier that summer: "The country [America] must be in a very ugly mood and it is hard to fathom from here [Moscow]. We also have a rough time trying to explain, defend, or what not and I really can't conceive of it all."[41]

Race riots, antiwar demonstrations, and the rise of the counterculture worried her, and that was what she found herself delivering her two younger daughters into when the girls returned to the United States in 1968. Jane herself was going back to Moscow. Andy was at the University of Vienna. Jenny was heading to Cornell University, and Sherry to a boarding school in New England. She had been asked to stay on at the Bolshoi Ballet School in Moscow, but Thompson, knowing he would be leaving early that year, had said "*Nyet.*" She was accepted at the School of American Ballet, with George Balanchine himself giving her the once-over, but Thompson and Jane were worried about the state of affairs in America and would not allow her to live in New York City, either. So they sent Sherry to an idyllic campus in a town not terribly far from Alice's Restaurant, where Arlo Guthrie set his popular folksong about getting arrested for littering and trying to use his "criminal record" as a reason to avoid being drafted and sent to Vietnam. All that should have been a clue for her parents.

On September 24, Thompson wrote an enigmatic cable back to the State Department.[42] Apparently some individuals in the Johnson administration were concerned that the Soviets might move into Romania and Yugoslavia, or even Austria, as the fever from the Prague Spring spread. Thompson assured the department that this was not likely. What was mysterious, though, was that he was planning a trip to Wiesbaden, West Germany, "ostensibly" he said, for medical treatment. He had previously made arrangements for a government plane to take him back from Germany to Moscow and "bring in 8,000 pounds of sensitive military equipment." This seems most unusual, and there is no indication as to what the equipment might have been, although it possibly consisted of supplies for a new bubble room. In his current cable, however, Thompson said he would not be taking that plane, but instead would fly back by a commercial airline a couple of days later, while recommending that the plane with the supplies go ahead as planned. This change in plans happened a month in advance of the event.

Jane believed it was an unscheduled trip to Wiesbaden because of a lung cancer scare, and she would make him quit smoking after that. Thompson did have a deferred physical while he was in Germany, and some benign polyps were found. The doctors in Wiesbaden told him he'd have to have a 5 cm section of his colon cut out, which would probably result in him needing a colostomy bag. The operation was scheduled for a week later,[43] but Thompson could not accept that. Instead, he and Jane returned to Washington, DC, where surgeons at the nearby Bethesda Naval Hospital performed a minor operation, avoiding the colostomy bag.

Thompson and Jane stayed in the United States that October, he for the UN General Assembly meetings in New York City, and she to see friends. She got herself into the newspapers' social pages by attending the seventeenth annual Washington International Stakes, a prestigious horse race. Their trip did not include a visit to the girls' schools.

One Last Try

LBJ finally agreed to halt all the bombing of North Vietnam in October 1968, and it looked as if meaningful discussions between the two warring countries would finally begin, but there was still no breakthrough. One of the reasons may have been Richard Nixon's intervention. Afraid that the peace talks in Paris might actually produce a settlement of the Vietnam War, which could jeopardize his presidential campaign, he solicited the help of Anna Chennault to pass a message to the South Vietnamese, encouraging them to withdraw from the talks and promising them a better deal once Nixon became president.[44] Just before LBJ announced the complete bombing halt, in a nationally broadcast speech on October 31, the president learned of Nixon's move through an FBI tap of the South Vietnamese ambassador's phone. In a conversation with Senator Everett Dirksen, LBJ said, "This is treason."[45] The president decided not to go public with what he knew, because it would mean revealing that the National Security Agency (NSA) was intercepting the South Vietnamese ambassador's communications with Saigon. Perhaps once again, a chance for peace was thwarted. In light of the recent revelations regarding NSA surveillance, it is instructive that LBJ and the US senators with whom he discussed this had been more reluctant to expose what the *FBI and NSA* were doing than what *Nixon* had done.

The talks dragged on for five years, until a "peace agreement" was signed in 1973 under the Nixon administration. The South Vietnamese, however, did not get the better deal Nixon had promised them. Tens of thousands more Vietnamese would die during Nixon's administration.[46]

Family Troubles

Sherry and Jenny were each going to a friend's home for Thanksgiving in 1968, since Thompson and Jane had returned to Moscow by then. Just after Thanksgiving, the Thompsons received a frantic call from Sherry's friend's parents (it was not so easy to phone Moscow in those days). Their daughter had called to say that she and Sherry were not going back to school. They were "alright and heading for San Francisco to see the Jefferson Airplane," a rock 'n' roll group. Thompson called Bohlen in Washington, DC, to ask for his help. Bohlen, in turn, contacted the FBI, who located Sherry and her friend in New York City's Grand Central Station a few days later.

In hindsight, the ballet school in New York City would have been a safer bet for Sherry. At boarding school, she was swept up in the fever of the youth movement. She was fascinated by her native country, which seemed altogether new, and she wanted to see what the California scene was all about. After her "capture," the boarding school principal said he would take the two girls back if they signed an affidavit stating they had never smoked pot on campus. Sherry's friend was readmitted, but Sherry refused to sign, because she told her mother it wasn't true.

Thompson wrote to Bohlen to thank him for his help and admitted that he was completely baffled by the whole affair. Bohlen wrote back that Sherry "seemed to be somewhat obsessed with the war in Vietnam and all of the current lines of thought among the youth." He went on, "I sometimes wonder who is teaching these kids, as the outcome seems to be fairly consistent."[47] Many of the sons and daughters of his colleagues were expressing these same sorts of ideas. The adults didn't seem to understand that this movement was an internal impulse against what seemed to be a *world* gone wrong, not just a Communist plot.

Thompson's world had certainly gone awry. Sherry's escapade and Jenny's Soviet boyfriend were both overshadowed by his stepdaughter's troubles. Andy had shown signs of mental instability in the past, but it was now getting worse. He and Jane worried that she could succumb to the Goelet family's legacy of mental illness. The Paris peace talks were going nowhere. The Prague Spring had scuttled the arms control talks. Nixon was the president-elect. Last, but not least, Thompson was, as always, worried about money, now that his prospects for the two-man think tank at Princeton had stalled, and his erstwhile partner, Bohlen, had signed a book deal for his memoirs.

Further Frustrations

The collateral damage from the Soviets' invasion of Czechoslovakia and the delay of the SALT talks was significant and long lasting. It meant that a potential cessation of MIRV programs in the United States and the USSR, which might have been negotiated in 1968, went past the point of no return.[48] Both the Soviet and the American participants in arms control issues would later rue missed chances: at Glassboro in 1967, when Johnson was ready, but Kosygin was not; and then in 1968, when Kosygin was prepared to go ahead, but Johnson no longer had enough authority to make that decision.

Toward the end of 1968, after Nixon had won the presidential election over Hubert Humphrey by a tiny margin but had not yet been sworn in, there were a few "hail Mary" attempts by the Johnson administration to rescue some vestige of the big Texan's legacy with arms talks and a Vietnam peace summit. A number of advisors, including Clark Clifford and Rusk, told LBJ to try to begin arms talks before the end of his presidency, because it would take too long for a new administration to gin up the process and, in waiting a year or more, the strategic situation would have changed for the worse.

When hints of arms control talks hit the press, however, a number of people objected vigorously. Perhaps the most impassioned was John McCloy, who had returned to New York as a private citizen. He penned a five-page memo to the president opposing any arms talks. Like many who were still in the US government, he held on to the notion that the United States had a right to maintain a strategic nuclear superiority, which, he argued, America would implicitly forego "the minute we touch our foot down in the meeting room."[49] Whether it was appropriate for LBJ at this stage in his lame-duck presidency to seek a summit is another issue. It really wasn't. His interests were clearly toward *his* legacy, and by now the Soviets were the ones who were again stalling and not responding. Yet Thompson was expected to try and arrange a summit he knew would not happen, and he did so while preparing for his own retirement.

38 ≋

"Retirement," So to Speak

The achievement by the two principal nuclear powers of
effective deterrence is probably the most important
military and political development of this decade.
—LLEWELLYN THOMPSON, speech, Vienna, 1964

The Thompsons left Moscow for the last time on January 14, 1969. When the press asked Thompson what his chief accomplishment was, he answered, "Not having done anything to make matters worse."[1] "Although," he added, "there are great opportunities for causing harm here." He explained that his formula for dealing with the Soviets was that "honesty was the best policy," and that it was never a good idea to resolve world problems in a hurry. He told reporter Edmund Stevens that his "bitterest disappointment" was the U-2 incident.[2]

Both Thompson and his friend Charles Bohlen officially retired on January 18, 1969. It was a simple but solemn ceremony, presided over by Dean Rusk at the State Department.[3] Rusk said: "I will not make individual speeches about these wonderful people. One doesn't need to talk about men who are legends while still on active duty." He called them his trusted advisors and said that they had made an imprint on history, as "they practiced the great virtues of classical diplomacy." For them, it was "never too early to anticipate a crisis or ever too late to take hold of a crisis and try to stop it." Bohlen made his remarks first. He noted that he and Thompson had served under seven secretaries of state and almost as many presidents. He then went to some lengths to praise his wife for her help and support throughout his career. When he finished, Thompson, "with a twinkle in his eye," said, "Well Chip, my wife is every bit as good as yours!" which helped to break the serious atmosphere. Thompson told the audience he was not meant to officially retire until the following month, but he said, fingering his "goodbye gift" (an American flag) from Rusk, "I figured a flag in the hand is worth two in the next administration." He chided the secretary in a friendly way, saying that Rusk was the worst vacation taker. He also acknowledged the persuasive powers of the secretary of state by recalling how Rusk "conned" Thompson into returning to Moscow for a third time.

Once the ambassador had formally retired, President Nixon would still ask Thompson to come in from time to time for consultations, and to sit in on NSC meetings. Thompson did research for the Board of Estimates at the CIA, served as a consultant for the RAND Corporation, and sat on several boards of directors. For this work, he would be paid far more than he had ever received as a US ambassador. Forever worried that something would happen to him before he had secured his family's future, Thompson tried to save as much money as he could. If anything, he kept his family on a tighter budget than before.

Thompson's retirement brought him institutional recognition. He obtained honorary degrees from both Yale University and the University of Colorado. During the latter occasion, he got to see his nephew, Bob Thompson, and catch up on Colorado news. In November 1971, the State Department gave Thompson the Director General's Cup for Civil Service.

On May 15, 1969, the White House and its new occupant held a tribute dinner to honor "famed American ambassadors."[4] This was the first presidential dinner in history to salute top Foreign Service officers. Thompson, Bohlen, Robert Murphy (who had served as ambassador to Belgium under Truman and then to Japan under Eisenhower), and David Bruce (as ambassador to West Germany under Eisenhower and then to the United Kingdom under JFK, LBJ, and Nixon) were the guests of honor,

Retirement speech by Llewellyn Thompson Jr. (*right*), at the Department of State, Washington, DC, January 17, 1969. The audience included Secretary of State Dean Rusk (*standing, center*) and family members (*seated, left to right*), stepdaughter Fernanda ("Andy") Goelet, and Jenny, Sherry, and Jane Thompson. Courtesy of James S. Wright, Department of State staff photographer.

and the after-dinner entertainment featured jazz pianist and conductor Peter Nero. Jane made her last grand appearance at this gala event, wearing an emerald-green silk dress. She looked remarkably well and happy.

The four ambassadors received their guests in different rooms. Bohlen was in the Blue Room, and Thompson got the Red Room. Seeing such a grand celebration for what was actually the end of four careers reminded him of a story, Thompson said: "A fellow went to the race track and saw a priest bless a horse before the race, so he bet on him. When that horse won, he bet on every horse the priest blessed and they all won. When the last race came, he decided to bet everything he had on the horse blessed for that race, but this horse lost. He asked the priest how such a thing could happen. 'The trouble with you Protestants,' said the priest, 'is you don't understand the difference between a blessing and the last rites.'"

In late July, the world sat in front of televisions and radios as US astronauts Buzz Aldrin and Neil Armstrong walked on the moon. The Thompsons set up their tiny, twelve-inch black-and-white television on the Venetian mirrored coffee table in their townhouse. They, their daughters Jenny and Sherry, and their guests Marie and Averell Harriman were crowded together on the long yellow sofa to watch. Averell, to whom the nickname "Crocodile" was frequently applied, really did look like a crocodile at that stage: he was very stooped and lined, and a little spittle formed at the corner of his mouth, despite his best efforts to keep it at bay. It could not have occurred to any of them that he would outlive Thompson by more than a decade.

SALT 1, 2, 3

Thompson's formal retirement would not last long, however. President Nixon would soon call on him to return. On the day of Nixon's inauguration, the Soviets contacted the new administration and indicated that they were ready to start strategic arms limitation talks.[5] In July 1969, Nixon's "Florida White House" announced that the US delegation to the SALT talks would include the former ambassador to Moscow, Llewellyn Thompson. This time he would not head the delegation—that was Gerard Smith's job—but instead would serve as an advisor.[6] The actual talks were announced in October, and they opened in Helsinki, Finland, on November 17.

On a chilly Sunday, the last day in November, Thompson was with Paul Nitze and Smith, returning to the Hotel Kalastajatorpa in Helsinki. They had come from a smorgasbord meal a few miles outside of the city, held in a beautiful, Russian-style house that had once been a famous bordello in the last days of the czars. Thompson was in a good mood. At long last, SALT was becoming a reality. The days were long, but the work was truly interesting and, as he told Jane in his letter home, "important."[7] Nonetheless, Thompson did think that there were too many people attached to the American delegation, which made for some bitterness, since various individuals, on occasion, were necessarily excluded from meetings. It was impossible to tell how it would all come out in the end, but, considering this was only the preliminary conference, Thompson estimated that the prospects didn't "look too bad."

From left to right, Raymond Garthoff, Llewellyn Thompson Jr., and Paul Nitze at the SALT talks, Helsinki, November 24, 1969. Kaius Hendenstrom, Helsinki, courtesy of Lehtikuva Picture Agency.

Thompson felt he was among friends in Helsinki. Besides Nitze and Smith, Raymond Garthoff was there and sat on his right during the meetings. Thompson's long-time secretary from the State Department, Lizzie Lee, was now stationed in Helsinki. On the Soviet side, there was Dobrynin, and Thompson also crossed paths with the head of the Soviet delegation, Vladimir Semonov, who had been the Soviet high commissioner to East Germany when Thompson was in Vienna. Semonov also had a hand in organizing the Berlin blockade in 1948–1949, as he was the senior Soviet political advisor there at that time. Then there was Georgi Kornienko, whom Thompson knew well and respected. A congenial atmosphere surrounded the delegates. The only thing that bothered everyone was when Nitze smoked his big cigar, which filled the small room they were in with a miasma of smoke.[8]

The weekend entertainment was a performance of *Swan Lake,* with a famous Soviet as the guest prima ballerina. Being a long-time expert in all things related to performances of this particular ballet, Thompson commented that the Russian danced quite well but was not attractive, as well as being a terrible actress, yet he was pleasantly surprised by the quality of the Finnish dancers, making yet another *Swan Lake* bearable. As he sat by the window, writing to his wife that he was "expanding rapidly" from the wonderful Finnish food, the first snow of the year began to fall, and he noticed that his old friend the ulcer had not appeared, at least not yet.[9]

The Soviets had reached the point where they truly wanted arms control, a situation that Thompson recognized, which contributed to his sense of optimism. It had taken a while for the Soviet leadership to understand the potential benefits of arms control for both sides. Like the Americans, there was opposition from the Soviets' conservative military leaders. When the Glassboro meetings took place, the Soviets had not yet had their own internal strategic arms debate.[10] Now, with the numerical increase in the Soviets' strategic forces and uncertainty about the evolution of their ABM system, they were ready to talk.[11]

The first round of SALT discussions in Helsinki (the location of the various rounds would alternate between there and Vienna) dealt as much with the "hows" as the "whats." Thompson saw this as an opportunity to structure the talks in a way he thought could be productive. He held, as he'd said many times before, that the United States ought to have a substantive position to offer, and Smith agreed. Nixon went along with this, although it was not because he agreed with Smith in holding that this action showed good faith, and not because, like Thompson, he reckoned that the Soviets would now be more likely to be serious about arms control talks. Nixon thought the proposal ought to "*appear* [emphasis added] serious   more for US public opinion than for showing good faith to the Soviets." Nixon believed the Soviets "don't care about world opinion" and instead "are worried about their security."[12]

Due to Thompson's initiative, the SALT talks would be held in the strictest confidence. Not only would neither side reveal the content of what was discussed to the press, but the Americans even established a separate communications system for cables back to Washington, DC, without going through the embassies in Helsinki or Vienna. In addition, the more sensitive talks took place in the bubble rooms of the Soviet and US embassies. Similar to the Trieste negotiations, delegates from both sides also took part in smaller, informal meetings over meals and the like. Both delegations maintained the rule of secrecy remarkably well. Eventually there would be some leaks, most of which could be traced to Washington, DC, colleagues.[13]

Thompson had very well-considered thoughts about what kinds of proposals the Americans should make, as well as on the various issues at hand, but he did not take hard positions, nor did he express his opinion in ways that might contribute to the difficulty of those delicate talks. His more-subtle contributions were first, to help "keep things on an even keel and moving forward,"[14] and second, to convince the Soviets, by his presence there, that the Nixon administration was actually ready to negotiate.

If Thompson had not been part of the delegation, the SALT negotiations might have ended with this first meeting. The Soviets had initially come to Helsinki not to negotiate, but to probe the seriousness of the Americans. They were not committed to the process and were prepared to pull out if they sensed it was only a ploy or mere window dressing. The Soviet delegation went back to the Kremlin to report on the first meeting, in order to allow a decision to be taken on whether to return or not. Garthoff believes that they chose to come back for the next meeting because Thompson was there.[15] The Soviets had seen him in action over so many years, during which time he'd always been direct and honest, and that helped them trust the Americans' intentions enough to continue.

Thompson left Finland just before Christmas. The delegations simply stated that their talks had been "businesslike," leaving the press scrambling for something to say. The participants could report, however, that the talks would go forward; that they had agreed, in general principal, on what the nature of the talks would be; and that the discussions would continue in Vienna in early spring 1970.

A day or two after Thompson got back to Washington, DC, he and Jane went to a "Colonial Christmas" weekend bash in Williamsburg, Virginia. It was a glittery affair that included the likes of Hubert Humphrey and Walter Cronkite, as well as socialites and minor royalty. The brochure Jane found, placed on the eighteenth-century bedstead in their room, said the party honored, in Williamsburg tradition, "acute men of business and [the] grace of living." The *Washington Star* gushed that the "doorways were lined with evergreens studded with polished red apples and Della Robbia wreaths hung from nearly every American brass knocker." Its reporter described Thompson as leaning back in his chair, legs outstretched, "pensively blowing silky smoke rings while the harpsichordist played softly."[16] That was the pose he would strike when deep in thought. Perhaps it was from jet lag. Perhaps he was thinking about the SALT talks and letting himself believe they might be more than "just nailing down radars and interceptors and that sort of thing," to become a process that might develop a better understanding between the two superpowers.[17] Perhaps he would finally have a forum in which he could put his years of experience to real use.

But that was not to be. Nixon's national security advisor, Henry Kissinger, had no intention of having the American SALT delegation—or any other—deal with issues that might have a political significance he wanted to reserve for himself. Kissinger virtually kidnapped the SALT talks, causing hard feeling and unnecessary difficulties. Importantly, it meant that there were really *two* negotiating teams: the one meeting first in Helsinki and then in Vienna, headed by Gerard Smith; and the other, where Kissinger met secretly in Moscow and Washington, DC, with the Soviet's ambassador, Dobrynin.[18] Neither Secretary of State William P. Rogers nor the delegates to the SALT talks were kept in the loop about these negotiations until the very end, when it was too late to give their input.[19]

Meanwhile, Thompson arrived in Vienna in April 1970 for the SALT 2 talks. "No other event in diplomatic history," claimed the *Department of State Newsletter*, "has been surrounded simultaneously by so much doubt and so much hope." The Austrian press, in particular, noted Thompson's attendance and recalled in words and images his role in the Austrian State Treaty negotiations, giving him a kind of celebrity.[20] To be back at the Belvedere Palace was especially poignant for Thompson. Just before the talks were officially convened, he stood by a window looking out over a cold gray day and, with eyes watering, he turned to a colleague standing next to him and said: "Fifteen years ago I looked down from this window on a sea of joyous faces as the State Treaty was signed and Austria took its place in the world once again as a sovereign country. I will never forget it."[21] That colleague later wrote to Jane: "That each face in this sea was in fact looking with gratitude at him never crossed [Thompson's] mind. I talked with many Austrians who stood in those grounds on that historic day and many who had not and I know their feelings. I don't think I ever met a man who had the respect of so many—a whole nation."

The stakes in SALT were even higher. At Hiroshima and Nagasaki in 1945, the explosive force of atomic bombs was measured in equivalent kilotons of TNT and the delivery time in hours; by 1970, it was measured in megatons—a thousand-fold increase—and delivery times were as low as four minutes. During the period of the early SALT talks, just one bomb was the equivalent of a freight train, loaded with TNT, that stretched from New York City to Los Angeles, all being held in check by the precarious doctrine of mutual deterrence, which was now being threatened by both ABMs and MIRVs.[22] MIRVs created the illusion of at least being able to knock out an enemy's second-strike ability and, unlike the large-scale footprint of a new missile silo, their locations would be difficult to verify. ABMs were also destabilizing and threatened to create an escalating arms race. The time was propitious, and the need was urgent. SALT had to happen when it did, because the two sides were at relative parity and could accept at least a nuclear arms freeze without substantially upsetting the strategic applecart.[23]

Sadly, in addition to Kissinger's extramural negotiations, the SALT delegates had to navigate intramural politics. Thompson was focused on moving the talks forward. According to Garthoff, Thompson approached the negotiations by advocating what he felt was best for the situation, not necessarily just for the State Department. That premise, he said, was "not true of others, especially the JCS or the DOD, with many of the differences [arising] between the military institutions."[24]

By the end of SALT 2 in Vienna, Thompson had become supremely frustrated. The negotiations were veering toward a track that encompassed nearly everything Thompson had said should *not* be done when negotiating with the Soviets.[25] He had counseled that surprise proposals never worked, and that patience was crucial. Nixon, however, stated, "I don't agree with Thompson['s] thesis."[26] The Kissinger-Nixon team was fast when creating and adjusting proposals, because it was small and did not send anything out for review to either the SALT delegation or Congress. The Soviets were not as flexible, and this caused stylistic differences. From the point of view of the American SALT delegation, the White House, in running the negotiations from afar, made a number of blunders. Dobrynin, too, in looking back, said that Kissinger, "for all his diplomatic talent and bureaucratic skills," was not able to deal with "all the details and minor nuances that arose."[27] The Soviets, Dobrynin said, had a single team in Moscow backing both the formal and the secret negotiators, but Kissinger chose to single-handedly "orchestrate the whole complex business." The White House also unilaterally inserted a last-minute clause into a proposal to ban the testing and deployment of MIRVs by linking them to onsite inspections—which the Soviets had never accepted—instead of the national verifications that the arms control establishment had carefully crafted over many years. It effectively destroyed the prospects for any agreement on MIRVs. This was probably what Nixon and Kissinger wanted, but the US delegation to the SALT talks did not know that, and they took it to be a colossal mistake.[28]

Despite all the stumbling blocks, Thompson stuck with it and planned to go to SALT 3, the next meeting in Helsinki, in fall 1970. Unfortunately, he had to sit out that session, because he'd suffered a mild heart attack late that summer. This third session didn't go very well, and Gerard Smith called it the "season of frustration" in his memoirs.[29] Thompson returned to SALT 4 in Vienna in spring 1971. By then, the Soviet position had hardened, and they sought to separate the ABM discussion from the offensive weapons discussion.[30] When the Soviets were the only ones who had an ABM system, they had insisted that any talks on limiting ABMs also had to include limits for offensive weapons. Now the Americans were moving ahead with their own ABM system, while the Soviets, who were cutting back on theirs, had more or less caught up with United States in terms of offensive weapons, so the tables were turned. Nixon and Kissinger agreed to separate the two issues, making some members of the US delegation, like Nitze, furious.

Thompson's participation in the SALT talks ended in 1971. The agreement collectively referred to as SALT I would not be signed until three months after his death. He had spent decades perfecting the art of negotiating with the Soviets and was dismayed that he could no longer bring it to bear in this important work. Aside from the specifics of what could have been accomplished in arms control at the SALT I series of talks, he rued the missed opportunity to improve understandings and relations between his "clients," as he called them, and to make some lasting difference in the peace and stability of the world.[31]

In October 1972, when the SALT treaty was eventually ratified, President Nixon paid a "personal tribute" to the Congress he'd sidelined.[32] He then said: "It would not be fair to mention the names of all [the people in both governments who worked on the agreement] . . . but I am sure that everyone would appreciate the fact that I would say that one name particularly comes to mind today . . . Ambassador Llewellyn Thompson. It can truly be said of him, as it can be said of so many others who have worked in this field, that he gave his life to the cause of peace."

During 1970 and 1971, Nixon hoped to link progress in the SALT talks to progress in Vietnam. That obviously went nowhere, causing the arms control talks to stall.[33] It was not until 1972, an election year, that the idea of signing the SALT agreement became a priority for Nixon. It would look good for the United States to sign a major deal with the Soviets, but Nixon was more interested in the *appearance* of an arms agreement than in actual arms control. He and Kissinger openly derided the arms control people, who these two men thought would "give it all away."[34] Even then, Nixon worried that the conservative wing of his Republican Party would criticize him for the agreement, so he wanted to be sure he could retroactively "build a record that we considered the thing [SALT]" before any of its terms were made public.[35]

Kissinger's method of handling diplomacy was far from what veteran diplomats like Thompson could accept.[36] Seeing how Kissinger treated Secretary of State Rogers, Thompson would tell young men thinking of joining the State Department—an institution he loved—not to do so unless they wanted to become innkeepers for Kissinger.[37] Thompson believed in the State Department and thought its role was indispensable to the running of foreign policy. He had faith in the painstaking information-gathering role its embassies played. It was teamwork, carefully coordinated by the secretary of state, that would provide the president with the best advice for his decision making. Thompson distrusted a situation where one individual usurped these duties. Thompson was not against opening relations toward China but was against Nixon and Kissinger's secret method of going about it. The president, who wanted to make bold foreign affairs moves, had begun looking for an approach to China since the beginning of his mandate.[38] Nixon's China initiative would take everyone by surprise, and it would change the global balance of power.

Shortly after Nixon had taken office, Thompson met with the new president and Kissinger on February 7, 1969, and warned them that the United States "should be careful not to feed Soviet suspicions about the possibility of our ganging up with Communist China against them."[39] He did not believe that rapprochement with the Chinese should be made at the expense of détente with the Soviets. In June, Thompson and Bohlen expressed similar concerns to the president when they heard that Nixon was going to ease trade restrictions with China. They warned the president to avoid "using" China against the Soviet Union. In December 1969, Thompson and Gerard Smith both proposed letting Dobrynin know that US-Chinese talks were resuming, "before it becomes public knowledge."[40] Nixon and Kissinger, however, brushed off all these advisors. Instead, both men agreed that "under no circumstances should we inform Dobrynin of the talks or their content."[41] In April 1971, the president scoffed that Thompson and other "State Department Foreign Service people" had opposed his China gambit because it would "make the Russians mad."[42] "Sure, it made the Russians mad," Nixon continued, adding, "If it makes them mad, it helps us." He thought the Kremlinologists had the idea that "we must do nothing that irritates the Russians."

Nixon, however, wanted to have his cake and eat it, too. At the same time as the president made overtures to the Chinese, he sought a summit with the Soviets, and he had discussed this briefly with Thompson in February 1969.[43] Nixon and Kissinger thought that a summit would be helpful in getting a better deal on SALT but bemoaned that "former peasant" Brezhnev was not responsive.[44] Kissinger said, "It's playing dangerously . . . but that's how you've got[ten to] where you are in foreign policy and in other things too. The thing to do is to tell . . . Dobrynin in early June, 'We've reviewed our . . . state of relations. Things are now moving on a number of fronts. Either you can commit yourself now for a summit in September or we won't have one this year.' " Kissinger described his move as an "ultimatum" and added, "Thompson would have had a heart attack."

Thompson and Kissinger had totally different approaches to diplomacy. Kissinger thought he knew how to handle the Soviets and, especially, Dobrynin. He would laughingly tell Nixon that at the opening of the Kennedy Center, when Dobrynin saw Kissinger, he came "dashing across the hall," with "Thompson trailing behind him." According to Kissinger, Thompson said, "God, you really have some relationship with Dobrynin." Kissinger then added: "I don't kid myself. I have no relationship with Dobrynin as an individual." The president agreed and said, "Thompson is naïve to think that a relationship is what does it."[45]

In a meeting with Dobrynin in June 1971, Thompson confided to him that there were two contradictory groups in both the White House and the State Department over foreign policy priorities.[46] One cohort gave importance to agreements with the Soviets, and the other to rapprochement with China, as these latter individuals thought the Chinese could help them with the situation in Vietnam. What Thompson was really trying to do was to let Dobrynin know that something was up, so when Kissinger's secret trip to China later that summer became known, it would not come as a complete surprise to the Soviets. Thompson expressed his uneasiness to the Canadian ambassador in Moscow, Robert Ford: "Things have certainly been active in the international field. . . .We seem to have managed to have offended just about everybody and I am particularly concerned about the people you are dealing with."[47] In July 1971, Kissinger secretly visited Beijing while on a trip to Pakistan and made the final arrangements for Nixon's trip to China, which would take place in February 1972, two weeks after Thompson died.

Chaga

Summer 1971 was supposed to be a quiet family holiday on Nantucket Island in Massachusetts. The family's troubles seemed to have resolved themselves. Sherry had finished high school and was set to go to University of Colorado. Jenny had abandoned the idea of returning to Moscow to marry the art student. Andy was in treatment for her bipolar disorder. The Thompsons had rented a house not far from where the Bohlens had theirs.

Jane and the three girls drove up, and they waited for Thompson to fly in to join them a few days later. The beach was a stone's throw away from the house. Thompson looked forward to golf with his friend and long conversations about everything and anything. It was all too good to be true. The night Thompson arrived by plane, the whole family went to the Bohlens' house for dinner. Thompson looked tired and seemed to sink into his chair, so they decided to leave shortly thereafter, skipping the bridge game. They would get together again when he had rested some.

That night Thompson knew something was very wrong, and he decided to fly back to Washington, DC. He had pancreatic cancer. Jane and Andy left the island by plane right away. Jenny and Sherry packed up the house and drove the two cars back home. All of a sudden, their world had become uncertain and insecure. The doctors told Jane the prognosis was that her husband had about nine months left. That autumn, Thompson began to tell people about his situation. He took William Bundy out to lunch and told him quite frankly about his illness. Bundy said: "He was in such good form that I foolishly decided to believe the two years he gave himself. It was typical of his directness and courage and ability to take life as it came."

A sort of invisibility cloak descends on people once they are diagnosed with a terminal illness. The invitations stopped coming, even from close friends. Between chemotherapy treatments, Thompson kept busy, mostly destroying certain papers and shipping others to the archives. He worried over his finances and tried to leave everything in good order. He also gave a few interviews, perhaps finally realizing that his story would either disappear altogether or be left for others to interpret.

In December 1971, Thompson received a letter from the US Golf Association, stating that the organization had exchanged correspondence with the Soviets, who had expressed some interest in golf. The head of the association remembered that Thompson "expressed the wish, however whimsical, that there be a modest course laid out somewhere near Moscow. The thought of a Soviet scorecard crediting the 'Royal and Ancient Golf Club of St. Andrews, Scotland' rules is delicious."[48] That was the last letter in Thompson's file. Although it took a while, the first golf club in Moscow was established in 1987, and the first nine-hole course opened in that city's suburbs in 1990.[49] In 1992, the Russian Golf Association was recognized by the Golf Club of St. Andrews.

Anecdotes aside, that last Christmas was special. It was very sad, but no one overtly showed it or cried or made a scene. When the pain got too bad, Jane would give her husband injections. He began walking with a cane and spent long hours sitting in his study or lying on his bed—fully dressed of course, including tie—ruminating but not sharing his thoughts. As always, he treated medical considerations as personal and almost embarrassing, not something to be communicated. It was as if he was sorry that his dying was going to cause discomfort, but there was little he could do about it. Thompson's illness was not a shock to him. Ever since his early days in Ceylon, he had known that his health was not good, and he had already dealt with the possibility of dying early. He had never been a religious man in the church-going sense, saying that he had had enough church as a youngster to last a lifetime.

When he was finally in the hospital, knowing it was only a matter of days or possibly hours that he had left, he suddenly turned to his daughters and said, "Promise me one thing." They bent over him. He had never asked them to promise anything, but now he said, "Promise you will love your father more each day." They looked at each other and smiled. "Of course we will," they said, completely misunderstanding him. A look of annoyance and almost of desperation flashed over his face, but he was too tired to go on, to explain, to add anything to his message. His expression said it all, and they understood which Father he was talking about.

One evening before he was hospitalized, there was a dinner being given at their friend Lily Guest's house for world-famous cellist Mstislav Rostropovich. Lily was one of the Kennedy Center founders, as well as chairman of the Friends of the Center. Jane, who had also worked hard for the Friends, wanted Thompson to come with her, but he was not up to it. He told her to go and pass on his regards to his old friend from Moscow days. When Rostropovich heard about Thompson's illness, he told Jane he wanted to see him right away. The two left the party immediately. Thompson was pleased by the visit, and the two men sat up until the early hours of the morning, talking and drinking a bottle of superbly well-aged whisky that someone had given Thompson as a goodbye present. Rostropovich told Thompson he would contact his friend Aleksandr Solzhenitsyn, who had cured his cancer with a magical fungus, a parasitic mushroom named chaga, which grew on trees in

Siberia.[50] The Russian author had written about chaga in his novel *Cancer Ward*, and it would surely help Thompson. Thompson thanked his friend but told him not to worry. Jane, however, did accept Rostropovich's offer, and so began a curious adventure.

Jacob Beam was the US ambassador to Moscow at the time and played a vital role. He sent the embassy counselor, Sherwood Demitz, to Mrs. Rostropovich's house.[51] It was a "secret mission," so Demitz had to sneak out of an embassy function, not telling anyone where he was going. Rostropovich's wife, Galina Vishnevskaya, a renowned opera singer, was residing in Moscow at that point, on a little street near the National Hotel. The apartment block where she lived was the usual drab, run-down Soviet building, but inside, her apartment was "spectacular," and was "decorated like something out of the nineteenth century." Demitz told her what his mission was and gave her a letter from her husband. She told him to return in a few days, when she would have the chaga available. He came back to collect it and was told to handle it carefully, as it was highly poisonous. He would have to return for directions on how to prepare it, however, because those were not ready yet. She also gave him a letter to pass on to her husband. Demitz hesitated, but under the circumstances, he decided to accept it. When he returned to pick up the instructions, he asked her if there was any expense involved, but "she absolutely refused to allow payment of any kind and said it was the least she could do for their good friend who was ill." He then passed everything on to Beam, who sent it via diplomatic pouch to Washington, DC.[52]

The package arrived in mid-January 1972. When Jane got it, she and her daughters took the chaga out into the backyard and, wearing thick rubber gloves, followed the instructions and prepared a drink made from the fungus. It had to sit in a dark place for several days before it could be taken, and Thompson died before he was able to try it. Jane gave the chaga and the mixture made from it to the National Institutes of Health, where it was analyzed and found to contain many of the properties that were used in chemotherapy.

Thompson died on February 6, 1972. His funeral took place in the National Cathedral in Washington, DC, and Charles Bohlen gave the eulogy:

> The eighteenth-century English writer, Sir Richard Steele, once wrote in the *Spectator*, "the noblest motive is the public good." This seems to epitomize Llewellyn Thompson's attitude toward his life and work. . . . His career stands and will continue to stand as an inspiration and model for all young diplomats. . . . His keen analytical intelligence, his "feel" for the other side's position, together with his tact and patience, made him one of our most effective diplomats and one of the ablest negotiators that the United States has ever had. He had the quality, so important to his profession, of being able to be firm when necessary without ever antagonizing those on the other side of the table. He could oppose without offending. . . . He would never claim credit for any success, even when it was clearly his. He never sought publicity. This was partly because of his own innate modesty, but also because he felt it was incompatible with his work as a diplomat. . . . I will remember him for his many fine qualities of mind and spirit; for the many hours of serious discussion, spiced with his inimitable stories; [and] for many happy encounters

on the golf course and at the poker table, where he excelled, as I learned to my cost. Tommy loved competition and enjoyed the clash of wits involved. But his most outstanding characteristic, to my mind, was his decency.[53]

Charles Bohlen would die two years later, on January 1, 1974, of the same pancreatic cancer that had felled Thompson.

Jane stayed on in Washington, DC, although at a remove from the city's political and social elite. In 1988, she moved to Florida to be near Sherry, and later followed her daughter to New Mexico. Jane died on February 3, 1999, and was buried three days later, on the anniversary of Thompson's death. "There are no coincidences," she used to say. The pair are both interred in the Las Animas cemetery in Colorado. As Jane used to quote about her husband, "Blessed are the peacemakers, for they shall be called the sons of God."

Perhaps it's best to end in Thompson's own words: "The most striking thing, when one looks at all the wonderful things that have been accomplished in the material field, is the little progress we have made in changing the nature of man. I should like to hope that we are entering the era of the rule of law, of disarmament, and of recognition of the brotherhood of man. As one looks around the world at today's disputes, virtually all of which are unnecessary and are capable of solution to the benefit of all parties concerned, I must confess I see little reason to be optimistic. Nevertheless we must keep on trying and hope that we can bring up future generations sufficiently free from our vices and weaknesses that they can deal with the world problems in a more rational way than we have been able to do."[54]

Notes

Abbreviations

CF   central file
DDEL   Dwight D. Eisenhower Presidential Library, Abilene, Kansas
Dulles-PL   Papers of John Foster Dulles, Princeton University Library
FA-ADST   Foreign Affairs Oral History Collection, Association for Diplomatic Studies and Training,
            Arlington, Virginia
FRUS   *Foreign Relations of the United States*, various volumes
GW-NSA   National Security Archives, George Washington University
JFKL   John F. Kennedy Presidential Library, Boston, Massachusetts
LBJL   Lyndon Baines Presidential Johnson Library, Austin, Texas
LC   Library of Congress, Washington, DC
MemCon   memo of conversation
MemConf   memo of conference
MFA   Ministry of Foreign Affairs of the Russian Federation, Moscow, Russia
NACP   National Archives, College Park, Maryland
NARA   National Archives and Records Administration
NSF   National Security File
RG   Record Group
RGANI   Russian State Archive of Contemporary History, Moscow, Russia
SecState   Secretary of State
State   US Department of State
TelCon   telephone conversation
TFP   Thompson Family Papers
TL   Harry S. Truman Library and Museum, Independence, Missouri

1 ≋ The Beginning

Epigraph. Werner Karl Heisenberg, "The Fundamental Concepts of Quantum Theory," in *Physical Principles of Quantum Theory*, introductory section 2 in the Kindle edition.

1. Thompson family tree and history, compiled by Roger and Kerry Kellermeyer, Linda Pointer and Ralph Sheely, and Eldridge Thompson, TFP.

2. Attributed to both William Byrd II and William Robert Hamilton. See Virgle Chappell, "Memories of an Oklahoma Farm Boy," www.usgennet.org/usa/ok/county/ellis/farmboy/hamilton.html.

3. Her actual name was Sarah, but everyone called her Sally.

4. Letter written by Flora Belle Thompson, TFP.

5. Llewellyn Thompson Sr. was born in Caldwell County, Missouri, on August 27, 1893.

6. Dorothy Boyd letter to Thompson, May 1962, TFP. Eli Butcher died Oct. 1936.

7. Her real name was Viddie Virginia.

8. MWood is pronounced "Em-wŏd."

9. One section of land covered approximately one square mile, or 640 acres. Part of their ranch was deeded land, and part of it included the rights to federal grazing leases. This is a typical arrangement for land in the western United States. Llewellyn Sr. and Nalda purchased the deeded land from Anglo and Hispanic settlers. The "great land grab" in New Mexico is still a highly sensitive issue, as many of the Spanish inhabitants were cheated out of their lands by unscrupulous prospectors, who had them sign away their property using English-language documents they could not read. The papers that Robert Thompson, Llewellyn Sr.'s nephew and the authors' cousin, gave us show that this was not the case for his uncle and Nalda, although some of the land they bought was sold to pay the tax debt the previous owners had accumulated, possibly accrued because they didn't know they owed their land, another sorry practice in those days.

10. The average annual rainfall is about thirteen inches.

11. She was also the first president of Chapter B of the Philanthropic Educational Organization. See *Bent County Chronicle*, 36th ed., Oct 2016–Feb 2017.

12. The authors interviewed the owner, Mrs. Perkins, shortly before her hundredth birthday. She still wrote the local gossip column, with her daughter's help, in 2006.

13. Comancheros were New Mexican Hispanic traders, whose best customers were the Comanche Indians.

14. The ranch was split in 1939. Half of Nalda's portion of the ranch is now the 28,000-acre New Mexico State University Range and Livestock Research Center.

15. The authors visited the ranch the same day that Campos's body was returned from Texas for reburial in Corona.

16. Authors' interview with Robert Thompson, Aug 27, 2007, TFP.

17. Authors' interview with Delores Plested [Bill's sister], Aug 27, 2007, TFP.

2 ≋ Into the World

1. While the official title is the Department of State, it is often referred to as the State Department. In this book, the authors use the latter term.

2. He believed he botched the oral exam, so the written exam had to make up for a lot. See Wallace Carroll, "Llewellyn E Thompson: The Diplomat and the Enigma," p. 39, in Kuhn and Kuhn, *Adventures in Public Service*.

3. Ruth Shipley was a famous fixture in the State Department.

4. Thompson correspondence with Norman Armour, 1959–1960, TFP.

5. Thompson uttered this statement in a film made when he received the President's Award for Distinguished Federal Civil Service, Nov 6, 1962, TFP.

6. Jack Ryan, "Meet Llewellyn Thompson: Our Expert at the Kremlin," *Family Weekly*, Jan 20, 1963, p. 6.

7. John Silva note to Thompson, TFP. *Bhikkliu* refers to an ordained male Buddhist monastic.

8. Muggeridge, in *Infernal Grove* (p. 13), wrote that it was as though "in some mysterious way just willing this would bring it about." It remained wishful thinking. As Benito Mussolini had observed, "The League is very well when sparrows shout, but no good at all when eagles fall out." In a sad irony, World War II began just as construction of the new Palais des Nations to house the League was being finished.

9. Ryan, "Meet Llewellyn Thompson." Thompson named Gilbert's wife, Charlotte, as godmother to his daughter Jenny and, later, Jacob Beam as her godfather.

10. Carroll, "Llewellyn E Thompson," in Kuhn and Kuhn, *Adventures in Public Service*, p. 40.

11. Weisbrode, *Atlantic Century*, location 487 in the Kindle edition.

12. Muggeridge, *Infernal Grove*, p. 8.

13. Geneva, 1934 efficiency report, Thompson personnel file, TFP.

14. Carroll, "Llewellyn E Thompson," p. 41.

15. "Frances Perkins (1880–1965)," Eleanor Roosevelt Papers Project, https://www2.gwu.edu/~erpapers/teachinger/glossary/perkins-frances.cfm.

16. In *Citizens of London*, Olson mistakenly credits Ambassador John Gilbert Winant with being the first American to serve in the ILO, when instead it was Thompson. FDR appointed Winant as head of the ILO in 1939.

17. "Report of the Director General of the International Labour Office," 185th Session, 1972, items 20 and 21, and correspondence with Jane Thompson, TFP.

18. Prentiss Gilbert, 1936 report on Thompson, Thompson personnel file, TFP.

19. Thirty years later, in 1970, when access to official evaluations was made available, Thompson was disappointed to learn that Gilbert, the man he so admired and whose influence had marked him so much, had actually been responsible for slowing down Thompson's advancement by his unfortunate remarks. It upset Thompson enough that he called Jonathan Rickert [his staff aide in Moscow from 1966 to 1968] into his office, fearing he may have committed the same error. "Out of the blue," Thompson told Jonathan the story that had impeded his progress in Geneva and added that he had persevered, working hard and building a successful career, despite this early setback. Jonathan did not realize the purpose of this unusual personal confidence sharing until he read his own evaluation report from Thompson later on. It was less than positive and had resulted in no promotion. The offhand remark that "my wife and daughters would give him low marks" was the offending phrase. To Jonathan's credit, he went on to have a long and successful career and bore no grudges. He was very helpful to the authors in this book project.

20. This included letters of appeal from Labor Secretary Frances Perkins and from James C. Dunn, in the State Department's Division of European Affairs, both in TFP.

21. Two years later, in 1939, Gilbert died in Berlin. He was only fifty-six years old.

22. Thompson's much-loved grandfather, Eli Butcher, died that October and became the last Confederate to be buried in the Las Animas Cemetery.

3 ≋ To Moscow

1. Thompson was promoted to Foreign Service Officer (FSO) class 7 in what, until 1943, was called the Division of European Affairs.

2. Sally Swift, Capital Whirl column, *Washington Post*, Oct 2, 1940, TFP.

3. After World War I, the Sudetenland (roughly 11,000 square miles) became part of Czechoslovakia. Hitler threatened to invade Czechoslovakia. To avoid war, on September 29, 1938, Adolf Hitler, Neville Chamberlain, Edouard Daladier, and Benito Mussolini signed the Munich Agreement, which transferred the Sudetenland to Germany.

4. The Soviets invaded Finland after a series of demands for access to Finnish military bases. Unexpectedly, the Finnish army put up an impressive defense, but after three months of intense fighting, Soviet forces defeated the Finns. The Finnish and Soviet governments then negotiated the Treaty of Moscow, resulting in the transfer of around 16,000 square miles to the USSR.

5. The US Army sent promising officers who were expected to rise to the rank of general to this program. Alumni have included Generals Dwight D. Eisenhower, Omar Bradley, and George S. Patton.

6. Thompson correspondence with his brothers, TFP.

7. Directive memo for Analytical Studies course, Army War College, Jan 12, 1940, TFP.

8. Memorandum from Undersecretary of State Welles to Assistant Secretary of State Berle, regarding Thompson's report on the Army War College's G-2 course, Feb 5, 1940, TFP. The War College closed after the United States entered World War II, due to the nation's need for officers in the field. It reopened in 1950.

9. Costigliola, *Roosevelt's Lost Alliances*, pp. 264–67.

10. *Yezhovshchina* was derived from the name of the head of the Soviet secret police, Nikolai Yezhov.

11. Costigliola, *Roosevelt's Lost Alliances*, chap. 7, "The Diplomacy of Trauma."

12. The lowest figures given are around 9 million, and the highest, about 60 million. The generally accepted number of Stalin victims is circa 20 million. Costigliola, in *Roosevelt's Lost Alliances* (p. 263), argues that the Soviet experts among the Americans the reacted to the clampdown personally and behaved like "spurned lovers." Yet their response to the purges can hardly be considered frivolous.

13. Bohlen, *Witness to History*, p. 51.

14. Kennan to SecState, telegram, Feb 22, 1946, 861.00/2-2246, GW-NSA.

15. After Moscow, Charles Bohlen was sent to Tokyo, and it is possible that this is where Thompson and Bohlen first met. After six years in Moscow, George Kennan, who never agreed with Ambassador Joseph Davies, accepted a transfer back to Washington, DC. Loy Henderson was sent to Iraq, under pressure from the White House.

16. Sally Swift, Capital Whirl column, *Washington Post*, Dec 13, 1940, TFP.

17. The poem came from a Christmas booklet that was presented to Thompson at the farewell party. This booklet is in TFP.

18. The poem, also from the farewell party, was attached to an Edward Page letter to Thompson, May 28, 1958, TFP.

19. Sally Swift, Capital Whirl column, *Washington Post*, Dec 18, 1940.

20. Tolly, *Caviar and Commissars*, p. 48.

21. Angus Ward would go on to serve in China, where he and other Americans were accused of inciting riots and espionage. They were held for over a year by Mao Zedong's People's Liberation Army during the Chinese revolution, after Ward refused to turn over the United States' coded transmitter.

22. State to Tokyo for Thompson, 1941 travel order 10940, Jan 31, 1941, Thompson 123 file, 1945–1949, stack 250, row 60, compartment 10, shelf 1, box 937, RG 59, NACP.

23. A balalaika is a Russian stringed instrument with a triangular body.

24. Charles Thayer would later be recruited by William J. "Wild Bill" Donovan, head of the Office of Strategic Services (the wartime espionage and sabotage agency), to parachute into Yugoslavia to both help and report on the Chetniks and Tito's Partisans, who were fighting the Germans as well as each other.

25. For more stories about how the community of foreigners saw Ambassador Steinhardt, see Moats, *Blind Date with Mars*. Thompson, according to the archives of the Soviets' main state security agency, the KGB, was offended by Moats's easy derision of the Soviets she encountered. See a draft article by Vasilii S. Khristoferov, TFP.

26. Thompson letter to Professor Travis Beal Jacobs, Middlebury College, Vermont, TPF; Mayers, *The Ambassadors*; and Harriman and Abel, *Special Envoy*.

27. The Arbat is a well-known street in the historical center of Moscow. It is one of the Russian capital's oldest surviving streets.

28. "Efficiency Rating: Political Work, February 1941 to _____" [blank on original], Thompson personnel file, TFP.

29. In the case of Yugoslavia, this tunnel vision ironically would lead the United States and the United Kingdom into supporting the Communist Partisans over the royalist anti-Communists (Chetniks), because reports from British intelligence at the time claimed that the Partisans were more effective against the Germans. This was a questionable decision, as it is now clear that the Partisans used most of the supplies and arms sent to them by the Allies not to fight the Germans, but to fight their civil war instead. See Lindsay, *Beacons in the Night*.

30. Tolly, *Caviar and Commissars*, p. 51.

31. The embassy would eventually evacuate from Moscow, but it did not relocate to Kazan.

32. Thayer, *Bears in the Caviar*, location 3092 in the 2015 Kindle edition.

33. CIA Center for the Study of Intelligence publication, vol. 48, no. 2, V. S. Khristoforov, article 12.

34. Thayer, *Hands across the Caviar*, p. 11.

35. Tzouliadis, *The Forsaken*; and Moats, *Blind Date with Mars*. "Potemkin" refers to the story of Grigori Potemkin, who set up a fake village in order to impress the Russian empress.

36. Robert Pickens Meiklejohn, World War II diary, Averell Harriman Papers, LC. Meiklejohn was Harriman's longtime secretary.

37. For a description of Harriman's rise in politics and the Foreign Service, see Olson, *Citizens of London*.

38. Thayer, *Bears in the Caviar*. Thayer explained that Lord Beaverbrook insisted the Soviet pilot fly higher than the usual low "contact flying" that country's pilots preferred. This caused the Soviet antiaircraft battery to mistake the planes for enemy aircraft, because the men could not see the Soviet markings on them.

39. Meiklejohn World War II diary, Averell Harriman Papers, LC.

40. Harriman and Abel, *Special Envoy*.

41. Ibid.

42. Ibid.

4 ≋ The Siege of Moscow

1. Until 1942, FDR relied on Sumner Wells, the undersecretary of state, more than on his secretary of state.

2. Cassidy, *Moscow Dateline*.

3. Ibid.

4. Vyacheslav Molotov was the Soviet foreign minister from 1939 to 1949. He was preceded by Maxim Litvinov and succeeded by Andrey Vyshinsky. Molotov had formed part of Stalin's close circle and helped Nikita Khrushchev come to power after Stalin's death. Molotov also plotted to remove Khrushchev, so he was reassigned from his Moscow post and sent as an ambassador to Mongolia. He was cosignatory to the Molotov-Ribbentrop Pact between the USSR and Germany. When Germany invaded the USSR, Molotov then negotiated with the British. See Cassidy, *Moscow Dateline*.

5. Annual efficiency report, Aug 31, 1942, Thompson personnel file, TFP.

6. Cassidy, *Moscow Dateline*.

7. General Zhukov claimed that 250,000 women and teenagers moved almost 3 million cubic meters of dirt to build trenches and moats by hand. See "Battle of Moscow," Wikipedia, https://en.wikipedia.org/wiki/Battle_of_Moscow/.

8. Moats, *Blind Date with Mars*.

9. For more on Kuybyshev, see Kemp Tolly, *Caviar and Commissars*.

10. Thayer, *Bears in the Caviar*, p. 228; Cassidy, *Moscow Dateline*; and Moats, *Blind Date with Mars*.

11. *Spaso House, 75 Years: A Short History*, Office of the Historian, US Department of State, 2008.

12. Loy Henderson inspection report, Sep 1, 1942, Foreign Service inspection reports file: Moscow 1942, RG 59, NACP.

13. William L. White, "Tommy," *Emporia [KS] Gazette*, Feb 10, 1972, TFP.

14. Authors' conversation with their mother; and Jane Thompson unpublished memoirs, TFP.

15. Thayer, *Bears in the Caviar*; and C. L. Sulzberger, "But This Is Moscow," *New York Times*, Dec 14, 1941, TFP.

16. Cassidy, *Moscow Dateline*.

17. Inspection report, Dec 18, 1942, Foreign Service inspection reports file: Moscow 1942, RG 59, NACP.

18. White, "Tommy."

19. William J. Jorden, "Quiet Diplomacy of Our Moscow Spokesman," *New York Times Magazine*, Jan 26, 1958.

20. Laura Bergquist, "Llewellyn Thompson: JFK's No. 1 Russian Expert," *Look*, Feb 12, 1963, TFP.

21. Thayer, *Moscow Interlude*.

22. Tolly, *Caviar and Commissars*, p. 64n; and Carroll, "Llewellyn E Thompson," in Kuhn and Kuhn, *Adventures in Public Service*, pp. 45–46.

23. Regarding the danger involved, see correspondence from the undersecretary of state to Messrs. Shaw and Atherton, and memo from Steinhardt to Henderson, both dated Dec 4, 1941, CF FW124.61/223a, RG 59, NACP.

24. Summer didn't improve things in Kuybyshev, with some of the Americans already showing signs of malnourishment and scurvy from the limited diet. Their misery was compounded by mud and malaria [contracted from giant mosquitoes].

25. Laurence Steinhardt letter to MWood Thompson, Dec 1, 1941, TFP.

26. F. Joseph Dresen, "Review of Rodric Braithwaite, *Moscow 1941: A City and Its People at War*," Jul 27, 2011, Kennan Institute, Wilson Center, Washington, DC. This refers to military deaths in the entire battle of Moscow, which were over 925,000, not just to the siege of the city. US and British military deaths in all of World War II were just 675,000. These numbers vary according to the source, but not enough to negate the statement.

27. An accounting of the siege by Vassily Pronin, chairman of the Moscow City Soviet, noted that 1,088 civilians were killed in the city; 35,000–40,000 incendiaries were dropped; nearly 2,000 heavy explosive bombs went off in Moscow and its suburbs; and 1,100 German planes were downed. See Henry Cassidy's article for the *St. Petersburg Times*, Aug 11, 1943, in Cassidy, *Moscow Dateline*. In the battle itself, between

300,000 and 750,000 Soviet casualties and over 200,000 German casualties were estimated. See "Battle of Moscow," World War II Database, http://ww2db.com/battle_spec.php?battle_id=37/.

28. C. L. Sulzberger, "Here Is Picture of Nazi Retreat from Moscow," *New York Times*, Dec 17, 1941; and Sulzberger, "But This Is Moscow."

29. Thompson paper, "The Concept of Soviet Foreign Policy," TFP.

30. Bergquist, "Llewellyn Thompson," pp. 21–25.

31. Jorden, "Quiet Diplomacy."

32. *Zakuski* is the Russian word for a wide selection of small hot and cold dishes that can either begin a meal or constitute the whole repast.

33. Anthony Eden returned from the front to Moscow on December 19, 1941.

34. Thompson to SecState, Dec 19, 1941, FRUS, 1941, vol. 1 (*Diplomatic Papers, 1941, General, the Soviet Union*), [doc. 211], p. 198. The FRUS volumes are also available online, at https://history.state.gov/historical documents/.

35. Ambassador Winant to SecState, Dec 19 and 21, 1941, FRUS, 1941, vol. 1, [doc. 212], p. 199, and [doc.] 214, p. 201.

36. Thompson to SecState, Dec 20, 1941, FRUS, 1941, vol. 1, [doc. 213], p. 200.

37. These prisoners were captured when the Soviets annexed western Poland, as a result of the USSR's invasion of that country with Hitler.

38. They became "Anders' Army," named after the dashing Polish leader they followed. Among the Poles released to fight was Menachem Begin, who later became prime minister of Israel. Many of those who were released immigrated to other countries and formed the Polish diaspora. Some of the Jewish soldiers, later known as "Anders' Aliyah," deserted the army when it got to Palestine and joined settlements there, but the Polish army refused to pursue them. Anders' Army consisted of only a fraction of the Poles who were imprisoned, since many never made it out of the gulags. For a colorful description of General Anders, see Moats, *Blind Date with Mars*. In summer 1942, more than 70,000 Polish soldiers and 40,000 civilians marched on foot across the vast Soviet Union and into Iran, where they entered British-controlled territory.

39. This behavior was not isolated to Moscow during the Roosevelt administration. According to Olson, in *Citizens of London*, John G. Winant, US ambassador to the United Kingdom, was bypassed in favor of his unofficial colleague, Averell Harriman. Also see Weisbrode, *Atlantic Century*, for a broader view of FDR's relations with the State Department. In addition, see Tolly, *Caviar and Commissars*, p. 61; and Mayers, *The Ambassadors*, preface.

40. James McCargar, "Llewellyn Thompson: Recollections," Feb 10, 2003, TFP.

41. Efficiency reports by Ambassador Standley on Thompson, Thompson personnel files, TFP.

42. Authors' correspondence with James McCargar, Feb 2007, TFP.

43. Inspection report, Dec 18, 1942, Foreign Service inspection reports file: Moscow 1942, RG 59, NACP.

44. Harry Hopkins made him chief of EUR in November 1943.

45. Bohlen, *Witness to History*, p. 125.

46. Loy Henderson inspection reports, 1942, Foreign Service inspection reports file: Moscow 1942, RG 59, NACP; and memo by Henderson, Jul 12, 1941, FRUS, 1941, vol. 1, [doc.] 940, pp. 987–88.

47. Tolly, *Caviar and Commissars*, p. 78.

48. Ibid., p. 184.

49. Ibid., pp. 61–68; and Meiklejohn World War II diary, Averell Harriman Papers, LC.

50. Tolly, *Caviar and Commissars*, p. 89.

51. Harriman and Abel, *Special Envoy*.

52. Cassidy, *Moscow Dateline*, pp. 250–51.

53. Loy Henderson inspection report, Sep 1942, Foreign Service inspection reports file: Moscow 1942, RG 59, NACP.

54. Standley to SecState, cable, Jul 2, 1942, CF 541.202/20, RG 59, NACP; SecState Hull to Standley, Sep 2, 1942, CF 541.202/21A, RG 59, NACP; and Standley to SecState, cable, Sep 6, 1942, CF 841.202/22, RG 59, NACP.

55. US Major General J. R. Dean met with Lieutenant General Fitin, head of the Soviet External Intelligence Service, and with the head of its Subversive Activities in Enemy Countries section, Colonel Ossipov.

See "Memoranda for the President: OSS-NKVD Liaison," docs. from Nov 5, 1943, through Nov 10, 1944, vol. 7, no. 3, Sherman Kent School for Intelligence Analysis, Central Intelligence Agency, https://www.cia.gov/library/center-for-the-study-of-intelligence/kent-csi/vol7no3/. For Hoover's intervention, see Grose, *Operation Rollback*.

56. Wendell Willkie had been FDR's Republican opponent in the presidential election but became his unlikely ally afterward, joining Roosevelt's administration as a special ambassador-at-large.

57. Dunn, *Caught between Roosevelt and Stalin*, p. 171.

58. Loy Henderson efficiency report on Thompson, Sep 28, 1942, Thompson personnel files, TFP.

59. W. A. Harriman report, Aug 1, 1944, 1940s file, with a cover note from Pie Friendly [the wife of journalist Alfred Friendly and a close friend of Sally Chase, who became the authors' nanny in 1960], TFP.

60. Hurley accused State Department officials of "losing China" to the Communists. This contributed to many experienced China hands being removed from the State Department.

61. "Indian Territory" eventually became the state of Oklahoma.

62. Correspondence between Thompson and Hurley, TFP; and Tolly, *Caviar and Commissars*, p. 156.

63. Thompson to SecState, cable 523, Dec 8, 1942, FRUS, 1942, vol. 3 (*Diplomatic Papers, 1942, Europe*), [doc.] 553, p. 668.

64. Meier, *Lost Spy*, p. 184. Also see FRUS, 1942, vol. 3, [doc.] 649, p. 765.

65. SecState to Standley, Jun 30, 1942, FRUS, 1942, vol. 3, [doc.] 649, p. 765n8. For more information on Oggins's story, see Meir, *Lost Spy*.

66. Stalin had no intention of ever setting Oggins free and was just trying to see how far the Americans would go. The Soviets had only "dangled" the American prisoner in front of the federal government. By 1947, however, when Oggins was officially due to be released, Senator McCarthy's hunt for Reds was on. If Oggins were to be released, he could be made to reveal the workings of Russia's underground and thus jeopardize the Kremlin's spy network. In summer 1947, the guards came to tell Oggins he was to have a medical examination before being released. The clinic where he was taken, however, was the Kamera, a toxicological laboratory under the direction of Dr. Grigory Moiseevich Mairanovsky, famous for developing the use of poison as an untraceable means of execution. It was here that Mairanovsky injected Oggins with a toxin extracted from a tropical plant, which acted by constricting every muscle one by one, including the heart. Death was excruciatingly painful, but Oggins was not able to shout or move, although he was conscious until his death, fifteen minutes after he was given the injection. See Meier, *Lost Spy*.

67. Carroll, "Llewellyn E Thompson," p. 46, in Kuhn and Kuhn, *Adventures in Public Service*.

68. Meier, *Lost Spy*, p. 279.

69. Joseph E. Davies, "Missions for Peace" manuscript, LC.

70. Associated Press, May 24, 1943, clippings in TFP.

71. Authors' correspondence and conversation with James McCargar, Feb 2007, TFP.

5 ≋ The Germans in Retreat

1. Thompson 123 file, 1940–1944, stack 250, row 60, compartment 10, shelf 1, box 642, RG 59, NACP.

2. Meiklejohn World War II diary, Averell Harriman Papers, LC.

3. This shipping corridor had come at the expense of a joint British-Soviet invasion of Iran in 1941 and the forced abdication of a too pro-German Reza Shah, who did not want Iran used to supply arms and equipment to the Soviet Union and the Allies. His son, Mohammad Reza Pahlavi, was installed in his place, until the Islamic revolution in 1979 deposed him.

4. In addition to Vyacheslav Molotov, the welcoming party included the Soviets' Deputy Foreign Minister Andrey Vyshinksy, Vice Commissar for Foreign Affairs Maxim Litvinov, and Vice Commissar for Foreign Affairs Ivan Maisky.

5. Meiklejohn World War II diary, Averell Harriman papers, LC.

6. The pact was signed by the conference principals: Secretary of State Cordell Hull for the United States, Foreign Secretary Anthony Eden for Great Britain, and Foreign Minister V. M. Molotov for the Soviet Union, plus the Chinese ambassador to the Soviet Union.

7. See C. Ben Wright interview with Thompson, Oct 2, 1970, Papers of C. Ben Wright, box 8, folder 20, George C. Marshall Foundation Research Library, Lexington, Virginia.

8. Harriman and Abel, *Special Envoy*, p. 229n.

9. See C. Ben Wright interview with Thompson, Oct 2, 1970, Marshall Foundation Library.

10. Reynolds, *Summits*, p. 107.

11. Authors' interview with Richard Davies, Feb 23, 2003, TFP.

12. Elizabeth W. "Wendy" Hazard interview with Isaac Patch, Sep 2006, TFP.

13. Over 20,000 Polish soldiers were shot and then interred in three burial sites near Katyn.

14. Ms. Harriman later repudiated her 1944 statement before the House Select Committee of the US Congress. The Soviets admitted responsibility for the atrocity in 1990. Documents released in 2013 confirmed that the Russians were responsible for the massacre and that the United States had helped to cover it up.

15. Mayers, *The Ambassadors*, p. 156.

16. Tzouliadis, *The Forsaken*, pp. 217–26.

17. Harriman to SecState, cable 2199, June 20, 1944, FRUS, 1944, vol. 4 (*Diplomatic Papers 1944, Europe*), [doc.] 878, p. 968.

18. William L. White letter to Jane Thompson, Feb 12, 1972; and White, "Tommy," TFP.

19. White, "Tommy," TFP. White's book was called *Report on the Russians*. Also see Jean Folgers, "The US Press and Russia: A Tortured History," *Huffington Post*, May 26, 2014, for White's story. He never told anyone Thompson was his source.

20. Thompson letter to Arthur Schlesinger Jr., 1967, TFP.

21. Thompson presentation at the Fourth Air Force–Civilian Seminar, Maxwell Air Force Base, Alabama, May 12–14, 1949, TFP.

22. Reynolds, *Summits*, chap. 3, "Yalta 1945."

23. Djilas, *Conversations with Stalin*, p. 105.

24. Churchill went along with FDR and the Atlantic Charter, with its insistence on self-determination, but this created difficulties for a colonial power like Britain. Churchill believed in realpolitik—such as, during the fourth Moscow Conference, making a percentages agreement with Stalin, in which the United Kingdom and the USSR agreed to divide the Balkan countries into spheres of influence. This was certainly not in the spirit of the Atlantic Charter. Roosevelt's other ally, Joseph Stalin, also signed the Atlantic Charter, but his real goal was to occupy and secure a wide belt of Soviet-controlled states, in order to protect his country from any further dangers in the future, as well as to allow him to isolate and insulate his domains. Stalin had no intention of honoring this high-minded but virtually powerless document.

25. Harriman cables, August 21, 1944, signed "George Kennan for Harriman," entry UD-3316, file 44, embassy personnel, RG 84, NARA.

26. Thompson, "Soviet Satellites," speech at the National War College, Washington, DC, Oct 6, 1949, TFP. Only four other copies of this speech were made, and they were not allowed to leave the War College, per a letter from Richard H. Werner, executive officer, National War College, Dec 27, 1949.

27. Ibid.; and Hazard, *Cold War Crucible*, p. 49.

28. See Hazard, *Cold War Crucible*.

29. Harriman to Roosevelt, "Personal for the President," Oct 10, 1944, FRUS, 1944, vol. 4, [doc.] 915, p. 1006.

30. Churchill historian and blogger Richard M. Langworth, "The Language: Some Issues over 'Issues,'" Jun 8, 1990, https://richardlangworth.com/the-language-some-issues-over-issues/.

31. Kennan letter to Thompson, Aug 1, 1945, TFP.

32. Thompson paper, "The Concept and Structure of Soviet Foreign Policy," 1944, TFP.

33. Since thousands had been imprisoned or executed merely for having contacts with foreigners, the Soviet diplomatic service "has not been considered a safe profession," and it did not attract many of the more able young Soviet officials.

34. The Telegraph Agency of the Soviet Union (Телеграфное агентство Советского Союза, or Telegrafnoye agentstvo Sovetskovo Soyuza; abbreviated TASS), was responsible for the collection and distribution of news for Soviet newspapers, radio, and television.

35. Andrey Yanuarevich Vyshinsky was a Soviet diplomat, state prosecutor at Stalin's show trials, and foreign minister from 1949 to 1953.

36. The Soviet secret police force was known as the People's Commissariat for Internal Affairs (Народный комиссариат внутренних дел, or Narodnyy komissariat vnutrennikh del; abbreviated NKVD).

37. Authors' conversation with Priscilla McMillan, Boston, Jul 2010.

38. Ibid.

6 ≋ Conferences

Epigraph. Arthur Schlesinger Jr., "Origins of the Cold War," *Foreign Affairs* (Council on Foreign Affairs), vol. 46, no. 1 (Oct 1967), pp. 22–52.

1. Kennan letter to Thompson, Aug 1, 1945, TFP.

2. Meiklejohn World War II diary, Averill Harriman Papers, LC. It was the fastest trip ever made between Moscow and Washington, DC.

3. Thompson 123 file, 1950–1954, stack 250, row 60, compartment 10, shelf 1, box 642, RG 59, NACP.

4. Ibid.

5. Thompson's immediate boss, Elbridge Durbrow, the chief of E-EUR, would have filled in for H. Freeman Matthews, the head of EUR. EEUR was reestablished in 1937.

6. Reynolds, *Summits*.

7. Thompson presentation at the Fourth Air Force–Civilian Seminar, Maxwell Air Force Base, Alabama, May 12–14, 1949, TFP.

8. The Treaty of Versailles, signed in June 1919, ended the war between Germany and the Allied powers. Germany was made to accept responsibility for all the damages and forced to pay the equivalent of $442 billion in today's dollars. This harsh treatment of Germany is considered one of the reasons for the subsequent rise of nationalism in Germany.

9. Harriman to SecState, cable 1198, Apr 16, 1945, FRUS, 1945, vol. 5 (*Europe*), [doc.] 183, p. 225.

10. This was known as the Curzon Line. See *Agreements Reached at the Cairo, Tehran, Yalta, and Potsdam Conferences*, Department of State, Division of Historical Policy Research Project No. 80, Sep 1948, TFP.

11. Although Churchill went along with the declaration, he had a moment of panic when he got the impression that it might apply to colonies in the British Empire.

12. Churchill wanted France—despite its Vichy government's cooperation with the Germans—in a zone of occupation, because FDR had revealed that the Americans would remove their army from Europe as quickly as possible, and Britain wanted a friendly partner in German lands. Stalin, in particular, did not feel as though France should have this concession, since it was merely a defeated country and had not shared the blood lost in fighting the Germans that the United States, Britain, and the USSR had.

13. See Tolstoy, *The Minister and the Massacres*; and Bethell, *The Last Secret*. Stalin was not the only Communist to eliminate returned compatriots. Between 20,000 and 40,000 Yugoslavs of various ethnic origins were repatriated to Tito's forces at the end of World War II, the majority of whom were slaughtered. Names such as the Kočevski Rog massacre and the Bleiberg incident in Yugoslavia, and the tragic repatriation of the Cossacks and other POWs to the Soviet Union, fill some of the darkest pages of history, which we are still reluctant to face. This is on top of more than 9,000 retreating Montenegrin monarchists (Chetniks) that Tito's army eliminated at Zelengora once the war was already over. See Michael Portmann, "Communist Retaliation and Persecution on Yugoslav Territory during and after World War II (1943–50)," *Tokovi istorije* (*Currents of History*), vol. 12 (2004), pp. 45–75, Central and Eastern European Online Library, www.ceeol.com.

14. Thompson, "Soviet Satellites," speech at the National War College, Washington, DC, Oct 6, 1949, TFP.

15. Thompson presentation at the Fourth Air Force–Civilian Seminar, Maxwell Air Force Base, Alabama, May 12–14, 1949, TFP.

16. Thompson letter to Arthur Schlesinger Jr., Oct 24, 1967, TFP.

17. CF 860C-0/4-145, RG 59, NACP; and Polish ambassador to SecState, Apr 4, 1945, FRUS, 1945, vol. 5, [doc.] 164, pp. 198–201.

18. Correspondence between Thompson and Arthur Schlesinger Jr., 1967, TFP.

19. S. Schlesinger, *Act of Creation*, chap. 1, "The Takeover."

20. The conference lasted from April 25 to June 26, 1945.

21. Memo from John D. Hickerson to Mr. Davis, regarding Thompson's performance in San Francisco, Thompson personnel file, TFP.

22. This was the time when the Soviets were still considered to be staunch allies, incapable of wrongdoing. Some of the Soviets' political problems were (a) their insistence on still trying to get as many Soviet

republics as possible recognized as separate voting entities, although only the original two attempts succeeded; (b) details of how the veto authority of the three Big Powers, agreed to at Yalta, would be exercised in the Security Council; (c) recognition of the Polish provisional government, with a seat at the table; and (d) the allowance of regional security organizations, also known as Article 51, which would later make the South-East Asia Treaty Organization (SEATO) and the North Atlantic Treaty Organization (NATO) possible.

23. S. Schlesinger, *Act of Creation*, pp. 147–48.

24. Bohlen, *Witness to History*, pp. 214–15. In his book, Bohlen mistakenly named Anthony Eden as the recipient of this information, not the US ambassador. See MemCon by Bohlen, May 4, 1945, FRUS, 1945, vol. 5, [doc.] 208, p. 282.

25. Bohlen was with Harry Hopkins in Moscow from May 27 to June 13, 1945.

26. For more on Truman and Poland, see Robert James Maddox, "Truman, Poland, and the Origins of the Cold War," *Presidential Studies Quarterly*, vol. 17, no. 1 (winter 1987), pp. 27–41.

27. Bohlen, *Witness to History*, p. 215.

28. Churchill's political defeat was due in great part to the situation after World War II, when people in Britain were in dire circumstances, and the country's physical and economic reconstruction required governmental intervention. Churchill's Conservative Party would not favor anything that smacked of a redistribution of wealth, while the Labour Party ran on a platform promising help. The same was true for the rest of Europe—a decided advantage for the Socialist and Communist Parties.

29. Djilas, *Conversations with Stalin*, p. 105.

30. McCullough, *Truman*, p. 509. The description of the flowers composing the red star is also from this book.

31. Ibid., p. 496.

32. Bohlen, *Witness to History*, p. 237. Also see Thompson, "Vital Interests and Objectives of the United States," speech at the Industrial College of the Armed Forces, Washington, DC, Aug 25, 1965, TFP.

33. Bohlen, *Witness to History*, p. 232.

34. Thompson, speech at the Foreign Service Institute, Washington, DC, Apr 12, 1971, TFP.

35. Thompson presentation at the Fourth Air Force–Civilian Seminar, Maxwell Air Force Base, Alabama, May 12–14, 1949, TFP.

36. Thayer, *Diplomat*, p. 96.

37. Stearman, *The Soviet Union*.

38. Holloway, *Stalin and the Bomb*, p. 117.

39. Authors' conversations with Priscilla McMillan, Boston, Jul 2010, regarding Holloway, *Stalin and the Bomb*.

40. The Soviets detonated their first atomic bomb in August 1949.

41. Thompson presentation at the Fourth Air Force–Civilian Seminar, Maxwell Air Force Base, Alabama, May 12–14, 1949, TFP.

42. Ibid.

43. A. Schlesinger, "Origins of the Cold War."

44. Thompson presentation at the Fourth Air Force–Civilian Seminar, Maxwell Air Force Base, Alabama, May 12–14, 1949, TFP.

45. G. Bernard Noble was the editor of *Foreign Relations of the United States* for the period covering the Potsdam summit.

46. Toward the end of the Yalta summit, Truman asked for the State Department's views "concerning the wisdom of attempting to secure agreement at [the upcoming Potsdam conference] on a twenty-five year treaty . . . to demilitarize Germany and to keep her demilitarized by force if necessary." Stettinius asked Thompson and his supervisor, John Hickerson, to each compose papers addressing this question. Thompson wrote that such an agreement might break the vicious cycle in which the Soviet Union was engaged. Otherwise, the USSR, fearful of its perceived enemies in the West, would take steps to ensure its security, which, in turn, would cause the very reactions from the Western powers (themselves fearful of Soviet expansionism) that the Soviets sought to avoid. He also thought a treaty might help ease European concerns over a US exodus from that continent. The Americans would, in fact, offer the Soviets such a treaty, but not until after the Potsdam conference. By that time, Stalin viewed the proposed accord with suspicion and thought it was an effort to make the Soviets withdraw their troops from Germany, which he could not accept. By keeping the Red Army

in eastern Germany, he still hoped for a reunified, pro-Soviet Germany. See SecState to Acting SecState, Jun 22, 1945, FRUS, 1945, vol. 3 (*European Advisory Commission, Austria, Germany*), [docs. 366–68], pp. 527–31; and Levering, Pechatnov, Botzenhart-Viehe, and Edmonson, *Debating the Origins*, including the documents therein.

47. Correspondence between Thompson and G. Bernard Noble, chief, Historical Division, State Department, Oct 1954; Thompson correspondence with Professor Ernest R. May, Institute of Politics, Harvard University, in reply to "A Case for Court Historians," Apr 1, 1969, TFP.

48. Thompson presentation at the Fourth Air Force–Civilian Seminar, Maxwell Air Force Base, Alabama, May 12–14, 1949, TFP.

49. "According to Gen. Dwight D. Eisenhower, when he was informed of the existence of the bomb at the Potsdam Conference . . . he told Stimson he thought an atomic bombing was unnecessary because 'the Japanese were very close to surrender and it wasn't necessary to hit them with that awful thing.' " Quotation in Bird and Sherwin, *American Prometheus*. These authors also suggest that Truman, too, believed this to be the case.

50. Bohlen, *Witness to History*, p. 238.

51. Kennan letter to Thompson, Aug 1, 1945, TFP.

7 ≋ The Hot War Ends and the Cold War Begins

1. Authors' correspondence and conversation with James McCargar, Feb 2007, TFP.

2. For example, Leonard Hankin was a colonel in the OSS and was working on the Russian occupation of lower Austria in 1945. He and Thompson remained lifelong friends. Hankin later went into business in New York City, becoming head of Bergdorf's Department Store and Fendi Furs. At the London meeting, through Charlie Thayer, who had gone behind the lines in Yugoslavia with British intelligence agents, Thompson met Frank Lindsay, who was parachuted into Yugoslavia during the war under the OSS. Lindsay later went on to be a right-hand man to Executive Director Frank Wisner in the early days of the Office of Policy Coordination, the organization set up for peacetime US covert operations. Lindsay subsequently was named head of the Covert Operations Study Group, set up by Richard Helms to promote this clandestine service to the president. See Weiner, *Legacy of Ashes*.

3. Thompson letter to MWood, Oct 1945, TFP.

4. There were three meetings: this one in October in London; one in December in Moscow, and a final one in Paris in 1946.

5. Bohlen, *Witness to History*.

6. Anne O'Hare McCormick, "American Experts Arrive in Britain," *New York Times*, Sep 11, 1945.

7. An insignificant contest between Vyacheslav Molotov and US Secretary of State James F. Byrnes perhaps best illustrates the mood. The meetings began at 11 a.m., and every time Byrnes arrived, Molotov would already be sitting at the circular table. Byrnes felt that Molotov was trying to assert the seniority of the Soviet delegation, so he stationed his military aide in the hallway that Molotov would use to enter the room. The aide would signal Byrnes, who was in the other hallway, so that he reached his chair and sat down at the exact moment Molotov took his seat. See correspondence between the authors and Frank Lindsay, Aug 2005, TFP. Lindsay was sent to the conference by General "Wild Bill" Donovan.

8. Jonathan Knight, "Russia's Search for Peace: The London Council of Foreign Ministers, 1945," *Journal of Contemporary History*, vol. 13, no. 1 (Jan 1978), pp. 137–63.

9. Bergquist, "Llewellyn Thompson," p. 25, TFP.

10. Bischof, *Austria in the First Cold War*, p. 106.

11. Thompson, "Soviet Satellites," speech at the National War College, Washington, DC, Oct 6, 1949, TFP.

12. MemCon, Jan 2, 1946, FRUS, 1946, vol. 5 (*British Commonwealth, Western and Central Europe*), [doc.] 185, pp. 283–85.

13. Thompson letter to Arthur Schlesinger Jr., Dec 1967, TFP.

14. Kennan to SecState, cable 5121, Feb 22, 1946, FRUS, 1946, vol. 6 (*Eastern Europe, the Soviet Union*), [doc.] 475, pp. 696–709. The telegram was typed by Martha Mautner.

15. Thompson paper, "The Concept and Structure of Soviet Foreign Policy," 1944, TFP.

16. Thompson letter to Arthur Schlesinger Jr., Oct 24, 1967, TFP.

17. Ibid. "Litvinov" is Maxim Maximovich Litvinov, Soviet diplomat and deputy commissar for foreign affairs. Also see Ambassador Walter Smith to SecState, cable 1964, Jun 21, 1946, FRUS, 1946, vol. 6, [doc.] 517, pp. 763–65. A. Schlesinger, in "Origins of the Cold War," p. 26, defined "universalist" this way: "The universalist view assumed that national security would be guaranteed by an international organization, as opposed to the sphere-of-interest view, which assumed that national security would be guaranteed by the balance of power."

18. Kennan's "X Article" was printed anonymously, as "The Sources of Soviet Conduct," in *Foreign Affairs*, vol. 25, no. 4 (Jul 1947), pp. 566–82.

19. See C. Ben Wright interview with Thompson, Oct 2, 1970, Marshall Foundation Library.

20. Levering, Pechatnov, Botzenhard-Viehe, and Edmonson, *Debating the Origins*, doc. 3, "George F. Kennan's 'Long Telegram,' February 1946."

21. In 1945, Igor Guzenko, a GRU cipher clerk, provided information that led to the arrest of Los Alamos scientist Karl Fuchs, as well as Julius and Ethel Rosenberg, for passing nuclear secrets to the Soviets. When it was revealed that so many Canadians from diverse walks of life, including the film industry, were actually working for the Russians, this probably helped precipitate the McCarthy hysteria in the United States.

22. Sergei Kudriavtsev came with the Soviet trade mission as an assistant to Major Sergei Sokolov, who was actually a GRU officer. Together they recruited the nucleus of a spy network in Canada, with agents in Toronto, Ottawa, and Montreal. Kudriavtsev would be posted to Vienna when Thompson was there, and he later became the Soviet ambassador to Cuba during the Cuban Missile Crisis. Kudriavtsev would be "quite friendly" to Jane when the Thompsons were posted to Moscow.

23. This occurred in November–December 1946.

24. Bertha Browne, report of travel of FSO Llewellyn E Thompson Jr., TFP.

25. Thompson's salary was increased by over 10 percent, to $9,017.40.

26. The wording comes from the citation that accompanied the Medal of Freedom. The original, dated Dec 11, 1946, was signed by Acting Secretary of State Dean Acheson, and a duplicate, dated Jan 1, 1947, was signed by Secretary of State James Byrnes and reissued as a copy in 1956. These, and two newspaper clippings, are all in TFP.

27. *Bent County [CO] Democrat*, Jan 17, 1947; and Thompson correspondence with MWood, TFP.

28. C. Ben Wright, "Mr. X and Containment," *Slavic Review*, vol. 35, no. 1 (Mar 1976), pp. 1–31.

29. Directive memo for Analytical Studies course, Army War College, Jan 12, 1940, TFP.

30. "Lecture by Mr. George Kennan and Mr. Llewellyn E Thompson, Walter-Johnson Building," Sep 17, 1946, box 298, folder 13, Mudd Manuscript Library, Princeton University.

31. Georgy Zhukov had led the Red Army through much of Eastern Europe to liberate the Soviet Union from the Axis powers.

32. Joint off-the-record speech by Kennan and Thompson to media representatives, Walker-Johnson building, Washington, DC, Sep 17, 1946, TFP. Another attempt at articulating these thoughts was made by Clark Clifford and George Elsey, who used a number of sources, including George Kennan, Dean Acheson, and James Forrestal. In Clifford and Elsey's September 1946 report, they talked about "restraining" the Soviet Union whenever and wherever possible. These authors later suggested that if their report had been made public before Kennan's "X Article" on containment appeared, the new policy might have been called "restrainment" rather than "containment." The Clifford and Elsey report was never published, because Truman considered it to be "too explosive" (Donovan, *Conflict and Crisis*, p. 222), since a substantial number of people still viewed the Soviets as allies.

8 ≋ The Truman Doctrine

Robert C. Tucker, "Emergence of Stalin's Foreign Policy," *Slavic Review*, vol. 36, no. 4 (Dec 1977), pp. 563–89.

1. Thompson presentation at the Fourth Air Force–Civilian Seminar, Maxwell Air Force Base, Alabama, May 12–14, 1949, TFP. A draft of the official transcript was supplied after the fact by the US Air Force, in which Thompson struck out one of his remarks, "That was the general hope; I certainly didn't share it myself" [which probably does not appear in the official transcript of the speech], TFP.

2. Tucker, "Emergence." Also see Friedman, *Fifty-Year War*, chap. 8, "Tito and Mao."

3. Wright, "Mr. X and Containment."

4. Address of the president to Congress, "Recommendation for Assistance to Greece and Turkey," Mar 12, 1947, Truman Doctrine Collection, Elsey Papers, TL, https://www.trumanlibrary.org/whistlestop/study _collections/doctrine/large/documents/index.php?documentdate=1947-03-12&documentid=5-9&page number=1/.

5. Carroll, "Llewellyn E Thompson," in Kuhn and Kuhn, *Adventures in Public Service*.

6. On reading George Kennan's draft memoirs of that time period, Loy Henderson wrote that Kennan seemed to be "claiming to have had a major influence on the decision to recommend aid to Greece and Turkey that night, although [Kennan] had not been present and had not then been aware of the British notes." See Robert Frazier, "Kennan, 'Universalism,' and the Truman Doctrine," *Journal of Cold War Studies*, vol. 11, no. 2 (Spring 2009), p. 30. Also see Joseph M. Jones, "Drafting the President's Message," a draft chronology for Jones's later book, *Fifteen Weeks*, attached to his letter to Thompson, Jun 23, 1954, TFP.

7. Thompson correspondence with Joseph M. Jones, the Graduate School, Yale University, Aug 1954, TFP; and Jones, "Drafting the President's Message," TFP.

8. Minutes of the first meeting to study assistance to Greece and Turkey, Feb 24, 1947, FRUS, 1947, vol. 5 (*The Near East and Africa*), [doc.] 32, pp. 45–47. The economist was Hubert F. Havlik.

9. Jones, "Drafting the President's Message," TFP; SecState to Truman, [Feb 27, 1947], FRUS, 1947, vol. 5, [doc.] 37, pp. 60–62; and SecState to Henderson, Feb 27, 1947, FRUS, 1947, vol. 5, [doc.] 38, pp. 63–64.

10. Ranelagh, *The Agency*, pp. 123–24.

11. Ibid., p. 123.

12. As an example of Dean Acheson's views in 1945, see Ranelagh, *The Agency*, p. 107. For George Kennan, see C. Ben Wright interview with Charles Bohlen, Sep 29, 1970, Marshall Foundation Library.

13. Senator Vandenberg's nephew was, at that time, the director of the newly formed CIA. See Jones, "Drafting of the President's Message," TFP; and "Drafting of the President's Message of March 12, 1947," Truman Doctrine Collection, Joseph M. Jones Papers, TL, https://www.trumanlibrary.org/whistlestop/study _collections/doctrine/large/documents/index.php?documentdate=1947-03-00&documentid=7-3&page number=1/.

14. "Meeting Notes," ca. Feb 1947, Joseph. M. Jones Papers, TL, https://www.trumanlibrary.org/whistle stop/study_collections/doctrine/large/documents/index.php?documentdate=1947-02-00&documentid =8-4&pagenumber=1/.

15. See Ferald J. Bryan, "George C. Marshall at Harvard: A Study of the Origins and Construction for the 'Marshall Plan Speech,'" *Presidential Studies Quarterly*, vol. 21, no. 3 (Summer 1991), pp. 489–502. This quote is disputed. It's not clear that Senator Vandenberg used these words, but he surely meant that the case needed to be made emotionally and forcefully.

16. For remarks by George Marshall at the Moscow conference of foreign ministers, Mar 10, 1947, see Jones, "Drafting of the President's Message," p. 4, TFP.

17. Ibid.

18. Francis Russell's summary of the State–War–Navy Coordinating Committee (SWNCC), Subcommittee on Foreign Policy Information meeting, Feb 28, 1947, Office of the Assistant Secretary for Public Affairs, Office of the Director of Public Affairs, subject files: 1944–1952, file: Greece—general, entry A1-1530 [also marked lot file 54 D 202, box 11569, but crossed out], RG 59, NACP, also in TFP. Thompson's suggestion is on p. 5 of this document. Thompson continued to worry about this new shift in policy and sent a memo to Henderson, cautioning him about it, in January the following year. See Thompson to Henderson, Jan 9, 1948, FRUS, 1948, vol. 4 (*Eastern Europe; The Soviet Union*), [doc.] 6, p. 15.

19. Memo by Russell on the genesis of Truman's March 12 speech, Mar 17, 1947, FRUS, 1947, vol. 5, [doc.] 87, p. 122.

20. Francis Russell's summary of the SWNCC, Subcommittee on Foreign Policy Information meeting, Feb 28, 1947, Office of the Assistant Secretary for Public Affairs, Office of the Director of Public Affairs, subject files: 1944–1952, file: Greece—general, entry A1-1530 [also marked lot file 54 D 202, box 11569, but crossed out], RG 59, NACP, also in TFP. Jones, in "Drafting of the President's Message" (in TFP), indicates that Kennan did not participate in the weekend work session.

21. Thompson correspondence with Joseph M. Jones, Aug 1954, TFP; and Jones, "Drafting of the President's Message," p. 2, TFP.

22. Robert Frazier, "Acheson and the Formulation of the Truman Doctrine," *Journal of Modern Greek Studies*, vol. 17, no. 2 (1999), pp. 229–51; Francis Russell's summary of the SWNCC, Subcommittee on Foreign Policy Information meeting, Feb 28, 1947, Office of the Assistant Secretary for Public Affairs, Office of the Director of Public Affairs, subject files: 1944–1952, file: Greece—general, entry A1-1530 [also marked lot file 54 D 202, box 11569, but crossed out], RG 59, NACP, also in TFP; and report by the SWNCC Subcommittee on Foreign Policy Information, Feb 28, 1947, FRUS, 1947, vol. 5, [doc.] 50, p. 77.

23. Frazier, "Acheson." Truman claimed that he changed the wording, but, according to Frazier, the draft Truman saw already had the new wording.

24. Ibid.; and Frazier, "Kennan, 'Universalism,'" p. 31.

25. Thompson correspondence with Joseph Jones and Loy Henderson, Aug 4, 1954, TFP. Despite what Jones had written about Thompson in his draft chronologies, Jones reduced Thompson's role to a footnote in his published book.

26. Thompson, notes for "Soviet Satellites" speech at the National War College, Washington, DC, Oct 6, 1949, TFP.

27. Thompson letter to A. Schlesinger Jr., Oct 24, 1967, TFP. A. Schlesinger, in "Origins of the Cold War," p. 26, defined "universalist" this way: "The universalist view assumed that national security would be guaranteed by an international organization, as opposed to the sphere-of-interest view, which assumed that national security would be guaranteed by the balance of power." This was opposed to what Kennan meant by "universal"—as in a doctrine applied universally—when disagreeing with the Truman Doctrine.

28. Ranelagh, *The Agency*, p. 131.

29. Nothing in Jones's "Drafting of the President's Message" (in TFP) or his later book (*Fifteen Weeks*) suggests that this was the case. Kennan would have received a similar request for input from Jones in 1954, and it may be that this is when the erroneous information, indicating that Kennan had been present at the initial meeting, made its way into history. Once Jones published *Fifteen Weeks*, placing Kennan at that meeting, Kennan, in his *Memoirs*, quoted Jones and asserted that he (Keenan) had been present. Kennan was corrected by Henderson (see Frazier, "Kennan, 'Universalism,'" p. 30), but this occurred too late to alter Jones's version. The reason all this is important is because it shows how something erroneous can become part of historical "truth," even unintentionally.

30. Frazier, "Kennan, 'Universalism,'" p. 24.

31. Thompson, "Vital Interests and Objectives of the United States," speech at the Industrial College of the Armed Forces, Washington, DC, Aug 25, 1965, TFP.

32. Miscamble, *George F. Kennan*, p. 170.

33. Bohlen, *Witness to History*, p. 274.

34. Robert Cecil, "Potsdam and Its Legends," *International Affairs: Journal of the Royal Institute of International Affairs*, vol. 46, no. 3 (Jul 1970), pp. 455–65.

35. Thompson presentation at the Fourth Air Force–Civilian Seminar, Maxwell Air Force Base, Alabama, May 12–14, 1949, TFP.

36. John D. Hickerson oral history, TL; Bohlen, *Witness to History*; and N. Thompson, *The Hawk and the Dove*.

37. See Jones, *Fifteen Weeks*.

38. Thompson presentation at the Fourth Air Force–Civilian Seminar, Maxwell Air Force Base, Alabama, May 12–14, 1949, TFP.

39. Judt, *Postwar*, p. 87.

40. John D. Hickerson oral history, TL.

41. Ibid. The Soviets spread a rumor that corn flour caused impotence, which didn't help make the bread any more palatable.

42. Judt, *Postwar*.

43. Ibid., p. 88.

44. Bryan, "George C. Marshall."

45. Kennan later made Paul Nitze his deputy [against the advice of Undersecretary of State Dean Acheson]. See N. Thompson, *The Hawk and the Dove*, p. 70.

46. For more detail on the origins of the Marshall Plan, see the memo by Charles Kindleberger [chief of the State Department's Division of Austrian and German Affairs, who worked on the Marshall Plan], Jul 22, 1947, FRUS, 1947, vol. 3 (*The British Commonwealth; Europe*), [doc.] 142, pp. 241–47.

47. Memo by the undersecretary of state for economic affairs about the European crisis, FRUS, 1947, May 27, 1947, vol. 3, [doc.] 136, p. 231.

48. Judt, *Postwar*, p. 90. This amount is over $121 billion in 2017 dollars.

49. Ambassador Winiewicz was sufficiently impressed by Thompson's efforts that he remembered them and wrote to Walter Stoessel, who was the US ambassador to Poland at the time of Thompson's death, stating that he "learned to appreciate [Thompson's] honesty and his great diplomatic abilities." See condolence note from Stoessel to Jane Thompson, 1972, TFP.

50. MemCon: Ambassador Winiewicz, Thompson, and Counselor Benjamin Cohen, [undated], 1947, FRUS, 1947, vol. 3, [doc.] 154, p. 260.

51. Miscamble, *George F. Kennan*, p. 56.

52. Klement Gottwald toppled President Eduard Benes on February 25, 1948, shortly after the respected non-Communist foreign minister Jan Masaryk was assassinated.

53. William Cromwell, "The Marshall Non Plan, Congress, and the Soviet Union," *Western Political Quarterly*, vol. 32, no. 4 (Dec 1979), pp. 422–43.

54. This plan to aid counties aligned with the USSR became the Council for Mutual Economic Assistance (COMECON).

55. Zubok and Pleshakov, *Inside the Kremlin's Cold War*, p. 111.

56. Thompson, "Vital Interests and Objectives of the United States," speech at the Industrial College of the Armed Forces, Washington, DC, Aug 25, 1965, TFP.

57. NATO was formally established on April 4, 1949. On May 14, 1955, the Communists created the Warsaw Pact.

58. Wright, "Mr. X and Containment"; and N. Thompson, *The Hawk and the Dove*.

59. See C. Ben Wright interview with Thompson, Oct 2, 1970, Marshall Foundation Library.

60. C. Ben Wright, a student of George Kennan, collected research material while writing a biography of Kennan. These items are located in the Marshall Foundation Library.

61. Wright, "Mr. X and Containment."

62. See C. Ben Wright interview with Thompson, Oct 2, 1970, Marshall Foundation Library. Wright interviewed many of Kennan's colleagues, and Thompson, Bohlen, and Nitze, at least, believed that Kennan thought about military containment. Thompson's interview was pulled from the Wright files in 1985 and was subsequently lost. It took the authors seven years of persistence until it was finally found by Jeffrey Kozak, a diligent archivist at the Marshall Library.

9 ≋ The Birth of Covert Operations

1. The National Security Act of 1947 reorganized the military, creating the US Air Force [which was formally part of the army before and during World War II] and the Joint Chiefs of Staff, as well as consolidating the military services, which were to be headed by the appointee to a newly created cabinet post: a secretary of defense, as opposed to the previous post of secretary of war.

2. Sherry Thompson interview with Marshall Schulman, Oct 2003, TFP. Thompson's wife learned about one of these trips when she stumbled on a packet of matches from a New York City bar after a supposedly "late night at the office."

3. This was the offspring of the State–War–Navy Coordinating Committee, which was in place before the NSC changes. SWNCC had been grappling with how to conduct psychological warfare since its formation in 1946, but focused on its deployment in wartime, not peacetime.

4. These documents were NSC 4 and super-secret annex NSC 4A. It is possible that Forrestal's sojourn in the world of espionage was partly responsible for his death in 1949, when he threw himself out of the window of the hospital where he was being treated for a mental breakdown.

5. Kennan even came up with the extraordinary recommendation that the Italian government should outlaw the Communist Party just prior to the elections, causing a civil war that would provide the excuse to permit the United States to reoccupy military facilities in Italy. Thompson's boss, Hickerson, opposed this scheme and, fortunately, prevailed. See Miscamble, *George F. Kennan*, p. 105. During those early years, Thompson and Kennan had been friends, but their relationship later grew less personal, with communication occurring more often in the form of letters and notes than one-on-one contact. For instance, unlike

Chip Bohlen or Frank Wisner, or even Paul Nitze, Kennan did not make informal visits to the Thompson house.

6. Over $1 million was given to centrist parties. See the congressional report by Pike and House Select Committee, *CIA*, pp. 204–5.

7. Grose, *Operation Rollback*, p. 96.

8. Numerous cryptic memos and notes in the NSC's SANACC files at NARA show a flurry of attempts in trying to fashion this new entity.

9. When this book was written, the CIA was still bifurcated into the Directorate of Intelligence and the National Clandestine Service, formerly the Directorate of Operations.

10. NSC directive on the Office of Special Projects, NSC 10/2, Jun 18, 1948, FRUS, retrospective volume (*Emergence of the Intelligence Establishment, 1945–1950*), doc. 292.

11. B. Hersh, *The Old Boys*, p. 213.

12. Grose, *Operation Rollback*, p. 104.

13. Ranelagh, *The Agency*, p. 135; and Hazard, *Cold War Crucible*, p. 194.

14. Thompson to Butler, "Top Secret Memo," Apr 7, 1948, Thompson lot file 64 D 563, stack area 150, row 68, compartment 8, shelf 6, box 11A, RG 59, NACP, also in TFP.

15. Miscamble, *George F. Kennan*, p. 109.

16. Ibid.

17. These individuals were George Kennan, Maynard Barnes, and John Davies of the Policy Planning Staff.

18. "List of Department of State and Foreign Service Personnel Having Knowledge of Political Warfare Operations," [undated], doc. 11-178, entry A1-558-B, folder: political and psychological warfare 1947–50, subject file: Policy Planning Staff / Council 1947–61, box 28, RG 59, NACP, also in TFP. The Thompsons and friends who were in the know referred to the OPC as the "pickle factory," and for a number of years the Thompson children really believed Uncle Wiz worked in a pickle factory.

19. "State Department–Office of Policy Coordination Agreement on Responsibility for Émigrés," Feb 21, 1949, International History Declassified Digital Archive, Wilson Center, http://digitalarchive.wilsoncenter.org/document/114323/.

20. The NCFE was a think tank, often influential on State Department policy, created by the Dulles brothers.

21. "Understanding between Office of Policy Coordination and National Committee for Free Europe," Oct 4, 1949, International History Declassified Digital Archive, Wilson Center, http://digitalarchive.wilsoncenter.org/document/114332/. Also see Hazard, *Cold War Crucible*, p. 204.

22. Voice of America was officially speaking for the US government. Radio Free Europe was ostensibly a private enterprise, under the umbrella of the NCFE, funded by private individuals, businesses, and foundations.

23. Thompson's future son-in-law, an anti-Tito Yugoslav émigré, would hear of this college offer while working in a London brick factory, where he had been sent from a displaced persons camp in Trieste. He managed to get into the program and completed a degree in physics.

24. For details, see Bethell, *Betrayed*; and Grose, *Operation Rollback*.

25. The Pond, under the War Department since 1943, continued its operations in peacetime as a semiprivate organization. Much of the Pond's activities were secret, even from the CIA, until late 2001, when Grombach's records of this intelligence organization were found in a barn in Virginia. The Pond became widely know publicly in an article published in summer 2010 in various newspapers and online blogs.

26. After being occupied by Italy and Nazi Germany during World War II, Albania became a Communist state under Enver Hoxha's Labour Party, with support from Yugoslavia's Tito. After breaking with Tito in 1948 and losing his patronage, Albania tied itself to the Soviet Union. Since 1946, the United States and Britain conducted an elaborate, multiyear covert operation to pull Albania out of the Communist sphere. It was poorly executed and ultimately unsuccessful.

27. MemCon by SecState, Sep 14, 1949, FRUS, 1949, vol. 5 (*Eastern Europe; The Soviet Union*), [doc.] 195, pp. 315–16.

28. B. Hersh, *The Old Boys*, p. 247; and authors' correspondence with James McCargar, Feb 2007, TFP.

29. These delegates were Midhat Frasheri and Said Kyushu.

30. Bethell, *Betrayed*, p. 100; and MemCon: Acting Chief, Division of Southeast European Affairs, FRUS, 1949, vol. 5, [doc.] 197, pp. 318–19.

31. McCargar, "Llewellyn Thompson: Recollections," Feb 2008, TFP. He would stymie McCargar yet again, when Thompson himself was posted to Vienna in 1957 and McCargar was working for the Free Europe Committee.

32. For a particularly colorful description of Offie, see Thomas, *The Very Best Men*, p. 34.

33. Gross, *Operation Rollback*, p. 155.

34. Thompson letter to Zbigniew Brzezinski, Feb 6, 1969, TFP.

35. See Miscamble, *George F. Kennan*.

36. Thompson, notes for "United States Foreign Policy," speech to students and faculty at the NATO Defense College, Mar 29, 1966, TFP.

37. N. Thompson, *The Hawk and the Dove*.

38. Report of conference on implementation of treaties of peace, Jun 14–21, 1948, FRUS, 1948, vol. 4, [doc.] 240, pp. 353–62. The Soviets were restricting military traffic between the western sectors of Germany and Berlin, which was in the eastern (Soviet) sector.

39. Thompson later passed through Belgrade on June 25, just three days before the Cominform kicked Tito out, making the Tito-Stalin split official.

40. Jane Thompson unpublished memoirs, TFP.

41. Just before the war broke out, Jane's father was sent to Germany on business and came back convinced that the Germans were producing some kind of lethal gas for chemical weapons. Uncertain whether this was true or simply part of his delusions, no one paid any attention. Unfortunately, two of his most notable contributions to his employer, the Dow Chemical Company, were phosphorous detergent and tetraethyl-leaded gasoline, both of which proved to be very bad for the environment but were hailed at the time.

42. Jane Thompson unpublished memoirs, TFP.

43. He concluded that there was little to be done about the Balkan nations' noncompliance with treaties, except to demand evidence of compliance should those countries ask to be admitted to the UN. As for human rights violations, not much could be done there either, apart from making people aware of them and protesting such violations.

44. Report of conference on implementation of treaties of peace, Jun 14–21, 1948, FRUS, 1948, vol. 4, [doc.] 240, pp. 353–62.

45. Authors' group interview with former Thompson colleagues at the home of Robert Martens, Washington, DC, Feb 2003, TFP.

46. Authors' interview with Kempton Jenkins, Feb 2004, TFP.

47. Comment by Marvin Kalb to Avis T. Bohlen [Charles Bohlen's daughter and herself an ambassador], TFP.

48. Rada Khrushcheva, "Recollections of Thompson and the '60s in Moscow," Aug 2010, TFP.

49. Actually, it was Stalin who liberated Belgrade.

50. Joseph Walter Neubert oral history, LC. Thompson never made it to his mission inspection in Bulgaria because of heavy flooding and washed-out roads. See Thompson letter to Jane Goelet, Jun 25, 1948, TFP.

51. Frank Wisner to Harriman, Jul 22, 1948, FRUS, 1948, vol. 4, [doc.] 716, pp. 1095–96.

52. The quotes are from letters between Thompson and Jane, TFP.

53. Ibid.

54. By "grass widow," he meant a divorced woman.

55. Philip C. Jessup, "The Berlin Blockade and the Use of the United Nations," *Foreign Affairs*, vol. 50, no. 1 (Oct 1971), pp. 163–73.

56. *St. Louis Post Dispatch*, Sep 27, 1948, with photo included, TFP.

57. "Interview with Martha Mautner," Aug 25, 1996, Iron Curtain: Episode 2, GW-NSA, http://nsarchive.gwu.edu/coldwar/interviews/episode-2/mautner1.html.

58. Schick, *Berlin Crisis*.

59. Thompson presentation at the Fourth Air Force–Civilian Seminar, Maxwell Air Force Base, Alabama, May 12–14, 1949, TFP.

60. Ibid.

61. It went from a bizone to a trizone when France was included in the equation.

62. Thompson, cable 1773, Mar 9, 1959, CF 762.00/3-959, RG 59, NACP.

1. Thompson memo to Kennan, May 3, 1949, FRUS, 1949, vol. 1 (*National Security Affairs; Foreign Economic Policy*), [doc.] 119, pp. 292–93.

2. Thompson address, Studentenclub, Vienna, Austria, Nov 19, 1952, TFP.

3. NATO was instigated by British Foreign Secretary Ernest Bevin. It was then taken up by the PPS and would be backed by Undersecretary of Defense Robert Lovett. See Miscamble, *George F. Kennan*.

4. PPS meeting, Dec 16, 1949, FRUS, 1949, vol. 1, [doc.] 156, pp. 413–16.

5. See Miscamble, *George F. Kennan*. On Kennan's opposition to NATO, see the correspondence between Miscamble and the authors, Feb 7, 2011, TFP. Also see N. Thompson, *The Hawk and the Dove*.

6. Clark's Island was owned at that time by a small group of families. It had no utilities, and motorized vehicles were not allowed. The island was reputed to be the staging area for the Pilgrims' landing at Plymouth, that is, the place where they left the women and children before the men went ashore to the mainland. There is a large rock in the island's interior that is inscribed as the site of the Pilgrims' first religious service, predating those in Plymouth. Whether or not this contention is authentic, it is a much bigger object than the more famous Plymouth Rock.

7. In 1949, Acheson authored what is referred to as the "China White Paper," which said that American intervention would not stop the Communists in China. This led many critics to accuse Truman and Acheson of having lost China. See *United States Relations with China*.

8. Hickerson to Smith, Jun 23, 1949, Thompson personnel file, TFP.

9. Hickerson efficiency report, Oct 15, 1948, TFP.

10. NSC 68 was not declassified until the 1970s.

11. N. Thompson, *The Hawk and the Dove*, p. 111.

12. Preparation of NSC 68, FRUS, 1950, vol. 1 (*National Security Affairs; Foreign Economic Policy*), [doc.] 85, pp. 234–92.

13. N. Thompson, *The Hawk and the Dove*, p. 113.

14. Thompson memo to SecState, Apr 3, 1950, FRUS, 1950, vol. 1, [doc.] 77, pp. 213–14.

15. Bohlen, *Witness to History*, p. 291.

16. Robert Jervis, "The Impact of the Korean War on the Cold War," *Journal of Conflict Resolution*, vol. 24, no. 4 (Dec 1980), pp. 563–92.

17. Anthony R. Garrett, "Was the Soviet Union Responsible for the Outbreak of the Korean War?," master's thesis, US Army Command and General Staff College, 1992, www.dtic.mil/dtic/tr/fulltext/u2/a2570 96.pdf.

18. Thompson oral history, Jun 29, 1966, Dulles-PL.

19. Mosely letter to Thompson, Jul 31, 1954, TFP.

20. This Italian national holiday, on August 15, coincides with a major Catholic holy day, Assumption Day.

21. Jane Thompson unpublished memoirs, TFP.

22. Villa Taverna was the US ambassador's residence in Rome, Italy. The gardens are the largest private gardens in that city.

23. Thompson address, Studentenclub, Vienna, Austria, Nov 19, 1952, TFP.

24. Mario Del Pero, "The United States and 'Psychological Warfare' in Italy, 1948–1955," *Journal of American History*, vol. 87, no. 4 (Mar 2001), pp. 1304–34.

25. The formation of NSC 68 and Truman's speech for the Campaign for Truth both occurred in April 1950. See Krugler, *Voice of America*, chap. 4, "Campaign for Truth."

26. The abbreviations stand for the United Nations (UN); United Nations Educational, Scientific and Cultural Organization (UNESCO); Economic and Social Council of the UN (ECOSC); Organisation for Economic Co-operation and Development (OECD); North Atlantic Treaty Organization (NATO); European Defense Community (EDC); International Labour Organization (ILO); and Economic Cooperation Administration (ECA), the agency that administered the Marshall Plan.

27. Thompson address, Studentenclub, Vienna, Austria, Nov 19, 1952, TFP.

28. Joseph Earle Jacobs letter to Elbridge Durbrow, Oct 7, 1951, TFP.

1. Authors' interview with Richard Davies, Feb 23, 2003, TFP.

2. James Marlow for the Associated Press, Mar 25, 1953, Newspapers.com, reprinted in *Courier News* [Blytheville, AR], TFP; Herman, *Joseph McCarthy*, p. 227; and Bohlen, *Witness to History*.

3. Authors' interview with Halvord Ekern, May 2005, TFP.

4. Authors' interview with John Mapother, spring 2004, TFP.

5. For example, GRU Major Pyotr Semyonovich Popov began providing information to the Americans in 1952 and continued to do so until his defection was discovered, resulting in his execution in Moscow in 1959.

6. Authors' interview with Halvord Ekern, May 2005, TFP.

7. Jane Thompson unpublished memoirs, TFP.

8. In 1952, the Soviets still had a military high commissioner. The first postwar Soviet ambassador to arrive in Vienna did so only after Stalin died in 1953, and he also had a double title.

9. This was the same John Connally who rode in the fateful motorcade with John F. Kennedy in 1963.

10. Sergei Kudriavtsev was the same GRU agent who helped set up the 1946 spy ring in Canada.

11. Loy Henderson was partly responsible for the State Department's consent to the operation, in that he had been warning Washington, DC, that Mosaddegh was in the hands of Iran's Communist Party, the Tudeh Party, and was looking to the Soviet Union for aid and commercial ties. In fact, Mosaddegh never legalized the Tudeh Party, although its members were in favor of his reforms. He was, however, decidedly anti-British and had a new vision for Iran.

12. Mohammad Mosaddegh would remain under house arrest until his death in 1967.

13. The information on Mosaddegh comes from B. Hersh, *The Old Boys*; Evans, *The Very Best Men*; Quigley, *Tragedy and Hope*; Loy Henderson oral history, TL; and Helms, *A Look over My Shoulder*.

14. He did not know then about Henderson's negative efficiency report on Thompson when they were both serving in Moscow in 1942.

15. Jane Thompson unpublished memoirs, TFP.

16. This appellation came from Ted Kaghan, who was on the embassy staff.

17. Thompson oral history, Jun 29, 1966, Dulles-PL.

18. Jane Thompson letters to her parents, 1953, TFP.

19. Thompson oral history, Jun 29, 1966, Dulles-PL.

20. The authors surmise that this was *History of the Communist Party of the Soviet Union (Bolsheviks): Short Course*. For a brief overview of the book and its contents, see the WorldCat online library catalog, www.world cat.org/title/history-of-the-communist-party-of-the-soviet-union-bolsheviks-short-course/oclc/575680536? referer=di&ht=edition/.

21. Jane Thompson letters to her parents, 1953, TFP.

12 ≋ The Trieste Negotiations

Epigraph. William Ralph Inge, *The End of an Age*, p. 127.

1. A grand jury had secretly indicted Holmes, along with seventeen other people and seven corporations, the previous April. The indictment was kept sealed, in the hopes that some of the accused who were overseas would come back to the United States, where they could be prosecuted. That ploy failed, however, and the indictment was publicly handed down by the Justice Department on February 23, 1954. Those being prosecuted were accused of having bought surplus US ships from the government at the end of World War II under false pretenses, with the intention of selling or leasing them to foreign concerns, which was illegal. The indictments indicated that the accused had made a profit of $3.35 million on an investment of $101,000. The defendants averred that the indictment was "politically motivated" and a "ghastly mistake," as well as claiming that this was just the Republicans going after prominent Democrats. According to the indictment, however, these corporations and their accounting firms filed false financial statements and balance sheets, in addition to lying in their statements about not selling or chartering these vessels to foreigners. One of the corporate defendants complained that the public had been misled in believing that surplus war ships were somehow

responsible for US military deaths in Korea, because the ships had been leased to deliver Rumanian oil to China. That rumor persists on Internet blogs, even today.

2. The Julian March (Serbo-Croatian and Slovene: *Julijska krajina*), or Julian Venetia (Italian: *Venezia Giulia*; Venetian: *Venesia Julia*; Friulian: *Vignesie Julie*; German: *Julisch Venetien*), is a term applied to an area of southeastern Europe, today split among Croatia, Italy, and Slovenia. It is a geographical term coined by the Italian linguist Graziadio Isaia Ascoli, in order to present the Austrian Littoral as a unified region and a historic part of Italy.

3. Slovenia was divided between Italy and Germany. Croatia became a separate kingdom under the Ustaše, a Fascist movement. Ante Pavelić, Croatia's Ustaše leader, took advantage of the situation to practice an ethnic cleansing of the Serbs in Croatia, killing, at a conservative estimate, 350,000. Serbia fell under German occupation, and Montenegro under the Italians.

4. This British group was known as the Special Operations Executive (SOE). See Lindsay, *Beacons in the Night*, for a personal account of Allied paramilitary operations in Yugoslavia.

5. Only now are these forgotten massacres being reexamined.

6. Clare Boothe Luce was a colorful, amazing, ambitious character, around whom intrigue, drama, and publicity always seemed to swirl. The daughter of a former chorus girl and a wandering musician [although official biographies say she was the "daughter of a successful New York businessman"], she graduated from college at age sixteen. She married and later divorced an abusive alcoholic, with whom she had a daughter. As a single mother, she pursued a writing career, literally forcing her way into a job at *Vogue* magazine and then working her way up to become editor for another periodical, *Vanity Fair*. In 1935, she married Henry Luce, a wealthy and powerful publisher who may have inspired her interest in politics. He was the founder and owner of *Time*, *Life*, and *Fortune* magazines, among others. Her marriage to Luce did not temper Clare's own ambitions. After she married him, she wrote several successful plays, became a wartime journalist, and later was the first woman elected to Congress (from Connecticut), as well as a diplomat and a doyenne of high society. She suffered a nervous breakdown when her daughter was killed in a car crash. It led her to a deep religious faith, and she became a devout Roman Catholic. The Luces were staunch conservatives who contributed generously to Dwight Eisenhower's election campaign, no doubt a factor in Claire Boothe Luce's appointment as ambassador to Rome. While in Rome, she supposedly had an affair with Allen Dulles, the head of the CIA. Wonderful as the story might have been, it is the opinion of the authors that Dulles was probably not the mystery man Luce would claim visited her during the Trieste negotiations.

7. Luce to president's special assistant, Sep 7, 1953, FRUS, 1952–1954, vol. 8 (*Eastern Europe; Soviet Union; Eastern Mediterranean*), doc. 106.

8. The American delegation to the talks included Professor Philip Mosely, who was part of the fact-finding mission in 1945 (see Bischof, *Austria in the First Cold War*, p. 106); military and legal advisors; and Leonard Unger, who had served as an economic adviser on the Italo-Yugoslav Border Commission and also had been a US political advisor to the British commanding general in Trieste's Zone A. Only Unger remained to assist Thompson until the negotiations ended.

9. Thompson oral history, Jun 29, 1966, Dulles-PL.

10. Thompson letter to Jane, Feb 14, 1954, TFP.

11. Campbell, *Successful Negotiations*, p. 393.

12. Thompson to State, cable 3488, Feb 13, 1954, box 3633B, RG 59, NACP. Also see Thompson letter to Woodruff Wallner, Mar 8, 1954, CF 750G.00/3-854, RG 59, NACP, also in FRUS, 1952–1954, vol. 8, doc. 171, and in TFP.

13. The EDC was to be supranational agency that would form a European army under joint European control. This never happened.

14. The allies were developing military relationships with Yugoslavia, Greece, and Turkey (the Balkan Pact) to close the gap in NATO defenses in the eastern Mediterranean region.

15. For more details, see Campbell, *Successful Negotiations*.

16. Thompson letter to Julius C. Holmes, Feb 9, 1954, enclosing full notes of the first, second, and third meetings with the Yugoslavs, CF 750.G.00/2-954, RG 59, NACP. Lancaster House is a large building used by the British Foreign Office (now called the Foreign and Commonwealth Ministry) for outside events. Presumably, this was so the participants would not be seen going into and out of the Foreign Ministry building itself.

17. Campbell, *Successful Negotiations*, chap. 3, "Vladimir Velebit."

18. Ibid., chap. 2, "Geoffrey Harrison," p. 50.

19. Thompson to James Bonbright Jr., Feb 16, 1954, FRUS, 1952–1954, vol. 8, doc. 169.

20. Thompson to SecState, cable 3536, 250/40/7/5, CF 750.G.00/2-1754, box 3633B, RG 59, NACP.

21. Ibid. In that cable, Thompson requested a meeting with Dulles. In a letter to his wife, Thompson told her he went to Paris on February 23 to see Dulles, although the authors found no record of that meeting in the files.

22. Thompson letter to Jane, Feb 23, 1954, TFP.

23. Campbell, *Successful Negotiations*; authors' correspondence with Leonard Unger, TFP; summary of negotiations [not for publication], Dec 2, 1954, Royal Institute of International Affairs, Chatham House, London; and Thompson oral history, Jun 29, 1966, Dulles-PL.

24. Nolan, *Notable US Ambassadors*, pp. 346–47.

25. Harrison letter to Thompson, Jan 24, 1972, TFP. Regarding Harrison and his Foreign Office duties, Thompson did keep Harrison informed at all times, and the two acted in unison. See "Reminiscences of Llewellyn Thompson," [undated], interview by John Campbell, Columbia Center for Oral History Collection, Columbia University, New York.

26. Thompson had already written this in the long paper he gave to Kennan to edit (see chapter 5).

27. Campbell, *Successful Negotiations*, p. 27.

28. The modifications were probably due to Thompson's meeting with Dulles in February. See Campbell, *Successful Negotiations*, p. 27; and Thompson oral history, Jun 29, 1966, Dulles-PL.

29. Campbell, *Successful Negotiations*, p. 27.

30. Thompson letter to Elbridge Durbrow, Mar 8, 1954, CF 750.G.00/3.854, box 3633B, RG 59, NACP.

31. Ibid.

32. Velebit also maintained his pressure for Trieste to remain a free port, a status it had had since 1719, and provisions for this were included in the final settlement. Also see Thompson letter to Elbridge Durbrow, Mar 8, 1954, CF 750.G.00/3.854, box 3633B, RG 59, NACP.

33. Editorial note, FRUS, 1952–1954, vol. 8, doc. 174. For more on Thompson seeking to create Italian-Yugoslav interdependence, also see Thompson to State, cable 4418, Apr 7, 1954, CF 750.G.00/4-754, RG 59, NACP.

34. Thompson letter to Jane, Mar 7, 1954, TFP.

35. Thompson letter to Hooker, Mar 19, 1954, CF 750.G00/3-1954, RG 59, NACP, also in TFP.

36. Yugoslavia claimed that it was due $50 million in reparations payments from Italy, because Yugoslavia had suffered under an unwanted occupation by that country when Italy was a willing partner of the Nazis during World War II. Thompson thought the Yugoslavs would settle for $30 million, but he did not think the lump-sum cash approach Velebit wanted would work. Instead, Thompson argued that if the United States could give Italy $20 million in aid, this then could be converted into $30 million worth of deliveries of goods and services from Italy to Yugoslavia under a general economic settlement. An added argument Thompson presented was that if the increased $20 million in US aid to Yugoslavia for port improvements ever became known, America would have already made a similar additional contribution to Italy.

37. Thompson to State, cable 4418, Apr 7, 1954, CF 750.G.00/4-754, RG 59, NACP, also in TFP.

38. SecState to Prime Minister Mario Scelba, Apr 10, 1954, FRUS, 1952–1954, vol. 8, doc. 182; and Thompson to State, cable 4418, Apr 7, 1954, CF 750.G.00/4-754, RG 59, NACP.

39. Thompson letter to Jane, Mar 29, 1954, TFP.

40. Thompson letter to Elbridge Durbrow, Mar 8, 1954, CF 750.G.00/3.854, box 3633B, RG 59, NACP.

41. Cyrus Sulzberger, "Trieste Formula Offered by Tito: Yugoslav President's Plan for Partition Follows That Drafted by U. S., Britain," *New York Times*, dateline May 8, published May 9, 1954.

42. On May 11, the Yugoslav newspaper *Borba* published the full transcript of the Tito-Sulzberger interview.

43. The State Department wanted to know how Sulzberger had come to learn the details of the negotiations. In a cable on May 11, Riddleberger implied that Tito had been Sulzberger's source, but this could not have been so, because Sulzberger had known the details before this interview took place. Riddleberger adroitly managed to leave out of the cable that it was Riddleberger himself who had confirmed the story for Sulzberger, at a dinner prior to the Tito interview, and that, according to Sulzberger's memoirs, Riddleberger

even "quipped with delight, 'I'll bet this will send Luce into a tizzy.'" See Sulzberger, *Long Row of Candles*, pp. 1005–6. Sulzberger goes on to say that Riddleberger agreed the negotiation settlements couldn't stay secret forever, and that he [Riddleberger] was surprised they hadn't been leaked before.

44. In a speech to future diplomats on negotiating tactics, Thompson said: "I would like to give one piece of advice which applies to all diplomacy as well as negotiation. . . . You will find it elaborated with great skill in Harold Nicholson's writings and it may be summed up by saying that no matter whom you are dealing with—honesty is the best policy." Thompson speech at the Foreign Service Institute, Washington, DC, Apr 12, 1971, TFP. Honesty almost halted the Trieste negotiations, but anything less would probably have derailed them forever.

45. MemCon 18: deputy undersecretary, ambassador, Robert Hooker, Mr. Williamson, Mr. Collins, and Mr. O'Sullivan, Sep 18, 1954, CF 750.G.00/9-7854, RG 59. NACP, also in TFP.

46. Unger and Segulja, *Trieste Negotiations*, p. 29. While Thompson was talking to Manlio Brosio in London, Luce contacted the Italian government in Rome with the same message. See editorial note, FRUS, 1952–1954, vol. 8, doc. 191.

47. Thompson letters to Jane, various dates, 1954, TFP.

48. Jane Thompson unpublished memoirs, TFP.

49. Campbell, *Successful Negotiations*, p. 118.

50. Acting Secretary Walter Bedell Smith to Thompson, London, cable 0959-08, Aug 26, 1954, CF 750G.00/8-2654, RG 59, NACP.

51. Thompson letter to Jane, Jul 31, 1954, TFP.

52. SecState to Belgrade Embassy, Urtel 38, Jul 15, 1954, FRUS, 1952–1954, vol. 8, doc. 226.

53. Thompson to SecState, cable 979, Aug 26, 1954, CF 750.G.00/8-2554, RG 59, NACP, also in TFP. Also see Campbell, *Successful Negotiations*, chap. 1, "The American Negotiator, Llewellyn E Thompson," and chap. 4, "The Italian Negotiator, Manlio Brosio."

54. Telegram 911 from London to SecState, Aug 23, 1954, CF 750.G.00/8-2354, box 3633C, RG 59, NACP. Also see Merchant to SecState, Aug 25, 1954, CF 750.G.00/8-2554, box 3633, RG 59, NACP; and scanned "Top Secret" memo from Dulles to American embassies in Belgrade, Rome, and London, Aug 25, 1954, TFP.

55. Clare Boothe Luce oral history, FA-ADST. [The Foreign Affairs Oral History Collection, at http://adst.org/oral-history/oral-history-interviews/, was put together by Stuart Kennedy, a retired Foreign Service officer who compiled over 700 oral histories of American diplomats.] Also see Rabel, *Between East and West*, pp. 157–58.

56. Thompson to SecState, cable 979, Aug 26, 1954, CF 750.G.00/8-2554, RG 59, NACP, also in TFP.

57. Livingston Merchant memo to SecState, status of Trieste negotiations, Aug 30, 1954, CF 750.G.00/8-3054, RG 59, NACP, also in TFP.

58. Thompson to SecState, cable 1177, Sep 6, 1954, CF 750.G.00/9-654, RG 59, NACP, also in TFP.

59. Editorial note, FRUS, 1952–1954, vol. 8, doc. 253, p. 514; and Murphy, *Diplomat among Warriors*, p. 471.

60. Murphy, *Diplomat among Warriors*, pp. 470–72.

61. Livingston Merchant memo to Acting SecState W. B. Smith, Sep 2, 1954, CF 750.G.00/9-254, RG 59, NACP, stating, "After discussions with Mrs. Luce, I suggest that we should plan for Mr. Murphy to go to Belgrade and Rome to present the US-UK proposal to Tito and Scelba." This memo implies that Merchant met with Luce and discussed the Murphy trip.

62. Knight memo to Merchant, Sep 3, 1954, CF 750.G.00/9-354, RG 59, NACP, also in TFP; Merchant memo to Acting SecState Smith, Sep 2, 1954, CF 750.G.00/9-254, RG 59, NACP, also in TFP, with the handwritten note "Sec Smith approved 9/2."

63. Authors' telephone interview with Robert Knight, Sep 13, 2006. Another piece of the puzzle that doesn't fit is that Acting Secretary of State Smith did not cable Eisenhower or Dulles, asking for permission to send Murphy, until the next day, September 3. Both Murphy and Luce knew about the proposed trip on September 2, and there is a cable from Merchant to Thompson, drafted on that day, to officially inform him of the decision to send Murphy. This implies that permission was sought from the president only after the decision had been made, which is unlikely. Lastly, Luce recalled that she spoke with Murphy at a ball in Washington, DC, while Murphy's account placed him at a dinner in New York City.

64. Unger and Segulja, *Trieste Negotiations*, p. 34. Unger cites cables from London to Washington, DC, Sep 1954, in Leonard Unger's private records. The authors could not find the relevant Thompson cable to Smith in the archives, but we discovered during our research that it is not unusual for cables to be missing or misplaced. Another possibility is that, due to the urgency of the matter, the issue may have been discussed by telephone.

65. Merchant to SecState, Oct 14, 1953, FRUS, 1952–1954, vol. 8, doc. 136, p. 319.

66. Thompson to SecState, cable 1138, Sep 3, 1954, CF 750.G.00/79-354, RG 59, NACP.

67. MemCon: Tarchiani and SecState, Aug 3, 1954, FRUS, 1952–1954, vol. 8, doc. 230.

68. Thompson to SecState, cable 1138, Sep 3, 1954, CF 750.G.00/79-354, RG 59, NACP.

69. "Exchange of Messages between the President and President Tito of Yugoslavia on the Trieste Agreement," Oct 5, 1954, American Presidency Project, www.presidency.ucsb.edu/ws/?pid=10079/.

70. That is, issues such as the Basovizza pit, or quarry.

71. Authors' interview with John Mapother, Sep 2013, TFP.

72. Campbell, *Successful Negotiations*, p. 136.

73. Murphy, *Diplomat among Warriors*, p. 473.

74. Ibid.

75. Murphy to SecState, cable 219, Sep 17, 1954, CF 750.G.00/9-1754, RG 59, NACP, also in TFP.

76. Thompson "personal and confidential" letter to Loy Henderson, Jan 3, 1957, TFP.

77. Campbell, *Successful Negotiations*, pp. 39–40.

13 ≋ The Austrian State Treaty Negotiations

1. See, for example, Carafano, *Waltzing into the Cold War*.

2. It was not until thirty-five years later, in 1989, when the Berlin Wall came down, that the issue of post–World War II Germany was finally settled and the country was reunited.

3. Authors' interview with Richard Davies, Feb 23, 2003, TFP; and Hendrik Van Oss oral history, FA-ADST.

4. Austrian historian Gerald Stourzh called the cables the "ping-pong" reports. See Stourzh, *Um Einheit und Freiheit*.

5. Sulzberger, *Last of the Giants*, pp. 125–26.

6. As it turned out, the Austrian example did influence Soviet relations with other countries. After the signing of the Austrian State Treaty, they invited West German chancellor Konrad Adenauer to Moscow for talks in 1955. They also sent a delegation to Yugoslavia to soften relations with that country, and they returned the Porkkala naval base to Finland. See Barraclough and Wall, *Survey of International Affairs 1955–56*, chap. 9, "Soviet Foreign Policy," pp. 125–27. More importantly, neutrality would form part of Khrushchev's strategy for relations with the Third World.

7. Don Cook, "1955 Diplomatic Corps Taught Future Strategy: Thompson's Technique in Austrian Treaty May Have Been Key to Accord on Berlin," *Los Angeles Times*, Aug 29, 1971.

8. Bohlen to State, cable 1690, Mar 31, 1955, FRUS, 1955–57, vol. 5, (*Austrian State Treaty; Summit and Foreign Ministers Meeting*), doc. 17.

9. Bohlen to State, cable 1808, Apr 14, 1955, FRUS, 1955–1957, vol. 5, doc. 24, p. 38; and Dulles to Thompson, cable 2904, Apr 18, 1955, FRUS, 1955–1957, vol. 5, doc. 29, p. 47.

10. Thompson to State, cable 2338, Apr 18, 1955, FRUS, 1955–1957, vol. 5, doc. 28, p. 45.

11. Cook, "1955 Diplomatic Corps."

12. These events were (a) Stalin's death, in March 1953; (b) Khrushchev's subsequent ascendancy and his desire to burnish the Soviets' image; (c) the Trieste settlement in October 1954; (d) the momentum provided by the Austrians' trip to Moscow in April 1955; (e) the Paris Accords, bringing Germany into NATO's embrace in May 1955; (f) the American military's satisfaction that Austria's gendarmerie, surreptitiously armed by the United States, could at least temporarily defend the country against the Red Menace; and (g) US estimates that the Austrian economic pump was primed.

13. See Executive Secretariat conference file, boxes 69–71, stack area 150, RG 51, NACP.

14. These were Articles 16 and 35 (later listed as Article 22).

15. See Tolstoy, *The Minister and the Massacres*.

16. Authors' interview with Halvord Ekern, May 3, 2005, abbreviated transcript in TFP, and original digital recording in authors' computer files, TFP. These conditions also occurred in the former Czechoslovakia, according to Sherry Thompson's interview with an eyewitness, Mar 2011.

17. See verbatim minutes, May 12, 1955, Executive Secretariat conference file, boxes 69–71, stack area 150, row 68, compartment 20, shelf 34, RG 51, NACP.

18. Ibid.

19. Allard, *Russia and the Austrian State Treaty*.

20. Thompson to SecState, cable 2618, May 5, 1955, incoming cable control no. 2901, May 6, 1955, TFP, also in NACP.

21. Cook, "1955 Diplomatic Corps."

22. See Bohlen, *Witness to History*, p. 362.

23. Dulles to Thompson, May 6, 1955, Thompson lot file 64 D 653, stack area 150, row 68, compartment 8, shelf 6, RG 59, NACP, also in TFP.

24. The final treaty allowed the return of "small property"—valued at not more than $10,000—as well as church property and property serving educational, cultural, or charitable concerns.

25. See verbatim minutes, May 12, 1955, Executive Secretariat conference file, boxes 69–71, stack area 150, row 68, compartment 20, shelf 34, RG 51, NACP.

26. Authors' correspondence with Gerald Stourzh, Dec 10, 2004, TFP.

27. Thompson correspondence with Julius Epstein, Hoover Institution, Aug–Oct 1965, TFP.

28. Jane Thompson unpublished memoirs, TFP.

29. Cook, "1955 Diplomatic Corps," although Cook confuses Article 35 with Article 16. The Article 16 issue had already been solved before Thompson met with Dulles.

30. Thompson to SecState, cable 2705, May 11, 1955, TFP, also in NACP .

31. According to Bischof, in *Austria in the First Cold War*, the oil companies had an agreement—quietly drawn up in 1950—that Western oil companies would be compensated by the Austrian government if their assets were not returned to them. The authors, however, did not come across such a document.

32. One of the largest oil fields in the Soviet zone belonged to a Canadian company—RK Van Sickle—and the others belonged to a joint Dutch-US company called Shell-Sacony-Vacuum.

33. It was not until 1958, when Austria showed signs of taking its neutrality seriously and being what the United States considered too friendly toward the Soviet Union, that the American government really put pressure on the Austrian government to negotiate the terms of the Vienna Memorandum. Thompson's successor, Ambassador H. Freeman Matthews, withheld US government loan guarantees as leverage, both to show Austria that the United States was not to be taken for granted, and to bring Austria back into the fold. The direct corporate negotiations continued until 1960, with the oil companies accepting $13 million plus stock interests as "satisfaction." This proved to be a shrewd maneuver, since the stocks gained considerably in value, and the oil companies ended up with quite a bit more than they could have hoped to negotiate for at the time of the treaty.

34. Note also the first point for negotiations, presented in the position paper prepared by Richard B. Freund, the State Department officer in charge of Austrian affairs, and reviewed by Livingston Merchant, the assistant secretary of state for European affairs: "Secure full information concerning any Austro-Soviet bilateral agreement in regard to concessions with respect to Art. 35 with a view to protecting the Austrians, to the extent possible, against onerous terms. If the Austrians are unable to arrange satisfactory terms bilaterally, attempt to obtain Soviet agreement to handling the concessions on Article 35 by amending the treaty." It does not mention Western oil interests and specifically refers to securing Austrian interests. Since this was a secret document, there was no need to lie about its intentions. See Richard Freund, "Austrian Treaty, Suggested Western Tactics," TFP.

35. Thompson to State, cable 404, May 9, 1955, FRUS, 1955–1957, vol. 5, doc. 58.

36. When Thompson was about to leave Vienna two years later, he wrote to Loy Henderson that his successor as ambassador to Austria would have to deal with the many claims still to be settled under the Austrian State Treaty and the Vienna Memorandum, the most important of which were those by the oil companies. That person, Thompson said, "should have the capacity for exercising restraint," because it would be wise not to endanger Austria's coalition government. There were many faults and weaknesses in the Austrian setup, and it was natural that any new American representative might get the urge to set things right. This, however,

could well furnish the straw that would break the coalition. See Thompson letter to Henderson, Jan 3, 1957, TFP.

37. Thompson to US delegation at North Atlantic Council, cable 425, May 11, 1955, FRUS, 1955–1957, vol. 5, doc. 66; and Thompson to US delegation at North Atlantic Council, cable 431, May 12, 1955, FRUS, 1955–1957, vol. 5, doc. 67.

38. Thompson to US delegation at North Atlantic Council, cable 411, May 10, 1955, FRUS, 1955–1957, vol. 5, doc. 60, p. 96n2.

39. Thompson to SecState, cable 2671, May 10, 1955, TFP. Also see Thompson to US delegation at North Atlantic Council, cable 411, May 10, 1955, FRUS, 1955–1957, vol. 5, doc. 60, p. 96n2.

40. Authors' interview with Halvord Ekern, May 3, 2005, abbreviated transcript in TFP, and original digital recording in authors' computer files, TFP.

41. Verbatim minutes, May 12, 1955, Executive Secretariat conference file, boxes 69–71, stack area 150, row 68, compartment 20, shelf 34,, RG 51, NACP.

42. Authors' interview with Halvord Ekern, May 3, 2005, abbreviated transcript in TFP, and original digital recording in authors' computer files, TFP.

43. Verbatim minutes, May 12, 1955, Executive Secretariat conference file, boxes 69–71, stack area 150, row 68, compartment 20, shelf 34, RG 51, NACP.

44. Authors' interview with Halvord Ekern, May 3, 2005, abbreviated transcript in TFP, and original digital recording in authors' computer files, TFP.

45. A painting was made for the occasion, one copy of which Thompson hung in his office. It is now at the history museum in Las Animas, Colorado.

46. Thompson correspondence with Julius Epstein, Hoover Institution, Aug–Oct 1965, TFP.

47. Thompson oral history, Jun 29, 1966, Dulles-PL.

48. With difficulty, we finally found the verbatim minutes, not in the lot file for the Austrian State Treaty, where they should have been, but buried in the Executive Secretariat conference file, boxes 69–71, stack area 150, row 68, compartment 20, shelf 34, RG 51, NACP.

48. See Barraclough and Wall, *Survey of International Affairs 1955–56*, p. 126.

50. Jane Thompson unpublished memoirs, TFP

14 ≋ Open Skies, Closed Borders

1. The delegation included Livingston Merchant, assistant secretary of state for European affairs; Eisenhower's son, Major John S. D. Eisenhower; Dillon Anderson, special assistant for national security affairs; Robert R. Bowie, director of the State Department's PPS; James Hagerty, White House press secretary; Douglas MacArthur II, counsel for the State Department; and Herman Phleger, legal adviser for the State Department.

2. Bulganin was the chairman of the Council of Ministers of the USSR. The other participants were the defense minister, Marshal Georgy K. Zhukov; Foreign Minister Vyacheslav M. Molotov; and Deputy Foreign Minister Andrei Gromyko.

3. On Khrushchev's insecurity, see Taubman, *Khrushchev*.

4. Ibid., pp. 352, 353.

5. Dobrynin was Molotov's assistant at that time.

6. Thompson speech at the Foreign Service Institute, Washington, DC, Apr 12, 1971, TFP.

7. Dobrynin, *In Confidence*.

8. Fursenko and Naftali, *Khrushchev's Cold War*, p. 285.

9. Dobrynin, *In Confidence*.

10. Bohlen, *Witness to History*, p. 386.

11. Taubman, *Khrushchev*, p. 352.

12. N. Khrushchev, *Khrushchev Remembers*, p. 400.

13. Jane Thompson unpublished memoirs, TFP.

14. Campbell, *Successful Negotiations*, p. 43.

15. The propaganda apparatus—both overt and covert—in Austria was immense. Approximately fifty Americans and over nine hundred Austrians were employed in the public US effort.

16. Thompson to State, cable 1022, Oct 31, 1956, FRUS, 1955–1957, vol. 25 (*Eastern Europe*), doc. 150, p. 352; and Thompson to State, cable 1268, Nov 11, 1956, FRUS, 1955–1957, vol. 25, doc. 181.

17. According to Taubman, Georgy Zhukov, Vyacheslav Molotov, and even Chinese Communist leader Mao Zedong had doubts about what action should have been taken. See Taubman, *Khrushchev*, p. 296.

18. Embassy status was not given to the Budapest legation until 1966.

19. Thompson letter to Bohlen, Nov 16, 1956, TFP.

20. Thompson oral history, Jun 29, 1966, Dulles-PL.

21. Thompson letter to Bohlen, Nov 16, 1956, TFP.

22. B. Hersh, *The Old Boys*, p. 371.

23. Hungary's Cardinal Mindszenty spent fifteen years in the American embassy.

24. See John P. C. Matthews, "John Foster Dulles and the Suez Crisis of 1956," *American Diplomacy*, University of North Carolina, www.unc.edu/depts/diplomat/item/2006/0709/matt/matthews_suez.html. One of the tactics Ike used was threatening to sell US reserves of the British pound sterling, which would cause that currency to fall, and refusing to provide oil when Saudi Arabia started an embargo against Britain and France. According to his memoir, Eisenhower instructed Dulles to cease all economic aid to Israel and call for a resolution in the UN to withdraw *all* troops, ban military shipments to the area, and reopen the Suez Canal. Lester Pearson, the Canadian secretary of state for external affairs, came up with a plan to form a UN emergency force to separate the opposing armies. Thus began the UN peacekeeping troops, for which Pearson received the Nobel Peace Prize. Ironically, the United States did not glean local credit from the Arab states for joining with Nasser and the Soviet Union to censure its own allies and demand that they remove themselves from the area around the canal. The Soviets, *after the UN vote*, threatened to drop atomic bombs on London and Paris if those countries' troops weren't withdrawn. Most people in the affected region did not know about the UN vote and assumed that it was the Soviets who delivered them from the occupying forces, not the United States.

25. Csaba Békés, "New Findings on the 1956 Hungarian Revolution," Bulletin No. 2 (Fall 1992), Cold War International History Project, Wilson Center, https://www.wilsoncenter.org/sites/default/files/CWIHPBulletin2.pdf.

26. Radio Free Europe was CIA funded, although it was nominally created by the National Committee for a Free Europe. Its financial support went from $10 million a year in 1950 to $50 billion by the end of the 1950s.

27. Thompson to State, cable 1268, Nov 11, 1956, FRUS, 1955–1957, vol. 25, doc. 181, p. 430; and "Policy Review of the Voice for Free Hungary Programming, October 23–November 23, 1956," Dec 5, 1956, doc. 10, GW-NSA, http://nsarchive.gwu.edu/NSAEBB/NSAEBB76/doc10.pdf.

28. Thomas, *The Very Best Men*, p. 146.

29. Jane Thompson unpublished memoirs, TFP.

30. Sebestyen, *1956 Hungarian Revolution*, p. 281.

31. See Thompson oral history, Jun 29, 1966, Dulles-PL.

32. Jane Thompson unpublished memoirs, TFP.

33. Thompson to State, cable 1268, Nov 11, 1956, FRUS, 1955–1957, vol. 25, doc. 181.

34. Thompson letter to Bohlen, Nov 14, 1956, TFP.

35. Such a message had been sent before, by Dulles through Bohlen, but it just reiterated what Dulles had said in public earlier, when he noted that the United States did not look on Eastern bloc countries as military allies, although that earlier statement was not very forceful.

36. Bohlen, *Witness to History*, p. 413.

37. Bohlen letter to Thompson, Nov 16, 1956, TFP.

38. From 1945 to 1948, and again from 1956 to 1970, Gomulka was able to convince the Soviets that Poland had no intention of abandoning Communism or its treaties with the Soviet Union. This allowed him to maneuver for some reforms and take power. His success no doubt encouraged the Hungarians.

39. Thompson letter to Bohlen, Nov 16, 1956, TFP.

40. Thompson letter to Bohlen, Nov 14, 1956, TFP.

41. Thompson letter to Bohlen, Nov 16, 1956, TFP.

42. Bohlen letter to Thompson, Nov 26, 1956, TFP.

43. Bohlen to State, cable 1199, Nov 14, 1956, FRUS, 1955–1957, vol. 25, doc. 188, p. 445.

44. Thompson letter to Bohlen, Nov 16, 1956, TFP.

45. These rules were laid out in the Immigration and Nationality Act of 1952, known as the McCarran-Walter Act.

46. Wolf Lehmann, "Politics and Refugees," given to the authors by Mr. Lehmann, TFP. Sebestyen's *1956 Hungarian Revolution* puts this number at 150,000.

47. Authors' interview and letters exchanged with Wolf Lehman, TFP.

48. Jane Thompson unpublished memoirs, TFP.

49. Ibid.

50. Ibid.

51. Meeting with Eisenhower, Dec 26, 1956, FRUS, 1955–1957, vol. 25, doc. 218, p. 534; and Thompson letter to Bohlen, Jan 17, 1957, TFP.

52. See Spaulding, *Ambassadors Ordinary and Extraordinary*, chap. 9, "The Pros."

53. Bunker would become the US ambassador to India when he left the Red Cross.

54. Thompson letter to Bunker, Sep 15, 1955, TFP.

55. Ibid.

56. Thompson resignation letter to Dulles, Aug 12, 1955, TFP.

57. Dulles letter to Thompson, Sep 1, 1955, TFP.

58. Ibid.

59. Thompson letter to Bunker, Sep 15, 1955, TFP.

60. Thompson letter to Henderson, describing his conversation with Dulles, Feb 11, 1957, TFP.

61. Thompson letter to Bohlen, Jan 17, 1956, TFP.

62. Ibid.

63. Thompson letter to Henderson, Jan 3, 1957, TFP.

64. Ibid.

65. Bohlen letter to Thompson, Jan 11, 1957, TFP.

66. Thompson letter to Bohlen, Jan 17, 1957, TFP.

67. Bohlen letter to Thompson, Jan 28, 1957, TFP.

68. Thompson letter to Henderson, Feb 11, 1957, TFP.

69. Bohlen, *Witness to History*, p. 442.

70. Thompson told his daughter this was the closest he had ever come to a breakdown.

71. Bohlen, eulogy for Thompson, Feb 1972, TFP.

72. Bohlen, *Witness to History*, 442. Also see Bohlen, eulogy for Thompson, Feb 1972, TFP.

73. Bohlen, eulogy for Thompson, Feb 1972, TFP.

74. The Communist Party members who had tried to oust Khrushchev for attacking Stalin in his "Secret Speech"—as well as for Khrushchev's pursuit of peaceful coexistence with the West, which they rejected—were dubbed the Anti-Party Group by Khrushchev. Khrushchev removed the group's leadership, but he was not able to purge all of its members from the Communist Party, at least not right away. The Anti-Party Group was led by the old Stalinists: Vyacheslav Molotov, Lazar Kaganovich, Kliment Voroshilov, Georgy Malenkov, Maksim Saburov, Mikhail Pervukhin, Nikolai Bulganin, and Dmitri Shepilov.

15 ≋ Khrushchev's Decade (1953–1964)

1. Thompson letter to A. Schlesinger Jr., Oct 24, 1967, TFP.

2. Thompson undated paper, "The Soviet System and Ours," 1970s, TFP.

3. Khrushchev used the phrase "we will bury you" at a later point in time, while addressing Western ambassadors at a reception at the Polish embassy in Moscow on November 18, 1956. See "Khrushchev Tirade Again Irks Envoys," *New York Times*, Nov. 19, 1956, p. 1.

4. Thompson undated paper, "The Soviet System and Ours," 1970s, TFP.

5. Thompson, "Vital Interests and Objectives of the United States," speech at the Industrial College of the Armed Forces, Washington, DC, Aug 25, 1965, TFP.

6. This policy had been announced by Dulles in a 1954 speech. See Campbell Craig, "Just Like Ike on Deterrence," *Santa Fe New Mexican*, Apr 8, 2010. Craig and Fredrik Logevall are the coauthors of *America's Cold War: The Politics of Insecurity*.

7. NSC 5707/8 stated that the United States would place its main reliance on nuclear weapons in the event of war with the Soviet Union. See basic national security policy, June 3, 1957, FRUS, 1955–1957, vol. 19 (*National Security Policy*), doc. 120, section B, [subsection] no. 11.

8. For a description of Eisenhower's "more bang for the buck" approach to defense spending, see "Dwight D. Eisenhower: Foreign Affairs," American President: A Reference Resource, Miller Center, http://millercenter.org/president/biography/eisenhower-foreign-affairs/.

9. National Intelligence Estimate NIE 11-5-58, released in August 1958, concluded that the USSR had "the technical and industrial capability . . . to have an operational capability with 100 ICBMs" sometime in 1960, and perhaps with 500 ICBMs "sometime in 1961, or at the latest in 1962." See Bureau of Intelligence and Research–National Intelligence Estimate (INR-NIE) files, "Top Secret," TFP. By 1959, the CIA concluded that the amount was only around 10 missiles, according to Perry, *My Journey*, p. 17n.

16 ≋ Moscow 2

1. Thompson letter to Edward Freers, general records, stack 150, box 7, RG 59, NACP, also in TFP.

2. A Tupolev Tu-104 had caused a stir during Nikita Khrushchev's state visit to London the year before, in 1956. The jet wasn't deemed safe enough to carry the entourage, but Khrushchev didn't want to miss the opportunity to show off one of the world's first passenger jet planes, so he came by ship and used the plane to deliver his mail.

3. Authors' interview with Ted Eliot, summer 2003, TFP.

4. Authors' group interview with former Thompson colleagues at the home of Robert Martens, Washington, DC, Feb 2003, TFP.

5. The poker players included Henry Shapiro, Irving R. Levine, Daniel Schorr, and Art Buchwald, when he was in town.

6. Authors' interviews with Robert Martens, Feb 2003, and Ted Eliot, summer 2003, both in TFP.

7. Authors' interview with Ted Eliot, summer 2003, TFP.

8. Authors' interview and email correspondence with Ted Eliot, Jul 27, 2003, TFP.

9. Authors' email correspondence and interview with Richard Davies, Feb 23, 2003, TFP. For an example of Thompson forwarding junior officers' opinions to the State Department, even when he disagreed with them, see David E. Mark oral history, FA-ADST.

10. Authors' email correspondence and interview with Richard Davies, Feb 2003, TFP.

11. Authors' interview with Richard Davies, Feb 23, 2003, TFP.

12. Constance Gagnon letter to Jane Thompson, describing her "favorite boss," Feb 11, 1972, TFP.

13. Authors' group interview with former Thompson colleagues at the home of Robert Martens, Washington, DC, Feb 2003, TFP.

14. Ibid.

15. Richmond, *Practicing Public Diplomacy*, p. 89.

16. Thompson to State, cable 107, Jul 15, 1957, FRUS, 1955–1957, vol. 24 (*Soviet Union; Eastern Mediterranean*), doc. 72. Thompson had arrived in Moscow on July 10.

17. By the time Sputnik burned up in the Earth's atmosphere on its return, it had travelled roughly 37 million miles.

18. Both Khrushchev and American politicians wasted no time in exploiting the event. In November 1957, the US Senate's Committee on Defense Preparedness declared that the United States was falling far behind the Soviets in its missile capabilities and urged a vigorous campaign to build fallout shelters to protect American citizens, which, in itself, would have repercussions in Moscow. Also that November, Khrushchev declared the Soviets' missile superiority and challenged the United States to a "shooting match" to prove his point. See "Khrushchev Invites U.S. to Missile Shooting Match," *New York Times*, Nov 15, 1957.

19. Thompson to State, cable 953, Nov 16, 1957, FRUS, 1955–1957, vol. 24, doc. 88.

20. Thompson to State, cable 895, Nov 3, 1957, FRUS, 1955–1957, vol. 24, doc. 84.

21. Thompson to State, cable 1903, Jan 18, 1960, FRUS, 1958–1960, vol. 10, pt. 1 (*Eastern Europe Region, Soviet Union, Cyprus*), doc. 141.

22. The chief of general staff, Marshal Vassily Sokolovsky, would resign in protest over Khrushchev's 1960 cuts, according to Zubok, *Failed Empire*, p. 135.

23. Thompson to State, cable 895, Nov 3, 1957, FRUS, 1955–1957, vol. 24, doc. 84.

24. Editorial note, quoting Thompson to State, cable 917, Nov 8, 1957, FRUS, 1955–1957, vol. 24, doc. 86.

25. Jane Thompson diary, TFP.

26. Mićunović, *Moscow Diary*, p. 335.

27. Jonathan Rickert, "Impressions of Ambassador Thompson," Nov 25, 2002, TFP.

28. Authors' interview with Valdimir Toumanoff, Jul 14, 2003, TFP. Toumanoff said that when Thompson left Moscow, Khrushchev lost one of the two people he could really trust—the other being his wife, Nina Petrovna.

29. Pugwash was the result of a manifesto by Bertrand Russell and Albert Einstein, delivered on July 9, 1955, in London. It began: "In the tragic situation which confronts humanity, we feel that scientists should assemble in conference to appraise the perils that have arisen as a result of the development of weapons of mass destruction, and to discuss a resolution." See "Statement: The Russell-Einstein Manifesto," Pugwash Conference on Science and World Affairs, https://pugwash.org/1955/07/09/statement-manifesto/. The first Pugwash Peace Conference took place in July 1957, with twenty-three scientists attending, including seven from the United States and three from the Soviet Union.

30. Hixon, *Parting the Curtain*, p. 157.

31. Quirk, *Bob Hope*, p. 209.

32. Valdislav M. Zubok, "Khrushchev and the Berlin Crisis (1958–1962)," p. 13, Woodrow Wilson International Center for Scholars, https://www.wilsoncenter.org/sites/default/files/ACFB7D.pdf.

33. MemCon, Washington, DC, Feb 11, 1958, FRUS, 1958–1960, vol. 8 (*Berlin Crisis, 1958–59*), doc. 7.

34. Draft of Thompson television speech, Apr 1958, TFP.

35. Authors' interview with Hans Tuch, Feb 25, 2003, TFP.

36. Hixon, *Parting the Curtain*, p. 156.

37. Thompson must have handled the delicate situation well, because in 1960, Cliburn, at a high point in his career, took the time to write and congratulate Thompson on the honorary degree the latter received from Harvard University. Cliburn also offered to come back to Moscow to attend a Fourth of July celebration at the American embassy there. See Cliburn letter to Thompson, Jun 30, 1960, TFP. For a complete description of Van Cliburn's Moscow trip, see Stuart Isacoff, *When the World Stopped to Listen*.

38. This was the first time the Eisenhower Doctrine of 1957, giving the United States the right to intervene in countries threatened by international Communism, was applied. At the same time, pro-Western King Faisal was overthrown by a military coup in Iraq, and Khrushchev threatened to use force to defend the "Iraqi revolution" if there was any Western interference.

39. Thompson to State, cable 201, Jul 23, 1958, FRUS, 1958–1960, vol. 10, pt. 1, doc. 49; and Jane Thompson unpublished memoirs, TFP.

40. Adlai Stevenson, "Khrushchev Stresses Ties to U.S," *New York Times*, Aug 28, 1958.

41. Thompson letter to Frederick "Fritz" Jandrey, acting assistant secretary for European Affairs, Aug 18, 1958, TFP; and Office of Soviet Union Affairs, Bureau of European Affairs: bilateral political relations, records relating to Soviet and American leadership and diplomatic personnel, 1929–1974, entry A1-5564, RG 59, NACP. The authors do not have the original inquiry from SecState Dillon to Jandrey, only Thompson's reply referencing it.

17 ≋ Khrushchev's First Gamble: Berlin Poker

1. For more information about the formation of and reasons for two Germanys, see Harrison, *Up the Wall*, p. 54.

2. Ibid., p. 42. Also see Zubok and Pleshakov, *Inside the Kremlin's Cold War*, pp. 161–62. Lavrenti Beria didn't think the USSR could afford to prop up East Germany, and he wanted to get in on the benefits of US postwar aid. Khrushchev used Beria's position on East Germany to call him a traitor and get rid of him.

3. Thompson, cable 1052, Nov 11, 1958, and Thompson, cable 1773, Mar 9, 1959, CF 762.00/3–959, RG 59, NACP.

4. It was during these years that the United States armed West Germany's federal defense forces, the Bundeswehr, with nuclear weapons, albeit under American custody. See Garthoff, *Assessing the Adversary*. What was not known at the time was that Operation Atom was underway, to put twelve medium-range nu-

clear Soviet missiles north of Berlin. The missiles became operational in April 1959, but the United States only had suspicions about their existence. The missiles were removed to Kaliningrad, on the Baltic Sea, just before Khrushchev's summit with Eisenhower in September 1959. By then, the Soviets had deployed new medium-range ballistic missiles in the USSR, which allowed them to hit the same targets as the missiles they had had stationed in East Germany.

5. The reference to a bone in Khrushchev's throat was used many times, but probably the origin was during Khrushchev's meeting with Senator Hubert Humphrey. See Humphrey to State, cable 1208, Dec 3, 1958, FRUS, 1958–1960, vol. 8, doc. 84, p. 151.

6. Trachtenberg, *History and Strategy*, p. 176.

7. For a discussion on Khrushchev's meeting with Poland's Władysław Gomułka, indicating that "above all else [Khrushchev's motivation for the ultimatum was] to gain international recognition of East Germany," see Douglas Selvage, "New Evidence on the Berlin Crisis, 1958–1962," p. 200, Bulletin No. 11 (Winter 1998), Cold War International History Project, Wilson Center, https://www.wilsoncenter.org/publication/bulletin -no-11-winter-1998/.

8. Thompson to State, cable 1052, Nov 11, 1958, FRUS, 1958–1960, vol. 8, doc. 25.

9. Thompson, noting that the *Pravda* article on Berlin should be taken seriously, cable 1106, Nov 18, 1958, item BC00317, GW-NSA.

10. Thompson to State, cable 1813, Feb 1, 1961, FRUS, 1961–1963, vol. 5, doc. 20.

11. Thompson to State, cable 1106, Nov 18, 1958, item BC00317, GW-NSA.

12. Thompson to State, cable 1226, Dec 5, 1958, FRUS, 1958–1960, vol. 8, doc. 85.

13. Thompson to State, cable 1080, Nov 14, 1958, FRUS, 1958–1960, vol. 8, doc. 33.

14. Thompson to State, briefing on the status of Berlin, cable 1128, Nov 21, 1958, FRUS, 1958–1960, vol. 8, doc. 55.

15. Thompson oral history, Apr 27, 1966, JFKL.

16. Fursenko and Naftali, *Khrushchev's Cold War*, pp. 201, 575; and Harrison, *Up the Wall*. These authors disagreed with each other on the level and specifics of Mikoyan's reaction, with Harrison thinking that Mikoyan merely disagreed with the move, and Fursenko and Naftali seeing it as a something greater—a power struggle.

17. For a full description of Mikoyan's efforts to soften the ultimatum, see Fursenko and Naftali, *Khrushchev's Cold War*.

18. Ibid., pp. 207, 208.

19. Valdislav M. Zubok, "Khrushchev and the Berlin Crisis (1958–1962)," p. 13, Woodrow Wilson International Center for Scholars, https://www.wilsoncenter.org/sites/default/files/ACFB7D.pdf.; and "Working Paper No. 6," May 1993, TFP.

20. State to US embassy in Germany, cable 1012, Nov 17, 1958, FRUS, 1958–1960, vol. 8, doc. 45, p. 82; and US embassy in UK to State, cable 2752, Nov 19, 1958, FRUS, 1958–1960, vol. 8, doc. 49, p. 86.

21. Thompson toyed with the idea that the allies might construct a bluff [which was not carried out], where the British and French would give indications that they were preparing for a countermeasure, using force, and then, if the Soviets moved toward them, the Western allies could propose a high-level meeting to diffuse the situation. It would, in practicality, have the same outcome: the high-level meeting that Khrushchev wanted. But with this bluff, the meeting would be at the West's initiative, and it would happen before the Soviets turned over their authority in East Germany to Ulbricht, not after the horse was already out of the barn. See Thompson to SecState, "Eyes Only," Nov 21, 1958, FRUS, 1958–1960, vol. 8, doc. 56; and Thompson to State, cable 1128, Nov 21, 1958, FRUS, 1958–1960, vol. 8, doc. 55.

22. Ed Hurwitz letter to the authors, Apr 2003, TFP.

23. The United States tested its first hydrogen bomb on November 1, 1952, in the Marshall Islands, with the legacy of elevated rates of cancer in that region in the Pacific Ocean, which are still present more than sixty years later.

24. Thompson to State, cable 1208, Dec 3, 1958, FRUS, 1958–1960, vol. 8, doc. 84, with verbatim notes by Senator Hubert Humphrey, but also with an introductory paragraph by Thompson, stating the senator's opinion on Khrushchev's motive for the conversation.

25. Thompson to State, cable 1226, Dec 5, 1958, FRUS, 1958–1960, vol. 8, doc. 85.

26. Mikoyan, however, had more flexibility than most.

27. Fursenko and Naftali, *Khrushchev's Cold War*.

28. Ibid., p. 218.

29. MemCon, Washington, DC, Jan 6, 1959, FRUS, 1958–1960, vol. 10, pt. 1, doc. 61.

30. Ibid.

31. The UAR was a political alliance between Egypt and Syria from 1958 to 1961. The event took place on February 24. See Thompson to State, cable 1686, Feb 25, 1959, CF 761.13/2-2559, RG 59, NACP, where he mentions going to the UAR reception.

32. Jane Thompson unpublished memoirs, TFP.

33. Harrison, *Up the Wall*, p. 118.

34. Thompson to State, cable 1649, Feb 19, 1959, FRUS, 1958–1960, vol. 8, doc. 180.

35. Newman, *Macmillan, Khrushchev*.

36. The draft treaty had been presented by the Soviets the previous January. See Fursenko and Naftali, *Khrushchev's Cold War*, p. 219.

37. Ibid., p. 222; and Taubman, *Khrushchev*, p. 410.

38. Eisenhower message to Macmillan, Feb 24, 1959, FRUS, 1958–1960, vol. 8, doc. 184, p. 387, which refers to Khrushchev's speech, given to workers in the Kalinin district.

39. Thompson to State, cable 1686, Feb 25, 1959, internal political office records, CF 761.13/2-2559, RG 59, NACP; and "Macmillan's Visit to the Soviet Union, 02-21 to 03-03-59, prepared by Office of Research and Analysis for Sino-Soviet Bloc," Mar 13, 1959, report 7969, box 319E, entry 449, Research and Analysis Branch (OSS) and Bureau of Intelligence and Research, RG 59, NACP.

40. Though agreeing to the lower-level meeting, Khrushchev's acceptance represented a toughening of the Soviet position, because it put East-West parity as a precondition for the meeting by insisting that Poland and Czechoslovakia be included, as well as East Germany, to offset the participation of West Germany, the United States, France, and Great Britain.

41. When Khrushchev backpedaled on the Berlin ultimatum in this speech, he offered to postpone it until June or July, if necessary. See Peterson, *Crisis Bargaining*, p. 153.

42. "Macmillan's Visit to the Soviet Union, 02-21 to 03-03-59, prepared by Office of Research and Analysis for Sino-Soviet Bloc," Mar 13, 1959, report 7969, box 319E, entry 449, Research and Analysis Branch (OSS) and Bureau of Intelligence and Research, RG 59, NACP.

43. Thompson to State, cable 1747, Mar 4, 1959, FRUS, 1958–1960, vol. 8, doc. 197. Also see Thompson to State, cable 1687, Feb 25, 1959, CF 761.13/2-2559, RG 59, NACP, stating that "it is quite clear he will not reveal his hand on any lower level."

44. Thompson to SecState, cable 1773, Mar 9, 1959, CF 762.00/3-959, RG 59, NACP, also in TFP.

45. Garthoff, *Assessing the Adversary*, p. 42n101.

46. Thompson to SecState, cable 1773, Mar 9, 1959, CF 762.00/3-959, RG 59, NACP, also in TFP.

47. Ibid.

48. Ibid.

49. Garthoff, *Assessing the Adversary*.

50. Thompson to Merchant, Apr 6, 1959, CF 762.00221/4-659, RG 59, NACP, also in TFP.

51. Thompson to SecState, Mar 31, 1959, CF 761.13/3-3159, RG 59; NACP, also in TFP.

52. Fursenko and Naftali, in *Khrushchev's Cold War*, chap. 17, "Meniscus," described this as meniscus tactics.

53. Thompson to State, cable 2204, May 6, 1959, FRUS, 1958–1960, vol. 8, doc. 285. Also see Thompson to State, cable 2034, Apr 9, 1959, FRUS, 1958–1960, vol. 8, doc. 257.

54. Sulzberger, *Last of the Giants*, pp. 571–72.

55. Harrison, in *Up the Wall*, cites Jack Schick on this point.

56. Ibid., p. 126.

57. Taubman, *Khrushchev*, p. 414; Thompson to State, Charles Thayer's notes on Averell Harriman's conversation with Khrushchev re. Berlin and Germany, cable 2653, Jun 25, 1959, FRUS, 1958–1960, vol. 8, doc. 417, p. 941.

58. Taubman, *Khrushchev*, p. 414. Also see Thompson to SecState, cable 2665, Jun 26, 1959, CF 611.6176-2659, microfilm C0015, reels 14, 15, NARA.

59. Averell Harriman letter to Thompson, Jul 21, 1959, TFP.

60. Thompson to State, cable 734, Jun 26, 1959, FRUS, 1958–1960, vol. 10, pt. 1, doc. 75.

61. MemCon by Thompson, subject: Ambassador C. E. Bohlen [authors' note: we believe that Bohlen is probably the recipient, not the subject], Sep 29, 1959, Executive Secretariat conference files, CF 1463, box 195, entry 3051B, RG 59, NACP, also in TFP.

62. Thompson to State, concerning Germany and Berlin [supplement to Thayer's report on his conversation with Khrushchev], cable 2665, Jun 29, 1959, CF 611.81/6-2959, RG 59, NACP, also in TFP.

63. Editorial note, FRUS, 1958–1960, vol. 10, pt. 1, doc. 85.

64. Ibid., p. 310.

65. Dulles became ill in February 1959, was replaced by Christian Herter in April, and then died in May.

66. Eisenhower must have seen both documents, making the subsequent "misunderstanding" between him and Murphy odd. See MemConf with Eisenhower, FRUS, 1958–1960, vol. 8, doc. 431, p. 977n3. Also see Eisenhower to Khrushchev, draft letter, [undated], FRUS, 1958–1960, vol. 10, pt. 1, doc. 89.

67. D. Eisenhower, *Waging Peace*, p. 407.

68. Eisenhower to Khrushchev, draft letter, [undated], FRUS, 1958–1960, vol. 10, pt. 1, doc. 89. Eisenhower's reply, accepting a September visit by Khrushchev to the United States, was handed to Ambassador Menshikov by Robert Murphy on July 29, 1959. See State to Herter, Jul 29, 1959, FRUS, 1958–1960, vol. 10, pt. 1, doc. 101; and Eisenhower to Khrushchev, draft letter, [undated], FRUS, 1958–1960, vol. 10, pt. 1, doc. 89.

69. The Russian children turned a long, narrow strip of snow into ice, then ran and slid to the end. They then came round to stand in line again to repeat the same action.

18 ≋ Dueling Exhibitions

1. Thompson wrote to Acheson on July 18, 1959, trying to stop or at least stall the resolution. He stated: "Congressional resolution coming at a time when we are probably approaching a turning point in world history will of course strengthen the hands of those Soviet leaders who think we are out to overthrow their government." See Thompson to SecState, Jul 18, 1959, stack area 150, row 68, compartment 1922, box 189, shelf 7, CF 1413–1416, RG 59, NACP, also in TFP.

2. Vladimir Toumanoff oral history, FA-ADST.

3. Garthoff, *Journey through the Cold War*, p. 72.

4. Ibid.; and Vladimir Toumanoff oral history, FA-ADST.

5. Hixson, *Parting the Curtain*, p. 167.

6. Enyd Blyton's main works are in the genre of young readers' novels, in which children have their own adventures, with minimal adult help.

7. The tunnels were built in 1914, under the direction of the owner of Spaso House, Nikolay Aleksandrovich Vtorov, a wealthy merchant and manufacturer.

8. Thompson and Charles Bohlen both died at age sixty-eight, and Walter Stoessel at age sixty-seven.

9. Lilienfeld et al., *Foreign Service Health Status Study*. Also see J. Mark Elwood, "Microwaves in the Cold War: The Moscow Embassy Study and Its Interpretation: Review of a Retrospective Cohort Study," *Environmental Heath*, vol. 11, no. 1 (2012), pp. 1–10.

10. Hixon, *Parting the Curtain*.

11. Jane Thompson unpublished memoirs, TFP.

12. Vladimir Toumanoff oral history, FA-ADST.

13. Jane Thompson unpublished memoirs, TFP.

14. George Feifer, "While Khrushchev and Nixon Debated, a Dialogue Was Born," commentary, Jul 23, 2009, Radio Free Europe, www.rferl.org/content/While_Khrushchev_And_Nixon_Debated_A_Dialogue _Was_Born_/1783945.html.

15. Beschloss, *May Day*. For their discussion, see MemCon: Nixon and Khrushchev, Jul 24, 1959, FRUS, 1958–1960, vol. 10, pt. 1, doc. 95.

16. Hixon, *Parting the Curtain*, p. 177.

17. Even Russian émigrés were chagrined by the resolution. See Tschebotarioff, *Russia, My Native Land*, p. 357.

18. Garthoff, *Journey through the Cold War*, chap. 6, "Intelligence Excursions in the Soviet Union."

19. The Soviets wanted to buy the color TV studio after the exhibit closed, but they were hampered in doing so because the Ampex tape used by the equipment there was on the restricted list of US exports.

20. Carlson, *K Blows Top*, pp. 24, 30, 38.

21. Authors' interview with Hans Tuch, Feb 25, 2003, TFP.

22. Thomas J. Niles oral history, FA-ADST.

23. MemConf with Eisenhower, Aug 5, 1959, FRUS, 1958–1960, vol. 10, pt. 1, doc. 106.

24. Ho Chi Minh visited Moscow that month, but it's not known if he attended the exhibit. See "Chronology of Significant Events Relating to Soviet Foreign Policy: 1959," Intelligence Report 8507.2, prepared Aug 16, 1961, Bureau of Intelligence and Research, TFP.

25. Vassili Kuznetsov called in Ed Freers to talk about the "book problem" and suggested that these items be placed under glass, since 600 were taken during the first day. Books that he asked to be removed included *Soviet Economic Growth in Comparison with the United States*, 85th Cong., 1st Sess. See authors' notes in TFP, taken from Sokolniki Park files, stack area 350, row 70, compartment 12, shelf 5, RG 84, NARA.

26. The guests included a wide array of famous personages: Buckminster Fuller, socialite Angier and Mrs. Biddle Duke, Helena Rubenstein, Admiral Hyman Rickover, Edward Steichen, impresario Sol Hurok, and IBM chief executive Tom Watson Jr.

27. Taubman, *Khrushchev*, p. 418.

28. MemCon: Nixon and Khrushchev, Jul 26, 1959, FRUS, 1958–1960, vol. 8, doc. 481, pp. 1064–66.

29. Thompson lecture at the National War College, Washington, DC, Sep 1, 1964, p. 6, TFP.

30. Ibid. Khrushchev's colleagues were Anastas Mikoyan, Frol Kozlov, Vassili Kuznetsov, and Yuri Zhukov.

31. Garthoff, *Journey through the Cold War*, chap. 6.

32. Authors' interview with Sergei Khrushchev, Feb 11, 2010, TFP.

33. Authors' correspondence with Vladimir Toumanoff, Feb 2003, TFP.

34. Nixon-Thompson correspondence; and transcript of Nixon talks to newsmen at the White House, May 1972, prior to the president leaving for Moscow to meet with Leonid Brezhnev, both in TFP.

35. Excerpts from notes taken by William H. Lawrence at a dinner given by Vice President Nixon, Aug 1959, original typed copy, TFP.

36. Vladimir Toumanoff oral history, FA-ADST; and M. Eisenhower, *The President Is Calling*.

37. Richmond, *Practicing Public Diplomacy*, p. 48; and Milton Eisenhower personal note to Jane Thompson, Aug 6, 1959, TFP.

38. Excerpt from notes taken by William H. Lawrence at a dinner given by Vice President Nixon, Aug 1959, original typed copy, TFP; and MemConf with Eisenhower, Aug 5, 1959, FRUS 1958–1960, vol. 10, pt. 1, doc. 106.

39. MemConf with Eisenhower, Aug 5, 1959, FRUS, 1958–1960, vol. 10, pt. 1, doc. 106.

40. Chronology of significant events relating to 1959 Soviet foreign policy, Aug 16, 1961, TFP.

19 ≋ The Russian Is Coming

1. Carl Hummelsine was a former FSO who had recently become president of the Colonial Williamsburg historic area.

2. The Tupolev Tu-114 was a remarkable-looking plane, long and sleek, with four turboprop engines, each with two sets of propellers, one behind the other. There was some concern about whether the plane would make it to the United States, having shown microcracks in the engines, but Khrushchev was confident enough to bring his family and, perhaps as insurance, the plane designer's son, too.

3. Memo: Mrs. Thompson, [undated], folder 3.4: Khrushchev visit, Office of Soviet Union Affairs, box 4, entry 3095, RG 59, NACP, also in TFP.

4. S. Khrushchev, *Nikita Khrushchev*, pp. 326–27.

5. Thompson was assigned to the car with Jane, but he did not ride with her that day, or even for most of the trip. It is not clear why his assignment was changed or where he ended up. See administrative arrangements from the Office of the Chief of Protocol, TFP.

6. Rada Khrushcheva, "Recollections," Aug 2010, TFP.

7. Memo: Mrs. Thompson, [undated], folder 3.4: Khrushchev visit, Office of Soviet Union Affairs, box 4, entry 3095, RG 59, NACP, also in TFP; Thompson observations of Khrushchev trip, TFP; and Thompson letter to Foy Kohler, Sep 28, 1959, DDEL, also in TFP.

8. S. Khrushchev, *Nikita Khrushchev*; and Thompson letter to Foy Kohler, Sep 28, 1959, DDEL, also in TFP.

9. Carlson, *K Blows Top*, pp. 176–77.

10. Ambrose, *Eisenhower*, p. 492.

11. MemCon, Sep 15, 1959, FRUS, 1958–1960, vol. 10, pt. 1, doc. 109.

12. S. Khrushchev, *Nikita Khrushchev*, p. 343.

13. Carlson, *K Blows Top*.

14. MemCon by Lodge, Sep 16, 1959, FRUS, 1958–1960, vol. 10, pt. 1, doc. 112.

15. Jane Thompson unpublished memoirs, TFP.

16. Later in the trip, Jane observed that Mrs. Khrushcheva did not react badly to photos of herself eating or drinking and so had surmised that the woman had realized such photos were not meant to be insulting.

17. Jane Thompson unpublished memoirs, TFP.

18. Carlson, *K Blows Top*, p. 118.

19. Not to be confused with Marshal Georgy Zhukov, who was removed by this time.

20. The joke went that someone in the audience of the Party's congress sent an anonymous note to the podium, asking Khrushchev what he was doing while Stalin was committing these crimes. Khrushchev purportedly asked the questioner to identify himself, and when no one did, Khrushchev supposedly answered, "Well, comrades, now you know what I was doing." Carlson, *K Blows Top*, p. 93.

21. Memo: Mrs. Thompson, [undated], folder 3.4: Khrushchev visit, Office of Soviet Union Affairs, box 4, entry 3095, RG 59, NACP, also in TFP.

22. Programs and lists from the Protocol Office, State Department, TFP.

23. Memo: Mrs. Thompson, [undated], folder 3.4: Khrushchev visit, Office of Soviet Union Affairs, box 4, entry 3095, RG 59, NACP, also in TFP.

24. MemCon, Sep 20, 1959, FRUS, 1958–1960, vol. 10, pt. 1, doc. 121.

25. Memo: Mrs. Thompson, [undated], folder 3.4: Khrushchev visit, Office of Soviet Union Affairs, box 4, entry 3095, RG 59, NACP, also in TFP; and Thompson letter to Foy Kohler, Sep 28, 1959, DDEL, also in TFP.

26. Memo: Mrs. Thompson, [undated], p. 10, folder 3.4: Khrushchev visit, Office of Soviet Union Affairs, box 4, entry 3095, RG 59, NACP, also in TFP.

27. Minutes of Soviet Presidium meeting, May 26, 1961, RGANI, also in TFP [a Russian-language version was provided to the authors by RGANI]; and N. Khrushchev, *Khrushchev Remembers*.

28. Authors' various conversations with Sergei Khrushchev. Also see N. Khrushchev, *Khrushchev Remembers*, p. 389.

29. Rada Khrushcheva, "Recollections," Aug 2010, TFP.

30. Memo: Mrs. Thompson, [undated], p. 10, folder 3.4: Khrushchev visit, Office of Soviet Union Affairs, box 4, entry 3095, RG 59, NACP, also in TFP.

31. MemCon, Sep 21, 1959, FRUS, 1958–60, vol. 10, pt. 1, doc 122, p. 439n2.

32. Carlson, *K Blows Top*, p. 205.

33. MemCon by Lodge, Sep 23, 1959, FRUS, 1958–1960, vol. 10, pt. 1, doc. 124.

34. N. Khrushchev, *Khrushchev Remembers*, pp. 399–400.

35. Ibid., p. 402.

36. Ibid., p. 411.

37. MemConf with Eisenhower, Sep 25, 1959, FRUS, 1958–1960, vol. 10, pt. 1, doc. 128, p. 454; and Thompson letter to Foy Kohler, Sep 28, 1959, DDEL, also in TFP.

38. Jane Thompson speech notes, card no. 24, inserted in Jane Thompson unpublished memoirs, TFP.

39. Jenny Thompson telephone interview with Georgi Arbatov, Jul 4, 2003.

40. MemConf with Eisenhower, Sep 25, 1959, FRUS, 1958–1960, vol. 10, pt. 1, doc. 128, p. 456.

41. MemCon: Camp David, Sep 26, 1959, FRUS, 1958–1960, vol. 10, pt. 1, doc. 129.

42. MemCon: Camp David, Sep 26, 1959, FRUS, 1958–1960, vol. 9 (*Berlin Crisis, 1959–1960; Germany, Austria*), doc. 13.

43. Eisenhower did characterize the situation in Berlin, as well as in Germany, as "abnormal and unjust" in his summary of the Camp David discussions, sent to Adenauer immediately following that morning's meeting. See Eisenhower to Adenauer, cable 694, Sep 28, 1959, FRUS, 1958–1960, vol. 9, doc. 18.

44. MemCon: Camp David, Sep 26, 1959, FRUS, 1958–1960, vol. 10, pt. 1, doc. 130.

45. Ibid., doc. 131.

46. Ibid., doc. 133.

47. Ibid.

48. N. Khrushchev, *Khrushchev Remembers*, p. 497.

49. Andrei Gromyko, *Memoirs*, p. 136.

50. MemCon: Camp David, Sep 27, 1959, FRUS, 1958–1960, vol. 9, doc. 14, p. 44.

51. MemCon: joint communiqué, Sep 27, 1959, FRUS, 1958–1960, vol. 9, doc. 16.

52. Memo: Mrs. Thompson, [undated], folder 3.4: Khrushchev visit, Office of Soviet Union Affairs, box 4, entry 3095, RG 59, NACP, also in TFP.

53. N. Khrushchev, *Khrushchev Remembers*, p. 330.

54. Personal letters, TFP.

55. Thompson letter to Foy Kohler, Sep 28, 1959, DDEL, also in TFP.

56. Memo to SecState from Thompson through Merchant, Sep 30, 1959, TFP.

57. Summary of US policy toward the Soviet Union, Oct 13, 1959, TFP.

58. Thompson memo to SecState, recapping a conference with Eisenhower, Oct 16, 1959, TFP.

59. In March 1958, the Soviets unilaterally halted nuclear testing and called for the Americans and the British to join them. Eisenhower agreed to stop for a year. This led to talks in Geneva on limiting nuclear testing. The issue of inspections couldn't be resolved, so Eisenhower suggested a ban on atmospheric testing, which would not require any inspections. This is the first time the idea of a "limited test ban" was seriously put forward, but Khrushchev rejected it.

60. Thompson memo to SecState, recapping a conference with Eisenhower, Oct 16, 1959, TFP.

61. Ibid.

62. "Libero Ricciardelli, who had served in the US Air Force, defected in August 1959. He lived in Kiev until returning to the United States in June 1963. Robert E. Webster had been working for the Rand [Research and Development] Corporation as a plastics technician at the American National Exhibition in Moscow when he disappeared in September 1959. He emerged a month later, on October 17, at the US Embassy, where he attempted to renounce his citizenship. Webster returned to the United States in May 1962. On September 5, 1959, Nicholas Petrulli of Long Island renounced his American citizenship in Moscow, but after being turned down for Soviet citizenship, he decided to return to the United States on September 21. Lee Harvey Oswald was the next to go, in October 1959. He was followed by Bruce Frederick Davis. After serving for 5 years in the US Army, Davis left his post in West Germany and defected to the Soviet Union in August 1960. He lived in Kiev before returning to the United States in July 1963." See John Simkin, "Oswald and the CIA Defection Program," Education Forum, http://educationforum.ipbhost.com/index.php?/topic/8068 -oswald-and-the-cia-defection-program/.

20 ≋ U-2: The End of Détente

1. The Italian representative was Luigi Longo, who did not speak Russian and hence did not participate at all in the ensuing conversation. Thompson and the French ambassador were clearly made uncomfortable by Longo's presence, and Khrushchev asked if they could not, for this one occasion, consider him simply as an Italian and not as a Communist. Later on, when Khrushchev was toasting the foreigners who were present, he proposed a toast to Longo. Thompson suggested that they also raise their glasses to Italy, which Khrushchev good-naturedly accepted.

2. "Secret: Priority. Received at 9:54 a.m. Repeated to London, Paris, and Bonn," Whitman file, international file, DDEL; and FRUS, 1958–1960, vol. 9, doc. 63. Also see Thompson to SecState, embtel 1774, Jan 8, 1960, CF 611.61/1-8-60, RG 59, NACP.

3. For a summary of Khrushchev's speech to the Supreme Soviet, see memo, of discussion at 432nd meeting of NSC, Jan 14, 1960, FRUS, 1958–1960, vol. 10, pt. 1, doc. 140.

4. Polaris was a nuclear armed missile that could be launched from a submerged submarine, making its warheads difficult to target and easy to move into a position closer to the Soviet Union.

5. Sulzberger, *Last of the Giants*, p. 929. In reporting his conversation with Thompson, Sulzberger took it further and wrote that in early 1960, the Soviet marshals told Khrushchev that they were not prepared for a showdown unless they got a bigger budget. According to Sulzberger, "They [the Soviet military] thought a summit meeting with Khrushchev was too dangerous and broke it up."

6. Thompson to SecState, cable 1904, Jan 18, 1960, CF 761.551/1-1860, RG 59, NACP, also in TFP.

7. Thompson to SecState, cable 1903, Jan 18, 1960, FRUS, 1958–1960, vol. 10, pt. 1, doc. 141.

8. Authors' undated telephone conversation with Maria Troyanovsky.

9. Rada Khrushcheva, "Recollections," Aug 2010, TFP.

10. Central to the success of Communist ideology was the idea that a new archetype would spontaneously emerge, creating a Soviet (and eventually global) citizen whose primary motive would be the collective good, with a "new ethics" that would be the same, regardless of culture, language, or ethnicity.

11. Current strains within the Soviet system, dispatch 412, Jan 29, 1960, presidential office file, box 125 A, JFKL, also in CF 761.60/1-2960, RG 59, NACP, and in TFP.

12. *The Fog of War: Eleven Lessons from the Life of Robert S. McNamara*, documentary film, directed by Earl Morris, 2003.

13. Lodge to State, cable 2098, Feb 9, 1960, CF 761.00/2-960, RG 59, NACP, also in TFP.

14. Authors' interview with Hans Tuch, Feb 25, 2003, TFP.

15. Ibid.

16. Yale Richmond, "Cultural Exchange and the Cold War: How the West Won," *Polish Review*, vol. 50, no. 3 (2005), pp. 355–60.

17. MemCon: Thompson and Menshikov, Apr 14, 1960, political relations, USSR, CF 611.61.4-1460, NACP, also in TFP.

18. Sulzberger, *Last of the Giants*, p. 663.

19. Thompson to State, cable 2613, Apr 23, 1960, 396.1-PA/4-2360, RG 43, NACP, also in TFP.

20. Ibid.; and Thompson to State, cable 2614, Apr 23, 1960, 396.1-PA/4-2360, RG 43, NACP, also in TFP.

21. "The Cold War: Return of the Airmen," *Time*, Feb 3, 1959.

22. "Cold War Reconnaissance and the Shootdown of Flight 60528," National Security Agency, https://www.nsa.gov/news-features/declassified-documents/c130-shootdown/assets/files/cold_war_recon_shootdown_60528.pdf.

23. Beschloss, *May Day*, p. 111.

24. For instance, on April 24, 1958, General Goodpaster had advised CIA director Allen Dulles to cease any and all flights over Soviet or other Communist territories, per Eisenhower's instructions. Goodpaster authorized a low-altitude reconnaissance flight into the Soviet Union on that very same day, "after checking" for authorization, but he failed to note checking with whom. See memo for the record, Apr 24, 1958, FRUS, 1958–1960, vol. 10, pt. 1, doc. 44, p. 163, including footnote. The implication is that Goodpaster checked with the president, but this is not clear.

25. Beschloss, *May Day*, p. 42.

26. Authors' interview with Hans Tuch, Feb 25, 2003, TFP.

27. The Skunk Works—named after a remote, falling-apart factory with a still that was used to brew "skonk oil" (made from dead skunks and worn shoes) in the comic strip *Li'l Abner*—was formed in 1943 by Lockheed Aircraft Corporation to develop a secret new jet fighter. Lockheed later got the contract for the U-2 spy plane. The U-2 started as a joint project between the CIA and the Strategic Air Command, although, after a bitter rivalry developed, Eisenhower decided to give this project to the CIA, because he thought it would constitute an act of war if it was a military operation. The US Air Force continued to provide support services, such as pilot training and weather reporting.

28. Brigadier General Goodpaster, "The Evolution of Relations between the United States and the Soviet Union," in K. Thompson, *Presidency and Foreign Policy*.

29. Chris Pocock, "The Early U-2 Overflights of the Soviet Union," presentation at the Allied Museum Conference, Apr 24, 2006, Cold War Museum, www.coldwar.org/articles/50s/early_u2.asp.

30. The Polaroid predated digital photography as the first "instant" camera, which produced images that self-developed in a few seconds. See Emma Cobb, "Instant History," *Invention and Technology*, vol. 22, no. 3, www.inventionandtech.com/content/instant-history-1/.

31. Gregory W. Pedlow and Donald E. Welzenbach, "The CIA and the U-2 Program, 1954–1974," pp. 72, 120, Center for the Study of Intelligence, Central Intelligence Agency, https://www.cia.gov/library/center-for-the-study-of-intelligence/csi-publications/books-and-monographs/the-cia-and-the-u-2-program-1954-1974/u2.pdf.

32. Garthoff, *Assessing the Adversary*, p. 42.

33. Authors' interview with Raymond Garthoff, Sep 22, 2009, TFP. He agreed with this conclusion.

34. Dulles personal note to Thompson, "Top Secret," May 13, 1958, Dulles-PL, copy in TFP; "The U-2 Incident," attachment 15 in "Damage Estimate: Foreign Policy Interests" [memo by Richard H. Davis, acting assistant secretary of state for European affairs], May 28, 1964, microphones Moscow folder, box 10, entry A1-5008, records of Ambassador-at-Large Thompson, 1961–1970, RG 59, NACP. Also see the reference in Thompson to Sec State, cable 2716, May 5, 1960, CF 761.5411/5-560, NACP, also in TFP.

35. Pedlow and Welzenbach, "CIA and the U-2 Program."

36. Ibid., p. 168.

37. James P. Pfiffner, "The Contemporary Presidency: Presidential Lies," *Presidential Studies Quarterly*, vol. 29, no. 4 (Dec 1999), pp. 903–17.

38. "Statement Concerning Francis Gary Powers," part of the CIA's "The U-2 Incident," [undated], written for General Eisenhower, with a cover letter from John McCone, doc. CIA-RDP33-02415A000800300001-8, Library, Central Intelligence Agency, https://www.cia.gov/library/readingroom/document/cia-rdp83-00764r000500100022-3.

39. Pedlow and Welzenbach, "CIA and the U-2 Program," p. 179; "Mayday 1960: Reassessing the U-2 Shoot Down," Apr 28, 2010, archived video, Cold War International History project, Wilson Center, https://www.wilsoncenter.org/event/mayday-1960-reassessing-the-u-2-shoot-down/.

40. Ambrose and Immerman, *Ike's Spies*, p. 274.

41. Beschloss, *May Day*, p. 9.

42. Editorial note, FRUS, 1958–1960, vol. 10, pt. 1, doc. 147.

43. Data from five weather-collecting stations closest to the target sites in Plesetsk, Kirov, Tyuratam, Sverdlovsk, and Kamyslov, based on longitude and latitude, indicate that visibility and precipitation for April 9 (the day of the previous flight) and for May 1 were similar, and that there wasn't materially better visibility for quite a few days between April 11 and 25. When the weather was reportedly still too bad to fly on April 25, permission was extended to May 1. There were also days without precipitation and good visibility between April 25 and May 1. The only days on which there was either precipitation or fog, or poor visibility otherwise, at any one of these site were April 12, 13, 15, 18, and 28, and, at one site, on May 1. So it would seem as though the planes should have been able to fly on April 14, 16, 17, and any day between April 19 and 24, as well as between April 25 and May 1. Data were obtained from the Global Historical Climatology Network, International Research Institute for Climate and Society, Columbia University, and from the National Climate Data Center, National Oceanic and Atmospheric Administration.

44. Arbatov and Oltmans, *Cold War or Détente?*, p. 59 of online version, www.dbnl.org/tekst/arba001cold01_01/arba001cold01_01.pdf.

45. Russell Warren Howe and Sarah Trott, "J. William Fulbright: Reflections on a Troubled World," *Saturday Review*, Jan 11, 1975, pp. 12–19.

46. The assigned plane was grounded, because it had flown for too many hours shuttling between its permanent base in Turkey and the Peshawar site.

47. Pedlow and Welzenbach, "CIA and the U-2 Program," p. 175.

48. See James Nathan, "A Fragile Detente," *Military Affairs*, vol. 39, no. 3, Oct., 1975, pp. 97–104.

49. Pedlow and Welzenbach, "CIA and the U-2 Program," p. 175.

50. Chris Pocock, "From Peshawar to Bodø—Mission Impossible?" in Lundestad, *U-2 Flights*.

51. Pedlow and Welzenbach, "CIA and the U-2 Program."

52. Authors' interview with Vladimir Toumanoff, Feb 2010, TFP.

53. Thompson to State, cable 2763, May 9, 1960, CF 761.5411/5-960, RG 59, NACP, also in TFP.

54. John Scanlan oral history, FA-ADST.

55. Thompson to SecState, cable 2716, May 5, 1960, CF 761.5411/5-560, RG 59, NACP, also in TFP.

56. Dulles personal note to Thompson, "Top Secret," May 13, 1958, Dulles-PL, copy in TFP; and "The U-2 Incident," attachment 15 in "Damage Estimate: Foreign Policy Interests," May 28, 1964, microphones Moscow folder, box 10, entry A1-5008, records of Ambassador-at-Large Thompson, 1961–1970, RG 59, NACP. Also see the reference in Thompson to SecState, cable 2716, May 5, 1960, CF 761.5411/5-560, RG 59, NACP, also in TFP.

57. Vladimir Toumanoff oral history, FA-ADST.

58. Although Beschloss, in *May Day* (p. 430nn53–54), reported that Thompson said he "overheard" this conversation, a cable from Thompson on May 5, 1958, does not say how he knew that Malik said those things. See editorial note, FRUS, 1958–1960, vol. 10, pt. 1, doc. 147. According to a conversation the authors had with Sergei Khrushchev, this phone call was intercepted by the KGB, so they knew about what Malik was telling the Swedish ambassador.

59. Thompson to SecState, cable 2716, May 5, 1960, CF 761.5411/5-560, NACP, also in TFP.

60. The authors determined this from embassy personnel when trying to figure out why it took so long for the transmission to reach Washington, DC. The Soviets had to do the same thing in the American capital. Anatoly Dobrynin tells a story about the bicycle courier they hired to send cables during the Cuban Missile Crisis, wondering if they would reach Moscow.

61. Thompson to SecState, cable 2716, May 5, 1960, CF 761.5411/5-560, RG 59, NACP, also in TFP.

62. Garthoff, *Assessing the Adversary*, p. 42.

63. Press Day was a major annual affair, commemorating the first publication of the Soviet newspaper *Pravda*.

64. Authors' email with Priscilla Johnson McMillan, Jan 22, 2010, TFP.

65. *Gospodin* means "Mister" in Russian.

66. Tuch, *Arias*, p. 82.

67. Tuch insisted to the authors (in an interview on Feb 25, 2003, and emails in 2010) that this happened on May 1, not on the day of the press reception, which was May 5. Also see Tuch, *Arias*, p. 82. The authors have not been able to find an incoming cable in the State Department's archives to support Tuch's claim. It does not make sense, however, that a cable with this sort of information would have languished in the embassy for an entire day, in order to be sent from Moscow as a normal cable on May 6, especially as Tuch went to the embassy on the night of May 5 to have his cable sent on a priority basis. The May 5 cable the authors found in the archives was signed not by Tuch, but by his boss, which surprised Tuch. Bohlen could support Tuch's account, saying (in *Witness to History*, p. 465) that the United States knew the plane went down in the middle of the USSR before the NASA announcements were made, although Bohlen could have learned of this through other sources (see note 68 below). If this is so, it is a crucial change in the history of the U-2 incident.

68. "Top Secret Chronological Account of Handling of U-2 Incident," [undated and unsigned], U-2 case folder, box 17, entry A1-1560, records of Ambassador Bohlen, 1942–1971, RG 59, NACP, also in TFP. The online version of the CIA's chronological account, while still partially redacted, now contains this quote. See https://www.cia.gov/library/readingroom/docs/CIA-RDP90T00782R000100110012-9.pdf. The CIA's chronology may have been given to Bohlen and thus was in his files, but it does not indicate that Bohlen was at the meeting, or that he took part in the decision to go ahead with the cover story. The version of this document that was in the NACP and CIA *files* at the time had this quote redacted. The *online* CIA version was released in 2012, after we found the relevant document in Bohlen's file and alerted the NACP archivist.

69. Tatu, *Power in the Kremlin*, p. 59.

70. Thompson to SecState, cable 2745, May 7, 1960, USSR post files, stack 350, RG 84, NARA; and Herter to Thompson, cable 2247, May 8, 1960, USSR post files, stack 350, RG 84, NARA.

71. It would be intriguing to find out if the photos shown during that meeting really were fakes, or if they were of such poor quality because Powers's plane actually did have [as was claimed] an inferior camera, something the analysts couldn't have known about.

72. Thompson to SecState, cables 2746 and 2750, May 7, 1960, TFP.

73. Ibid., p. 515. Khrushchev made the statements in his May 7 speech, after a visit with Charles de Gaulle in late March, during which the French president told the Soviet leader that there would be no change in the

allies' position on the Berlin question, coupled with hard-line remarks by the acting US secretary of state, Douglas Dillon, in April and a NATO communiqué on May 4, all taking a pre–Camp David stand on Berlin.

74. Ibid.

75. Statement by the New China agency, May 14, 1960. See Tatu, *Power in the Kremlin*, p. 48.

76. Newman, *Macmillan, Khrushchev*.

77. Tatu, *Power in the Kremlin*, p. 53.

78. Thompson to SecState, cable 2750, May 7, 1960, FRUS, 1958–1960, vol. 10, pt. 1, doc. 148.

79. Thompson to State, May 9, 1960, FRUS, 1958–1960, vol. 10, pt. 1, doc. 150.

80. Salisbury, *Journey of Our Times*, pp. 489–90.

81. Thompson to State, May 9, 1960, FRUS, 1958–1960, vol. 10, pt. 1, doc. 151. Powers was to begin his overflight in Peshawar, Pakistan, and end up in Bodø, Norway.

82. John Scanlan oral history, FA-ASDT.

83. James Reston, "The Summit Tragedy," *New York Times*, sent from Paris on May 18, 1960, printed on May 19.

84. Thompson to SecState, cable 2750, May 7, 1960, FRUS, 1958–1960, vol. 10, pt. 1, doc. 148.

85. Taubman, *Khrushchev*, p. 448.

86. Newman, *Macmillan, Khrushchev*.

87. Ibid., pp. 1, 187n1.

88. Taubman, *Khrushchev*.

89. Authors' conversations with Priscilla Johnson Macmillan, Jan 2010, TFP; and Tatu, *Power in the Kremlin*, p. 63.

90. Thompson to State, cable 5276, May 12, 1960, CF 396.1/5-1260, RG 43, NACP, also in FRUS, 1958–1960, vol. 9, doc. 153.

91. Sulzberger, *Last of the Giants*, p. 673.

92. Thompson to State, cable 698, Sep 8, 1960, FRUS, 1958–1960, vol. 10, pt. 1, doc. 163. Khrushchev's son Sergei, however, asserts that his father hadn't considered such diplomatic implications at that point and was only following protocol, in that de Gaulle was the host of the summit and therefore should be informed of Khrushchev's position. See authors' telephone interview with Sergei Khrushchev, Mar 2010, TFP.

93. MemConf with Eisenhower, May 15, 1960, FRUS, 1958–1960, vol. 9, doc. 164.

94. Herter to State, Oct 14, 1960, FRUS, 1958–1960, vol. 9, doc. 167.

95. Ed Crankshaw letter to Thompson, Sep 11, 1963, TFP.

96. MemCon, Paris, May 16, 1960, FRUS, 1958–1960, vol. 9, doc. 168.

97. Bohlen, *Witness to History*.

98. Sulzberger, *Last of the Giants*, p. 669.

99. Bohlen, *Witness to History*.

100. MemCon, Paris, May 17, 1960, 10 a.m., FRUS, 1958–1960, vol. 9, doc. 175.

101. For Harold Macmillan's reaction, see Taubman, *Khrushchev*, p. 464; and Fursenko and Naftali, *Khrushchev's Cold War*, p. 288. For the British delegation's concern, see Sulzberger, *Last of the Giants*, p. 672.

102. MemCon, Paris, May 17, 1960, 3 p.m., FRUS, 1958–1960, vol. 9, doc. 178.

103. Taubman, *Khrushchev*, p. 465. On p. 466, Taubman writes that Khrushchev had actually "been on his best behavior, considering the circumstances; only later, at a meeting of Eastern European ambassadors, did all his hurt and rage show through."

104. On Walter Ulbricht's support for the *modus vivendi* (i.e., a temporary or provisional diplomatic accord) in Berlin until May 1960, see Newman, *Macmillan, Khrushchev*, p. 12.

105. Beschloss, *May Day*, p. 302.

106. Thompson to State, cable 5276, May 12, 1960, FRUS, 1958–1960, vol. 9, doc. 153.

107. On the flight that resulted in Powers's death, his fuel gauge, which had been broken for some time, was repaired, but no one told him about it, so he misread the amount of fuel that was left in the tank. He was buried in Arlington Cemetery, and he eventually received the Silver Star from the US Air Force in 2012. His name was placed on the wall of honor at the CIA, some very small comfort for his surviving family, considering the way he was received in 1962.

108. Bureau of Intelligence and Research report, "Analysis of Soviet Behavior at the Conference," Jul 25, 1960, FRUS, 1958–1960, vol. 9, doc. 195.

109. Tatu, *Power in the Kremlin*, p. 122.

110. McGhee Harvey interview with Nikita Khrushchev, *Life*, Dec 18, 1970, cited in Kempe, *Berlin 1961*.

111. On Khrushchev's primacy in decision making prior to 1960, see Newman, *Macmillan, Khrushchev*, pp. 11, 12.

21 ≋ Picking Up the Pieces

1. They arrived on May 28, 1960. Thompson had to return as well, since the Soviets would not allow the plane with supplies for the embassy to land at the Moscow airport unless he was on it. See authors' notes from US-USSR political relations, 1960–1963 file, microfilm reel 7, stack 250, row 3, compartment 26, shelf 6–7, CF 611.61/6197, NACP; and Jane Thompson letter to "Dear Family," Jun 1, 1960, TFP.

2. Freers to SecState, cable 2903, control 15095, May 20, 1960, CF 611.61/5-2060, RG 59, NACP.

3. Thompson to SecState, cable 3047, control 3212, Jun 4, 1960, CF 761.13/6-460, RG 59, NACP, also in TFP.

4. Taubman, *Khrushchev*, p. 469.

5. Thompson to SecState, cable 3047, Jun 4, 1960, CF 761.13/6-460, NACP, also in TFP.

6. Thompson to State, cable 3072, Jun 7, 1960, US-USSR political relations, 1960–1963 file, microfilm reel 7, stack 250, row 3, compartment 26, shelf 6–7, CF 611.61/6197, NACP.

7. Taubman, *Khrushchev*, p. 471.

8. US delegation chairman's letter to SecState Herter, Jul 25, 1960, FRUS, 1958–1960, vol. 3 (*National Security Policy; Arms Control and Disarmament*), doc. 258.

9. Stanford Arms Control Group, *International Arms Control*.

10. Thompson's University of Colorado degree came in the mail.

11. Jane Thompson letter to "Dear Family," Jun 13, 1960, TFP.

12. Bounce, the Thompsons' old boxer dog, had died the previous year.

13. White, *Little Toy Dog*.

14. The Soviet officials included Anastas Mikoyan, deputy premier; Frol Kozlov, Central Committee secretary; and Nikolay Ignatov, Communist Party of the Soviet Union secretary. See John McSweeney memo to Richard Davis, Jul 15, 1960, US-USSR political relations file, microfilm reel 7, stack 250, row 3, compartment 26, shelf 6–7, CF 611.61/6197, NACP.

15. "Halfway Coexistence," *Time*, Jul 18, 1960.

16. Thompson speech on Soviet television, Jul 4, 1960, TFP.

17. White, *Little Toy Dog*.

18. Thompson to SecState, cable 236, Jul 1, 1960, TFP, also in NACP.

19. *Chicago Daily Tribune*, Jul 15, 1960; *Register Guard* [Eugene, OR], May 22, 1960, TFP.

20. Thompson to Richard Davis, EUR, Aug 29, 1960, CF 611.61/6-160, RG 59, NACP.

21. On July 13, the Democratic national convention nominated JFK as its presidential candidate.

22. Gill had left to marry Michael Bordeaux, a British exchange student. Now Rev. Canon Dr. Bordeaux, he has dedicated his life to helping fight religious persecution, has written a number of books, and founded the Centre for the Study of Religion and Communism, which has become the Keston Institute.

23. Sally fell in love with a British diplomat but was pressured by her family to return and marry her fiancé.

24. Thompson to SecState, cable 698, Sep 8, 1960, FRUS, 1958–1960, vol. 10, pt. 1, doc. 163.

25. Nixon personal letter to Thompson, Sep 8, 1960, TFP, also in the Richard Nixon Presidential Library and Museum, Yorba Linda, California.

26. Beschloss, *Crisis Years*, p. 35.

27. N. Khrushchev, *Khrushchev Remembers*, pp. 488–90.

28. Thompson to State, cable 686, Sep 7, 1960, CF 611.61/79-760, RG 59, NACP; and Thompson to State, cable 688, Sep 8, 1960, CF 611.61/9860, RG 59, NACP, also in TFP.

29. Khrushchev initiated this conversation with Thompson on the U-2 incident, in the presence of the entire diplomatic corps, during a Kremlin reception on September 7 for the vice president of the United Arab Republic. See Thompson to State, cable 686, Sep 7, 1960, CF 611.61/79-760, RG 59, NACP, also in TFP; and Thompson to State, cable 688, Sep 8, 1960, CF 611.61/9860, RG 59, NACP, also in TFP.

30. Thompson to SecState, cable 688, Sep 8, 1960, CF 611.61/9860, RG 59, NACP, also in TFP.

31. RGANI documents, Sep 8, 1960, TFP; Thompson to State, cables 692, 698, and 699, Sep 8, 1960, FRUS, 1958–1960, vol. 10, pt. 1, docs. 162, 163, and 164; and Thomson to State, cable 713, Sep 9, 1960, FRUS, 1958–1960, vol. 10, pt. 1, doc. 165.

32. It was never definitively proven whether the flyers did or did not violate Soviet air space. The discrepancy between the testimony of the young MIG fighter plane pilot [Vasiliy Ambrosheivich Polyakov, who was twenty-eight years old] who shot them down and that of the two Americans indicates that perhaps the Soviet pilot may have been overzealous in following the Soviet Ministry of Defense's directive, issued in May, to shoot, on the spot, at any airplane that was cruising over Soviet territory. Polyakov was possibly hoping for praise, or perhaps he was afraid he could be blamed for incompetence and the subsequent consequences of his actions. Nonetheless, his choice led to his receiving the Order of the Red Banner. It was also clear that there was a divergence from the projected RB-47 flight plan and the one actually carried out, but the Americans claimed that their plane was still well outside the twelve-mile limit. Unlike the U-2, this aircraft certainly was never meant to have crossed into Soviet territory, since Eisenhower had subsequently ordered that no US plane approach more than a hundred kilometers from Soviet borders.

33. He cited the flight plan of the U-2 and a US flight over neutral Austria without permission during the Lebanon crisis. See Thompson to State, cable 692, Sep 8, 1960, FRUS, 1958–1960, vol. 10, pt. 1, doc. 162.

34. Khrushchev's remarks about the dead cat were not reported in this way in the Soviet transcript. For that statement, see Thompson to State, cable 713, Sep 9, 1960, FRUS, 1958–1960, vol. 10, pt. 1, doc. 165.

35. Once Thompson left the meeting, however, he recorded what he remembered.

36. Foreigners were not allowed beyond a forty-kilometer radius of Moscow's center without permission.

37. Thompson to State, cable 699, Sep 8, 1960, FRUS, 1958–1960, vol. 10, pt. 1, doc.164, also in TFP.

38. Willard L. Thorp, "Soviet Economic Growth and Its Policy," pp. 571–88, and Walt W. Rostow, "Summary and Political Implications," pp. 589–607, both in *Comparisons of the United States and Soviet Economies: Papers Submitted by Panelists Appearing before the Subcommittee on Economic Statistics*, part 3, 86th Cong., 1st sess., 1960, https://www.jec.senate.gov/reports/86th%20Congress/Reports%20and%20Other/Comparisons%20of%20the%20United%20States%20and%20Soviet%20Economies%20(158).pdf.

39. This is quoted from the Soviet report, thanks to RGANI. Thompson reported it slightly differently. "In my opinion the president had probably not specifically authorized the U-2 flight." See Thompson to State, cable 698, Sep 8, 1960, FRUS, 1958–1960, vol. 10, pt. 1, doc. 163.

40. RGANI documents, Sep 8, 1960, TFP; and Thompson to State, cables 692, 698, 699, and 713, FRUS, 1958–1960, vol. 10, pt. 1, docs. 162, 163, 164, and 165.

41. RGANI documents, Sep 8, 1960, TFP; and memo of TelCon: Gore calling JFK, Feb 25, 1961, notes made by Evelyn Lincoln, JFKL.

42. Gromyko's report on his conversation with Thompson on Aug 25, 1960, MFA; and meeting with Khrushchev, Sep 8, 1960, RGANI documents, TFP.

43. William Taubman, "Did He Bang It? Nikita Khrushchev and the Shoe," *New York Times*, Jul 23, 2003, www.nytimes.com/2003/07/26/opinion/did-he-bang-it-nikita-khrushchev-and-the-shoe.html.

44. The British and the Belgians had vested interests in keeping as much control as possible over the copper industry in that area, and they were concerned about its possible nationalization. They backed the secession of the copper-rich province of Katanga, which was led by Moïse Tshombe. Khrushchev then supported Patrice Lumumba in his struggle against Katanga, and even the UN got involved.

45. Lumumba was killed on January 17, 1961; Hammarskjöld died on September 18, 1961.

46. Weiner, *Legacy of Ashes*, pp. 162–63.

47. Fursenko and Naftali, *Khrushchev's Cold War*, p. 313.

48. This was the same conference that divided Vietnam into North Vietnam and South Vietnam and ended French colonial rule in the region.

49. The efforts of Souvanna Phouma, prime minister of Laos, to form a neutralist government failed, in large part due to the opposition of a right-wing faction, backed by the CIA, that took over the capital. Souvanna, who was still recognized as the legitimate leader by the Soviets, China, and India, was forced to flee. He joined forces with his half brother Souphanouvong [who was leading the Communists] and the Pathet Lao, and he then asked the Soviets for military aid. Soon the coalition of neutralists and Communists began to take on the Royal Laotian Army in a civil war.

50. The authors never saw her again.

51. MemCon: Khrushchev and Salinger, May 13, 1962, JFKL.

52. This took place on November 30, 1960. See Hope M. Harrison "Ulbricht and the Concrete Rose: New Archival Evidence on the Dynamics of Soviet–East German Relations and the Berlin Crisis, 1958–61," p. 33, Working Paper No. 5, Woodrow Wilson International Center for Scholars, https://www.wilsoncenter.org/sites/default/files/ACFB81.pdf.

53. Ibid., p. 37.

54. Ibid., p. 38.

55. Thompson speech at the Naval War College, Newport, Rhode Island, Jan 8, 1964, TFP.

56. Beschloss, *Crisis Years*.

22 ≋ Working for the New President

Epigraph. Thompson to State, cable 1813, Feb 1, 1961, FRUS, 1961–1963, vol. 5, doc. 20.

1. Jane Thompson letter to "Dear Family," Jan 20, 1961, TFP.

2. Thompson to SecState, Moscow, cable 1682, Jan 19, 1961, JFKL, also in TFP.

3. See Beschloss, *Crisis Years*, p. 61; and Garthoff, *Journey through the Cold War*, p. 132.

4. This information comes from Raymond Garthoff's report of discussions with Thompson at the time, as well as with former Soviet officials some years later. See authors' telephone conversation with Garthoff, Sep 2014, TFP.

5. Thompson to State, airgram G-504, Jan 24, 1961, FRUS, 1961–1963, vol. 5 (*Soviet Union*), doc. 13.

6. The Karl Marx reference applied to circumstances in the second half of the nineteenth century, when the US labor movement was formed in response to terrible working conditions, such as in sweat shops and dangerous mines, as well as to the nefarious company stores, which created a kind of indentured servitude. Workers in remote areas, who generally were all employed by one company (which also owned the store), had nowhere else nearby where they could purchase necessary goods. These items were sold on credit, at extortionate prices, often creating enough debt that employees were forced to remain with a firm until it could be paid off.

7. Thompson to State, airgram G-504, Jan 24,1961, FRUS, 1961–1963, vol. 5, doc. 13, also in TFP, with the notation "President has seen," and in JFKL.

8. A British reporter trailed Tuch around the Moscow airport, asking questions. Finally, as the plane took off, he asked Tuch if the two men he had seen in the waiting room were the American airmen, and Tuch said, "Yes." The headlines the next day read "*London Express* journalist witnesses the release of the RB-47 flyers!" Authors' interview with Hans Tuch, Feb 25, 2003, TFP.

9. MemCon: President Eisenhower, president-elect Kennedy, and their chief advisers, White House, Jan 19, 1961, written by Clark Clifford and dated Jan 24, 1961, TFP. Rusk said that Eisenhower did not use the briefing paper prepared by the State Department for his meeting with JFK and did not "even mention Berlin during the meeting." See Rusk letter to JFK, Jan 28, 1961, FRUS, 1961–1963, vol. 14 (*Berlin Crisis, 1961–1962*), doc. 2, p. 4n4. Also see Dwight D. Eisenhower, Jan 17–Dec 9, 1961, presidential office files, JFKL. For a discussion on Laos, see JFK notes, Jan 19, 1961, FRUS, 1961–1963, vol. 24 (*Laos Crisis*), doc. 7. For a general discussion on what went on that day, based on various sources, see Fred Greenstein and Richard Immerman, "What Did Eisenhower Tell Kennedy about Indochina? The Politics of Misperception," *Journal of American History*, vol. 79, no. 2 (Sep 1992), pp. 568–87. Also see Clifford, *Counsel to the President*, pp. 342–45.

10. Thompson to State, cable 1784, Jan 28, 1961, FRUS, 1961–1963, vol. 5, doc. 17.

11. Thompson to State, cable 1797, Jan 30, 1961, FRUS, 1961–1963, vol. 5, doc. 19, with the notation "President has seen," also in TFP.

12. N. Khrushchev, *Khrushchev Remembers*, p. 536.

13. Thompson to State, cable 1797, Jan 30, 1961, FRUS, 1961–1963, vol. 5, doc. 19.

14. Thompson to State, cable 1813, Feb 1, 1961, FRUS, 1961–1963, vol. 5, doc. 20.

15. Ibid.

16. US Senate, Foreign Relations Committee, "Relations with the Soviet Union," Monday, Feb 13, 1961, Thompson testimony, beginning on p. 135, microfiche files, New Mexico State Library, Santa Fe, also in TFP.

17. This also infuriated the Chinese and the East Germans, who wanted more aid from the USSR and thought they deserved consideration over non–Warsaw Pact nations.

18. Thompson to State, cable 1813, Feb 1, 1961, FRUS, 1961–1963, vol. 5, doc. 20.

19. Ibid.

20. Anatole Shub, "Thompson's Negative Success in Moscow," *Paris Herald Tribune*, Jan 1969, TFP; Thompson to SecState, cable 1773, Mar 9, 1959, CF 762.00/3–959, NACP.

21. US Senate, Foreign Relations Committee, "Relations with the Soviet Union," Thompson testimony, also in TFP.

22. "Current Strains within the Soviet System," dispatch 412/2, box 125 A, presidential office files, JFKL.

23. Thompson to State, cable 1839, Feb 4, 1961, FRUS, 1961–1963, vol. 14, doc. 4.

24. Thompson's handwritten notes, attached to a transcript of his speech at the Naval War College, Newport, Rhode Island, Jan 8, 1964, TFP.

25. Trachtenberg, *History and Strategy*, p. 176.

26. This conclusion is also supported by a conversation between Khrushchev and Gomulka on November 10, 1958, just before Khrushchev's speech that started the Berlin Crisis. See Douglas Selvage, "New Evidence on the Berlin Crisis, 1958–62," Bulletin No. 11 (Winter 1998), Cold War International History Project, Wilson Center, https://www.wilsoncenter.org/publication/bulletin-no-11-winter-1998/. Also see Haslam, *Russia's Cold War*, p. 177; Harrison, *Up the Wall*; and Zubok, *Failed Empire*.

27. Dean Acheson advocated for nuclear war with regard to the Berlin issue. See Goduti, *Kennedy's Kitchen Cabinet*.

28. Authors' interview with Kempton Jenkins, Feb 2004, TFP.

29. Bohlen letter to Thompson, Mar 10, 1961, TFP.

30. Thompson oral history, Mar 25, 1964, JFKL, also in TFP.

31. Thompson appreciated that JFK actually read the cables and papers the ambassador sent to the president.

32. Thompson oral history, Mar 25, 1964, JFKL, also in TFP.

33. Notes on discussion, "The Thinking of the Soviet Leadership," Feb 11, 1961, drafted by McGeorge Bundy, Feb 13, 1961, FRUS, 1961–1963, vol. 5, doc. 26, also in McGeorge Bundy Papers, JFKL.

34. The one-of-a-kind, circular Moskova Pool had a diameter of 129.5 meters (424 ft. 10 in.). Jane would take her daughters there, even in winter. When the Soviet Union was dissolved, the Cathedral of Christ the Savior was built on the site of the pool.

35. Bohlen letter to Thompson, Mar 10, 1961, TFP.

36. Notes on discussion, "The Thinking of the Soviet Leadership," Feb 11, 1961, drafted by McGeorge Bundy, Feb 13, 1961, FRUS, 1961–1963, vol. 5, doc. 26.

37. He would not be officially reappointed under the new administration until May.

38. See Goduti, *Kennedy's Kitchen Cabinet*.

39. US Senate, Foreign Relations Committee, "Relations with the Soviet Union," Thompson testimony, also in TFP.

40. Bohlen, *Witness to History*, p. 479; and Thompson to State, Jan 28, 1961, FRUS, 1961–1963, vol. 5, doc. 17.

41. Thompson oral history, Mar 25, 1964, JFKL.

42. Intelligence assessment on Khrushchev, marked "confidential," [undated and unsigned], TFP. This document does not appear to have been written by Thompson.

43. Thompson to State, cable 1784, Jan 28, 1961, FRUS, 1961–1963, vol. 5, doc. 17; and JFK and Thompson conversation, Aug 8, 1962, Miller Center, *John F. Kennedy*, vol. 1, pp. 261–71.

44. Notes on discussion, "The Thinking of the Soviet Leadership," Feb 11, 1961, drafted by McGeorge Bundy, Feb 13, 1961, Feb 11, 1961, FRUS, 1961–1963, vol. 5, doc. 26.

45. O'Donnell and Powers, *We Hardly Knew Ye*.

46. JFK letter to Khrushchev, Feb 22, 1961, FRUS, 1961–1963, vol. 6 (*Kennedy-Khrushchev Exchanges*), doc. 7.

47. Thompson to State, cable 2065, Mar 3, 1961, Thompson 123 files, 600.0012/3-261, NACP, also in TFP. The cable is mentioned in an editorial note, FRUS, 1961–1963, vol. 5, doc. 38.

48. Jane Thompson letter to "Dear Family," Feb 7, 1961, TFP.

49. Beschloss, *Crisis Years*, p. 66.

50. Thompson to State, cables 2136 and 2146, Mar 10, 1961, airgrams G-665 and G-666, Mar 14, 1961, and editorial note, all in FRUS, 1961–1963, vol. 5, docs. 42–46; and Beschloss, *Crisis Years*, pp. 81–83.

51. Beschloss, *Crisis Years*, pp. 80–81.

52. JFK was forty-three years old at that time.

53. All of the cited cables are from Thompson to State, dated Mar 10, 1961. On the Novosibirsk meeting, see cables 2135, 2136, and 2146, FRUS, 1961–1963, vol. 5, docs. 41–43, also in JFKL. On Laos, see cable 2138, FRUS, 1961–1963, vol. 24, doc. 27, also in JFKL; and cable 2139, CF 751J/00/73–1061, NACP, also in JFKL and in TFP. On the nuclear test ban conference, see cable 2140, JFKL, also in TFP. On disarmament, see cable 2142, JFKL, also in TFP. On the Congo, see cable 2145, FRUS, 1961–1963, vol. 20 (*Congo Crisis*), doc. 47, also in JFKL and in TFP. On trade, see cable 2146, JFKL, also in TFP. On Germany and Berlin, see cable 2147, FRUS, 1961–1963, vol. 14, doc. 8, also in JFKL.

54. Thompson to State, cable 2136, Mar 10, 1960, FRUS, 1961–1963, vol. 5, doc. 42.

55. JFK letter to Khrushchev, Feb 22, 1961, FRUS, 1961–1963, vol. 6, doc. 7.

56. State to Thompson, cable 1402, Feb 28, 1961, FRUS, 1961–1963, vol. 14, doc. 7.

57. Thompson to State, cable 2139, Mar 10, 1961, CF 751J/00/73-1061, NACP, also in JFKL and TFP.

58. Thompson to State, cable 2145, Mar 10, 1961, FRUS, 1961–1963, vol. 20, doc. 47.

59. Thompson to State, cable 2140, JFKL, also in TFP.

60. Thompson to State, cable 2147, Mar 10, 1961, FRUS, 1961–1963, vol. 14, doc. 8.

61. Thompson to State, airgram G-665, Mar 14, 1961, FRUS, 1961–1963, vol. 5, doc. 44.

62. Thompson to State, cable 2147, Mar 10, 1961, FRUS, 1961–1963, vol. 14, doc. 8.

63. Thompson to State, airgram G-666, Mar 14, 1961, FRUS, 1961–1963, vol. 5, doc. 45.

64. A year later, in March 1962, Dobrynin would be named the USSR's ambassador to the United States.

65. State to Moscow, telegram 1518, Mar 17, 1961, CF 611.61/3-176, RG 59, NACP. Also see Thompson to State, FRUS, 1961–1963, vol. 14, doc. 8, p. 20n4[n5 in online version].

66. Thompson to SecState, telegram 2219, Mar 18, 1961, McGeorge Bundy Papers, JFKL, also in TFP. The authors asked Mr. Schorr about this in an interview, but, even fifty years later, he declined to tell them anything more.

67. Thompson to State, cable 2209, Mar 16, 1961, FRUS, 1961–1963, vol. 14, doc. 11, also in TFP; McGeorge Bundy Papers, JFKL; and Beschloss, *Crisis Years*, p. 175.

68. Thompson to State, cable 2209, Mar 16, 1961, FRUS, 1961–1963, vol. 14, doc. 11, also in TFP.

69. Ibid.

70. Fursenko and Naftali, *Khrushchev's Cold War*, p. 352. Robert F. Kennedy claimed that Bolshakov led him to believe there would be a test ban agreement in the Vienna meeting. See Guthman and Shulman, *Robert Kennedy*, pp. 260–63.

71. Thompson oral history, Mar 25, 1964, JFKL.

72. Ibid.; and Guthman and Shulman, *Robert Kennedy*, p. 260.

73. Sergei Khrushchev email to the authors, Apr 19, 2012, TFP.

74. Authors' telephone interview with Sergei Khrushchev, Apr 2012, TFP.

75. Dobrynin, *In Confidence*, p. 53.

23 ≋ Meeting in Vienna

1. Thompson to State, cable 2209 (in two parts), Mar 16, 1961, doc. 34, McGeorge Bundy Papers, JFKL.

2. Fursenko and Naftali, *Khrushchev's Cold War*, pp. 350–51.

3. Thompson to State, cable 2354, Apr 1, 1962, FRUS, 1961–1963, vol. 24, doc. 46; and Thompson to State, cable 2362, Apr 1, 1962, CF 611.61/4-161, RG 59, NACP, also in USSR general files in JFKL, also in TFP.

4. Thompson to State, cable 2459, Apr 11, 1961, CF 611.61/4-1161, RG 59, NACP.

5. In addition to the U-2 overflights, under Eisenhower, Bissell orchestrated plans for the removal of the heads of the governments of Guatemala (Jacobo Árbenz), the Congo (Patrice Lumumba), and the Dominican Republic (Raphael Trujillo). See, for example, Evan Thomas, *The Very Best Men*.

6. Brandon, *Special Relationships*, p. 168.

7. See Freedman, *Kennedy's Wars*, pp. 127–46.

8. Fursenko and Naftali, *Khrushchev's Cold War*, p. 349.

9. Delegates from foreign Communist parties, as well as Soviet Communists, were to participate in this congress. The Chinese Communists were more revolutionary and therefore were willing to go into any war—large, small, or even nuclear—to further their cause, which is why it was important to do whatever possible to make the split between China and the USSR stay that way.

10. Thompson to SecState, cable 2714, May 4, 1961, FRUS, 1961–1963, vol. 5, doc. 66, also in TFP, and microfilmed in 1964 for JFKL.

11. Thompson to SecState, cable 2887, May 24, 1961, CF 611.61/5–2461, RG 59, NACP.

12. Khrushchev had publicly let loose his anger and bluster over the U-2 incident at the opening of the Paris summit. He came as the injured party, yet it was Eisenhower's standing in the United States and in most of Europe that improved the situation afterward and actually served to solder Western cohesion. Khrushchev had been criticized for the way he handled himself at the Paris summit and no doubt wanted to avoid this in Vienna.

13. Thompson to SecState, cable 2887, May 24, 1961, CF 611.61/5–2461, RG 59, NACP.

14. Presidium meeting, May 26, 1961, in Fursenko et al., *Prezidium TSK KPSS 1954–1964*.

15. Ibid.

16. Zubok and Pleshakov, *Inside the Kremlin's Cold War*, p. 247. Thompson's quote is redacted in the relevant document in FRUS (MemCon, May 31, 1961, 12:30 p.m., vol. 14, doc. 30). Zubok and Pleshakov thanked William Burr for making the excised portion available, as do we. In Burr's review of FRUS, 1961–1963, vol. 14 (*Berlin Crisis, 1961–1962*) in *International History Review*, vol. 17, no. 3 (Aug 1995), on p. 634 he notes, "Rather than show how an ambassador tried to make a foreign leader more comfortable by emphasizing shared concerns about the German question only sixteen years after the Second World War, departmental censors snip away, worrying that publication in FRUS will somehow impair current relations with Bonn."

17. Thompson to State, cable 2889, May 24, 1961, FRUS, 1961–1963, vol. 14, doc. 25.

18. Thompson, cable 2890, May 24, 1961, CF 611.61/5–2461, RG 59, NACP.

19. McGeorge Bundy memo to the president, subject: specific answers to your questions of May 29 relating to the USSR, May 29, 1961, McGeorge Bundy Papers, JFKL, also in TFP. Bundy was Acheson's son-in-law.

20. Berlin Mission to State, cable 572, May 25, 1961, FRUS, 1961–1963, vol. 14, doc. 27.

21. Authors' correspondence with Martha Mautner, Mar 15, 2004, TFP; and "Interview with Martha Mautner," Aug 25, 1996, Iron Curtain: Episode 2, GW-NSA, http://nsarchive.gwu.edu/coldwar/interviews/episode-2/mautner1.html. With hindsight, an interim agreement might have worked. In 1971, the Four Powers signed a Berlin Agreement that established the sovereignty of two Germanys, expanded contact between the two, and improved communication and travel. This held until the Berlin Wall fell. The wall was officially opened in November 1989 and completely demolished by 1992.

22. Thompson to SecState, cable 2939, May 27, 1961, CF 762.00/5–2761, RG 59, NACP, also in TFP and in GW-NSA, www.gwu.edu/~nsarchiv/nsa/publications/berlin_crisis/bcdoc1.jpg.

23. Ibid.

24. Authors' telephone interview with Sergei Khrushchev, Mar 2010, TFP.

25. Thompson to State, cable 2941, May 27, 1961, FRUS, 1961–1963, vol. 5, doc. 79.

26. Thompson to SecState, cable 2939, May 27, 1961, CF 762.00/5–2761, RG 59, NACP.

27. Fursenko and Naftali, *Khrushchev's Cold War*; Smyser, *Kennedy and the Berlin Wall*; and Kempe, *Berlin 1961*.

28. Freedman, *Kennedy's Wars*, p. 54.

29. "Special Message to the Congress on Urgent National Needs," May 25, 1961, JFKL, https://www.jfklibrary.org/Asset-Viewer/Archives/JFKPOF-034-030.aspx.

30. Fursenko and Naftali, *Khrushchev's Cold War*, p. 355.

31. Ibid. Also see notes on a meeting of the Presidium, May 26, 1961, in Fursenko, *Prezidium TSK KPSS 1954–1964*; and Dobrynin, *In Confidence*, pp. 44–45.

32. Fursenko and Naftali, *Khrushchev's Cold War*, p. 596n71.

33. Ibid., p. 353.

34. A. Schlesinger, *A Thousand Days*, p. 350.

35. Thompson to State, cable 1959, Jan 15, 1959, box 5, folder 12, Martin Hillenbrand Papers: series 4, Richard B. Russell Library for Political Research and Studies, University of Georgia, also in TFP; and Fursenko and Naftali, *Khrushchev's Cold War*, pp. 206, 389.

36. JFK's daily diary, Jun 2, 1961, JFKL.

37. Taubman, *Khrushchev*, p. 49; Jane Thompson unpublished memoirs, TFP; and Beschloss, *Crisis Years*, p. 209.

38. Thompson oral history, Apr 27, 1966, JFKL.

39. N. Khrushchev, *Khrushchev Remembers*, p. 495.

40. MemCon: JFK and Khrushchev, Vienna meeting, Jun 3, 1961, FRUS, 1961–1963, vol. 5, doc. 83.

41. On the "nothing new" comment, see Thompson oral history, Apr 27, 1966, JFKL. On the ankle kick, see Bohlen, *Witness to History*, p. 482.

42. Guthman and Shulman, *Robert Kennedy*, p. 28.

43. Reeves, *President Kennedy*, p. 162.

44. Ibid., p. 167.

45. See Taubman, *Khrushchev*, p. 499; Beschloss, *Crisis Years*, pp. 214–15; and MemCon: JFK and Khrushchev, Vienna meeting, Jun 3, 1961, FRUS, 1961–1963, vol. 5, doc. 87.

46. Harrison, "Concrete Rose," p. 43.

47. Dobrynin, *In Confidence*, p. 46.

48. Sorensen, *Kennedy*, p. 543.

49. Ted Sorensen, "Als Kennedys Politscher Berater: Personliche Einblicke," in Karner et al., *Der Wiener Gipfel*.

50. Thompson oral history, Apr 27, 1966, JFKL. Some have stated that JFK said: "Then there will be war. It will be a long cold winter." But others have averred that this comment was added later on, for more drama. Ted Sorensen and Alexander Akalovsky claim those words were not said.

51. S. Hersh, *Dark Side of Camelot*, p. 252.

52. Sorensen, "Als Kennedys Politscher Berater," in Karner et al., *Der Wiener Gipfel*.

53. Bohlen, *Witness to History*, p. 482.

54. JFK and Thompson conversation, Aug 8, 1962, Miller Center, *John F. Kennedy*, vol. 1, p. 266; and Thompson oral history, Apr 27, 1966, p. 39/26, JFKL.

55. N. Khrushchev, *Khrushchev Remembers*, pp. 492, 495.

56. JFK and Thompson conversation, Aug 8, 1962, Miller Center, *John F. Kennedy*, vol. 1, p. 267.

57. Ibid.

58. Ibid., p. 266; and Thompson oral history, Apr 27, 1966, JFKL.

59. Sorensen, *Kennedy*.

60. Authors' interview with Ted Sorensen, winter 2011, TFP; and Slusser, *Berlin Crisis of 1961*, p. 81.

61. Thompson oral history, Apr 27, 1966, JFKL.

62. Thompson correspondence with Jane, Jun 10, 1961, TFP.

63. One tangible result of the Vienna meeting was an agreement to hold a conference on the subject of Laos, which resulted in a neutral Laos in 1962.

64. Due to the political climate, Khrushchev's appearance never took place.

65. Khrushchev letter to JFK, Sep 29, 1961, FRUS, 1961–1963, vol. 6, doc. 21.

66. The Berlin Task Force was formally known as the Interdepartmental Coordinating Group on Berlin Contingency Planning, See record of meeting, Jun 16, 1961, FRUS, 1961–1963, vol. 14, doc. 42.

67. Goduti, *Kennedy's Kitchen Cabinet*.

68. Beschloss, *Crisis Years*, p. 244.

69. Thompson to SecState, Jun 19, 1961, CF 160.00/6-1961, RG 59, NACP, also in TFP.

70. Report by Dean Acheson, Jun 28, 1961, FRUS, 1961–1963, vol. 14, doc. 49.

71. Thompson to State, cable 341, Jul 31, 1961, FRUS, 1961–1963, vol. 14, doc. 88. Also see notes in box 5, folder 12, Martin Hillenbrand Papers, University of Georgia.

72. Kempe, *Berlin 1961*, p. 283.

73. Thompson oral history, Apr 27, 1966, JFKL.

74. Thompson to SecState, cable 258, Jul 24, 1961, CF 162.00/7-2461, NACP, also in TFP.

75. Ibid.

76. Clifford, *Counsel to the President*, p. 136.

77. Jane Thompson letter to "Dear Family," Jul 26, 1961, TFP.

78. Authors' interview with Kempton Jenkins, Feb 2004, TFP.

79. This is a Russian expression for "clever girl."

80. Dobrynin, *In Confidence*, p. 62.

81. Dean Rusk interview with Martin Hillenbrand, p. 22, Dean Rusk Papers, Richard B. Russell Library for Political Research and Studies, University of Georgia.

82. "United States Note in Reply to the Soviet Aide-Mémoire of 4 June, 17 July 1961," in Watt, *Documents on International Affairs 1961*, pp. 323–29.

83. Thompson to SecState, cable 166, Jul 17, 1961, CF 762.00/7-2461, RG 59, NACP, also in TFP.

84. The official aide-mémoire was sent on July 17. Fursenko and Naftali, in *Khrushchev's Cold War*, p. 373, say it was July 18, but Thompson's report (in cable 166, see note 83) said it was July 17.

85. See Harrison, "Concrete Rose"; and Bundy, *Danger and Survival*.

86. Thompson to State, cable 323, Jul 28, 1961, FRUS, 1961–1963, vol. 14, doc. 84.

87. Ibid.; and Thompson to State, cable 324, Jul 29, 1963, FRUS, 1961–1963, vol. 14, doc. 85.

88. Harrison, "Concrete Rose."

89. MemCon: SecState meeting with European ambassadors, doc. 9, p. 8, entry 12, GW-NSA, http://ns archive.gwu.edu/NSAEBB/NSAEBB354/8-9-61%20Secy%20meeting.pdf; and "Khrushchev's Secret Speech on the Berlin Crisis, August 1961," Cold War International History Project, https://www.mtholyoke.edu/acad/intrel/khrush.htm.

90. They met from 10:42 to 11:24 a.m., Aug 14, 1961. See JFK's daily diary, JFKL.

91. Beschloss, *Crisis Years*, p. 275.

92. Ibid.

93. Ibid., p. 277.

94. Fursenko and Naftali, *Khrushchev's Cold War*, p. 391.

95. Jane Thompson letter to "Dear Family," Sep 22, 1961, TFP.

96. The Pioneers was the name a Soviet Communist youth organization for children between the ages of ten and fifteen. Older children were supposed to become members of the Komsomol, and eventually, when they became adults, they would join the Communist Party.

97. Rada Khrushcheva, "Recollections," Aug 2010, TFP.

98. Fursenko and Naftali, *Khrushchev's Cold War*, p. 390.

99. Slusser, *Berlin Crisis of 1961*, p. 207.

100. Sulzberger, *Last of the Giants*, entry for Sep 6, 1961, p. 803. Sulzberger should have known that the Soviets had remote listening devices, using microwaves, that could easily have picked up the conversation.

101. Ibid., entry for Sep 9, 1961, p. 806.

102. Cecil B. Lyons letter to Sorenson, Sep 10, 1961, JFKL, also in TFP.

103. Fursenko and Naftali, *Khrushchev's Cold War*, p. 397.

104. Kempe, *Berlin 1961*, p. 412.

105. Slusser, *Berlin Crisis of 1961*, p. 207; Kempe, *Berlin 1961*, pp. 412–13; and Fursenko and Naftali, *Khrushchev's Cold War*, p. 397.

106. See Sulzberger, *Last of the Giants*; Slusser, *Berlin Crisis of 1961*; Beschloss, *Crisis Years*; Fursenko and Naftali, *Khrushchev's Cold War*; and Salinger, *John F. Kennedy*, p. 58.

107. William Burr and Hector Montford, eds., "The Making of the Limited Test Ban Treaty, 1958–1963," Aug 8, 2003, GW-NSA, http://nsarchive.gwu.edu/NSAEBB/NSAEBB94/. For Rusk's request to Thompson, Sep 7, 1961, and Thompson's reply to Rusk, cable 847, Sep 9, 1961, see "Policy Planning Council—JCS Joint Staff Meeting," Sep 14, 1961, GW-NSA, http://nsarchive.gwu.edu/NSAEBB/NSAEBB94/tb34.pdf.

108. "Current Intelligence Weekly Review," Sep 14, 1961, FRUS, 1961–1963, vol. 5, doc. 118.

109. State to US embassy in France, cable 1691, Sep 22, 1961, FRUS, 1961–1963, vol. 14, doc. 156.

110. Khrushchev letter to JFK, Sep 29, 1961, FRUS, 1961–1963, vol. 6, doc. 21, pp. 25–38.

111. Slusser, *Berlin Crisis of 1961*, p. 244.

112. Ibid., p. 247.

24 ≋ The Twenty-Second Congress of the Communist Party

1. Taubman, *Khrushchev*.

2. Jane Thompson letter to "Dear Family," Nov 13, 1961, TFP.

3. Taubman, *Khrushchev*, p. 513.

4. For example, he had cars and convoys stopped on the Autobahn, sometimes detaining travelers for hours.

5. Garthoff, "Berlin 1961: The Record Corrected," *Foreign Policy*, vol. 84 (Fall 1991), pp. 142–56; and William Burr, "New Sources on Berlin Crisis, 1958–62," Bulletin No. 2 (Fall 1992), Cold War International History Project, Wilson Center, https://www.wilsoncenter.org/sites/default/files/CWIHPBulletin2.pdf.

6. "Interview with Alexei Adzhubei and Rada Khrushcheva," p. 12, GW-NSA, http://nsarchive.gwu .edu/NSAEBB/NSAEBB400/docs/Interview%20with%20Adzhubei%20&%20Rada.pdf.

7. Smyser, *Kennedy and the Berlin Wall*; and Garthoff, "Berlin 1961."

8. S. Khrushchev, *Nikita Khrushchev*, pp. 463–67.

9. Fursenko and Naftali, *Khrushchev's Cold War*, p. 404; and Slusser, *Berlin Crisis of 1961*, p. 422.

10. Fursenko and Naftali, *Khrushchev's Cold War*, p. 404.

11. S. Khrushchev, *Nikita Khrushchev*, pp. 463–67.

12. The Soviet leader's comment was made the following summer, when Thompson visited Khrushchev at his private dacha.

13. Garthoff, "Berlin 1961."

14. See Beschloss, *Crisis Years*, p. 356.

15. INR, research memo RSB-53, TFP.

16. Taubman, *Khrushchev*.

17. Ibid., p. 525.

18. Tatu, *Power in the Kremlin*, p. 127.

19. Khrushchev was able to reaffirm the central terms of the settlement with the Anti-Party Group but failed to extend it to the degree to which he might have hoped. As Tatu summarized in *Power in the Kremlin*, p. 139, "Khrushchev was not so weak that he could not purge his notorious opponents from the local Party apparatus; but on the other hand, he could not save his most outspoken allies from suffering the same fate."

20. Thompson notes for a speech at the National War College, Washington, DC, Oct 15, 1962, TFP.

21. Khrushchev's plan to increase crop production was to bring huge amounts of semiarid tracts of unused lands under cultivation. At first his plan did increase production, but the decline in crop yields and the farmers' inexperience proved to be a net loss.

22. Tatu, *Power in the Kremlin*, pp. 127–28.

23. Jane Thompson letter to "Dear Family," Nov 13, 1961, TFP.

24. Zubok and Pleshakov, *Inside the Kremlin's Cold War*, p. 264.

25. Ibid., pp. 263–65; and Taubman, *Khrushchev*, p. 521.

26. S. Khrushchev, *Nikita Khrushchev*, p. 501.

27. According to Dobbs (*One Minute to Midnight*, p. 54) and Zubok and Pleshakov (*Inside the Kremlin's Cold War*, p. 264), Pliyev knew very little about missiles. Sergei Khrushchev, however, in an email to the authors (Apr 25, 2017, TFP) told them that this was not accurate. Most likely Khrushchev picked Pliyev not for his knowledge of missiles, but because he was absolutely sure of Pliyev's loyalty to him and knew the marshal would keep the secret.

28. Khrushchev letter to JFK, Sept 29, 1961, FRUS, 1961–1963, vol. 6, doc. 21.

29. Jane Thompson letter to her mother, Dec 8, 1961, TFP.

30. "Remarkable Remarks," *Des Moines Register*, Jan 2, 1962, and several similar versions in TFP.

31. Thompson to State, cable 1714, Dec 9, 1961, CF 601.6111/12–961, RG 59, NACP, also referenced in an editorial note, FRUS, 1961–1963, vol. 5, doc. 138.

32. The authors have not been able to determine who Thompson's contact was.

33. Presidium meeting, Jan 8, 1962, in Fursenko et al., *Prezidium TSK KPSS 1954–1964*.

34. State to Thompson, cable 1520, Dec 28, 1961, FRUS, 19671–1963, vol. 14, doc. 248.

25 ≋ Up the Down Escalator: The Thompson-Gromyko Talks

1. State to Thompson, cable 1520, Dec 28, 1961, FRUS, 1961–1963, vol. 14, doc. 248, p. 710n3.

2. State to Thompson, cable 1520, Dec 28, 1961, FRUS, 1961–1963, vol. 14, doc. 248.

3. State to Thompson, cable 1523, Dec 29, 1961, FRUS, 1961–1963, vol. 14, doc. 249.

4. The Thompson-Gromyko talks were followed by the Rusk-Gromyko talks during the UN-sponsored Eighteen-Nation Committee on Disarmament conference on March 11–27, 1962, and the Rusk-Dobrynin meetings from April 16 to May 30, 1962.

5. Authors' interview with Kempton Jenkins, Feb 2004, TFP.

6. Kempton Jenkins remembered that it was the Soviets' deputy minister of foreign affairs, Vladimir Semyonov, who was with Gromyko, but the newspapers named Ilychev. See Seymour Topping, "Khrushchev and Vienna," New York Times, Jan 3, 1962.

7. Thompson to SecState, cable 1832, Jan 2, 1962, 762/1-262, GW-NSA, also in TFP; and Jenkins, Cold War Saga, p. 192.

8. Thompson to State, cable 1840, Jan 2, 1962, FRUS, 1961–1963, vol. 14, doc. 251.

9. Ibid.

10. Topping, "Khrushchev and Vienna."

11. Ibid.

12. State to Thompson, cable 1615, Jan 10, 1962, FRUS, 1961–1963, vol. 14, doc. 259.

13. State to Thompson, cable 1616, Jan 10, 1962, FRUS, 1961–1963, vol. 14, doc. 260.

14. Presidium meeting, Jan 8, 1962, in Fursenko et al., Prezidium TSK KPSS 1954–1964.

15. Ibid. Also see Wilke, Path to the Berlin Wall.

16. Thompson to SecState, cable 1922, Jan 11, 1962, and cable 1933, Jan 12, 1962, GW-NSA, also in TFP; and Thompson to SecState, cable 1936, Jan 12, 1962, FRUS, 1961–1963, vol. 14, doc. 264, also in TFP.

17. Thompson to SecState, cable 1936, Jan 12, 1962, FRUS, 1961–1963, vol. 14, doc. 264, also in TFP.

18. Thompson to SecState, cable 1932, Jan 12, 1962, GW-NSA, also in TFP.

19. Kempton Jenkins, "Reflections: A Confrontation in Moscow," Foreign Service Journal, vol. 86, no. 2 (Feb 2009), p. 72.

20. Jenkins, Cold War Saga, p. 198.

21. Thompson to State, cable 1959, Jan 15, 1962, FRUS, 1961–1963, vol. 14, doc. 267.

22. JFK memo to SecState, Jan 15, 1962, FRUS, 1961–1963, vol. 14, doc. 268.

23. Henry Owen was a National Security Council staff member until December 1961, and thereafter a member of the State Department's Policy Planning Council.

24. Henry Owen memo to Bundy, Jan 10, 1962, McGeorge Bundy Papers, JFKL, also in TFP.

25. Thompson to SecState, cable 2097, Feb 1, 1962, CF 611.61/2-1-62, RG 59, NACP, also in TFP; and Thompson to State, cable 2175, Feb 9, 1962, CF 762.0221/2-962, RG 59, NACP, also in FRUS, 1961–1963, vol. 14, doc. 284.

26. Ausland, Kennedy, Khrushchev. John Ausland was member of Berlin Task Force.

27. Thompson to State, cable 2186, Feb 12, 1962, FRUS, 1961–1963, vol. 14, doc. 288.

28. Kennedy letter to Khrushchev, Feb 15, 1962, FRUS, 1961–1963, vol. 6, doc. 34.

29. For the text of this address, see Public Papers of the Presidents; and editorial note, FRUS, 1961–1963, vol. 5, doc. 166.

30. The tests began on April 25, 1962.

31. Thompson to State, cable 2255, Feb 21, 1962, FRUS, 1961–1963, vol. 5, doc. 158.

32. Jenkins, Cold War Saga.

33. Thompson to State, cable 2350, Mar 6, 1962, FRUS, 1961–1963, vol. 14, doc. 314.

34. Authors' email correspondence with Georgi Kornienko, Apr 2004, TFP.

35. Smith memo to SecState, CF 762.00/3-962 and CF 611.61/600.0012/662.001, RG 59, NACP. Gerard Smith was part of the State Department's Policy Planning Group from 1957 to 1961, but he signed the memo sent in 1962 with the title of that group. The authors don't know why he did so.

36. Thompson to State, cable 1773, Mar 9, 1959, CF 762.00/3.959, RG 59, NACP, also in GW-NSA, https://nsarchive.gwu.edu/coldwar/documents/episode-9/01.pdf.

37. Thompson correspondence about the Princeton job, Mar 13, 1962, TFP.

38. MemCon, March 11, 12, 18, and 20, FRUS, 1961–1963, vol. 15 (Berlin Crisis, 1962–63), docs. 6, 8, 16, and 18. These documents show that Thompson was present at the Geneva meetings with the American and the Soviet delegates on those dates.

39. JFK to Rusk, Mar 9, 1962, FRUS, 1961–1963, vol. 15, doc. 1. In diplomatic parlance, a *modus vivendi*, literally meaning a "way of life," generally refers to a temporary or provisional accord that is intended to later be replaced by a more permanent agreement.

40. Rusk to State, Geneva, Mar 14, 1962, 11 p.m., FRUS, 1961–1963, vol. 15, doc. 13.

41. Draft paper prepared in the US delegation in Geneva, [undated], FRUS, 1961–1963, vol. 15, doc. 20. The footnote to this FRUS entry states that the document was attached to a March 21 memo from Kohler to Rusk that bears the handwritten notation "As handed [to] Gromyko," but there is no explanation as to whether this happened before the paper was given to the West Germans.

42. Thompson memo to SecState, Apr 3, 1962, FRUS, 1961–1963, vol. 5, doc. 175. On p. 398n2, it states: "The source text bears an 'OK DR' [suggesting that the secretary of state approved it] but other than an entry in the president's log, no record of his meeting with Thompson at 10:30 a.m., April 6, has been found." There is an entry in the president's daily diary for April 6 at 10:30 a.m., however, and photos show that this meeting occurred. See JFK's daily diary, JFKL.

43. MemCon: Thompson and Dobrynin, Apr 6, 1962, FRUS, 1961–1963, vol. 5, doc. 179.

44. Thompson to State, cable 2848, May 4, 1962, FRUS, 1961–1963, vol. 5, doc. 188.

45. Thompson to State, cable 2935, May 13, 1962, FRUS, 1961–1963, vol. 5, doc. 195; Thompson to State, cable 2942, May 13, 1962, CF 611.61/5-1362, XR-751J-00, RG 59, NACP, also in TFP, and (microfilmed in 1964) in McGeorge Bundy Papers, JFKL; and MemCon: Khrushchev lunch for Salinger, airgram A-886, May 15, 1962, McGeorge Bundy Papers, JFKL, also in TFP.

46. State to US embassy in Moscow, cable 2571, May 12, 1963, FRUS, 1961–1963, vol. 5, doc. 193.

47. Salinger was accompanied by Ted Sorensen and Alexander Akalovsky.

48. Thompson to State, May 13, 1962, FRUS, 1961–1963, vol. 5, doc. 195. Salinger spent the night with Aleksei Adzhubei [Khrushchev's journalist son-in-law], Mikhail Kharlamov [the Soviet Foreign Ministry's press aide], Leonid M. Zamyatin [deputy chief of the American Countries Division in the Soviet Foreign Ministry], and the Sukhodrevs [Khrushchev's official translator and his wife].

49. State to US embassy, Moscow, cable 2571, May 12, 1963, FRUS, 1961–1963, vol. 5, doc. 193.

50. MemCon: Salinger and Khrushchev, JFKL.

51. Stewart Alsop, "Kennedy's Grand Strategy," *Saturday Evening Post*, Mar 31, 1962.

52. MemCon: Thompson and Dobrynin, Apr 6, 1962, FRUS, 1961–1963, vol. 5, doc. 179.

53. It is also intriguing that Khrushchev said he had come up with the Cuban missile idea during his trip to Bulgaria, which took place just after Salinger's visit. Khrushchev knew that Soviet missiles were not particularly reliable in accurately delivering their payloads. Perhaps JFK's words about the missiles in his interview with Alsop had sparked the idea in Khrushchev's head. In any case, the idea of a possible preemptive attack by the United States certainly could have done so.

54. Tatu, *Power in the Kremlin*, p. 218.

55. Salinger to SecState, cable 2935, May 13, 1962, FRUS, 1961–1963, vol. 5, doc. 195.

56. MemCon: Khrushchev lunch for Salinger, airgram A-886, May 15, 1962, McGeorge Bundy Papers, JFKL, also in TFP.

57. Ibid.

58. Ibid.

59. During the first week in May 1962, Pathet Lao forces attacked the Royal Laos troops at Nam Tha.

60. Thompson to SecState, cable 2942, May 13, 1962, 611.61/5-1362, JFKL, also in TFP.

61. Thompson to SecState, May 14, 1962, McGeorge Bundy Papers, JFKL, also in TFP.

62. Beschloss, *Crisis Years*, p. 396. The coalition government was represented by Souvanna Phouma and Souphanouvong, with Souvanna as Prime Minister.

26 ≋ Goodbye Moscow, Hello Washington

1. Thompson met with the president on June 8, from 5:15 until 6:03 p.m. See JFK's daily diary, JFKL.

2. Foy Kohler replaced Thompson as US ambassador in Moscow, and Martin Hillenbrand replaced Kohler on the Berlin Task Force.

3. Fidel Castro interview, in Blight, Allyn, and Welch, *Cuba on the Brink.*, pp. 202, 180.

4. Ibid., pp. 345, 348.

5. Beschloss, *Crisis Years*, p. 409.

6. Rada Khrushcheva, "Recollections," Aug 2010, TFP.

7. Thompson to SecState, cable 170, Jul 19, 1962, CF 611.61/7-162, XR-600.0012, 711.5611, 911.8296, and 600.00121, RG 59, NACP, also in TFP.

8. MemCon from MFA, translation in TFP. Also see Thompson cables 224, 225, 227, 228, and 229, Jul 25 and 26, 1962, TFP, some of which are also in CF 600.0012/7-2562 and 600.0012/7-2662, NACP, and some in McGeorge Bundy Papers, JFKL.

9. Thompson to SecState, cable 227, Jul 26, 1962, McGeorge Bundy Papers, JFKL, also written as note 123, Thompson, Llewellyn E, CF 600.0012-7-2662, 611.61, XR-121.612, NACP. Also see minutes of conversation between Khrushchev and Thompson, Jul 25, 1962, p. 3 (of translation), RGANI doc. no. 25.07.1962 B, B/N List 17 F.52, on 1 D[ec], 582 L, 41–57, TFP.

10. Khrushchev could not allow this, because he knew what Thompson said was true. It would be increasingly difficult to hide that weakness, and, once it was evident, all the leverage he had attained though his nuclear bluff would disappear. This is another reason why his Cuba scheme was important to the Soviet leader. If he had bases in Cuba, it would make a substantial difference. Maybe then he could go ahead with an agreement on disarmament, and subsequently get the West to respond to his other needs. Even if the missiles in Cuba didn't make the nuclear arsenals of the United States and the USSR equal, they provided a practical parity, and negotiations on any subject would then be totally different. The United States couldn't be so "high-handed" anymore.

11. Minutes of conversation between Khrushchev and Thompson, Jul 25, 1962, p. 3 (of translation), RGANI doc. no. 25.07.1962 B, B/N List 17 F.52, on 1 D[ec], 582 L, 41–57, TFP.

12. Thompson to SecState, cable 227, Jul 26, 1962, CF 600.0012/7-2662, RG 59, NACP, also in TFP.

13. Thompson to SecState, cable 228, Jul 26, 1962, McGeorge Bundy Papers, JFKL, also in TFP.

14. Thompson to SecState, "Eyes Only," cable 230, Jul 26, 1962, McGeorge Bundy Papers, JFKL, also in TFP.

15. Memo to president, Jul 31, 1962 [it's not clear who sent the three-page memo; the signature looks like "D Klein"], JFKL, also in TFP. The document (on p. 2) quotes Thompson on the issue.

16. Thompson to SecState, "Eyes Only," cable 225, Jul 25, 1962, McGeorge Bundy Papers, JFKL, also in TFP.

17. Thompson to SecState, Jul 25, 1962, cable 224, McGeorge Bundy Papers, JFKL, also in TFP.

18. This dacha later became Dmitry Medvedev's country retreat. When the authors first recalled the trip we had made to Khrushchev's dacha as children, we thought it was his private dacha, but in talking more recently to Viktor Sukhodrev and Sergei Khrushchev, they insisted it must have been the official government dacha. We couldn't understand why these two men were so certain, until they explained that there was only one bathroom in the private dacha.

19. Comments to the authors from a Russian friend, 2010, TFP.

20. Authors' telephone interview with Viktor Sukhodrev, Feb 22, 2010, TFP.

21. Ibid.

22. Minutes of conversation between Khrushchev and Thompson, , Jul 25, 1962, p. 16 (of translation), RGANI doc. no. 25.07.1962 B, B/N List 17 F.52, on 1 D[ec], 582 L, 41–57, TFP.

23. Transcript of JFK and Thompson meeting, Aug 8, 1962, Miller Center, *John F. Kennedy*, vol. 1, p. 262.

24. David Eisenhower letter to Jenny Thompson, Jan 15, 2010, TFP.

25. Thompson oral history, Mar 25, 1964, JFKL. Other recipients of this award included Waldo Lyon, who made it possible for a submarine to go under the Arctic ice, and Robert Gilruth, who oversaw the first US manned orbit of the earth.

26. Transcript of JFK and Thompson meeting, Aug 8, 1962, Miller Center, *John F. Kennedy*, vol. 1, pp. 261–71.

27. Ibid., p. 264.

28. Ibid., p. 267.

29. Ibid., p. 269.

30. At that point, Andy was at the University of Vienna, studying opera and opera production, although she did join the rest of the family in Washington, DC, later. After her university studies, Andy went to Italy, working as an apprentice assistant to Giorgio Strehler, an Italian opera and theater director.

31. Richard Davis was the deputy chief of mission in Moscow, and his daughter entered school at the same time Thompson's two younger girls did.

32. Max Holland, "A Luce Connection: Senator Keating, William Pawley, and the Cuban Missile Crisis," *Journal of Cold War Studies*, vol. 1, no. 3 (Fall 1999), pp. 139–67.

33. Message from Khrushchev to JFK, Sep 28, 1962, FRUS, 1961–1963, vol. 6, doc. 56.

34. Sherry Thompson conversations with Stuart Udall, Santa Fe, New Mexico, 2009.

35. Reeves, *President Kennedy*, pp. 350–52.

36. The transcript of the full conversation is in Miller Center, *John F. Kennedy*, vol. 2, pp. 182–214.

37. Authors' interview with Sergei Khrushchev, Jul 2010, TFP. He made this statement and said that it created an obligation for the Soviets to defend a "war of liberation." Prior to that point, he added, Nikita Khrushchev had said, "Let's be cautious because we don't know about this Castro fellow."

38. The term "general war" was a euphemism for an all-out nuclear conflagration.

39. "Thompson Takes Oath as Envoy," *Boston Herald*, Oct 8, 1962, TFP.

40. Perkins letter to Thompson, Aug 9, 1962, TFP. Frances Perkins died a few years later.

41. Dobrynin to Ministry of Foreign Affairs, USSR, cable, Nov 26, 1962, about a conversation with Walter Lippmann on Nov 1, 1962. The authors express their thank for this information to Svetlana Savranskaya at GW-NSA.

27 ≋ Thirteen Days in October

Epigraph. Joseph S. Nye, discussing lessons learned from the Cuban Missile Crisis, in Allyn, Blight, and Welch, *Back to the Brink*, p. 172.

1. Vladimir Toumanoff oral history, FA-ADST.

2. Cuban Missile Crisis meeting, Oct 16, 1962, Miller Center, *John F. Kennedy*, vol. 2, pp. 396, 422.

3. JFK did not particularly want to bring in either the OAS or NATO at this point.

4. Cuban Missile Crisis meeting, Oct 16, 1962, Miller Center, *John F. Kennedy*, vol. 2, p. 406.

5. Ibid., p. 418. It is remarkable that, after the Bay of Pigs affair, anyone in the room could entertain such an idea. Their attitude is a frightening precursor of the parallel misconception that, two score years later, American troops would be welcomed as liberators and embraced in Iraq.

6. Ibid., p. 422.

7. See Dobbs, *One Minute to Midnight*, p. 28; and Martin Tolchin, "U.S. Underestimated Soviet Force in Cuba during '62 Missile Crisis," *New York Times*, Jan 15, 1992.

8. According to National Security Archive documents, there were a total of 98 tactical nuclear warheads on Cuban territory for fifty-nine days, until the departure of the *Arkhangelsk* cargo ship on December 1, 1966. There were 80 warheads for the land-based FKR-1 cruise missiles, 12 warheads for the dual-use Luna launchers, and 6 nuclear bombs for the IL-28 bombers; 24 R-14 IRMBs were never unloaded from the *Aleksandrovsk* ship. See Svetlana Savranskaya and Thomas Blanton, eds., with Anna Melyakova, "Last Nuclear Weapons Left Cuba in December 1962," Dec 11, 2013, GW-NSA, www2.gwu.edu/~nsarchiv/NSAEBB/NSAEBB 449/. There were also 32 antiaircraft missiles, one of which would shoot down an American U-2 plane. See Munton and Welch, *Cuban Missile Crisis*, p. 36.

9. Office schedule for Rusk during the Cuban Missile Crisis, general office files 1952–1995, subseries A, alpha files, box 11, folder 2, Dean Rusk Personal Papers: series 4, University of Georgia.

10. There was also a sense that nations in Europe, having lived in the shadow of Soviet missiles that were within striking distance, would not share the Americans' outrage over this development and would pressure the United States to capitulate. So secrecy was important, until the Americans had figured out how they would respond.

11. Vladimir Toumanoff oral history, FA-ADST.

12. Cuban Missile Crisis meeting, Oct 16, 1962, Miller Center, *John F. Kennedy*, vol. 2, p. 448.

13. Ibid., p. 462.

14. Bundy, *Danger and Survival*, p. 422.

15. Dobbs, *One Minute to Midnight*, p. 218; and Kempe, *Berlin 1961*, p. 497. Mikoyan was quoted in Dobbs's book as saying Khrushchev, at least, recognized that what he was doing in Cuba was an adventure. Also see Mikoyan, *Soviet Cuban Missile Crisis*, p. 246.

16. RFK would later repeat the analogy with Pearl Harbor, to persuasive effect.

17. Cuban Missile Crisis meeting, Oct 16, 1962, Miller Center, *John F. Kennedy*, vol. 2, p. 466.

18. John McCone meeting schedule, Oct 17–23, 1962, CIA CREST database, RDP803B01676R001900 100014-8, NACP. The secretary of state's office was located on the seventh floor, and it was a completely different world than the rest of the building.

19. Office schedule for Rusk during the Cuban Missile Crisis, Dean Rusk Personal Papers, University of Georgia; and Rusk letter to Sherry Thompson, Oct 28, 1987, TFP.

20. Rusk, *As I Saw It*, p. 232.

21. Dean Rusk letter to Sherry Thompson, Oct 28, 1987, TFP; Dean Rusk oral history, series 1, p. 11, and Rusk interview with James Blight and David Welch, May 18, 1987, both in Richard B. Russell Library for Political Research and Studies, University of Georgia; and Rusk correspondence with Stephen S. Rosenfeld, deputy editorial editor, *Washington Post*, Nov 16, 1987, TFP.

22. Interview with Robert McNamara and Ted Sorensen, moderated by Tom Oliphant, Oct 2002, JFKL.

23. Rusk, *As I Saw It*, p. 242.

24. Rusk interview with James Blight and David Welch, May 18, 1987, University of Georgia; Blight and Welsh, *On the Brink*, p. 175; summary, Cuban Missile Crisis meeting, Oct 18, 1962, Miller Center, *John F. Kennedy*, vol. 2, pp. 512–13. Although this information appears in the summary for October 18, it refers to the meeting at the State Department between the Joint Chiefs of Staff on October 17. Also see McCone memo for the files, Oct 17, 1962, FRUS, 1961–1963, vol. 11 (*Cuban Missile Crisis and Aftermath*), doc. 23.

25. See Robert Kennedy handwritten list of blockade and strike proponents, "Declassified RFK Documents Yield New Information on Back-Channel to Fidel Castro to Avoid Nuclear War," Oct 12, 2012, *National Security Archive Electronic Briefing Book No. 395*, GW-NSA, http://nsarchive.gwu.edu/NSAEBB/NSAEBB395/.

26. This was mentioned by someone on Bundy's staff, but the authors cannot locate that citation. The point was reiterated in the CIA's top-secret briefing paper, "Soviet Military Buildup in Cuba," Oct 21, 1962, doc. 74, p. 11, in McAuliffe, *CIA Documents*, also at https://www.cia.gov/library/center-for-the-study-of-intelligence/csi-publications/books-and-monographs/Cuban%20Missile%20Crisis1962.pdf.

27. Frank Sieverts report, "The Cuban Crisis, 1962," NSF, series 1: Countries, box 49, folder: Cuba, subject: history of the Cuban crisis, 1/9/63–9/1/63, John F. Kennedy Papers, JFKL.

28. McCone memo for the files, Oct 19, 1062, docs. 57 and 60, in McAuliffe, *CIA Documents*. One of these documents is also in FRUS, 1961–1963, vol. 11, doc. 28.

29. Bohlen's decision to stick with a time-consuming mode of transport made no sense to the authors or to Bohlen's daughter, Avis T. Bohlen, who said she did not know why he did not stay longer in Washington, DC, during the Cuban Missile Crisis. [Instead of taking a ship, Chip Bohlen could have flown to Paris and gotten there at the same time as his scheduled arrival by boat. As an excuse for leaving the United States later than planned, Bohlen could have said that he had a family emergency.] This crisis was a defining career moment, and Bohlen was said to hover over the ship's radio daily, miserable at not being in the thick of things. In their memoirs, Jackie Kennedy and RFK rather harshly criticized Bohlen for leaving when he did, which was unfair of them, but Bohlen never did reveal a satisfactory reason. This was told to the authors by Avis T. Bohlen. Thompson was dubbed the "in-house Russian" by Sorenson in his conversations with the authors and was referred to as such by Douglas Dillon and Dean Rusk. See authors' telephone interview with Ted Sorenson, Feb 2010, TFP.

30. Cuban Missile Crisis meeting, Oct 18, 1962, Miller Center, *John F. Kennedy*, vol. 2, p. 516. This was not quite true, however. According to Mikoyan, in *Soviet Cuban Missile Crisis*, the missiles could reach Atlanta, but not Chicago.

31. Cuban Missile Crisis meeting, Oct 18, 1962, Miller Center, *John F. Kennedy*, vol. 2, p. 532.

32. Mikoyan, *Soviet Cuban Missile Crisis*, p. 114.

33. Cuban Missile Crisis meeting, Oct 18, 1962, Miller Center, *John F. Kennedy*, vol. 2, p. 532.

34. See Thompson comments to INR, "Ikle Report for the Arms Control and Disarmament Agency," Feb 4, 1966, TFP; and Thompson oral history, Apr 27, 1966, JFKL.

35. Cuban Missile Crisis meeting, Oct 18, 1962, Miller Center, *John F. Kennedy*, vol. 2, p. 534; and Thompson oral history, Apr 27, 1966, JFKL.

36. Khrushchev was referring to the Bay of Pigs, as well as to Operation Mongoose—ongoing covert operations to overthrow the Communist regime in Cuba—and harassment operations using Cuban-Americans.

37. Cuban Missile Crisis meeting, Oct 18, 1962, Miller Center, *John F. Kennedy*, vol. 2, p. 534.

38. Leonard Meeker oral history, Aug 25, 1989, FA-ADST.

39. Beschloss, *Crisis Years*, p. 455.

40. Ibid.

41. Allyn, Blight, and Welch, *Back to the Brink*, p. 54.

42. Sieverts, "Cuban Crisis, 1962," JFKL.

43. Mikoyan, *Soviet Cuban Missile Crisis*, p. 117; and JFK summary of late-night meeting, Oct 18, 1962, Miller Center, *John F. Kennedy*, vol. 2, p. 576.

44. See Fidel Castro's comments on the Soviets' intervention in Blight, Allyn, and Welch, *Cuba on the Brink*.

45. This was the Inter-American Treaty of Reciprocal Assistance, which was signed in 1947 and came into effect in 1948.

46. Thompson oral history, Apr 27, 1966, JFKL; and record of meeting, Oct 19, 1962, FRUS, 1961–1963, vol. 11, doc. 31.

47. JFK's recollection of the meeting, Oct 18, 1962, Miller Center, *John F. Kennedy*, vol. 2, p. 576.

48. Rusk's office schedule states that Thompson was present at the dinner. See office schedule for Rusk during Cuban Missile Crisis, Dean Rusk Personal Papers, University of Georgia. Sieverts, in "Cuban Crisis, 1962," p. 59, JFKL, indicates that a briefing occurred afterward.

49. Leonard Meeker oral history, FA-ADST.

50. Rusk did not say if the ultimate decision occurred in this meeting, in the previous one with the president, or in the congressional briefing to come.

51. George W. Ball oral history, Apr 16, 1965, JFKL. For Thompson's participation in that meeting, see Thompson's daily diary, TFP.

52. Meeting with JCS, Oct 19, 1962, Miller Center, *John F. Kennedy*, vol. 2, pp. 578–98.

53. Cuban Missile Crisis meeting, Oct 16, 1962, Miller Center, *John F. Kennedy*, vol. 2, p. 16.

54. Record of meeting, Oct 19, 1962, FRUS, 1961–1963, vol. 11, doc. 31.

55. Authors' telephone interview with Ted Sorensen, Feb 2010, TFP.

56. Ibid.

57. Record of meeting, Oct 19, 1962, FRUS, 1961–1963, vol. 11, doc. 31.

58. Leonard Meeker oral history, FA-ADST.

59. See Blight and Welch, *On the Brink*, p. 314.

60. JFK interview for television, Dec 1962. It appears in "Fiftieth Anniversary of the Cuban Missile Crisis" video, pt. 2 of 3, at 13:55 minutes, JFKL, https://www.jfklibrary.org/Asset-Viewer/txVKGLZQWUy1s396Rx4HkA.aspx.

61. Leonard Meeker oral history, FA-ADST.

62. Record of meeting, Oct 19, 1962, FRUS, 1961–1963, vol. 11, doc. 31.

63. This UN resolution was a requirement of a provision in the Rio Treaty. See Leonard Meeker oral history, FA-ADST.

64. Rusk, *As I Saw It*, p. 236.

65. Robert S. McNamara, "Forty Years after 13 Days," *Arms Control Today*, Nov 20, 2002, Arms Control Association, https://www.armscontrol.org/act/2002_11/cubanmissile/.

66. Cuban Missile Crisis meeting, Oct 22, 1962, Miller Center, *John F. Kennedy*, vol. 2, pp. 3, 6.

67. As told to the authors by Jane Thompson.

68. The meeting was with George Ball, McGeorge Bundy, Roswell Gilpatric, U. Alexis Johnson, RFK, Paul Nitze, Kenneth O'Donnell, Dean Rusk, and Ted Sorensen.

69. SecState telephone log, Oct 22, 1962, 2:24 and 2:35 pm, JFKL.

70. Rusk, *As I Saw It*, p. 234.

71. Meeting with congressional leadership on Cuban Missile Crisis, Oct 22, 1962, Miller Center, *John F. Kennedy*, vol. 3, pp. 40–58.

72. JFK speech to the nation, Oct 22, 1962, https://www.mtholyoke.edu/acad/intrel/kencuba.htm.

73. Conversation between JFK and Macmillan, Oct 22, 1962; and meeting with congressional leadership on Cuban Missile Crisis, Oct 22, 1962, both in Miller Center, *John F. Kennedy*, vol. 3, p. 99.

74. For all the postmortem conference transcripts on the Cuban Missile Crisis, containing numerous

assertions by the Soviet counterparts for this belief, see Blight and Welch, *On the Brink* [re. the Hawks Cay and Harvard conferences]; and Allyn, Blight, and Welch, *Back to the Brink* [re. the Moscow conference].

75. Nor was this just discussed during the Kennedy administration. As late as June 1965, Admiral William Raborn, the director of the CIA at the time, recommended that President Lyndon Johnson reactivate covert paramilitary operations against Cuba, over the objections of Thompson, McGeorge Bundy, and Cyrus Vance, who was then the deputy secretary of defense. See Bundy memo to LBJ on June 10, 1965, meeting of 303 Committee, Jun 25, 1965, NSF: McGeorge Bundy 1965, box 3, vol. 11, folder 1 of 3, LBJL, also in FRUS, 1964–1968, vol. 32, doc. 303.

76. Office schedule for Rusk during the Cuban Missile Crisis, Dean Rusk Personal Papers, University of Georgia.

77. Khrushchev letter to JFK, Oct 23, 1962, FRUS, 1961–1963, vol. 6, doc. 61.

78. "Marine Air in October 1962," Cuban Missile Crisis, MOFAK, www.mofak.com/cuban_missile_cri sis.htm.

79. Cuban Missile Crisis meeting, Oct 23, 1962, Miller Center, *John F. Kennedy*, vol. 3, p. 127.

80. Thompson oral history, Apr 27, 1966, p. 12, JFKL; and Cuban Missile Crisis meeting, Oct 25, 1962, Miller Center, *John F. Kennedy*, vol. 3, p. 248.

81. The Washington Ambassadorial Group (WAG) consisted of the French, British, and German ambassadors to the United States and representatives of the US government.

82. Cuban Missile Crisis meeting, Oct 23, 1962, Miller Center, *John F. Kennedy*, vol. 3, p. 127.

83. Some have suggested that this showed JFK was being tough and overriding a "weaker" solution to stop the convoys, but it actually illustrates the opposite.

84. Paper agreed to by Berlin-NATO subcommittee, Oct 24, 1962, FRUS, 1961–1963, vol. 15, doc. 142.

85. Thompson's objections in the Nitze subcommittee meeting are noted in a memo from David Klein and Lawrence Legere to Bundy, Oct 29, 1962, FRUS, 1961–1963, vol. 15, doc. 146.

86. Authors' email correspondence with David Klein, Dec 9, 2012, TFP.

87. Bundy, *Danger and Survival*, p. 241.

88. Thompson letter to Rusk, Nov 22, 1964, LBJL, also in TFP; and summary notes in TFP.

89. For example, in Allyn, Blight, and Welsh, *Back to the Brink*, p. 79, Dobrynin is quoted as saying. "After all, who if not the brother of the president would know what the president was thinking. Consequently, those statements I sent to Moscow were received as quite authoritative."

90. Ibid., p. 143.

91. Khrushchev letter to JFK, Oct 24, 1962, FRUS, 1961–1963, vol. 6, doc. 63.

92. For the description of JFK's conversation with Macmillan that afternoon, discussing a summit option, see May and Zelikow, *Kennedy Tapes*, p. 243.

93. Authors' interview with Svetlana Savranskaya, Jun 19, 2013, TFP. Also see S. Khrushchev, *Nikita Khrushchev*; and minutes of Presidium meetings, in Fursenko et al., *Prezidium TSK KPSS 1954–1964*.

94. Authors' interview with John Mapother, Feb 2004, TFP. Mapother, a CIA officer, had briefings from an intelligence officer [named Maple] for the Berlin Command who was monitoring the Soviet military forces. Those in the Berlin Command thought that if the Soviets were going to do anything in Cuba, they'd need to move their forces from East Germany, so the Americans were using this as a signal for possible action. The Soviet forces in East Germany were moved out of their barracks and into staging areas on October 20. They remained there until they were moved back to their barracks on October 25, the same day that Khrushchev decided to end the crisis.

95. Sieverts, "Cuban Crisis, 1962," JFKL.

96. Adlai Stevenson was widely hailed for his statements at the UN, both this one to the Security Council and the more public ones in coming days.

97. See summary of Stevenson-Yost phone call, Oct 26, 1962, Miller Center, *John F. Kennedy*, vol. 3, p. 316.

98. May and Zelikow, *Kennedy Tapes*, pp. 292–93; and TelCon: JFK and Rusk, Oct 26, 1962, Miller Center, *John F. Kennedy*, vol. 3, pp. 331–32.

99. Walter Lippmann, "Blockade Proclaimed," *New York Herald Tribune*, Oct 25, 1962.

100. See Uslu, *Turkish-American Relationship*, p. 144.

101. Abel, *Missile Crisis*, p. 189.

102. Hare to State, cable 587, Oct 26, 1962, SecState lot file 65 D 438 (Jupiter-Cuba), NACP; and "The Cuban Missile Crisis, 1962: The Documents," The Cuban Missile Crisis, 1962: The 40th Anniversary, GW-NSA, http://nsarchive.gwu.edu/nsa/cuba_mis_cri/docs.htm.

103. Authors' interview with Sergei Khrushchev, Jul 10, 2010, TFP; and Naftali and Fursenko, *One Hell of a Gamble*, pp. 263–65.

104. TelCon: JFK and Macmillan, Oct 26, 1962, FRUS, 1961–1963, vol. 11, doc. 87.

105. Dobbs, *One Minute to Midnight*, p. 117; and authors' interview with Svetlana Savranskaya, Jun 19, 2013, TFP.

106. Authors' interview with Svetlana Savranskaya, Jun 19, 2013, TFP.

107. Authors' interview with Richard Davies, Feb 23, 2003, TFP. Foy Kohler, the ambassador, did not take part in these exchanges because, Davies said, he'd "hit the bottle again" and was not available late in the day, when all the action took place.

108. The translation the State Department saw is the one for Oct 26, 1962, Miller Center, *John F. Kennedy*, vol. 3, pp. 349–55. The version in FRUS, 1961–1963, vol. 6, doc. 66, has subsequent edits to the "official translation."

109. Summary record of seventh meeting of ExCom, Oct 27, 1961, FRUS, 1961–1963, vol. 11, doc. 90.

110. Authors' interview with Svetlana Savranskaya, Jun 19, 2013, TFP, to establish the correct order of the letters. Savranskaya translated a book by Sergo Mikoyan that led her to research both the Russian and the American literature, in order to reconstruct the chronology surrounding the various letters.

111. Ibid.

112. Georgi Kornienko, the Soviet deputy chief of mission, met with the reporter.

113. Authors' interview with Svetlana Savranskaya, Jun 19, 2013, TFP. Khrushchev habitually thought that the American press was much more under the US government's control than it actually was. Therefore, he was prone to take articles written by the media as coming from official sources, even when they were not.

114. Ibid. Also based on S. Khrushchev's accounts [in Russian] in *Reformator*; Korniyenko, *Holodnaya Voyina*; and Mikoyan, *Soviet Cuban Missile Crisis*.

115. Weiner, *Legacy of Ashes*.

116. Cuban Missile Crisis meeting, Oct 27, 1962, Miller Center, *John F. Kennedy*, vol. 3, p. 471. According to a paper in TFP [no other source information is on the paper], JFK sent a message to the prime minister of Turkey on October 27, 1962, warning him that it could become necessary for the United States to attack Cuba. Since the most likely Soviet action in response would be to attack Turkey, JFK would announce the removal of the NATO missiles in that country to avoid such an action.

117. Dobbs, *One Minute to Midnight*, p. 291.

118. Mikoyan, *Soviet Cuban Missile Crisis*; and all the conferences in both Blight and Welch, *On the Brink*, and Allyn, Blight, and Welch, *Back to the Brink*. The Americans assumed, until they met decades later with their Soviet counterparts, that it was the Cubans who ordered the U-2 to be shot down.

119. "Robert McNamara's Feud with Admiral George Anderson," in David Coleman, *The Fourteenth Day*, http://jfk14thday.com/tape-mcnamara-anderson/.

120. Munton and Welsh, *Cuban Missile Crisis*, p. 100.

121. Summary record of seventh meeting of ExCom, Oct 27, 1961, FRUS, 1961–1963, vol. 11, doc. 90.

122. There are photos of the *Grozny*, with captions claiming that the Americans fired across its bow, but the authors cannot find any corroboration for this. All indications are that the Soviet ship finally stopped just short of the line and then turned back.

123. See Rusk, *As I Saw It*, p. 240; Dean Rusk oral history, University of Georgia; and *The Fog of War: Eleven Lessons from the Life of Robert S. McNamara*, documentary film, directed by Earl Morris, 2003.

124. Cuban Missile Crisis meeting, Oct 27, 1962, Miller Center, *John F. Kennedy*, vol. 3, p. 471.

125. Ibid., p. 427.

126. Ibid. p. 428.

127. Authors' email correspondence with David Klein, Dec 8, 2012, TFP.

128. This ploy, named after an incident in an Anthony Trollop novel, refers to a situation in which an offer by the proposing party is deliberately misinterpreted by the receiving party, generally to the latter's advantage.

129. State to NATO mission, Oct 28, 1962, FRUS, 1961–1963, vol. 11, doc. 100.

130. According to Bundy, it was JFK, RFK, Bundy, Ball, McNamara, Rusk, Sorensen, and Thompson. See Jim Hershberg, "Anatomy of a Controversy: Anatoly F. Dobrynin's Meeting with RFK, Saturday, October 27, 1962," Bulletin No. 5 (Spring 1995), Cold War International History Project, Wilson Center, http://nsar chive.gwu.edu/nsa/cuba_mis_cri/moment.htm.

131. Arnold R. Horelick, "The Cuban Missile Crisis: An Analysis of Soviet Calculation and Behavior," memorandum RM-3779-PR, Sep 1963, for US Air Force Project Rand, https://www.rand.org/content/dam /rand/pubs/research_memoranda/2008/RM3779.pdf. Horelick (p. 55) cited "the speed and impressive-ness of the U.S. conventional military build-up in the southeastern states and of the alert measures taken by U.S. strategic forces around the world . . . [which] no doubt were carefully noted by Moscow," and adds that this reflected "Khrushchev's December 12, 1962, statement that he took his decision to withdraw Soviet missiles from Cuba after receiving urgent word that a US attack was imminent."

132. It was important that RFK was explicit in stating this letter to Khrushchev wasn't an ultimatum. See Dobrynin, In Confidence.

133. Office schedule for Rusk during the Cuban Missile Crisis, Dean Rusk Personal Papers, University of Georgia.

134. Ibid.; Blight and Welch, On the Brink, p. 174 [this is where, when RFK left the room for a phone call, Dobrynin states that he thought the call was with JFK]; and Garthoff, Reflections on the Cuban Missile Crisis, p. 87. Allyn, Blight, and Welch, in Back to the Brink, p. 93n23, indicate that the phone call was actually from Dean Rusk. It seems to us that Dobrynin may have mixed up his meeting with RFK at the embassy on Octo-ber 26 with his meeting with RFK at the Justice Department on October 27. Blight and Welch, in Back to the Brink, p. 81, note that Dobrynin says his meeting on October 26 was at the Justice Department, when it was the meeting on October 27 that took place there.

135. Rusk, As I Saw It, p. 240.

136. Blight and Welch, On the Brink, p. 174.

137. Rusk, As I Saw It, p. 231; and authors' interview with Tom Hughes, Jun 2013, TFP. Hughes remarked that the secretary of state detested the attorney general.

138. Cable from Dobrynin to Kremlin, Oct 27, 1962, as printed in the appendix of Gross Stein and Lebow, We All Lost, p. 524.

139. Allyn, Blight, and Welsh, Back to the Brink, p. 143n. In this compendium of the proceedings from a 1989 Moscow conference on the Cuban Missile Crisis, Dobrynin claimed that his meeting with RFK was on Friday, October 26. But after a careful scrutiny of the literature, the authors have concluded that Dobrynin had confused it with the one on October 27. Dobrynin uses similar language to describe both occasions. Dobrynin's own book, In Confidence, came out some years after the Moscow conference, and he does not mention the Friday meeting. Further, he states that his book is the "authoritative version of events."

140. Allyn, Blight, and Welsh, Back to the Brink, p. 143.

141. Intriguingly, Dobrynin reported that RFK told him that, besides the Kennedy brothers, only Rusk and Thompson knew about the trade. See Dobrynin to Soviet Foreign Ministry, telegram, Oct 30, 1962, Wilson Center Digital Archive, http://digitalarchive.wilsoncenter.org/document/112633.pdf?v=4cc2dd26cd838141 752bfaee/.

142. Ibid; Garthoff, Reflections; and Mikoyan, Soviet Cuban Missile Crisis.

143. Blight and Welch, On the Brink, p. 174.

144. Mikoyan, Soviet Cuban Missile Crisis, pp. 229–30.

145. "Interview with Alexei Adzhubei and Rada Khrushcheva," p. 5, GW-NSA, http://nsarchive.gwu.edu /NSAEBB/NSAEBB400/docs/Interview%20with%20Adzhubei%20&%20Rada.pdf., also in TFP.

146. Ibid., p. 13.

147. Dobbs, One Minute to Midnight, p. 322.

148. "Interview with Oleg Troyanovski," Episode 10: Cuba, GW-NSA, www.gwu.edu/~nsarchiv/cold war/interviews/episode-10/troyanovski2.html; and Freedman, Kennedy's Wars, p. 217.

149. Raymond L. Garthoff, "Cuban Missile Crisis: The Soviet Story," Foreign Policy, vol. 72 (Fall 1988), pp. 61–80. As Garthoff put it: "Once the exigencies of the situation shifted to a withdrawal of the Soviet missiles, the operative rationale had to be a U.S. guarantee of Cuba's security as a quid pro quo justifying the withdrawal of the Soviet missiles. A reciprocal missile withdrawal was an additional desideratum but not the central element."

150. Dobbs, *One Minute to Midnight*, p. 323.

151. The U-2 was shot down by Colonel Georgy Voronkov, by order of Lieutenant General Stephan Gretchko, who took it upon himself to allow this action after he was unable to find General Issa Pliyev.

152. Mikoyan, *Soviet Cuban Missile Crisis*.

153. N. Khrushchev, *Khrushchev Remembers*, pp. 497–98. The Soviet leader wasn't entirely wrong. The JCS were champing at the bit to strike. For JFK, having drawn a "red line" in not allowing offensive weapons in Cuba, as well as keeping in mind the upcoming midterm elections in the United States, the JCS argument for a preemptive strike on the missiles before they became operational seemed rational.

154. "Interview with Oleg Troyanovski," Episode 10: Cuba, www.gwu.edu/~nsarchiv/coldwar/interviews /episode-10/troyanovski2.html.

155. Authors' interview with Svetlana Savranskaya, Jun 19, 2013, TFP.

156. Mikoyan asserted that it was this, more than the Armageddon letter, that prompted Khrushchev's urgent reply. See Mikoyan, *Soviet Cuban Missile Crisis*, p. 230.

157. "Interview with Oleg Troyanovski," p. 2, Episode 10: Cuba, www.gwu.edu/~nsarchiv/coldwar/inter views/episode-10/troyanovski2.html.

158. Khrushchev letter to JFK, Oct 28, 1962, FRUS, 1961–1963, vol. 6, doc. 68.

159. "Chronologies of the Crisis," Cuban Missile Crisis, 1962: The 40th Anniversary, GW-NSA, http:// nsarchive.gwu.edu/nsa/cuba_mis_cri/chron.htm.

160. See Dobrynin to Soviet Foreign Ministry, telegram, Oct 30, 1962, Wilson Center Digital Archive, http://digitalarchive.wilsoncenter.org/document/112633.pdf?v=4cc2dd26cd838141752bfaee/; Dobbs, *One Minute to Midnight*, p. 338; and S. Hersh, *Dark Side of Camelot*, p. 382.

161. N. Khrushchev, *Khrushchev Remembers*.

162. Authors' interview with Svetlana Savranskaya, Jun 19, 2013, TFP.

163. Authors' telephone interview with Sergei Khrushchev, Oct 29, 2012, TFP.

164. Bundy, *Danger and Survival*, pp. 409–10.

165. The story told to the authors was that JFK wanted to give each of the ExCom members something to remember their days in it by. He instructed his personal secretary, Mrs. Evelyn Lincoln, to find something they'd keep but that would not cost much.

166. Memo from Nitze to Kennedy, [undated], FRUS, 1961–1963, vol. 15, doc. 149, p. 411n1.

167. Memo from Rostow to Bundy, Nov 9, 1962, FRUS, 1961–1963, vol. 15, doc. 151, with attachment "Possible Berlin Solutions," drafted by Thompson.

168. His idea was the possibility of leasing the Autobahn, in an arrangement modeled after the Soviet lease of the Finnish Canal.

169. Memo from Rostow to Bundy, Nov 9, 1962, FRUS, 1961–1963, vol. 15, doc. 151, with attachment "Possible Berlin Solutions," drafted by Thompson.

170. Authors' interview with Sergei Khrushchev, Jul 10, 2010, TFP.

171. Thompson letter to SecState, Oct 31, 1962, folder: chron file, Ambassador Thompson 1962, box 22, entry AI-5008, records of Ambassador-at-Large Thompson, 1961–1970, RG 59, NACP.

172. John J. McCloy was also chairman of the Coordinating Committee for US-Soviet Negotiations over Cuba at the UN.

173. Garthoff, *Reflections*, p. 108; and Chang and Kornbluh, *Cuban Missile Crisis, 1962*, p. 396.

174. Bundy, *Danger and Survival*, 407.

175. Mikoyan, *Soviet Cuban Missile Crisis*, p. 169.

176. For a thorough description of this series of events, see Mikoyan, *Soviet Cuban Missile Crisis*.

177. Thompson oral history, Mar 25, 1964, JFKL.

178. The suggestion was in Khrushchev's telegram to Mikoyan on November 22, 1962. See Mikoyan, *Soviet Cuban Missile Crisis*, p. 493; and Thompson telephone call to Bundy, Nov 28, 1962, JFKL.

179. The official reason for not providing the noninvasion guarantee was that Cuba would not allow US inspections to verify that all weapons had been removed.

180. A Cuba invasion was still on the table as late as 1975, proffered by Secretary of State Henry Kissinger, after Castro's decision to send troops to Angola. See LeoGrande and Kornbluh, *Back Channel to Cuba*.

181. Thompson [and other witnesses to JFK's encounter with Khrushchev at their 1961 meeting] never

believed that JFK had been "beaten" in the Vienna summit. On the contrary, Thompson thought JFK's resolve over Berlin and Germany had sent the right message to Khrushchev.

182. One such advisor was Marshal Rodion Malinovsky, the Soviet minister of defense. See Allyn, Blight, and Welsh, *Back to the Brink*, p. 38.

183. Thompson letter to Undersecretary of State, Dec 12, 1966, folder: chron file, Jan 1966, box 20, entry A1-5008, records of Ambassador-at-Large Thompson, 1961–1970, RG 59, NACP, also in TFP.

184. Authors' interview with Sergei Khrushchev, Jul 10, 2010, TFP.

185. Although this idea was variously attributed to McGeorge Bundy, RFK, Ted Sorensen, and probably others, in later years both Robert McNamara and Dean Rusk said it was a proposal by Thompson, stated in a closed meeting, that was later presented to the entire ExCom group. Thompson would have claimed that this idea was widely discussed, and that where it originated was not as important as the final decision that was taken to follow it.

186. Svetlana Savranskaya statement to the authors, Feb 2015.

187. See the cable for George Ball, in New York City, in Garthoff, *Reflections*, pp. 212–13. Garthoff helped to draw up the State Department's position on the IL-28s and would become an important colleague of Thompson's during the disarmament negotiations.

188. Thompson oral history, Mar 25, 1964, JFKL.

189. Authors' email correspondence with David Klein, Dec 9, 2012, TFP.

190. Stewart Alsop, "Affairs of State: Let the Poor Old Foreign Service Alone," *Saturday Evening Post*, Mar 11, 1967.

191. Dobbs, *One Minute to Midnight*, p. 353.

28 ≋ Limited Test Ban

1. Thompson oral history, Apr 27, 1966, JFKL.

2. Andreas Wender and Marcel Gerber, "John F. Kennedy and the Limited Test Ban Treaty: A Case Study of Presidential Leadership," *Presidential Studies Quarterly*, vol. 29, no. 2 (June 1999), pp. 460–487.

3. Thompson to SecState, subject: Khrushchev's speech, Jan 16, 1963, JFKL, also in TFP [first page only]

4. Ibid.

5. Thompson to SecState, Mar 7, 1963, and Mar 26, 1963, FRUS, 1961–1963, vol. 15, docs. 180 and 182.

6. Thompson to SecState, Jan 9, 1963, FRUS, 1961–1963, vol. 15, doc. 166.

7. Thompson to SecState, on his last meeting with Khrushchev, cable 227, Jul 26, 1962, 611.61, XR-121.612, RG 59, NACP, also in TFP.

8. Thompson memo to William Foster, Nov 23, 1963, TFP. Although written later than the events discussed here, the memo summarizes Thompson's thoughts on the matter.

9. Seaborg, *Test Ban*, p. 8. It turned out to be much more powerful than predicted—a thousand times more powerful than the bomb dropped on Hiroshima.

10. National Cancer Institute and Centers for Disease Control and Prevention, "Report on the Health Consequences to the American Population from Nuclear Weapons Tests Conducted by the United States and Other Nations," 2001, Centers for Disease Control, https://www.cdc.gov/nceh/radiation/fallout/default.htm; and William Burr and Hector Montford, eds., "The Making of the Limited Test Ban Treaty, 1958–1963," Aug 8, 2003, GW-NSA, http://nsarchive.gwu.edu/NSAEBB/NSAEBB94/.

11. Editorial note, Apr 13, 1959, FRUS, 1958–1960, vol. 3 (*National Security Policy; Arms Control and Disarmament*), doc. 212.

12. To signal his seriousness, JFK established the Arms Control and Disarmament Agency within the State Department and set up a new cabinet position: a special advisor on disarmament, filled by John J. McCloy.

13. Thompson memo to Rusk, Jun 8, 1961, FRUS, 1961–1963, vol. 7 (*Arms Control and Disarmament*), doc. 33.

14. A. Schlesinger, *A Thousand Days*.

15. Seaborg, *Test Ban*, p. 76.

16. A. Schlesinger, *A Thousand Days*, p. 459.

17. Bundy memo, Jul 28, 1961, FRUS, 1961–1963, vol. 7, doc. 46.

18. JFK to Harold Macmillan, Aug 3, 1961, FRUS, 1961–1963, vol. 7, doc. 50.

19. A. Schlesinger, *A Thousand Days*, p. 459; and US delegation to Geneva conference to State, Jun 12, 1961, FRUS, 1961–1963, vol. 7, doc. 34.

20. Seaborg, *Test Ban*, p. 84.

21. A. Schlesinger, *A Thousand Days*, p. 459.

22. Tal, *American Nuclear Disarmament Dilemma*, p. 182.

23. JFK, "Address to the United Nations General Assembly," Sep 25, 1961, JFKL, https://www.jfklibrary .org/Asset-Viewer/DOPIN64xJUGRKgdHJ9NfgQ.aspx.

24. The concern was that the 1961 Soviet tests had made progress toward an antimissile missile, so the United States had to catch up.

25. JFK meeting with Thompson, Aug 8, 1962, in Miller Center, *John F. Kennedy*, vol. 1, pp. 261–72.

26. Foster to Bundy, [undated], and editorial note, FRUS, 1961–1963, vol. 7, docs. 223 and 224.

27. Khrushchev to JFK, Sep 4, 1962, FRUS, 1961–1963, vol. 6, doc. 53; and JFK to Khrushchev, Sep 15, 1962, FRUS, 1961–1963, vol. 6, doc. 55.

28. The Pugwash conferences "seek to bring scientific reason to the threat of weapons of mass destruction." See Pugwash Conferences on Science and World Affairs, https://pugwash.org/about-pugwash/.

29. Meeting on the Soviet Union, Sep 29, 1962, Miller Center, *John F. Kennedy*, vol. 2, pp. 208–14.

30. JFK to Khrushchev, Oct 28, 1962, FRUS, 1961–1963, vol. 6, doc. 69.

31. Khrushchev to JFK, Oct 30, 1962, FRUS, 1961–1963, vol. 6, doc. 71. Also see Voijtech Mastny, "The 1963 Nuclear Test Ban Treaty," *Journal of Cold War Studies*, vol. 10, no. 1 (Winter 2008), pp. 3–25.

32. Khrushchev letter to JFK, Dec 19, 1962, FRUS, 1961–1963, vol. 6, doc. 85.

33. Wiesner tried to set up a bargain where Khrushchev would propose three or four inspections, then JFK would come back with seven or eight, and they would settle for something in the middle. See Seaborg, *Kennedy, Khrushchev*, p. 180. Thompson also thought that only a very small number of inspections were needed, because he believed that the Soviets would not run the risk of exposure. See Thompson oral history, Apr 27, 1966, p. 18/5, JFKL. On Arthur H. Dean's resignation at the end of the year, see editorial note, FRUS, 1961–1963, vol. 7, doc. 252.

34. MemCon, Jan 9, 1963, FRUS, 1961–1963, vol. 7, doc. 255.

35. MemCon, Jan 20, 1963, FRUS, 1961–1963, vol. 5, doc. 281, p. 611n1.

36. MemCon by Thompson to SecState, Bundy, and Foster, Jan 19, 1963, in Thompson-Dobrynin talks, TFP; and Dobrynin talks, [dated Jan 21, 1963, at top of page], NSF: countries series, JFKL.

37. Dobrynin, *In Confidence*, p. 100.

38. JFK letter to Khrushchev, Dec 28, 1962, FRUS, 1961–1963, vol. 6, doc. 87.

39. Thompson oral history, Apr 27, 1966, JFKL.

40. Thompson, comments on draft paper about intelligence disclosure to the Soviets, "Top Secret," Feb 13, 1963, TFP; and Thompson to U. A. Johnson, Feb 21, 1963, TFP.

41. Dobrynin claimed that Seaborg told him, with regret, that he had been the one who had convinced JFK to bargain for more inspections. If Seaborg had known that Khrushchev would take back even the three he had offered, Seaborg would have advised the president to accept. See Dobrynin, *In Confidence*, p. 102.

42. Notes of JFK's remarks, Jan 22, 1963, FRUS, 1961–1963, vol. 11, doc. 271.

43. Coordinator of Cuban affairs memo to ExCom, Jan 24, 1963, FRUS, 1961–1963, vol. 11, doc. 272.

44. Summary record of thirty-eighth ExCom meeting, Jan 25, 1963, FRUS, 1961–1963, vol. 11, doc. 274.

45. Thompson to Rusk, Mar 2, 1963, FRUS, 1961–1963, vol. 5, doc. 301.

46. Thompson to Rusk, Mar 21, 1963, FRUS, 1961–1963, vol. 5, doc. 306.

47. This argument is presented by Tal, *American Nuclear Disarmament Dilemma*, p. 223.

48. Seaborg, *Test Ban*, p. 208.

49. Macmillan's ambassador to the United States, David Ormsby Gore, had left the letter with Carl Kaysen. See editorial note, FRUS, 1961–1963, vol. 7, doc. 267.

50. TelCon with Kaysen and Ball, Mar 19, 1963, 4:25 p.m., JFKL.

51. Thompson to Rusk, Mar 21, 1963, FRUS, 1961–1963, vol. 7, doc. 268.

52. Germany would gain nuclear capability either through a Franco-German treaty or a multinational NATO force.

53. JFK to Macmillan, Mar 28, 1963, FRUS, 1961–1963, vol. 7, doc. 269.

54. The mission members were Averell Harriman and Lord Hailsham.

55. RFK memo to JFK, Apr 3, 1963, FRUS, 1961–1963, vol. 6, doc. 94.

56. Thompson to Dean Rusk, George Ball, LBJ, and Tom Hughes, "Top Secret," Apr 2, 1963, TFP.

57. Meeting on nuclear test ban, Apr 5 [mislabeled Apr 2], 1963, tapes 79.2 and 79.3, Miller Center, secret White House tapes, https://millercenter.org/the-presidency/secret-white-house-tapes/meeting-nuclear-test-ban-0/ and https://millercenter.org/the-presidency/secret-white-house-tapes/meeting-nuclear-test-ban-1/; and White House memo for the record, April 6, 1963, TFP, also in McGeorge Bundy Papers, JFKL.

58. Meeting on nuclear test ban, Apr 5 [mislabeled Apr 2], 1963, tapes 79.2 and 79.3, Miller Center, secret White House tapes, https://millercenter.org/the-presidency/secret-white-house-tapes/meeting-nuclear-test-ban-0/ and https://millercenter.org/the-presidency/secret-white-house-tapes/meeting-nuclear-test-ban-1/; and White House memo for the record, April 6, 1963, TFP, also in McGeorge Bundy Papers, JFKL.

59. Thompson memo to Rusk, Apr 5, 1963, entry A1-5196, special US-USSR file, pen-pal series, 963l, vol. 2, presidential SecState correspondence with heads of state 1943–72, RG 39, NACP.

60. MemCon: Dobrynin and Thompson, Apr 6, 1963, TFP.

61. JFK to Khrushchev, Apr 11, 1963, FRUS, 1961–1963, vol. 6, doc. 95.

62. Macmillan to JFK, Apr 3, 1963, FRUS, 1961–1963, vol. 7, doc. 271.

63. Norman Cousins visit to Soviet Union, Apr 22, 1963, TFP.

64. Douglass, *Kennedy and the Unspeakable*, p. 345.

65. Ibid.; and Norman Cousins visit to Soviet Union, Apr 22, 1963, TFP.

66. Norman Cousins visit to Soviet Union, Apr 22, 1963, TFP.

67. Thompson to Rusk, "Eyes Only," with copies to Ball and Bundy, Apr 24, 1963, TFP.

68. Fursenko and Naftali, *Khrushchev's Cold War*, p. 520.

69. State to US embassy in Moscow, cable 2191, April 15, 1963, FRUS, 1961–1963, vol. 6, doc. 96. It was not delivered to Khrushchev until April 24, by Kohler and British Ambassador Humphrey Trevelyan. See Kohler to State, cable 2719, Apr 24, 1963, FRUS, 1961–1963, vol. 7, doc. 280.

70. The lectures were part of the commitments [which had been postponed during the Cuban Missile Crisis] attached to Thompson's Rockefeller Public Service Award.

71. Summary record of 512th NSA meeting, Apr 20, 1963, FRUS, 1961–1963, vol. 24, doc. 459.

72. Several scholars have concluded that Averell Harriman was the special JFK representative that resulted from the April 5 meeting, but he was not. Harriman's trip to Moscow was related to Laos, and he was not given instructions to talk about the other matters that were bothering Khrushchev. That was left to Rusk.

73. MemCon: nuclear test ban and Germany, Apr 26, 1963, FRUS, 1961–1963, vol. 15, doc. 186.

74. Khrushchev to JFK, [undated], FRUS, 1961–1963, vol. 6, doc. 98.

75. TelCon with Thompson and Ball, Apr 29, 1963, JFKL.

76. Ibid.; and Dobrynin, *In Confidence*, p. 101. Dobrynin said that Rusk was also Thompson's choice.

77. See Thompson letters to Kohler, May 1, 10, and 23, 1963, as well as Thompson letter to Bohlen, May 27, 1963, all in TFP.

78. Dobrynin, *In Confidence*, p. 102.

79. Khrushchev to JFK, May 8, 1963, FRUS, 1961–1963, vol. 6, doc. 99.

80. Carl Kaysen oral history, second session, pp. 117–18, JFKL. According to Kaysen, John J. McCloy was the first choice, but McCloy didn't want it, because he didn't think the administration was serious. See TelCon with Bundy and Ball, Jun 11, 1963, JFKL. Rusk then suggested Harriman. Jane was angry that her husband had not been picked, but Thompson said that it was "awkward for his [Thompson's] successor for an ambassador to return on a special mission of that sort." See Thompson oral history, Apr 27, 1966, JFKL. Given Harriman's experience, it was quite natural that he was selected.

81. Thompson letter to Kohler, May 1, 1963, TFP.

82. Thomas Godby oral history, JFKL. Godby was incorrect in saying that Thompson had rejected an attempt *at an LTB* back in March and April. Thompson had only pointed out that the Soviets would not accept *a CTB agreement* (which would require inspections) while their quarrel with the Chinese was going on, which took precedence for them.

83. Thompson-Dobrynin talks, May 17, 1963, TFP, also in LBJL; and Thompson oral history, Apr 27, 1966, JFKL.

84. See Thompson to Rusk, May 20, 1963, TFP.

85. MemCon: Rusk and Dobrynin, May 18, 1963, FRUS, 1961–1963, vol. 7, doc. 287, also in FRUS, 1961–1963, vol. 5, doc. 323; and Rusk, *As I Saw It*, p. 257.

86. Carl Kaysen oral history, JFKL.

87. Authors' telephone interview with Ted Sorensen, Feb 2010, TFP.

88. According to Bundy's assistant, Carl Kaysen, who was the one tasked with getting the speech looked at, these individuals were Dean Rusk, Adrian S. Fisher, probably Adam Yarmolinsky from the Pentagon, Arthur M. Schlesinger, McGeorge Bundy, and Carl Kaysen. Also see memo for the record, Jun 13, 1963, McGeorge Bundy Papers, JFKL.

89. Thompson oral history, Apr 27, 1966, p. 20/7, JFKL.

90. Commencement address at the American University, Washington, DC, Jun 10, 1963, JFKL, https://www.jfklibrary.org/Asset-Viewer/BWC7I4C9QUmLG9J6I8oy8w.aspx.

91. Seaborg, *Test Ban*, p. 218.

92. Reeves, *President Kennedy*, pp. 538–39.

93. For an intriguing paper on the way psychological gestures initiated by one nation will be reciprocated by others, with the effect of reducing international tension, see Amitai Etzioni, "The Kennedy Experiment," *Western Political Quarterly*, vol. 20, no. 2, pt. 1, (June 1967), pp. 361–80.

94. Editorial note, Jul 2, 1963, FRUS, 1961–1963, vol. 7, doc. 309.

95. Thompson oral history, Apr 27, 1966, JFKL.

96. Summary record of 515th NSC meeting, Jul 9, 1963, FRUS, 1961–1963, vol. 7, doc. 318, including p. 784n10.

97. TelCon with Ball and Thompson, Jun 25, 1963, 6:05 a.m., JFKL.

98. TelCon with Thompson and Ball, Jul 16, 1963, 3:10 p.m., JFKL.

99. See JFK's daily dairy, JFKL.

100. Executive secretary memo to Rusk, Ball, Thompson, and Foster, Jul 10, 1963, TFP.

101. Reeves, *President Kennedy*, p. 545; and Carl Kaysen oral history, JFKL.

102. Seaborg, *Test Ban*, p. 245. For example, peaceful uses of nuclear detonations could be for mining and construction projects, such as those proposed in Operation Plowshare.

103. With China in mind, the clause sought to establish a procedure to withdraw from the treaty if some country set off a nuclear detonation that jeopardized national security. The Soviets felt it was their right to abrogate *any* treaty that jeopardized their national security and therefore did not need to have this spelled out.

104. For the kids' version: The only memories the authors have of that weekend was that Sherry didn't want to play with Caroline Kennedy, because all Caroline wanted to do was hide from her Secret Service escort. Jenny only remembers that she didn't want to eat the clams and got menacing looks from her mother.

105. Newspaper articles in TFP; JFK's daily dairy, JFKL; Thompson oral history, Apr 27, 1966, JFKL; and authors' interview with Ted Sorensen, Feb 2010, TFP.

106. Besides the JCS, many others were opposed the treaty simply because it would be a plus for JFK, or because they were opposed to his policy on civil rights.

107. Timothy Naftali presentation for Arms Control Association panel, 50th Anniversary of the Limited Test Ban Treaty, part 1, http://www.youtube.com/watch?v=x_OgBTJOV5M/.

108. JFK address to the nation on the test ban treaty, Jul 26, 1963, JFKL.

109. TelCon: Ball and Thompson, Jul 25, 1963, JFKL.

110. The original drafters were Thomas Pickering and James Goodby.

111. See Thompson conversation with JFK on the Rusk trip, Aug 15, 1963, tape 106, presidential recordings, JFKL. Also see Rusk to State, Moscow, Aug 9, 1963, FRUS, 1961–1963, vol. 5, doc. 345.

112. Rusk to State, Aug 10, 1963, FRUS, 1961–1963, vol. 5, doc. 348.

113. Thompson memo, "Miscellaneous Information Garnered during Secretary's Visit to the Soviet Union, August 3–10," Aug 12, 1963, TFP.

114. Editorial note, FRUS, 1961–1963, vol. 5, doc. 349.

115. This process began on August 8, 1963.

116. Taylor, *Swords and Plowshares*, p. 286.

117. Khrushchev letter to JFK, Aug 17, 1963, FRUS, 1961–1963, vol. 6, doc. 115.

118. State to US embassy in Vietnam, cable 243, Aug 24, 1963, FRUS, 1961–1963, vol. 3 (*Vietnam, January to August 1963*), doc. 281. Roger Hilsman was the assistant secretary of state for Far Eastern affairs.

119. MemCon, Aug 26, 1963, FRUS, 1961–1963, vol. 5, doc. 350.

120. Thompson memo to Bundy, Jan 28, 1963, TFP.

121. The Soviets used the USSR's UN teletype line for any of their urgent business, but the Americans had nothing comparable in Moscow.

122. Thompson memo for JFK, Oct 8, 1963, TFP.

123. Johnson, *Vantage Point*, p. 287.

124. Dobrynin, *In Confidence*, p. 106.

125. Schick, *Berlin Crisis*.

126. Jean Edward Smith, "Berlin: The Erosion of a Principle," *Reporter*, Nov 21, 1963, pp. 32–37, https://www.unz.org/Pub/Reporter-1963nov21-00032/. In the article, Smith reports that the US troops were in a rush, because they were to join Vice President Johnson in Berlin at noon.

127. State to US embassy in Moscow, FRUS, 1961–1963, vol. 15, doc. 220, p. 594n1.

128. Gromyko used the term "spirit of Moscow" during his talk with JFK, referring to the atmosphere after the LTB treaty. See Oct 10, 1963, tape 115/A51, reel 3, presidential recordings, JFKL.

129. Ibid., tape 115/A51.l.

130. Ibid., tape 115/51.2.2.

131. A full combat brigade was still in Cuba, but it would not be "discovered" until 1979, during Jimmy Carter's administration.

132. Thompson-Dobrynin conversation, Oct 11, 1963, JFKL, also in TFP.

133. MemCon: Thompson and Dobrynin, holdup of US convoy on Autobahn, Oct 11, 1963, JFKL, also in TFP.

134. MemConf with JFK, Oct 11, 1963, FRUS, 1961–1963, vol. 15, doc. 224. The authors listened to a tape of this conversation. It illustrates Thompson's participation, which is not reflected in the FRUS document.

135. Schick, *Berlin Crisis*. The trouble started when the Soviets stopped a test convoy that should have complied with the recently agreed-upon procedures, but the Americans refused to dismount. Thompson suggested that the British and the French send similar convoys, so the Soviets would either have to engage all the allies or let these nations' vehicles proceed. The Soviets let the British and French convoys through first, and eventually the American one as well. Shortly thereafter, the Soviets forwarded slightly amended but still acceptable rules. Theirs was the last word, and this was the last incident. See John Ausland, "Six Berlin Incidents, 1961–64: A Case Study in the Management of U.S. Policy Regarding a National Security Problem," Senior Seminar in Foreign Policy, 1965, GW-NSA; and Ausland, *Kennedy, Khrushchev*.

136. Thompson oral history, Apr 27, 1966, JFKL.

137. "The committee [US House of Representatives, Select Committee on Assassinations] believes, on the basis of the evidence available to it, that President John F. Kennedy was probably assassinated as a result of a conspiracy. The committee is unable to identify the other gunman or the extent of the conspiracy." See "Summary of Findings in the Assassination of President Kennedy," National Archives, https://www.archives.gov/research/jfk/select-committee-report/summary.html#kennedy/.

138. Dobrynin, *In Confidence*.

139. Thompson letter to David Bruce [US ambassador to the United Kingdom], Nov 23, 1963, TFP, also in JFKL.

140. Thompson testimony, Warren et al., *Hearings*, vol. 5, p. 572. Also see Dobrynin, *In Confidence*, p. 108: "Oswald was deemed quarrelsome and shiftless. . . . He was left alone because of his mediocrity and shrewishness."

141. Dobrynin, *In Confidence*.

142. Thompson memo to Rusk, Nov 24, 1963, FRUS, 1961–1963, vol. 5, doc. 379.

143. Dobrynin, *In Confidence*, p. 109.

144. It would be an instructive project for some scholar to get all the memos of conversations between Thompson and Dobrynin, written by both men, and compare them. The authors tried, without success, to get the Soviet MemCons from the Russian archives.

145. Bundy memo for the record, Dec 18, 1963, FRUS, 1961–1963, vol. 5, doc. 388.

1. Stewart Alsop, "The Face of the President, 1966," *Saturday Evening Post*, Sep 24, 1966, pp. 23–25.

2. David Halberstam interview with Thompson, Halberstam Papers, Howard Gotlieb Archival Research Center, Boston University, also in TFP.

3. LBJ said this when he expressed reluctance to have Thompson leave Washington, DC, and go to Moscow as an ambassador to the USSR, because the president was comfortable with him as his advisor on Soviet affairs. See conversation, Sep 29, 1966, tape WH6609.13, Miller Center, secret White House tapes, https://millercenter.org/the-presidency/secret-white-house-tapes/conversation-robert-mcnamara-september -29-1966/, transcript in TFP.

4. Great Society programs included the Civil Rights Act; the War on Poverty; federal funding for elementary and secondary education; Head Start; Medicare and Medicaid; welfare; and food programs, such as food stamps and school nutrition programs. It also went further, with something for everyone, encompassing the arts and culture, protections for consumers and the environment, and even mass transit projects.

5. This metaphor is borrowed from Francis M. Bator, "The Politics of Alliance: The United States and Western Europe," in Gordon, *Agenda for the Nation*, pp. 335–36.

6. See Thompson memos to Rusk, [no subject], Jan 26, 1963, and "US Political, Economic, and Military Policy in Europe," Feb 27, 1963, TFP, also in Thompson lot file 64 D 653, RG 59, NACP.

7. General Charles de Gaulle made a number of other unfriendly moves. For example, he thwarted US actions toward a North Atlantic free trade area and in monetary reforms; pushed for replacing the dollar by gold in the International Monetary Fund's Central Bank reserves; refused to grant the United Kingdom membership in the European Economic Community; and, regarding the fate of Europe, made overtures to explore a German-French alliance, cutting out the United States, as well as a unilateral one with the Soviet Union.

8. Secretary of State Rusk, Undersecretary George Ball, and Deputy National Security Advisor John McCloy made up this powerful lobby. See Bator, "Lyndon Johnson and Foreign Policy," in Lobel, *Presidential Judgment*, pp. 51–55.

9. Thompson to SecState, Jan 26, 1963, TFP; and Thompson to SecState, Feb 27, 1963, TFP, also in Thompson lot file 64 D 653, RG 59, NACP.

10. Bohlen, *Witness to History*, pp. 508–9.

11. Thompson to Rusk, Jan 26, 1963, TFP, also in Thompson lot file 64 D 653, RG 59, NACP.

12. Ibid.

13. Bator, "Politics of Alliance," in Gordon, *Agenda for the Nation*, p. 335. Bator also stated (p. 339n1), "We tend to forget that, while Europe is rich, it is not nearly as rich as the United States."

14. Thompson letter to Fulbright, with attached talking points, Feb 6, 1964, TFP.

15. "Microphones Found in U.S. Embassy," *Southeast Missourian* [Cape Girardeau, MO], May 20, 1964. Also see Kohler to State, embtel 3241, April 29, 1964, FRUS, 1964–1968, vol. 14, doc. 30.

16. Thompson speech to members of the Foreign Ministry and Parliamentary Foreign Relations Committees, Vienna, Jun 10, 1964, TFP.

17. The secret committee was established under Eisenhower, to deal with covert activities that had begun before the approval of NSC 5412/2. See National Security Council directive on covert operations, NSC 5412, Mar 15, 1954, and NSC directive 5412/2, [undated], both in FRUS, retrospective volume, *The Intelligence Community, 1950–1955*, docs. 171 and 250. This group was where Robert F. Kennedy later led the planning for illegal activities against Fidel Castro.

18. Peter Jessup, an NSC staff member, stated that the group was exposed in Wise and Ross's *The Invisible Government* and suggested that "there seems to be some merit in changing the name of the Special Group." See Jessup memo to Bundy, FRUS, 1964–1968, vol. 33 (*Organization and Management of Foreign Policy; United Nations*), doc. 203. The 303 Committee was rumored to have been named for the room number where it met (see Ranelagh, *The Agency*, p. 279; and Goldman, *Central Intelligence Agency*, p. 362), with its original designation having come from the number of the National Security Action memo that created it. See NSA memo no. 303, FRUS, 1964–1968, vol. 33, doc. 204.

19. When expedient, however, the US intelligence apparatus would bypass the 303 Committee for certain activities that met these criteria. See testimony for the Frank Church Committee hearings, May 1976, in

Church and Senate Select Committee, *Final Report*. For a full explanation and proof of the defensive nature of the 303 Committee meetings, see Richard Helms speech, Oct 14, 1965, TFP.

20. The authors have made several Freedom of Information Act requests for these notes but have never received a reply.

21. For example, Thompson opposed the reactivation of the CIA's paramilitary effort against Cuba in 1965 and was in favor of ending US involvement in the Congo in 1966. During the 1964 attempt by the United States to influence the elections in Chile, documents show that Thompson's limited participation was cautionary. On Cuba, see excerpt from the minutes of the 303 Committee, Jun 10, 1965, attached to Gordon Case memo to Bundy, Jun 25, 1965, and memo to the president, Jun 26, 1965, both in NSF: McGeorge Bundy file, box 3, vol. 2, LBJL. On the Congo, see Jessup memo to Rostow, subject: 303 Committee, Nov 2, 1966, NSF: Intel file, box 2, 303 Committee, LBJL. On Chile, see Jessup memo for the record, FRUS, 1964–1968, vol. 31 (*South and Central America; Mexico*), doc. 267, p. 589n5; and editorial note, FRUS, 1964–1968, vol. 31, doc. 269.

22. TelCon: Harriman and Thompson, Sep 11, 1964, Averell Harriman Papers, LC.

23. This experience in the art world helped Jane after Thompson died and she needed a real income.

24. Ray Cline memo for the record, Oct 16, 1964, FRUS, 1964–1968, vol. 14 (*Soviet Union*), doc. 53.

25. Thompson letter to Myron Rush, RAND Corporation, Sep 6, 1963, TFP.

26. Briefing by Thompson, Oct 20, 1964, FRUS, 1964–1968, vol. 14, doc. 61.

27. Ray Cline memo for the record, Oct 16, 1964, FRUS, 1964–1968, vol. 14, doc. 53.

28. MemCon, Oct 16, 1964, FRUS, 1964–1968, vol. 14, doc. 55; and briefing by Thompson, Oct 20, 1964, FRUS, 1964–1968, vol. 14, doc. 61.

29. See aggregated official results of all past US presidential elections, Dave Leip's Atlas of U.S. Presidential Elections, http://uselectionatlas.org/RESULTS/.

30. David Halberstam interview with James Lloyd Greenfield, Halberstam Papers, Boston University.

30 ≋ Strand One: Vietnam (1962–1967)

1. For books on Vietnam, see Gibbons, *U.S. Government and the Vietnam War*, vols. 2, 3, and 4; Halberstam, *Best and the Brightest*; VanDeMark, *Into the Quagmire*; and Hoopes, *Limits of Intervention*.

2. See Goldstein, *Lessons in Disaster*.

3. Ibid., p. 167.

4. "Mr. McNamara's War," *New York Times*, Apr 12, 1995.

5. Afghans, armed with the same types of scanty equipment, were also a formidable force against the Soviets and, later, the Americans.

6. Lee Lescaze, "My Vietnam Policy Was a Terrible Mistake" [reviewing McNamara's book, *In Retrospect*], *Wall Street Journal*, Apr 14, 1995; McNamara, *In Retrospect*, appendix.

7. McNamara, *In Retrospect*, preface, p. xx.

8. Ibid., p. 32; and *The Fog of War: Eleven Lessons from the Life of Robert S. McNamara*, documentary film, directed by Earl Morris, 2003.

9. McNamara, *In Retrospect*, p. 101.

10. Stephen Kinzer, *The Brothers*, pp. 126, 203, 218 [for the quotation].

11. The Geneva Conference, which ended in the signing of these accords, took place from April 26 to July 20, 1954.

12. This might explain why Hanoi showed a stubborn refusal to negotiate, believing that a settlement would not necessarily be honored. This idea was put forth by Fulbright, *Arrogance of Power*, p. 117.

13. One should not underestimate the role Cardinal Spellman played in rallying support for Ngo Dinh Diem, a Roman Catholic.

14. Halberstam, *Best and the Brightest*, p. 77.

15. Beschloss, *Crisis Years*, p. 676.

16. Madame Nhu's letter appeared in the *Chicago Tribune*, Nov 25, 1963.

17. South Vietnam had eight heads of state between 1963 and 1969.

18. Bundy condolence letter to Jane, 1972, TFP. Talking to his advisors, LBJ referred to Vietnam as "a piddling, piss-ant little country."

19. Halberstam, *Best and the Brightest*, p. 523. In Halberstam's notes from his interview with Thompson, the wording is slightly different, as "He regrets he didn't fight harder at the time." See David Halberstam interview with Thompson, Halberstam Papers, Boston University, also in TFP.

31 ≋ Thompson's Vietnam

Epigraph. Francis Bacon, aphorism 46, *Novum Organum Scientarium*, 1620.

1. Thompson was in Colorado from the end of July to August 20, 1964, but he was recalled to Washington, DC, on August 4 for five days. See Thompson's daily diary, TFP.

2. The name DESOTO stands for DEHAVEN Special Operations off Tsingtao, after the first such patrol to gather signal-based intelligence in hostile waters.

3. Memo for Bundy and Thompson, operation plan 34-A for approval of leaflet dropping, NSF: Vietnam, box 52, vol. 3, LBJL.

4. The reference is to a document prepared at the time, with a chronology of the incident, by the Department of Defense's Joint Reconnaissance Center and sent to the White House on August 10, as cited in Gibbons, *US Government and the Vietnam War*, vol. 2, p. 284.

5. The decision to send the USS *Maddox* was made on Wednesday, July 15, 1964, by the NSC, but the 303 Committee was not scheduled to meet until Thursday, July 16. The Thursday meeting was crossed out as canceled in Thompson's daily dairy, so he would not have attended the July 16 meeting, if one did indeed take place. For more details on the *Maddox*, see Gibbons, *US Government and the Vietnam War*, vol. 2, p. 285.

6. Ibid., pp. 282–86.

7. "History of Cold War Intelligence Activities," Nov 14, 2008, *National Security Archive Electronic Briefing Book No. 280*, GW-NSA, http://nsarchive.gwu.edu/NSAEBB/NSAEBB260/index.htm.

8. The August 10, 1964, resolution gave LBJ the authority to assist any Southeast Asian country whose government was considered to be jeopardized by Communist aggression.

9. Thompson's daily dairy, TFP, also in NSF: NSC meetings, vol. 3, tab. 20, LBJL; and summary notes of 538th meeting of NSC, FRUS, 1964–1968, vol. 1 (*Vietnam, 1964*), doc. 278.

10. Thompson memo to Bundy, Feb 1, 1965, FRUS, 1964–1968, vol. 14, doc. 89; and Raymond Garthoff, "The Aborted US-USSR Summit of 1965," *Brookings Institution Newsletter*, Jun 2001, also in TFP.

11. As an example, see Gibbons, *US Government and the Vietnam War*, vol. 2, pp. 216–17.

12. Lyndon B. Johnson, "Why We Are in Viet-Nam," president's news conference, Jul 28, 1965, American Presidency Project, www.presidency.ucsb.edu/ws/index.php?pid=27116/.

13. The South Vietnamese government's name for the National Liberation Front was the Viet Cong. The two were, in effect, the same thing.

14. TelCon: Bundy and Ball, Feb 3, 1965, George Ball Papers, box 7, Vietnam file 1 (1/5/65–5/24/65), LBJL, also in TFP.

15. David Halberstam interview with Thompson, Halberstam Papers, Boston University.

16. There had been previous attacks directed against Americans—at Bien Hoa Airport on November 1, 1964, and Brinks Billet on December 24, 1964—where LBJ had not acted, underscoring the US response to the attack at Pleiku as a virtual change in policy.

17. VanDerMark, *Into the Quagmire*, p. 62.

18. TelCon, Feb 6, 1965, George Ball Papers, box 7, Vietnam file 1, LBJL, also in TFP. In that phone call, Smith told Ball it would be an off-the-record meeting, and Ball said he would bring Thompson along with him. There was, however, a record made of that meeting. See McCone memo for the record, Feb 6, 1965, FRUS, 1964–1968, vol. 2, doc. 77.

19. According to William Bundy, his brother recommended reprisal strikes before he had actually gone to Pleiku. William dispelled the idea that McGeorge made the recommendation solely because of an emotional reaction to what he saw there. See William Bundy oral history, LBJL.

20. McNamara, *In Retrospect*, p. 171.

21. Summary notes of 546th meeting of NSC, Feb 7, 1965, FRUS, 1964–1968, vol. 2 (*Vietnam, January–June 1965*), doc. 80.

22. MemCon: Thompson and Dobrynin, Feb 7, 1965, FRUS, 1964–1968, vol. 2, doc. 82.

23. TelCon: Greenfield and Ball, Feb 7, 1965, George Ball Papers, Vietnam file 1, LBJL, also in TFP.

24. Goldstein, *Lessons in Disaster*, p. 155; and Halberstam, *Best and the Brightest*.

25. VanDeMark, *Into the Quagmire*, p. 67; and Bundy to LBJ, en route from Saigon to Washington, DC, Feb 7, 1965, FRUS, 1964–1968, vol. 2, doc. 84.

26. William Bundy oral history, p. 12, LBJL.

27. Mansfield memo to LBJ, Feb 8, 1965, FRUS, 1964–1968, vol. 2, doc. 92.

28. Memo for the record, NSC meeting, Feb 8, 1965, FRUS, 1964–1968, vol. 2, doc. 88.

29. Stewart Alsop, quoting one of LBJ's aides, in "The Face of the President, 1966," *Saturday Evening Post*, Sep 24, 1966.

30. William Bundy oral history, p. 14, LBJL.

31. VanDeMark, *Into the Quagmire*, p. 69.

32. Thompson-Dobrynin talk, Feb 9, 1965, LBJL, also in FRUS, 1964–1968, vol. 14, doc. 91.

33. Ball, *The Past Has Another Pattern*, p. 390.

34. Summary record of 548th NSC meeting, Feb 10, 1965, FRUS, 1964–1968, vol. 2, doc. 98.

35. Ball, *The Past Has Another Pattern*, p. 391; and draft joint memo to LBJ, Feb 13, 1965, with handwritten note by Ball, LBJL, also in FRUS, 1964–1968, vol. 2, doc. 113, p. 525n2.

36. Authors' interview with Tom Hughes, Jun 2013, TFP.

37. George Ball oral history, p. 22, LBJL.

38. Bundy left a note on the paper, saying that this was not his view. He wanted to leave the US objectives unformulated. Ball could not agree to going further "into the mire" without acknowledging where the United States was going and on what basis a halt would be called. See Ball, *The Past Has Another Pattern*, p. 505n8.

39. Ibid., p. 391.

40. VanDeMark, *Into the Quagmire*, p. 75.

41. Authors' interview with Tom Hughes, Jun 2013, TFP.

42. William Bundy oral history, p. 13, LBJL.

43. Goldstein, *Lessons in Disaster*, p. 183.

44. It would be instructive to do a study on the influence (or lack thereof) of their children on LBJ's advisors. The Rusk, McNamara, Bohlen, Wisner, and Thompson children are a few such individuals who were against the war in Vietnam.

45. Dobrynin-Thompson talk, Feb 15, 1965, NSF: Europe and USSR, box 227, LBJL, also in TFP [printed version and digital photo].

46. Paper prepared by Rusk, Feb 23, 1965, FRUS, 1963–1968, vol. 2, doc. 157.

47. Up to that point, the State Department was the agency expressing misgivings. To have the secretary of state make this strong statement removed objections and let the escalation go forward without obvious dissent.

48. Gibbons, *US Government and the Vietnam War*, vol. 3, p. 115.

49. David Halberstam interview with Thompson, Halberstam Papers, Boston University.

50. Summary notes of 550th meeting of NSC, Mar 26, 1965, FRUS, 1963–1968, vol. 2, doc. 217.

51. Goldstein, *Lessons in Disaster*, p. 169; and McNamara, *In Retrospect*, p. 183.

52. Alsop, "The Face of the President, 1966," *Saturday Evening Post*, Sep 24, 1966.

53. Goldstein, *Lessons in Disaster*, p. 181.

54. MemCon: Thompson and Alsop, sent to Rusk, Apr 20, 1965, TFP. For the US military's version of Thompson's position, see memo for the record, Honolulu, Apr 4, 1965, FRUS, 1963–1968, vol. 2, doc. 240.

55. U Thant proposed a three-month cease-fire. Seventeen nonaligned countries met in Yugoslavia and also called for negotiations. These events coincided with increased pressure from US allies. See *Pentagon Papers*, Mar 12–18, 1965, https://www.archives.gov/research/pentagon-papers.

56. See *Pentagon Papers*, Senator Gravel edition, vol. 3, chap. 3, "The Air War in North Vietnam: Rolling Thunder Begins, February–June, 1965," https://www.mtholyoke.edu/acad/intrel/pentagon3/pent7.htm.

57. The United States was obviously not against self-determination per se, but was opposed to it being formulated by the Viet Cong. The Viet Cong program had such laudable goals as universal suffrage, freedom of speech, and freedom of the press, but it also included a redistribution of farmland to the peasants and the seizure of certain foreign assets.

58. Ball, *The Past Has Another Pattern*, p. 393.

59. Thompson's daily diary, TFP.

60. A flower lover in the upper echelons of the State Department apparently gave the peace initiatives their names. After Mayflower would come the Marigold, Sunflower, and Buttercup initiatives. See Oberdofer, *Tet!*, p. 63n3.

61. William Bundy oral history, LBJL.

62. Bundy to SecState, May 11, 1965, FRUS, 1963–1968, vol. 2, doc. 291; and *Pentagon Papers*, Senator Gravel edition, vol. 3, chap. 3, https://www.mtholyoke.edu/acad/intrel/pentagon3/pent7.htm.

63. This remark was made by John McNaughton to McGeorge Bundy. See VanDeMark, *Into the Quagmire*, p. 143.

64. Dobrynin-Thompson talk, May 18, 1965, LBJL.

65. Ball, *The Past Has Another Pattern*, p. 404.

66. Dobrynin, *In Confidence*, p. 139.

67. A document in the Russian archives, dated January 2, 1968, refers to a meeting between Thompson and Gromyko on December 28, 1967. See RGANI; and meeting between Thompson and Gromyko, Dec 1967, TFP.

68. General Westmoreland had wanted ground troops, but General Taylor previously had argued against them, preferring to rely on air assaults.

69. McNamara, *In Retrospect*, p. 187.

70. General William Westmoreland was the deputy commander of the Military Assistance Command, Vietnam (MACV).

71. McNamara, *In Retrospect*, p. 196.

72. Thompson memo to William Bundy, "Top Secret," Jul 10, 1965, TFP.

73. The "Wise Men" were a bipartisan group of elder statesmen who had previously played important roles in government and, as VanDeMark points out in *Into the Quagmire*, p. 173, they were the very men who had perpetuated the policy of global containment.

74. Bundy, notes of meeting, Jul 8, 1965, FRUS, 1963–1968, vol. 3 (*Vietnam, June–December 1965*), doc. 55; and Thompson's daily diary, TFP.

75. In June 1967, the Soviet ship *Turkestan* was hit near Haiphong. One Soviet crew member was killed and several were injured. The Soviet government took the incident very seriously, and Gromyko accused the United States of "bandit-like" actions. See Guthrie to State, cable 5322, Jun 2, 1967, NSF: embassy files, Europe and USSR, LBJL; and John Chancellor, "Foul-Ups in the Pentagon," *Washington Post*, Mar 15, 1970. Former Pentagon official Phil G. Goulding, in *Confirm or Deny*, wrote that the commander-in-chief of the Pacific Command (CINPAC) told the Pentagon that no American planes were in the harbor, and the Pentagon went public with a denial. Two weeks later, McNamara discovered that American planes were there and probably did hit the Soviet ship. See Chancellor, "Foul-Ups." For additional information, see "Russ Ship Bombed by U.S.: File Protest of Incident in Viet Port," *Chicago Tribune*, Jun 3, 1967; "U.S. Admits It May Have Hit Soviet Ship," *Chicago Tribune*, Jun 19, 1967; and "Russ Protest Ship Attack in N. Viet Port," *Chicago Tribune*, Jul 1, 1967. Also see *Pentagon Papers*, Senator Gravel edition, vol. 4, chap. 1, "The Air War in North Vietnam, 1965–1968"; and editorial note, FRUS, 1964–1968, vol. 5, doc. 188.

76. Ball, *The Past Has Another Pattern*, p. 401.

77. Notes of meeting, Jul 21, 1965, FRUS, 1964–1968, vol. 3, doc. 71.

78. General Franco to LBJ, FRUS, 1964–1968, vol. 12 (*Western Europe*), doc. 184.

79. Thompson memo to Ball, "Top Secret," May 28, 1965, TFP.

80. John Prados, "The '65 Decision: Bombing Soviet SAM Sites in North Vietnam," *Veteran*, Jan/Feb 2006, Vietnam Veterans of America, http://archive.vva.org/archive/TheVeteran/2006_01/featureSAM.htm. Thompson added, however, that if a choice was made to bomb the sites, the Soviets should not be warned, contrary to what Ambassador Kohler had suggested. Thompson thought that cautioning the Soviets not to use the Ilyushin IL-28s would seem like an ultimatum and cause them to do just the opposite. In the end, the advisory group decided not to bomb the SAM sites.

81. From 1965 through all of 1966, nearly the entire total of forty-eight US jet aircraft shot down by SAMs over North Vietnam were downed by Soviet missile operators. See "Surface-to-Air Missile," Wikipedia, http://en.wikipedia.org/wiki/Surface-to-air_missile/.

82. Notes of meeting, White House Cabinet Room, Jul 26, 1965, FRUS, 1964–1968, vol. 3, doc. 90.

83. Thompson to Tom Hughes at INR, re. Special National Intelligence Estimate (SNIE) 10-12-65, Dec 13, 1965, TFP.

84. VanDeMark, *Into the Quagmire*, p. 208.

85. Thompson memo for Ray Cline, CIA, "Secret," Oct 5, 1965, TFP.

86. Thompson, "Vital Interests and Objectives of the United States," speech at the Industrial College of the Armed Forces, Washington, DC, Aug 25, 1965, TFP.

87. SNIE 10-11-65 is still classified, but its contents are relayed in Gibbons, *US Government and the Vietnam War*, vol. 3, p. 77–80.

88. Ibid., pp. 78–79; and McNamara, *In Retrospect*, p. 213.

89. Thompson paper, Oct 11, 1965, FRUS, 1964–1968, vol. 3, doc. 164.

90. McNamara, *In Retrospect*, p. 223.

91. Thompson to Bundy, pros and cons of a bombing pause, Nov 13, 1965, LBJL; and Thompson paper, Oct 11, 1965, FRUS, 1964–1968, vol. 3, doc. 164.

92. Thompson to Bundy, pros and cons of a bombing pause, Nov 13, 1965, LBJL.

93. Rostow to LBJ, Dec 23, 1965, FRUS, 1964–1968, vol. 3, doc. 243.

94. McNamara, *In Retrospect*, p. 216.

95. This was right after the Battle of Ia Drang Valley, on November 14–17, 1965. See McNamara memo to LBJ, Nov 30, 1965, FRUS, 1964–1968, vol. 3, doc. 212.

96. Bundy to LBJ, Dec 4, 1965, FRUS, 1964–1968, vol. 3, doc. 215.

97. MemCon attachment to Bundy memo to LBJ, FRUS, 1961–1963, vol. 3, doc. 225.

98. Thompson-Dobrynin talk, Dec 23, 1965, LBJL.

99. Gibbons, *US Government and the Vietnam War*, vol. 4, p. 125.

100. Hershberg, *Marigold*, p. 21.

101. Bundy to LBJ in Texas, Dec 27, 1965, FRUS, 1964–1968, vol. 3, doc. 252; and Gibbons, *US Government and the Vietnam War*, vol. 4, pp. 125–27.

102. Robert Komer to LBJ on Thompson-Dobrynin talk, Dec 28, 1965, LBJL.

103. Hoopes, *Limits of Intervention*, p. 48; and Hershberg, *Marigold*, p. 21.

104. Kraslow and Loory, *Secret Search for Peace*, p. 147.

105. Summary notes of 556th meeting of NSC, Jan 29, 1966, FRUS, 1964–1968, vol. 4, doc. 55, p. 187n2.

106. Notes of meeting, Jan 28, 1966, FRUS, 1964–1968, vol. 4, doc. 52; and Thompson letter to Bohlen, Feb 4, 1966, records of Ambassador Bohlen, 1942–1971, box 27, entry A1-1560, RG 59, NARA.

107. William Bundy oral history, p. 18, LBJL.

108. Hershberg, *Marigold*, p. 66.

109. McNamara, *In Retrospect*, p. 235.

110. Halberstam, *Best and the Brightest*, p. 636.

111. Ibid., p. 628.

112. Hoopes, *Limits of Intervention*, p. 61.

113. Gibbons, *US Government and the Vietnam War*, vol. 4, p. 615.

114. Now it was the Rostow brothers, instead of the Bundy brothers.

115. "The Uncounted Enemy: A Vietnam Deception," television documentary, *CBS Reports*, Jan 23, 1982; McNamara, *In Retrospect*, pp. 241–42; and Halberstam, *Best and the Brightest*, pp. 467–68.

116. Thompson letter to Bohlen, Feb 4, 1966, TFP; and Bohlen, *Witness to History*, p. 524.

117. Talking points for Thompson talk, 1968, TFP.

118. Thompson to Bohlen, records of Ambassador Bohlen, 1942–1971, box 27, entry A1-1560, RG 59, NARA.

119. Rostow memo to LBJ, Dec 23, 1965, FRUS, 1964–1968, vol. 3, doc. 243; and Thompson paper, "Soviet Reaction to Possible Bombing of POL in North Viet-Nam," Dec 22, 1965, TFP.

120. Walt Rostow identified aerial bombing targets for the OSS during World War II and was convinced that bombing was the decisive factor in the Allied victory, although later studies clearly showed that this was not the case. He brought this mistaken lesson with him to Vietnam. See Milne, *America's Rasputin*. In an argument about the Vietnam War bombing, LBJ's undersecretary of state, Nicholas Katzenbach, remarked: "I finally understand the difference between Walt and me. . . . I was the navigator who was shot down and spent

two years in a German prison camp, and Walt was the guy picking my targets." See Todd S. Purdum, "Walt Rostow, Adviser to Kennedy and Johnson, Dies at 86," *New York Times*, Feb 15, 2003.

121. Thompson paper, "Soviet Reaction to Possible Bombing of POL in North Viet-Nam," Dec 22, 1965; and Thompson letter to Bohlen, Feb 4, 1966, TFP.

122. Notes of LBJ's meeting with NSC, Jun 22, 1966, FRUS, 1964–1968, vol. 4, doc. 161.

123. Editorial note, FRUS, 1964–1968, vol. 4, doc. 226.

124. Gibbons, *US Government and the Vietnam War*, vol. 4, p. 370. In light of Harold Wilson's opposition to bombing POL sites, LBJ did not want him to visit Washington, DC, as had been planned.

125. Thompson letter to Bohlen, Feb 4, 1966, TFP; and Bohlen, *Witness to History*, p. 524.

126. Notes of meeting, Jan 22, 1966, FRUS, 1964–1968, vol. 4, doc. 35.

127. Hanoi had anticipated just such a campaign and had dispersed the majority of its POL stocks in fifty-gallon drums across the length of the country. See the section on "Changing Priorities and POL Strikes," Operation Rolling Thunder, Wikipedia, http://en.wikipedia.org/wiki/Operation_Rolling_Thunder#Changing_priorities_and_POL_strikes/.

128. Thompson-Dobrynin talks, given to Rostow for LBJ to see, Jul 2, 1966, LBJL.

129. Thompson memo to LBJ, Jul 15, 1966, FRUS, 1964–1968, vol. 14, doc. 167.

130. Morocco, *Thunder from Above*.

131. Other participants were U. Alexis Johnson, William Bundy, Leonard Unger, Joseph Sisco, Benjamin Read, Chester Cooper, Montego Sterns, and someone from Rostow's staff.

132. Milne, *America's Rasputin*, p. 174.

133. Theodore Draper, "A Special Supplement: How Not to Negotiate," *New York Review of Books*, May 4, 1967, https://www.nybooks.com/articles/1967/05/04/a-special-supplement-vietnam-how-not-to-negotiate/.

134. Thompson to Unger, in reaction to Bundy paper on "Possible Sequence of Actions toward a Settlement in South Viet-Nam," Aug 11, 1966, FRUS, 1964–1968, vol. 4, doc. 209.

135. Memo of meeting, Aug 2, 1966, FRUS, 1964–1968, vol. 4, doc. 197.

136. It's unclear why Harriman believed this. Perhaps it was because he knew LBJ did. Or perhaps Harriman hoped it was true, as, having been marginalized by both JFK and LBJ, this would put him back in the center of the action.

137. Gibbons, *US Government and the Vietnam War*, vol. 4, p. 443.

138. Dobrynin said this in several places in his book. For example, see Dobrynin, *In Confidence*, p. 170.

139. Thompson memo to LBJ, [undated], FRUS, 1964–1968, vol. 14, doc. 177; Rostow note to LBJ, Oct 10, 1966, NSF: Walt Rostow files, box 11 (1 of 2), LBJL; and Harriman memo to LBJ and SecState, Oct 7, 1966, NSF: Walt Rostow files, box 11 (1 of 2), also in TFP.

140. Thompson draft of his undated memo to LBJ, Sep 29, 1966, TFP. For the undated memo citation, see endnote 139.

141. MemCon: delegation to UN General Assembly, Sep 24, 1966, FRUS, 1964–1968, vol. 4, doc. 247.

142. MemCon, Oct 10, 1966, FRUS, 1961–1968, vol. 4, doc. 264.

143. Dobrynin, *In Confidence*, p. 144.

144. MemCon, Oct 10, 1966, FRUS, 1964–1968, vol. 14, doc. 179.

145. LBJ and Fulbright, Oct 11, 1966, citation 10941, tape WH6610.04, https://millercenter.org/the-presidency/secret-white-house-tapes/conversation-william-fulbright-october-11-1966-1.

146. Thompson memo to Rusk, Nov 4, 1966, FRUS, 1964–1968, vol. 14, doc. 184.

147. LBJ, however, was concentrating on the upcoming presidential elections at the time and feared that any peace moves could help his opponent, Barry Goldwater, who was calling for greater military toughness in Vietnam. Also, the Johnson administration did not want to negotiate from a weak position. Adlai Stevenson, just before he died, told reporter Eric Sevareid that the United States had turned down an offer by Hanoi, made through U Thant, to open direct talks during a time when the Communists seemed to have the upper hand. When U Thant's efforts came to light, the White House denied that Hanoi had wanted talks, but U Thant was convinced that Hanoi's offer was genuine, and he would come to doubt the sincerity of the United States in its Vietnam diplomacy.

148. Rusk to LBJ, "Top Secret," Jul 10, 1967, NSF: Walt Rostow files, box 11, Rusk-Dobrynin file, LBJL.

149. MemCon, Oct 17, 1966, FRUS, 1964–1968, vol. 4, doc. 275; and Bromley Smith note to LBJ, Mar 16, 1966, FRUS, 1964–1968, vol. 4, doc. 97.

150. Memo of meeting, Jan 5, 1967, FRUS, 1964–1968, vol. 5, doc. 7.

151. Editorial note, FRUS, 1964–1968, vol. 4, doc. 281.

152. McNamara, *In Retrospect*, p. 260.

153. Rostow memo to LBJ, Dec 27, 1965, FRUS, 1964–1968, vol. 3, doc. 243.

154. For a very detailed and thorough book on this initiative, see Hershberg, *Marigold*.

155. Ball to Rusk, cable 1773, July 5, 1955, FRUS, 1964–1968, vol. 4, doc. 173.

156. William Bundy oral history, p. 19, LBJL.

157. See LBJ letter to Kosygin, Dec 6, 1966, FRUS, 1965–1968, vol. 4, doc. 330; and Herschberg, *Marigold*, chap. 5, "Something Big Has Happened."

158. McNamara, *In Retrospect*.

159. Hershberg, *Marigold*, chap. 9, "The Americans Have Gone Mad."

160. Rusk to LBJ, Jul 10, 1967, NSF: Walt Rostow files, box 11, Rusk-Dobrynin file, JFKL.

161. Hershberg, in *Marigold*, convincingly argues that it was a lost opportunity.

162. Ibid., p. 385.

163. MemCon: Dobrynin and Thompson, Dec 30, 1966, FRUS, 1964–1968, vol. 4, doc. 354.

32 ≋ Strand Two: Nonproliferation (1962–1967)

1. Efforts to control nuclear weapons had begun almost as soon as the first atomic bomb was detonated in wartime. The initial nonproliferation idea, which was favored by the father of the bomb, J. Robert Oppenheimer, was to share nuclear advances with the world through an international agency. In September 1946, the Clifford-Elsey report [for many years credited solely to Clark Clifford, but really written mostly by George Elsey] recommended that US policy should be aimed at checking Soviet expansion, not engaging in disarmament or arms limitations. The Acheson-Lilienthal report, written in March 1946, proposed the international control of fissile materials and an abandonment of the US monopoly on nuclear weapons. The Baruch plan, presented to the UN Atomic Energy Commission in June 1946, was based on the Acheson-Lilienthal plan but altered it in such a way (e.g., by including a provision for unrestricted inspections) as to guarantee its rejection by the Soviets, while still maintaining a public opinion advantage. For a thorough description of the Oppenheimer-Acheson-Lilienthal, and, later, Baruch plans, see Bird and Sherwin, *American Prometheus*. For the attacks on Oppenheimer, also see McMillan, *The Ruin of J. Robert Oppenheimer*. The nonproliferation idea effectively died through a combination of vested interests (individual, corporate, and national) and bureaucracy. Instead, the United States went the way of control and secrecy, through the Atomic Energy Act of 1946. When the Soviet Union developed its own nuclear weapons, however, with Britain following soon after, it became clear that this approach wasn't working very well, as it prevented the United States from participating in the civilian nuclear marketplace for processes such as power generation or desalinization. So in 1953, Eisenhower initiated the Atoms for Peace Program, designed to share nuclear technology with non–nuclear weapons states for peaceful purposes, in exchange for them accepting safeguards on the materials and technology they received. This was a nice idea, but it was not well monitored or coordinated, and it only added to the proliferation of nuclear materials in the end. For more background on nonproliferation, see Maddock, *Nuclear Apartheid*; and Gardner, *Nuclear Nonproliferation*.

2. The main players were members of the Eighteen-Nation Disarmament Committee, headquartered in Geneva, which consisted of representatives of NATO, the Warsaw Pact, and nonaligned nations. The ENDC was the negotiating body for arms control, except when the subject was brought directly to the UN Security Council or the UN General Assembly. Within the United States, there were four groups. First, there was the Arms Control and Disarmament Agency (ACDA), established in 1961 to engage in research, advise on policy, and conduct negotiations. It was headed by William C. Foster and his deputy, Adrian "Butch" Fisher, and was seen as advocating the primacy of disarmament and nonproliferation. Second, there was the Committee of Principals, consisting of the US secretaries of state and defense, as well as the heads of NASA, the CIA, the ACDA, the USIA, the JCS, and the Atomic Energy Commission. Third, there was the Committee of Deputies, which, as its name suggests, was the next level down. It was chaired by Adrian Fisher of the ACDA and tasked with doing the groundwork for the Committee of Principals. Fourth, there were offices and departments and other committees, formed within each of the agencies and the armed services, that attempted to influence and guide policy development.

3. Thompson memo to Rusk, talking points for LTB signing, Jul 29, 1963, TFP.

4. The British could not use IRBMs, because the land mass of Britain was too small to hide the silos well enough to ensure a defensive launch, and they had not been able to develop other missiles that had a practical range. Skybolt used the British V-bomber force as a delivery system for shorter-range nuclear missiles, as well as for free-fall bombs.

5. Bohlen, *Witness to History*, pp. 500–501. Bohlen suspected that George Ball's trip and the MLF's advocacy had pushed de Gaulle into rejecting membership for Britain.

6. Thompson to Rusk, Jan 26, 1963, TFP.

7. National *control* was an important distinction, because it would allow the United States to provide a nuclear deterrent to its allies as long as America maintained control of it.

8. Notes of meeting, Jan 18, 1964, FRUS, 1964–1968, vol. 11 (*Arms Control and Disarmament*), doc. 4. The JCS were concerned that the Soviets could press for nuclear-free zones in Western Europe, which the Americans did not want, because they needed a nuclear umbrella for West Germany.

9. The international crew would come from NATO nations and be under the command of the Allied Command Operations. The Allied Command Operations and the Allied Command Transformation are headed, respectively, by the Supreme Allied Commander, Europe (SACEUR) and the Supreme Allied Commander, Transformation (SACT).

10. Thompson letter to Bohlen, May 27, 1963, TFP.

11. Thompson to Rusk, US policy in Europe, Feb 27, 1963, TFP.

12. See Seaborg, *Stemming the Tide*, for his view of Rusk and the MLF.

13. Mikoyan, *Soviet Cuban Missile Crisis*.

14. Thompson-Dobrynin talks, May 17, 1963, TFP. Dobrynin found the MLF to be such a nonstarter that he didn't even mention it in his memoirs.

15. As historian Amitai Etzioni observed in 1967, "the US position on MLF for a while attempted to assure the Russians that there would be no proliferation of arms while at the same time encouraging the West Germans to hope for some control of nuclear weapons." See Etzioni, "The Kennedy Experiment," p. 376, TFP.

16. For example, the JCS tried hard to stop a treaty concerning the nonproliferation of nuclear weapons on the seabed. They asserted that it would inhibit the option of placing nuclear launchers on the bottom of the sea, despite a technical consensus that this would never be feasible, as well as the practical reason that there were no plans to do this.

17. Thompson to Fisher, May 20, 1964; and, more specifically, Thompson memo to SecState, Aug 25, 1964, Thompson lot file 67 D 2, box 25, RG 59, NACP, also in TFP.

18. Thompson memo to ACDA, subject: six-point program, Nov 28, 1964, Thompson lot file 67 D 2, box 25, RG 59, NACP, also in FRUS, 1964–1968, vol. 11, doc. 52.

19. Authors' interviews with Raymond Garthoff, Sep 2009 and Oct 2013, TFP.

20. Thompson to Rusk, Aug 25, 1964, Thompson lot file 67 D 2, box 25, RG 59, NACP, also in TFP. In this instance, Thompson used "case-by-case" to differentiate between the specific national or regional, politico-military nonproliferation calculations. He did not refer to allowing case-by-case exceptions to nonproliferation, for which the term "case-by-case" became a general shorthand.

21. Thompson to Rusk, Aug 25, 1964, Thompson lot file 67 D 2, box 25, RG 59, NACP, also in TFP.

22. Ibid.; and Thompson to Fisher, May 20, 1964, Thompson lot file 67 D 2, box 25, RG 59, NACP, also in TFP.

23. Thompson to Rusk, Aug 25, 1964, Thompson lot file 67 D 2, box 25 RG 59, NACP, also in TFP. This idea—that Thompson's main objection was an unlikely early acceptance by the Soviets—was also pointed out in a dissenting memo from Leonard Meeker. See Meeker to SecState, Aug 25, 1964, Thompson lot file 67 D 2, box 25, RG 59, NACP, also in TFP.

24. The idea behind the Thompson Committee was to "develop specific recommendations for further action that should be taken by the US to prevent the proliferation of nuclear weapons capability." See editorial note, FRUS, 1964–1968, vol. 11, doc. 45.

25. Authors' email correspondence with NSA historian William Burr, Nov 6, 2013, TFP.

26. Thompson memo to SecState, Jul 2, 1965, TFP; and Thompson to SecState, attachment B: "Attitudes of Selected Countries on Accession to a Non-Proliferation Agreement," Jul 21, 1965, DEF 18, box 35–36, NACP.

A draft of this attachment also appears in a research memo from Hughes to SecState, Jul 15, 1965, Wilson Center, http://digitalarchive.wilsoncenter.org/document/134060/.

27. Authors' interview with Tom Hughes, Jun 2013, TFP. Hughes characterized Israel as "jerking the US inspectors around" by refusing them admittance at the last minute, insisting on advance warning, blocking off certain parts of the facility, and the like.

28. Ibid.

29. The North Koreans would sign the NPT, but they also understood the usefulness of the bomb in upholding their regime. Therefore, they changed their minds about giving up on their weapons program. Today, we are faced with the possibility of Iran and perhaps Egypt seeking that same security.

30. Thompson-Dobrynin talk, Sep 11, 1964, LBJL; and Bundy memo for the record, Sep 15, 1964, FRUS, 1964–1968, vol. 30 (China), doc. 50, p. 95n3. There was a discrepancy between the INR's estimate of an imminent test and the CIA's, which concluded that the Chinese would not detonate a bomb before the end of the year. See "The Chances of an Imminent Communist Chinese Nuclear Explosion," Special National Intelligence Estimate (SNIE) 13-4-64, Aug 26, 1964, GW-NSA, https://www.cia.gov/library/readingroom/docs/DOC_0001095915.pdf, also in LBJL.

31. Thompson memo to SecState, May 29, 1963, TFP.

32. William Burr and Jeffrey T. Richelson, "Whether to 'Strangle the Baby in the Cradle': The United States and the Chinese Nuclear Program, 1960–1964," International Security [MIT Press], vol. 25, no. 3 (2000–2001), pp. 54–99.

33. See, for example, Bundy memo for the record, on a meeting between LBJ and top advisors on China's nuclear test, Sep 15, 1964, FRUS, 1964–1968, vol. 30, doc. 49, also in LBJL. For the possibility of a preemptive attack, see G. W. Rathjens report to 49 CDA, Dec 14, 1964, summarizing an earlier study by Robert H. Johnson for the Gilpatric Committee, recommending against a preemptive strike, which was not included in the Gilpatric Committee's report. Both are detailed in William Burr, ed., "The United States, China, and the Bomb," National Security Archive Electronic Briefing Book No. 1, GW-NSA, http://nsarchive.gwu.edu/NSAEBB/NSAEBB1/. Thompson's minutes of the committee meeting also show that this was considered and rejected. See Committee of Principals, Aug–Dec 1964, lot file 68 D 452, NACP; S/S-NSC files, Committee on Nuclear Weapons, lot file 70 D 265, NACP; and Garthoff, Journey through the Cold War, p. 193.

34. As examples of this hysteria, Bundy claimed that a nuclear-armed China would be the "greatest single threat." See Bundy memo to JFK, Nov 8, 1962, FRUS, 1961–1963, vol. 7, doc. 243. McCloy stated that unless the China threat were met, nuclear war was "almost inevitable," cited by Francis Gavin in "Blasts from the Past: Proliferation Lessons from the 1960s," International Security [MIT Press], vol. 29, no. 3 (Winter 2004–2005), p. 102. Mao Zedong's rhetoric that "we must not fear nuclear war" was also cited by Gavin, "Blasts from the Past," p. 101.

35. Authors' interview with Tom Hughes, Jun 2013, TFP.

36. The Gilpatric Committee was staffed by Spurgeon Keeney of the NSC and Raymond Garthoff, with support from outside experts. The committee met three times: twice in December 1964, and once in a two-day meeting in early January 1965.

37. Authors' interview with Raymond Garthoff, Oct 2013, TFP.

38. DEF 18-10, nonproliferation, Nov–Dec 1964, with tab. A, "Meeting of the Committee of Principals, Nov 23, 1964," and tab. B, "US Nuclear Assistance to Pacific-Asian Countries," [undated], entry A1-5180, records relating to arms control and disarmament, 1961–1966, RG 59, NACP.

39. Authors' interview with Raymond Garthoff, Oct 2013, TFP. Garthoff said that he thought Thompson did not favor selective proliferation.

40. Report by Committee on Nuclear Proliferation, Jan 21, 1965, FRUS, 1964–1968, vol. 11, doc. 64.

41. Seaborg, Stemming the Tide, pp. 143–45.

42. Thompson wrote to Bohlen that he thought the Gilpatric Committee "came down on the wrong side of this question" and was pleased that their report was going to be "closely held." Thompson letter to Bohlen, Jan 30, 1965, records of Ambassador Bohlen, 1942–1971, box 27, entry A1-1560, RG 59, NACP, also in TFP.

43. Thompson memo to Rusk, "Talking Points for Meeting with the Gilpatric Committee," Jan 7, 1965; and "Notes on Secretary of State's Meeting with Gilpatric Committee on Non-Proliferation," Jan 7, 1965, drafted by Garthoff, both in Thompson lot file 64 D 653, RG 59, NACP, also in TFP.

44. Thompson memo to Rusk, "Talking Points for Meeting with the Gilpatric Committee," Jan 7, 1965; and "Notes on Secretary of State's Meeting with Gilpatric Committee on Non-Proliferation," Jan 7, 1965, drafted by Garthoff, both in Thompson lot file 64 D 653, RG 59, NACP, also in TFP.

45. Authors' interview with Raymond Garthoff, Oct 2013, TFP.

46. Thompson letter to Bohlen, May 6, 1965, records of Ambassador Bohlen, 1942–1971, box 27, entry A1-1560, RG 59, NACP, also in TFP.

47. Letters between Bohlen and Thompson, Jul 1965, records of Ambassador Bohlen, 1942–1971, box 27, entry A1-1560, RG 59, NACP.

48. Thompson memo to SecState, "Our Non-Proliferation Program," Jul 2, 1965, drafted by Garthoff, TFP.

49. For a description of the demise of the MLF, see Seaborg, *Stemming the Tide*, pp. 169–80; and Bator, "Lyndon Johnson and Foreign Policy," in Lobel, *Presidential Judgment*, p. 45.

50. Safeguards were the way in which the treaty would be enforced. These safeguards included procedures for tracking fissionable material that non–nuclear weapons states had for their nuclear power programs. This controlled how the material was inventoried, moved, and stored, and it made sure that no material was processed into weapons-grade U-235 or plutonium. Adrian Fisher stated, "The reason a treaty wasn't tabled [i.e., brought to the table] until January 18, 1968, was because we were fighting for a verification article—an article on inspection that kept open a respectable role for Euratom." See Adrian Fisher oral history, LBJL.

51. The European Atomic Energy Community (Euratom) and the International Atomic Energy Agency had similarly robust safeguards, though they were not as strong as the US bilateral ones. See Seaborg, *Stemming the Tide*, p. 275.

52. It wouldn't be until 1974 that a committee, which had been formed under Swiss professor Claude Zangger in 1971, defined the safeguards clause of the NPT. See https://www.scribd.com/document/25078 9698/Zangger-Committee-pdf; and Gardner, *Nuclear Nonproliferation*.

53. TelCon: LBJ and Rusk, Sep 16, 1966, FRUS, 1964–1968, vol. 33 (*Organization and Management of Foreign Policy; United Nations*), doc. 93.

54. LBJ telephone conversations, in order, all in Miller Center, secret White house tapes: Rusk and LBJ, Sep 17, 1966, citation 10795, https://millercenter.org/the-presidency/secret-white-house-tapes/conversation -dean-rusk-september-17-1966-0/; LBJ and McNamara, Sep 29, 1966, citation 10850, https://millercenter .org/the-presidency/secret-white-house-tapes/conversation-robert-mcnamara-september-29-1966/; and LBJ and Crockett, Oct 1, 1966, citation 10908, https://millercenter.org/the-presidency/secret-white-house-tapes /conversation-william-crockett-october-1-1966-0/. Also in LBJL, https://www.discoverlbj.org/exhibits/show /loh/telecon/.

55. Bohlen, *Witness to History*, p. 526.

56. LBJ and McNamara, Sep 29, 1966, citation 10850, Miller Center, secret White house tapes, also in LBJL; and Drew Pearson and Jack Anderson, "Pact May Open Ports to Russia," *Washington Post*, Dec 24, 1966, p. B11, TFP.

57. LBJ and McNamara, Sep 29, 1966, citation 10850; and LBJ and Crockett, Oct 1, 1966, citation 10908, both in Miller Center, secret White house tapes, also in LBJL.

58. LBJ and Crockett, Oct 1, 1966, citation 10908, Miller Center, secret White house tapes, also in LBJL.

59. Bundy to Thompson, Oct 18, 1966, personal file, box 114, McGeorge Bundy Papers, JFKL.

60. Correspondence between Thompson and Bohlen, Oct–Nov 1966, Thompson lot file, box 20, RG 59, NACP, also in TFP; and Bohlen lot file, box 27, entry A1-1560, RG 59, NACP.

61. The Consular Treaty with the USSR would be held up by the Americans, causing some friction.

62. Thompson to Rusk, Nov 4, 1966, Thompson lot file 64 D 653, RG 59, NACP.

63. Much of the meeting was expected to deal with the topic of Vietnam, but some suggestions for broaching nonproliferation were effectively squelched by Rostow's advice, which appeared in the form of a cover note. He counseled the president to simply state the US position regarding an MFL veto [never mind that the MLF was effectively dead by then] and leave the rest to Rusk to deal with, either at dinner or in later correspondence with Kosygin. LBJ thus missed an opportunity to move the ball forward a little. See LBJ doc. 57, Oct 10, 1966, cover note with attached memos from Harriman and Thompson on Oct 7 and 10, respectively, NSF: Walt Rostow files, box 11 (1 of 2); and memo for LBJ, subject: meeting with Gromyko, [undated], FRUS, 1964–1968, vol. 14, doc. 177. Also see correspondence between Thompson and Bohlen, Oct–Nov 1966, Thompson lot file, box 20, RG 59, NACP, also in TFP.

64. For an overview of the NPT, see Gardner, *Nuclear Nonproliferation*. For the text of the treaty and more details, see "Treaty on the Non-Proliferation of Nuclear Weapons (NPT)," United Nations Office for Disarmament Affairs, https://www.un.org/disarmament/WMD/Nuclear/NPT.shtml. For a critical view of the NPT, see Amitai Etzioni, "Nuclear Nonproliferation Treaty Is Obsolete," special to *National Law Journal*, Apr 25, 2005, https://www2.gwu.edu/~ccps/etzioni/A331.pdf.

65. For a list of states that have signed or ratified the Comprehensive Test Ban Treaty, see that organization's website, www.ctbto.org.

66. This was what the ball was dubbed in *Vanity Fair*'s article on the event.

67. Thompson FBI dossier, TFP. Colonel Ivan D. Yeaton went on to author a right-wing political blog that no longer exists. Yeaton was an acquaintance of John "Frenchy" Grombach, the notorious chief of the Pond, a super-secret but questionable spy organization. See Mark Stout, "The Pond: Running Agents for State, War, and the CIA," The Hazards of Private Spy Operations, CIA, https://www.cia.gov/library/center-for-the-study-of-intelligence/kent-csi/vol48no3/pdf/v48i3a07p.pdf.

33 ≋ Strand Three: The Road to SALT (1962–1967)

1. Authors' interview with Raymond Garthoff, Oct 2013, TFP.

2. Authors' conversations with Avis T. Bohlen, winter 2010.

3. Newhouse, *Cold Dawn*, p. 21.

4. Seaborg, *Stemming the Tide*, pp. 395–98.

5. Thompson speech at the French National War College, State Department, Washington DC, Mar 25, 1963, TFP; and Thompson speech, "USSR National Strategic Alternatives," at Maxwell Air Force Base, Alabama, May 15, 1963, TFP.

6. There was a parochial interest within DOD's very powerful Research and Development Department to advocate for funding to develop more and more whiz-bang ideas.

7. The name was derived from the area around the city of Tallinn, Estonia, where the United States first observed this Soviet defense system.

8. MIRV was still on the engineers' drawing board at that point, but it would be ready by 1970.

9. During Khrushchev's September 1959 visit to the United States, at a dinner in Los Angeles, the city's mayor, Norris Paulson, delivered a somewhat sanitized but still-provocative speech (see chapter 19). Khrushchev, in response, told the gathering that the Soviets were turning out missiles "like sausages." Film footage of that event is part of "Cold War Roadshow," a documentary in PBS's *American Experience* television series. The program was aired on November 18, 2014.

10. Memo from Bundy to McNamara, Jan 14, 1964, FRUS, 1964–1968, vol. 11, doc. 2.

11. Authors' interview with Raymond Garthoff, Oct 2013, TFP.

12. ACDA review paper, "The US Arms Control and Disarmament Agency during the Johnson Administration, II: Policy and Negotiations," first draft, full document digitized at LBJL, and partial printout in TFP; and Keeney to Bundy, Dec 16, 1964, FRUS, 1964–1968, vol. 11, doc. 57.

13. Thompson to Adrian Fisher, Nov 28, 1964, Thompson lot file 67 D 2, box 25, RG 59, NACP.

14. Thompson memo to ACDA, re: Six-Point Program, Nov 29, 1964, Thompson lot file 67 D 2, box 25, RG 59, NACP, also in TFP.

15. Memo to Foster, drafted by Garthoff but sent under Thompson's name, Dec 10, 1964, FRUS, 1964–1968, vol. 11, doc. 55; and Thompson to Adrian Fisher, Nov 28, 1964, Thompson lot file 67 D 2, box 25, RG 59, NACP.

16. ACDA review paper, "The US Arms Control and Disarmament Agency during the Johnson Administration, II: Policy and Negotiations," first draft, pp. 95–97, full document digitized at LBJL, and partial printout in TFP; and Thompson to Foster, "Comments on the ACDA Draft Proposal for a Freeze and Reduction of SNDV," Jun 16, 1965, which are described in the cited ACDA review paper. For Thompson's and the State Department's other concerns at this time about the president's statements at the ENDC conference, see Thompson to SecState, meeting with LBJ on ACDA proposals, Jul 19, 1965, DEF 18, box 35–6, NACP, also in TFP.

17. ACDA review paper, "The US Arms Control and Disarmament Agency during the Johnson Administration, II: Policy and Negotiations," first draft, pp. 97–98, full document digitized at LBJL, and partial printout in TFP.

18. Meeting of Committee of Principals, [undated], FRUS, 1964–1968, vol. 11, doc. 87.

19. Suggested letter to Kosygin, May 2, 1966, FRUS, 1964–1966, vol. 11, doc. 126; and Fisher memo to LBJ, May 12, 1966, FRUS, 1964–1968, vol. 11, doc. 129.

20. Thompson to Rusk, "Suggested Letter to Mr. Kosygin on a Truce in the Deployment of Offensive Strategic Missiles and Antiballistic Missile Launchers," May 2, 1966, Thompson lot file 67 D 2, box 20, RG 59, NACP.

21. ACDA review paper, "The US Arms Control and Disarmament Agency during the Johnson Administration, II: Policy and Negotiations," first draft, pp. 95–97, full document digitized at LBJL, and partial printout in TFP.

22. Thompson to Zbigniew Brzezinski, Jul 6, 1966, TFP; and Thompson report on West German trip, Jul 11, 1966, TFP.

23. Thompson presentation to Germany specialists in the State Department, "Ambassador Thompson's Report on His German Trip, June 9–22, 1966," Jun 24, 1966, TFP.

24. Thompson memo to U. A. Johnson, subject: ABMs, "Top Secret," Sep 9, 1966, Thompson lot file 67 D 2, box 20, RG 59, NACP.

25. This overture was made through William Foster, according to Dobrynin. See Thompson-Dobrynin conversation, Dec 6, 1966, Soviet Union files, box 227, doc. 50, LBJL.

26. The DOD had already spent $6 billion developing an ABM, and a sum five times greater than that was anticipated for its deployment.

27. Thompson-Dobrynin conversation, Dec 6, 1966, Soviet Union files, Thompson-Dobrynin talks, box 227, doc. 50, LBJL; and MemCon: Thompson and Dobrynin, Dec 7, 1966, FRUS, 1964–1968, vol. 11, doc. 168.

28. Conversation with McNamara in Austin, Dec 6, 1966, LBJ's daily diary, LBJL.

29. Draft notes of meeting, Austin, TX, Dec 6, 1966, FRUS, 1964–1968, vol. 10 (*National Security Policy*), doc. 150.

30. Ibid. McNamara made a recommendation against ABMs for three reasons: (1) it would force the Soviets to react by increasing the number of their offensive weapons; (2) it would not lessen any risk of a Soviet attack on the United States; and (3), if they did attack, damage to the United States would not be brought down to an acceptable level by the ABM system. The JCS disagreed. To them, an ABM system would save 30–50 million lives in the event of an attack. General Earl Wheeler argued that (1) it was not possible to predict how the Soviets would react; (2) deterrence was not just weapons, but a "state of mind"; and (3) the abandonment of the ABM system would suggest that the United States was not willing to maintain its present nuclear superiority. McNamara got a fourth point in: the Soviet ABM system would not save any lives in the USSR, since the Americans had "more than insured that we can still maintain our assured damage capability." That was the important factor. It was what made deterrence work.

31. Thompson personal letter to Rusk, Dec 8, 1966, Thompson lot file 67 D 2, box 20, RG 59, NACP, also in FRUS, 1964–1968, vol. 10, doc. 152.

32. Place and timing of phone call, Dec 7, 1966, LBJ's daily diary, LBJL; LBJ telephone conversation, citation 11114, tape WH6612.01, program 14, length 2:47, LBJL. A transcript of the recording is in TFP. Also see Robert McNamara oral history, pt. 1 of 2, pp. 59–61, LBJL.

33. Draft notes of meeting, Austin, TX, Dec 6, 1966, FRUS, 1964–1968, vol. 10, doc. 150.

34. For LBJ's letter to Kosygin, see FRUS, 1964–1968, vol. 4, doc. 330. It should be noted that this FRUS document, on p. 908n1, incorrectly states that Thompson said in his memo of that conversation that he handed the letter to Kosygin, which is impossible. This is most likely a typo, which meant to say that Thompson handed the letter to Dobrynin. This caused John Clearwater to make this mistake in his book, *Johnson, McNamara, and the Birth of SALT*.

35. LBJ telephone conversation, citation 11114, tape WH6612.01, program 14, length 2:47, LBJL. A transcript of the recording is in TFP.

36. Thompson-Dobrynin conversation, Dec 7, 1966, pt. 5 of 5, Soviet Union files, Thompson-Dobrynin talks, box 227, doc. 45, LBJL.

37. Thompson personal letter to Rusk, Dec 8, 1966, Thompson lot file 67 D 2, box 20, RG 59, NACP, also in FRUS, 1964–1968, vol. 10, doc. 152.

38. Authors' interview with Raymond Garthoff, Sep 2009, TFP.

39. Personal letters (sent to Thompson's home) between Fulbright and Thompson, Nov 2 and 5, 1966, TFP.

40. Thompson-Dobrynin talks, Dec 30, 1966, TFP; and MemCon: Dobrynin and Thompson, Dec 30, 1966, FRUS, 1964–1968, vol. 4, doc. 354.

41. "Reply to President's Letter to Kosygin," Thompson-Dobrynin meeting, Dec 30, 1966, Soviet Union files, Thompson-Dobrynin talks, LBJL, also in TFP; and editorial note, FRUS, 1964–1968, vol. 5, doc. 80.

34 ≋ Moscow 3

1. Thompson to State, on his meeting with Kosygin, cable 3560, Feb 18, 1967, CF 1967–69, POL US-USSR, RG 59, NACP; and Walt Rostow files, box 10, LBJL.

2. Bohlen, *Witness to History*, p. 528.

3. Thompson to Bohlen, Feb 1, 1967, TFP; and Thompson to State, cable 3465, Feb 13, 1967, FRUS, 1964–1968, vol. 14, doc. 200.

4. In his efficiency report on David Klein, Thompson indicated his initial concerns and subsequently commented that he was impressed with how well it worked with his political counselor. For his part, Klein said that he admired Thompson more than the latter realized, later writing that of the three major figures handling Soviet affairs at the time, Thompson "was the shyest of the three but in [Klein's] judgment, the wisest of the three." Authors' email correspondence with David Klein, Dec 9, 2012, TFP.

5. Thomas Niles oral history, Jun 5, 1998, FA-ADST; and Jonathan Rickert, "Impressions of Ambassador Thompson," Nov 25, 2002, TFP.

6. LBJ read Barbara Ward's *Rich and Poor Nations* "over and over again" and accepted her argument that the West should "steal Communism's thunder in the developing world by investing there," according to LBJ historian Dumbrell, in *Lyndon Johnson and Soviet Communism*, p. 6. Sharing the burden might also help the emerging US balance of payments problem.

7. Edward P. Morgan radio address, Jan 12, 1967; "Hoover Scuttles Johnson's Consular Treaty with USSR, Rusk Caught Unawares," *Washington Post*, Jan 30, 1967; and TelCon: LBJ and Attorney General Ramsey Clark, on consular treaty, FRUS, 1964–1968, vol. 14, doc. 192.

8. TelCon: Harriman and Goldberg, Feb 2, 1967, Harriman Personal Papers, LC, also in TFP.

9. "Remarks by Ambassador Thompson on the Occasion of Presentation of Credentials to the Chairman of the Presidium of the Supreme Soviet of the USSR," Jan 23, 1967, TFP; and Jane Thompson letter to her mother, Jan 24, 1967, TFP.

10. Editorial note, FRUS, 1964–1968, vol. 14, doc. 196.

11. Newhouse, *Cold Dawn*, p. 87.

12. Ibid.

13. Kosygin press conference, *Pravda*, Feb 9, 1967.

14. Thompson to State, cable 3465, Feb 13, 1967, FRUS, 1964–1968, vol. 14, doc. 200.

15. Ibid., although Thompson's exact words were: "Khrushchev was a prolific source of information on Soviet policies and the thinking that lay behind them. Now there is remarkably little contact between the diplomatic corps and the political leadership and such as there is, is not generally rewarding."

16. Information in this section was taken from Gibbons, *US Government and the Vietnam War*, vol. 4, pp. 500–59; Sunflower chronology and Sunflower Plus chronology, NSF: Vietnam country file, box 256 S, LBJL; backup cables and documents in the Sunflower chronology files, LBJL; and FRUS, 1964–1968, vol. 5, docs. 1–83.

17. Draper, "How Not to Negotiate"; and Gibbons, *US Government and the Vietnam War*, vol. 4, pp. 496, 496n47. See Halberstam, *Best and the Brightest*, for an analysis of why Walt Rostow clung so tightly to the notion that aerial bombing of North Vietnam was the key to winning in Vietnam. For an exhaustive account of the Marigold initiative, see Hershberg, *Marigold*.

18. Gibbons, *US Government and the Vietnam War*, vol. 4, pp. 497–98.

19. Ibid., pp. 499–501.

20. This was a four-point plan by North Vietnam's premier, Pham Van Dong. Rusk said three points were acceptable to the United States but took issue with the item that, as he interpreted it, meant that the NLF had to represent South Vietnam. Draper, in "How Not to Negotiate," claimed that Rusk used tortuous logic to

arrive at this interpretation of the plan's fourth point and argued that this was used as an excuse to stymie negotiations. Therefore, dropping this requirement was a breakthrough.

21. Gibbons, *US Government and the Vietnam War*, vol. 4, pp. 502–4; and Sunflower chronology and Sunflower Plus chronology, NSF: Vietnam country file, box 256 S, LBJL.

22. Sunflower chronology, p. 8, NSF: Vietnam country file, box 256 S, LBJL.

23. Gibbons, *US Government and the Vietnam War*, vol. 4, p. 504; and Sunflower chronology, NSF: Vietnam country file, box 256 S, LBJL.

24. Thompson to SecState, cable 3231, Jan 28, 1967, NSF: Vietnam country file, box 147, doc. 5, LBJL; and Sunflower chronology, p. 14, NSF: Vietnam country file, box 256 S, LBJL.

25. Thompson reasoned that the Russian chauffeur would have reported Guthrie's movements, in the American's attempts to make arrangements with the North Vietnamese, to the KGB. Thompson also assumed that the North Vietnamese embassy was almost certainly bugged.

26. Thompson to SecState, cable 3231, Jan 28, 1967, NSF: Vietnam country file, box 147, doc. 5, LBJL; and Sunflower chronology, pp. 14, 15, NSF: Vietnam country file, box 256 S, LBJL, also in TFP.

27. Sunflower chronology, pp. 16–19, NSF: Vietnam country file, box 256 S, LBJL; and Gibbons, *US Government and the Vietnam War*, vol. 4, p. 509.

28. Sunflower chronology, pp. 22–23, NSF: Vietnam country file, box 256 S, LBJL.

29. Ibid., p. 24.

30. Herring, *Secret Diplomacy*; and Jack Anderson, "Nixon's Tacit Understanding in Russia," *Washington Post*, Jun 9, 1972, B-15, TFP.

31. The game of telephone consists of a statement being passed along a line from one to another to still another, with each of the players repeating what they thought they heard. The end statement, however, is usually quite different from the initial one.

32. Gibbons, *US Government and the Vietnam War*, vol. 4, pp. 503–11.

33. LBJ to Ho Chi Minh, 2:15 p.m., Feb 7, 1967, FRUS, 1964–1968, vol. 5, doc. 40; and Rostow memo to LBJ, 8 p.m., Feb 7, 1967, FRUS, 1964–1968, vol. 5, doc. 41.

34. State to US embassy in the United Kingdom, FRUS, 1964–1968, Feb 11, 1967, vol. 5, doc. 60.

35. TelCon: LBJ and Rostow, Feb 11, 1967, 9:15 a.m., FRUS, 1964–1968, vol. 5, doc. 55; and Rusk memo to LBJ, Feb 11, 1967, FRUS, 1964–1968, vol. 5, doc. 58. The ongoing hatred between LBJ and RFK had instigated some sparring on the best way to seek peace in Vietnam. With the Kennedy family's connections in London, LBJ had some fears that, should the London Sunflower initiative bloom, RFK would try to take credit for it.

36. State to Thompson, cable 135734, Feb 12, 1975, FRUS, 1964–1968, vol. 5, doc. 68; Sunflower chronology, pp. 24–38, NSF: Vietnam country file, box 256 S, LBJL; and Gibbons, *US Government and the Vietnam War*, vol. 4, pp. 514–17.

37. Thompson to State, cable 3503, Feb 15, 1067, FRUS, 1964–1968, vol. 5, doc. 81; and Ho Chi Minh to LBJ, attachment to memo from Rostow to LBJ, Feb 15, 1967, FRUS, 1964–1968, vol. 5, doc. 82.

38. Dobrynin, *In Confidence*; and Anderson, "Nixon's Tacit Understanding."

39. Thompson memo to Walt Rostow, Jun 16, 1967, NSF: USSR country file, box 223, vol. 15, LBJL.

40. POL 27-14 VIET/SUNFLOWER, Moscow, cable 3533, Feb 17, 1967, NSF: Vietnam country file, box 256 S, LBJL, also in TFP; and Thompson to State, cable 3562, Feb 18, 1967, FRUS, 1964–1968, vol. 5, doc. 85, p. 186n2.

41. Thompson, regarding his meeting with Kosygin, cables 3560–3568, Feb 18, 1967, CF 1967–69, POL US-USSR, RG 59, NACP; and Rostow cover memo to LBJ, Feb 18, 1967, NSF: Rostow files, box 10, Kosygin, LBJL.

42. Sunflower chronology, p. 49, NSF: Vietnam country file, box 256 S, LBJL, referencing POL 27-14 VIET/SUNFLOWER, Moscow, cable 3533, Feb 17, 1967, NSF: Vietnam country file, box 256 S, LBJL, also in TFP.

43. Draper, in footnote 11 to "How Not to Negotiate" [unpaginated], called for a "thorough examination of this dubious justification," and he cited evidence that the situation was vastly exaggerated. Unfortunately, Thompson would not have known this.

44. Thompson to State, cable 3562, Feb 18, 1967, FRUS, 1964–1968, vol. 5, doc. 85.

45. Thompson to State, cable 3564, Feb 18, 1967, FRUS, 1964–1968, vol. 14, doc. 203.

46. Thompson to State, cable 3559, Feb 18, 1967, FRUS, 1964–1968, vol. 14, doc. 201, p. 451n2.

47. Thompson to State, cable 3568, Feb 18, 1967, LBJL, also in TFP; and Sunflower chronology, p. 55, NSF: Vietnam country file, box 256 S, LBJL.

48. Gibbons, *US Government and the Vietnam War*, vol. 4, p. 560.

49. There are numerous cables and memos Thompson sent back, expressing his objections to the mining of Haiphong, as well as to the bombing of Hanoi and the surrounding airfields and oil depots. For example, see Thompson to State, Vietnam, Dec 13, 1966, and Apr 6, 1967, CF POL 27, NACP. Gibbons, in *US Government and the Vietnam War*, vol. 4, p. 639n88, cites a CIA estimate from May 1967. The CIA came to essentially the same conclusion Thompson had.

50. Draper, "How Not to Negotiate."

51. Thompson to Rostow, cable 3674, Feb 28, 1967; Thompson to Rostow, translation of Kosygin letter to LBJ, cable 3676, Feb 28, 1967; Thompson to Rostow, Gromyko's oral statement to Thompson, cable 3675, Feb 28, 1967; and Rostow cover note summary to LBJ, Feb 28, 1967, all in NSF: Walt Rostow files, box 10 (3 of 7), Kosygin, LBJL. For Thompson's analysis of the meeting, see Thompson to State, cable 3682, Feb 28, 1967, NSF: USSR country file, box 223, vol. 14 ("cables and memos" file), LBJL.

52. Thompson letter to Kohler, Mar 13, 1967, UD-UP 63-B, box 22, RG 84, NACP, also in TFP.

53. Newhouse, *Cold Dawn*, pp. 90–91.

54. Draft instructions to Thompson on US-Soviet strategic weapons talks, Mar 17, 1967, NSF: USSR country file, box 223, vol. 14 ("cables and memos" file), LBJL.

55. Thompson to Bohlen, Apr 27, 1967, records of Ambassador Bohlen, 1942–1971, box 27, entry A1-1560, RG 59, NACP, also in TFP.

56. Khrushchev, in *Khrushchev Remembers*, vol. 2, p. 367, wrote that he was "touched" by Nixon's attempt to see him in 1965. Also see Associated Press, "Nixon, Snubbed by Kremlin, Sees Moscow as Tourist," *New York Herald Tribune–Washington Post*, March 18–19, 1967, TFP.

57. Jonathan Rickert, "Impressions of Ambassador Thompson," Nov 25, 2002. TFP.

58. Jane Thompson letter to her mother, Apr 1967, TFP.

59. Dobrynin later asked Thompson if the president's letter to Ho Chi Minh had been signed. It had not, because it was relayed from Washington, DC, by cable. Thompson had not put a cover note on the communications, because the North Vietnamese ambassador had specifically stated that they would not deal with Thompson. Thompson "concluded [correctly] that North Vietnam had used the lack of signature as an excuse to the Soviets [for] why it had been rejected."

60. Thompson to Rusk, cable 4310, Apr 7, 1967, NSF: USSR country file, box 223, vol. 15, LBJL, also in TFP. The authors did not find evidence that this letter was ever sent.

61. On the heels of its Great Leap Forward, which had killed tens of millions of its citizens, China initiated its Cultural Revolution, creating instability. In January 1967, the purges were accelerating, and even high-ranking party officials were affected, making it seem as though that country might be spinning apart.

62. Thompson to State, cable 4491, April 19, 1967, FRUS, 1964–1968, vol. 5, doc. 137.

63. Thompson personal letter to Bohlen, Apr 27, 1967, TFP, also in records of Ambassador Bohlen, 1942–1971, box 27, entry A1-1560, RG 59, NACP.

64. Rostow note to LBJ, Thurs, Apr 20, 1967, 8:05 p.m., NSF: USSR country file, box 223, vol. 15, LBJL.

65. Sunflower chronology, p. 69, NSF: Vietnam country file, box 256 S, LBJL.

66. Eugene Rostow to Thompson, May 1, 1967, Harriman Personal Papers, LC, also in FRUS, 1964–1968, vol. 14, doc. 212, and in NSF: USSR country file, vol. 15, LBJL. Benjamin Read, the special assistant to the secretary of state, forwarded a copy of the letter to Walt Rostow, under cover of a May 5 memo.

67. Thompson to Eugene Rostow, May 8, 1967, Harriman Personal Papers, LC, also in TFP.

68. Thompson personal letter to Bohlen, May 15, 1967, records of Ambassador Bohlen, 1942–1971, box 27, entry A1-1560, RG 59, NACP.

69. State to Thompson, cable 197662, May 18, 1967, NSF: USSR country file, box 223, vol. 15, LBJL.

70. Thompson to Rusk, cable 5015, May 19, 1967, TFP.

71. Rusk to Thompson, cable 198583, May 19, 1967, FRUS, 1964–1968, vol. 14, doc. 215.

72. Thompson to State, cable 5033, NSF: USSR country file, box 223, vol. 15, LBJL; and editorial note, FRUS, 1964–1968, vol. 5, doc. 179.

73. Rostow to LBJ, May 20, 1967, NSF: Walt Rostow files, box 10 (1 of 7), Kosygin, LBJL.

74. Editorial note, FRUS, 1964–1968, vol. 5, doc. 181.

75. Thompson to SecState, cable 5214, May 29, 1967, NSF: USSR country file, box 223, vol. 15, LBJL, written in reference to Vientiane, cable 7381 to State, and Saigon, cable 26983 to State.

35 ≋ The Six-Day War: Hotline Diplomacy

1. The UAR was a political alliance between Egypt and Syria from 1958 to 1961, but Egypt kept that name from 1961 until 1971.

2. Helms, *A Look over My Shoulder*, p. 301.

3. Uri Bar-Nol, "The Soviet Union and the Six-Day War: Revelation from the Polish Archives," Cold War International History Project, Wilson Center, https://www.wilsoncenter.org/publication/the-soviet-union-and-the-six-day-war-revelations-the-polish-archives.

4. The MIG is a Russian fighter jet named after the Mikoyan and ("I" in Russian) Gurevich military aircraft design bureau, founded by Artem Mikoyan and Mikhail Gurevich.

5. Thompson to State, cable 5125, May 25, 1967, FRUS, 1964–1968, vol. 19 (*Arab-Israeli Crisis and War*), doc. 59.

6. "The Washington-Moscow Hotline," Electrospaces.net, http://electrospaces.blogspot.com/2012/10/the-washington-moscow-hot-line.html.

7. Dobrynin, *In Confidence*, p. 161.

8. McNamara, *In Retrospect*, p. 278.

9. For example, see LBJ's daily brief, Jun 9, 1967, FRUS, 1964–1968, vol. 19, doc. 230, in which it notes that the Soviets "are finding it hard to conceal their shock." This document also quotes a Soviet source, who stated that the USSR could not understand "how our intelligence could have been so wrong" and asked, "how could we have gotten into such a mess?"

10. Thompson-Dobrynin conversation, subject: Soviet-American relations, Jun 19, 1967, Walt Rostow files, Thompson-Dobrynin talks, box 17, LBJL.

11. Thompson address at University of Colorado, Boulder, Colorado, Jun 6, 1969, TFP.

12. LBJ's daily diary, Jun 5, 1967, LBJL.

13. Editorial note, Jun 5, 1967, FRUS, 1964–1968, vol. 19, doc. 152; and LBJ to Kosygin, Jun 5, 1967, 8:15 a.m., FRUS, 1964–1968, vol. 19, doc. 157.

14. Viktor Sukhodrev comment, "Cold War Hotline Recalled," BBC News, http://news.bbc.co.uk/2/hi/europe/2971558.stm. The hotline was first officially used by the United States when JFK was assassinated.

15. Robert McNamara oral history, special interview I, LBJL, www.lbjlibrary.net/assets/documents/archives/oral_histories/mcnamara_r/McNamara-SP1.PDF. The teletype machine was moved to the White House, to make it easier for the president to use. See Helms, *A Look over My Shoulder*.

16. Kosygin and LBJ messages, June 5, 1967, FRUS, 1964–1968, vol. 19, docs. 156, 157, and 159.

17. Nathaniel Davis interview with Thompson, "The Hotline Exchanges," Nov 4, 1968, FRUS, 1964–1968, vol. 19, doc. 245, also in LBJL and in TFP; and Thompson address at University of Colorado, Boulder, Colorado, Jun 6, 1969, TFP. The Davis interview with Thompson took place at the Bethesda Naval Hospital in Maryland, where Thompson was being checked after he had undergone abdominal surgery.

18. Dobrynin, *In Confidence*, p. 160.

19. MemCon: Thompson and Dobrynin, Jun 16, 1967, FRUS, 1964–1968, vol. 14, doc. 218.

20. Kosygin to LBJ, Jun 6, 1967, 5:34 a.m., FRUS, 1964–1968, vol. 19, doc. 173.

21. LBJ to Kosygin, Jun 6, 1967, 10:21 a.m., FRUS, 1964–1968, vol. 19, doc. 175.

22. Nathaniel Davis interview with Thompson, "The Hotline Exchanges," Nov 4, 1968, FRUS, 1964–1968, vol. 19, doc. 245, also in LBJL and in TFP.

23. Kosygin to LBJ, Jun 6, 1967, 6:07 p.m., FRUS, 1964–1968, vol. 19, doc. 182.

24. LBJ to Kosygin, Jun 6, 1967, 8:23 p.m., FRUS, 1964–1968, vol. 19, doc. 183.

25. Kosygin to LBJ, Jun 7, 1967, 8:18 a.m., FRUS, 1964–1968, vol. 19, doc. 188; and LBJ to Kosygin, Jun 7, 1967, 11:18 a.m., FRUS, 1964–1968, vol. 19, doc. 193.

26. Nathaniel Davis interview with Thompson, "The Hotline Exchanges," Nov 4, 1968, FRUS, 1964–1968, vol. 19, doc. 245, also in LBJL and in TFP.

27. Rusk, *As I Saw It*.

28. Authors' interview with Raymond Garthoff, Sep 2009, TFP. Also see Helms, *A Look over My Shoulder*, p. 301.

29. Authors' interview with Raymond Garthoff, Sep 2009, TFP.

30. "Dead in the Water," BBC Four documentary, broadcast Jun 10, 2002; and Bamford, *Body of Secrets*. There are a number of books and articles that deal with this incident.

31. State to US embassy in Israel, cables 209890 and 209964, Jun 9, 1967, FRUS, 1964–1968, vol. 19, docs. 238 and 239. It also happened to be the day Paul Nitze was sworn in as secretary of the navy.

32. Nathaniel Davis interview with Thompson, "The Hotline Exchanges," Nov 4, 1968, FRUS, 1964–1968, vol. 19, doc. 245, also in LBJL and in TFP; and Jack Anderson, "LBJ Recalls Kosygin Backdown in '67," *Washington Post*, Oct 7, 1971, G-7.

33. Memo for the record, Oct 22, 1968, FRUS, 1964–1968, vol. 19, doc. 244. Those present were Richard Helms, Nicholas Katzenbach, Robert McNamara, Clark Clifford, McGeorge Bundy [although no longer a national security advisor, he had been called back to the White House during this crisis], and Walt Rostow.

34. Kosygin to LBJ, Jun 10, 1967, 8:48 a.m., FRUS, 1964–1968, vol. 19, doc. 243.

35. Memo for the record, Oct 22, 1968, FRUS, 1964–1968, vol. 19, doc. 244.

36. Nathaniel Davis interview with Thompson, "The Hotline Exchanges," Nov 4, 1968, FRUS, 1964–1968, vol. 19, doc. 245, also in LBJL and in TFP.

37. Helms, *A Look over My Shoulder*, p. 303.

38. Ibid.; and McNamara, *In Retrospect*, p. 278.

39. Nathaniel Davis interview with Thompson, "The Hotline Exchanges," Nov 4, 1968, FRUS, 1964–1968, vol. 19, doc. 245, also in LBJL and in TFP.

40. LBJ to Kosygin, Jun 10, 1967, 9:39 a.m., FRUS, 1964–1968, vol. 19, doc. 246.

41. Kosygin to LBJ, June 10, 1967, 9:44 a.m., FRUS, 1964–1968, vol. 19, doc. 247.

42. LBJ to Kosygin, June 10, 1967, 10:58 a.m., FRUS, 1964–1968, vol. 19, doc. 252.

43. LBJ to Kosygin, June 10, 1967, 11:58 a.m., FRUS, 1964–1968, vol. 19, doc. 255.

44. John Guthrie, Thompson's number-two man at the US embassy in Moscow, cabled the State Department, saying that Chinese accusations of Soviet collusion with Israel and the imperialists to betray the Arabs may have been a factor in this dramatic gesture, as well as in requesting an emergency session of the UN General Assembly. See Guthrie to State, cable 5451, June 15, 1967, NSF: Walt Rostow Papers, box 17, doc.70-A, LBJL, also in TFP.

45. Dobrynin, *In Confidence*, p. 160.

46. The emergency meeting would take place on June 17, 1967.

36 ≋ Glassboro: The Summit That Wasn't (June 23–25, 1967)

1. MemCon: Thompson-Dobrynin, Jun 16, 1967, FRUS, 1964–1968, vol. 14, doc. 218, also in LBJL, and in TFP.

2. Thompson memo for W. Rostow, Jun 16, 1967, NSF: USSR country file, box 223, vol. 15, LBJL, also in TFP.

3. Thompson letter to Jane, Jun 16, 1967, TFP.

4. Thompson-Dobrynin conversation, Jun 16, 1967, with Rostow cover note dated Jun 19, 1967, NSF: Walt Rostow Papers, box 17 (3 pts.), LBJL.

5. Zbigniew Brzezinski was then on the State Department's Policy Planning Council.

6. Rostow memo, Jun 21, 1967, NSF: USSR country file, Hollybush, box 230, LBJL; and McNamara memo, Jun 21, 1967, NSF: Walt Rostow Papers, box 11, Soviet missile talks [it should be in the Hollybush files, but the authors found it here], LBJL, also in TFP.

7. Thompson's response to two questions from LBJ, dictated over the phone to Rostow, Jun 21, 1967, NSF: USSR country file, Hollybush, box 230, LBJL.

8. Rusk to State, Jun 22, 1967, FRUS, 1964–1968, vol. 14, doc. 227.

9. Robert McNamara oral history, LBJL.

10. It would be instructive if someone studied the influence of ex-presidents on current ones.

11. The details were provided by LBJ's personal secretary, in his daily diary. See LBJ's daily diary, LBJL.

12. The traffic was so bad that Kosygin, after having insisted that the Soviet entourage be able to drive to the meeting, accepted LBJ's invitation to go back to New York City by helicopter.

13. Newspaper clipping, [undated], "Thompson, Summitry Veteran, on Job Again," noted as an "exclusive to the *Times*" [although it is not clear which newspaper this is], TFP.

14. MemCon, Glassboro meeting, Jun 23, 1967, FRUS, 1964–1968, vol. 14, doc. 229.

15. Before the UN General Assembly meeting, Rusk and Thompson had met with Dobrynin. Rusk assured the Soviet ambassador they had had no previous knowledge of the Israeli surprise attack on the UAR. Dobrynin wanted to know why the United States now opposed an Israeli withdrawal from the territory they had just occupied. Rusk replied that it was difficult to tell the Arabs that "we supported territorial integrity if they won't recognize the existence of Israel." See MemCon, Jun 16, 1967, FRUS, 1964–1968, vol. 19, doc. 301. At the UN meeting, Kosygin tried to persuade the UAR's foreign minister to accept a compromise that would officially recognize the existence of Israel, in exchange for the return of the occupied territories, but the minister would not budge.

16. Dobrynin, *In Confidence*, pp. 165–66. McNamara said Dobrynin had approached him before, in April 1967, and seemed interested in discussions on deterrent forces. See Robert McNamara oral history, LBJL.

17. Dobrynin, *In Confidence*, pp. 165–66. Dobrynin believed that the reason McNamara wanted the meeting to be private was to avoid exposing his position to those who favored the development of an ABM system.

18. As told to Raymond Garthoff and relayed to the authors in an interview with him, Oct 2013, TFP.

19. McNamara also mentioned this talk. See Robert McNamara oral history, LBJL. The presidential secretary's note taking is mentioned in LBJ's daily diary, LBJL.

20. MemCon: luncheon, Jun 23, 1967, FRUS, 1964–1968, vol. 14, doc. 231. Another record of the luncheon discussions, made by the president's secretary, is included in LBJ's daily diary, LBJL. Thompson reported Dobrynin's opinion in a letter to Rusk, Aug 4, 1967, TFP. Also see Dobrynin, *In Confidence*.

21. MemCon, Glassboro meeting, Jun 23, 1967, FRUS, 1964–1968, vol. 14, doc. 232.

22. Bundy was present, in his capacity as executive secretary of the Special Committee of the National Security Council from June–August 1967.

23. Francis M. Bator, "No Good Choices: LBJ and the Vietnam / Great Society Connection," *Diplomatic History*, vol. 32, no. 3 (Jun 2008), pp. 309–40.

24. Rostow memo to LBJ, Jul 19, 1967, FRUS, 1964–1968, vol. 34, doc. 164, p. 292n2. Eisenhower librarian Mary Burtzloff checked his post-presidential appointment book. See Burtzloff email to the authors, Sep 18, 2013, TFP.

25. TelCon: LBJ and Eisenhower, Jun 25, 1967, 9:44 p.m., FRUS, 1964–1968, vol. 14, doc. 237. LBJ stated that had mentioned this scheme to Kosygin during their conversation earlier that day. The Soviet had heard him out, but he kept insisting that before anything else could be discussed, the Israelis had to withdraw.

26. Ibid., p. 561. Eisenhower merely told LBJ that Thompson gave him a briefing on Vietnam, and then Ike proceeded to talk only about his water scheme.

27. See Rusk memo to LBJ, Jun 24, 1967, FRUS, 1964–1968, vol. 14, doc. 233; and Benjamin Reed oral history, LBJL.

28. MemCon, June 23, 1967, FRUS, 1964–1968, vol. 14, doc. 230; and MemCon, June 25, 1967, FRUS, 1964–1968, vol. 14, doc. 235. Also see Dobrynin, *In Confidence*. Thompson enquired about the Soviets' reply to LBJ's communiqué when the ambassador returned to Moscow, but he was given no answer. See Kornienko to Thompson, relayed in Thompson cable 450, Aug 5, 1967, and Rusk message to Thompson, Aug 6, 1967, both in NSF: Walt Rostow Papers, box 10, Hollybush, LBJL.

29. MemCon, June 25, 1967, FRUS, 1964–1968, vol. 14, doc. 234, p. 538n2.

30. Thompson appointment diary, Jun 25, 1967, Thompson lot file 67 D 2, box 20, RG 59, NACP, also in TFP.

31. See the relevant undated documents in the Glassboro file, LBJL, including a note to Rostow from Richard Moose, a special assistant the national security advisor, along with Moose's typewritten notes from the meetings. Also see Dumbrell, *Lyndon Johnson and Soviet Communism*, p. 73.

32. MemCon, Jun 25, 1967, FRUS, 1964–1968, vol. 14, doc. 236.

33. Thompson to State, cable 34, Jul 24, 1967, NSF: USSR country file, special committee, box 8, LBJL, also in TFP.

34. Authors' email correspondence with David Klein, Dec 8, 2012, TFP.

35. Thompson to SecState, cable 1492, Oct 18, 1967, NSF: USSR country file, box 224, vol. 16, LBJL, also in TFP. The next round would happen in 1973. The humiliation of their defeat by Israel would induce the Arabs to try to regain their lost territories. They launched the Yom Kippur War (October 6–26, 1973), and although they did not win against Israel, this time it was not so easy for the Israelis. Once again, the United States and the Soviet Union would become dangerously involved. One of the results of this 1973 war was the withdrawal of Israeli forces from the Suez Canal, which allowed Egypt to finally reopen the waterway.

36. Paper prepared by Bundy, Jul 18, 1967, FRUS, 1964–1968, vol. 19, doc. 374.

37. The term "land for peace" was first used as the basis for Israel's peace treaty with Egypt in 1979, when Israel withdrew from the Sinai Peninsula, and it was repeated again in 1994, in an Israel-Jordan peace treaty, where both sides agreed on an international boundary.

38. Bilateral and multilateral peace conferences took up where Gunnar Jarring left off. The Suez Canal was reopened in 1975. A peace treaty was signed between Israel and Egypt in 1979. This agreement included mutual recognition, Israel's return of the Sinai Peninsula to Egypt, and the granting of free passage for Israeli ships through the Suez Canal. In 1994, a similar peace treaty was signed between Israel and Jordan, which included solving water disputes and boundaries. The question of Jerusalem, however, was left open. Today, both the Palestinians and the Israelis claim it as their capital. The 1993 Oslo Accords established that the Palestinian Authority controls part (11 percent) of the West Bank, with 61 percent under Israeli control, and the rest subject to joint Israeli military control and Palestinian civilian control. The major problem in this area is the continuous building of Israeli settlements on the West Bank, which makes the idea of a two-state solution for the Palestinians increasingly difficult. Syria still does not recognize Israel.

39. Bohlen letter to Thompson, Jun 14, 1967, records of Ambassador Bohlen, 1942–1971, box 27, entry A1-1560, RG 59, NACP.

40. Kornienko to Thompson, relayed in Thompson cable 450, Aug 5, 1967, NSF: Walt Rostow Papers, box 10, Hollybush, LBJL.

41. Thompson to State, cable 2404, reflecting on his past year in Moscow, Jan 11, 1968, NSF: USSR country file, box 224, LBJL, also in TFP and in FRUS, 1964–1968, vol. 14, doc. 261.

42. Jane Thompson letter to Sally Chase, Jan 28, 1967, TFP.

43. Jonathan Rickert, "Impressions of Ambassador Thompson," Nov 25, 2002, TFP.

44. Ibid.

45. Thompson to State, cable 3465, Feb 13, 1967, FRUS, 1964–1968, vol. 14, doc. 200; and Thompson to State, cable 2404, Jan 11, 1968, NSF: USSR country file, box 224, LBJL, also in TFP and in FRUS, 1964–1968, vol. 14, doc. 261.

46. Jonathan Rickert, "Impressions of Ambassador Thompson," Nov 25, 2002. TFP.

47. Ibid.; Charles Stuart Kennedy interview with William T. Pryce, FA-ADST, https://cdn.loc.gov/service/mss/mfdip/2007/2007pry01/2007pry01.pdf; and Ed Hurwitz correspondence with the authors, Apr 4, 2004, TFP.

48. Yaroslavl is a city known for its beautiful churches, and its historic center is now a World Heritage Site.

49. Thompson to Bohlen, Jul 20, 1967, records of Ambassador Bohlen, 1942–1971, box 27, entry A1-1560, RG 59, NACP.

50. See, for example, Newhouse, *Cold Dawn*, pp. 21, 24, 128.

51. For comments by Rostow and Rusk regarding this point, see Dumbrell, *Lyndon Johnson and Soviet Communism*, p. 85; and Garthoff, *Journey through the Cold War*, p. 262.

52. Thompson letter to Rusk, Aug 4, 1967, Thompson lot file, 67 D, RG 59, NACP, also in TFP.

53. When Foy Kohler became the US ambassador in Moscow, he apparently had replaced the Checker limousine (see chapter 22) with a new Cadillac.

54. These were actually comb jellies (known as sea gooseberries, or *Pleurobrachia pileus*), not true jellyfish This sighting by the Thompsons is not to be confused with the jellyfish "invasion" of *Mnemiopsis* in the 1980s, thought to have begun with a US ship disgorging infected ballast water.

55. A Moskvich is a Soviet copy of a Fiat.

56. Thompson to State, cable 896, Sep 2, 1967, FRUS, 1964–1968, vol. 11, doc. 207.

57. "McNamara Speech on U.S. Nuclear Strategy," *CQ Almanac 1967*, ed. 23 (1968).

58. For Thompson's thoughts on the "Chinese Communists" reference in a draft of McNamara's speech, see Thompson to State, Sep 2, 1967, cable 896, FRUS, 1964–1968, vol. 11, doc. 207, also in NSF: USSR country file, box 224, vol. 16, LBJL. On Garthoff, see Spurgeon Kenny memo to Rostow, Aug 28, 1967, NSF: USSR country file, ABM negotiations, box 231, LBJL. For McNamara's speech, it is important to look at the complete speech, since there are abbreviated copies online that do not reflect this. See "McNamara Speech on U.S. Nuclear Strategy," *CQ Almanac 1967*, ed. 23 (1968).

59. Newhouse, *Cold Dawn*, pp. 95–98.

60. Thompson-Kennan correspondence, Apr 1966, TFP. Also see Thompson to Kennan, cable 259, Jul 19, 1967, FRUS, 1964–1968, vol. 14, doc. 240. In part because of the intense Soviet reaction to Svetlana Alliluyeva's *Twenty Letters to a Friend*, Thompson had tried but failed to convince George Kennan to postpone publication of his own memoirs until after the jubilee. Kennan, who helped Alliluyeva get asylum in India, in the US embassy in New Delhi, and then temporarily put her up in his country home in the United States, professed that he only did it as a kindness to her. The Soviets, however, assumed it was a deliberate action on Kennan's part to discredit them, because they had expelled him as a persona non grata years before. Kennan once again either did not anticipate the Soviets' practical reaction to his behavior, which they found offensive in the extreme, or did not care, because he then helped Alliluyeva publish her book. Kennan subsequently published his own memoirs on US-USSR relations from 1925 to 1950, covering the Stalin purges.

37 ≋ 1968: A Year of Frustrated Promise

1. Dobrynin, *In Confidence*, p. 170. Also see MemCon, Jan 12, 1968, FRUS, 1964–1968, vol. 6, doc. 10, p. 26.

2. Thompson to State, cable 2404, Jan 11, 1968, FRUS, 1964–1968, vol. 14, doc. 261.

3. Thompson personal letter to Bohlen, Dec 29, 1967, records of Ambassador Bohlen, 1942–1971, box 27, entry A1-1560, NACP, also in TFP.

4. Dumbrell, *Lyndon Johnson and Soviet Communism*, pp. 166–67.

5. Thompson personal letter to Rusk, Jan 29, 1968, TFP.

6. This phase of the Tet Offensive lasted from January 31 to March 28, 1968.

7. Hoopes, *Limits of Intervention*, p. 147.

8. Clark Clifford became the US secretary of defense on January 19, 1968.

9. The meetings took place on March 25 and 26, 1968. Members of the Senior Advisory Group on Vietnam were John McCloy, Dean Acheson, Arthur Dean, McGeorge Bundy, Douglas Dillon, and Robert Murphy.

10. Thompson letter to Jane, Apr 1, 1968, TFP.

11. "Lyndon Baines Johnson, 'Withdrawal Speech' (March 31, 1968)," Voices of Democracy: The U.S. Oratory Project, http://voicesofdemocracy.umd.edu/lyndon-baines-johnson-withdrawal-speech-31-march-1968/.

12. Rostow's memo to LBJ on April 4—when Thompson had a meeting with the president to discuss the ambassador's role in the Vietnam talks—indicates that this was to follow up on LBJ's earlier conversation with Thompson, although the authors found no record of an earlier discussion in LBJ's daily dairy. See diary backup, box 95, LBJL, also in TFP.

13. Rostow, memo for the record, Mar 31, 1968, NSF: Walt Rostow Papers, box 10, Rusk-Dobrynin file, LBJL, also in FRUS, 1964–1968, vol. 6, doc. 168.

14. It was not until the end of October 1969, with Clark Clifford's support, that LBJ stopped all the bombing of North Vietnam.

15. LBJ telephone call to Fulbright, Apr 1, 1968, tape WH6804.01, Miller Center, secret White House tapes, https://millercenter.org/the-presidency/secret-white-house-tapes/conversation-william-fulbright-april-1-1968/, also in FRUS, 1964–1968, vol. 6, doc. 171.

16. Notes of meeting, Apr 3, 1968, FRUS, 1964–1968, vol. 6, doc. 178. A UPI report published on the same day lists Thompson and Harriman as the president's special representatives to the talks.

17. Thompson wanted to clarify the wording of the San Antonio formula, which was used by the president in a speech in San Antonio, Texas, on September 29, 1967. In it, LBJ had offered to stop the US bombing of North Vietnam if Ho Chi Minh agreed both to begin serious negotiations for a peaceful settlement of the conflict and to not use the bombing halt to increase the infiltration of troops and supplies into South Viet-

nam. The president restated this on March 31, 1968, after the Tet Offensive and his decision not to seek a second full term as president.

18. LBJ's daily diary, Apr 4, 1968, LBJL. Rostow's memo to LBJ shows that Thompson met with the president at 7 p.m. on April 4.

19. For the CIA's memo, see Dumbrell, *Lyndon Johnson and Soviet Communism*, pp. 168–69. For Jacob Beam, see Beam to State, cable 2825, Aug 4, 1968, FRUS, 1964–1968, vol. 17 (*Eastern Europe*), doc. 77. For Thompson's views, see Thompson to State, cable 4614, Jul 11, 1968, FRUS, vol. 17, doc. 65; and Thompson to State, cable 4732, July 21, 1968, and cables 4751 and 4752, Jul 22, 1968, all three in NSF: USSR country file, box 226, vol. 21, LBJL.

20. Dumbrell, *Lyndon Johnson and Soviet Communism*, p. 82.

21. "Boxcar" was the largest hydrogen bomb test in Nevada. See Keith Rogers, "Scientists Conducted First Atomic Bomb Test in 1951, Last in '92," *Las Vegas Review-Journal*, Jan 12, 2014, www.reviewjournal .com/nevada-150/scientists-conducted-first-atomic-bomb-test-1951-last-92/.

22. Moscow to State, cable 4111, Jun 5, 1968, NSF: USSR country file, box 226, vol. 20, LBJL. For Sirhan Sirhan's motive, see "Sirhan Felt Betrayed by Kennedy," *New York Times*, Feb 20, 1989, www.nytimes.com /1989/02/20/us/sirhan-felt-betrayed-by-kennedy.html.

23. Authors' email correspondence with David Klein, Dec 9, 2012, TFP.

24. Rostow memo to LBJ, Jun 5, 1968, FRUS, 1964–1968, vol. 6, doc. 262.

25. Notes of meeting, LBJ with foreign policy advisers, FRUS, 1964–1968, vol. 6, doc. 265; and Tom Johnson notes of meetings, box 3, LBJL, also in TFP. For the official reply, see LBJ to Kosygin, Jun 11, 1968, FRUS, 1964–1968, vol. 6, doc. 269.

26. Merle Pribbenow, "North Vietnam's 'Talk-Fight' Strategy and the 1968 Peace Negotiations with the United States," Apr 16, 2012, Cold War International History Project, Wilson Center, https://www.wilson center.org/publication/north-vietnams-talk-fight-strategy-and-the-1968-peace-negotiations-the-united -states/.

27. Dobrynin, *In Confidence*, p. 174.

28. Kosygin's failed effort to help the Americans (see chapter 34) was probably a contributing factor in the ascendancy of Brezhnev and the diminishing place of Kosygin in the Soviet power structure.

29. Thompson to State, cable 4614, Jul 11, 1968, FRUS, 1964–1968, vol. 17, doc. 65.

30. After Thompson's death, Jenny was told in an interview with an American intelligence official that her reports constituted one of the reasons why the US government believed an invasion of Czechoslovakia was imminent.

31. Thompson to State, cable 4614, Jul 11, 1968, FRUS, 1964–1968, vol. 17, doc. 65. Regarding the letters, see Beam, *Multiple Exposure*, p. 182.

32. Dobrynin, *In Confidence*, p. 145.

33. Bohlen, *Witness to History*, p. 528.

34. Thompson letter to Jane, Jul 25, 1968, TFP.

35. Lawrence Roberts, an art historian and an expert on Japanese antiquities, was the head of the American Academy in Rome, and Villa Aurelia is a historic home that was the director's residence at that time.

36. Jane Thompson letter to her mother, Aug 15, 1968, TFP.

37. Navratil, *Prague Spring 1968*, pp. 189–90.

38. Beam to State, cable 2825, Aug 4, 1968, FRUS, 1964–1968, vol. 17, doc. 77. For Rusk's comment, see Dumbrell, *Lyndon Johnson and Soviet Communism*, p. 171. According to one of the Communists inside the Dubček regime, the Soviet invasion could have been avoided, had Dubček agreed to Brezhnev's proposed "four steps." See Navratil, *Prague Spring 1968*, p. 320.

39. Thompson to State, cable 4910, Aug 2, 1968, FRUS, 1964–1968, vol. 17, doc. 76.

40. Summary of NSC meeting, Sep 4, 1968, FRUS, 1964–1968, vol. 17, doc. 93; and Thompson undated paper, "The Soviet System and Ours," 1970s, TFP.

41. Jane Thompson letter to her mother, Jul 17, 1968, TFP.

42. Moscow to SecState, cable 5648, Sep 24, 1968, NSF: USSR country file, box 226, vol. 21, LBJL, also in TFP.

43. Thompson letter to Jane, Oct 22, 1968, TFP.

44. Anna Chennault is a Chinese-American member of the Republican Party, had been an advisor for Richard Nixon's presidential campaign, and is the widow of Lieutenant General Clare Chennault, a World War II aviation hero who died in 1958.

45. See LBJ conversation with Everett Dirksen, Nov 2, 1968, tape WH6811-01-13706, LBJL, with a transcript at http://prde.upress.virginia.edu/conversations/4006123/notes_open/; and summary in David Taylor, "The Lyndon Johnson Tapes: Richard Nixon's 'Treason,'" Mar 22, 2013, BBC News magazine, www.bbc.com/news/magazine-21768668/. This episode was later published in Fulsom, *Treason*.

46. Ronald H. Spector, "Vietnam War, 1954–1975," Encyclopædia Britannica online, https://www.britannica.com/event/Vietnam-War/.

47. Letters between Thompson and Bohlen, Nov–Dec 1968, records of Ambassador Bohlen, 1942–1971, box 27, A1-1560, RG 59, NACP, also in TFP.

48. Dumbrell, *Lyndon Johnson and Soviet Communism*, p. 85; and Newhouse, *Cold Dawn*, pp. 181–82.

49. McCloy to LBJ, Dec 12, 1968, NSF: strategic missile talks, box 11, file 3 of 3, LBJL, also in TFP.

38 ≋ "Retirement," So to Speak

1. Anatole Shub, "Thompson's Negative Success in Moscow," Jan 1969, *Paris Tribune*, TFP.

2. Edmund Stevens, "Interpretive Report: Thompson's Moscow Key; Honesty," *Washington [DC] Star*, Jan 13, 1969.

3. James Foster, "Rusk Bids Farewell to 3 Top Diplomats," *Rocky Mountain News* [Denver, CO], Jan 18, 1969.

4. Marie Smith, "A Tribute to American Ambassadors," Style section, *Washington Post*, May 16, 1969, TFP.

5. "Strategic Arms Limitation Talks (SALT I)," Oct 26, 2011, Nuclear Threat Initiative, www.nti.org/learn/treaties-and-regimes/strategic-arms-limitation-talks-salt-i-salt-ii/. SALT was divided into a series of talks: SALT I, in Helsinki; SALT II, in Vienna; SALT III, in Helsinki; through to SALT VII (some held in Helsinki and some in Vienna). The subsequent series of SALT talks that began in November 1972 were then called SALT II, and the name SALT I was retroactively given to all of the first set of talks, thus confusing the names. Therefore, the individual sessions of SALT I are herein referred to as SALT 1, SALT 2, SALT 3, and so forth.

6. "Thompson Will Join in Arms Curb Talks," *Denver Post*, Jul 6, 1969, TFP.

7. Thompson letter to Jane, Nov 31, 1969, TFP.

8. Authors' interview with Raymond Garthoff, Sep 2009, TFP.

9. Thompson letter to Jane from Helsinki, Dec 1969, TFP.

10. Dobrynin, *In Confidence*.

11. Authors' interview with Raymond Garthoff, Oct 2013, TFP.

12. Minutes of NSC meeting, Jun 25, 1969, FRUS, 1969–1976, vol. 32 (*SALT I, 1969–1972*), doc. 22.

13. John Newhouse, *Cold Dawn*, p. 6.

14. Authors' interviews with Raymond Garthoff, Sep 2009 and Dec 2009 [by telephone], TFP.

15. Authors' telephone interview with Raymond Garthoff, Dec 2009, TFP. Garthoff's comments were based on his conversations with senior Soviet officials after the fact.

16. Betty Beale, "Colonial Christmas Like It Was," *Washington [DC] Star*, Dec 24, 1969, reprinted in *Miami Herald*, Jan 4, 1970, TFP.

17. Authors' interview with Raymond Garthoff, Sep 2009, TFP.

18. Editorial note, FRUS, 1969–1976, vol. 32, doc. 45.

19. Conversation: Nixon and Kissinger, FRUS, 1969–1976, vol. 32, doc. 247.

20. Nicholas Ruggieri, "The World Hopes as U.S. and U.S.S.R. Talk at Vienna," *Department of State News Letter*, no. 109 (May 1970), p. 10; *Die Presse* [Vienna, Austria], Apr 25–26, 1970, TFP; and several other newspaper and magazine clippings, TFP.

21. Rollie White letter to Jane, Feb 9, 1972. White was an FSO in Moscow during 1957–1958 and later was a special assistant to Undersecretary of State Averell Harriman.

22. Scoville and Osborne, *Missile Madness*, pp. 3, 4, 23.

23. Authors' interview with Raymond Garthoff, Oct 7, 2013, TFP.

24. Ibid. For example, according to Garthoff, Nitze and the DOD were interested in using the talks to work out controls for radar, while the staff was more interested in the broader strategic nuclear issues. Also see Newhouse, *Cold Dawn*, pp. 12, 33, 46–48, 83, 180. Newhouse cited the DOD's Office of Research and Engineering as being problematic.

25. Various Thompson speeches to Foreign Service Institute classes (e.g., Foreign Service Institute, Washington, DC, Apr 12, 1971), TFP.

26. Minutes of NSC meeting, Jun 25, 1969, FRUS, 1969–1976, vol. 32, doc. 22. In this meeting, Nixon said he thought Congress and the allies should not know what the initial proposals were. Also see Raymond Garthoff, "Negotiating SALT," *Wilson Quarterly*, vol. 3, no. 4 (Autumn 1977), p. 82; and Newhouse, *Cold Dawn*, pp. 190–192.

27. Dobrynin, *In Confidence*. As an example, John Newhouse, in *Cold Dawn*, states that Kissinger offered a proposal that would allow each side to maintain an ABM system around its capital, which John Newhouse claimed the White House later acknowledged as "an intellectual blunder" (*Cold Dawn*, p. 184). First, the US negotiators were divulging their maximum bargaining chip to the Soviets initially, which made it harder to go back to a preferred, zero-AMB position. Second, Kissinger failed to see that protecting Moscow and Washington, DC, were not equivalent. The Soviets already had Galosh deployed, and they had ICBM sites within the Galosh's boundaries, which would, therefore, also be protected. Washington, DC, had no ABM system surrounding it, and Congress wasn't likely to fund such a project. Even if it did, America's ICBMs were all located out in the hinterland and could not be protected by any system set up around Washington, DC. In the end it was agreed that each country would have the right to one site and could choose whether to protect the capital or the ICBMs. The Soviets deployed missile defenses around Moscow; the U.S. decided not to deploy any around DC because at that time it considered such defenses ineffective. Reagan's SDI proposal later placed all this in a different light.

28. For the nature of the Kissinger Nixon decision making, the last-minute change, and the SALT delegation's reaction, see Newhouse, *Cold Dawn*, pp. 178–80.

29. Smith, *Doubletalk*, chap. 5, "Season of Frustration."

30. N. Thompson, *The Hawk and the Dove*, pp. 232–33.

31. Authors' interview with Raymond Garthoff, Sep 2009, TFP.

32. "Exchange of Remarks between President and Foreign Minister Andre Gromyko, East Room," White House press release, Oct 3, 1972, TFP, also in "334: Remarks at a Ceremony Marking Entry into Force of the Treaty on the Limitation of Anti-Ballistic Missile Systems and the Interim Agreement on the Limitation of Strategic Offensive Arms," Oct 3, 1972, American Presidency Project, www.presidency.ucsb.edu/ws/index .php?pid=3613/.

33. Dobrynin, *In Confidence*, p. 201.

34. In this instance, "it" was the ability of the United States to somehow win the nuclear arms race, or at least to maintain a vast superiority over the Soviets. See conversation: Nixon and Kissinger, Apr 19, 1972, FRUS, 1969–1976, vol. 32, doc. 260.

35. Conversation: Nixon, Gerard Smith, and Alexander Haig Jr., Mar 21, 1972, FRUS, 1969–1976, vol. 32, doc. 242.

36. The State Department had changed under the Nixon administration. Secretary of State William Rogers was left out of important meetings, as Kissinger took on the role of handling all diplomatic issues. For example, the US ambassador to Moscow, Jacob Beam, was virtually kept in the dark and did not even know that Kissinger had come to Moscow in April 1972 for his secret SALT negotiations with the Soviets. Leaving Beam out of the picture, to the extent of not even staying at the ambassadorial residence, was a humiliation for Beam and rendered him ineffective as an ambassador.

37. This advice was given to one of the authors' friends, who was thinking about joining the Foreign Service. Thompson used less-colorful wording with other young people seeking his advice on joining the Foreign Service, but the content was the same.

38. Nixon told his close advisors—Kissinger, White House chief of staff H. R. "Bob" Haldeman, and special consultant John Scali—that he and he alone began the China initiative "20 months ago." See conversation: Nixon, Kissinger, Haldeman, and Scali, Apr 13, 1971, FRUS, 1969–1976, vol. 13 (*Soviet Union, October 1970–October 1971*), doc. 174.

39. William Rogers's office files, lot 73 D 443, box 4, White House correspondence, 1969, RG 59, NACP, also in Thompson memo to Rogers, Feb 7, 1969, FRUS, 1969–1976, vol. 12, doc. 11.

40. Helmut Sonnenfeldt [NSC staff member] memo to Kissinger, Dec 11, 1969, FRUS, 1969–1976, vol. 12 (*Soviet Union, January 1969–October 1970*), doc. 105.

41. Ibid., p. 319n2.

42. Conversation: Nixon, Kissinger, Haldeman, and Scali, Apr 13, 1971, FRUS, 1969–1976, vol. 13, doc. 174.

43. Thompson memo to Rogers, Feb 7, 1969, FRUS, 1969–1976, vol. 12, doc. 11.

44. Conversation: Nixon and Kissinger, May 27, 1971, FRUS, 1969–1976, vol. 13, doc. 240.

45. Conversation: Nixon, Kissinger, and Haldeman, May 28, 1971, FRUS, 1969–1976, vol. 13, doc. 243.

46. Dobrynin, *In Confidence*.

47. Thompson letter to Robert Ford, Aug 20, 1971, TFP.

48. Frank Hannigan [assistant director of the US Golf Association] letter to Thompson, Dec 7, 1971, TFP.

49. "Golf in Russia," Wikipedia, https://en.wikipedia.org/wiki/Golf_in_Russia/.

50. For more information on chaga, see "*Inonotus obliquus*," Wikipedia, https://en.wikipedia.org/wiki/Inonotus_obliquus#Medicinal_research/.

51. The details of this story come thanks to Sherwood Demitz's correspondence with the authors, Sep 2007, TFP.

52. There is a sequel to this story. Many years later, when Jane was alone in Washington, DC, and feeling more and more isolated and abandoned by friends, Rostropovich was again in that city. Jane invited him to her house for a meal, in gratitude for all he had done. He accepted and said he would arrive with his secretary. A young woman who had worked with Jane heard about the planned lunch with the famous cellist and asked Jane to include her. Jane obliged. When Rostropovich arrived, he looked incredibly uncomfortable and, after a few minutes, mumbled some excuse about having to leave right away, so just his secretary finished the meal with Jane, her daughter, and their other guest. It was not until much later that the truth of what occurred came out. The young woman who had worked with Jane had had a short affair with Rostropovich, and he had subsequently broken it off. When the cellist arrived and saw her at Jane's house, he thought it was a trap. The authors do not know whether he believed Jane was a deliberate party to the young woman's machinations, but Jane would wonder for years what had caused Rostropovich to flee her home.

53. Charles Bohlen eulogy for Thompson, TFP.

54. Thompson speech to members of the Foreign Ministry and Parliamentary Foreign Relations Committees, Vienna, Jun 10, 1964, TFP.

Bibliography

Abel, Elie. *The Missile Crisis*. J. B. Lippincott, 1966.

Acheson, Dean, and board of consultants David E. Lilienthal (chairman), Chester I. Barnard, J. R. Oppenheimer, Charles A. Thomas, and Harry A. Winne. *A Report on the International Control of Atomic Energy*. US Government Printing Office, 1946.

Allard, Sven. *Russia and the Austrian State Treaty: A Case Study of Soviet Policy in Europe*. Pennsylvania State University Press, 1970.

Alliluyeva, Svetlana. *Twenty Letters to a Friend: A Memoir*. Hutchinson, 1967.

Allyn, Bruce J., James G. Blight, and David A. Welch. *Back to the Brink: Proceedings of the Moscow Conference on the Cuban Missile Crisis, January 27–28, 1989*. Center for Science and International Affair, Harvard University, 1991.

Ambrose, Stephen. *Eisenhower: Soldier and President*. Simon & Schuster, 1991.

Ambrose, Stephen, and Richard H. Immerman. *Ike's Spies: Eisenhower and the Espionage Establishment*. University Press of Mississippi, 1999.

Arbatov, Georgi, and Willem Oltmans. *Cold War or Detente? The Soviet Viewpoint*. Zed Books, 1983.

Ausland, John C. *Kennedy, Khrushchev and the Berlin-Cuba Crisis, 1961–1964*. Aschehoug, 1996.

Ball, George W. *The Past Has Another Pattern: Memoirs*. W. W. Norton, 1983.

Bamford, James. *Body of Secrets: Anatomy of the Ultra-Secret National Security Agency*. Anchor Books, 2002.

Barraclough, Geoffrey, and Rachael F. Wall. *Survey of International Affairs, 1955–1956*. Chatham House Series. Oxford University Press, 1960.

Beam, Jacob. *Multiple Exposure: An American Ambassador's Unique Perspective on East-West Issues*. W. W. Norton, 1978.

Beschloss, Michael R. *The Crisis Years: Kennedy and Khrushchev, 1960–1963*. Edward Burlingame Books, 1991.

Beschloss, Michael R. *May Day: Eisenhower, Khrushchev and the U-2 Affair*. Harper & Row, 1986.

Bethell, Nicholas. *Betrayed*. Times Books, 1984.

Bethell, Nicholas. *The Last Secret: Forcible Repatriation to Russia, 1944–1947*. Andre Deutsch, 1974.

Bird, Kai, and Martin J. Sherwin. *American Prometheus: The Triumph and Tragedy of J. Robert Oppenheimer*. Alfred A. Knopf, 2005.

Bischof, Günter. *Austria in the First Cold War, 1945–55: Leverage of the Weak*. St. Martin's, 1999.

Blight, James G., Bruce J. Allyn, and David A. Welch. *Cuba on the Brink: Castro, the Missile Crisis, and the Soviet Collapse*. Rowman & Littlefield, 2002.

Blight, James G., and David A. Welch. *On the Brink: Americans and Soviets Reexamine the Cuban Missile Crisis*. Hill & Wang, 1989.

Bohlen, Charles E. *Witness to History*. W. W. Norton, 1973.

Brandon, Henry. *Special Relationships: A Foreign Correspondent's Memoirs from Roosevelt to Reagan*. Scribner, 1989.

Bulgakov, Mikhail. *The Master and Margarita*, trans. by Michael Glenny. Collins, 1967.

Bundy, McGeorge. *Danger and Survival: Choices about the Bomb in the First Fifty Years*. Vintage Books, 1990.

Campbell, John Creighton, ed. *Successful Negotiations, Trieste, 1954: An Appraisal by the Five Participants*. Princeton University Press, 1976.

Carafano, James Jay. *Waltzing into the Cold War: The Struggle for Occupied Austria*. Texas A&M University Press, 2002.

Carlson, Peter. *K Blows Top: A Cold War Comic Interlude Starring Nikita Khrushchev, America's Most Unlikely Tourist*. Public Affairs, 2009 (paperback ed.).

Cassidy, Henry C. *Moscow Dateline, 1941–1943*. Houghton Mifflin, 1943.

Chang, Laurence, and Peter Kornbluh, eds. *The Cuban Missile Crisis, 1962: A National Security Archive Documents Reader*. New Press, 1992, 1998 (rev. ed.).

Church, Frank, and Senate Select Committee, US Congress. *Final Report of the Select Committee to Study Governmental Operations with Respect to Intelligence Activities*. US Government Printing Office, 1976.

Clearwater, John Murray. *Johnson, McNamara, and the Birth of SALT and the ABM Treaty, 1963–1969*. Dissertation.com, 1999.

Clifford, Clark. *Counsel to the President: A Memoir*. Random House, 1991.

Clifford, Clark, [and George Elsey]. *American Relations with the Soviet Union: A Report to the President by the Special Counsel to the President, September 24, 1946*. White House, 1946.

Coleman, David. *The Fourteenth Day: JFK and the Aftermath of the Cuban Missile Crisis; Based on the Secret White House Tapes*. W. W. Norton, 2013.

Costigliola, Frank. *Roosevelt's Lost Alliances: How Personal Politics Helped Start the Cold War*. Princeton University Press, 2014.

Craig, Campbell, and Fredrik Logevall. *America's Cold War: The Politics of Insecurity*. Harvard University Press, 2012.

Davies, Joseph E. *Mission to Moscow*. Simon & Schuster, 1941.

Djilas, Milovan. *Conversations with Stalin*. Hart Davis, 1962.

Dobbs, Michael. *One Minute to Midnight: Kennedy, Khrushchev, and Castro on the Brink of Nuclear War*. Alfred A. Knopf, 2008.

Dobrynin, Anatoly. *In Confidence: Moscow's Ambassador to America's Six Cold War Presidents*. University of Washington Press, 1995.

Donovan, Robert J. *Conflict and Crisis: The Presidency of Harry S. Truman, 1945–1948*. University of Missouri Press, 1977.

Douglass, James W. *Kennedy and the Unspeakable: Why He Died and Why It Matters*. Orbis Books, 2008.

Dumbrell, John. *President Lyndon Johnson and Soviet Communism*. Manchester University Press, 2004.

Dunn, Dennis J. *Caught between Roosevelt and Stalin: America's Ambassadors to Moscow*. University of Kentucky Press, 1998.

Eisenhower, Dwight. *Waging Peace, 1956–1961*, vol. 2 in *The White House Years*. Doubleday, 1965.

Eisenhower, Milton. *The President Is Calling*. Crown, 1974.

Freedman, Lawrence. *Kennedy's Wars: Berlin, Cuba, Laos, and Vietnam*. Oxford University Press, 2000.

Friedman, Norman. *The Fifty-Year War: Conflict and Strategy in the Cold War*. Naval Institute Press, 2007.

Fulbright, J. William. *The Arrogance of Power*. Random House, 1966.

Fulsom, Don. *Treason: Nixon and the 1968 Election*. Pelican, 2015.

Fursenko, Aleksandr, and Timothy Naftali. *Khrushchev's Cold War: The Inside Story of an American Adversary*. W. W. Norton, 2006.

Fursenko, A[leksandr] A., et al. *Prezidium TSK KPSS 1954–1964: Chernovye protokol'nye zapisi zasedanii͡, stenogrammy, postanovleniia* [Presidium of the Central Committee of the Communist Party of the Soviet Union, 1954–1964: Draft Minutes from Meetings, Transcripts, Decisions], 3 vols. ROSSPĖN, 2003.

Gardner, Gary T. *Nuclear Nonproliferation: A Primer*. Lynne Rienner, 1994.

Garthoff, Raymond L. *Assessing the Adversary: Estimating by the Eisenhower Administration of Soviet Intentions and Capabilities*. Brookings Institution Press, 1991.

Garthoff, Raymond L. *Journey through the Cold War: A Memoir of Containment and Coexistence*. Brookings Institution Press, 2001.

Garthoff, Raymond L. *Reflections on the Cuban Missile Crisis*. Brookings Institution Press, 1987, 1989 (rev. ed.).

Gibbons, William Conrad. *The US Government and the Vietnam War: Executive and Legislative Roles and Relationships*, 4 vols. Princeton University Press, 1986–1995.

Goduti, Phillip A., Jr. *Kennedy's Kitchen Cabinet and the Pursuit of Peace: The Shaping of American Foreign Policy, 1961–1963*. McFarland, 2009.

Goldman, Jan. *The Central Intelligence Agency: An Encyclopedia of Covert Ops, Intelligence Gathering, and Spies*, 2 vols. ABC-CLIO, 2015.

Goldstein, Gordon M. *Lessons in Disaster: McGeorge Bundy and the Path to War in Vietnam*. Holt Paperbacks, 2008.

Gordon, Kermit, ed. *Agenda for the Nation: Papers on Domestic and Foreign Policy Issues*. Brookings Institution Press, 1968.

Goulding, Phil G. *Confirm or Deny: Informing the People on National Security*. Harper & Row, 1970.

Gromyko, Andrei. *Memoirs*. Doubleday, 1990.

Grose, Peter. *Operation Rollback: America's Secret War behind the Iron Curtain*. Mariner Books, 2001.

Gross Stein, Janice, and Richard Ned Lebow. *We All Lost the Cold War*. Princeton University Press, 1994.

Guthman, Edwin O., and Jeffrey Shulman, eds. *Robert Kennedy: In His Own Words; The Unpublished Recollections of the Kennedy Years*. Bantam Books, in cooperation with Twenty-First Century Books, 1989.

Halberstam, David. *The Best and the Brightest*. Random House, 1969.

Harriman, W. Averell, and Elie Abel. *Special Envoy to Churchill and Stalin, 1941–1946*. Random House, 1975.

Harrison, Hope. *Driving the Soviets Up the Wall: Soviet-East German Relations, 1953–1961*. Princeton University Press, 2005.

Haslam, Jonathan. *Russia's Cold War: From the October Revolution to the Fall of the Wall*. Yale University Press, 2012.

Hazard, Elizabeth W. *Cold War Crucible: United States Foreign Policy and the Conflict in Romania, 1943–1953*. Columbia University Press, 1996.

Helms, Richard. *A Look over My Shoulder: A Life in the Central Intelligence Agency*. Presidio Press, 2004.

Heisenberg, Werner Karl. *The Physical Principles of the Quantum Theory*, trans. by Carl Eckart and Frank C. Hoyt. University of Chicago Science Series 1. University of Chicago, 1930.

Herman, Arthur. *Joseph McCarthy: Reexamining the Life and Legacy of America's Most Hated Senator*. Free Press, 1999.

Herring, George C., ed. *The Secret Diplomacy of the Vietnam War: The Negotiating Volumes of the Pentagon Papers*. University of Texas Press, 1983.

Hersh, Burton. *The Old Boys: The American Elite and the Origins of the CIA*. Tree Farm Books, 2001.

Hersh, Seymour. *The Dark Side of Camelot*. Back Bay Books, 1998.

Hershberg, James G. *Marigold: The Lost Chance for Peace in Vietnam*. Stanford University Press, 2014.

History of the Communist Party of the Soviet Union (Bolsheviks): Short Course, ed. by commission of the Central Committee of the Communist Party of the Soviet Union. International Publishers, 1939.

Hixon, Walter. *Parting the Curtain: Propaganda, Culture, and the Cold War*. St. Martin's Press, 1998.

Holloway, David. *Stalin and the Bomb: The Soviet Union and Atomic Energy, 1939–1956*. Yale University Press, 1994.

Hoopes, Townsend. *The Limits of Intervention: An Inside Account of How the Johnson Policy of Escalation in Vietnam Was Reversed*. David McKay, 1970.

Inge, William Ralph. *The End of an Age and Other Essays*. Putnam, 1947.

Isacoff, Stuart. *When the World Stopped to Listen: Van Cliburn's Cold War Triumph, and Its Aftermath*. Knopf Doubleday, 2017.

Jenkins, Kempton. *Cold War Saga*. Nimble Books, 2010.

Johnson, Lyndon Baines. *Vantage Point: Perspectives of the Presidency, 1963–1969*. Holt, Rinehart & Winston, 1971.

Jones, Joseph. *Fifteen Weeks (February 21–June 5, 1947)*. Harbinger Book No. 47. Harcourt, Brace & World, 1964.

Judt, Tony. *Postwar: A History of Europe since 1945*. Penguin, 2006.

Karner, Stefan, et al., eds. *Der Wiener Gipfel, 1961: Kennedy-Chruschtschow*. StudienVerlag.

Kempe, Fred. *Berlin 1961: Kennedy, Khrushchev, and the Most Dangerous Place on Earth*. Berkley Books, 2012.

Khrushchev, Nikita Sergeyevich. *Khrushchev Remembers*, 2 vols., trans. and ed. by Strobe Talbott. Little, Brown, 1970.

Khrushchev, Sergei N. *Nikita Khrushchev and the Creation of a Superpower*. Pennsylvania State University Press, 2000.

Khrushchev, Sergei [N.] *Reformator*, 3 vols. Vriemia, 2010.

Kinzer, Stephen. *The Brothers: John Foster Dulles, Allen Dulles, and Their Secret World War*. Times Books, 2013.

Korniyenko, Georgy. *Holodnaya Voyina* [Cold War]. Olma Press, 2001.

Kraslow, David, and Stuart H. Loory. *The Secret Search for Peace in Vietnam*. Random House, 1968.

Krugler, David. *The Voice of America and the Domestic Propaganda Battles, 1945–1953*. University of Missouri Press, 2000.

Kuhn, Delia, and Ferdinand Kuhn, eds. *Adventures in Public Service: The Careers of Eight Honored Men in the United States Government*. Vanguard Press, 1963.

LeoGrande, William M., and Peter Kornbluh. *Back Channel to Cuba: The Hidden History of Negotiations between Washington and Havana*. University of North Carolina Press, 2015.

Levering, Ralph D., Vladimir O. Pechatnov, Verena Botzenhart-Viehe, and C. Earl Edmonson. *Debating the Origins of the Cold War: American and Russian Perspectives*. Rowman & Littlefield, 2002.

Lilienfeld, A. M., J. Tonascia, S. Tonascia, C. H. Libauer, G. M. Cauthen, J. A. Markowitz, and S. Waida. *Foreign Service Health Status Study: Evaluation of Health Status of Foreign Service and Other Employees from Selected Eastern European Posts*, contract no. 6025-619073. Department of Epidemiology, School of Hygiene and Public Health, Johns Hopkins University, 1978.

Lindsay, Franklin. *Beacons in the Night: With the OSS and Tito's Partisans in Wartime Yugoslavia*. Stanford University Press, 1993.

Lobel, Aaron, ed. *Presidential Judgment: Foreign Policy Decision Making in the White House*. Hollis, 2000.

Lundestad, Svein, ed. *U-2 Flights and the Cold War in the High North: Report from the Cold War Forum Conference on the Cold War in Bodø*. Bodø College, in cooperation with the Norwegian Aviation Centre, 1995.

Maddock, Shane J. *Nuclear Apartheid: The Quest for American Atomic Supremacy from World War II to the Present*. University of North Carolina Press, 2010.

May, Ernest R., and Philip Zelikow. *The Kennedy Tapes: Inside the White House during the Cuban Missile Crisis*. W. W. Norton, 2002.

Mayers, David. *The Ambassadors and America's Soviet Policy*. Oxford University Press, 1995.

McAuliffe, Mary S., ed. *CIA Documents on the Cuban Missile Crisis, 1962*. CIA History Staff, 1992.

McCullough, David. *Truman*. Simon & Schuster, 1992.

McMillan, Priscilla. *The Ruin of J. Robert Oppenheimer and the Birth of the Modern Arms Race*. Viking, 2005.

McNamara, Robert, with Brian VanDeMark. *In Retrospect: The Tragedy and Lessons of Vietnam*. Vintage Books, 1996.

Meier, Andrew. *The Lost Spy: An American in Stalin's Secret Service*. W. W. Norton, 2008.

Mićunović, Vejko. *Moscow Diary*. Doubleday, 1980.

Mikoyan, Sergo. *The Soviet Cuban Missile Crisis: Castro, Mikoyan, Kennedy, Khrushchev, and the Missiles of October*, ed. by Svetlana Savranskaya. Stanford University Press, 2014.

Miller Center. *The Presidential Recordings: John F. Kennedy*, 6 vols. W. W. Norton, 2001 (vols. 1–3), 2016 (vols. 4–6).

Milne, David. *America's Rasputin: Walt Rostow and the Vietnam War*. Hill & Wang, 2009.

Miscamble, Wilson D. *George F. Kennan and the Making of American Foreign Policy, 1947–1950*. Princeton University Press, 1992.

Moats, Alice. *Blind Date with Mars*. Doubleday, Doran, 1943.

Morocco, John. *Thunder from Above: Air War, 1941–1968*. Boston Publishing, 1984.

Muggeridge, Malcolm. *The Infernal Grove*. Fontana/Collins, 1981.

Munton, Don, and David A. Welch. *The Cuban Missile Crisis: A Concise History*. Oxford University Press, 2006, 2011 (2nd ed.).

Murphy, Robert. *Diplomat among Warriors: The Unique World of a Foreign Service Expert*. Doubleday, 1964.

Naftali, Timothy, and Aleksandr Fursenko. *One Hell of a Gamble: Khrushchev, Castro, and Kennedy*. W. W. Norton, 1997.

Navratil, Jaromir. *The Prague Spring 1968: A National Security Archive Documents Reader*. Central European University Press, 1998.

Newhouse, John. *Cold Dawn: The Story of SALT*. Holt, Rinehart & Winston, 1973.

Newman, Kitty. *Macmillan, Khrushchev, and the Berlin Crisis, 1958–1960*. Routledge, 2007.

Nolan, Cathal J., ed. *Notable US Ambassadors since 1775: A Biographical Dictionary*. Greenwood Press, 1997.

Oberdofer, Don. *Tet!: Turning Point of the Vietnam War*. Johns Hopkins University Press, 2001.

O'Donnell, Kenneth, and David F. Powers. *Johnny, We Hardly Knew Ye: Memories of John Fitzgerald Kennedy.* Pocket Books, 1973.

Olson, Lynne. *Citizens of London: The Americans Who Stood with Britain in Its Darkest, Finest Hour.* Random House, 2011.

Perry, William J. *My Journey at the Nuclear Brink.* Stanford University Press, 2015.

Peterson, Susan. *Crisis Bargaining and the State: The Domestic Politics of International Conflicts.* University of Michigan Press, 1999.

Pike, Otis, and House Select Committee on Intelligence, US Congress. *CIA: The Pike Report.* Spokesman Books, for the Bertrand Russell Peace Foundation. 1977.

Public Papers of the Presidents of the United States: John F. Kennedy. US Government Printing Office, 1961–1964.

Quigley, Carroll. *Tragedy and Hope: A History of the World in Our Time.* Macmillan, 1966.

Quirk, Lawrence J. *Bob Hope: The Road Well Traveled.* Applause Books, 2000.

Rabel, Roberto G. *Between East and West: Trieste, the United States, and the Cold War, 1941–1954.* Duke University Press, 1988.

Ranelagh, John. *The Agency: The Rise and Decline of the CIA.* Cambridge Publishing, 1987.

Reeves, Richard. *President Kennedy: Profile of Power.* Simon & Schuster, 1993.

Reynolds, David. *Summits: Six Meetings That Shaped the Twentieth Century.* Basic Books, 2007.

Richmond, Yale. *Practicing Public Diplomacy: A Cold War Odyssey.* Berghahn Books, 2008.

Rusk, Dean. *As I Saw It.* Penguin Books, 1991 [first published by W. W. Norton, 1990].

Salinger, Pierre. *John F. Kennedy, Commander in Chief: A Profile in Leadership.* Gramercy Books, 2000.

Salisbury, Harrison E. *A Journey of Our Times: A Memoir.* Harper & Row, 1983.

Schick, Jack M. *The Berlin Crisis, 1958–1962.* University of Pennsylvania Press, 1971.

Schlesinger, Arthur M., Jr. *A Thousand Days: John F. Kennedy in the White House.* Houghton Mifflin, 1965.

Schlesinger, Stephen C. *Act of Creation: The Founding of the United Nations.* Westview Press, 2003.

Scoville, Herbert, and Robert Osborn. *Missile Madness.* Houghton, Mifflin, 1970.

Seaborg, Glenn T. *Kennedy, Khrushchev, and the Test Ban.* University of California Press, 1983.

Seaborg, Glenn T., with Benjamin S. Loeb. *Stemming the Tide: Arms Control in the Johnson Years.* Lexington Books, 1987.

Sebestyen, Victor. *Twelve Days: The Story of the 1956 Hungarian Revolution.* Vintage Books, 2007.

Slusser, Robert M. *The Berlin Crisis of 1961: Soviet-American Relations and the Struggle for Power in the Kremlin, June–November 1961.* Johns Hopkins University Press, 1973.

Smith, Gerard. *Doubletalk: The Story of SALT I.* Doubleday, 1980.

Smyser, W. R. *Kennedy and the Berlin Wall.* Rowman & Littlefield, 2009.

Solzhenitsyn, Aleksandr. *Cancer Ward.* Farrar, Straus & Giroux, 1968.

Sorensen, Ted. *Kennedy: The Classic Biography.* Harper Perennial Political Classics, 1965.

Spaso House, 75 Years: A Short History. Office of the Historian, US Department of State, 2008.

Spaulding, E. Wilder. *Ambassadors Ordinary and Extraordinary.* Public Affairs Press, 1961.

Stanford Arms Control Group. *International Arms Control: Issues and Agreements.* Stanford University Press, 1984 (2nd ed.).

Stearman, William. *The Soviet Union and the Occupation of Austria: An Analysis of Soviet Policy in Austria, 1945–1955.* Siegler, 1961.

Stourzh, Gerald. *Um Einheit und Freiheit: Staatsvertrag, Neutralität und das Ende der Ost-West-Besetzung Österreichs 1945–1955* [For Unity and Freedom: State Treaty, Neutrality, and the End of the Allied Occupation of Austria 1945–1955]. Böhlau, 1998.

Sulzberger, C. L. *The Last of the Giants.* Macmillan, 1970.

Sulzberger, C. L. *A Long Row of Candles: Memoirs and Diaries (1934–1954).* Macmillan, 1969.

Tal, David. *The American Nuclear Disarmament Dilemma, 1945–1963.* Syracuse University Press, 2008.

Tatu, Michel. *Power in the Kremlin: From Khrushchev to Kosygin.* Viking Press, 1969.

Taubman, William. *Khrushchev: The Man and His Era.* W. W. Norton, 2003.

Taylor, Gen. Maxwell D. *Swords and Plowshares: A Memoir.* Da Capo Press, 1972.

Thayer, Charles. *Bears in the Caviar.* J. B. Lippincott, 1951.

Thayer, Charles. *Diplomat.* Harper, 1959.

Thayer, Charles. *Hands across the Caviar.* J. B. Lippincott, 1952.

Thayer, Charles. *Moscow Interlude: A Novel.* Harper, 1962.

Thomas, Evan. *The Very Best Men: The Daring Early Years of the CIA.* Simon & Schuster 2006.

Thompson, Kenneth W., ed. *The Presidency and Foreign Policy.* University Press of America and Miller Center, 1997.

Thompson, Nicholas. *The Hawk and the Dove: Paul Nitze, George Kennan, and the History of the Cold War.* Henry Holt, 2009.

Tolly, Kemp. *Caviar and Commissars: The Experiences of a U.S. Naval Officer in Stalin's Russia.* Naval Institute Press, 1983.

Tolstoy, Nicolai. *The Minister and the Massacres.* Century Hutchinson, 1986.

Trachtenberg, Marc. *History and Strategy.* Princeton University Press, 1991.

Tschebotarioff, Gregory P. *Russia, My Native Land.* McGraw Hill, 1964.

Tuch, Hans. *Arias, Cabalettas, and Foreign Affairs: A Public Diplomat's Quasi-Musical Memoir.* New Academia / Vellum Books, 2008.

Tzouliadis, Tim. *The Forsaken: An American Tragedy in Stalin's Russia.* Penguin, 2008.

Unger, Leonard, and Kristina Segulja. *The Trieste Negotiations.* University Press of America, 2000.

United States Relations with China, with Special Reference to the Period 1944–1949; Based on the Files of the Department of State. US Government Printing Office, 1949.

Uslu, Nasuh. *The Turkish-American Relationship between 1947 and 2003: The History of a Distinctive Alliance.* Nova Science, 2003.

VanDeMark, Brian. *Into the Quagmire: Lyndon Johnson and the Escalation of the Vietnam War.* Oxford University Press, 1991.

Ward, Barbara. *Rich and Poor Nations.* Canadian Broadcasting Corp., 1961.

Warren, Earl, et al. *Hearings Before the President's Commission on the Assassination of President Kennedy,* 5 vols. US Government Printing Office, 1964.

Watt, Donald C., ed. *Documents on International Affairs, 1961.* Chatham House Series. Oxford University Press, 1965.

Weiner, Tim. *Legacy of Ashes: The History of the CIA.* Doubleday, 2007.

Weisbrode, Kenneth. *The Atlantic Century: Four Generations of Extraordinary Diplomats Who Forged America's Vital Alliance with Europe.* Da Capo Press, 2009.

White, William L. *The Little Toy Dog: The Story of the Two RB-47 Fliers, Captain John R. McKone and Captain Freeman B. Olmstead.* E. F. Dutton, 1962.

White, William L. *Report on the Russians.* Harcourt, Brace, 1947.

Wilke, Manfred. *The Path to the Berlin Wall: Critical Stages in the History of Divided Germany,* trans. by Sophie Perl. Berghahn Books, 2014.

Wise, David, and Thomas B. Ross. *The Invisible Government.* Random House, 1964.

Zubok, Vladislav. *Failed Empire: The Soviet Union in the Cold War from Stalin to Gorbachev.* University of North Carolina Press, 2009.

Zubok, Vladislav, and Constantine Pleshakov. *Inside the Kremlin's Cold War: From Stalin to Khrushchev.* Harvard University Press, 1997.

Index

Guthrie, John, 414; and negotiations with the North Vietnamese, 417

Hailsham, Quinton, 346, 348
Halberstam, David, 365, 369
Hammarskjöld, Dag, 230
Hare, Raymond, 316–17, 322
Harlem Globetrotters, 159
Harriman, Averell, 21, 24–25, 26, 39, 74, 238, 351, 362, 415, 467; as ambassador to the USSR, 40–41, 42, 43, 44; and concerns over a divided Germany, 176; and nuclear test ban negotiations, 344–46, 348–49; as Thompson's ally, 35–36, 41, 42; and the Vietnam War, 381, 386–88, 418, 453, 454, 455
Harriman, Kathleen, 39; at the American embassy in Moscow, 41–42
Harriman, Marie, 467
Harrison, Geoffrey W., 414; and the Trieste negotiations, 103, 104, 106, 108, 110, 114, 115
Harvard University: Thompson awarded an honorary doctorate from, 224
Heisenberg, Werner Karl, 5
Hellman, Lillian, 444
Helms, Richard, 247, 433
Hemry, Isaac Newton, 6
Hemry, Sally Thompson, 6
Henderson, Loy, 19–20, 32, 33, 35, 36, 41, 62, 143, 145; as ambassador to Iran, 97–98; at the US embassy in Austria, 98
Henkle, Monica, 260
Herter, Christian, 176, 177, 195, 197, 198, 215, 218, 229
Hickerson, John D., 50, 62, 81
Hilsman, Roger, 351
Hitler, Adolf, 16, 19, 24, 54, 102, 235; Stalin's pact with, 31
Ho Chi Minh, 186, 368, 380, 383, 412, 423; and the Sunflower initiative, 416, 418, 419
Holmes, Julius, 101
Hoover, J. Edgar, 192, 415
Hope, Bob, 159, 193
Hopkins, Harry, 24–25, 26, 33, 36, 51
hotline: between the US and the Soviet Union, 352, 429, 430
Houghton, Laura, 220
Hoxha, Enver, 71, 72
Hughes, Howard, 456
Hughes, Tom, 360, 375, 376, 397, 456
Hull, Cordell: as secretary of state, 39, 40
Hummelsine, Carl, 190
Humphrey, Hubert, 169, 429, 464; and the Vietnam War, 374
Hungarian refugees, 137, 141–42; Jane Thompson's involvement with, 139–40, 142

Hungary: aftermath of the crisis in, 141–42; Communism in, 234; revolt in, 135, 136–37, 140–41; and the Suez crisis, 138
Hurley, Patrick J., 37
Hurok, Sol, 206, 444–45
Hurwitz, Ed, 169, 446

Ilyichev, Ivan I.: and the Austria State Treaty negotiations, 120–21, 122–23, 124–25, 127–28; and the Thompson-Gromyko talks, 275, 277
India: and American concerns about China, 397; as nuclear power, 402
Inge, William Ralph, 101
INR. *See* Bureau of Intelligence and Research
intercontinental ballistic missiles (ICBMs): Soviet stockpile of, 151, 156, 187, 405, 407; and U-2 spy planes, 209
International Geophysical Year, 156
International Labour Organization (ILO): Thompson as representative to, 18
international organizations: growing involvement of, after World War II, 86
Iran, 297, 402, 458; CIA activity in, 97–98
Israel: as nuclear power, 395–96, 402; and ongoing tensions with the UAR, 443; and the Six-Day War, 428–34; and the Suez crisis, 137–38
Italy: Communist presence in, 63, 66, 69–70; Thompson family in, 458–60, 461; US aid to, 109. *See also* Rome, Italy; Trieste
Ivanov, Seymon, 325

Jarring, Gunnar, 443
Jebb, Gladwyn, 71–72
Jenkins, Kempton, 238, 274, 276, 277
Jernegan, John, 62
Johns, Jasper, 363
Johnson, Eric, 193
Johnson, Lyndon B., 256, 260; and the Cuban Missile Crisis, 300, 312–13; Franco's advice to, 380; at the Glassboro summit, 436–42; global economic crisis faced by, 358; and Gromyko, 387–89; after Kennedy's assassination, 354, 358; and Kosygin, 390, 436–42; and nuclear nonproliferation, 397–98, 464; and peace negotiations with North Vietnam, 454–55, 456–57; Rostow as advisor to, 382, 383–84, 385, 402; and the Six-Day War, 429–34; and the Sunflower peace initiative, 416–19; Thompson as advisor to, 357, 370, 371, 372–76, 377, 381–83, 384–86; Thompson's impressions of, 357; and the Vietnam War, 365, 366–68, 371, 372–376, 377–78, 379–84, 385, 387–90, 439–41, 462–63; and withdrawal from the 1968 presidential election process, 454
Johnson, Priscilla, 213, 217–18
Johnson, U. Alexis, 301, 307, 308, 313, 361, 383

Joint Chiefs of Staff (JCS), 69; and the Cuban Missile
Crisis, 307–8; and disarmament negotiations, 404,
407; and the Nike-X system, 410; and nuclear test ban
treaty negotiations, 336

Jones, Joseph, 63, 64

Jordan, 443; and the Six-Day War, 428, 429, 432

Kádár, János, 136, 137

Kalb, Marvin, 274–75

Kasavubu, Joseph, 230

Katzenbach, Nicholas, 384, 390, 410; and the Six-Day
War, 429, 433

Kaysen, Carl, 341

Keating, Kenneth, 295, 298

Keeney, Spurgeon, Jr., 406

Kelley, Robert F., 19–20

Kennan, George, 19, 20, 33, 36, 44, 45, 47, 62, 64, 81, 149,
238, 260, 425; as ambassador to the USSR, 91–92,
155; and containment policy, 67–68; Long Telegram
by, 55, 57–58; and the Marshall Plan, 66; at the
National War College, 59–60; and the OPC, 69, 70,
72; Thompson's assessment of, 41

Kennedy, Jackie, 369

Kennedy, John F., 94, 199, 217, 229; and the aftermath of
the Cuban Missile Crisis, 331–32; and his American
University speech, 347–48; assassination of, 328, 353–
54; and the Bay of Pigs invasion, 247; and the Berlin
question, 231–32, 255–57, 258–60, 277, 278–79, 293;
and the Cuban Missile Crisis, 298–331; and Dobrynin,
351–52; elected president, 231; foreign policy decision
making of, 236, 245; and Khrushchev, 233–34, 235,
240, 251–54, 294–97, 328; Khrushchev's impressions
of, 253; and meetings with Gromyko, 352–53; meeting with Khrushchev proposed by, 240–41, 243; and
nuclear test ban negotiations, 243, 337–39, 340–46,
347–51; as presidential candidate, 223, 225; public
perceptions of, 331; and release of the RB-47 flyers,
235; Soviet experts' advice to, 238–39; speech on the
Cuban Missile Crisis, 312–13; and tensions with
Khrushchev, 295–97; Thompson as advisor to, 238–
40, 260, 266, 292–93, 295–97, 298–314, 318–23, 326,
328–29, 334, 347, 348–49; Thompson as supporter of,
231; and Vietnam, 368–69

Kennedy, Robert F., 245, 252, 268, 278, 296; assassination of, 456; and the Cuban Missile Crisis, 300, 302,
308, 314, 315, 322–25; and nuclear test ban negotiations, 342; as presidential candidate, 454

Kennedy Center, 362

Kharlamov, Mikhail, 254, 264

Khrushchev, Nikita, 10, 22, 94, 122–23; and the Austrian
State Treaty, 130; Berlin as issue for, 164, 165–77, 189,
197–98, 203, 217, 218, 231–32, 237–38, 242, 248–51,

253, 255–57, 258–60, 276–77, 328; at Camp David
with Eisenhower, 197–201; challenges faced by, 220–
21, 271–72, 281, 293, 340; at the Communist Party
Twenty-Second Congress, 269; concerns about ideological speech by, 233–34; and consolidation of power,
135, 145, 149; and Cuba, 246, 247; and the Cuban
Missile Crisis, 301, 302–6, 309, 312, 313, 315, 317–19,
321–27; descriptions of, 132–33; Eisenhower's impressions of, 291–92; first US visit by, 190–201; at the
Four-Powers summit, 217–19; at the Geneva summit
(1955), 132–35; and the Hungarian Revolt, 136–37,
138; and his impressions of Eisenhower, 202, 205; and
Kennedy, 233–34, 235, 240, 295–97, 328; Kennedy's
invitation extended to, 240–41, 243; and missiles
installed in Cuba, 285; and Nixon, 226; and Nixon's
visit to Moscow, 180, 182, 183–86, 187–88; and
nuclear test ban negotiations, 243, 245, 296, 336, 339–
40, 341–46, 348, 349, 350–51; and nuclear threat as
deterrent, 150–51, 156; and possible visit to the US,
164, 176–78; and Salinger, 281–82; and Jane Thompson, 162–63, 203, 205, 257–58; and relationship with
Thompson, 158–59, 162, 163, 176, 186, 202–3, 216,
222–23, 227–29, 234–35, 240, 242–43, 285–91;
removed from office, 364; and Sulzberger interview,
262–64; and tensions over East Germany, 157, 165–
70, 173–75, 186, 222; Thompson's observations and
assessments of, 163–64, 174–75, 237, 351; at the
United Nations, 193, 230; and the U-2 incident, 208,
211–12, 213, 214–15, 216, 220–21, 228, 287; and the
Vienna summit, 248–54; on Vietnam, 368; and Zhukov, 156–57

Khrushchev, Sergei, 130, 190–91, 268, 327, 328

Khrushcheva, Julia, 192, 204

Khrushcheva, Nina Petrovna, 232, 285; at the Soviet
dacha, 204; in the US, 192, 197

Khrushcheva, Rada, 76, 152, 350; in the US, 191, 192,
193, 197, 204, 205, 262

King, Martin Luther, Jr., 451

Kissinger, Henry: and the Vietnam War, 367; and SALT,
471–72; Thompson's impressions of, 473–74

Klein, David, 314, 322, 333, 414, 442, 456

Klosson, Boris, 204, 241, 271

Klosson, Harriet, 271

Knight, Robert, 113

Kohler, Foy, 256, 453; as ambassador to the Soviet
Union, 262, 288, 345, 350, 400

Konev, Ivan, 268

Korea, 171, 375

Korean War, 83; Eugene Rostow's beliefs about, 425

Kornienko, Georgi, 279, 444, 468

Kosygin, Alexei, 223, 412; and arms control negotiations,
420, 421–22, 464; declining status of, 450; at the

Middle East: Eisenhower's perspective on, 440; Six-Day
War in, 428–34; Soviet interests in, 428–34, 438, 442–
44; and UN Security Council Resolution 242, 443–44
Mijailović, Draža, 102
Mikoyan, Anastas, 158, 162, 183, 202, 205, 224, 257, 257,
271, 350–51; and the Cuban Missile Crisis, 301, 304,
317, 325, 329–31; after Kennedy's assassination, 354;
and tensions over a divided Germany, 168, 170–72, 250
Mikoyan, Sergo, 304, 330
Minh, Duong Van, 369
MIRVs. *See* multiple independent reentry vehicle
(MIRV) system
missile systems. *See* antiballistic missile (ABM) system;
intercontinental ballistic missiles (ICBMs); multiple
independent reentry vehicle (MIRV) system
Moats, Alice, 26
Mobutu, Joseph, 230
Molotov Plan, 67
Molotov, Vyacheslav, 27, 31, 33, 35, 40, 43, 44, 50, 51, 145,
169, 235; and the Austrian State Treaty negotiations,
116, 118, 119, 120, 128, 129, 130
monetary policy, international: and the Bretton Woods
accord, 358
Monroe, Jane. *See* Thompson, Jane Monroe
Monroe, Kenneth Potter, 74
Morgan, Edward P., 428
Morgenthau, Henry, 39, 65
Morrison, Norman, 382
Moscow: Annual World Youth Festival in, 156; the chal-
lenges of air travel to, 39–40; German invasion of, 24;
German retreat from, 30–31; golf club in, 475; Hubert
Humphrey's visit to, 169; ice follies in, 203–4; North
Vietnamese embassy in, 412; siege of, 26–31;
Tchaikovsky Piano Competition in, 161–62; the
Thompson family's departure from, 284–85; Thomp-
son's impressions of, 153–54, 414. *See also* Soviet
Union; Spaso House; Thompson, Llewellyn E, Jr.
Moscow Conferences, 24, 35, 40–41, 44–45
Moscow Memorandum, 119, 124, 125–27
Moscow Pact, 40
Mosely, Philip, 57, 83
Mossadegh, Mohammad, 97–98
Moyers, Bill, 384
multilateral force: opposition to, 398–99; proposed for
Western allies, 392–94, 396; Thompson's view of, 393
multiple independent reentry vehicle (MIRV) system,
405–6, 422, 446. *See also* strategic arms limitation
talks
Multiple Reentry Vehicles (MRVs), 446
Murphy, Robert, 113–14, 177, 178, 466
Mussolini, Benito, 101
Mydans, Carl, 271

Nagy, Imre, 136
Nalda, Gratien, 10
Nalda, Mike, 6–7, 9–10
Nalda, Pete, 1
NASA: role of, in the U-2 cover story, 211, 213, 214
Nasser, Gamal Abdel, 137; and the Six-Day War, 428
Nathan, James, 515n48
National Committee for Free Europe (NCFE), 70–71
National Security Act (1947), 69
National Security Agency (NSA): surveillance by,
462–63
National Security Council (NSC), 69, 150, 256, 299; and
nuclear test ban negotiations, 340, 344–45. *See also*
Executive Committee of the National Security
Council
NATO. *See* North Atlantic Treaty Organization
Nero, Peter, 467
New York City: Khrushchev in, 193, 230
Newman, Kitty, 217
Nhu, Madame, 369
Nike-X ABMs, 409–10, 411
Nitze, Paul, 73, 81, 82, 254, 256, 327, 413, 468; and the
Cuban Missile Crisis, 308, 313–14, 319; farm owned
by, 311, 334–35; at the SALT talks, 467, 468
Nitze, Phyllis, 413
Niven, David, 193
Nixon, Pat, 182–83, 188
Nixon, Richard, 141, 142, 159, 171, 456; and Khrushchev,
180, 182, 183–86, 187–88, 191, 203, 226; in Moscow,
180–89, 423; and the Paris Peace Talks, 462–63; in
Poland, 188; as president, 358; as presidential candi-
date, 225, 226, 231; and rapprochement with China,
473, 474; and SALT, 469, 471–72; Thompson as advisor to, 466; and the Vietnam War, 367
NKVD (Soviet secret police), 37, 47
Noble, G. Bernard, 54
North Atlantic Treaty Organization (NATO), 61, 67, 79,
83, 256, 360; creation of, 80–81; and the Cuban Missile Crisis, 300, 303, 305, 306, 309, 316–17, 319–20,
321–22; European countries' ambivalence toward,
358; fragmentation of, 359–60
North Korea, 402
North Vietnam: bombing halt in, 378–79, 382–83; Chinese influence in, 375, 379–80, 425; covert operations
in, 370–71; mining of harbors in, 421; peace talks with,
454–55; SAM missile sights in, 380; US bombing of,
372, 373, 374, 375–76, 377, 381, 383, 384–85, 389,
390, 416, 418, 420, 421, 424, 426–27, 439–41, 455, 457.
See also Vietnam War
Novikov, Nikolai, 58
Novosibirsk: Thompson and Khrushchev's meeting in,
241–44

Princeton University: Thompson offered a job at, 279
Pryce, William, 445–46